BARRON'S
Legal-Ease

Probate and Settling an Estate

STEP · BY · STEP

BARRON'S
Legal-Ease

Probate and Settling an Estate
S·T·E·P · B·Y · S·T·E·P

James John Jurinski, J.D., CPA

BARRON'S

This publication is designed to provide accurate and
authoritative information in regard to the subject
matter covered. It is sold with the understanding
that the publisher is not engaged in rendering legal,
accounting, or other professional services. If legal
advice or other expert assistance is required, the
services of a competent professional person should
be sought.

All inquiries should be addressed to:
Barron's Educational Series, Inc.
250 Wireless Boulevard
Hauppauge, New York 11788

International Standard Book No. 0-7641-0167-6

Library of Congress Catalog Card No. 97-25801

Library of Congress Cataloging-in-Publication Data
Jurinski, James.
     Probate and settling an estate step-by-step /
James John Jurinski.
       p.   cm.—(Barron's legal-ease)
     Includes index.
     ISBN 0-7641-0167-6
     1. Probate law and practice—United States—
Popular works. 2. Executors and administrators—
United States—Popular works. I. Title. II. Series.
KF765.Z9J87   1997
346.7305'2—dc21   97-25801
                              CIP

PRINTED IN THE UNITED STATES OF AMERICA

987654321

Contents

6 UNDERSTANDING WILLS

7 MANAGING PROPERTY

8 PAYING CREDITORS AND TAXES

9 CLOSING THE ESTATE

10 INTESTACY—WHEN THERE IS NO WILL

11 WILL CONTESTS

Introduction

WHAT THIS BOOK IS ALL ABOUT

Y ou're probably reading this book because
you have been named as executor or personal representative in the will of a friend or family
member. Or perhaps you are a surviving spouse or
relative of the deceased, and you need to get a better
understanding of the probate process and your role
in that process. This book has been written specifically with you in mind.

Probate is one of the most feared words in the
English language. Many people have heard horror
stories about probate, and even more people are
aware that the probate process can be grueling and
unpleasant. Best-sellers have been written on how to
avoid it. Although settling an estate and guiding it
through probate is fairly complicated and time-
consuming, it is hardly the ordeal that many people
fear. Like any complicated journey, your progress
will be faster and far easier if you have a roadmap.
This book has been written to serve as a roadmap
through the legal system and the probate process.
The book is designed to guide you through the
process step-by-step.

PROBATE STEP-BY-STEP

The executor or personal representative will also
have primary responsibility for dealing with family
members and other heirs. The executor or personal
representative will be overseeing the deceased's
property, paying off outstanding debts, and distributing the deceased's property according to the directions in the will. However, there is more to the job
than just dealing with property. The death of a family member or close friend is always traumatic for
family and friends. It is even more so when unex-

pected. An important role of the executor is to help
people deal with their grief and move on with their
lives.

Executors and personal representatives don't
have to make this journey alone. You will be working with one or more attorneys who will be guiding
the estate through the court system. You will probably also be working with an accountant, an
appraiser, and other individuals who will be helping
at each step. Family members may also be willing to
help out when needed. As executor or personal representative your job will be to coordinate these individuals' efforts in settling the estate.

The length of time needed to settle the estate
will depend on a number of factors. If the decedent's
affairs were in good order at the time of death, then
the process will be relatively straightforward. On the
other hand, if the deceased had been seriously ill for
some time, it is likely that his financial affairs may be
in disorder because he simply couldn't keep up with
the day-to-day management of his personal finances.
If this is the case, the executor or personal representative will have to spend extra time putting those
affairs in good order.

Similarly, the length of time to settle the
estate will depend on how much and what kind of
property the decedent held at death. If the deceased
left only a small estate, the probate process will be
relatively simple. On the other hand, if the deceased
owned lots of real estate or owned a business, the
probate is likely to be much more complicated. But
even if the settlement of the estate is complicated, it
is never impossible. The process just needs to move
forward step-by-step.

HOW TO USE THIS BOOK

Although you might read this book cover to cover, it is more likely that you will be reading chapters as you go along in the probate process. The chapters have generally been arranged in "chronological" order—in the order of events as they will most likely occur. Thus, the early chapters deal with the executor's or personal representative's initial duties; later chapters deal with property management and other management issues, and continue with the distribution of property to the heirs, and closure of the estate. After you have read the first three chapters you may want to continue reading the entire book, or you may want to save the material in later chapters until your probate has progressed and you need more information.

The first three chapters of the book will give you an overview of what follows. You should certainly read the first four chapters right away: "Last Illnesses and Other Preprobate Matters"; "Funerals"; "Understanding the Probate Process"; and "The Executor."

Following is a brief synopsis of each of the book's chapters as well as the appendices and other contents. By familiarizing yourself with this outline, you will be able to determine which chapters will be most useful to you at any given point of the probate process.

CHAPTER 1, "LAST ILLNESSES AND OTHER PREPROBATE MATTERS"

This first chapter deals with what to do immediately after a person's death. Someone—perhaps you—needs to step forward to notify family members and other concerned parties and to care for the deceased's belongings. If you have not had to cope with this situation before, this material is especially helpful.

CHAPTER 2, "FUNERALS"

Funeral and burial arrangements need to be made very quickly after a person's death. There is normally very little time to carefully investigate the best course of action. This chapter will let you know what to expect and what problems to watch out for. It also can help you make some quick decisions.

CHAPTER 3, "UNDERSTANDING THE PROBATE PROCESS"

Chapter 3 describes what happens during a "normal" probate. Although no two probates will be exactly alike, this chapter will give you an idea of the steps involved in settling the estate. The chapter also discusses how a will operates (Chapter 6, "Understanding Wills," gives more details on this point), and what happens if there is no will, or if there is a living trust in place of a will.

CHAPTER 4, "THE EXECUTOR"

This chapter provides a general description of the duties expected of an executor (sometimes referred to as a personal representative). The chapter also discusses how the executor works with the attorney and communicates with family members throughout the probate process. The chapter also gives some of the pros and cons of serving as an executor, and it should help you decide whether you should accept the appointment or whether you should decline and let someone else assume these duties.

CHAPTER 5, "COURT APPOINTMENT OF THE EXECUTOR AND PROBATE INITIATION"

This chapter details the basic qualifications necessary to serve as an executor and describes how the court appoints the executor or personal representative. The chapter also describes the importance of letters testamentary and their legal significance. In addition, the chapter discusses circumstances in which the executor may be required to furnish a bond. The chapter describes ancillary probate, a special procedure to be followed if the deceased owned out-of-state property, as well as the executor's duties immediately after being appointed by the court, including what the executor must do if the will is lost or if there are multiple wills. The chapter also describes the executor's responsibility to give notice of the death to both heirs and to creditors.

The executor must also prepare a formal inventory of the deceased's assets for the court. The chapter describes how this inventory is prepared and also discusses typical valuation issues that arise in preparing the inventory.

CHAPTER 6, "UNDERSTANDING WILLS"

To the uninitiated wills can be confusing. Additionally, state law adds another level of complexity. Chapter 6 describes many common will provisions. The chapter also describes the surviving spouse's elective share, which protects the surviving spouse if the will leaves little or nothing to him. The chapter also describes what happens when a child is disinherited, accidentally or intentionally. Finally, the chapter describes what happens when the will makes a gift of property but the property no longer exists or the beneficiary has already died.

CHAPTER 7, "MANAGING PROPERTY"

Chapter 7 explains the executor's duties in safeguarding property. The chapter also describes the legal guidelines for investing estate funds, borrowing money for the estate, and selling property. The chapter concludes with a discussion of managing the deceased's business.

CHAPTER 8, "PAYING CREDITORS AND TAXES"

This chapter provides detailed guidance about paying creditors and taxes. The chapter begins with a discussion of notice to creditors. The chapter next describes how claims against the estate are handled, and concludes with an overview of the estate's duty to pay both income taxes and death taxes.

CHAPTER 9, "CLOSING THE ESTATE"

Chapter 9 provides a description of the final steps in the probate process in which the executor or personal representative closes the estate. The chapter explains how the executor prepares an accounting for the court. The chapter also describes the procedures for making distributions of money and property to the heirs. Finally, the chapter details the steps to follow before the executor can be discharged and collect the executor's fee.

CHAPTER 10, "INTESTACY—WHEN THERE IS NO WILL"

Most people die intestate—without a will. Dying without a will raises a number of issues, some of which are complex. This chapter describes what happens when a person dies without a will.

CHAPTER 11, "WILL CONTESTS"

Occasionally wills are challenged—most often by disappointed heirs. This chapter details how and why a will may be challenged. The chapter examines how the court will determine if a will is valid and describes how challenges normally proceed through the court system.

CHAPTER 12, "UNDERSTANDING TRUSTS"

Many wills contain or are coordinated with a *testamentary trust,* a trust created by a will that goes into effect at the time of death. This chapter describes the essentials of such trusts in layman's terms. The chapter also discusses typical trust provisions.

CHAPTER 13, "ESTATE AND GIFT TAX BASICS"

Estates over $600,000 may be subject to federal estate and gift taxes. This chapter provides an overview of the federal *transfer tax* system that imposes both the estate and gift taxes.

CHAPTER 14, "STREAMLINED PROBATE"

In many states smaller estates may qualify for a streamlined probate process that is much simpler and less costly than normal probate. This chapter describes the process and provides a state-by-state summary of streamlined probate rules.

CHAPTER 15, "AVOIDING PROBATE"

Although most estates pass through probate, some property may pass outside probate. In some cases a deceased may have arranged his affairs by using a living trust to avoid probate entirely. This chapter describes how probate may be avoided and the procedures that will take place as a substitute for the probate process.

BACK MATTER

Following Chapter 15 are Appendix A, which consists of a sample will, and Appendix B, which contains information on deadlines, spousal elective shares, claims, taxes, and other information for all 50 states. Appendix C contains various federal tax forms used during the probate process.

Although many terms will be defined as you read through the chapters, there is also a glossary that will help you understand many of the unfamiliar terms you will meet during the probate process.

A section featuring commonly asked questions and answers also appears at the end of the book. If you have a specific question, you may find the answer there.

DEALING WITH THE LEGAL SYSTEM

To the layman the legal system can look like a conspiracy to keep people confused and lawyers in business. Most people find the legal system intimidating because they are unfamiliar with the language used by lawyers and unsure how to proceed in legal matters. Although this book is written by a lawyer, the book is written specifically for nonlawyers. The book contains numerous tips and helpful hints on how to deal with the legal system.

Unfortunately legal rules are not uniform throughout the United States. Because probate is a local rather than a national matter, the rules are governed by state, not federal, law. Although the rules surrounding probate are similar in all states, there is a good deal of variation from state to state. States

have different filing requirements and forms. There can even be variations within a state because of local rules in certain counties. Many of these differences are illustrated in Appendix B. Because of these state-to-state differences, it is important that the executor or personal representative gets advice from a competent attorney who is knowledgeable about local law.

WARNING *Although the material in this book concerns legal issues, the information you find here should not be regarded as legal advice and should not be substituted for legal advice. The discussions in the text are, of necessity, generalized, and a slight change of fact or local law for any of the described scenarios might change the legal implications. Probate law does vary from state to state, so it is essential that you determine whether a particular rule applies in your state.*

Additionally, although every effort has been made to ensure that this material is accurate at the time of writing, the law constantly changes. It is often wise to seek legal counsel from an attorney familiar with state and local probate matters.

CHAPTER 1

Last Illnesses and Other Preprobate Matters

INTRODUCTION

This chapter will discuss many of the matters that must be attended to even before an executor is named by the court. The chapter is concerned with two main issues: medical and financial concerns. The chapter starts with a discussion of certain issues relating to a person's last illness and medical decisions that must be made prior to death. The second part of the chapter deals with issues that are primarily, although not exclusively, financial. This includes predeath planning issues. Chapter 2 deals with planning the funeral and burial or cremation and a number of other details that must be taken care of immediately after a person's death.

Who Has Power to Make Decisions?

When a person dies, his or her property normally passes into an artificial entity known as the *probate estate*. The law recognizes many other artificial entities, such as trusts and business corporations. The probate estate is supervised by an *executor*. In many states the executor is called the *personal representative*. For simplicity's sake we will use the term *executor*. The executor may be an individual or a corporate entity, such as the trust department of a bank. The executor—with the help of the estate's attorney—is responsible for settling the estate. The executor will essentially be making most of the decisions in handling the estate.

Decisions for the Family

However, as a matter of law, the executor is only empowered to act once appointed by a probate court, or other court with jurisdiction over the probate. There are a number of very important decisions that must be made even before the executor is appointed.

The law in most states provides that family members—not necessarily the executor—will be making the initial decisions. These include:

1. medical decisions;
2. funeral arrangements; and
3. burial or cremation decisions.

WHEN DEATH IS NEAR

When an individual is near death, family members may be called upon to make several hard decisions. Some of these are medical decisions, some are financial. If the ill individual still has his mental faculties, and is able and willing to participate, there are several matters that the family may want to resolve. If the family does not know the whereabouts of a will, or what funeral and burial arrangement the individual prefers, this is the best time to ask. Most terminally ill patients will want to get their affairs in order rather than leaving the chore to their loved ones.

PLANNING TIP *If the ill individual has no will it may be a good idea to have an attorney visit the hospital to write one. If the ill individual lacks the legally required mental capacity, then it is too late to make a will. This topic is discussed in more detail later in the chapter.*

MEDICAL DECISIONS BEFORE DEATH
Who Can Make Decisions?

An individual with a life-threatening illness or medical condition may still have his mental faculties, in which case he can continue to make his own decisions about the level of medical care he receives. Once he loses consciousness or is mentally or physically unable to make decisions, decisions about the proper level of care are left to medical professionals. However, an exception to this general rule is made when an individual has executed either a *living will* or an *advance healthcare directive* (sometimes called a *healthcare proxy*).

Living Wills

A living will is a legal document that expresses the patient's wishes about medical treatment if he becomes terminally ill. A living will allows the person to express a preference about whether heroic efforts should be made to preserve his life if it merely prolongs life for a brief period. Some states have statutory living wills that are likely to be respected.

Advance Healthcare Directives (Healthcare Proxies)

A number of states allow a patient to execute an advance healthcare directive, sometimes called a healthcare proxy. This allows a named individual or individuals to make medical choices when the patient is unable to do so. For example, an individual who is not in terminal condition can often be asked about whether she desires to have a particular treatment. If the patient is unconscious or otherwise unable to make such a decision, the person named in the directive or proxy is able to make the decision on behalf of the patient. Healthcare directives may also express a person's desires should she be in a persistent vegetative state (PVS). Some states have adopted a special form for these proxies and health-

care providers will only accept the form that is recognized by their state.

WARNING *The laws regarding both living wills and advance healthcare directives vary state by state. Unfortunately there is not one form that is accepted in every state. Moreover, the laws pertaining to living wills and healthcare directives comprise a new area of law, and states seem to change them with surprising frequency. If the patient wants his wishes regarding medical care respected, the hospital providing that care should be contacted to make sure that the form expressing those wishes will be respected. If the form is not acceptable, the hospital will be able to provide a form that is acceptable and that will be respected by both attending physicians and hospital staff.*

WARNING *The hospital should have copies of either a living will or an advance healthcare directive. Attending physicians will not limit treatment or consult with non-patients unless such a form is actually on file at the hospital.*

Overlap Between Living Wills and Advance Healthcare Directives

Although the scope of living wills and advance healthcare directives overlaps, most states allow a patient to have both. Unlike a living will, the advance healthcare directive is effective even when the patient is not terminally ill.

Durable Power of Attorney

About 30 states allow a person to have a durable power of attorney that allows the holder to make medical decisions on behalf of the patient, including the decision to withdraw life support. The durable power of attorney for healthcare is a different form of advance healthcare directive.

Federal Patient Self-Determination Act

The Federal Patient Self-Determination Act requires hospitals, nursing homes, home health agencies, health maintenance organizations (HMOs), and hospices to actively bring up the subject of advance healthcare directives such as living wills. If the patient does not have a living will or healthcare directive he can sign one in the hospital if he is able.

....

WARNING *There are a number of problems in having an individual's healthcare wishes respected. If the healthcare directive is not state-mandated, healthcare providers may simply ignore the document. Compliance with the document is less likely if the document is couched in vague terms such as "without heroic measures." Finally, if the patient is in a hospital or other facility away from home, the doctors will not have access to the document and may not know the patient's actual wishes. For example, if the patient is hospitalized while on vacation or a trip, it is unlikely that the hospital will have access to the form. What's more, if the hospital is in a different state than the patient's home state, the hospital may not recognize the out-of-state form even if a copy is provided.*

....

HOSPICE CARE

Although long ago most people died at home, more recently people are brought to hospitals immediately before death. Although hospitals can provide needed medical care, in some cases medical procedures are useless or not desired. Hospice care during a patient's last illness is an alternative that all families should consider. Hospice care is available at the patient's home or in a hospice.

Hospice Care Emphasis

A hospice is a nursing facility that serves patients who have terminal diseases and are in their final stage of life. A hospice provides an alternative to dying at the hospital. Hospice care attempts to make the patient's final days pain-free without much medical intervention. The focus is on care rather than cure. Instead of aggressive medical measures to sustain life, the emphasis is on making the patient as comfortable as possible in a more homelike setting.

Hospice care is more family-centered and hospice workers help the family cope with the loss of their loved one. Trained counselors can help the family with both emotional and financial counseling. The hospice often arranges for a member of the clergy to attend to the spiritual needs of both the patient and her family. Many hospices can arrange for care to be given at the patient's own home. Nor-

mally, family and friends provide care in a person's home with assistance from a hospice team member who is available on an around-the-clock basis.

Medicare Funding for Hospice Care

Medicare does fund hospice services performed by an approved provider. However, specific preapproval by Medicare is required for an individual to receive hospice care, even if the provider has been approved by Medicare. Deductibles and co-payments are waived except for the 5 percent co-payment (with a $5 maximum) for prescription drugs. Hospice care normally extends for two 90-day periods and a final 30-day period. However hospice care can continue indefinitely even after these time limits elapse. The periods are designed to allow a patient to switch back to standard Medicare coverage if he desires it. Medicare Part B coverage (coverage for care other than hospitalization) is not affected. A patient may transfer from one hospice to another once within each period.

Medicare Eligibility

An elderly client may have Medicare pay for hospice care if she is eligible for Part A coverage and if her doctor certifies that she is terminally ill and has six months or less to live. The patient must also accept care in a Medicare-approved hospice in place of standard Medicare benefits. The provider must establish a written plan of care that must be regularly reviewed by a Medicare representative.

What Medicare Covers

Medicare covers nearly all of the expenses associated with hospice care, including physician services, nursing care, medical appliances and supplies, outpatient drugs for pain relief and symptom management, home health aide and homemaker services, physical therapy and speech and language pathology services, medical social services, and counseling.

Respite Care

Respite care allows a hospice patient staying at home to move back to an inpatient facility for up to five consecutive days to give the caregiver a break. Patients covered by Medicare are responsible for 5 percent of the cost of the respite care, up to the current $716 hospital deductible for each of the three hospice care periods.

....

PLANNING TIP *If the three hospice care periods are consecutive, in calculating the respite care deductible they are considered one period. Accordingly, only one hospital deductible must be met.*

....

MEDICAL BILLS FROM THE LAST ILLNESS

The last two weeks of a person's life can be the most expensive if he spends that time in the hospital. The costs of heroic medical measures can be astronomical. Medical bills from the last illness are solely the responsibility of the patient unless family members have agreed—in writing—to be responsible as well. For elderly patients, most of the costs should be borne by Medicare. Low-income patients are normally covered by Medicaid. Deductibles and other fees not covered by insurance will be an expense of the deceased's estate.

PREDEATH FINANCIAL PLANNING

If the individual is still mentally competent during the last illness, it may be advisable for him to do some predeath planning with the goal of setting his affairs in order. This type of planning may also minimize death taxes, which in turn maximizes the amount that will go to family members and other heirs.

Update Will and Estate Plan

If the ill individual has not updated his will or estate plan in some time—or has never had a will—then this is the time to update or write one. Many people who do have a will have not updated it for many years. Although a lapse of time does not in itself invalidate a will, the document and overall estate plan may need updating. Generally an estate plan or will needs to be updated if:

- there have been family changes (new children or grandchildren, or a marriage or divorce in the family);
- heirs named in the will have died;
- property listed in the will is no longer owned by the testator or no longer exists;

- the individual's assets have changed significantly (increased from an inheritance, decreased because of business losses, etc.);
- the individual has moved to a new state;
- five or more years have elapsed since the document was created.

Consider Executing a Living Trust

If the individual's illness is likely to continue for some time, it may be a good idea to consider a living trust in place of a will. A living trust works as a will substitute—it functions differently from a will in the way it shifts ownership of property to the heirs. Essentially ownership of all of the ill person's property will vest in the trust controlled by the trustee. On the individual's death ownership passes to the heirs. There are two distinct advantages of a living trust in this situation:

1. ability of trustee to manage property during the individual's disability;
2. ability to postpone gifts.

Because the ill individual will be unable to take care of day-to-day business, the trustee can step in and perform this function. Also, the trust terms can specify that some property be held in trust for a period of time after the individual's death. This would be appropriate if the individual thought that a property transfer should be postponed.

EXAMPLE Paul wants to set up a living trust both to manage his property during his last illness and also to transfer his property to family members. One of Paul's sons is still in college and Paul does not feel that he is ready to handle a large amount of cash or manage investments. Paul can have the trust written so that it continues after his death. The trust could continue until the youngest son reaches age 30, at which time the trust's assets would be distributed to Paul's son and the trust would terminate.

Trusts are discussed in more detail in Chapter 12, "Understanding Trusts."

Consider Predeath Transfers of Jointly Held Property

If an ill individual owns property jointly with his spouse, he should consider a property transfer before death because it has the potential for significant income tax savings. This technique may appear counterintuitive, because it transfers ownership of jointly owned property to the ill spouse. However, in calculating income taxes, there is no tax on the transfer. When the ill spouse dies, the will can provide that the entire property go to the surviving spouse. If the surviving spouse turns around and sells the property, there will be absolutely no income tax due, because the tax basis on which gain is computed will rise to fair market value. This is a wonderful technique for property that has risen steeply in value. For example, if a husband and wife own property jointly—such as stock or investment real estate that has risen in value dramatically—significant amounts of income tax can ultimately be saved by having the property transferred into the name of the terminally ill spouse. However, there is no need for such transfers in the nine community property states (Arizona, California, Idaho, Louisiana, Nevada, New Mexico, Texas, Washington, and Wisconsin). In those states spouses achieve this favorable result without making any transfers. There is more discussion of this topic in Chapter 15, "Avoiding Probate."

Consider Predeath Gifts to Charity

Terminally ill individuals should also consider making gifts to charity while still living rather than make them in their will. Such a gift will generate an income tax deduction, which can be applied to the person's last income tax return. The gift will also be removed from the estate, which may lower both probate fees and death taxes, both of which are based on the value of the estate.

This topic is discussed in more detail in Chapter 13, "Estate and Gift Tax Basics."

Consider Predeath Gifts to Family Members

Predeath transfer of property to family members can have several advantages. A predeath gift allows early enjoyment and use of the property by the heirs and facilitates communication between the donor (the person making the gift) and the recipient. Also, for federal tax purposes, it is normally less costly to make a lifetime gift than to leave property in the

estate, which may be subject to death taxes. Only individuals with more than $600,000 of property need to worry about this tax, however. Predeath gifts generally provide no advantage when calculating state inheritance taxes, though, because these taxes generally disregard transfers made three years prior to death. Death taxes are discussed in more detail in Chapter 13, "Estate and Gift Tax Basics."

Review Beneficiary Designations

Along with reviewing the will and the estate plan, there should be a thorough review of beneficiary designations in other documents. Beneficiary designations control the disposition of certain property at death, including:

- life insurance policies;
- certain annuities;
- pensions;
- IRAs;
- U.S. savings bonds.

Very often these beneficiary designations need to be updated.

EXAMPLE 1 Mary started work with her employer 20 years ago when she was unmarried, and named her parents as beneficiaries on a group term life insurance policy and pension plan. Mary has long since forgotten about either of these beneficiary designations and nobody at the company has suggested to her that she review them. If Mary has since married she will probably want to change the designations—and certainly she should if her parents are dead.

WARNING *It is impossible to change beneficiary designations in a will. The only way beneficiary designations can be changed is through the issuer. For example, assume that Sam has a terminal illness. He writes a new will that gives all of his property to his brother. The will also directs that the proceeds from any life insurance should go to his brother. This last instruction will be ineffective because Sam's brother is not named beneficiary in the insurance policy itself. The insurance company is legally obligated to pay any proceeds to the person named in its records, notwithstanding Sam's clear intent in the will for it to do otherwise.*

EXAMPLE 2 John purchased a life insurance policy several years ago. The policy is paid up and John no longer needs to make premium payments but merely gets a report about the value of the policy from the company each year. When John bought the policy he named his first wife, Sara, as beneficiary, but he neglected to change the beneficiary designation when they divorced ten years ago. If John has since remarried he will probably want to change the beneficiary designation.

WARNING *It is common for divorce agreements to specify that a spouse must keep his ex-spouse as beneficiary of a life insurance policy. Before any changes are made, check any divorce decrees.*

Tax Problems

Although life insurance is frequently sold with the assurance that it is "tax free," that notion is only partially correct. Although life insurance proceeds can normally be received free of income tax charges, those proceeds may be subject to federal estate tax. The federal estate tax rate can exceed 50 percent, so the taxes are not a trivial concern. Estate tax problems can sometimes be avoided with advance planning. Tax problems with life insurance are discussed in more detail in Chapter 13, "Estate and Gift Tax Basics."

Life Insurance Planning

- review and update beneficiary designations if needed
- repay life insurance policy loans
- check for "waiver of premium" clause during disability
- consider conversion of whole life policy to term policy

Letter of Instructions

If an individual has not done so and is able during an illness, this is a good time for him to dictate a letter of instructions to the family. The letter should contain any details not covered in the will, but that the family should know. If the individual led a fairly complex life and did not share a lot of information, this letter can be extremely helpful to both the family and the executor. The letter of instructions will typically include any of the following matters:

- existence of a living will and/or an advance healthcare directive;
- identity of personal doctor;
- desires about funeral and burial arrangements;
- list of organ donations;
- location of will;
- identity of executor;
- existence and location of trusts;
- identity of trustee(s);
- location of deeds, life insurance contracts, and other important documents;
- location of safe-deposit box;
- location of post office box;
- identities of attorney, accountant, stock brokers, insurance agents, and financial advisors.

The letter may also include additional information about financial matters, such as:

- amounts owed to the writer of the letter itself;
- unpaid bills or contract amounts;
- business interests;
- investments and/or collectibles;
- real estate holdings;
- life insurance policies;
- bank and brokerage accounts;
- pensions and annuities;
- lawsuit or other legal or tax information.

Practical information about the family home should be included in the letter, such as:

- location of deed;
- location of key(s);
- burglar alarm details;
- yard and maintenance information.

The disposition of personal property to specific individuals (if not detailed in the will), should be itemized in the letter, including who will get specific items, such as:

- antiques;
- autos;
- books;
- collectibles;
- family Bible;

- family records;
- furniture;
- guns;
- hobby equipment;
- household furnishings;
- mementos;
- musical instruments;
- pets;
- photos, family videos.

Finally, the letter of instructions should contain any other information about the deceased's estate that the family may not know.

WARNING *Depending on your state's law, the instructions in this letter may not be legally binding on either the family or the executor. These are the deceased's wishes and the survivors may or may not decide to carry them out.*

ANATOMICAL GIFTS

Many individuals wish to donate their hearts, livers, kidneys, corneas, or other body parts to others. In some cases they may wish to donate their entire body to a medical school. Such gifts are allowed in every state.

Donor Cards

An anatomical gift is typically identified on a donor card. Although such donor cards do not have to be filed with an agency in most states, many require that the donor's signature on a card be witnessed by two people. Some states have a form that may be filled out when a person renews her state driver's license. Donor cards are sent to the charity or non-profit organization that will receive the organ.

Although a donor may have made a gift of an organ, several organs, or the entire body to one or more organizations, these organizations can decline the gift. The organs may be unusable because of the deceased's advanced age or medical condition. In some cases there may simply be no recipients who need the organs.

PLANNING NOTE *It may be possible to arrange with a medical school to have a donated body cremated after*

the school has finished with it. The ashes will be returned to the family a year or two after death.

The Family Decides

Whatever the deceased's wishes, it is up to family members, not the executor or the court, to make decisions about anatomical gifts, funerals, and burial. Of course if the executor is a family member, she will be involved in making these arrangements. Note that these decisions have to made promptly after death and often before the executor is formally empowered by the court. In all states the law gives the family the power to make these decisions.

WARNING *The law may require that anatomical gifts be honored or an autopsy performed even if the family objects.*

The Need for Haste

If organs are to be "harvested" to enable another person to use them, the procedure must be done within just a few hours of death. In practical terms this means that there must be coordination between the institution to receive the organs and the hospital or other facility where the person dies. If there is any delay the organs will normally be unusable.

WARNING *Although family members may be grieving, they need to take quick action. If the family knows that a donor card has been filled out and wishes to honor the donor's wishes, the family must immediately contact the organization holding the card and notify the hospital, nursing home, or other facility where the body is located in order to start the process. Failure to act quickly will frustrate the procedure.*

WARNING *In some cases family wishes may conflict with those of the deceased. Although the deceased may have executed an organ donor's card to make an anatomical gift at death, family members may be opposed. Although the law provides that the deceased's wishes must be followed, in practical terms the family may drag its feet until it is too late to make the donation. Although this type of behavior is illegal, it is rarely challenged in the courts.*

OTHER DUTIES
Support of Surviving Spouse and Dependent Children

If the deceased died leaving a surviving spouse or dependent children, they will need financial support. It is important to get in touch with the estate's attorney to handle this matter. If there is no attorney for the estate, the executor needs to hire one. The attorney can go to court to free up cash for the survivors.

Notifying Relatives

When a person is in his or her last illness, someone needs to notify relatives, friends, and clergy. Relatives in distant states may want to fly in to say their goodbyes while the person is still alive. If the person owned a business, the managers or employees are probably already aware of the illness, but they may not be aware of its severity. Someone needs to make sure that the managers know that the person is likely to die. They would probably want to pay their respects, and they also have to make arrangements to keep the business functioning.

Protection of Property

Someone needs to make sure that the ill person's home, auto, and any other property is secured and cared for. Lawn and other yard maintenance needs to be attended to. If the individual's home appears vacant because of a hospital stay, precautions should be taken against burglars. Stop newspaper, mail service, and utilities if appropriate. If the ill person has a pet, it will need care. Finally, it is a good idea to try to determine if there are any payments needed on installment debts or if other obligations need to be met.

Locating the Will

One of the first tasks after a death is to search for a will and other documents. In some cases—especially where death was not unexpected—someone will know the whereabouts of the will. An executor will most likely have a copy of the will and know the whereabouts of the original—often in a safe-deposit box.

WARNING *Safe-deposit boxes are a poor place to keep a will because banks "seal" the box to limit access after death. If an individual has a spouse or other close family members, they will typically know the whereabouts of the will. If there are no close family members living nearby, the deceased's neighbor, attorney, or doctor may know where to find the will. In some states individuals can file their wills with the probate court so they will be easier to find.*

Lost Wills

Occasionally it is impossible to find any trace of a will although family members recall having seen one. In other cases someone—typically the executor—may have a copy, but the original cannot be found. This problem is referred to as a *lost will.* This subject is discussed in more detail in Chapter 10, "Intestacy—When There Is No Will."

WARNING *It is not unusual to recover more than one version of a will. However, only one will at a time can be binding. Although the latest document is usually the legally valid document, this is not always true. A more recent will may actually be legally defective for one reason or another, which means that an earlier version is actually the legally valid will. If there appears to be more than one document, the best course is to gather all of the documents and have them examined by an attorney to determine which one is in fact the legally valid will. When there is more than one will, disappointed heirs sometimes challenge the will that is declared valid. This is called a* will contest. *This topic is discussed in some detail in Chapter 11, "Will Contests."*

Checklist of Initial Duties
Predeath Questions
- Has home hospice care or a stay in a hospice been considered as an alternative to the hospital?
- Has the patient considered making anatomical gifts?
- Has the ill person executed a living will?
- If so, does the doctor and hospital or hospice have a copy?
- If they have a copy, do they consider it legally binding?

- Has the patient signed the living will at the hospital?
- Who should make the medical decisions outlined on the patients healthcare directive?

Predeath Financial Checklist

Determine location of the following items. (There may be more than one in any category.)

- safe-deposit box
- will
- letter of instructions to heirs/family
- trust documents
- insurance policies
- deeds
- military records
- marriage, birth certificates
- stocks, bonds, brokerage account records
- bank account records
- marital/divorce agreements
- tax returns
- pension information
- lawsuit information

Predeath Financial Planning

- update will/estate plan
- consider executing a living trust
- consider predeath transfers of jointly held property
- consider predeath gifts to charity
- consider predeath gifts to family members

Other Duties

- Notify relatives, friends, and clergy of patient's illness
- Notify managers if patient owns a business
- Secure home, auto, and any other property
- Stop newspaper, mail service, and utilities if appropriate
- Provide care or financial support for surviving spouse or children if necessary
- Provide care for pets
- Arrange payments on installment or other debts

Advisors

Identify the following legal, financial, and spiritual advisors. (There may be more than one in any category.)

- attorney
- accountant
- financial planner
- trust officer
- insurance agent
- clergy

Grief

Although this topic closes the chapter, it is by no means the least significant one. Grief is both inevitable and unavoidable. Each person must accept the reality of death as part of the human condition and must try to move on and find purpose with his own life. The loss of a loved one diminishes the quality of one's life, and life will no longer be the same. People are simply not replaceable. People need to remember, however, that the deceased would have wanted them to continue with their lives. Family, friends, and religion can be comforting for those who are grieving. It will take time to get over the pain and loneliness. Those who don't have a large number of people for support are in special need of understanding.

CHAPTER 2 Funerals

INTRODUCTION

This chapter will discuss planning the funeral and arranging for burial or cremation. There are a surprising number of other details that must be taken care of immediately after a person's death. Although the family, not the executor, is responsible for making funeral arrangements, the executor will often be called upon to help with funeral planning. Of course when the executor is the surviving spouse or child, he or she will be handling many of the funeral arrangements. This chapter is designed to alert family members about what they will need to know about funeral and burial arrangements.

FUNERAL ARRANGEMENTS
Who Decides What Is Appropriate?

Like anatomical gifts, the family, not the executor, will determine the funeral arrangements. Although a decedent may indicate his or her wishes about anatomical gifts, funeral arrangements, and burial in the will, these wishes are often expressed in letters or other documents. If there is no mention made in the will or other formal documents, the next most likely source of information may be a funeral director with whom the deceased may have left instructions. Family members or friends may also know the deceased's wishes about these matters.

WARNING *In most states the deceased's wishes are not binding on the family. For example, if the deceased specified that he wanted a funeral of a certain sum, it may be an impossibly low figure, simply because of inflation. Likewise, his wishes may be too expensive given the size of the estate.*

What Needs to Be Decided?

There are a large number of issues that may need to be decided by the family. These include decisions regarding the following details:

- funeral home
- embalming
- internment or cremation
- casket and outer case
- casket cover
- open or closed casket at service
- apparel in which body will be dressed
- cosmetics
- type of service
- clergy
- music
- hearse, limousine, motorcycle escort services
- memorial folders, or cards
- publication of funeral notices
- copies of death certificates
- cemetery location

- transport of body if burial takes place somewhere other than place of death
- disposition of cremated remains

....

WARNING *All of these decisions must be made promptly. State laws normally require burial or cremation within seven to ten days after death. Most state laws also require embalming or refrigeration of the body 24 hours after death. Note that many religions find embalming objectionable. Additionally the family may be pressured by the hospital to proceed with funeral arrangements because they have no room to refrigerate the body. Nursing homes typically don't have refrigeration facilities for the deceased.*
....

WARNING *In some cases, family members may disagree about what type of funeral is appropriate. Such disagreements frequently occur when the family is broken into factions and they fight about other matters as well. For example, if the deceased has remarried, the children from the first marriage may resent the second spouse, and the spouse and children from the prior marriage may not agree on funeral and burial arrangements. In some states the law does not specify who is really in charge. In other states the surviving spouse has control over final arrangements. In a few cases relatives have completely excluded other relatives from participation, leading to severe emotional distress and lawsuits.*
....

FUNERAL HOME SERVICES

The funeral director performs a number of services including providing the casket, embalming, and burial. There may be a time when friends and family pay their last respects to the deceased. In addition there may be a memorial service at the funeral home and another service at the gravesite. The funeral director will arrange all of these details, including coordinating activities with florists, musicians, clergy, and the motorcade to the cemetery.

Embalming

One of the first decisions that must be made is whether the deceased's body should be embalmed. If the deceased was an Orthodox Jew or a member of another religion that frowns on embalming, the answer will probably be no. Embalming involves

draining the blood and replacing it with preservative. However, the embalming process is not permanent, so the corpse must be interred or cremated within about two weeks. Most states have laws requiring that bodies either be embalmed or refrigerated. If the body is to be transported to another state, it will have to be embalmed. The body will also be made up cosmetically and restorative services are available if needed.

Choices

There are a wide variety of funeral choices. If a traditional funeral is chosen, the body will be embalmed and prepared cosmetically. The funeral home will provide a room for public viewing of the body, which will be in an open casket for several nights. There will probably be a memorial service at the funeral home on one of those nights. A public service will be held at the cemetery after a funeral procession.

....

PLANNING TIP *If the deceased was a public figure, such as a politician or civic leader, members of the public may also wish to view the body and pay their respects. Public feelings for the deceased are sometimes underestimated when funeral arrangements are being made. For example, the outpouring of genuine affection by the general public for the late Jacqueline Kennedy Onassis stunned the Kennedy family and surprised the press.*
....

There are other options. The family can choose a closed casket service and limit viewing to one night or only to family members. The body can be cremated or interred and a service can be held later. Some families prefer no formal service whatsoever. Different family members may have strong feelings about these choices. Older individuals may prefer the more traditional approach while younger family members may want a simpler funeral. These preferences may be hard to reconcile but each family must eventually settle the issue for better or worse.

Funeral Expenses

Funerals are costly. There are a surprising number of items that must be taken care of by the funeral director and of course the funeral director will charge for each of these. Typical items include the cost of the:

- casket
- grave liner
- embalming
- cosmetic preparation of the body
- cosmetic restoration of the body
- special clothing for the body
- flowers at the funeral home
- rental of a room or the funeral home chapel for public viewing
- rental of the funeral home chapel for a memorial service
- honorarium for clergy at the service
- honorarium for musician(s) at the service
- visitor's register
- acknowledgment cards
- transportation of the body from the place of death to the funeral home
- hearse to the cemetery
- limousine(s) for mourners to the cemetery
- motorcycle escort
- pall bearers
- cemetery plot
- grave marker
- opening and closing grave
- honorarium for clergy at the cemetery
- honorarium for musician(s) at the cemetery
- preparing and publishing the obituary notice
- preparing Social Security and life insurance benefit requests
- preparing death certificate requests

Last Requests

Before a person dies, he may indicate to his executor or other family member which funeral home he wishes the family to use. The funeral may be fully or partially paid in advance, but if no payments have been made, the family needs to decide whether to honor the deceased's request. Unless some legally enforceable arrangement has been made in writing, the request is not binding on the family, who can then select a funeral home that is more convenient or more appropriate.

Funeral Home Pricing

Family members should try to comparison shop for the best deal. Although that is easy to say, it may be difficult in practice. Time will be short, and making arrangements will be emotionally draining. There are several other problems. Funeral directors are reluctant to give price quotes over the phone because they feel that such quotes lead to misunderstandings. Additionally, the way funerals are priced makes comparison difficult. Many funeral homes will give the family a single dollar figure for the "standard adult funeral." This is called *unit pricing*. Others will break the quote down between the casket and the many other services rendered by the funeral director. This is sometimes called *two-unit pricing*. Other funeral homes will give an itemized estimate which will break down the charge for each service. This is called *item pricing*. Obviously item pricing gives the family the best opportunity to compare the services and pricing of different funeral homes.

EXAMPLE Funeral Home A's bid estimates the casket will cost $5,000, the grave liner $3,000, and the memorial service $2,000. Funeral Home B quotes the price of a similar casket at $6,000, the liner at $5,000, and a similar memorial service at $1,000. These itemized quotes allow family members to try to negotiate the best price for each item with the funeral director. Item pricing also gives the family the most detailed information about exactly what services they will be buying.

Funeral Costs in Perspective

Although the expenses of a last illness can be overwhelming, funeral expenses can also loom large. Many people spend vast sums on elaborate funeral services. Although this may be appropriate for some families, other families overspend for a variety of reasons. It has been suggested that families spend too much because they are compensating for not spending enough time with the deceased during his or her lifetime. In some cases, families spend too much because they are not very knowledgeable about what they are buying. Unfortunately, some funeral directors manipulate grieving family members into spending far more than they need to. Unethical funeral directors have given the industry a bad reputation, and their practices have resulted in federal regulations to curb unethical practices.

What to Watch Out For

When individuals make a large purchase—such as a car or a major appliance—they normally have enough time to make an informed decision. A person will think carefully about his or her needs, get recommendations from friends, conduct consumer research, and shop around for the best deal. When funeral arrangements are made, however, family members are typically in a state of emotional shock, they have little knowledge of what they are actually buying, and most feel pressured to decide almost immediately. Given these disadvantages it is not surprising that many families live to regret their decisions concerning funeral arrangements.

How Costly Should the Funeral Be?

As a rule of thumb, 10 percent of a deceased's property is an upper limit of what the funeral should cost.

EXAMPLE George died owning $30,000 of property. The funeral should cost no more than $3,000 maximum. Funeral directors have an ethical obligation not to suggest overly expensive caskets and services to families that simply cannot afford them.

Who Pays the Funeral Expenses?

If funeral expenses are not already prepaid, they are normally paid out of the property in the estate. In other words, the bill is paid from the deceased's property rather than from family funds.

WARNING *Despite this general rule, funeral directors will typically require the person arranging the funeral to sign a contract that obligates them personally to pay the bills if the estate does not have enough funds to pay. If it ultimately turns out that the deceased died without enough funds to pay the funeral bills, then the person(s) who signed the contract will have to pay the expenses of the funeral.*

WARNING *Just because a family member has contracted for an expensive funeral, that doesn't mean the funeral director will always be paid from the estate. Funeral costs are a priority expense against the estate—funeral homes get paid for the cost of funerals before other creditors get paid, or before heirs receive their share of the estate. A probate judge can refuse to approve payment to a funeral home if the bill is too high in relation to the assets of the deceased. If the bills are too high, the family member who signed the contract may be liable for the excess. However, in some egregious cases, courts have ordered funeral directors to lower their bills.*

Burial Benefits

Burial benefits are available from a number of sources. The amounts of coverage may be rather small, but they can help defray funeral costs. Burial benefits may be available from:

- the Veterans Administration;
- Social Security;
- unions;
- fraternal organizations;
- life insurance policies.

If the deceased was a veteran, the family may be eligible for funeral and burial benefits including burial in a national cemetery. Eligibility information is available from your local Veterans Administration office.

PLANNING TIP *The executor should closely scrutinize all life insurance policies to determine if they include burial benefits. Inquiry should be made of any fraternal organizations to which the deceased belonged to see if they provide a burial benefit that can be applied against the cost of the funeral.*

HOW TO REDUCE THE COST OF FUNERALS

There is nothing especially tasteful about having an overly expensive funeral. In fact, many people find a simple service more dignified and respectful.

Also, it is important to understand that the amount of the estate going to the funeral director directly reduces the amount going to the heirs. For families of modest means, economizing will be essential. There are a number of ways to cut down funeral expenses, some of which have been mentioned:

- Comparison shop. One funeral home may bid thousands of dollars less than another. If funeral directors know you are comparing prices, their bids will probably be lower.
- Resist subtle pressure. Although the funeral director will be helping you, they also profit by steering you to more expensive caskets and services which may be inappropriate for your situation. Be especially watchful for sales ploys that try to make you feel guilty for not spending more money on the funeral.
- Consider using a simple minimum container or pine casket. Many mourners find this more dignified and the casket can be always be draped or covered with flowers. Ask for a grave liner rather than an expensive outer burial container (formerly called a *coffin vault*).
- Hold a memorial service without the body. The service does not have to be held at a funeral home. The body could be cremated or buried without embalming or being placed in a fancy casket.
- Consider cremation as an alternative.

PRENEED ARRANGEMENTS

The deceased may have already planned—and paid for—funeral arrangements. These plans—typically offered as a "package" by funeral homes—may be referred to as *preneed* or *prearranged* plans. Typically, the deceased will have arranged not only the funeral plan but also the burial or cremation details. If the deceased has attended to these details, then the cost of the funeral and burial will be paid by the plan.

CEMETERIES

All states have laws governing cemeteries. Cemeteries are operated by religious organizations, nonprofit associations, and for-profit businesses. In some parts of the country there are also private family cemeteries. Most state laws require that persons be buried only in established cemeteries.

Plots

The family, or the estate, must purchase a cemetery plot or mausoleum. For the burial of spouses, many families wish to purchase adjacent plots. In some cases a family may own a number of plots in anticipation that family members be interred together.

Markers

At one time, families had unlimited choice in selecting a marker. A visit to an older cemetery will reveal that there was once a great variety of markers. Early in the twentieth century, markers in the shape of tree stumps enjoyed some popularity. Today, many cemeteries insist that only brass nameplates be used as markers. This reduces both the cost of maintenance for the cemetery and the need for the family to purchase an expensive marker.

WARNING *The family should search for a cemetery deed among the deceased's effects. Many individuals buy cemetery plots during their lifetime.*

CREMATION

An increasing number of individuals specify that they would prefer to be cremated rather than interred. Cremation involves reducing the body to ashes by intense heat. The remains—referred to as "ashes"—generally weigh between six and twelve pounds. The ashes are put in a sealed urn. Typically the urn is kept in a columbarium, which is a building that holds the remains and makes them available for viewing, much like a mausoleum. Most columbariums will be connected to a mausoleum or will be located at a cemetery.

WARNING *The deceased may have already arranged with a funeral director for cremation. The fee may or may not have been prepaid.*

Scattering of Ashes

Although a will or letter of instructions may specify that the deceased wants his ashes scattered in a certain way, this can be difficult given the quantity of ashes. Even in states where there is no explicit law on the subject, it may be illegal to scatter the ashes on private property. Scattering ashes at sea beyond the three-mile limit is one alternative.

EXAMPLE A baseball fan wanted his ashes scattered at his favorite ballpark. The park owners prohibited a friend from scattering the ashes on the infield.

....

WARNING *In some states, like California, scattering ashes outside a cemetery is illegal inside city limits. California does allow the scattering of ashes from planes flying over 5,000 feet or at sea beyond the three-mile limit. Special permits may be needed however.*

....

Cremation Expenses

In theory cremation should be less expensive than interment because there is no need for embalming, a casket, or a grave liner. However, some funeral directors insist that the family purchase a casket for the memorial service anyway. Some funeral directors insist that the body also be embalmed prior to cremation. No states have laws requiring that a body be put in a casket or embalmed prior to cremation. But if there is only one funeral home in your area, or if all of the local funeral directors take the same position, it may be difficult to avoid this expense.

AUTOPSIES

An autopsy is an investigation of a body by a medical examiner (or coroner) to find evidence of the cause of death. An autopsy is normally required when death is thought to be a result of foul play, or suicide. Autopsies are also performed when it is necessary to prove that a person died as a result of an accident, on or off the job, or from drug use. The autopsy also determines the approximate time of death. Most bodies are not subjected to an autopsy because there is no need for one. The family member who controls disposition of the body can normally place some limits on when and how the autopsy is performed.

OTHER DETAILS
Insurance and Social Security Benefits

If the funeral director has not already helped process claims for Social Security benefits and life insurance policy proceeds, the executor should make these requests promptly. The funeral director will sometimes only be willing to file these claims before he receives the amounts due so they can be applied against the cost of the funeral. The funeral directors know that these amounts will be paid, even though the Social Security check will not be mailed promptly. There is one advantage to having the executor process these requests. If the executor processes them, the final bill from the funeral director will be higher. However, the executor can deduct the expenses on the federal estate tax return, which can in turn reduce taxes and thereby maximize the amount of property available to the heirs.

Death Certificates

The funeral director will normally offer to obtain several copies of the death certificate. The executor and or surviving spouse will need several copies of the death certificate to make legal transfers of ownership. For example, a copy of the death certificate will need to be sent to the Department of Motor Vehicles before they will change the name on a car title. Also, life insurance companies demand a death certificate before they will issue a check to a life insurance policy beneficiary. Sometimes the funeral director will charge a small amount to obtain these, so the surviving spouse or family member may want to order several at this time. An even better idea is to order ten copies and give them to the executor. Additional copies can be obtained later through the local office of vital statistics or similar office. In a large city the office may be close, but if the deceased lived in a rural area, the office may be some distance away. Although it will invariably be possible to obtain additional copies of the death certificate later, it may take a surprisingly long time for the government office to process the request. Therefore, it is a good idea to obtain the ten copies from the funeral director immediately.

CHAPTER 3 # Understanding the Probate Process

INTRODUCTION

Although most family members at some point must deal with the complications of probate, the probate process remains mysterious for most people. Even persons who have served as executors are sometimes confused about how probate operates.

This chapter will explain
- the probate process
- the role of the probate court
- the role of the will
- what happens when there is no will
- avoiding probate
- will substitutes, including living trusts

WHAT IS PROBATE?

Probate is probably one of the most emotionally laden words in the English language. Indeed, horror stories abound about the expense and complication involved in probating a deceased's estate. Friends, relatives, and co-workers may have shared stories about endless delays, excessive attorney's fees, and disappointed heirs. Although some of these stories are well-founded, some of the criticism leveled at the probate process exists because of ignorance about it.

Although an aura of mystery surrounds the probate process, the goals of probate are rather simple. There are four basic steps of the probate process:

1. identification of the decedent's will, if any, and the executor;
2. identification and collection of the decedent's property;
3. identification, validation, and payment of creditors' claims, including taxes; and
4. distribution of property to the heirs.

Although many people are fearful of probate, the probate system exists to protect property for both heirs and creditors alike. Probate is not just a process concocted to make lawyers richer. Although the procedures are often time-consuming, they are in place to protect creditors and heirs and to ensure that the deceased's lasts wishes are carried out.

Step 1: Identification of the Will and the Executor

The first step in the probate process is identification of the decedent's will. In some cases this may be straightforward. Many people put their wills in their bank safe-deposit box for safekeeping—but be aware that access to a safe-deposit box can be difficult. Others let relatives know where the will is kept. Unfortunately, some people make out wills but fail to tell anyone where they have left them. In some cases there are multiple wills and the executor and the court must determine which will—if any—is legally

16

valid. Wills are discussed in more detail in Chapter 5, "Court Appointment of the Executor and Probate Initiation," and in Chapter 6, "Understanding Wills." Unfortunately, many people simply die before they ever get around to making a will. This problem will be discussed later in the chapter.

The will normally names the executor. The executor will have responsibility for "settling" the estate, which requires: establishing the will, identifying and valuing the property, seeing that debts and taxes are paid, and distributing property to the heirs. The named person is not always willing to serve. In such cases the court will determine who is to serve as executor to settle the estate. The court will also name someone if there is no will.

Step 2: Identification and Inventory of the Property

The executor must identify, inventory, and value the decedent's property. This step may be relatively easy or quite difficult depending on the complexity of the holdings and how well-organized the decedent's records are. If the deceased merely owned a home, a car, and a few investments, then the process will be relatively simple. On the other hand, if the deceased owned one or more businesses and perhaps real estate or other investments, then the inventory process may be time-consuming. The executor can rely on experts—attorneys, accountants, and appraisers—to help in this step. More details on handling property are found in Chapter 7, "Managing Property."

Step 3: Payment of Debts

After inventorying the assets, the next step is the payment of debts and taxes. Generally, debts are not discharged on the debtor's death. In other words, when a person dies, his or her debts are not forgiven but become a claim against the estate. Creditors will be repaid from the estate before any property is distributed to the heirs. In fact, if the amount of the debts at the time of death exceeds the amount of property in the estate, the estate will be insolvent and the heirs will get nothing. Large medical bills during a last illness are one type of claim that can be made against an estate. If the decedent's net estate (after the payment of debts and expenses)

exceeds $600,000, federal estate tax will be due. This topic is discussed in Chapter 8, "Paying Creditors and Taxes."

Step 4: Distribution of Gifts to Heirs

The final step in the probate process is the distribution of property to the heirs, a step normally accomplished with court approval.

....
OBSERVATION *As a rule of thumb, few estates can be wound up in less than six months, and most take about a year to resolve. In some cases—normally when a lawsuit of some sort erupts—probate can drag on for a number of years.*
....

More detail on making distributions is found in Chapter 9, "Closing the Estate."

THE ROLE OF THE PROBATE COURT

Probate is conducted under court supervision. Some states have a special *probate, surrogate,* or *chancery* court, while others have a special department of the court to handle probate matters. Although a layperson can handle the details in an uncomplicated case, normally an executor will work with an attorney to settle the estate.

....
CAUTION *Although it is tempting to avoid using an attorney to escape paying attorney's fees, it may be impossible to attend to property transfers without an attorney's help. Likewise, the attorney will be knowledgeable about how to efficiently navigate the local court rules for filings.*
....

All states have local legal forms that need to be filed by certain deadlines and local courts often have their own procedural rules for filing documents. Although the executor does not normally need to make any actual appearances in court, the executor does have to make frequent reports to the court. The executor is responsible for settling the estate and it is important to meet all deadlines promptly.

Why Does Probate Exist?

Probate has a bad reputation among the public. This naturally begs the question, "Why does probate exist?" There is a simple answer to this question. The probate system exists to keep executors, family members, and others from looting an estate.

Years of experience have demonstrated that distribution of property without court supervision leads to unhappy results for all involved. Disgruntled friends, relatives, and employees have been known to abscond with property after a person's death.

EXAMPLE 1 John dies with a will leaving all of his property to his three daughters. Thousands of dollars worth of expensive antiques mysteriously disappear from John's home. Many people had a key to the home and had the opportunity to abscond with the antiques. A disgruntled family member—who had been left out of the will—was eventually found to be the culprit.

EXAMPLE 2 Mary was mentally incompetent during her last few years of life. A relative persuaded her to turn over all of her cash and put it into savings accounts with joint names. At Mary's death, all of this cash passed automatically to the unscrupulous relative and the balance of the estate consisted of only a few sticks of furniture.

EXAMPLE 3 Sara died naming Roger as executor of her estate. Roger had control over the estate's funds and "loaned" money to his own firm. Although he intended to pay the loan back with interest, his own business had a cash flow problem and he was unable to repay the loan. The estate, therefore, was unable to make the gifts provided in the will.

PROBATE COSTS

Probate fees are high and much of the cost is attributable to legal costs. The attorney has to complete a large number of legal forms and may have to appear in court from time to time, depending on the complexity of the issues involved. The more time the attorney spends helping the executor, the higher the legal bills will be. Keep in mind that these bills get paid by the estate, which decreases the amount available for the heirs.

OBSERVATION *Although there may be a strong temptation to let the attorney's staff do much of the executor's work, this can be costly. There is a good deal of work— especially surrounding the management of property—that can be done by the executor.*

Calculation of Attorney Fees

Different states have varying rules regarding attorney fees for probating an estate. Some states have adopted a percentage system. In such a state, the attorney will be paid a flat fee based on the value of the estate. The higher the value, the lower the percentage. In other states the attorney will get a *reasonable fee*. This fee is based on the number of hours the attorney works and the difficulty of the work.

OBSERVATION Reasonable *means what other attorneys of similar experience and competence would charge in similar circumstances, not what the clients view as reasonable. In most parts of the country, attorney fees range between $120 to $200 an hour. However, much of the work can be done by paralegals and other staff people in the law office, and they will have a lower billing rate. An attorney's request for fees may be reduced by the probate judge if it seems unreasonable or unjustified.*

Other Expenses

Attorney fees aren't the only expense of probate. Property must be assessed for the court, so appraisers often have to be hired to do valuations. Tax returns must be filed for both the deceased and the estate, so accountants must be hired. If the decedent died owning over $600,000 worth of property, there will probably be death taxes levied. This type of tax work can be expensive, especially if the estate is audited by the Internal Revenue Service. In general, the larger the probate estate, the larger the costs and the longer the delays. Information on death taxes is found in Chapter 13, "Estate and Gift Tax Basics."

COURT HEARINGS

Some estates can be probated without any court hearings. However, it may be necessary to appear before a judge in some cases. Typically, an attorney is present to advise the executor. The probate court does not sit to hinder resolution of the estate, but it does sit to protect everyone's interest. If, for example, an executor wants to distribute cash to an heir to meet an emergency before creditors have been paid, the court will probably want some explanation for the distribution and assurances that all creditors will be paid.

Occasionally estates and executors become involved in lawsuits. For instance, someone may sue the estate over unresolved business dealings with the deceased before his or her death. Sometimes the executor may have to file a lawsuit.

Additionally, if the decedent ran a business, it is not unusual for lawsuits to be brought against the business after the person's death. Plaintiffs may think that they have better luck after the decedent is no longer present to contest the suit.

EXAMPLE 1 John died in January. In March, Debra, a business associate of John, filed a claim against the estate alleging that John owed her $200,000, representing her share of the profits from a business deal. The executor rejected Debra's claim because there was little paperwork to support it. Debra responded by suing the estate for the $200,000.

EXAMPLE 2 After reviewing the deceased's business records, the executor concludes that the deceased was owed $100,000 on a land sale contract. The debtor refused to pay, offering a number of excuses. The executor was forced to file a lawsuit to recover the money for the heirs.

Streamlined Probate

Many states have a system of *streamlined probate* for estates with modest amounts of property. This procedure does not require an attorney and involves simplified court filings. (See Chapter 14, "Streamlined Probate.")

Will Contests

If a will is contested by a disappointed heir, the cost and delay of probate will increase greatly. Normally, a will is contested in order to have it set aside by the court in favor of an earlier will. In other cases, the challengers want the court to determine that the deceased died without a valid will.

There are a number of grounds upon which wills are contested, including the decedent's mental incompetence at the time the will was signed. Other grounds include the belief that the decedent was subjected to fraud, duress (use of threats), and/or undue influence—the overuse of persuasion by a trusted person when the deceased was in a vulnerable state of mind. These types of complications are considered in Chapter 11, "Will Contests."

Probate Jurisdiction

Generally, probate will take place in the state where the decedent was *domiciled,* or living, at the time of death. The concept of *domicile* requires not only physical presence in the state, but also the intent to reside there.

EXAMPLE John lives in New York, but is vacationing in Florida when he dies. Florida would not necessarily be the jurisdiction to administer the probate because John probably did not intend to reside in Florida permanently.

If a person has retired to a new area, his new home will probably be his domicile as long as he intends to stay there permanently. When retirees split their time between two homes in different states, it can be difficult to determine domicile.

Factors that establish domicile include:
- the amount of time spent at a location
- the state in which the individual is registered to vote
- the state issuing the deceased's driver's license
- the address where Social Security checks are delivered
- the address where bank and brokerage statements are delivered
- the location of a safe-deposit box
- the location of the deceased's church or temple
- the address on tax returns
- the certificate of domicile (in some states only)

Out-of-State Probate (Ancillary Probate)

Additional proceedings and an ancillary administrator may be necessary because a state court and personal representative only have power within one state. For example, suppose that a resident of New York dies and his executor starts a probate proceeding in New York's Surrogate's Court. Although the New York court has power over the decedent's property in New York, the New York court and the New York state executor have no special legal powers in Florida. Therefore, if the deceased owned a vacation home in Florida, an ancillary proceeding in the Florida probate court would be required to administer that property. Not surprisingly, ancillary administration adds substantial costs to the probate bill because there is duplication of efforts and of legal bills.

Assets Passing Outside Probate

Finally, keep in mind that some assets are not subject to probate, namely, property held in joint names, such as joint bank accounts, real estate property held in joint names, property held in *inter vivos* (living) trusts, and life insurance. These "will substitutes" will be discussed in more detail below.

ROLE OF THE WILL

If the decedent died with a legally valid will, the will controls disposition of the decedent's property and many other details of probate administration. Many people die without a will, however; the consequences of such an event are discussed later in the chapter.

A person who makes a valid will is not only able to carefully control posthumous distribution of her property, but is also able to designate the executor who will administer the estate after death and who will also have the responsibility to take possession of all the deceased's property and distribute it according to the deceased's wishes.

The will allows the decedent to specifically designate who should receive property and how and when they should receive it. Absent a will, state law controls the distribution of property, which will normally be awarded to the nearest relatives. Necessarily, state statutes cannot make special provisions for needy relatives, or relatives who have fallen into disfavor, or relatives who simply do not need bequests because of their personal wealth. Precise distribution of a decedent's property is only possible if the person had made a will or a trust. Wills are discussed in more detail in Chapter 6, "Understanding Wills."

IN THE ABSENCE OF A WILL

It is not enough to plan and write a will. A will must be signed and properly witnessed before it can operate as a will. If the decedent did not complete this procedure, the will is invalid. If there is no valid will, the estate is intestate, and the intestacy statute controls the distribution of property. In other words, when a person dies without a legally valid will, the state law of the decedent's domicile will control the distribution of property. As mentioned earlier, a person's domicile is the state in which she resides and intends to make her permanent home. If a person has two homes in different states, only one state will be her domicile.

If a person fails to write a will, the law, in effect, writes one for her. Because it is impossible for the law to tailor a will to a person's particular family circumstances, the law attempts to write a generic will that would reflect the circumstances of the average person.

Although some individuals believe that the state automatically receives intestate property, this is simply not true in any state. In every state, property is distributed to the next of kin under the intestacy statute. In other words, because most people leave their property to close relatives, if a person dies without a will, the law will distribute her property to her closest blood relatives. If, however, a person dies without a will and she has no close family members, then her property will go to the state government. When this happens, the property is said to "escheat" to the state. If a decedent dies without a valid will, is the last of a family line, and has no surviving family, then the property would escheat to the state.

Scheme of Distribution

In most states the intestacy statute will award property to either *lineal* or *collateral* relatives. A lineal relative is a direct relation, such as a grandfather, father, son, or grandson. A collateral relative is one who shares a common ancestor, such as brothers and sisters, cousins who have a common grandparent, and uncles, aunts, nephews, and nieces. Individual states vary as to the degree of kinship that constitutes these relationships. In some states, distribution will be made to parents, children, grandparents, grandchildren, great-grandchildren, uncles, and aunts, but not to cousins.

Unmarried Couples

Although distributing property to close relatives is appropriate for most decedents, it can work a real hardship on unmarried partners. If one person in an unmarried couple dies without a will, the other partner may get nothing because he is not a legal relative under the law. It is essential that both partners in an unmarried couple have a will to prevent this.

State-by-State Variations

States vary somewhat in their treatment of distribution in intestacy.

EXAMPLE Assume that Jane Brown dies without a will. Though her two children are not living, Jane is survived by three grandchildren. The first grandchild is a daughter of Jane's first child, and the second and third grandchildren are the children of Jane's other child. In some states, each of the grandchildren would receive a one-third share of the estate because there are three heirs. In other states, the first grandchild would receive one-half of the property; the second and third grandchildren would each receive one-quarter. The estate is divided in this way because each grandchild traces his or her inheritance through his or her deceased parent.

Adopted, Illegitimate, and Posthumous Children

Adopted children, illegitimate children, and posthumous children (children conceived but not born before the death of the deceased), are treated as any other children under the intestacy statutes in most states. However, some states have special rules in this area. Also, many states have special rules for step-children and "half-bloods." A half-blood shares only one common ancestor with the deceased, such as a half-brother, whose mother was also the deceased's mother, but whose father was not the deceased's biological father.

AVOIDING PROBATE: USING WILL SUBSTITUTES AND LIVING TRUSTS

Because probate has such a bad reputation, many

people are attracted to the idea of avoiding probate. With advance planning, many people can help avoid their heirs probate or at least minimize its cost and duration. The main tools to avoid probate are will substitutes and living trusts.

Will Substitutes

Any transfer of property that occurs outside the estate probate process operates as a will substitute. Because the property's title is transferred without falling into the probate estate, the property skirts around probate. There are three primary advantages to this technique. First, the transfer of title is immediate upon the death of the decedent. Transfers from probate estates take many months, or years in extreme cases.

Second, the title transfer will go unpublicized. Because the transfer is not made in the will, it will be difficult and in some cases impossible for the public to learn the details of the transfer. If property is left in a will, which is a public document, the will's contents are available for the general public to see at the probate court.

Finally, and most importantly, will substitutes reduce probate fees. Fees are often calculated on a percentage of the value of the estate. When property changes title outside the estate, fees go down—sometimes drastically. Even in states in which attorneys charge by the hour rather than as a percentage of the estate's value, will substitutes can reduce legal fees because property transfers will be simplified. This in turn reduces the amount of time an attorney spends working on a probate case.

Joint Ownership

In some states, the costs associated with probating even a small estate are so high that it is far more economical to leave most of property in will substitutes. The most common type of will substitute is joint ownership. Newly acquired property titles can be put in joint names or existing property can be retitled in joint names. Joint titles pass to the co-owner(s) automatically at the time of death, and consequently never pass through the estate.

EXAMPLE Mary opens a joint bank account with her brother Martin, and the account agreement specifies that the co-owner of the account is a joint owner with right of survivorship. In most states, Martin would automatically become the owner of the account on Mary's death. This is true even if Mary's will provides that all of her property is to go to a particular charity. Note carefully that ownership must be taken as "joint owners with right of survivorship" rather than as "tenants in common."

Various kinds of property can be jointly owned. In addition to joint bank accounts with rights of survivorship, bank account trusts, often referred to as "Totten trusts," and U.S. Savings Bonds are often owned jointly.

Although spouses and other family members commonly hold property jointly, there is no legal limitation on who may be a joint owner. Additionally, an individual may make a gift of a fractional interest in property. For example, a person could give a deed to a one-half interest in a piece of real estate.

Although joint ownership is the most common type of will substitute, it is hardly the only one. Other types of will substitutes include:

- life insurance proceeds;
- U.S. Savings Bonds with a payable-on-death designation;
- annuities;
- custodial accounts for minors; and
- trusts.

Each of these will substitutes has a beneficiary designation that takes precedence over any stipulations in a will. Moreover, when the person dies, title to the property automatically vests in the beneficiary without going through probate. Because in many states both the executor's fee and attorney fees are calculated based on the value of the estate, such will substitutes can effectively reduce probate fees.

Disadvantages of Joint Ownership

Creating joint interests in property is not always advisable, even between spouses. Property can be lost if one spouse files for bankruptcy—or worse, divorce. Property laws vary state by state and can be complicated. Although beneficiary designations can be handled by laypersons, retitling property in joint names should only be done with the advice of an attorney.

The disposition of joint property at the time of death depends on the technical designation of the co-ownership. State laws distinguish between a "tenancy in the entireties," a "tenancy in common," and "joint tenancy with right of survivorship." These legal designations of ownership supersede any designation in a will. For example, assume that two sisters own a parcel of real estate as joint tenants. On the death of the first sister the property becomes the property of the second sister. This would be true even if the deceased sister's will leaves all her real estate to her husband. The jointly held property passes outside the estate and the will simply does not apply to that parcel.

Future Interests

Besides concurrent joint ownership, it is possible for an individual to give away so-called future interests in property during his lifetime or in a will. A person who has a future interest has an ownership interest in property but with delayed possession.

EXAMPLE Grey wants his son to have his farm after his death, but Grey wishes to live on the property for the remainder of his life. Grey could retain a *life estate* in the property and give his son a *remainder* interest. Both Grey and his son would be owners but only Grey would have current possession. Grey would have the right to use the property for his life, but it would automatically become his son's property on Grey's death. This type of ownership is also an effective will substitute and the property can bypass probate. There are a number of different future interests that can be tailored to meet particular needs.

Tax Implications

There may be federal estate tax implications even though property passes outside the jurisdiction of state probate laws. There is also a federal gift tax that may apply to gifts greater than $10,000 in value (see Chapter 8, "Paying Creditors and Taxes"). Transferring a joint interest in property may create a taxable gift. This sort of tax determination should be made by an attorney.

Living Trusts

Another type of will substitute is a living trust (also referred to as a *loving trust*) which holds all of your property. Living trusts have become increasingly popular because they avoid the delay and expense of probate. However, in some states, because probate costs are not as high as generally perceived, a living trust may provide little in the way of savings.

There are both advantages and disadvantages in using a living trust. A living trust operates as a will substitute. Instead of using a will to distribute property at death, a person transfers legal title to her property to the living trust during her life. When she dies, the trustee who administers the trust will distribute the property to those parties that the decedent designated in the trust. Although many trusts are irrevocable, trusts used as will substitutes are typically set up as revocable trusts so that they may be easily changed or even canceled.

Advantages of Living Trusts

The biggest advantage of a living trust is the avoidance of state probate fees and delays. Because legal title to the property has been transferred to the trust, the property will pass outside probate. Accordingly, there will be little delay in distributing the assets, and probate fees will largely be eliminated.

Another advantage of the living trust is the absence of publicity. Unlike a will, a living trust is not normally a court document, and there is often no need to file the trust in a courthouse. Accordingly the provisions of a living trust are not normally made part of the public record. If a person wants to escape public attention, using a living trust makes sense. If a person wants to make a gift that might prove embarrassing to his family, the trustee can make the distribution privately. (The person could also set up a small trust for this purpose, without substituting a living trust for a will.) Additionally, because of the confidential nature of the living trust, it is hard for disgruntled relatives to challenge.

Disadvantages of Living Trusts

There are some disadvantages to living trusts that are not always apparent. First, there are set-up costs and trustee's fees. In states where probate fees are relatively low, the costs associated with the trust will be about the same as those that would arise in the probate of a will, assuming that the person's affairs are in good order.

Selecting a Trustee

A person must select a trustee who will be absolutely honest. The person establishing the trust is free to select either an individual or an institution, such as a trust company or bank, to serve as trustee. Although a trustee has a fiduciary duty to protect the trust's assets, individuals have on occasion stolen trust assets. Because the trust will not be supervised by the probate court, there is no one to supervise the handling of the property other than the trustee.

Because the trustee of the living trust will be working closely with the family and other heirs during their bereavement, the trustee's personal qualities are important. If possible, the person establishing the trust should take the time to introduce the heirs to the trustee and make sure that they understand how the trust will work after the decedent's death.

Deciding Between a Will and a Living Trust

Setting up a living trust is not terribly complicated, and in fact, the terms of most living trusts will closely parallel the provisions in a typical will. Attorneys who prepare wills also typically prepare living trusts for clients upon request.

The fee for establishing a trust typically will be higher than for preparing a will, and additional costs will be incurred related to transferring legal title to the assets. However, because the trust will be outside probate, the fees after death should be minimal.

....
WARNING *Unfortunately some mail-order and seminar promoters are selling expensive living trust packages that promise more than they can deliver. For a large fee these promoters sell a book or booklet and a set of legal forms to complete. Although the forms may be legally sufficient, simply filling them out does not put property into the trust and thereby avoid probate. Only actual legal transfer of the assets to the trust can accomplish this (for example, by changing the name on a deed to real property). Although a person buys one of these packages assuming that their expensive living trust will bypass probate and estate taxes, the opposite is true. Without the legal transfer of assets to the trust, there will be no tax savings and probate fees will not be avoided. Additionally, the individual will have spent hundreds or even thousands of dollars needlessly.*
....

PROBATE TIMELINE

Preliminary Matters

- Locate will, letter of instructions
- Arrange funeral and burial or cremation
- Meet with other survivors
- Court appoints executor

Executor's Duties

- Claims for pensions, life insurance, Social Security filed
- Identify and collect and secure decedent's property
- Inventory and appraise the property
- Invest liquid funds
- Commence or defend lawsuits if needed
- Identify creditors and evaluate debts
- Provide support for surviving spouse and dependents
- Manage assets and/or business
- Pay debts
- File tax returns and pay taxes
- Determine gifts to heirs
- Provide probate court with plan of distribution
- Distribute assets to heirs
- Pay executor and attorney
- Provide probate court with final accounting
- Discharge of executor

CHAPTER 4

The Executor

INTRODUCTION

The probate process is carried out by the executor or personal representative. This chapter explains the role of the executor in the probate process, including the executor's basic duties and a description of how the executor works with the attorney. The chapter also discusses the executor's role in communicating with family members during the probate process. The chapter concludes with a discussion that should help you decide whether you should serve as executor. The basic qualifications necessary to serve as executor and details on court appointment of an executor are found in the next chapter, Chapter 5, "Court Appointment of the Executor and Probate Initiation."

This chapter will describe:

- the executor's role
- the executor's compensation
- the executor's duties
- working with the attorney
- the importance of communicating with family members
- how to decide if you should accept appointment as executor

ROLE OF THE EXECUTOR

The executor, who is normally named in the will, is in charge of "settling" the estate. The executor must see that the four basic goals of the probate process are carried out, namely:

1. identification of the decedent's will, if any;
2. identification and collection of the decedent's property;
3. identification, validation, and payment of creditors' claims, including taxes; and
4. distribution of property to the heirs.

Seeking Assistance

Although the executor is responsible for overseeing the entire probate process, the executor will typically be working with an attorney and other experts, such as an accountant and appraiser. Some executors have a great deal of expertise and will be working with little assistance, while others will be doing little more than signing papers prepared by the estate's attorney. The majority of executors fall somewhere in between these two extremes.

At times the probate process can be confusing. There is often a maze of legal rules and procedures and little written guidance for laypersons. At times the executor may not be sure what to do next. If the executor is unsure how to proceed, he or she should check with the estate's attorney, who will be able to help guide the executor through the probate process.

EXAMPLE The will provides that a family member should receive the deceased's car. The heir approaches the executor and asks for the keys. The executor should consult with the estate's attorney to determine if the heir should get custody of the car during the probate proceedings.

Court Appointment

Even though an executor is named in a will, she is only empowered to act after being appointed by the court. By law, some persons are not qualified to serve. For example, in some states a person convicted of a felony cannot serve as an executor. In some states a surviving spouse has the right to ask the court to appoint her executor even if the deceased's will names someone else. Even though a will names an executor, this choice can be challenged and the court may decide to name someone else if good cause is established for replacing the original executor. Many wills provide for "contingent executors." They name a party who they expect will settle the estate, but they also name an alternate in case the first party is unable of unwilling to serve. It is possible to name a bank or a trust company as executor. Qualification and appointment of executors are discussed in Chapter 5, "Court Appointment of the Executor and Probate Initiation."

Note carefully that a codicil to a will may also name an executor. *Codicil* means "little will" and it is used to update a will. For example, a person may want to change the disposition of one item of property, such as the family car. In the past, instead of typing up an entirely new will, an attorney might produce a one-page codicil renaming the person who will receive the car. The codicil must be signed and witnessed with the same formalities as a regular will.

Previously, codicils were popular because they eliminated the chore of retyping and proof-reading a multipage will typed on a typewriter. Today codicils are becoming more rare because wills are produced on word processors and a revised version can easily be run off in a few minutes. However, there are still wills that have codicils.

When there is an executor named in a will and a different executor named in a codicil, the document with the later date controls, assuming that it's in proper legal form. If you find two codicils that each name a different executor the same rule applies: the document with the most recent date is valid. This is because wills—unlike contracts—are "ambulatory," that is, they can be changed at any time before death. Wills and codicils are discussed in greater detail in Chapter 6, "Understanding Wills."

Terminology

The feminine form of executor is *executrix*. The official title now used in most states is *personal representative,* which applies to persons of either gender. This book will use the term executor. Although the titles are different, executors and personal representatives have identical duties; personal representative is merely a more modern term.

Potential executors should keep in mind that the terms *executor* and *personal representative* are generally interchangeable in the same way that the terms *shareholders* and *stockholders* are; they essentially mean the same thing. Even in a state that uses the term "personal representative," a funeral director or insurance agent may talk about checking with the executor. They are merely being imprecise. There will not be a separate executor *and* a personal representative. There will be one or the other. State law will decide if the correct legal title is executor or personal representative.

Administrators

An estate may be settled by an administrator. An administrator will be named if the deceased died without a will or with a will that is declared invalid. The administrator has the same duties as an executor.

OBSERVATION *The majority of Americans die without a valid will. Accordingly, most estates are actually settled by an administrator.*

Administrators may be appointed for a variety of reasons. The court may be called upon to appoint an administrator even though an executor is named in the will. This might happen when the executor is in some way "disqualified" from serving. An executor might be disqualified because of lack of mental capacity, conviction of a crime, or even non-residence in the state (state laws vary on this point). This type of administrator may be referred to as an "administrator with the will annexed," or "administrator c.t.a." *(cum testamento annexo).*

Sometimes an administrator must be named because the original executor cannot complete the job for one reason or another. This type of administrator is referred to as an "administrator *de bonis non*"—or simply "D.B.N."—which means administrator of "goods not administered." If the executor dies and is replaced by an administrator, the administrator is known as an "administrator c.t.a.d.b.n."

Courts may also appoint a *special administrator* at the beginning of a probate case. The special administrator is authorized to act before the actual executor is confirmed by the court. The special administrator is a temporary appointment and will normally be replaced by the executor. For example, a court might appoint a special administrator to sell perishable inventory in the deceased's store.

In most states courts must follow state law in appointing administrators. Preference is typically given to a surviving spouse. Next in line are children, with preference going to the child who gets the largest share of the estate. If there is no surviving spouse or children, a creditor may be named administrator.

RESPONSIBILITIES OF THE EXECUTOR
Liability Concerns

Depending on the provisions of the will, the executor may or may not be held personally liable for actions taken on behalf of the estate, and may or may not be required to post a bond that will be paid from the estate. An executor can be sued personally for actions she takes on behalf of the estate. Some wills provide that the executor will not be held personally responsible for debts. When the will and probate court require the executor to post a bond, the bonding company will satisfy any legal judgments against the executor, but the executor may have to indemnify (repay) the bonding company for amounts paid out.

In many states a will may waive the requirement to have a bond. However, the court always has the power to require a bond to protect creditors and other interested parties, if it determines that one is

needed. State law determines the exact requirements. In many states the amount of the bond is twice the actual value of the "personal property" (non–real estate in the estate).

Fiduciary Duty

The executor has a strict "fiduciary duty" to protect the property in the estate and to avoid all improprieties and conflicts of interest with respect to the assets in the estate. In most states the executor owes this duty *both* to the estate and to the heirs. Generally an executor has the same sort of duty as the trustee of a trust—a duty that goes beyond mere honesty. A person with a fiduciary duty must actively look out for the best interests of the persons that he serves.

To understand this concept better, consider the process of selling a used car. If you sell the car to a stranger, it is your duty to be honest. You have no special duty to speak up and tell the potential buyer that the car is sluggish and guzzles gas. On the other hand, you do have to truthfully answer any questions the prospective buyer poses. If your sister wants to buy the car, however, you might dissuade her if you had concerns about the car. You would want to go beyond answering her questions honestly, and actively look out for her best interests. This is what a "fiduciary duty" requires—the executor must actively look out for the best interests of the estate, the creditors, and the heirs.

Accounting for Funds

An executor has an absolute duty to account for all the funds in his care. The court will not discharge the executor from his duties or close the probate case until the executor has made a full "accounting" of all cash and other property under his supervision and control.

The executor must reimburse heirs and/or creditors for any missing cash or property. Executors are sometimes tempted to "borrow" estate funds for personal purposes. This is considered theft and as such is illegal. Even honest people are sometimes driven to desperate acts by drug and alcohol abuse, job or family stress, depression, or a financial emergency. For this reason many wills name co-executors. Although executors operate under court supervision that does not always prevent an executor from stealing from the estate.

There are also less obvious breaches of duty; even innocent mistakes may be a breach of duty. Executors must scrupulously account for every dollar of estate assets. All paperwork must be retained because missing records may cast doubt on the integrity of the executor. The executor must also invest any spare cash to make it productive. For example, an executor might invest the estate's excess cash in a money market account. However, some states still have very restrictive laws that prohibit the executor from investing cash in short-term investments such as money market accounts, even though most prudent business people would consider them a safe and prudent investment.

FEES

The executor is normally compensated for his time and work, and in most states receives a fee based on a percentage of the estate's value. Because court probate rules vary from state to state, fee arrangements also differ. In some states the law requires a reasonable fee, which comes from the estate.

There is no clear-cut definition of reasonable, but courts look at the following factors:
- time and work required to settle the estate
- complexity of the problems
- skills required
- customary fees for such services
- dollar value of the estate
- results obtained

In most states, if the will appoints more than one executor, the co-executors split the fee. In a few states each co-executor receives the full fee.

Executor's Fee

Executors receive a handsome fee for their work—based either on the size of the estate or on a state-regulated "reasonable" basis.

Executor's fees are typically higher than attorney's fees. In many states, the executor will receive a fee calculated on the size of the estate. For example, in California, the executor gets a fee based on the following formula:

4 percent of the first $15,000;
3 percent of the next $85,000;
2 percent of the next $900,000;
1.5 percent of the next $2,000,000; and
1 percent on any excess.

New York uses a slightly different formula:

5 percent of the first $100,000;
4 percent of the next $200,000;
3 percent of the next $700,000;
2.5 percent of the next $4,000,000; and
2 percent of any excess.

On a $1 million estate, the executor would receive $21,150 in California, and $34,000 in New York. These fees can be increased if the executor has to handle any matter that is out of the ordinary. As mentioned previously, many other states' laws limit the executor to a reasonable fee, but it will probably not be much different from the fees calculated by formula.

WARNING *Heirs may feel that the executor does not deserve to receive anything other than nominal compensation. This feeling may be the result of pure greed on their part because the executor's compensation typically reduces the gifts to the heirs. However the animosity may result because the heirs have no idea of the amount of time the executor must devote to the estate. Problems can be minimized by keeping heirs aware of the extent and difficulty of the executor's work.*

An executor can agree to waive either all or a portion of the compensation. This would most likely occur when a family member assumes the executor's duties. If a surviving spouse is named executor, it does not make sense for him to receive compensation.

Spouses typically receive the "residue" of the estate. The residue is all the property that is not specifically given away in the will. In this situation, the executor's fee merely reduces the property the spouse/executor would have received as a gift from the estate. However, the executor's fee is subject to income tax while a distribution from an estate is not. Accordingly, by waiving the fee the surviving spouse can minimize her own income taxes to increase the net amount available from the estate.

In larger estates (those with over $600,000) the executor's fee will reduce death taxes, so a fee may be advantageous. These taxes run between 37 and 55 percent, so the tax savings to the estate can be impressive and may actually exceed the executor's income tax costs. The attorney or the CPA preparing the federal estate tax return should decide whether to waive or exact the executor's fee. Estate taxes are discussed in more detail in Chapter 13, "Estate and Gift Tax Basics."

WORKING WITH AN ATTORNEY

Unless the executor tries to settle the estate without legal advice, he will work closely with the attorney. The will may name a specific attorney to help probate the estate. However, the executor will normally have power to select a different attorney if he wishes. It is important to have a good working relationship with the attorney, so the attorney's personality is an important consideration. If the deceased provided for a particular attorney, the attorney is probably familiar with the deceased's affairs and desires, and may be the best qualified lawyer to serve. An attorney named in a will may decline to serve because he is too busy or because he has retired from active practice. In this case, the executor will be responsible for finding another competent attorney.

The division of work between the executor and the attorney depends on the expertise and the inclination of the executor. Although the executor is normally "responsible" for performing certain duties, in many cases the attorney—or more typically, someone in the attorney's office—actually performs much of the work.

EXAMPLE The executor has responsibility for paying the estate's debts and for keeping records of those payments. If the executor is actively involved in settling the estate the executor will be handling all of these details with the attorney's advice. However, it is not uncommon for an executor to let someone in the attorney's office handle such details.

DUTIES OF THE EXECUTOR

As mentioned above, the executor has four basic duties: 1) identification of the decedent's will, if any; 2) identification, collection, and management of the decedent's property; 3) identification, validation, and payment of creditors' claims, including taxes; and 4) distribution of property to the heirs.

The extent of the executor's duties will depend on a number of factors including:
- complexity of the deceased's affairs
- existence of significant investments
- existence of a business
- extent of predeath estate planning
- organization of the deceased's property and records

If the deceased was relatively well-to-do and had significant investments and/or a business, the executor will have to manage those properties which could take a fair amount of time. On the other hand, if the deceased only had a house, a car, and a few investments, then the administration should not be too time-consuming. If the deceased had engaged in estate planning and died leaving a well-planned will, the executor's job will be easier. Similarly if the deceased had his or her property in order and left detailed and easy-to-follow records, this will simplify the executor's job.

WARNING *The executor is not automatically appointed guardian of any orphans. The will designates the guardian of any minor children. In some cases the will may name the executor as guardian. If the will does not appoint a guardian or if the deceased died without a will, the court will have to appoint a guardian. In most states there is a legal preference to name blood relatives as guardians.*

WARNING *When there is a surviving spouse or children, state laws provide that the executor must provide for them during the pendency of the probate proceeding. The executor should consult with the estate's attorney about support obligations.*

Identification of the Will

The first step in the probate process is identification of the will. The will typically names a person or institution as executor. If the executor does not have a copy of the will for some reason, the executor will need to find the will and present it to the court. In some cases more than one version of a will may be found. It is ultimately up to the probate court to determine which version is the deceased's legal will.

If no valid will is found, the court will appoint someone to oversee the probate process. This person will have the title "administrator" in most states. An administrator essentially has the same duties as an executor.

Collection and Management of Property

After the will is found and the court formally appoints the executor, she must then gather together the decedent's property and provide an inventory for the court. The executor must identify and pay any bills and taxes due, and finally distribute the remaining property to the heirs in accordance with the will. Unless the executor chooses to go it alone, she will be working with an attorney who will help at each step in the process.

The executor's very first duty, then, is to identify and protect the assets of the estate. This is referred to as "marshalling" the assets of the estate. If the property is well-organized and documented, the job of the executor will be far easier.

When a person dies, much of his property will fall into his "estate." The property in the estate is first applied to pay any debts of the decedent. Only then is the remaining property distributed to the deceased's heirs. If the decedent died leaving a valid will, the property will be distributed according to the instructions left. If the decedent died without a legally valid will, the decedent dies "intestate," and state law will control how the property is distributed.

Identifying and Paying Creditor Claims

After establishing the will, the executor must identify and validate creditor claims, and then use assets from the estate to pay those claims. Most, but not all, states require the executor to give notice of the death to creditors by publication in local newspapers. Known creditors of the deceased should get personal notice. Finally, the executor must distribute whatever property is left in the estate after all debts and taxes

have been paid, according to the provisions of the will. All this is done under court supervision.

The executor may be called upon to perform additional duties, often with the assistance of an attorney. For example, the executor will have to ensure that a surviving spouse and any dependent children are cared for while the will is being probated. The executor may have to petition the court to authorize funds for the support of the dependents during the probate proceedings.

If the estate contains a business, the executor must oversee its management, or hire competent managers to do so. Additionally, the executor must see to it that the terms of any binding contracts will be performed. Somewhat surprisingly, estates are often sued. The executor must defend the estate in the event of a lawsuit, and may sue to recover assets on behalf of the estate.

Distribution of Property to the Heirs
Communicating with Family Members
An important duty of the executor is to communicate with family members during the settlement of the estate. This can be a difficult duty because family members may be bereaved, in shock, or in denial about the death. A number of decisions have to be made fairly promptly and may prove difficult for certain family members. Decisions must be made about the time and type of funeral and about burial arrangements. In some cases the executor may be forced to sell a family home to pay debts against the estates, even though the home was left to one of the heirs in the will. Other heirs may be disappointed because they are not mentioned in the will, or were left property that no longer exists. Promises may have been made by the deceased but not kept. All of these scenarios emphasize the need for communication between the executor and surviving family members.

· ·

WARNING *When family members become angry about the estate settlement, the executor—not the deceased—may become the target for their anger. Those who are not knowledgeable about the probate process may mistakenly think the executor has power to change the will, or that the executor, rather than the decedent's will or intestacy statutes, is responsible for determining property distribution.*

· ·

The executor has a duty to act efficiently and unemotionally, but she may have to deal with distraught family members who are not only in no hurry, but resent the executor's desire to move the process along.

A family may not be emotionally prepared to sort through the deceased's property. The executor is required to have the property inventoried and valued, and assets must be sold to pay off the deceased's creditors in a matter of months. If the family is grieving, they may resent the executor's actions.

On the other hand, some heirs who are unfamiliar with the probate process may not understand why they can't get their inheritances the day after the funeral. They probably suspect that the executor and the attorneys are plotting to deprive them of their property. Of course, nothing of the sort will happen. Delays occur because property must be inventoried and creditors—including the tax collectors—must be paid before the heirs get their distributions.

Coping with Grief

The executor must be prepared to deal with the grief of family members—especially that of a surviving spouse. Most people die when they are over age 65, and husbands tend to predecease their wives. Beyond their initial shock and grief, these surviving spouses may face severe loneliness and depression in the months following the spouse's death. The spouse may be asked to make a number of decisions that would be very difficult at any time, let alone when she is grieving.

EXAMPLE The decedent's last illness ran up extraordinary medical bills that were not reimbursed by insurance. The hospital is pressing for payment and the only solution is sale of the home that has been in the family for thirty years. The sale of the family home can be very traumatic at any time. Losing a home on the heels of losing a spouse could be psychologically crushing. The surviving spouse may need extra support from family and friends, or even professional counselling.

WARNING *Although the executor can help survivors deal with grief, the executor is probably not a professional psychologist. The executor needs to be alert for heirs who need professional counselling to address their loss and also address the demands and joys of life.*

Dealing with Family Conflicts

A death in the family may bring a family together, but it may also revive or create family conflicts. Ideally a death may make family members recall all the memories and experiences they've shared and may cause them to put aside their differences. However, a death or funeral may also revive past animosities among family members. Long dormant rivalries may resurface—especially when one family member is perceived to be favored over another.

The will itself may ignite a family feud. Relatives who have gotten along over the years may suddenly be at odds when a will leaves a disproportionate amount to one part of the family.

EXAMPLE A father died, survived by three married daughters. Intending to ensure that the daughters have equal levels of comfort and security in life, the father's will provided that his youngest daughter, married to a schoolteacher, would get significantly more than her sisters, both of whom are married to successful businessmen. The two older sisters felt that they had been slighted by their father and resented the youngest daughter's windfall.

It Helps to Have a Thick Skin

The perfect executor needs not only business sense but also the ability to communicate with a variety of people under sometimes stressful circumstances. It probably helps to have a thick skin and the ability to shrug off criticism from those who are not knowledgeable about the probate process, or those whose emotional state leads them to say or do things they would not normally say or do.

SHOULD YOU ACCEPT APPOINTMENT?

The person named as executor has an absolute right to decline the appointment. She does not need any excuse not to serve—she can decline for any reason or no reason at all. The individual named as executor should consider the pros and cons before she accepts appointment. Being named in a will as executor doesn't mean that person should serve.

There may be others more willing or capable to serve the estate.

Declining Appointment

It is easier for the named executor to decline at the outset than to resign part way through the probate process. An executor named in a will has a right to decline appointment. However, the named person must communicate this desire to the estate's attorney at the outset. If not, the court will appoint the person named in the will. Once the court appoints the executor, the executor must get the court's approval to resign.

Attributes of a Good Executor

The choice of an executor is an important one because the executor controls the tenor of the probate process. The executor will be called upon to make decisions with business and legal consequences; but more importantly, the executor will be dealing closely with bereaved family members and should understand family relationships and expectations. Although legal and business experience are helpful, the ability to work with family members is probably even more important. An executor without technical knowledge will have access to the attorney, accountants, and appraisers should any technical questions arise.

A good choice for an executor would be a competent and knowledgeable relative, such as the surviving spouse or next of kin, such as children, parents, grandchildren, brothers and sisters, and nieces and nephews. In fact, most people name their spouse as executor. Alternatively, many people name a close friend or business advisor, such as a CPA. Still other people prefer to name a trust department as executor because of its greater expertise.

Using an Outsider

Sometimes someone outside the family may be the best executor, especially when the family has a history of conflict. Sibling rivalries and parent-child conflicts often persist into adulthood. If one or more children are not on good terms with their mother, for example, having the mother serve as executor of her spouse's estate may exacerbate family conflicts. Even an adult child may feel that he will not be given a fair share by a parent or sibling he dislikes or distrusts. Someone outside the family may be perceived as a neutral party who would be able to settle the estate without favoring any particular individuals.

Institutional Executors

A bank's trust department can act as executor of the estate. In fact many wills name a bank as executor, or list a bank as a contingent (backup) executor in the event the named executor cannot or will not serve. A bank or trust company is a good choice when a number of investments or a business must be sold. A bank will have a staff that specializes in overseeing investments, collecting property, and valuing and selling investments and business assets.

Joint Executors

Some wills appoint joint executors who serve together. This can create problems if the two do not agree.

EXAMPLE A successful businessman appointed several executors to settle his estate. Unfortunately, the executors resented one another and a power struggle erupted for control of the estate. The estate used several hundred thousands of dollars of the heirs' property to pay the subsequent legal fees.

Replacement

An executor must agree to serve and can decline or even resign for almost any reason. Accordingly, most decedents name an executor only after that person has agreed in advance to serve. Because the executor may be unwilling or unable to serve, it is a good idea for the will to name a contingent executor. If none is named, the court will appoint an administrator to settle the estate. Courts will usually select a family member for this duty.

Time Considerations

Settling an estate can be quite time-consuming, although in most cases it is only a part-time job. Most estates take about a year to settle. Some estates are wound up sooner, although some can remain pending for a number of years. The amount of time that will be required depends on the complexity of the estate. If the estate is comprised of just a home, personal property, an auto, and a few investments, then the amount of time required should not be too great and should occupy the executor for only a number of months. On the other hand, if the decedent owned a business and many investments, there may be a good deal of work, and settling the estate may be a full-time job.

REASONS TO DECLINE

The estate will be probated in the deceased's state of domicile. If the executor lives far away, it will be harder to settle the estate because she won't have immediate access to property, the local attorney, the courthouse, or the heirs and family members. The executor also needs to consider whether any potential conflicts of interest exist that would prevent her from serving the estate without bias or favoritism. If the executor has a history of feuding with some, but not all, of the heirs, this could influence decisions that may pit one heir against the other. This becomes especially tricky if the executor is an heir herself; as executor she may have to make a decision that could be construed as self-serving.

For example, assume that an estate provides that the executor will receive the residue of the estate after other gifts have been distributed. In other words, the executor will get any property not mentioned in the will. Suppose a decedent's brother appears with a letter to him from the deceased. The brother argues that the letter contains an acknowledgment of indebtedness, and that he is owed $20,000 from the decedent's estate. As a legitimate creditor, the brother should be paid before any property is distributed to heirs. Suppose, however, that after reading the letter, the executor is not convinced that the decedent made any promises at all, and didn't acknowledge any debt to his brother. Because of the lack of evidence, the executor denies the brother's claim. This creates a delicate situation because the estate's residue will not be reduced, and the executor will profit at the brother's expense. The issue may become explosive because the brother may tell other family members that the executor is stealing what's rightfully his, and of course he may believe it. What's worse, other family members without full information may believe him. Although most executors do not run into such problems, others have described their role as executor as the worst period of their life.

If an individual is already overwhelmed by his own family or business commitments, taking on the responsibility of executorship may be too much. The additional work and responsibility of settling an estate can create both physical and emotional stress. If the named executor doesn't have adequate time and energy to devote to the task, he will be letting down the heirs and other family members who are depending on him. He should decline and let somebody else settle the estate.

For some executors, settling an estate is not a pleasant experience because they have to deal with attorneys and the court system, unhappy business associates of the deceased, or angry or disappointed heirs. If the deceased's will leaves property to an ex-spouse as well as a current one, the executor may have to handle family friction. If the deceased was in the middle of a divorce at the time of death, this may create further difficulties in settling the estate. Such possibilities should be considered before a person agrees to act as executor.

Will Contests

Occasionally disappointed heirs bring a "will contest" to set aside a will. This typically happens when there is a new "deathbed will" that disinherits one or more family members. The will contest is a lawsuit which may take years to resolve. If it appears that the will may cause major problems with certain family members, the executor may have an unpleasant experience. Will contests are described in detail in Chapter 11, "Will Contests."

Lawsuits Against the Executor

Executors sometimes get sued. Executors can be liable for mismanagement of assets, whether intentional or through carelessness. The executor may have to reimburse the estate for any losses. The executor may also be liable to third parties with whom he deals. The executor may be sued for what he does personally or for what his "agents" do. An agent is someone the executor hires. For example, suppose an executor decides to sell some nonproductive property and hires a real estate agent. Suppose the realtor tells the buyer that the property is at least two acres in size. After the sale, the buyer has the property surveyed and finds that the property is well under two acres, and decides to sue. If the executor was careless in describing the property to the real estate agent, the executor may be personally liable to the buyer for the misrepresentation. Suppose, however, that the real estate agent was careless or even intentionally misrepresented the property as being at least two acres. Even then, the executor may be personally liable for this misrepresentation by the agent. The legal doctrine here is known as "respondeat superior," which imposes liability for the actions of those under someone else's control. Businesses, pursuant to the doctrine of respondent superior, are typically liable for the wrongful acts of their employees.

When an executor is held liable to a third party, she may be entitled to reimbursement from the estate. But some states deny any reimbursement where the executor has been negligent.

Just as important, an executor may be personally liable for contracts entered into on behalf of the estate. This is true even if the executor gets no benefit from the contract. Typically, a third party will sue the executor if there is a breach of contract. If the estate is *insolvent* (that is, it has no funds) the executor may be personally liable for contracts that the executor signed on behalf of the estate. Obviously the executor needs to be extremely careful in signing such contracts.

Breach of Duty

If the executor succumbs to temptation and "borrows" property from the estate or fails to carefully segregate the estate's property from his own property, he has breached his duty. However, other behaviors may be considered breaches of duty and give rise to lawsuits as well. If the decedent died leaving investments, the executor must decide about selling those assets and such decisions can create problems.

For example, suppose that a decedent died owning $50,000 of XYZ Corporation's stock. Unfortunately, the stock is declining in value. If the executor holds the stock expecting a price rebound that never occurs, the heirs may be extremely unhappy with the executor. If the executor sells because the XYZ price appears to be declining, and the stock's price does rebound, the heirs will be even more unhappy because of the lost profits. The estate will shoulder any legal costs should the heirs sue the executor. If the estate has significant investments and the executor has no experience in this area, he should consider declining to serve.

Running a Business

If the deceased owned a business, the executor will be called upon either to continue the business or to wind it up. The executor can, of course, hire others to do this, but the executor will be called upon to make a number of business decisions. If the deceased was in a partnership or owned an interest in a small corporation, the interest has to be sold. In many cases there will be a buy/sell agreement that controls disposition of the deceased's interest in the business. If there is no agreement, then the executor will have to negotiate the sale with an eye to maximizing the return to the heirs.

These transactions can be complex and involve large stakes of money. Experience—or the advice of an attorney and CPA—are helpful in this type of situation. If the executor feels that the demands of running, liquidating, or selling a business are beyond him, then he might consider declining to serve as executor in favor of a party with more business experience.

Personal Skills

Don't ignore the importance of a potential executor's people skills. As mentioned above, such skills—or lack thereof—may be even more important than business skills. An executor who knows family members personally will understand family relationships and expectations. This can be very helpful in dealing with them. If a person feels that he has the respect of family members and can work well with most of them, then he will probably do well as executor. If, on the other hand, he doesn't really get along well with a number of the heirs, he might want to let someone else accept the appointment.

Compensation

The executor is paid for the time involved in settling the estate, and this should be considered by the prospective executor. Usually the amount is set by law and is fairly generous. In some states, the law provides for a reasonable executor's fee. In other states, the fee is calculated as a percentage of an estate which ranges between two and five percent of the estate. For example, suppose a state provides that the executor is to receive three percent of the estate. If the decedent had a $100,000 home, a $20,000 car, $30,000 worth of furniture and personal property, and $50,000 in investments, the estate is worth $200,000. The executor's fee would be a flat $6,000 ($200,000 × 3%).

Who Is an Alternative Executor?

There is one last question to consider. If an individual declines to serve, who will replace her? Sometimes the choice is spelled out in the will. Most wills written by attorneys will provide for a contingent executor—a party that will serve if the named executor declines. If an executor knows that her backup will do a poor job, maybe she should step up and serve for the good of the family. If the contingent executor seems capable—not just because he has good business judgment but also because he is able to maintain family harmony—then he may be a better candidate than the named executor, especially if she is uncertain about her own abilities or has other pressing business or family duties.

CHAPTER 5

Court Appointment of the Executor and Probate Initiation

INTRODUCTION

This chapter details how the court appoints the executor and the executor's initial duties after the appointment. The chapter discusses in some detail the importance of finding the will to determine who it has appointed executor. The chapter also discusses who is qualified to be executor, and what happens if a surviving spouse or other family member wants to serve even though they are not named as executor in the will. The executor derives his power to act for the estate through "letters testamentary" and these are described in the chapter. There is also a description of initial duties including securing a bond if needed, giving notice of probate proceedings to heirs and creditors, and starting the inventory of assets.

INITIAL STEPS

Probate is initiated by filing a "petition" with the appropriate court to admit a will to probate. A petition is a legal document that asks the probate court to open a case, admit the will to probate, and appoint the person named in the will—or some other person—to act as executor. Once the court has accepted the petition and issued an order, the executor will be empowered to act on behalf of the estate.

Before the petition can be filed, the will must be located, the legal petition must be drawn up (usually by an attorney), and signed. All this must be done promptly after death.

LOCATING THE WILL

Although finding the will is usually routine, occasionally a will cannot be located. At other times, more than one will is found and it may not be clear which is the legal will. In other cases, no one knows if the deceased died with a will or not.

The will is important not only because it provides instructions for the disposition of the deceased's property, but also because it names the person the deceased wanted to serve as executor. As discussed earlier, the deceased had the option of selecting any legally competent individual to serve as executor. In most states this means that the person selected is over age 18, and is not mentally incapacitated. Several states have additional requirements. Many states also require that the person has never been convicted of a felony. In other states, a felony conviction is not an absolute bar to serving as executor. A few states require that the executor be a resident of the state conducting the probate. A list of state-by-state requirements is found in Appendix B.

The will may also name two or more co-executors who must work together as a team. The deceased may have named a bank or trust company to serve as executor. Most wills name a contingent executor in case the first-named executor cannot serve for one reason or another.

All of these details about the executor will be found in the will, so it is vital that it be located promptly.

Lost Wills

Although most wills are easily found, it is not unusual for a will to be lost. Someone in the family or an heir may know that there was a will, but may have no idea where to find it. Although some states require wills to be filed in the local courthouse, many states have no such requirement. Individuals retain their own copies. Although wills are frequently kept in a safety deposit box, many people keep their will at home along with other important documents such as deeds, insurance policies, and bank records. If the deceased was a sloppy record keeper, it may be difficult to find the will, especially if it was executed some time ago.

In many states it can be difficult to gain access to a person's safety deposit box after his death. Once the bank learns of the death the box will be sealed and can only be opened with a court order—from the probate court. Even after the court order is obtained, access is allowed only in the presence of a representative of the state revenue department. All of this takes time to arrange. Obviously a safety deposit box is not the best place to keep a will. However, if the will can't be found elsewhere, the safe-deposit box is a good place to look for it.

If the will can't be located at the person's home, there are other places to look. Close family friends and family members may have been given a copy of the will or may know its whereabouts. In some states, law firms are required to keep copies of wills they have drawn up, just in case the originals are lost. However, problems can still arise. The attorney who drafted the will may have died, and it may be difficult to find where the copy of the will actually is. It is not always clear which attorney the deceased used to draw up the will. Someone may have to do some detective work to find out which attorney the deceased used. There may be a receipt or a canceled check that would provide a clue. However, if the will was written a number of years ago, this may be an unfruitful trail. The deceased's accountant, clergyman, or funeral director may know the whereabouts of the will, or they may know which attorney drafted the will. As a last resort, an advertisement can be placed to try to find the lost will. There are newspapers and journals that lawyers read, and these regularly carry ads searching for "lost wills."

Multiple Wills

The will search may yield more than one will. Of course, if the wills are identical, then they are simply copies of the same document. If the wills are different, however, the finders must determine which is the valid will. This is a major decision because in most cases the wills probably differ in some material way. For instance, the deceased may have changed a will to deprive someone from an inheritance. Obviously the disinherited person will be unhappy. In some cases, the later, most recent will may be challenged in court. If the later will is proved invalid, then the prior will controls. In some cases these disputes turn into real battles between contesting heirs. The topic of "will contests" is mentioned again in Chapter 6, "Understanding Wills," and is covered in detail in Chapter 11, "Will Contests."

No Will

If no will is found, if the will found is invalid for one reason or another, or if there never was a will, then the property will pass *intestate,* which means "without a will." It does not mean that the property will go to the state. It does mean that the property will pass to closest relatives according to an order devised by state laws. This scheme may or may not resemble what the deceased wished.

Foreign Wills

A will that was drafted and signed in another state or in a foreign country is usually treated like any other will. Legal advice may be needed in the case of an international will, although most courts accept them.

PROBATE COURT

The will and petition must be filed in the correct court. Generally a will is probated where the deceased lived permanently, not necessarily in the state where the deceased lived when the will was drawn up and signed. There are actually two issues involved in filing the petition, *jurisdiction* and *venue*.

Jurisdiction

Jurisdiction is a legal term meaning the *power* to hear a case. Some courts only hear special matters. For example, traffic court may only have jurisdiction to hear cases involving traffic tickets. Some states have a special court—sometimes called surrogate's court—that handles probate cases. Other states handle probate through special departments of their general trial courts. Normally only one court will have jurisdiction over probate cases. It is important to identify the correct court in which to file the petition and will. A state-by-state list of courts is found in Appendix B.

Venue

Venue is the physical location of the court. For example, in most states there will be a probate court in each county. It is important that the petition and will be filed in the probate court having proper venue. Generally the proper venue is where the deceased had a permanent place of residence (called *domicile*). Some state statutes are more flexible and provide other options such as where the deceased died or owned property.

PLANNING TIP *If the state statute does allow some flexibility in filing, the executor should choose the location that will be most convenient for the executor and the estate's attorney. Travel time should not be underestimated. Legal fees will be reduced if the attorney does not have to travel long distances to the courthouse to file papers or attend hearings.*

DOMICILE

Some state statutes require that the proper venue is the decedent's last domicile. Legal domicile has two requirements:

1. physical presence and
2. intent to permanently reside in the state.

EXAMPLE John, who owns a home in New Jersey, died while on an extended vacation in Florida. Although John was physically present in Florida, his legal domicile is in New Jersey because that is where his permanent home is located.

Factors Suggesting Intent

There are a number of factors that determine domicile. Each of these factors suggests that the individual had permanent ties to a particular state, which in turn suggests that he intended to reside there more or less permanently. These factors include, but are not limited to:

- home ownership
- location of real estate investments
- time spent at location
- driver's license
- vehicle registration
- voter registration
- church or temple membership
- mailing address for Social Security
- mailing address on tax returns
- residency status claimed on state tax returns (i.e., resident or nonresident)

OBSERVATION *A reference to residency in a will is good evidence of intent. It is even better evidence if the will is relatively recent.*

Difficulties in Determining Domicile

Occasionally it can be difficult to determine the proper domicile because the facts lead to conflicting conclusions. Determining domicile can be difficult when people are in the process of moving from one state to another, for example. Determining domicile is also difficult in the case of so-called snowbirds—retired individuals who winter in the South but spend their summers in the North.

EXAMPLE Helen maintains two homes, one in Massachusetts and another in South Carolina. She spends almost exactly half the year in one home and half the year in the other. Helen has her driver's license and car registered in Massachusetts, but she votes in South Carolina because she is normally there on election day. She is a parishioner in a church in both states. It is difficult to know where Helen has established her domicile.

The Importance of Domicile

Domicile is important because laws differ state by state. A good example is the right to disinherit a spouse. All states give a surviving spouse some sort of protection against disinheritance, but the extent of that protection varies greatly. Creditors also have different rights to estate assets in different states.

Moreover, domicile can be important for tax reasons. All states impose an estate tax and some states also have inheritance taxes. If the deceased is a resident of a state with inheritance taxes, the state can impose its tax on all of the property in the estate. The heirs will have to pay tax on whatever property they receive.

EXAMPLE Shawn, a widower, owned a home in Michigan and a home in Florida. Michigan has an inheritance tax while Florida does not. Shawn winters in Florida and spends about half the year in Michigan. If Shawn is found to be a Michigan resident, his heirs will have to pay inheritance tax to the state of Michigan.

Taxes are discussed in more detail in Chapter 8, "Paying Creditors and Taxes," and Chapter 13, "Estate and Gift Tax Basics."

OBSERVATION *Occasionally two or more states will claim that a deceased individual was a resident at the time of death and will try to impose their inheritance taxes. An interesting example involves Howard Hughes, the founder of TWA Airlines and Hughes Tools. Hughes, a billionaire, was a recluse during the last years of his life, and only had contact with his close advisors for several years. There was great speculation at the time about his whereabouts or whether he was actually still alive.*

When Hughes did die in 1976, three states, California, Nevada, and Texas, all claimed Hughes as a resident. The greed was not confined to the state revenue departments, however; several bogus wills and bogus relatives also surfaced as people tried to cash in on the reclusive Hughes' enormous estate.

PLANNING TIP *It is best if individuals establish domicile before their death. A court will usually assume that the person has proper domicile in the state if the individual owns property there and wrote and signed the will while in the state.*

ANCILLARY ADMINISTRATION

When the deceased owned real estate in a state other than the state of domicile, there must be a second probate proceeding in the state where the real estate is located. This second proceeding is called ancillary administration and an executor, usually called an ancillary administrator, would be appointed. Most states allow the executor to act as the ancillary administrator.

EXAMPLE Paul, a resident of Chicago, owns a vacation home in Wisconsin. If Paul's estate is being probated in Illinois, there must also be an ancillary probate proceeding in Wisconsin to dispose of the property there. The court in Illinois has no jurisdiction (power) to order disposition of the property in another state. Accordingly, the executor must arrange a second probate proceeding in Wisconsin.

The additional proceeding and ancillary administrator are necessary because a state court and executor only have power within one state. Not surprisingly, ancillary administration adds substantial costs to the probate bill because there is a lot of duplication of effort and of legal bills. Additionally, the state in which the real estate is located may impose its estate tax and possibly also its inheritance tax if it has one. Such taxes are imposed only on the property located in that state.

PETITION

Once the will is located, probate can be commenced by filing the will and a petition with the court. As mentioned earlier, the petition is essentially a request by an individual that the will be admitted to probate and that the person named in the will, or another person, be appointed as executor of the estate.

In most states the petition must include most or all of the following information:

- deceased's full name
- mailing address (this information establishes venue with the court)
- age
- date of birth
- place of birth
- domicile
- date of death
- place of death
- Social Security number (or taxpayer identification number)
- facts showing the named executor's qualifications to serve
- heirs' and devisees' names, mailing addresses, relationship to the deceased, and the ages of any minor heirs
- existence of other wills or knowledge that the enclosed will may be invalid
- whether there was a "contract to make a will" or a promise not to revoke a will
- nature and extent of assets, including real estate
- information about known creditors
- estate attorney's name and address (if an attorney is used)

Additionally, the executor will have to include a copy of the will and possibly a copy of the death certificate. Funeral directors usually help in obtaining copies of the death certificate (see Chapter 2, "Funerals"). Additional copies are available from the vital records branch of state or local government offices.

Who Can File a Petition?

In most states, any interested party may file the petition. Interested parties include, but are not limited to, a surviving spouse, next of kin, a named heir, or even a creditor. However, in most cases the executor named in the will is the one who will commence the probate proceedings by filing the petition. Most often, the estate's attorney will draft the petition. As a rule, the petition is a brief, standardized document, and the law firm essentially "fills in the blanks."

Executors working without an attorney should be able to purchase a blank legal form and

fill in the necessary material themselves. In some states the probate court will supply the forms free of charge.

If the probate court thinks material is missing from the petition, the court clerk will return it with a list of missing items and the executor can simply correct and refile it. In most states there is no actual court hearing to start the probate proceedings. The judge merely reviews the petition and signs an order. Normally the petitioner must also prepare the order for the judge's signature. The estate attorney will be preparing the order along with the petition. An executor working without an attorney will also have to prepare an "order admitting the will to probate." In some states the exact wording on the order may differ. Blank legal forms should also be available for this purpose.

PLANNING TIP *Executors working without an attorney still need to comply with all the court filing requirements that apply to estates. Since probating an estate is a common action, blank legal forms should be available to fill in and file with the court. Blank legal forms are sold by legal stationery stores, which generally cater to lawyers. Sometimes these forms are not in view, and must be asked for. A list of the forms can be helpful to determine what is needed. The store may even carry a packet of commonly used probate forms at a discount. Unlike tax returns, the government does not usually supply these forms. However, some courts, like those in New York, do assist the executor by providing free forms.*

PLANNING TIP *Before the petitioner buys any forms, she should call the clerk of the local probate court, identify herself as an executor, and ask if the court supplies the forms free of charge.*

PLANNING TIP *Before typing up the petition and other forms that must be filed with the court, it is a good idea to make a copy to prepare a "rough draft" to make sure all the information fits on the form.*

PLANNING TIP *Court personnel are normally under strict orders not to give out legal advice to individuals who are filing forms. They can, however, explain filing requirements.*

PLANNING TIP *If the executor is acting without an attorney and has no idea how to fill out a particular form, there is a source of help close at hand. Probate files—like other court records—are open to the public for inspection. If the executor knows the name of another individual who is recently deceased, she can ask to see the file. She can see how the law firm for that individual filled out the forms, which should provide a good model.*

Who Must Sign the Petition?

In most states the executor must sign the petition. If the petition is prepared by an attorney, the attorney must also sign it. There is no need for the heirs or creditors to sign.

REVIEW OF PETITION: PROOF OF WILL

The judge reviews the petition and will to determine if the will should be admitted to probate. Wills, of course, must be witnessed. This is to ensure that the deceased wanted the document to be his or her will. Most modern wills are *self-proving*—under oath, the witnesses sign a statement on the will itself that they believe the document is the testator's last will and testament. They must normally have seen the deceased sign the will or have heard him describe the document as his will. These affidavits by the witnesses on the will itself are generally sufficient to establish the validity of the document. If there is any question on this point, the witnesses can be summoned to court to testify about the document.

Once the judge determines that the will is valid and that there are no objections to the executor by interested parties, the judge will sign an "order" admitting the will to probate. The judge will also decide at this time if a bond will be required.

PREFERENCE

Although the will may name an executor, most state laws provide that a surviving spouse or other family member be appointed if they want to serve.

Many states have enacted the "Uniform Probate Code," which provides the following order of priority for selecting an executor:

1. person(s) named in the will

2. surviving spouse who receives real property under the will
3. other individuals who receive real property under the will
4. surviving spouse or a person selected by the surviving spouse
5. other heir or a person selected by an heir
6. any creditor

In states having this hierarchy, the judge will normally follow it and first name the person mentioned in the will. Sometimes that person may be unwilling or incapable of performing the duties of executor, and the judge must appoint someone else. The judge will simply work down the list of preferences to find someone to serve.

OBSERVATION *States using this statutory scheme may make a distinction between* devisee *and* heir. *Although these terms are increasingly used interchangeably, technically speaking, a devisee is a party who is left property in the will. Heirs are sometimes called* distributees *in statutes and legal documents. An heir is a person who would receive property if the deceased died intestate (without a will). Note that an heir may be a devisee if the will leaves him property.*

NOTICE TO INTERESTED PARTIES

The party petitioning the court to initiate probate and appoint an executor must provide notice to interested parties. The purpose is to notify family members and other parties that the deceased has died, that a will has been presented to the court, that someone has requested to act as executor, and that probate proceedings are about to begin. If the interested parties object to the selection of executor for any reason, they need to come forward at this time.

Interested Parties

In most states, the following individuals and firms are considered "interested parties" and are entitled to be notified of the probate proceedings:

- spouse
- next of kin
- devisees (persons named in the will as beneficiaries)

- heirs (those who would receive property if there was no will, but who are not necessarily mentioned in the will)
- creditors

Notification of Parties—Practical Difficulties

It is the executor's duty to locate all of these parties promptly. If the deceased has left a letter of instructions, the executor may be able to find addresses there or among the deceased's personal effects. However, it may not be so simple. Because creditors are entitled to notice of the proceedings, the executor needs to review the deceased's financial records to determine who those creditors are.

To complete giving the required notices, the executor also needs to determine which family members must be notified and where they currently live. Persons named in the will must also be notified. This can produce even more problems. These people may be old friends who are unfamiliar to local family members. Luckily most lawyers try to identify at least the hometown of people mentioned in the will when it is drawn up. Although this makes the job of locating such individuals somewhat easier, problems arise if they have moved, especially if they have a fairly common last name.

EXAMPLE A provision in George's will left his photo albums and other mementos to Joe Smith of St. Louis. The executor learns that Joe was George's old army buddy, but nobody in the family has seen him for ten years. Because the will only mentions that Joe lives in St. Louis without giving a street address, the executor may have to engage in some serious detective work to find Joe. There may be a whole page of Joe Smiths in the St. Louis phone book. The research escalates if Joe has retired and moved away.

How to Find Missing Interested Parties

Executors facing problems finding all the interested parties may want to use the Internet to help locate them. If that fails, there are companies listed in the phone book that trace missing heirs for a fee. Often they will not charge a fee if they cannot locate the person. Any fees for the search will be paid by the estate.

What Interested Parties Need to Receive

In most states, the interested parties must be provided with:

- a copy of the petition
- a copy of the will
- notice of when and where the hearing will be (if any)
- notice of how to make objections to the proceeding

Hearings

In some states an executor is appointed without any court hearing at all. The petition and will are merely dropped off at the probate court. If no objections are made, the court notifies the executor by mail to come to the court office to pick up the letters testamentary—the legal documents empowering the executor to act on behalf of the estate—to start administration of the estate. Other states require a brief hearing, and in some the executor is appointed without prior notice to interested parties.

Challenges

Although it is unlikely, an interested person may challenge probate of a will. Objections may be based on the following:

- existence of a later and different will
- challenge to the particular will offered for probate
- challenge to the person petitioning to act as executor

The purpose of the notice to interested parties is to assure that the proper will is being probated, and that the proposed executor is the proper party to act in that capacity. An interested party may know of the existence of a later will with different provisions. On the other hand, an interested party may attack the will being offered for probate, arguing that the deceased was not legally capable of making a valid will at the time because the decedent was mentally incompetent. Another common objection to a will is the belief that the deceased was tricked into making certain provisions. These topics are covered in more detail in Chapter 11, "Will Contests."

An interested person may also challenge the appointment of the executor. For example, if a son or daughter is petitioning the court for appointment as executor, a surviving spouse may come forward and claim the right to act as executor. Interested parties may also come forward to challenge the petitioner's qualifications on somewhat technical grounds. In many states the executor must be a resident of the state. A nonresident is simply barred from serving even though he lives right across the state line and relatively near the courthouse. Interested persons may also claim that the petitioner has a conflict of interest. This situation might arise if the estate does not have sufficient assets to pay everyone and the executor's fee is taken out of the estate, or if the petitioner is a creditor.

OBSERVATION *Problems can also arise when two or more potential executors have equal priority under a state law. For example, suppose there is no spouse and the law provides that next-of-kin are next in line to serve as executor. There are two sons, both of whom get equal shares in the will, and each insists on serving as executor. The judge is likely to appoint them as co-executors, which of course can lead to a deadlock if they fail to agree with one another while administering the estate.*

LETTERS TESTAMENTARY

The judge reviews the petition and the will. If all seems in order and there are no objections from interested parties, the judge will order the executor to receive *letters testamentary*. These are the actual legal documents issued by the court empowering the executor to act on behalf of the estate. In some states these are referred to as *letters of appointment* or as *letters of authority,* because they give authority to the executor to act. The executor has no legal authority to act on behalf of the estate before the letters testamentary are in hand. A number of states do empower the executor to carry out written instructions left by the deceased about funeral arrangements and disposition of their remains.

The executor will need to give copies of letters testamentary to banks, insurance companies, brokerage houses, and other entities that deal with the deceased's property. Each institution wants to make sure that the executor is actually empowered by the court to dispose of the deceased's property.

Because they will want to retain a copy of the letters testamentary to document the executor's authority, the executor needs to obtain a number of copies from the court. The more complex the deceased's financial affairs are, the more copies of the document will be needed.

OBSERVATION *Letters testamentary are either sealed or unsealed. A sealed copy has an embossed seal from the court and is more expensive. The seal provides added assurance that it came directly from the court. Letters made on a copy machine without a seal are also obtainable. Some third parties will insist on having the more expensive kind, while some are satisfied with unsealed letters.*

PLANNING TIP *Executors can obtain copies of the letters from the court. It is a good idea to obtain at least six copies at the outset. If more are needed, they can be obtained later.*

Ancillary Probate

When ancillary (out-of-state) probate proceedings are required, normally because the deceased owned out-of-state real property, the out-of-state court will issue letters testamentary in that state, empowering the executor to deal with the deceased's property in that state.

EXAMPLE Paul, a resident of Illinois, dies owning a vacation home in Wisconsin. Paul's executor will initiate probate proceedings in Illinois by filing a petition with the local court in Illinois. Additionally, Paul's executor must file a petition and copy of the will in court in Wisconsin. It is possible to have a second executor, "the ancillary administrator," appointed to deal with the Wisconsin property if that is more convenient than having Paul's executor travel to Wisconsin to deal with the property.

BONDS

The probate court will normally require a bond to be filed by the executor. A bond is a suretyship arrangement—the bonding company will indemnify (pay back) the estate if the executor loses property through fraud, theft, or carelessness. The bond is in place to protect both the heirs and creditors.

EXAMPLE John, an executor, has a gambling problem. As executor, John has access to all the cash in the estate and gambles nearly all of it away before he is exposed. All of the cash was expected to pay professionals working on the estate, creditors of the deceased, and the heirs. Because John was required to post a bond at the outset of probate, the bonding company will repay the misappropriated cash to the estate so the heirs and creditors can be paid.

PLANNING TIP *Bonds are available directly from bonding companies or through insurance agents. The higher the value of the estate, the larger the required bond and the higher the cost. Rates do vary between bonding companies.*

PLANNING TIP *The bonding company needs to be notified when the estate is closed. Most bonds renew automatically for an additional 12-month period unless the company hears otherwise.*

Waiving a Bond

The will may provide that the executor need not post a bond. This will save costs and will increase the amount of property available to the heirs and creditors. However, the probate court may decide to require a bond despite the clear language in the will. The judge might do this if he or she feels that it will best protect the interest of the heirs and creditors of the estate. A person who is to receive property under the will or a creditor may also petition the court to require the executor to obtain a bond.

OBSERVATION *At one time the law in most states required the executor to get court approval before doing almost anything. Many states have since greatly reduced the amount of court supervision. The executor generally carries out her duties with no supervision, making only annual accountings to the court and petitioning for permission to act only for major undertakings. This topic is discussed in more detail in Chapter 7, "Managing Property."*

Notice to Heirs and Devisees

As discussed earlier, the executor's first official duty after appointment is to notify interested parties, including the heirs and devisees. The devisees are persons named in the will and heirs are individuals who receive the property if there is no will. In most states these parties need to receive the following information:

- executor's name and address
- estate attorney's name and address (if any)
- whether a bond has been filed
- acknowledgment that the recipient has an interest in the estate
- notice that the administration of the probate will generally be without court supervision
- notice that the recipient will be entitled to information about the probate from the executor
- notice that the recipient may petition the court in any matter

Notice to Creditors

The executor needs to provide each known creditor with essentially the same information sent to the heirs and devisees mentioned above. Additionally, in most, but not all, states, the executor needs to publish notice about the probate proceeding to all creditors in a local newspaper. Most states require the notice to run for three weeks.

INVENTORY OF ASSETS

The executor is required to prepare a precise inventory of the estate's property and debts. An inventory is a listing and valuation. Preparing inventory is a good deal easier if the deceased started the job before death.

The deceased may have left a letter of instructions with the will that includes a listing of all his property and debts with up-to-date valuations. The executor merely has to double check and update this information to prepare the inventory. However, the deceased may have prepared nothing at all. This is common if the deceased has been in poor health for some time. In this case, the executor will have to start from scratch and assemble all the information himself. Although such a task is difficult and time-consuming, it is certainly not impossible. The executor can also get a lot of help from family members and professionals along the way.

Where to Begin

Assuming the deceased has left a listing of property and debts, the executor's first step is to prepare a rough inventory of the deceased's property. This inventory should also include a rough valuation of the property. In some cases, the executor may know or can easily determine the value of the property. For example, in some areas, the local taxing authority prepares a fair market value appraisal of real estate on a fairly regular basis. In other areas, the property tax appraisal may represent only a percentage of the property's real value. Even if there is no completely accurate appraisal of the property, putting an estimated value on each item provides some idea about the property's value, and these estimates can be verified later. (An inventory checklist is provided at the end of Chapter 7, "Managing Property.")

OBSERVATION *The purpose of the rough inventory is two-fold. The executor has to prepare and present to the court a formal inventory of all the property and debts. Even before this happens, however, the executor is responsible for safeguarding the property and seeing to it that bills are paid as they fall due.*

WARNING *In most states the inventory normally needs to be completed and filed with the court three months after the executor's appointment. In practical terms this is a very short time. The executor needs to start the inventory process immediately after appointment.*

Care of Property

Although the executor does not take title to the deceased's property, he is responsible for safeguarding the property and has a duty to take steps to manage, preserve, and protect it. The executor needs to decide who should have custody (possession) of the property subject to its ultimate distribution to the devisee and heirs.

The will may provide that survivors are entitled to remain in the family home. The executor needs to decide who should have custody of other items, such as autos and boats. Generally the executor will give custody of an item of property to the person who will ultimately receive it. The executor needs to make clear, however, that this is not a final distribution and that the executor may have to reclaim the property. This needs to be stated in writ-

ing, because the person receiving custody of the property may consider the property his, and may not pay much attention to the legal nuances.

EXAMPLE Ed's will provides that his brother Howard is to receive the Ed's Oldsmobile. During the administration of the estate, the executor lets Howard drive the car. However, the executor needs to get a receipt from Howard acknowledging that he may have to return the car. Additionally, the executor needs to verify that Howard has maintained adequate auto insurance on the vehicle.

Mail

Besides securing the residence and other property, the executor needs to attend to the deceased's mail. A surviving spouse who resides at the deceased's home can collect and sort mail as it comes in. The postmaster will forward the deceased's mail directly to the executor upon presentation of the death certificate and/or letters testamentary. The executor needs to carefully sort through the mail. Social Security and Veterans Administration checks must be returned to those agencies.

WARNING *Neither the estate nor the surviving spouse is entitled to Social Security and/or Veterans Administration checks for the month of death, even if the deceased lived nearly until the end of the month. These checks must be returned.*

Paying Bills

The executor needs to pay bills as they fall due. Utility bills, mortgage payments, and property taxes all need to be paid. Paying creditors is discussed in more detail in Chapter 8, "Paying Creditors and Taxes." The executor needs to open a checking account for this purpose. Bank accounts are discussed in Chapter 7, "Managing Property."

Support of Family

There are several protections built into the law to protect families of the deceased. The executor needs to understand these important rights because the family will look to the executor for both emotional and financial support during the probate process.

Homestead Right

In most states the family has a homestead right, which allows them to remain in the family home during the probate proceedings even if the deceased left the home to someone else in the will.

Family Allowance

Most states provide a family allowance to continue supporting a surviving spouse and other dependents, for which the probate court orders the executor to use estate assets. In some cases, this family support may deplete the assets in the estate so that neither creditors nor persons named in the will receive anything. In most states the family allowance is not automatic, nor is the allowance amount fixed. The judge has discretion about how much to award, or whether any allowance at all should be awarded.

Election Against the Will

An important protection for surviving spouses is the "election against the will." This rule allows a surviving spouse to receive a set percentage of the estate—typically between 33 and 50 percent—no matter what the deceased's will provides. This effectively makes it impossible for the deceased to disinherit his or her spouse. This is exactly what the law is designed to prevent. On the other hand, it is possible to disinherit anyone else, including children, in all states except Louisiana. Election against the will is discussed in detail in Chapter 6, "Understanding Wills."

TAX ISSUES

The executor will also be responsible for filing tax returns. The executor must see that the deceased's final Form 1040 is filed. Additionally, the estate itself must file a tax return, using Form 1041, to report any income such as interest or rents that are received after the deceased's death. Finally, if the deceased owned more than $600,000 in property, the executor will have to file a Federal Estate Tax Return (Form 706). Copies of these forms appear in Appendix E. The executor will need to know the details of property ownership to complete these returns. Of course the executor can hire an accountant to help prepare the returns. Details on filing is found in Chapter 8, "Paying Creditors and Taxes."

Preparing the Formal Inventory

Details on property ownership and how to prepare the formal inventory for the court are found in Chapter 7, "Managing Property." That chapter also includes an inventory checklist.

ROLE OF THE ESTATE LAWYER

Although it is possible to probate an estate without a lawyer, it can be difficult because of the court procedures involved. Unfortunately, court rules vary state to state, and even county to county in some areas.

Executors who choose to proceed without an attorney can try to garner advice from clerks at the probate court and from friends who have been through the process. A friend who happens to be a lawyer might be a good source of information about dealing with the court—but executors should not abuse such friendships.

TIPS ON FILLING OUT BLANK LEGAL FORMS

Although it is preferable to use an attorney in probating an estate, it is possible for the executor to probate the estate without one. If so, the executor will have to file the legal forms normally drafted and filed by the attorney. Blank probate forms are frequently available from legal stationery stores.

Here are are number of tips to help fill out these forms. The executor should:

- make sure the form is what he needs—there are often different versions of the same form.
- make a copy of the form to use as a rough draft and fill in the blanks on the rough copy by hand. The executor will find out if he has the information necessary to fill out the form. If not, he will have to find the information before he can complete the form. Using a rough copy will also give an idea of how much information will fit on a typed form.
- ask court clerks how many copies of the form are required. If multiple copies are needed, each requires original signatures.
- make sure to notarize his signature if the form has a place for a notary's seal, before filing the form with the court.
- always make at least one copy of the forms after completing them. Put them in a file by date, with the most current form on the top.

CHAPTER 6 Understanding Wills

INTRODUCTION

The will controls the distribution of the deceased's property. One of the executor's primary jobs is to determine how the property gets divided and distributed. Although this seems straightforward, there are a remarkable number of rules and exceptions that can complicate the executor's job. Accordingly, executors need to have a complete and accurate understanding of wills. This chapter will discuss the essential elements of a will and many common will provisions. The chapter will also discuss the spouse's elective share, which protects a spouse from being disinherited. Wills are also discussed in Chapter 10, "Intestacy—When There Is No Will." You will also find a longer discussion of validity of wills in Chapter 11, "Will Contests."

LEGAL REQUIREMENTS FOR A VALID WILL

Generally, wills are controlled by state statutes. These laws create certain legal requirements for a will. Additionally, they validate the document's control over the disposition of property after death. In all states, the right to inherit property is controlled by statute, not from the common law. Accordingly, strict compliance with the law is required.

For example, because of the obvious potential for fraud, wills are required not only to be written documents, but also to be witnessed. Some states require two witnesses while others require three. A list of different state requirements is found in Appendix B. If a will is not properly witnessed, it will not be enforced at death and the individual will die without a legal will. This topic is discussed in detail in Chapter 10, "Intestacy—When There Is No Will." If a person dies without a valid will, his property will be distributed by state law to his closest relatives, which may or may not have been the deceased's intent. This will happen even if it is obvious that he wanted his property distributed according to the failed will.

THREE TYPES OF WILLS

There are three different types of wills:

1. holographic wills;
2. nuncupative wills; and
3. written and witnessed wills.

Holographic Wills

Holographic and *nuncupative wills* are valid only in a minority of states. A *holographic will* is completely handwritten by the deceased, and typically lacks witness signatures. In some states, a holographic will might be admitted to probate and will be effective even if not witnessed properly. A holographic will might be written by a person during his last illness, or while he is in the hospital.

Nuncupative Wills

Oral wills, called *nuncupative wills*, are valid in some states if made during the deceased's last illness. Typically, they are not valid to bequeath real estate, but only a limited amount of personal property. Oral wills known as "soldiers and sailors wills" are effective during wartime in some states. To prevent problems, a person should avoid using both holographic and oral wills even if they are valid in his state. He should only rely on a properly signed and witnessed will.

Written Wills

Written and witnessed wills are by far the most common form of wills. They are relatively easy to prepare, yet a surprising number of people die without any will at all.

BASIC LEGAL CRITERIA FOR WRITING A WILL

There are three basic requirements to make a will:

1. intent to make a will;
2. strict compliance with the statutory requirements; and
3. legal capacity to make a will.

The law demands strict compliance with the legal requirement for a will. Only a document that meets all of the requirements will be allowed to operate as a person's will. This is true even if it is clear that an individual wanted a document to operate as his will. Although a court sometimes enforces other kinds of legal agreements even if all the formalities are not satisfied, a court typically requires strict compliance with all of the requirements for a will.

Intent to Make a Will

In most cases, intent to make a will is demonstrated by the document itself, which is labeled as a will and typically states that it is the will of the testator.

Compliance with State Statutes

The will must be written (handwritten, typed,

preprinted, or a combination of the three) and signed by the testator. Additionally, it must be witnessed. In some states two witnesses are required but in others three are needed. See Appendix B for a list of state-by-state requirements. In all states the witnesses must be legally competent. In some states a person who receives property in the will cannot serve as a witness. Failure to comply with any of the statutory requirements can pose many problems.

Legal Capacity

Finally, the testator must be "legally competent" at the time the will was made. Four basic criteria must be met to establish legal capacity to make a will:

1. the testator must understand the nature and extent of his or her property;
2. the testator must recognize the "natural objects of his or her bounty" (i.e., he must be able to remember who is a member of his family);
3. the testator needs to understand the testamentary act; and
4. the testator must understand the relation of the first three elements to one another.

A person who is seriously ill may have diminished legal capacity and may simply be unable to make a legally valid will. Problems in this area can arise when an elderly person makes a will.

If it can be proved that a person was tricked into signing or modifying a will, a court will declare the will invalid. Similarly, if a testator was forced into signing a will against his better judgment, the will may be set aside. Legal capacity and fraud issues are often the subject of will contests, which are detailed in Chapter 11.

Effect of Moving to a New State

Generally, if a testator moves from one state to another, it will have no effect on the validity of her will. American states recognize the validity of wills drawn up in other states. However, the will must have been valid in the state in which it was made at the time it was made. Most states also recognize a foreign will that was legally sufficient in the foreign country of origin.

EXAMPLE Assume that Mr. Black has died, leaving behind a handwritten will. When the will is examined, it is found to be entirely in Black's handwriting, and it is signed and dated at the end. However, the will has not been properly witnessed. State law where Black died does not recognize a will unless it is properly witnessed. However, if the executor can show that the will was made while Black was a resident of another state that, at the time the will was made, recognized Black's will as legal, then the state of Black's final residence must also recognize the will.

A question of validity occasionally arises because different states have different witness requirements. Some states require more than two witnesses and some states will not allow a person to be a witness if that person is to receive anything under the will. As a general rule, if the will was legal when and where it was made, it will be recognized in any other state.

EXAMPLE Bob Wilson, a resident of New York, writes a will and has it properly witnessed by two witnesses, satisfying the requirements of New York law. Later in life Wilson moves to Connecticut, but he never writes a new will. Wilson dies a resident of Connecticut; his will, made years ago in New York, will be admitted to probate despite the fact that Connecticut requires not two witnesses to a will but three. The Connecticut court will recognize that the will was valid when written in New York. A similar rule applies to marriages. If a couple residing in one state elopes to another state to be married, the couple's resident state must recognize the marriage even though it had a longer waiting period.

JOINT AND MUTUAL WILLS
Joint Wills

A joint will is a will written on a single piece of paper and executed by two parties, normally a husband and wife. The provisions made by the signers are usually reciprocal. The will may provide that each spouse leaves all his or her property to the other, or to their children if both spouses die. For example, suppose that John and Mary have been married for a number of years. Years ago they exe-

cuted a joint will. In it John left all his property to Mary, but in the event that Mary predeceased him, all his property at the time of his death would go to their sole child, Virginia. Mary left all her property to John with the same provision in favor of Virginia. Both John and Mary signed the single joint will.

In many states, a joint will is probated when the first party to the will dies, thus preventing the will from being changed in the future. A husband and wife may feel that freezing the will on the death of the first spouse is appropriate because it makes a binding commitment. However, if one spouse significantly outlives the other, the will may be entirely inappropriate in the future. If one spouse dies at an early age, for example, the other spouse is likely to remarry, in which case the old will may prevent the survivor from leaving her property to the second spouse. Some, but not all, states will relax the strict enforcement of a joint will to prevent any injustice.

Mutual Wills

While a joint will is made on one piece of paper, mutual wills are two identical wills normally drawn in favor of the other mutual party. Like joint wills, mutual wills are most commonly made by husbands and wives. Unlike joint wills, in most states, mutual wills do not prevent one party from making changes. Because wills are ambulatory and can be changed at any time, even after the first party dies, the second party can change a mutual will.

Mutual wills are preferable to joint wills. A husband and wife can demonstrate their commitment to one another by making reciprocal promises about the disposition of their property. And if the wills remain appropriate until both parties' deaths then they can be carried out. If one spouse dies unexpectedly or long before the other, the surviving spouse will be free to change the will should the need arise.

OPERATING RULES

The executor will be dealing with relatives and other individuals who are named in the will. They will frequently have questions about how the will operates. The executor needs to understand a number of operating rules relating to wills.

What Can't a Will Do?

An individual cannot give away what he does not own at the time of his death. Accordingly, a provision in a will that attempts to give away property that the deceased did not own at death will be ineffective.

Moreover, a will cannot control the disposition of life insurance, savings bonds, annuities, and retirement plans with beneficiary or due-on-death designations. Even if the deceased tried to control these designations in the will, this attempt will fail because beneficiary designations supersede provisions in a will.

Gifts in a Will

A will may contain various types of gifts. A general legacy is one payable out of the general assets of the estate. For example, a will may provide that Baxter is to receive $10,000. On the other hand, a specific legacy is one that can be satisfied only by particular property. For example, suppose that Ames' will contained the following language: "I give my 1936 Buick to Baxter." Only the delivery of the Buick satisfies the will. A demonstrative legacy is one that must be satisfied out of a particular fund or a particular asset. For example, if Ames' will provides that Baxter is to receive $10,000 out of a particular brokerage account, then this is a demonstrative legacy. Finally, a residuary gift is one that comes out of property that has not been otherwise disposed of in the will. These different gifts are discussed in further detail later in this chapter.

Mortgages, Auto Loans, and Liens

At one time liens and mortgages on property would be paid off before the encumbered property was distributed to heirs. For example, if a car was subject to a car loan, the estate would pay off the loan before distributing the car to an heir. Today, in most states property will be inherited with "encumbrances" attached. For example, suppose that Ames has left his farm to Jones and the farm is subject to a $50,000 mortgage. Jones will take title to the land, but must assume the mortgage debt.

A testator can prevent this by purchasing adequate life insurance to pay off any encumbrances on property left in a will. This strategy has the added advantage of reducing probate costs because title transfers are far easier if no liens are involved. Additionally, this will relieve the executor of the need to borrow funds during the probate proceedings to service the estate's debts.

The Residuary Clause

Most wills provide that the residue of the estate, or the property that is not specifically left to named individuals, goes to a named party or parties. If the testator had a spouse, it is common to leave the residuary to the surviving spouse. Note that many of the expenses of probate are paid out of this residuary.

Ademption

A basic rule to remember is that a will can only give away what the testator owned at the time of death. If specific property is no longer owned when the testator dies, the potential recipient is not entitled to some other property. This concept is called "ademption." The recipient may have already received the property during the testator's life, or the testator may simply no longer own the property.

EXAMPLE 1 Sam's will provides that his brother Jack is only to receive one item of property, Sam's 1990 Buick. If Jack was given the Buick previous to Sam's death, the property is considered "adeemed" and Jack is not entitled to anything else.

EXAMPLE 2 Sam's will provides that his brother Jack is only to receive one item of property, Sam's 1990 Buick. Assume that Sam traded in the 1990 model and a 1997 Buick is sitting in Sam's garage at the time of his death. Jack will receive nothing and the 1997 auto will most likely fall into the residue of the estate. Had the will provided that Jack would receive "my car at the time of my death," then Jack would have taken the 1997 auto.

EXAMPLE 3 Sam's will provides that his brother Jack is only to receive one item of property, Sam's 1990 Buick. Sam dies in an auto accident in which the car is completely destroyed. The insurance company pays the estate $3,000, which represents the value of the auto. Jack does not receive the cash in lieu of the car.

Abatement

Sometimes an executor faces a serious problem: the estate does not have sufficient assets to carry out all the gifts in the will. This might happen because creditors or tax collectors have made claims against the estate (see Chapter 8, "Paying Creditors and Taxes"). It can also occur if the surviving spouse "elects against the will," which will be discussed later in this chapter.

EXAMPLE Sam's will provides that each of his children are to receive $300,000. Although Sam died owning $1 million of property, creditor claims of $200,000 have reduced the amount available for distribution among the three children to only $800,000. They will not get the full amount specified in Sam's will.

When there are insufficient assets in the estate to carry out the gifts, not everyone is going to get what the testator intended. The law provides special rules to prioritize the gifts to determine whose share is decreased and by how much. This procedure is called "abatement."

In most states, the will controls the order of abatement with the caveat that the surviving spouse has a right to elect against the will. The testator's will can, however, provide that all gifts will abate before gifts given to the surviving spouse (who normally receives the residue).

If the will fails to provide for a specific order of abatement, most state laws provide that gifts are reduced in the following order:

1. gifts that pass through intestacy
2. residue
3. general legacies
4. demonstrative legacies
5. specific legacies

Gifts to Charity

Many individuals make charitable bequests to religious, educational, and charitable organizations in their wills. Hospitals and other civic institutions like libraries and parks are also favorite recipients of generous charitable giving. Besides making an unrestricted cash gift to a charity, wills have allocated money to plant trees in parks, establish book collections on a particular subject in a public or university library, or to establish a small scholarship for a student from the decedent's hometown. Well-to-do testators often make charitable gifts as part of their estate plan because charitable gifts reduce the amount of estate tax due at death.

Conditional Gifts

Testators sometimes try to control events even from the grave. A testator may give away property only on the condition that the devisee changes his behavior. For example, a father may think that his adult son should be married, employed, or both; because the father is reluctant to have his estate used to perpetuate what he perceives as his son's leisure, he would like to make the son's inheritance conditional to marriage or employment.

A testator may even condition the gift on the heir's changing his marital partner, or perhaps his religion. For example, a father may try to leave property to his son on the condition that he divorce his present wife. Similarly, the father might try to condition a son's bequest on the son's returning to the family's traditional religion.

In most states, conditional gifts will be enforced unless they are against public policy. Gifts that would promote divorce or would force a person to desert his present religion are considered to be against public policy in most states, and will not be enforced. In the example above, the father's attempt to condition a gift on the son's divorce or on his renunciation of his current religion would fail. If the son challenged the condition, the probate court would most likely award the property without requiring the son to fulfil the will's condition.

MODIFICATIONS

Wills are often modified or revoked. The executor needs to understand how these changes take place. There are also circumstances when a modification is not permitted.

Modifications by the Deceased

Wills are *ambulatory,* which means that the testator (the person making up the will) may change his or her will at any time and for any reason. Generally, an individual may change his will even if his heirs know the contents of his will. Similarly, a will is not invalidated because a testator has misled family members about its contents.

Codicils

Before law firms used word processors to create wills, a common way to change a will was by adding a codicil. A codicil—which is Latin for "little will"—is simply an addition that changes one or more provisions in a will.

EXAMPLE After Sara wrote a will, she inherited some real estate that she wanted a particular person to have after her death. Sara added this desire to her will without making out an entirely new will, but by adding a short codicil.

A codicil must be executed with the same formalities as a will. Accordingly, the codicil must be signed and witnessed in the same way as a will and must comply with any special requirements in the testator's state.

When Can't a Will Be Changed?

Although a will may usually be changed, there are a few exceptions. A common exception occurs when an individual has agreed to make out a will in a certain way. Such an agreement is in the form of a written contract separate from the will. Nonetheless, an oral agreement to make certain provisions in a will can be deemed valid and enforceable.

Prenuptial and Postnuptial Agreements

Spouses could agree either before or after their marriage to include certain provisions in a will. A husband might agree to leave his wife a fixed amount of money in his will. This kind of contract to make a will is enforceable in most states. Such contracts will be discussed in more detail toward the end of this chapter.

Divorce Decrees

Similarly, divorce decrees sometimes obligate one of the parties to provide for the ex-spouse or their children in a certain manner. These decrees are also enforceable in most states and usually prevent a will from being changed so as to be contrary to the terms of the decree.

Contract to Make a Will

Most states will also respect a "contract to make a will," which can basically freeze certain provisions in a will. These contracts typically occur when one party agrees to make a will in favor of another if that person performs certain acts. For example, an older relative who wants to be cared for later in life might promise to make a will in favor of the relative who promises to provide the care.

EXAMPLE A grandfather promises to leave his granddaughter half of his property on his death if she promises to care for him for his remaining years. If the granddaughter provides the agreed services, but the will makes no provision for her, she will be able to sue the estate based on the contract. This is an area for a skilled attorney to address.

Mere Promises Distinguished

Contracts to make a will should be distinguished from mere promises. A promise to make a gift in a will is unenforceable, even if someone detrimentally relies on the promise—that is, even if someone is hurt because he relied on an unkept promise. However, the promise may be respected posthumously if a charity is involved or if there was foreseeable detrimental reliance. For example, assume that a father orally promises his son that he will leave the family home to the son in his will. After the father's death, the will provides that the house goes to the father's brother. Although the father made a promise the promise was not kept. If the family home is of little value, and the son has pursued a lucrative career on the other side of the country, he has not relied to his detriment on the promise. Therefore, no enforceable agreement has occurred.

REVOCATION (CANCELLATION) OF WILLS

Usually, a will can be revoked (canceled) at any point during the testator's lifetime. Of course, exceptions to this general rule were just discussed above. If the testator has signed a prenuptial or postnuptial agreement, a divorce decree, or entered into a contract to make a will, then the will can neither be modified nor revoked. Aside from these circumstances, the testator can simply revoke the will altogether.

Although there must be a formal execution of a will, there are no special formalities required to revoke a will. Generally, a will may be revoked by tearing, burning, or marking up the old will.

EXAMPLE John writes "canceled" and "void" over each page of his will. He has canceled the will.

More commonly, an individual will merely execute a new will. The new will has language to the following effect: "This is my last will and testament and supersedes and revokes any prior wills."

Partial Revocation

Although most states allow partial revocations, some do not. In other words, in many states the testator can cross out specific provisions in a will. However in other states crossing out a sentence or paragraph, or marking "revoked" next to a particular paragraph may revoke the entire will. Even if it is obvious that the testator probably only intended that part of the will to be revoked, some court cases have held that this sort of partial revocation revokes the entire will. Because of the possibility of fraud, courts often interpret the rules in this area quite strictly.

When an individual tries to revoke a gift in a will he must be extremely careful to specifically identify to whom the property will go. In many wills, once a gift is canceled the gift will go to the person who is left the residue of the estate. This may or may not be what the testator intended. Generally, using a codicil or making a new will is neater and will create less problems than relying on a partial revocation.

Inadvertent Revocations

Although most revocations are intentional, a will can also be inadvertently revoked. This can happen as a result of the actions of the testator or by the operation of state law. As mentioned above, in some states, if a testator attempts to cross out a sentence or paragraph, he can revoke the entire will. In some states, if the testator gets divorced, that can revoke the will in whole or in part, while in other states the divorce has no effect on the validity of the will. Similarly, in some states getting married may revoke a will in whole or part.

DISINHERITING A SPOUSE OR CHILD
Disinheriting a Spouse

Perhaps the most important limit on testation is a spouse's statutory "election against a will," or forced share. This rule prevents a decedent from disinheriting a spouse. In England, wives were traditionally entitled to a dower right, which was a life interest in one-third of their husbands' real estate. In other words, the law gave the wife during her life a one-third interest in all of her husband's land. A husband had a reciprocal right called "curtesy."

Electing Against the Will: The Forced Share

Most states have abolished the dower right, replacing it with a statutory election which is sometimes called a forced share. This election allows a surviving spouse to either take the property left to her in the deceased spouse's will, or to elect to take a statutory share, which is usually one-third of the entire estate, although the percentage share varies from state to state.

In many states, the estate is first subject to creditors, claims and in some states, the estate may be reduced by lifetime gifts. In many states, then, creditors' claims and lifetime gifts to the spouse both reduce the amount of the forced share.

EXAMPLE Suppose that David was married to Karla. Although David assured Karla that she was well provided for in his will, in fact, David left Karla only $1.00, leaving the rest of the estate to his brother, Robert. Karla, as a surviving spouse, may elect against the will, and take a statutory share of the estate. In most states, this share would be one-third, although it may be as low as one-quarter or as high as one-half in some states. In other words, Karla will get one-third of the estate and Robert, David's brother and preferred heir, will only receive two-thirds of the estate.

Note that a spouse may elect to take a forced share even if he has been provided for by being named the beneficiary of a large life insurance policy on the deceased. In some states insurance proceeds also reduce, but normally do not eliminate, the amount that may be distributed under the statutory forced share.

Appendix B contains a state-by-state list of each state's rules concerning election against the will (the spouse's forced share).

Disinheriting Children

Although it is almost impossible to disinherit a spouse, it is relatively easy to disinherit children. However, not all attempts at disinheriting a child are successful. Most states have "pretermitted heir" statutes which provide that when a child is not named in a will, the child is presumed to have been overlooked and will receive her intestate share. In other words, if a parent omits any reference to a child in a will, the law presumes that the child has been overlooked, and the child will receive the same amount as if there was no will and the property passed to the family through the laws of intestacy in that jurisdiction.

NEWLY BORN CHILDREN

Newly born or newly adopted children are often not included in their parents' wills. For example, assume that Mr. and Mrs. Green have two children. After the birth of their second child the Greens each made up a will. Two years later, the Greens had a third child, but neglected to change their wills, so the new baby was not mentioned in either will. If Mr. and Mrs. Green were to die together in an auto accident, would the newly born third child get anything, since the child is not mentioned in the wills?

In this type of situation, the law provides that the omitted child will get a share of the parents' estates. All states have a "pretermitted heir" statute that covers this situation because it is so common. This law presumes that parents who have omitted a

child from their will have done so inadvertently, which is usually the case. The law steps in to give the omitted child a share of the estate. These statutes will give a share of the estate not only to natural children, but also to adopted children, children from a prior marriage, and to illegitimate children.

When the pretermitted heir statute comes into play, the omitted child will receive a share of the estate that is equal to what she would have received if the parent had died intestate—without a will. Most state intestacy statutes are generous to children, and the omitted child will normally get a sizeable share of the estate. In some cases, the pretermitted heir statute might actually give the omitted child more than the other children. The omitted child's share is made up of contributions from the other heirs. In other words, the other heirs will each get a smaller amount, the remainder of which then goes to the omitted child.

PRENUPTIAL AND POSTNUPTIAL AGREEMENTS

As mentioned earlier, a valid prenuptial agreement or postnuptial agreement limits what the testator can give away in a will. The contract takes precedence over the gifts in the will. This is true whether the will was executed before or after the agreement.

Prenuptial Agreements

A prenuptial agreement is a contract entered into between a couple about to be married, in which each makes certain promises to the other. Parties enter into prenuptial agreements for a variety of reasons, financial and otherwise, and these agreements are generally enforceable in a court of law. Wealthy individuals have long used prenuptial agreements to protect themselves against unscrupulous individuals who might marry them merely for their money. For example, a wealthy woman might insist that a would-be husband sign an agreement specifying the amount he would receive on divorce. Additionally, the agreement might specify exactly what he would get in the event of her death. Such agreements are especially common when a spouse is entering a second marriage, and one or both parties have families from a previous marriage.

Generally, a prenuptial agreement can legally restrict the amount of property that will be given in a will. For example, a couple who both have children from prior marriages might agree that any property that they bring into a marriage will go exclusively to their respective children. Additionally, an agreement can settle estate planning problems for the newly married couple, assuming both sides agree with the terms of the agreement. Both parties will enter the marriage knowing in advance how their property will be handled. Like other contracts, the parties can normally modify the contract later if they both agree to the changes.

A prenuptial agreement can also be used to establish a fixed sum rather than a maximum amount that a spouse might receive in a will. For example, an individual might agree to get married only on the condition that she will receive a set amount in the event of the other spouse's death. Although such an arrangement might be unappealing to some people, the courts will enforce this type of agreement, which is normally called a "contract to make a will." When such a prenuptial agreement is in force, it supersedes a will that provides contrary terms.

Postnuptial Agreements

A postnuptial agreement is one that is written after marriage, and that can restrict the amount a party will receive in a will. Postnuptial agreements generally have the same purpose as prenuptial agreements. In a postnuptial agreement, the spouse who is to receive the testamentary gift must give something or make a promise to the other spouse in return to make the agreement an enforceable contract. This is the concept of "consideration." If the spouse who is to receive the testamentary gift makes no new promises and provides no consideration for the promise, the agreement is merely a promise to make a gift in the future, and cannot be enforced.

Many states have enacted strict rules governing both prenuptial and postnuptial agreements. These rules are enacted to protect a spouse from unwittingly signing away important legal rights. Generally, these states require full disclosure of all material facts. Some states will not enforce such an agreement unless both spouses were represented by an attorney. In nearly all states, such agreements will be unenforceable if the protesting spouse can show fraud. For example, if a wealthy spouse claimed to have only $5 million at the time of the agreement, but in fact owned much more, the agreement would probably be unenforced because of the fraud.

....

WARNING *An executor discovering either a prenuptial agreement or a postnuptial agreement must determine its legal validity. This question will probably have to be resolved by the probate court itself.*

....

OTHER MATTERS
Effect of a Divorce or Remarriage

If the testator has either divorced or remarried since his will was drawn up, the executor needs to determine to what extent the will is still effective.

In some states, a divorce automatically revokes (cancels) a spouse's will. In other states, a divorce revokes only the portions of the will made in favor of the testator's ex-spouse. In other words, if the divorcing spouse had a will at the time of the divorce, but died before he made a new will, the old will would still be legally valid. However, if the old will contained gifts to his ex-spouse, these will not be enforced.

In many states the law considers both marriage and divorce to be major events in an individual's life. In some states a marriage will revoke a premarital will entirely. Most spouses leave the bulk of their estate to their spouse and an old will written before the marriage would be inappropriate in most cases. In other states, a marriage will not automatically revoke a will, but it may revoke any specific bequest made to the spouse, on the premise that the earlier bequest would no longer be sufficient. State laws vary on this point and the executor should get competent legal advice.

Besides reviewing a will after a divorce or a remarriage, the testator should be sure to review the beneficiary and payable-on-death designations of life insurance policies, annuities, pensions, brokerage accounts, and government bonds. Although state law may modify the will, these beneficiary designations are not normally affected by a divorce or remarriage. In other words, the old designations will not change unless the holder requests a change from the company that issued the policy or plan. If the testator dies without making the necessary changes, the property could unexpectedly go to an ex-spouse.

A beneficiary designation on will substitutes such as an insurance policy, an annuity, a pension, a brokerage account, or a bond will control over any contrary provisions in a will. In other words, even though an individual made a recent will leaving all his property to his new spouse, the insurance company and other providers are legally bound to pay over these will substitutes to the designated beneficiary. This is true even if the individual mentioned the particular policy or annuity in his will.

EXAMPLE Assume that Brown has left a will leaving all his property to his new spouse. The will, which was quickly drawn up at the hospital, mentions that the proceeds of his life insurance should also go to his new wife. Unfortunately for Brown, the insurance company is legally bound by the beneficiary designation Brown made earlier, and the more recent designation in Brown's will is not enforced even though the deceased's intentions were clear.

Powers of Appointment

An often overlooked device that can be included in a will or a trust is called a power of appointment. A power of appointment is an authorization for another individual (frequently the executor) to exercise judgment and discretion about how a particular matter should be handled. This type of power is somewhat unusual because the executor's typical rule is to follow the precise instructions for the distribution of the estate's property set out in the will. Exercising a power of appointment is discussed more fully in Chapter 9, "Closing the Estate."

Estate Tax Consequences

Although a discussion of the estate tax consequences of powers of appointment is beyond the scope of this book, it should be noted that the holder of a general power of appointment is considered to own the property for estate tax purposes. The tax code specifies that in certain cases the holder of a special power of appointment need not include the value of the power in his or her own estate.

Disclaimers

When reading the deceased's will, the executor should bear in mind that an heir can disclaim a gift. In such an event, if the will provides for an alternate person to receive the gift, it will pass to that individual. If no provision for an alternate has been made, the gift will normally pass to the residue of the estate. Almost any property can be disclaimed, including joint interests in bank accounts, real estate, and even community property. The law also allows partial disclaimers. Disclaimers are addressed in more detail in Chapters 9 and 13.

CHAPTER 7

Managing Property

INTRODUCTION

One of the executor's important duties is managing the property in the estate. Depending on the complexity of the deceased's affairs, this could be either a relatively simple job or an extremely time-consuming one. If the deceased had substantial investments or a business, administering the estate may be almost a full-time job. This chapter details the executor's duties with regard to managing property, including the executor's duty to safeguard assets. The chapter will also discuss the executor's duties and responsibilities as they pertain to investing funds, borrowing money, and selling property. The chapter will also discuss running the deceased's business. Finally, the chapter concludes with a discussion of community property laws.

SAFEGUARDING PROPERTY

The executor's primary duty is to safeguard the deceased's property. This includes securing the family home and other property. If the executor is familiar with the deceased's affairs, this job will be far easier than if he is not. The executor has ultimate responsibility for all of the assets.

WARNING *Some criminals scan the obituary columns for information about easy burglary opportunities. The executor needs to take basic precautions against break-ins, such as locking up the deceased's house if unoccupied, and*

stopping newspaper and mail deliveries. An unoccupied home may invite unwanted attention from criminals. It is the executor's duty to safeguard these assets.

Custody of Assets

The executor needs to decide whether to take physical custody of assets. Family members or other trustworthy persons may already have custody. For example, a surviving spouse or other family member may be residing in the family home. This is probably a good idea, because property is safeguarded. If the deceased lived alone, then the executor will need to make arrangements to safeguard the house or apartment. If there are valuable items like watches, jewelry, paintings, televisions, and other electronic equipment in the home, they should be removed and stored in a secure place.

Insurance

The executor is responsible for seeing to it that all property continues to be properly insured. If insurance is insufficient or missing altogether, the executor needs to get the property insured promptly.

Taxes

The executor has a duty to pay all taxes on the deceased's property. These taxes should be paid out of the estate's checking account. If the property itself earns income—for example an apartment building—the taxes and other expenses should be paid with that income. If the property does not produce income, then the executor should use general estate funds.

Repairs

The executor has a duty to keep the deceased's property in good repair. However, only repairs, not "improvements," should be made.

EXAMPLE The deceased's home is in bad repair. For example, the deck has several missing boards and dry rot. The executor should see that the deck is repaired to preserve the home's value. The executor should not demolish the old deck and replace it with a larger one with a spa. This would go beyond a repair and would be considered an improvement.

LOCATING ASSETS

The executor has a duty to locate all of the deceased's property. If the deceased was well-organized this may be no problem. In other cases this job can be both frustrating and time-consuming. Fortunately, (at least for an executor), most property triggers some kind of paperwork. For example, if the deceased owned real estate, a utility bill, a mortgage bill, or a real estate tax bill will eventually arrive. These clues can help the executor make an accurate inventory of all of the property.

Life Insurance Policies

The executor can help collect any life insurance proceeds. Although the insurance proceeds are not usually part of the estate's assets, the executor will want to help the beneficiaries collect the death benefits.

Although family members and business partners may own policies on the life of the deceased, in most cases individuals own their own life insurance policies and name beneficiaries who are to receive the cash death benefit. These life insurance policies are typically found with the deceased's other important papers.

OBSERVATION *The deceased may have been covered by a number of policies—some large and some small. Do not overlook group policies provided by employers, frater-*

nal associations, and even the American Automobile Association. If the deceased died in an accident many policies include a double indemnity clause, *which provides that the beneficiaries receive twice the normal death benefit.*

Federal Tax Form 712

If a life insurance policy is legally part of the estate, the proceeds may be subject to federal estate tax. If the estate will be filing a Federal Estate Tax Return, Form 706, the executor must get an IRS Form 712 from each insurance company. This form reports the amount of the death benefit and who received it. If the deceased had no ownership interest in the policy at death (for example, a policy owned by a business partner who paid the premiums on it) then no Form 712 will be needed for that particular policy.

Most insurance companies will mail a check promptly once they are properly notified. The executor should call the insurance agent who sold the policy if that individual is known to the executor. The agent will help gather the documents and prepare the forms. Be sure to make a photocopy of the insurance policy, because the insurance agent will probably need to return the policy to the company. The insurance company will send the check in a few weeks.

OBSERVATION *If there is a very large policy, the insurance company may be a bit slow in paying it off—especially if the company has any doubts about its obligation to pay (for example, if it suspects fraud for some reason). Each state has a law requiring the company to pay interest on late payments. If the insurance proceeds are over two months late, the executor should check with the state insurance department to see what interest is due from the insurance company.*

Social Security and Veteran's Benefits

Like life insurance proceeds, Social Security and veteran's benefits are not part of the probate estate. However, the executor is in a good position to help grieving survivors file the paperwork to collect these benefits. Contact the local Social Security Administration and Veterans Administration offices to inquire about benefits.

RECORD KEEPING

The executor is expected to keep exact records of all property and money coming into and out of her possession. Although the executor may be grieving, this important responsibility cannot be overlooked.

The basic tool for financial record keeping is the estate's checking account, which is described in the next section. The executor is expected to be able to account for every penny of the deceased's property. This is a far more rigorous procedure than most individuals employ in their own lives.

EXAMPLE An executor meets several times with the estate's lawyer at the lawyer's downtown office to discuss issues surrounding the inventorying of property. The executor pays for parking in a parking garage. Because the parking fees are an expense of estate administration, the executor must keep accurate records, such as dated receipts. It is insufficient for the executor to write herself a check for $100 and record the expense as "Miscellaneous." Greater precision is required because the executor will have to account to the court for all monies, and the court will be reviewing each check and description of each expense. When in doubt, the executor should err on the side of keeping too much information rather than too little.

OPENING BANK ACCOUNTS

The executor needs to open a checking account for the estate immediately. The executor should ask the bank manager for an estate account because the bank will then provide a special check register (the portion of the checkbook in which you record the checks and deposits) that will make it easy to record the name and address of each recipient and the purpose of each payment. The executor will need these details to prepare the final accounting for the court; it will be far easier to prepare if the checkbook is in proper order.

The executor should choose a bank that is conveniently located because she may have to make numerous deposits. The executor can use her own

bank but a separate estate account must be opened. Bank personnel may be more helpful in resolving problems if they know the executor personally. Bank fees in a local area do vary, although probably not by very much.

WARNING *The executor must be very careful never to commingle funds. Never write a personal check for an estate expense and never write an estate check for a personal expense, even if you plan to reimburse the estate's account. Never deposit personal funds in the estate's account and* never, ever *deposit money of the estate in your personal account. The executor has a strict fiduciary duty and commingling funds may land the executor in serious trouble with the probate judge, even if the executor had no dishonest intent.*

If the deceased had substantial cash on hand at death, the executor should not keep it all in the checking account. The executor should establish one or more insured bank accounts that receive a higher rate of interest. If additional cash is received as insurance proceeds are paid out, assets are sold, or debts are collected, this cash should be promptly deposited into these additional accounts.

SAFE-DEPOSIT BOX

The executor needs to determine if the deceased had one or more safe-deposit boxes. Most people don't have more than one. The executor needs to examine and inventory the contents of the box. People often keep copies of important records in the box, such as a copy of their will, deeds to property, or the deed to a burial plot.

OBSERVATION *The best source of information about safe-deposit boxes is family members. However, even family members may not know if an individual had a safe-deposit box. People normally have a box at a bank in which they have other accounts. The executor should ask each bank in which there is evidence of an account if there is any record of the deceased having a box at the bank.*

Although the deceased was given a key to the box, it may be hard to find. If necessary, the bank can drill open the lock. In many states, state law requires the bank to "seal" the decedent's box to prevent removal of valuable items. Bank personnel will allow the executor to open the box in their presence, but will not allow removal of items. In a few states, bank safe-deposit boxes can only be opened in the presence of a state official.

....

WARNING *As soon as the executor discovers the whereabouts of a safe-deposit box, the executor should promptly notify the bank of the deceased's death so the bank can secure the box to bar entry to others. Family members with access to safe-deposit boxes have been known to wrongfully remove jewelry, cash, and other valuables before the bank has "sealed" the box.*

....

INVESTING ESTATE FUNDS

If the deceased had substantial investments, the executor is expected to maintain them. Although the executor can get professional help—from an investment advisor or stockbroker—the executor is ultimately responsible for making investment decisions.

Some states specifically limit the types of investments that can be made by executors. These states prohibit the executor from putting the estate's money in risky investments even though they promise a high return. The will itself may provide explicit directions. For example, the will may direct the executor to sell certain investments in the event of the deceased's death.

Standard of Care in Investing

In many states the probate court will require the executor to meet a special standard when making investments on behalf of the estate. The executor must act like a "prudent person" in investing estate assets. Under this standard, the executor must give equal regard to probable income and probable safety of the principle. Other states, such as New York, have adopted a "prudent investor" rule. The executor should check state laws to comply with the required standard of care.

BORROWING MONEY

In most states the executor has power to borrow money when needed to pay estate expenses. Executors are typically faced with a surprising number of

bills that must be paid. In many cases, although the deceased owned a lot of valuable property, the estate will not contain enough ready cash to pay bills including debts, taxes, medical bills, funeral expenses, and estate administration expenses. The executor may also need to borrow money to support the surviving spouse and dependents who have lost the regular salary the deceased earned.

The executor needs to consider several factors before borrowing money to pay expenses. Borrowing is often an alternative to selling estate assets to pay the estate's bills. Of course, borrowed money has to be paid back. If income or debts will be collected in the next few months, repayment may not be a problem. On the other hand, estate assets may have to be sold to raise cash to repay the loan. There may be a risk that the assets' value may drop unexpectedly. For example, the stock market may fall and stocks may lose a substantial portion of their value. The executor also needs to be prudent in selecting assets to be sold. Care should be taken not to inadvertently "disinherit" a beneficiary by selling off their inheritance before they receive it.

....

OBSERVATION *It may be possible to borrow money from family members who have received life insurance proceeds on the death of the deceased. Trusts are another source of funds. If these are not available, the executor will have to use more conventional sources, such as short-term bank loans.*

....

SELLING PROPERTY

If the estate needs money to pay its bills or taxes, the executor is normally empowered to sell assets. The executor may also need to raise cash to pay the support of a surviving spouse or other dependents. The executor needs to be careful to avoid selling property that is given to a specific person in the will. It is a good idea to notify—in writing—the beneficiaries of the estate that items are to be sold, and give them the opportunity to object.

Household Items

If the deceased lived alone, the executor must dispose of the contents of the deceased's house—furniture, bedding, and other household goods. The persons sharing the estate need to be consulted in this process. If those persons are to share the estate equally, then theoretically they should receive property of equal value. Typically, these persons will tour the home or apartment and try to come to some agreement about who will take what. If there is a dispute, the executor will have to resolve it.

Unwanted items can be sold in an "estate sale" at the home and the cash used to pay the estate's bills or distributed to the beneficiaries. If items have little value they may be donated to the Salvation Army or Goodwill Industries. The executor should keep a receipt because the charitable donation can be claimed on the estate's tax return.

The executor will also need to have the house or apartment cleaned out. If family members are unavailable to do this, the executor will have to hire people to help.

Obtaining a Fair Price

Sometimes there is no ready market for property that is obviously valuable. Although estates are typically settled within a few months or a year, this time frame may not be reasonable for a profitable sale of some property. For example, undeveloped land can be difficult to sell at a fair price. Similarly, selling an interest in a small business requires judgment and can be time-consuming. Although it may be tempting to accept the first offer for such property if no other offers have been made, the executor has a duty to maximize the amount that will go to the will's beneficiaries.

RUNNING THE DECEASED'S BUSINESS

If the deceased owned a business at the time of his death, the executor may have to step in to run it or find a competent manager to do so. If the business has managers in place because the owner was not active in the day-to-day operations, then the executor's duties will be correspondingly diminished.

Learning about a business and then managing it can be a major undertaking, and discussing the details involved is beyond the scope of this book. Details on selling the deceased's business are provided later in this chapter.

PREPARING THE INVENTORY

Executors must prepare a detailed inventory listing of all the deceased's property and its fair market value for the probate court. The inventory must normally be filed with the court just a few months after the deceased's death. The time period varies from three to nine months in most states. Three months after death is a very short time to get this work done, and many courts will allow an extension if more time is needed.

The checklist at the end of the chapter will help the executor in preparing this inventory.

LEGAL TITLE

In preparing the inventory, it is important to understand the concept of legal title.

Importance of Legal Title

The law considers the owner of property to be the party who holds legal title. This is true even though the property has been held and used by a party other than the legal title holder for a number of years. In most cases, if the deceased held legal title to property at the date of death, the property is part of the estate. The executor may need to consult with the estate's attorney about the ownership of certain property.

Generally, the will can only give away property that the decedent owned at death. Surprisingly, ownership of property is not always entirely clear. Memories fade over time and records are sometimes missing. Additionally, if the deceased lived in one of the community property states, legal advice should be sought regarding ownership. If there have been any lawsuits or other disputes regarding ownership of property, the executor may have to resolve these thorny disputes as part of the probate process.

Jointly Owned Property

The deceased may have owned property jointly with another person or persons. Many older people put property in joint names for a variety of reasons. One common reason is that when one of the owners dies, the property passes to the co-owner without going through probate. However, this is not always the case. The form of legal ownership will determine whether or not the property passes without going through probate. In most states there are two ways to put property in joint names: tenancy in common and joint tenancy. It is important to know the difference between these two forms of ownership. The consequeneces at death can be quite different depending on which legal term was used on the title.

EXAMPLE 1 Assume two brothers, John and Paul, own a vacation home as "joint tenants." John is married to Mary and his will provides that on his death Mary will receive all of his property. On John's death the vacation home will be owned by Paul because property held in joint tenancies do not become part of the probate estate and ownership vests in the joint tenant, in this case Paul.

EXAMPLE 2 Assume two brothers, John and Paul, own a vacation home as "tenants in common." John is married to Mary and his will provides that on his death Mary will receive all his property. On John's death the vacation home will be owned by Mary and Paul. An interest in a tenancy in common may be devised, or bequeathed, in a will and Mary will receive the interest in the vacation home along with John's other property.

VALUING THE DECEDENT'S PROPERTY

The probate court also needs to know the value of the property in the estate. The executor needs to provide the property's "current fair market value," which may be very different from the price the deceased paid for it. In most cases the value of property decreases with age and use. For example, a household appliance like a stove or refrigerator will only be worth a fraction of its original retail price. Other property—like paintings, real estate, or collectibles—can actually increase in value over time.

Where to Start

Valuation can be difficult and time-consuming. You can find the value of stocks and other investments by consulting the *Wall Street Journal* or by calling a stockbroker. You can find the value of a home by consulting a real estate agent, or by using the

county's tax value, although in some places the value used for real estate taxes may differ quite a bit from the property's true value. There are car valuation guides such as Kelly's *Blue Book*. If it isn't available at the newsstand or library, the executor can ask a loan officer at her bank or a car insurance agent to use theirs. If the deceased owned potentially valuable jewelry, antiques, or artwork, the executor will probably need an appraisal to back up her valuation. If unrealistic values are placed on property, the executor may have to explain them in court.

Some life insurance policies have a cash value. The executor needs to ask the deceased's insurance agent or the company to help get this figure. Notice that the "value" is different from the amount the policy will pay out should the insured die.

Valuing personal items—such as older cars, boats, household goods, and clothing—is a good deal less precise. The executor should do a little homework by visiting thrift stores or by looking in the newspaper's classified ads for similar items. Although you need to give a good faith effort at establishing a reasonable value, there is no "right" answer to these valuation questions.

INVENTORYING DEBTS

The executor must also detail all of the deceased's debts for the probate court. This inventory needs to be as precise as the one detailing the deceased's property.

MANAGING DIFFERENT TYPES OF PROPERTY
Cash

The executor needs to look carefully for any currency stored at the deceased's home or in a safe-deposit box. The executor should carefully account for the money, making a note of the exact amount and where it was found, and deposit it into the estate's checking account.

....
OBSERVATION *Older people who lived through the bank failures of the Great Depression are more likely to have cash hidden away in the home. Ask a family member if the deceased ever mentioned having a box or a hiding place at home.*
....

Bank Accounts

Locate and make a list of all of the deceased's bank accounts. The executor needs to verify each account's balance at the date of death for the court and for the IRS. The executor should mail a letter to each bank, identifying herself as executor, and include the deceased's full name, social security number, and account number, if known. The letter should request each bank to provide the exact balance in each separate account on the day the deceased died.

If the deceased kept money in a certificate of deposit (CD) or other term account, determine if the account renews automatically.

EXAMPLE Mary owned a $10,000 six-month certificate of deposit. The account automatically renews for another six months unless the bank hears otherwise.

The executor should cancel any such accounts and deposit the money in similar accounts in the name of the estate. This allows the estate the use of the funds and does not delay distribution of the money to the persons named in the will.

Jointly Owned Accounts

If the deceased owned the bank account with another individual as "joint owners with right of survivorship," legal ownership of the account passes automatically to the co-owner and the account does not come into the estate. The executor needs to determine the correct legal ownership. This topic is discussed later in the chapter.

Stock Brokerage Accounts and Other Investments

The executor needs to identify all brokerage accounts and other investments. Stock held in "street name" (stock in the name of a broker who trades in securities and is a member of an exchange) can be sold promptly if the estate is in need of funds. If the will makes gifts of stock, the stock should not be sold.

Automobiles

In many states jointly titled cars can be transferred to the co-owner by sending a copy of the death certificate along with an appropriate state form to the Department of Motor Vehicles. If there is only one name on the auto title, the auto will have to be disposed of through the will. Physical custody of the car can normally be given to the individual who will ultimately receive the car from the estate. The executor needs to get a receipt from that person acknowledging that they merely have custody, not full ownership of the vehicle, until the estate is fully settled and closed.

The executor also needs to make absolutely certain that this person obtains "full coverage" auto insurance and keeps it in force. There needs to be collision and comprehensive coverage on the auto, not just liability coverage. Liability coverage only pays for damage to other cars, whereas collision and comprehensive coverage pays for damage to the insured car.

Keepsakes and Heirlooms

The will may contain explicit directions on the distribution of heirlooms and keepsakes. In some cases, the will may merely provide that personal property is to be divided among certain persons. The deceased may have left a letter of instructions about such property. In some states such letters are binding on the executor and heirs. In other states such a letter stands just as a suggestion.

There may be problems if the deceased made any promises in the past about certain items. It is not unusual for bad feelings to arise because promises about keepsakes were forgotten when a will was drafted. The will may provide for a different final distribution of these items. The executor cannot change the distribution scheme from that stated in the will, even if it seems unfair.

Family Home

The family home also presents a number of potential problems. For many individuals, the family home is by far the most valuable asset in the estate. Husbands and wives typically own their homes jointly, with each owning a one-half interest. If this is the case, at death the surviving spouse will automatically become the owner of the home and the home will not pass through the probate estate. If only one spouse owns the family home then the will provides whether the house is left to the surviving spouse or to other heirs, such as the children.

For a widow or widower, the family home is likely to be the most significant asset in the estate, but if there is more than one heir, it may be impossible to keep the house in the family.

EXAMPLE Assume that Mary is a widow living in the family home and that she would like her three surviving children to share her estate equally. Because of appreciation in real estate prices, the home will probably comprise 70 percent of Mary's estate.

Because the home is such a large asset in comparison to the rest of the estate, it will be very difficult to equalize the distributions and keep the home in the family—that is, to give the house to one child and also provide the other two with shares of equal value. Unless one of the three children can raise enough cash by mortgaging the home or supply it from personal assets to equalize the three shares, the house will most likely have to be sold and the proceeds split between the three heirs. Alternately, the three heirs may be willing to co-own the home for a number of years with one heir paying off the other two over time.

OBSERVATION *If the heirs are forced to sell the family home, at least such heirs will not have to pay income tax on the sale. The heirs will take a "basis" in the house equal to the fair market value. Accordingly, if they sell the home for its market value then they will have no taxable gain and no income tax will be due on the sale of the home.*

A similar problem may arise when a farm or business makes up the bulk of an estate which is to be shared equally among three heirs. Unless one of them can raise enough cash through a mortgage or from personal assets to equalize the three shares, the farm or family business will most likely have to be sold.

Advance planning by the deceased can minimize such problems. If the deceased got good advice before death, he may have planned ahead by pur-

chasing life insurance whose death benefit could be used to equalize the heirs' shares of the property.

Rental Real Estate
If the deceased owned rental properties, the executor will have to manage them. This can be a major undertaking no matter what the size and extent of the rentals. The executor will be responsible not only for collecting rents, but also for paying bills, mortgage payments and taxes, as well as for keeping the property properly insured. The executor will also be responsible for renting the buildings and making sure that the properties are well-maintained.

If the rentals are extensive, the deceased may have had one or more employees helping to manage and maintain the properties. These people will have to be paid along with payroll taxes. If the executor has no knowledge of rental properties it may be a good idea to hire a company that specializes in managing rental properties. Even though they charge a fee, their experience may actually save money for the estate. They may be better able to maximize income by keeping the properties fully rented. Because they have on-staff maintenance people, they may be able to make repairs for less than an outside contractor would charge. Tenants will call the management company rather than the executor if they have lost their key or have a broken pipe on Saturday at 2:00 in the morning.

FAMILY FARMS AND BUSINESSES
If the deceased owned a farm or business, the executor may be called upon to manage it. It is important to examine the will carefully to determine if the deceased left instructions about the business. If the deceased owned a farm or business it is more likely that she may have done estate planning before death. The executor may be called upon to help a family resolve important issues about the ownership and management of the family farm or business.

Instructions Left in the Will
In some cases the will provides that the executor should liquidate—sell—the farm or business; in other cases the will may specifically provide that the

business be continued. When there are explicit instructions, the executor needs to follow them unless they are unreasonable and will harm the interests of the beneficiaries. If the will commands the executor to continue the business, but the executor concludes that this is an unwise decision, the executor should petition the probate court for permission to sell it.

EXAMPLE Paul's will instructs his executor to continue to run his small retail store. After a few weeks it becomes obvious that the business's success was built on Paul's personal abilities. Without Paul behind the counter, many old customers started shopping elsewhere. The executor concludes that the business cannot be run profitably, at least not in the foreseeable future. The executor should petition the court for permission to sell the business assets for the benefit of the will's beneficiaries.

No Instructions in the Will

If the will contains no explicit instructions about operating or selling the business, the executor needs to decide if continuing the business is the best course of action.

WARNING *This is an area of risk for the executor. Beneficiaries of the will may disagree with the executor's decision, especially if it produces a bad result. For example, if the will contains no instructions about the deceased's business and the executor decides to continue managing it, and it then posts a loss, a beneficiary might sue the executor for "wasting" the estate's property. Because legal rules vary state by state, it would be a good idea for the executor to consult with the estate's attorney (or another attorney if the estate has none) to determine what to do under the relevant state's laws.*

When no instructions are given in the will the executor's basic duty is to maximize the return for the beneficiaries of the will.

WARNING *Note carefully that the executor's duty is to the beneficiaries of the will, not to the employees, customers, or other owners of the business. If the conclusion is that the best interests of the beneficiaries will be served by closing the business, other persons may be harmed by the decision. The executor's legal duty is to maximize the beneficiaries' wealth.*

In deciding whether to continue a business or to liquidate it, the executor needs to consider a number of variables. Normally a business is worth far more as a "going concern." If the business assets are sold, they may only bring a fraction of the former value of the business. The beneficiaries may be better off if the business is continued. They could either continue to own it after the estate is closed or perhaps sell it at a later time.

The competence of the present managers is a big factor in the business's eventual success. If the remaining managers are competent and can carry on without the deceased, then the prospects for the business to remain profitable may be good. On the other hand, if the deceased was the real sparkplug in the business, it is less likely that the business will remain as profitable. There is also no guarantee that competent managers will remain with the business after the deceased's death. Customers, suppliers, and lenders who had a close personal relationship with the deceased will also reevaluate their relationships with the business and may go elsewhere.

If there are a number of uncertainties, the executor should consult with the beneficiaries about their desire to continue the business. They may also be a good source of information about the business's prospects of success. If one or more of the heirs are currently employed in the business, they may be eager to have the business continue operations.

Reconciling Different Desires

If there are outsiders who are co-owners of the business, their needs and desires must also be considered. A co-owner may decide that this is the time to liquidate or to retire. A co-owner may also approach the executor and offer to buy the deceased's share of the business from the estate.

If there are a number of beneficiaries, the situation can become more complex. This is especially so when the beneficiaries have different expectations of the estate.

EXAMPLE At the time of his death, John, a widower, owned a substantial family business. One of John's two sons works full-time in the business and has for a number of years. He would like to continue the business. The other son is a doctor and has no particular interest in the family business. This son is not interested in getting a one-half interest in the family business, but prefers to get cash as soon as possible.

The need to "cash out" an heir can present a significant issue for the estate. If the business represents the bulk of the estate, it is unlikely that enough cash and other liquid assets can be raised to equalize the shares of the two sons. There are a number of options available, however. If the uninvolved son is willing, he could receive his share over a number of years from the earnings of the company. However, this may be impossible if the company does not generate sufficient annual cash flow. Alternately, the company could borrow the money by mortgaging its assets, or could even sell some of them. However, either of these courses could financially weaken the business. If the deceased had planned ahead, he may have purchased life insurance to help finance the buy-out, and thereby help keep the business in the family.

Buy/Sell Agreements

Many business owners execute buy/sell agreements during their lives. These contracts cover the sale of the business when a triggering event—such as death—occurs. The executor may find that the deceased had planned for an orderly disposition of the business by negotiating a buy/sell agreement before death. If no evidence of such an agreement is found at the deceased's home, a search should be made of the business premises. The executor needs to consult with the business's accountant and attorney about the possibility that there is an existing buy/sell agreement.

Valuation

If the business is to be sold, professional advice needs to be sought to enable the estate to maximize the amount available for the heirs. The business will also need to be appraised by a professional business appraiser. This is required by both the probate court and the IRS.

Duties

The executor has some special duties in connection with the operation of a business. If the business is to be continued, the executor needs to make sure that all taxes—especially payroll taxes—are being paid. The executor needs to consult with the bookkeeper and accountant to ensure that taxes continue to be paid. If the deceased was a professional, a doctor, for example, the executor needs to secure client records. Patients need to be notified and arrangements made to turn over their files to whichever new doctor they choose. The executor needs to try to collect any fees that were earned by the deceased before death. Careful bookkeeping is essential.

Finances

The executor needs to keep in mind that the business and the estate are two separate entities, and that their financial affairs must be kept separate. Even though the executor is running both, money must be kept in separate bank accounts. Estate money should not be used to pay the bills of the business.

COMMUNITY PROPERTY SYSTEMS

Nine states—Arizona, California, Idaho, Louisiana, New Mexico, Nevada, Texas, Washington, and Wisconsin—have community property systems. If the deceased lived or owned property in any of these states, the executor needs to understand how the community property system operates.

Although the details of the state systems differ in some respects, the general scheme is similar. Community property only applies to married couples. In a community property state, spouses typically own community property as well as individual property. Each spouse has a one-half undivided interest in each item of community property. At death, a spouse can dispose of all of his separate property, but only his one-half interest in the community property. In some states a spouse cannot make a lifetime gift of community property without the other spouse's consent.

Classification of Property

To effectively create an estate plan in a community property state, the couple's property must be systematically classified as either separate or community property. Community property is property that is onerously (not gratuitously) acquired during the course of the marriage. This includes the salaries and the earned income of each spouse. Separate property—which can be owned by either a husband or wife—is property acquired before marriage, or gifts, inheritances, or life insurance proceeds received individually during the marriage. In Texas and Idaho, income from separate property is considered community property, while in the other seven states it is classified as separate property.

Commingling

Most states presume that property acquired during marriage is community property. Without careful segregation or record keeping, a couple may lose track of which property is separate property. In such cases, all of the couple's property may be considered community property. In some states, such as Washington, the couple can easily convert separate property to community property and community property to separate property. Texas, Idaho, and Washington recognize statutory community property agreements, which operate as will substitutes.

PLANNING NOTE *The executor, together with the estate's attorney, should accurately classify each item of property as community property or separate property. In several states, an agreement between the spouses can control classification.*

Income Tax Advantage of Community Property

Under current federal tax codes, community property has a major income tax advantage over jointly held property. The entire tax basis of the property is "stepped up" to fair market value on the death of either spouse. In non-community property states, only the deceased's share of jointly held property receives the favorable step-up. Well-to-do couples often engage in predeath planning to take advantage of these rules.

EXAMPLE A husband and wife own a parcel of property with a fair market value of $2,000,000

and a tax basis of $500,000. If the property is community property, on the death of the first spouse, the tax basis of $500,000 increases to $2,000,000. In a non-community property state, only one-half of the property receives a step-up. Accordingly, the tax basis for income tax purposes only rises to $1,250,000: one-half of the property rises from $250,000 to $1,000,000, and the other half retains its $250,000 basis (one-half of $500,000).

PLANNING NOTE *Although the "step-up" rule is generally favorable, it can be a disadvantage if property values have fallen. In such cases separate ownership of the property would be preferable.*

EXAMPLE A husband and wife own a parcel of property with a tax basis of $2,000,000 and a current fair market value of $500,000. If the property is community property, on the death of the first spouse the tax basis falls to $500,000. This minimizes any loss and tax advantage on disposition of the property. In a non-community property state, the basis would only fall to $1,250,000, which allows a greater write-off on the sale of the property by the surviving spouse.

Transitory Estates

It is not uncommon for a couple to have lived in many states in the course of their marriage. They may have lived in both community property and noncommunity property states. Even in a noncommunity property state, community property retains its unique status. Merely moving into a noncommunity property state will not change the community property ownership status of the couple. Accordingly, a spouse will have a one-half interest in the community property even in a noncommunity property state. A number of states have adopted the Uniform Disposition of Community Property at Death Act, which provides that the noncommunity property state shall apply community property law in probating the estate.

PLANNING NOTE *Attorneys in noncommunity property states are not always sensitive to community property* *issues and may ignore community property categorization. Though this does not constitute malpractice, such ignorance is disadvantageous to the client because community property is tax-advantaged.*

Quasi-Community Property

California and Washington have statutory schemes that recognize a special class of community property at the time of death. Quasi-community property is property that is not technically community property, but is treated as such when a spouse dies. Quasi-community property is property acquired in a common law state that would have been community property had the couple resided in California and/or Washington at the time.

Widow's Election

Although community property states do not have a "forced share" law, a widow or widower may elect to take their one-half share of community property in lieu of the disposition their spouse made for them in the will. This protects the surviving spouse when the deceased's will attempts to give away all or most of the community property. Since the deceased spouse had the right only to dispose of one-half of the community property, the surviving spouse can elect to take their one-half share despite any provision in the will.

OBSERVATION *California, a community property state, also allows a forced share of any quasi-community property.*

EXECUTOR'S INVENTORY CHECKLIST

The following checklists can be used in preparing the initial and final inventories of the decedent's property for the court.

Worksheet: Property Inventory

	Current Fair Market Value	Original Purchase Price	Source of Valuation
REAL PROPERTY			
Home	_____	_____	_____
Vacation Home	_____	_____	_____
Condominium	_____	_____	_____
Co-op Apartment	_____	_____	_____
Mobile Home	_____	_____	_____
Home Lot	_____	_____	_____
Burial Plot	_____	_____	_____
Rental Properties	_____	_____	_____
Vacant Land	_____	_____	_____
Farm Land	_____	_____	_____
PERSONAL PROPERTY			
Cash On Hand	_____	_____	_____
Bank Accounts	_____	_____	_____
	_____	_____	_____
	_____	_____	_____
	_____	_____	_____
	_____	_____	_____
Household Goods	_____	_____	_____
	_____	_____	_____
	_____	_____	_____
	_____	_____	_____
Hobby/Recreational Items	_____	_____	_____
	_____	_____	_____
	_____	_____	_____
	_____	_____	_____
	_____	_____	_____
Boats	_____	_____	_____
	_____	_____	_____

Worksheet: Property Inventory (Continued)

	Current Fair Market Value	Original Purchase Price	Source of Valuation
PERSONAL PROPERTY (Continued)			
Clothing			
Jewelry/Watches			
Investments			
Pensions			
Life Insurance Policies			
Amounts Due to Deceased (Accounts Receivable)			
Business Equipment			
Business Inventory			

Worksheet: Property Inventory (Continued)

	Current Fair Market Value	Original Purchase Price	Source of Valuation
PERSONAL PROPERTY (Continued)			
Farm Equipment	_____	_____	_____
	_____	_____	_____
	_____	_____	_____
	_____	_____	_____
Livestock/Animals	_____	_____	_____
	_____	_____	_____
	_____	_____	_____
	_____	_____	_____
Crops	_____	_____	_____
	_____	_____	_____
	_____	_____	_____
	_____	_____	_____
Other Property	_____	_____	_____
	_____	_____	_____
	_____	_____	_____
	_____	_____	_____
	_____	_____	_____
	_____	_____	_____
	_____	_____	_____
	_____	_____	_____
	_____	_____	_____

Worksheet: Debt Inventory

	Creditor, Address, Account #	Balance Owed	Monthly Payments	Amount in Arrears (overdue)	Value of Collateral (if any)
Mortgages					
2nd Mortgages					
Home Equity Loans					
Rent					
Car Loans					
Boat Loans					
Student Loans					
Credit Cards					

Worksheet: Debt Inventory (Continued)

	Creditor, Address, Account #	Balance Owed	Monthly Payments	Amount in Arrears (overdue)	Value of Collateral (if any)
Medical Bills					
Utility Bills					
Taxes					
Other Debts					

CHAPTER 8

Paying Creditors and Taxes

INTRODUCTION

The executor has several important basic duties: gathering together the deceased's property, paying creditors, and distributing the remaining property to those mentioned in the will.

Most people are familiar with distributing the property, but few people think much about paying creditors. However, this is a very important function of the probate process and one of the most important jobs that the executor will be called upon to perform. The executor must take care to pay creditors properly and promptly.

The executor must pay creditors and see to it that taxes are paid and tax returns are filed. This chapter will discuss the basics of dealing with "claims" made by creditors and taxing authorities. The chapter details the executor's duty to provide notice to creditors and how to evaluate claims made against the estate. There is also a discussion of what to do when there are insufficient assets to pay all claims and to make gifts described in the will. Finally, the chapter discusses the executor's responsibility for filing income taxes for both the deceased and the estate.

CREDITOR CLAIMS

Unfortunately, death does not eliminate an individual's debts. Instead, the deceased's estate becomes liable for the debts. Nearly all the deceased's property will ordinarily flow into the estate, where it can be reached by creditors. For example, if Green owed the IRS $3,000 for back taxes, his death does not eliminate the tax bill, and Green's estate will be liable to pay the debt. In fact, any property in the estate will go first to the testator's creditors. After all the bills are paid, whatever is left will go to the heirs. It is the executor's duty to evaluate creditor claims against the estate and pay those that prove legitimate and that are properly filed. If a creditor is not paid, it can sue the estate.

WHAT IS A CLAIM?

A *claim* is a debt of the deceased that is properly filed by a claimant. The executor has to pay all valid claims. If a creditor has actual notice or "constructive notice" (normally a newspaper ad) of the probate proceedings, he has to present his claim within a limited time period. If the claim is legitimate, the executor will pay it, assuming the estate contains sufficient assets. In most states a claim must be in writing, although local law may allow an oral claim in some cases. Additionally, if the deceased used property as collateral for a loan, then no formal claim for payment of the loan need be filed with the executor.

EXAMPLE 1 Alex, the deceased's brother, tells the executor that he was a "partner" in the deceased's Christmas tree farm, although there is no paperwork supporting this assertion. In most states, Alex's statement would not be considered a claim. If Alex writes a letter to the executor describing this alleged partnership, then it would be a claim.

EXAMPLE 2 The deceased bought a car and financed it through Friendly Finance Company. The finance company took a security interest in the car (the deceased agreeing that the finance company could repossess the car if he failed to pay the car loan). Friendly Finance does not have to make a formal claim with the executor because its interest in the car is a matter of public record.

The claim may not be paid if the creditor is late filing the claim, if the executor determines that the claim is invalid, or if there are insufficient assets in the estate. Notice to creditors is discussed in more detail on pages 77–78.

COMMON TYPES OF CLAIMS

All of the following categories of bills are properly paid out of estate assets. If the estate lacks cash, then property can be sold to raise the cash. The executor needs to be careful to sell property that is not specifically left to an individual in raising the cash. This topic is discussed on page 80.

Medical Expenses

The expenses of the deceased's last illness are typical claims. Note that many if not all of these expenses may be covered by insurance. Insurance coverage is discussed later in the chapter under the heading "Evaluating Creditor Claims."

Funeral Expenses

One of the biggest bills—and often the biggest—is for funeral expenses. Actually, a funeral may generate a number of bills. One from the funeral home for the funeral, and perhaps others for the religious ceremony, cremation, and gravestone if those items were not included in the funeral home's bill.

Tax Bills

The deceased may receive a number of tax bills. If the deceased owned a home or other real estate, then real estate taxes will need to be paid. Income tax returns must be filed and taxes paid for income earned by the deceased in the year of his death. The executor needs to take care of these matters. Taxes and filing requirements are discussed on pages 81–83.

Professional Fees for the Estate

Attorney and accounting fees for work done on behalf of the estate can be substantial. If the estate will be open for over a year, these professionals will be making progress billings before the estate is wrapped up and closed. These fees are properly paid out of estate assets.

The executor needs to be careful in paying these fees because the probate court will be examining the amount of the fees when the estate is closed. If the fees are excessive for the size and complexity of the estate, the judge may not approve them. If the executor has already paid the fees, and the professionals refuse to refund them, the executor may find himself liable for the fees.

Although most attorneys and other professionals will not overbill an estate, the executor needs to be alert for such a possibility. A large law firm might use the estate as a training exercise for new attorneys, who will research every issue and bill the estate for the time. Although legal work is often necessary, it also needs to be cost-effective. If the attorney knows that the executor will be sensitive to legal charges and ask for detailed billing records, the bills are apt to be lower than if the executor merely pays any bills presented without comment.

A few states do not allow the payment of attorney fees before the estate is closed. In those states the attorney will not be presenting bills to the estate until that time.

Executor's Fee

The executor also earns a fee for work performed on behalf of the estate. The executor—like the attorney—is a creditor of the estate and will get paid before any gifts are distributed. In fact, the executor's fee is a "priority claim" and will be paid before most other creditors (this topic is discussed in detail later in the chapter).

In most states the executor cannot advance himself funds. The executor should set aside an amount of cash equal to his fee, which is then paid when the estate closes.

Other Bills

The executor should expect to pay the deceased's bills including: mortgage payments, utility bills, consumer loan payments, and credit card bills. Additionally the executor needs to pay household bills for yard care, housecleaning, and alarm systems.

Common Creditors

Common creditors include:
- lenders (normally banks)
- credit card companies
- gasoline companies
- finance companies
- doctors
- hospitals
- dentists
- utilities

Unusual Claims

Although most claims presented to the executor will be normal bills for daily living expenses, the executor needs to anticipate that there may also be more unusual claims. For example, if the deceased was jointly liable on a debt of some sort, the co-debtor may make a claim on the estate.

EXAMPLE 1 The deceased and a friend, Alice, jointly bought a parcel of real estate. They financed the purchase by entering into an "installment contract" with the seller, whereby Alice and the deceased agreed to make monthly payments to the seller for a ten-year period. Three years later the deceased died. Alice is likely to make a claim against the estate for one-half of the remaining debt.

EXAMPLE 2 After probate commences, the deceased's housekeeper sends a letter to the execu-

tor. She claims that she is owed $100,000. She has a letter from the deceased promising her $100,000, and in return she agreed to live with and provide care for the deceased for the rest of his life. The executor would have to evaluate this claim.

EXAMPLE 3 Gene, the deceased's cousin, presents a letter to the executor. The deceased and Gene had a dispute about some family property. They evidently resolved the dispute by the deceased's taking possession of the property. However, the deceased promised Gene in writing that he would leave the property to Gene in his will. The deceased's will makes no mention of Gene. This is a special kind of claim called a "contract to make a will," which may or may not be valid under state law. In most states such a claim is not subject to the normal time restrictions for making claims.

EXAMPLE 4 Marty bought some property for "no money down." According to sales terms, the full purchase price of $100,000 is due in three years. One year after the purchase, Marty died. The $100,000 is not legally due for another two years. In many states, however, the creditor can present this claim as if it were due at the date of death. Many, but not all, contracts contain an "acceleration" clause, which makes the debt fully due in case of the debtor's death.

Protection of the Family

Although not strictly a claim, the executor needs to be mindful of the rights of dependent family members to the assets of the estate. In fact, the family will be first in line to receive the estate's assets, even before beneficiaries of the will or creditors are paid. In some cases, the executor will have to completely deplete the estate to support the family.

There are two separate rights that may be exercised by family members. The first is the "elective share"—the right of the surviving spouse to take a share of the estate no matter what the will says. The amount of the share varies, state by state, but the share typically runs between one-third and one-half of the estate. If the elective share is much greater than the gift left to the spouse in the will, the election can obviously imperil gifts to beneficiaries and payment to creditors.

EXAMPLE A husband's will left his wife only keepsakes because he had provided for her by making several substantial gifts to her during his life. The value of the estate is $500,000. The will made a gift of $200,000 to the deceased's brother and creditors' claims totaled $300,000. If the wife elects against the will and the state law provides that she will receive half the estate, that leaves only $250,000. $50,000 of the creditors' claims will go unpaid and the brother will receive nothing.

Other family rights against the estate include the family allowance and the homestead right. In most states the probate court will empower the executor to invade the estate for cash and even to sell estate assets to support the surviving spouse and dependents of the deceased. Additionally, in many states, the family has an automatic ownership interest—up to a set dollar amount—in the family home even if the will provides it is to be left to another individual. These rights are separate and additional to the spouse's right to elect against the will.

NOTICE TO CREDITORS

The executor's responsibility for paying creditors really starts with giving proper notice to creditors of the probate action. Different types of creditors are legally entitled to different types of notice. Known creditors are entitled to *actual notice* while other creditors are entitled to *constructive notice*.

Actual Notice

Creditors of the deceased that are actually known to the executor are entitled to actual notice. In most states, they must receive a court-approved form notifying them that the probate proceedings are commenced and inviting them to submit a claim to the executor.

Constructive Notice

Because there might be other creditors in addition to the ones known by the executor, in many states, the law requires the executor to give constructive notice to the public. Constructive notice is also known as *notice by publication* because it requires the executor to place an ad in the local newspaper informing the public of the probate proceedings. Creditors are presumed to read such notices and to present their claims to the probate court.

In states where notice by publication is required, the notice must usually appear in a newspaper for at least three consecutive weeks. Most states have a standardized form for the notice. Local newspapers are familiar with the form and can help prepare the ad.

OBSERVATION *The executor should verify that the ads have actually run and should retain a copy of one of the ads.*

Due Diligence

The executor must exercise *due diligence* to locate all creditors of the deceased and send them notice. This requires a real effort on the part of the executor. The executor needs to take active steps to identify who is owed money by the deceased.

Legal Effect of the Notice

It is important for the executor to understand the legal effect of giving notice. Creditors are under a legal obligation to pay attention to their affairs. If they are owed money, they are expected to look at the obituary notices or legal notices in the local newspaper. Once notices of the probate proceedings are given, creditors have a short time period to present a claim to the executor. In many states this time period is four months after the notice is received or appears in the newspaper.

At one time the cut-off period—typically four months—was a real cut-off. Creditors who did not submit claims by that date had their rights extinguished completely. Executors could ignore late-filed claims. Today the rule is different. A claim may be filed after the normal cut-off period. In some states these claims may be presented for payment up to two years after the deceased's death.

OBSERVATION *Late-filed claims create a dilemma for the executor. Most estates are settled in a year or less. If a claim is submitted to the executor after the estate is* *closed and property is distributed, the executor may have to seek return of the property to pay the creditors in the event the claim is upheld.*

EVALUATING CLAIMS

The executor has a duty to pay valid claims made against the estate, but the executor needs to carefully evaluate the claims. Not all claims are valid. Someone may present a claim when he is not really owed money, or he may bill for a larger amount than he is due. The executor has a duty to protect the assets of the estate and must be alert to such problems.

When medical bills arrive, the executor must determine if they are covered by insurance. There is often a delay between the time medical services are provided and when the insurer pays for them. If the executor pays the bill and the insurer also pays the bill the provider will be paid twice. An executor may never learn of the provider's windfall. Even if the double payment is discovered, it may be difficult to get the provider's bookkeeping department to make the refund. Many medical bills for the elderly are now covered by Medicare.

EXAMPLE Charles, serving as executor for his deceased father, who died at age 70, opens a bill sent to his father for $1,200 from a local anesthesiologist. The bill is for medical services during his father's last illness. Charles is uncertain whether the service is covered by Medicare or his father's Medigap coverage. It is possible that the insurers evaluated the bill and paid part of it, or perhaps declined to pay any of it. It is likely that the anesthesiologist's office sent the bill to Charles' father as a matter of course, even though the bill will ultimately be paid by Medicare.

Bogus Claims

If the deceased was involved in business activities, it is not unusual for persons to appear who assert that they are owed money for various business deals that took place before the deceased's death. This type of claim can be very difficult to evaluate.

EXAMPLE Fran was a real estate developer and was engaged in a number of real estate investments

at the time of her death. As her estate was being probated, Howard submitted a claim alleging that he was a silent partner in one of Fran's deals. He alleged that he had scouted out a property and negotiated the deal. Howard claims that he is half-owner of a parcel of Fran's real estate, although his name is not on the deed or the mortgage and records show that Fran supplied all of the funds for the down payment to buy the parcel. Although Howard may be telling the truth, the executor needs to be skeptical and should obtain some trustworthy collaboration of Howard's statement.

Documentation

The executor must be extremely careful in evaluating claims. The executor owes a duty to pay valid claims but must also preserve property for the beneficiaries of the estate. The executor should demand documentation from any claimant to support the claim for payment. Obviously evidence from a disinterested third party will be more reliable than that submitted by the claimant. Whenever possible, written, rather than oral, evidence should be obtained.

OBSERVATION *Claims for personal services to the deceased are seldom made in writing and there is often no documentation to support them. These claims can be difficult to evaluate. It is hard to know if the claimant was really acting as a volunteer or was promised payment.*

DENIAL OF CLAIMS

If the executor determines that a claim is bogus or questionable because of a lack of documentation or other evidence, the executor has a duty not to pay it.

Appeal by Claimant

If the executor denies a claim, the claimant has a right to petition the probate court for a hearing on the matter. In most states the probate judge, sitting without a jury, will determine if the claim should be allowed or denied based on the evidence provided by both the executor and the claimant.

Compromise

The executor also has the power to *compromise* a claim. If a claimant has a questionable claim, the executor may want to reach some sort of settlement.

EXAMPLE A creditor presents a claim for $10,000 to the executor, stating that the deceased bought property and never paid for it. The creditor has little paperwork to document the claim itself, or evidence proving the proper amount of the claim. However, there is evidence that a debt may have been owed. The executor can try to "cut a deal" with the creditor for a lesser amount. This is advisable if there is some basis for the claim and it appears that the creditor will opt to complain to the probate court.

WARNING *Because the executor has a duty to preserve the property in the estate for the beneficiaries, he should be cautious in settling claims. Those beneficiaries can sue the executor if he or she pays a bogus claim. In most states, settled claims must be approved by the probate court. Even in states where this is not required, the executor should ask the court for "instructions" about how to proceed.*

QUESTIONS CREATED BY CLAIMS

Creditor claims can create confusion. The following section details some of the more common issues that are likely to arise in probating an estate.

Managing Encumbered Assets

An *encumbered asset* is an item of property that has a debt associated with it. For example, a car may be encumbered by a car loan. When a debt is associated with particular property, then the debt "follows" that property unless the will directs otherwise. For example, if Green leaves his auto to his son, and the auto is subject to a car loan, then the son will receive the auto but will also be responsible for paying off the loan.

In many cases an individual will have life insurance in force which will alleviate the burden on the beneficiary. For example, if Green had a life insurance policy equal to the value of the outstanding car loan and that named the creditor as beneficiary of the policy, on Green's death the proceeds of the life insurance policy would be applied to pay off the car loan, and his son would get the car free and clear. Alternately, if Green does not have life insurance in force, he could still provide in his will that his estate should use any available cash to pay off the car loan on his death.

Effect of Large Creditor Claims

Although an individual may own a house, a car, and investments at death, that property may not be available to distribute to heirs if that individual died with sizable debts. If the debts are large enough, creditors' claims could render the estate insolvent. Insolvency means that the individual died with more debts than property. The estates of even prosperous people may be rendered insolvent because of business deals or investments that have gone sour or because of huge medical bills.

EXAMPLE Brown owns three apartment buildings at his death. Brown's will leaves each of his three sons an apartment building. Unfortunately, at the time of his death, Brown owed his business partners $700,000. Before any property can be distributed to Brown's heirs, the executor of Brown's estate must first pay administrative expenses and creditors' claims. The executor is also obligated to pay any income tax or estate tax liability before distributing any property to the sons. The executor may be forced to sell the apartment buildings to pay these bills.

Can Beneficiaries Be Liable for the Deceased's Bills?

Although the heirs' gifts may be reduced because of creditors' claims, beneficiaries of the estate will never have to pay the deceased's bills unless they in some way obligate themselves to pay, which would be very unusual. If the deceased incurred significant medical bills during his last illness, his estate, rather than the estate's beneficiaries, will be responsible for paying them. If the estate has insufficient assets to pay the creditors, claims will not be fully repaid.

INSUFFICIENT ASSETS IN THE ESTATE

It is important to understand what happens if there is insufficient property in the estate. This may occur because the deceased's financial circumstances changed for the worse between the time he wrote the will and the time he died. It can also occur because the executor has had to sell assets to provide support for a surviving spouse and other dependents. Finally, assets may be insufficient because the surviving spouse has "elected against the will" to take his or her "forced share" of the estate, which leaves less for beneficiaries named in the will.

Of course, there may be ample assets to pay all creditors and still distribute property to those named in the will. If the property in the estate is insufficient to do so, the creditors will be paid first and the gifts will be reduced. Each state has a law determining how the gifts will be reduced. This is discussed later in the chapter.

In some cases there may not be enough money even to pay the creditors. This is called an *insolvent estate*. In this case the gifts made in the will are not made at all. Since there is not enough property to pay all of the creditors, some creditors will not get fully paid. The law in each state determines who gets paid and who doesn't. These rules are also discussed below. At worst, the deceased may die penniless, and creditors and beneficiaries alike will go away empty-handed.

Assets Sufficient to Pay Creditors but Not Beneficiaries

When the estate's assets are sufficient to pay all creditors but insufficient to fund all the gifts made in the will, the law provides specific rules regarding who will receive property and who will not. This process is called *abatement*.

In most states, *specific legacies* will be paid first. A specific legacy is a gift of a particular item of property. For example, if the will leaves an heir the property at "342 Elm Street," this is a specific legacy. *General legacies* will be paid second, pro-rata. A general legacy is a gift of property in quantity, and is not distinguished from other property of the same kind. For example, if the testator left an heir "all my real estate" he made a general legacy. Finally, if there are still excess assets after the specific and general legacies have been paid, *residuary gifts* will be made.

If there are insufficient assets in the estate, creditor claims will be paid out of the estate's residue—any property other than specific and general bequests. Because the residue normally includes cash and other liquid items, this is a practical rule. If the residue is insufficient to pay the outstanding bills, then the heirs who get general legacies will have their gifts reduced and they will do so pro-rata. In other words, they will each have their gifts reduced by a certain percentage. A general legacy is a gift that comes from the general assets of the estate. If the residue and the general property are still not enough to pay the bills, then heirs who have been given specific property will have their gifts reduced.

Insolvent Estates: Assets Insufficient to Pay Creditors and Beneficiaries

If the deceased's debts exceed the value of the property in the estate, the estate will be insolvent. In an insolvent estate the heirs typically get nothing even though the will provides that they get generous gifts. In fact, the creditors may get little or even nothing.

EXAMPLE Kevin, who was once quite wealthy, made a will which made substantial cash gifts to a number of relatives. In the 20 years after the will was written, Kevin's business failed and he was forced to sell many of his assets. Additionally, he had a number of costly hospital stays which further depleted his assets. After his death family members were surprised to learn that not only would they receive nothing from his estate, but that the estate had so little funds that even the funeral director was not fully paid.

When the estate is insufficient to pay all of the creditors, the law provides rules about which creditors get paid first. Creditors first in line for payment are known as "priority creditors."

PRIORITY CREDITORS

When there is not enough property in the estate to pay all the creditors, they will not be paid in full.

All states have rules that provide which creditors get paid first. Although the rules are fairly similar, there is some variation among the states. For example, some states provide that funeral homes get paid first, while others provide that administrative expenses or taxes must be paid before the funeral home. In some states the will can control the order of abatement.

States typically have a system with five to ten classes of priority claims. All claims within a class are to be satisfied in full before moving on to the next class. For example, a typical state system might establish six classes of priority claims:

1. administrative expenses
2. funeral expenses
3. debts with preference under federal or state law
4. property taxes assessed against deceased prior to death
5. judgments and decrees against deceased prior to death
6. other debts

EXAMPLE Jason's estate is comprised of $12,000 of cash and other property that can be easily sold for cash. Administrative expenses of the estate are $2,000, and these will be paid in full. Funeral expenses are $6,000 and these will be paid in full. Jason owes $5,000 of unpaid state tax at the time of his death. Because there is only $ 4,000 available ($12,000 – $2,000 – $6,000 = $4,000), $2,000 of the state tax will not be paid. If there were two "category 3" debts of $6,000 each, the $4,000 would have been split evenly between them. If Jason had any category 4, 5, or 6 debts, they would go completely unpaid.

Administrative Expenses

Administrative expenses include any expenses of operating the estate. These include court fees, the cost of the executor's bond, appraiser's fees, miscellaneous expenses of managing property, accounting fees, attorney fees, and the executor's fee.

Funeral Expenses

Funeral expenses include the cost of the funeral director's services, the casket, the burial or cremation, the cemetery plot and the headstone or marker, as well as other costs associated with the funeral.

Family Allowance

The family allowance, available in many states, is an amount the court awards to a surviving spouse and dependents of the deceased.

Expenses of Last Illness

Expenses of the last illness include doctors, nurses, and hospital bills related to the deceased's last illness. It also includes drugs, therapy, and medical equipment, such as wheelchairs or oxygen tank rentals.

Debts with Preference under Federal Law

This category of debts includes debts owed to the federal government. Typical items include unpaid income tax and Social Security tax, student loans, and fines.

Debts with Preference under State Law

This category includes debts to the state itself and to its subdivisions. The most typical items are state and local taxes due before death.

Mortgages and Other Secured Loans

This category includes not only home loans but any loan that is backed by collateral. A typical car loan is a secured loan because the car is put up as collateral—the lender has a security interest in the car.

Judgments

This category includes legal judgments against the deceased. When a party loses a lawsuit, the winner is usually awarded a judgment against the loser, obligating the loser to pay the damages specified by the court.

INCOME TAX ISSUES

Death does not eliminate a person's bills, including income taxes. A final income tax return (Form 1040) will have to be filed for the deceased. When there is a surviving spouse, a joint return can be filed even if the deceased lived only a day or two during the year. However, when filing a final tax return, the advantages of filing a separate tax return need to be weighed. Even if a final joint return has been filed, an executor may cancel that joint return by filing a separate return for the decedent within one year from the due date of the return.

Tax Returns

There are a number of income tax elections that can minimize the tax due in connection with the decedent's final Form 1040. In the case of a single taxpayer, the last return will normally be a short tax year covering the period from January 1 up until the date of death. Although the decedent may die early in the calendar tax year, the final tax return is not due until April 15 of the year following the decedent's death. If the decedent was married a joint return may generally be filed.

Signing the Return

Of course the deceased cannot sign the final tax return. If the deceased left a widow or widower, the executor will sign the return along with the surviving spouse. The estate itself is considered a taxpayer and the executor must file a special tax return on its behalf, Form 1041. It is the executor's duty to see that this return is properly prepared and filed. Normally an executor will have the estate's attorney arrange to have the return filed.

WARNING *The executor is ultimately responsible for seeing that the Federal Estate Tax Return (Form 706) and the Fiduciary Income Tax Return (Form 1041) are filed. When the estate employs both an attorney and an accountant, there is some potential for miscommunication about filing the tax returns. Each may assume the other will be preparing the returns. The executor needs to verify which professional will be preparing which return and also needs to check to see that the returns are timely filed.*

Claiming Medical Expenses

The medical expenses associated with a taxpayer's last illness can be substantial. Due to anticipated cutbacks in Medicare and Medicaid, the unreimbursed portion of such expenses may be deductible. Unpaid medical expenses are deductible for federal estate tax purposes on the Estate Tax Return, Form 706. Additionally, the executor may elect to treat medical expenses paid by the estate within one year after death as having been paid by the decedent; therefore, the executor can deduct such medical expenses on the decedent's final Form 1040. However, the medical expenses cannot be deducted on

both forms. If no estate tax is due, then the expenses should be deducted on the Form 1040.

How to Deduct Medical Expenses

For both income tax and estate tax purposes, medical expenses are only deductible to the extent they exceed 7½ percent of adjusted gross income (AGI). However, it is not uncommon for an older person to have a low AGI because most of his income is tax-exempt income. To maximize the benefit of the deduction the executor must compare the decedent's personal income tax rate and the decedent's estate tax rate before making the election. Because estate tax rates generally exceed income tax rates, it is generally more advantageous to claim the expenses on the Federal Estate Tax Return.

EXAMPLE Assume a decedent has a marginal income tax bracket of 28 percent and an estate tax bracket of 37 percent. In addition, the decedent had $1,000 of unpaid medical expenses that exceed 7½ percent of adjusted gross income. If the $1,000 of medical expenses are deducted on Form 1040, it will result in a tax savings of $280 as opposed to a savings of $370 if deducted on Form 706. Additionally, by claiming the $1,000 as an income tax deduction, the executor will reduce the debts of the estate by $1,280 (the $1,000 of medical expenses + $280 of income tax expense). Multiplying this $1,280 by the decedent's 37 percent estate tax rate results in an increase in estate tax of $474.

Income in Respect of a Decedent

Planners also need to consider the issue of "income in respect of a decedent." Income in respect of a decedent, also known as "IRD," is income that is accrued (earned) by a cash basis taxpayer before death, but is not includable on the decedent's last Form 1040. Typical IRD items include salary and commissions, investment income, and proceeds from the installment sales of property. Additionally, income from S Corporations and partnerships can also be treated as IRD.

PLANNING NOTE *If local law allows, items of IRD should be distributed in the year of receipt because the* *estate pays a flat federal tax of 39.6% on any income in excess of $7,500.*

Missing Returns

It is not uncommon for a person who is in his last illness to fail to file income tax returns. The executor is responsible for filing any missing returns.

EXAMPLE Jim had been ill for a number of years and in and out of the hospital. Jim continued to receive substantial income from his real estate investments which were handled by a real estate management company. Jim usually prepared his own tax returns but for the last three years of his life he neglected to do so. Jim's executor needs to search for the returns. Any missing tax returns from prior years need to be prepared and any tax owing needs to be paid. The executor will probably need to find a skilled tax accountant to help in this chore.

Priority of Tax Claims

Federal tax claims are a priority claim for the estate.

The executor needs to determine if the IRS has filed a tax lien against any of the deceased's property. If so, the lien must be paid off. Tax liens will be on record at the courthouse in the county in which the property is located. The IRS may also be helpful in identifying such liens for an executor. Overdue taxes are still a claim against the estate even when no lien is imposed by the IRS.

Tax Audits

If the IRS or a state revenue department sends an audit notice to the deceased, the executor is responsible for overseeing the audit. The executor can hire an accountant or an attorney to handle the matter.

Death Taxes

This chapter has discussed income taxes as claims against the estate. The estate may also have liability for federal estate tax, which is an entirely different tax than the federal income tax. The estate tax is discussed in Chapter 13, "Estate and Gift Tax Basics." Notably, the beneficiaries of the estate may be liable for state inheritance tax.

CHAPTER 9

Closing the Estate

INTRODUCTION

T he executor's final duties are to provide an accounting to the probate court, to distribute the property to the beneficiaries named in the will, and to close the estate. This chapter will detail accounting and the partial and final distributions of property. The chapter will then discuss the executor's procedures for closing the estate and receiving a discharge from the probate court. Finally, the chapter will briefly address issues that might require an estate to be reopened.

CLOSING THE ESTATE: AN OVERVIEW

The last major job of the executor is to close the estate. Once all of the debts owed to creditors by the deceased and the estate have been paid, the executor will know what remains to be distributed to those persons named in the will. At this point, the estate is ready for what is known as *final settlement*. There are really two parts to this job:

1. preparing an accounting for the probate court, and
2. distributing the assets to those named in the will.

After these tasks have been done, the estate is closed and the executor will be discharged from further duty and further potential liability.

ACCOUNTINGS
Petition

In most states the executor must petition the probate court to file an accounting. There is a standardized legal form for this purpose. At the same time, the executor will file a plan to distribute the estate's remaining property for approval from the probate court, and the executor will also ask the probate court for a discharge.

Notice Requirements

In many states, the petition describing the accounting must be mailed to all interested parties, including those named in the will, other legal heirs, and any unpaid creditors or those with any claims against the estate. This gives interested parties an opportunity to visit the courthouse to examine the accounting for themselves and to raise any questions.

OBSERVATION *Typically no objections will be raised at this point. Few people will take the time to visit the probate court to look at the accounting. The most likely objection might come from the clerk of the court regarding some aspect of the forms submitted.*

First Accounting

If the estate is open more than one year, in many states a *first accounting* will be required at the end of the first year. (In some states accounting may be required more frequently.) The probate court requires this accounting in its role of supervisor of the administration of the estate.

Preparing an accounting is a fairly time-consuming process, so if possible the executor should try to wrap up the estate before the first year elapses to avoid having to prepare two accountings to the court. Of course, there may be very good reasons why the estate cannot be closed. Indeed, many estates are open for a number of years because of unpreventable delays. For example, if there are a number of investment properties or a business in the estate, it is very likely that these will not be sold within the first year. More cash will be realized for beneficiaries if such assets are sold in an orderly manner.

Final Accounting

The final accounting is filed with the probate court when the estate is ready for final settlement and final distribution of the property. If the estate is closed within the first 12 months, this will be both the first and final accounting.

If all the creditors have been paid, the only claims against the estate will be for income taxes due, the attorney's fee, and the executor's fee and expenses. The rest of the property will be ready for distribution to the individuals named in the will.

The Accounting Document

The accounting is a financial reconciliation of income and disbursements (inflows and outflows) to and from the estate. It is similar to, but more complicated than, a bank reconciliation that is prepared to reconcile a checkbook balance.

The probate court will be auditing (checking) the figures and the information provided by the executor. If all is in order, the judge will sign an order permitting distribution of the remaining assets and discharging the executor. If there are questions, the probate court will ask the executor for explanations before signing the order.

Although an executor can prepare it, most executors will have the estate's attorney or an experi-

enced accountant prepare the accounting. Having a professional prepare the accounting has several advantages and the fee will be an expense of the estate. A professional will know the format that the court clerk will be looking for. Additionally, a professional is far less likely to make errors in preparing the document.

The accounting normally should include the following information:

- time period covered by the accounting
- initial inventory value of each item of property
- all money and property received during the time period
- all disbursements made during the time period (including voucher numbers—see below)
- all money and property currently in possession of the executor
- reconciliation of cash balances
- any other information the court may need to know including:
  sale of property
  advancements
  disclaimers
  fee information

Additionally, the court may require that bank statements (from the estate's bank accounts) and vouchers be attached to the accounting.

Vouchers

Vouchers are the special receipts attached to the checks in the estate's checking account. Some but not all states require the executor to use these special vouchers. There is typically a place on the voucher not only for the name of the payee of the check, but also for his address, the purpose of the disbursement, and a place for a signature of the payee acknowledging receipt of the check.

The probate court will typically require the executor to submit vouchers accounting for every penny of the estate's money along with the accounting.

Taxes

When submitting the accounting, the executor will have to include a statement that all federal and state income taxes have been paid as well as state inheritance taxes and federal estate taxes.

STRUCTURING THE DISTRIBUTION PLAN

The executor must decide on the proper distribution of the property remaining in the estate after all claims have been paid. As mentioned above, this plan must be approved by the court before distributions take place. Beneficiaries under the will must be given a chance to examine the distribution plan to see if their interests are protected.

If the will was prepared shortly before the testator's death, chances are that the distribution planning will be relatively easy. The deceased probably had a good idea of the extent of his property and about who would be getting it.

Out-of-Date Wills

On the other hand, if a legally valid older will does not appropriately reflect the assets and circumstances of the decedent at the time of his death, the law has rules directing the executor to respond to the changed circumstances.

An older will may not really provide for the deceased's actual family. For example, the people named in the will to receive the property may all be dead. On the other hand, there may be several new grandchildren or even children who are simply not mentioned in the will. Executors sometimes find that the will is so old that the deceased's spouse is not mentioned at all. When there are such "gaps," the law provides directions.

A will might contain descriptions of property that are not accurate. For example, the will may mention property that the deceased no longer owns at death. The will may have been written many years ago when the deceased was wealthy. Decades of poor investments, or bad business decisions, or the expenses of a major illness or nursing home care may have reduced the estate substantially. The distribution plan in the will may be completely unrealistic.

The opposite can also be true. The will written years ago may only mention a few assets. However, the estate may actually contain millions of dollars in assets. Again, the law provides a way to fill these gaps.

DISTRIBUTION RULES

The law provides specific rules regarding the distributions in a will. Generally speaking, the law tries to carry out the desires of the deceased as spelled out in his will. However, the executor needs to keep in mind that there are several important limitations on the deceased's rights to give away property in the will. For example, a spouse cannot be disinherited. These topics are discussed in more detail in Chapter 6, "Understanding Wills."

Gifts in a Will

A will may contain various types of gifts. Common gifts include:
- specific legacy
- demonstrative legacy
- general legacy
- residual legacy

Order of Gifts

Gifts are paid in the following order. Specific legacies are paid first, then demonstrative legacies. If the estate still contains sufficient assets, general legacies (usually money) are paid. Finally, if the estate contains "excess" property, this excess falls into the "residuary" and is paid to the residuary beneficiary named in the will. Specific and general legacies are explained in detail in Chapter 6.

Demonstrative Legacy

A *demonstrative legacy* is one that is payable first from particular property and then from the estate's general funds. A will might provide that "Jack is to receive $10,000, and I direct that 100 shares of Microsoft stock be sold to pay this legacy." Unless abatement applies, Jack will receive $10,000; if the sale of the Microsoft stock fails to produce $10,000, the remainder will come from general estate funds.

Residuary

A *residuary gift* is one that comes out of property which has not been otherwise disposed of in the will. After all of the other legacies have been paid, whatever is left in the estate falls into the residuary. If all of the property has already been given away, there may be very little in the residue. Also, the executor and attorney fees—and sometimes estate taxes—are paid out of the residue. On the other hand, if the will does not make many legacies, the bulk of the estate may fall into the residue. If the will is an older one, the residue may be substantial.

Most wills provide that the residue of the estate, in other words, the property that is not specifically left to named individuals, will go to a named party or parties. If the testator had a spouse, it is common to leave the residuary to the surviving spouse.

Mortgages, Auto Loans, and Liens

At one time, liens and mortgages on property would be satisfied, or paid, out of the will's residuary. In most states today, property will be inherited with these "encumbrances" attached. For example, assume that Ames has left his farm to Jones and the farm is subject to a $50,000 mortgage. Jones will take title to the land but the mortgage debt does not disappear.

Ademption

A will can only give away what the testator owned at the time of death. If specific property is no longer owned at death, the potential recipient is not entitled to some other property. This concept is called ademption. The recipient may have already received the property during the testator's life, or the testator may simply no longer own the property. (See Chapter 6 for examples of ademption.)

Abatement

Sometimes an executor faces an acute problem: the will does not have sufficient assets to carry out all the gifts in the will. This might happen because creditors or tax collectors have made claims against the estate (see Chapter 8, "Paying Creditors and Taxes"). It can also occur when the surviving spouse "elects against the will" (discussed later in this chapter).

As discussed in Chapter 6, "Understanding Wills," the law provides special ordering rules to determine whose share is decreased and by how much when there are insufficient funds. This procedure is called *abatement*. However, if the will contains a specific abatement scheme, the will can control the order of abatement with the caveat that the surviving spouse has a right to elect against the will. The testator's will can, however, provide that all gifts will abate before the gifts are given to the surviving spouse (who normally gets the residue).

Order of Abatement

If the will fails to provide for a specific order of abatement, most state laws provide that gifts are reduced in the following order:

1. gifts that pass through intestacy
2. residue
3. general legacies
4. demonstrative legacies
5. specific legacies

Lapse

If a person named in the will has predeceased the testator, the executor needs to determine how to dispose of gifts to that person. At one time the gift would have automatically lapsed—terminated on the death of the beneficiary, but that is no longer the case. The will may provide that a beneficiary may only receive a gift if she outlives the testator by a number of days—typically 120. If there is no such provision in the will, state law will control. Many states have an anti-lapse statute. This law directs the executor to distribute the property to the heirs of the deceased beneficiary. For example, suppose the will provides that $1,000 should go to the deceased's brother, Fred. However, Fred died one year before the testator. If the anti-lapse statute applies, the $1,000 would go to Fred's closest surviving relatives—typically a surviving spouse, his children, or both. Most anti-lapse statutes do not specify how long the beneficiary must survive the testator.

GIFTS REQUIRING EXECUTOR'S JUDGMENT

The executor may be called upon to use judgment in making gifts. For example, the will may make a "conditional gift" that is only to be made if the beneficiary has fulfilled some condition or promise. The executor will have to determine if the condition has been met. (See Chapter 6 for a discussion of conditional gifts.) The executor may also be called upon to exercise a "power of appointment," which directs the executor to decide how property should be distributed.

Powers of Appointment

A power of appointment is an authorization for another person (usually the executor) to exercise judgment and discretion about how a particular matter should be handled. This type of power is somewhat unusual because the executor normally follows the precise instructions set out in the will for the distribution of the estate's property.

A power of appointment gives the holder the power to use his discretion in distributing certain property to the deceased's beneficiaries. Sometimes a power is arranged so that the person holding the power can only exercise the power in his (the holder's) own will.

EXAMPLE A father's will gives a general power of appointment over certain property to his son. However, the power may only be exercised in the son's will. Although the son will have the power to dispose of the property to anyone he sees fit, the son can only leave the property to those heirs in his own will.

The advantage of a power of appointment is its flexibility. Consider a gift to grandchildren. The testator's will is drawn up many years before his death, and there is no way for him to determine which of his grandchildren could best benefit from a large gift from the estate, and which will not deserve or not need a large gift. If the grandfather selects a trusted individual to hold a power of appointment over the property intended for the grandchildren, the holder will be able to exercise the discretion that the testator himself would have exercised had he lived.

General and Special Powers

There are two types of powers of appointment: general powers and special powers. A general power of appointment gives the holder broad latitude in the distribution of assets. Although there may be some suggestions in the will, the holder of a general power of appointment is not legally restricted in the distribution of the property.

In contrast, the holder of a special power of appointment is limited to distributing the property within a specified class. If the power is a nonexclusive special power, the holder must give something to everyone in the class. If the special power is exclusive, the holder typically has the power to give property to one or more of the class members.

For example, if a will vests the executor with an exclusive special power of appointment in favor of all of a testator's grandchildren, the executor has the right to determine which, if any, of the grandchildren are deserving of a gift. The holder is limited to the class "grandchildren" in making the gift, however. If the holder was given a general power of appointment then there would be no such limitation and the holder could distribute the property as she saw fit.

LIMITS ON THE DECEASED'S POWER TO DISPOSE OF PROPERTY

Although the law generally allows an individual to dispose of property in a will as he sees fit, there are a few very important limitations to this concept. First, of course, creditors must be paid before property can be distributed. Second, family members are protected from being left destitute. The law provides for family allowances and/or homestead rights. All of these concepts are detailed in Chapter 8, "Paying Creditors and Taxes."

Additionally, the law sets up some limits on the deceased's right to dispose of property. The law tries to prevent an individual from disinheriting a spouse. There is also protection for a child who has not been mentioned in the will.

Electing Against the Will: The Forced Share

At one time the law provided a surviving widow a "dower" right to prevent her from being disinherited in a will. Today, most states have a statutory election, which is sometimes called a forced share. This election allows a surviving spouse to either take the property left to him or her in the deceased spouse's will, or to elect to take a statutory share, which is usually one-third of the entire estate although the percentage share varies from state to state.

In many states, the estate is first subject to creditors' claims and in some states, the estate may be reduced by lifetime gifts. In other words, creditors' claims and lifetime gifts to the spouse both reduce the amount of the forced share.

Note that a spouse may elect to take a forced share even if he or she has been provided for by being named the beneficiary of a large life insurance policy on the deceased. In some states, insurance proceeds also reduce, but normally do not eliminate, the amount that may be distributed under the statutory forced share.

Disinheriting Children

Most states have "pretermitted heir" statutes which provide that when a child is not named in a will, the child is presumed to have been overlooked and will receive his intestate share. In other words, if a parent omits any reference to a child in a will, the law presumes that the omission was not intentionally, and the child will receive the same amount as if there was no will and the property passed to the family through the laws of intestacy in the jurisdiction. To intentionally disinherit a child, the will must name the child and provide that he gets nothing or a nominal amount, typically the customary one dollar.

Newly Born Children

Newly born or newly adopted children are often not included in their parents' wills. In this case, the law provides that the omitted child will get a share of the parents' estates. All states have a pretermitted heir statute that covers this situation because it is so common. These statutes will give a share of the estate not only to natural children, but also to adopted children, children from a prior marriage, and also to illegitimate children. In some states, when the pretermitted heir statute comes into play, the omitted child will receive a share of the estate that is equal to what they would have received if the parent had died intestate—without a will.

Prenuptial and Postnuptial Agreements

A valid prenuptial agreement or postnuptial agreement will take precedence over the gifts in the will. This is true whether or not the will was executed before or after the agreement. If such an agreement is in place, the executor must see that the terms of the agreement are fulfilled.

Disclaimers

Although the will provides a scheme for distributing the deceased's property, it is possible to change the result by the use of a *disclaimer*. A person does not have to accept property that she is left in a will: she can simply disclaim it. If the will provides for an alternate person to receive the gift, the gift will pass to that individual. If no provision for an alternate has been made, the gift will normally pass to the residue of the estate.

Almost any property can be disclaimed, including joint interests in bank accounts, real estate, or community property. The law also allows partial disclaimers. For example, if Ames left the entire residue of his estate to his son Robert, Robert can effectively disclaim all or perhaps 50 percent of the residue. A common use of qualified disclaimers is to minimize death taxes. Family members can increase or reduce the size of a surviving spouse's estate for this purpose.

Settlement Agreements

In most states the beneficiaries can get together and change the distribution scheme. This is sometimes done to prevent a will contest, in which case it may be called a *compromise*. If all the beneficiaries agree, they can simply decide to distribute property as they see fit. For example, assume a father with a sizable estate died leaving three adult children, as his only heirs. The father took an irrational dislike toward one of his children late in life, and left that child one dollar. If the other children agree, the three may share the estate equally despite the provisions of the father's will.

DISTRIBUTIONS TO HEIRS
Partial Distributions

Many states allow partial distributions to be made from the estate to the beneficiaries. In some states the executor must file a petition with the court to allow the distribution. Because creditors and taxes are paid out of the estate's assets before gifts are made, the court will only allow a distribution if it does not impair the rights of the creditors.

If a partial distribution has been made and it later turns out that there are insufficient assets to pay creditors, the executor will have to retrieve the asset from the beneficiary. This could be troublesome—especially if the beneficiary sold the asset and spent the money. For this reason, the executor should not suggest that beneficiaries receive partial distributions, but should wait a few months for their gifts until the estate is settled.

OBSERVATION *Beneficiaries who know the contents of a will normally want their property immediately. Some may go out and purchase a house thinking they will get a quick distribution of cash to help them with the down payment. When the down payment does not arrive as quickly as expected they blame the executor. The executor can be put under substantial pressure from beneficiaries—especially when they are the executor's relatives.*

In some cases the court will allow a partial distribution if the beneficiary is willing to post a bond to protect the rights of creditors.

WARNING *The executor needs to get a receipt from the recipient whenever a partial distribution is made. This receipt is particularly important because property that is distributed in a partial distribution may have to be reclaimed by the executor if estate assets ultimately prove insufficient to pay creditors. The executor needs to account for all property in the estate.*

Final Distribution
Once the court approves the final distribution plan, the executor may make the final distribution, the last step before receiving a discharge from the court.

Deeds and Titles
If real property is to be distributed, a deed is needed to transfer legal title. The executor should probably rely on an attorney in preparing the deeds to ensure that legal transfer is done properly. When an asset has a legal title—such as an automobile—there will be a transfer portion on the certificate that must be signed and completed. The state Department of Motor Vehicles may have an additional form that needs to be filled out.

Stock and bond transfers are best completed with the help of the deceased's stockbroker, who will be knowledgeable about transferring title to the beneficiary.

WARNING *The executor must be sure to get a signed receipt from each person receiving a gift. In some states there is a standardized form for this purpose. Check with your local probate court clerk on this point.*

Minors and Others Under a Disability
The executor needs to be careful in making distributions to certain individuals. Such individuals include minors (those under the age of 18), and those who are "protected" under the law, such as mentally impaired individuals and older persons who may have a court-appointed conservator to help them manage their affairs.

In many states the term *conservator* is used when a person, bank, or trust company is appointed to care for an adult, while the term *guardian* is used when the person needing protecton is a minor. The duties of a conservator and guardian are often quite similar.

The executor should see to it that a gift made to a minor is paid to the legal guardian. Usually, the guardian is the child's parent(s), but not always. If the parents are not alive, then the minor usually has a legal guardian appointed by the court to handle his legal affairs. If none is found, the executor needs to contact the probate court for further instructions.

Similarly, if a person named in the will has a conservator appointed to manage his affairs, the gift should go to the conservator. If no conservator has been appointed, but the person is obviously mentally ill, the executor should consult with family members of the person, and then consider petitioning the court for appointment of a conservator for that person.

DISCHARGE OF EXECUTOR
After all of the estate's property has been distributed and all fees paid, the probate court will formally discharge the executor. The probate court will issue a formal "order of discharge" (the title may vary in some states). Typically, this is a standard form that

must be presented to the court for the judge's signature. The order of discharge is an important legal document. The executor should keep it in a safe place with other important papers.

THE EXECUTOR'S FEE

The executor is entitled to a fee for his services. Fees are a matter of state law and vary state by state. In some states, the fee is based on a percentage of the estate's value. In other states, the fee is simply a "reasonable" fee. Appendix B contains a state-by-state listing of fee information.

REOPENING THE ESTATE

In rare cases, an estate may be "reopened" even after there is a final distribution and the executor has been discharged. This might happen if there are newly discovered assets, or a will is found after it was thought that there was no will.

Newly Discovered Assets

If assets of the deceased are discovered after the estate is closed, the executor needs to petition the probate court to reopen the estate to administer the assets. In most states this procedure will not be a full-blown probate. As a rule, creditors will have no claim on the newly discovered assets—the assets merely need to be distributed according to the terms of the will. If the assets are substantial and complicated, the executor should consult an attorney before proceeding with the distribution.

Newly Discovered Will

A newly discovered will only causes problems if the deceased was believed to have died intestate—without a will. If a will is admitted to probate and the estate has been settled and distributed, the new will does not change the result. In all states there is a brief time period at the commencement of probate where other wills can be produced—generally just a few months. Once this time period has elapsed it is simply too late to revisit the validity of the will used to probate the estate.

This result may seem unjust. If there is a later will it probably reflects the deceased's wishes at the end of his life, especially if it expressly revokes the will used to probate the estate. However, the law is also intended to establish certainty for both creditors and beneficiaries.

If the deceased was treated as having died intestate, there is a longer time period in which a newly discovered will can be produced. However, there is a time limit—normally one year, although this varies state by state. If the newly discovered will is valid, the probate will recommence and the executor named will probably be confirmed by the court and will settle the estate.

If the estate's assets have already been distributed under the intestacy statute and the estate closed, there will obviously be problems if the provisions in the new will are contrary to the actual distribution. For example, if a person died intestate, their property would have been distributed to their next of kin. What if the newly discovered will leaves most of the property to friends and charities rather than to close relatives? The relatives who received the property will have to return the property to the estate. If they received money and spent it, they become unexpected debtors. This is obviously a problem for an experienced probate lawyer to handle. Luckily, it is rare that a newly discovered will is found—and even more uncommon for such a will to provide in great contradiction with the state's intestacy laws.

RECORD KEEPING

The executor should retain copies of all paperwork for at least five years. Questions about how the estate was handled may arise from time to time. For example, beneficiaries may need to know the value of property they received when they sell it and have to report the income on their tax returns.

The best policy is to keep the records forever. If the executor ever needs to probate another estate, the paperwork will come in handy.

CHAPTER 10

Intestacy—When There Is No Will

INTRODUCTION

Many individuals die intestate, which means without a will. In these cases the deceased's property is distributed by state law. Each state has a law that attempts to distribute the property just as the deceased would have wished had she made a will. Of course these statutes cannot duplicate what the deceased could have done herself. But in cases of intestacy, what the deceased really wanted is irrelevant. Despite intestacy statutes, there are a surprising number of complications in this area.

INTESTACY
Dying Intestate

If an individual dies leaving a valid will, he dies *testate,* which is Latin for "with a will." If he dies without a valid will, he dies *intestate.* Although some individuals believe that the state will automatically get their property if they die without a will, this is not true. However, if a person dies without a will and there are absolutely no surviving blood relatives, then the property does go to the estate. This reversion of the property is called *escheat.*

The Administrator

When an individual dies without a will, the estate still needs to be administered. The probate court will appoint an "administrator" rather than an executor.

The administrator has the same duties as an executor. The big difference is that the administrator will distribute the estate according to the state's intestacy statute rather than a will.

Intestacy Statutes

All states have an intestacy statute that controls the distribution of a person's property if he dies without a will. In fact, many people do die without a will, either because they failed to plan ahead or because their will was invalid for one reason or another. Generally if an individual fails to write a will, the law will write one for her. Because it is impossible for the law to tailor a will to every individual's family circumstances, the law attempts to write a will that the average person would have written.

Which State Law Controls?

Intestacy statutes vary from state to state. For example, in some states, surviving parents of the deceased get a share of the estate while in other states they do not. So, in some states a surviving spouse may unexpectedly have to share an estate with her mother-in-law. The state law of the decedent's domicile controls. Domicile is the place where the deceased resided on a permanent basis. Domicile includes two elements, physical presence and the intent to reside permanently. Domicile is not always clear if an individual has two or more residences in different states. A more detailed discussion of domicile is found in Chapter 5, "Court Appointment of the Executor and Probate Initiation."

OBSERVATION *Because of state variations in the laws, certain family members may benefit financially by a particular determination of the location of the probate proceedings.*

Disadvantages of Intestacy

A person who dies without a valid will not only has no control over the distribution of property, but also is unable to designate the executor who will administer the estate after death. Accordingly, an individual who dies intestate cannot choose who will take possession of all the deceased's property and distribute it according to the deceased's wishes.

Only a will or a living trust can direct property to go to specific heirs. The intestacy statute cannot make a special provision for a child with medical problems, nor can it provide any estate tax savings. For an unmarried couple, if either partner dies without a will, there are disastrous consequences for the surviving partner because he will probably receive nothing.

CAUSES OF INTESTACY

Intestacy statutes apply in three situations:

1. when there is no will,
2. when there is a "lost" will that cannot be found, and
3. when there is a will, but it is not legally valid.

No Will

There are two reasons that explain why an individual might die without a will:

1. he or she never wrote a will, or
2. he or she wrote a will but revoked it and never replaced it with a new one.

Will Never Written

A surprising number of people die without having ever written a will, including many lawyers. Even Abraham Lincoln died intestate. Although it is rela-

tively easy to make a will, sign it, and get it witnessed, people procrastinate for a variety of reasons. Dealing with death is never easy, and few people consider their own death unless they discover they have a terminal illness.

Revoked Will

An extremely troublesome area of probate administration involves revoked (canceled) wills. There are a lot of evidentiary problems involved and many state-by-state variations in what constitutes a valid revocation. If it appears that the deceased did have a will but revoked it, it is essential to understand some of the rules that determines what happens in probate.

Wills are considered ambulatory, which means that they can be changed or revoked (canceled) at any time. This is true even though other individuals know the will's contents and have relied on anticipated gifts for financial security.

Methods of Revocation

A will can be revoked in a number of ways. A will can be revoked by a physical act—by tearing, burning, or marking "revoked" or "canceled" on the will. Somewhat surprisingly, no witnesses need be present for the act of revocation. However, many states require the deceased to have had testamentary capacity at the time of the revocation. If the revocation occurs when the individual did not have full mental capacity, the revocation would be ineffective. In fact, at a certain point, a person with diminished mental capacity is neither capable of making a new will nor of revoking an old one.

WARNING *The fact that no witnesses are required to revoke a will could lead to a counterfeit revocation by a family member who stands to gain from having the deceased die intestate.*

The most common way to revoke a will is by the execution of a later will that expressly revokes the earlier will. Even if the second will does not expressly state that the first will is revoked, the courts interpret the mere execution of the later will as revocation of the earlier one. A will is also revoked in many states by remarriage, although the laws of states vary on this point.

Irrevocability

There are a few exceptions to the rule that a will can be revoked. For example, when the deceased entered into a "contract to make a will" that obligated him to put certain provisions in a will. In some states a joint will is irrevocable after the death of one of the parties. A joint will is really two wills written on one piece of paper (typically by a husband and wife leaving all their property to one another).

A will is not revocable when a spouse enters into a divorce decree that obligates him to leave certain property to his ex-spouse in his will. He has obligated himself by a contract—here the divorce decree—to write the will in a certain way. In the absence of such a contract, a will can be changed or revoked entirely. When a will is revoked and not replaced, the individual has no will. If the person dies before a new will is written, the person dies intestate.

Although these rules seem relatively straightforward, the legal system has created some more exceptions (or perhaps exceptions to the exceptions).

Revival of Revoked Wills

In many states a revoked will may be "revived" by re-signing the will and having the signature properly witnessed. Many state laws also provide that a revocation of a will can be *conditional*, that is, the revocation will not be effective unless a specific event occurs.

In addition to the revival doctrine, a number of states recognize the doctrine of "dependent relative revocation." This doctrine revives a revoked will if the revocation was induced by a mistake of law or fact. A few courts have gone so far as to revive a will if the deceased anticipated executing a new one but failed to do so.

EXAMPLE Harold revokes his will, telling his spouse that he intends to visit his lawyer the next day to write a new one. Harold dies in his sleep. The court may revive the revoked will on the basis that Harold indicated his intention to execute a new will and on the belief that he would have preferred dying with the old will rather than without any will. Not all courts would make a similar ruling.

Lost Wills

Individuals sometimes draft a legally effective will, but the family is unable to locate it at the time of the person's death. A few states have a registry of wills at the courthouse, but many states do not. Although most people give a copy of their will to close family members, other individuals are secretive and don't want family members to know the exact contents of the will. There are a number of reasons for such secrecy. The testator may want to avoid any hard feelings that might be engendered by revealing the will. They may expect to change the will in the future, and the new will would cause a hardship on beneficiaries who are expecting a windfall. Whatever the reason, some individuals don't share copies of a will and this secrecy can cause problems.

The executor and family members may simply be unable to locate the will even though the deceased mentioned that he had one. If an exhaustive search through the family home, business office (if any), and bank safe-deposit box reveals nothing, the will may well be lost. Attorneys often keep copies of wills they draft—in some states this is required—but lawyers die, and law firms disband over time. The older the will, the less likely it will be found. Legal newspapers (special publications aimed at lawyers) typically run advertisements for "lost wills." The process of placing such an ad is referred to as a will search. If the lost will cannot be found, the deceased will be considered to have died intestate.

OBSERVATION *The will could have been wrongfully destroyed by a family member who stands to inherit more through intestacy than through the will. If wrongful destruction of the will is suspected, beneficiaries can petition the court for help, especially if there is any evidence of the original will, even an unsigned, unwitnessed copy. Testimony must be introduced by individuals who witnessed the lost will. This is a very difficult kind of case to prove in court. Clearly, the most trustworthy evidence of a will's existence could only be provided by the decedent. Moreover, witnesses may be unknown, or dead.*

Invalid Wills

Although intestacy normally occurs when no will has been written, it also occurs when a will has been written but the document is legally invalid for one reason or another. There are three common reasons for a will to be invalid:

1. lack of formalities,
2. lack of testamentary capacity, or
3. fraud or undue influence.

When a will is presented for probate, interested parties (usually relatives) may come forward to challenge the will, arguing that it should not be probated because the document lacks the required formalities, because the deceased lacked testamentary capacity, or because the will was the product of fraud or undue influence.

Lack of Formalities

It is not enough for the deceased to have planned and written a will. The will also must be signed and properly witnessed according to state laws before it can operate as a will. If the deceased did not complete this procedure, the document will not be legally valid and the intestacy statute passed by the decedent's state of domicile will control the distribution of his property.

....
OBSERVATION *Wills that lack the proper formalities are often drawn up without the aid of an attorney. The fact that the deceased genuinely believed that the will was valid does not make the document legally binding. There is no requirement that a will be drafted by an attorney. Indeed the will can be handwritten in pencil as long as it is properly signed and witnessed. A handwritten will—often referred to as a holographic will—that is properly witnessed is valid in all states. A handwritten will without proper witnesses is valid in only a minority of states.*
....

The law is quite strict about legal formalities, and if a will is not properly signed and witnessed, it cannot legally operate. This topic is discussed in more detail in Chapter 11, "Will Contests."

Lack of Testamentary Capacity

A document that has all the legal formalities—including proper signatures by the deceased and witnesses—will still not operate as a will if the deceased lacked "testamentary capacity" at the time the will was made.

Many wills are made in the hospital. There are no special rules for these wills, but they must be properly signed and witnessed. If the individual is physically incapable of signing, he may not be able to complete the will. Most states do allow someone to help the testator sign if he is too frail to do so himself, but this obviously invites a challenge from someone who will be financially disadvantaged by the will.

A more common problem with wills made during a last illness involves testamentary capacity. Essentially, the deceased must have a sound mind when the will is made. In most states, the testator must satisfy all of the four distinct requirements that demonstrate legal capacity to make a will:

1. the testator must understand the nature and extent of his or her property;
2. the testator must recognize the "natural objects of his bounty" (i.e., he they must be able to remember family members);
3. the testator needs to understand the testamentary act; and
4. the testator must understand the relation of the first three elements to one another.

A person who is seriously ill may have diminished legal capacity and may simply be unable to make a legally valid will. This topic is discussed in more detail in Chapter 11, "Will Contests."

Fraud and Undue Influence

A challenger may allege that the will was not the product of the deceased's own free will, or that there was a lack of "volitional consent." The challenger will allege that the testator did not voluntarily execute the will, but was tricked or pressured into signing the document. Normally the challenger will argue that the will was a product of either fraud or undue influence.

To prove fraud, a challenger must prove that someone made a false representation to the testator with an intent to deceive him. Moreover, the testator must have relied on the deception to the detriment of the challenger. However, if the challenger can provide "clear and convincing evidence" of fraud, then the court will set the will aside.

Another and even more frequent challenge to a will is based on undue influence. Undue influence occurs when someone uses overpersuasion or coercion to overcome the testator's free will. Most undue influence cases arise when the overreaching party enjoys a confidential relationship or a relationship of trust with the testator whose illness or stress renders him vulnerable.

APPOINTMENT OF THE ADMINISTRATOR

When a person dies intestate, his property still flows into a probate estate. The estate is run by an administrator rather than an executor, but her duties are much the same and she is held to the same high fiduciary standard.

Since there is no will to appoint the administrator, the law provides a list of possible individuals. The individuals at the top of the list have first priority. A typical list includes:

- a surviving spouse
- other "heirs at law" (family members who inherit a deceased's property)
- creditors

In appointing an administrator, the probate court will attempt to appoint the relative who is the most closely related to the deceased. If none of the parties listed above will serve, the court will appoint a stranger to serve.

Bonding

The probate court may require the administrator to buy a bond with the estate's finds. This protects the interests of both the heirs at law and the creditors.

INTESTATE DISTRIBUTION SCHEME

Under every state's intestacy statute, the deceased's property will be distributed to the next of kin. In other words, because most people leave their property to close relatives, if a person dies without a will, the law will distribute her property to those most closely related by blood.

Lineal and Collateral Relatives

In most states the intestacy statute awards property to either lineal or collateral relatives. A lineal relative is a direct relation, such as a grandfather, father, son, or grandson. A collateral relative is one who shares a common ancestor with the deceased, such as brothers and sisters, cousins who have common grandparents, and uncles, aunts, nephews, and nieces. States vary as to the degree of relationship that is required to inherit under the intestacy statute. In some states, distribution will be made to parents, children, grandparents, grandchildren, great-grandchildren, uncles, aunts, nephews, and nieces, but not to cousins.

Typical Scheme

Many, but not all, states have adopted the distribution scheme promoted by the Uniform Probate Code. This distribution system sets up a nine-step procedure. In interpreting Figure 1 on page 97, *issue* includes the deceased's children, grandchildren, and great-grandhildren. *Parents' issue* includes the deceased's brothers, sisters, nephews, nieces, grandnephews, and grandnieces. *Grandparents' issue* includes the deceased's aunts, uncles, first cousins, and distant cousins.

The administrator needs to start at the top of the list and work down until all property is distributed.

....

WARNING *Note that intestacy distribution rules vary from state to state.*

....

The following examples illustrate the operation of the rules listed in Figure 1 on page 97.

EXAMPLE 1 Todd dies intestate. Todd is survived by his wife, Mary. The couple's son, Harry, predeceased Todd. Mary takes the entire estate. (See rule 4.)

EXAMPLE 2 Todd dies intestate. Todd is survived by his two sons, Peter and Paul. Mary, the boys' mother and Todd's wife, predeceased Todd. Peter and Paul will share the estate. (See rule 5.)

EXAMPLE 3 Todd dies intestate. Todd has outlived his wife Mary and his two sons, Peter and Paul, but Todd is survived by one son, Harry. Both Peter and Paul had two children each (Todd's four grandchildren). The surviving son, Harry, will share the estate with Peter's and Paul's children. In most states Harry

FIGURE 1: UNIFORM PROBATE CODE

Deceased is survived by	Property distribution
1. spouse and issue born to both the deceased and spouse	spouse takes first $50,000, plus ½ of remainder*; issue take ½ of remainder
2. spouse and issue born to deceased alone	spouse takes first $50,000, plus ½ of remainder*; issue take ½ of remainder
3. spouse and parents but no issue	spouse takes first $50,000 plus ½ of remainder; parents take ½ of remainder
4. spouse only, but no issue	spouse takes all
5. issue only, but no spouse	issue take all
6. parents, but no spouse or issue	parents take all
7. parents' issue, but no spouse, issue, or parents	parents' issue take all
8. grandparents or their issue, but no spouse, issue, parents, or siblings	paternal grandparents or issue take ½ maternal grandparents or issue take ½
9. no relatives	all property "escheats" to the state

* In a community property state, the spouse would also take half of all the community property.
A state-by-state summary of intestacy laws is found in Appendix B.

---

will get one-third, and the grandchildren will each receive one-sixth of the estate. (See rule 5 above.)

EXAMPLE 4 Todd dies intestate. He died in an auto accident in which his wife Mary and only child Harry were also killed. Todd is survived by his parents, who have divorced. The parents will share his estate equally. (See rule 6 above.)

EXAMPLE 5 Todd dies intestate. He died in an auto accident in which his wife Mary and only child Harry were also killed. Todd's father died some time ago. Todd is survived by his mother and his brother Ted. His mother will take the entire estate and Ted will get nothing. (See rule 6 above.)

EXAMPLE 6 Todd dies intestate. He died in an auto accident in which his wife Mary and only child Harry were also killed. Todd's mother and father both died some time ago. Todd is survived by his brother Ted. Ted has a son, Gene (Todd's nephew). Todd also had a sister, Ann, who died a year ago. She had two daughters, Alison and Briana (Todd's nieces). In most states, the estate will be shared by his brother Ted, who will get one-half, and his nieces Alison and Briana, who will each get one-fourth. Gene, Todd's nephew, will get nothing. (See rule 7 above.)

EXAMPLE 7 Todd dies intestate. He died in an auto accident in which his wife Mary and only child Harry were also killed. Todd's mother and father died some time ago. Todd is survived by both of his maternal grandparents and his grandfather on his father's side. The grandparents will share the estate. The maternal grandparents will each get one-fourth and the grandfather on his father's side will get one-half of the estate. (See rule 8 above.)

EXAMPLE 8 Todd dies intestate. He died in an auto accident in which his wife Mary and his only child Harry were also killed. Todd's mother and father died some time ago. Todd is survived by both of his maternal grandparents and his mother's sister Doris (his aunt). Both grandparents on his father's side are dead. His father's brother Bob, however, is still living. Todd's Uncle Bob will receive one-half of the estate and the surviving grandparents will share the remaining half. Thus, the maternal grandparents will each take one-fourth. (See rule 8 above.)

State-by-State Variations

The states vary somewhat in their treatment of distributions in intestacy. For example, assume that Brown dies without a will and is not survived by his two children. He is survived by three grandchildren. The first grandchild is a daughter of Brown's oldest child and the second and third grandchildren are the children of Brown's other child. In some states, each of the grandchildren would receive a one-third share because there are simply three heirs. In other states, the first grandchild would receive one-half of the property, and the second and third grandchildren would each receive one-quarter because they trace their inheritance through their deceased parent.

Per Capita and Per Stirpes Distributions

The state intestacy statute may provide that the distribution among the beneficiaries be *per capita* or *per stirpes*. Administrators should understand the distinction between *per capita* and *per stirpes* distribution as applied to intestate gifts. These terms indicate the manner in which the property will be distributed among class members in the event that one of the members of the class predeceases the deceased. *Per capita* merely means "per person," and *per stirpes* means "from the root."

EXAMPLE Assume that Smith had two sons, Peter and Paul, who each have two children. Peter's children are named Alison and Briana, and Paul's children are named Chelsea and Darren. Smith dies intestate. The closest surviving relatives are his grandchildren, because Peter and Paul predeceased him. The law provides that the grandchildren shall receive their shares *per capita*, but at the time of Smith's death, Darren, one of the grandchildren, has predeceased Smith. Because state law calls for *per capita* distribution, the property will be divided into thirds and paid to Alison, Briana, and Chelsea in equal shares. A *per capita* distribution divides the property equally by the number of surviving persons in the class.

Using the example above, assume that the intestacy statute provides that the grandchildren share the property *per stirpes*. In some states, because Darren has predeceased his grandfather, the property will be divided at the "root level,"—in this example, the grandchildren's parents, Peter and Paul. Thus, the property would be divided into two parts, one for each root, and one-fourth of the proceeds would be paid to Alison, one-fourth to Briana, and one-half to Chelsea, the sole survivor of that root.

Additional complications can arise when the beneficiary is long-lived. Assume that in our example both sons, Peter and Paul, and one grandson, Darren, predecease Smith. Moreover, Darren is survived by two sons, Smith's great-grandchildren. State law, which varies, will determine exactly who is to receive Smith's property when the law dictates a *per stirpes* distribution. In many states the root level is determined at the first generation in which there is a survivor. In this case, since the sons have not survived, then the root level is the grandchild level. Because there are three surviving grandchildren there will be three roots. Accordingly, Alison, Briana, and Chelsea will each get a one-third share, and the great-grandchildren will get nothing.

In other states, however, the root level is determined at the level closest to the deceased, regardless of survivorship. In this case the root level would be at the parent level and there would be two roots, because Smith had two sons, Peter and Paul. Peter's children, Alison and Briana, would each get a one-fourth share, and Paul's child, Chelsea, would get one-half, and the great-grandchildren nothing. (In a few states, the result may be that Chelsea and the great-grandchildren would get one-quarter, one-eighth, and one-eighth shares respectively).

OBSERVATION *Administrators must determine the law in their state and seek legal advice on structuring complex distributions to avoid personal legal liability.*

Adopted and Posthumous Children

Adopted children, posthumous children (children conceived but not born before the death of the deceased), and illegitimate children are treated as any other children under the intestacy statutes in most states. However, some states have special rules for step-children and half-bloods, children who share only one common ancestor with the deceased.

Unmarried Couples

While distributing property to close relatives is appropriate for more traditional families, it can work a real hardship on unmarried couples. If one partner in an unmarried couple dies without a will, the other partner may get nothing because they are not legal relatives. It is essential that both partners in an unmarried couple have a will to prevent this.

Some states have enacted laws that protect the rights of unmarried couples who live together. At the time of this writing, these statutes usually require the partners to be of opposite sexes, although this requirement may become increasingly flexible in the future. In some states, the laws require the couple to have lived together for a specific period of time. For example, the Oregon statute requires a man and woman to have lived together for 10 years, and to have lived in Oregon for at least the last two years. Additionally, the couple must have "mutually assumed marital rights" and acquired a "general reputation of husband and wife."

OBSERVATION *When an unmarried co-habitant attempts to take a spouse's share under an intestacy statute, he or she may face opposition from surviving blood relatives. For example, children from a previous marriage may allege that the unmarried couple's relationship was too casual to satisfy the requirements of the state statutes. The executors of the estates of several well-known entertainers have been embroiled in such disputes.*

Escheat to State

If an individual dies without a will and leaves no close family members, the property will go to the state government. When this happens, the property is said to *escheat* to the state. If a person who dies intestate is the last of a family line and leaves no surviving family, then the property would automatically escheat to the state.

IDENTIFYING AND FINDING THE HEIRS AT LAW

The administrator of an intestate will has two tasks concerning heirs at law. The administrator must identify the individuals who qualify as heirs. If the administrator is familiar with the decedent's family, this may not be troublesome. On the other hand, if the family is large and does not keep in close touch, it may be more difficult. The best course may be to identify a few people in the family who seem the best-versed in family history and enlist them to help construct a family tree. The administrator then needs to show the family tree to various family members until some consensus is reached about who the family members are and how they are related.

The second step is to find the heirs at law. This may be a considerable task. Although in some families everyone lives close to one another, in other families, members are scattered not only around the country but around the globe. It may take considerable creativity and research on the part of the administrator to track down these people. If they have a fairly common name like "Robert Johnson," the task may be all the more difficult.

PLANNING TIP *There are firms that specialize in finding lost heirs. Genealogists can be useful in identifying and locating lost heirs.*

ADDITIONAL CONSIDERATIONS
Advancements

An heir's share of the intestate distribution will be reduced by any advancement. An advancement is a share of the estate that is received during the deceased's lifetime, and which is clearly identified as an advance payment of the recepient's inheritance.

EXAMPLE Sara has three children. Ron, the eldest son, asks Sara for $100,000 to start a business. Sara gives Ron the money but makes it clear to him that this $100,000 is an advancement from the amount he can expect to receive on her death. If Sara dies intestate, the administrator shall reduce Ron's inheritance by the $100,000. In some states, advancements must be acknowledged in writing by the heir or the deceased.

Qualifications to Inherit

There are some miscellaneous rules with which the executor needs to be familiar. In most states the right to inherit property is conditioned on the heir surviving the deceased by 120 days if there is no will. Some states have different rules.

EXAMPLE Todd dies intestate. State law provides that the right to inherit is conditioned on the heir surviving the deceased by 120 days. Todd is survived by two brothers, Peter and Paul, who are his sole heirs at law and are expected to share his estate. Peter, who has been ill for a number of years, dies 110 days after Todd. Paul will inherit all of Todd's estate. None of Todd's property will flow into Peter's estate.

Similarly, the heir must be conceived at the time of the death of the intestate. For example, a grandchild who is conceived after the deceased's death would not qualify as an heir at law.

Most states provide that if there is no evidence of the order of death of two individuals, no one is presumed to have died first. This avoids circularity in intestate proceedings. For example, assume a husband and wife both die together in a car crash. The estate of the husband will pass as though the wife died first. Her estate will pass as though her husband died first. This prevents one spouse's property from passing through the other's estate.

Most states have "slayer's statutes" that prevent a person who intentionally kills another from receiving a share of the victim's estate. Similarly, state law may prevent a person who has participated in fraud or undue influence in regard to the deceased from sharing in the estate.

PLANNING TIP *Although at common law an individual could not disclaim (renounce) an intestate share, most states now allow an heir to disclaim his share. This can be useful in avoiding estate tax problems. See Chapter 13, "Estate and Gift Tax Basics."*

CHAPTER 11

Will Contests

INTRODUCTION

If a will is contested or challenged by a disappointed heir, the cost and delay of probate will expand greatly. A will contest will normally try to have a will set aside by the court in favor of an earlier will. In other cases, the challenger would like the court to determine that the deceased died without a valid will.

There are a number of grounds on which to contest a will, including lack of mental capacity at the time the will was signed. Other grounds include fraud, duress (use of threats), and undue influence (use of overpersuasion by a person of trust when the deceased was in a vulnerable state of mind).

WHAT IS A "WILL CONTEST"?

Disappointed heirs and family members sometimes challenge the validity of a will. These challenges are usually referred to as *will contests* and are generally confined to the local probate court. Once the legality of a will is challenged, the local probate judge will determine if the will is legally effective.

Second Will

A similar but slightly different set of events takes place if a second will is found after probate has started. Even though the first will has been admitted to probate, if a later will is found and is determined to be the legal will of the testator, it will control the disposition of the deceased's property. This is true even though heirs and creditors have relied on the validity of the first will. A second will can cause a major disruption in the probate process.

EXAMPLE Mary died and her will was admitted to probate. Mary, a widow, left all of her property in equal shares to her two children, Peter and Paul. Anticipating a large windfall from the estate, Paul bought a new and expensive home. Although Paul could not afford the home, the builder sold it to him after he was shown a copy of Mary's will and a copy of the order admitting it to probate. Three months later, while searching through Mary's records to compile the inventory for the court, the executor discovers another and more recent will. This will gives almost all of Mary's property to the Salvation Army, and only modest amounts to her two sons. If the second will is Mary's last will and declared valid, Paul's gift under the first will becomes invalid even though he and the builder both relied on it and on the fact that it had been admitted to probate.

WHO CAN CHALLENGE A WILL?

In most states only an "interested" person can contest a will. That is, the challenger must have some financial interest at stake. As a rule, this will be someone who stands to gain financially if the will is set aside, namely disappointed relatives or persons who had received more in an earlier will.

In most states a creditor cannot contest a will, although in many states a "judgment creditor" (in this context, a creditor who has a court judgment against an heir under a prior will) is eligible to contest a later will.

Surprisingly, in a number of states a person who would receive more if there was no will at all, cannot contest the validity of a will. Similarly, if a person receives the same amount either way, most states won't allow that person to contest the will.

WHEN CAN THE CHALLENGE TAKE PLACE?

In most states there are strict limits about will contests. Challengers must be prompt in coming forward. In most states such challenges must take place within four months after the will is admitted to probate.

The short time limit for challenging a will may not apply if a second will is found. In many states anyone can bring forward a more recent will for probate even though the time period for bringing a will contest has elapsed.

WHY WOULD THE WILL BE CHALLENGED?

Wills are most commonly challenged by family members and friends who have been disinherited by a recent will. Testators sometimes change their wills and omit relatives after they have retired and moved to a new area. Once they have new friends and are away from their family, they feel that their wills are no longer appropriate. Contrary to the old adage that blood is thicker than water, it is not unusual for older people to cut out gifts to family members they seldom see once they have retired.

Family members frequently allege that the new will was a product of fraud, undue influence, or a mistake. They also may allege that the testator lacked the requisite testamentary capacity to make a new will.

WHAT HAPPENS IF THE CHALLENGE IS SUCCESSFUL?

If a will is successfully challenged, one of two things may happen. If the deceased had no other will, then the deceased's property will be distributed according to the state's intestacy statute (see Chapter 10, "Intestacy—When There Is No Will"). Generally, the law will cause the property in the estate to go to the deceased's closest living relatives.

Alternatively, if the deceased had a prior will, in many states the prior will would be revived. Accordingly, will contests are usually brought by relatives or friends who would benefit if the later will is ignored and the estate distributed either by intestate succession or by an earlier will. For example, disinherited children are often likely challengers to a will made in favor of a second spouse.

Chances for Success

Challenging a will is difficult. A challenger has only a short period, typically a few months, to contest a will. In many states, the grounds for challenging a will are quite limited. Unfairness is not sufficient grounds for challenging a will. A will that leaves no property to relatives is no less valid than one that leaves all property to the immediate family. However, a will that attempts to disinherit a spouse will be ineffective, as discussed in Chapter 9 and elsewhere.

In many states the only ground for challenging a will is some defect in its legal validity. A challenge could be based on some defect in the way the will was executed. For example, the challenger could try to argue that the will was not properly signed or witnessed. Other typical grounds for challenging a will include lack of testamentary capacity, fraud, undue influence, and/or a mistake made by the testator.

HOW DOES A WILL CONTEST AFFECT THE EXECUTOR?

Unfortunately the executor will be caught in the middle of the will contest. The executor will be named as a defendant in the lawsuit. The estate will have to retain a lawyer if none has been retained. And even if the estate has a lawyer, she may feel that she needs additional assistance with the lawsuit. Some lawyers who do estate work don't usually go to court and will want the assistance of a litigator—a lawyer who specializes in trying cases. Although the lawyer(s) will be taking care of the case, the executor will have to make a number of decisions on behalf of the estate about how the case should be handled.

If the executor knew the deceased, the executor will be involved and questioned under oath—either in court, out of court, or both—about the circumstances under which the will was made.

Emotional Toll

Will contests take a great emotional toll on everyone involved. These lawsuits are similar to divorces in that they can be exceptionally nasty. They often pit one branch of a family against another. Although the basic issue is often money, underlying resentments and jealousies fuel the fire. Long-dormant sibling rivalries may be revived. If a father's will has left more to one son than another, the disadvantaged son may see this as another insult in a long line of humiliations at the hands of his father. Because his father is no longer alive and cannot be confronted, the brother's rage may be directed toward his brother. Indeed, the real reason for the lawsuit could be to harass certain members of the family.

How Long Will the Lawsuit Last?

In some cases the probate court may be able to resolve the challenge without much difficulty. On the other hand, the lawsuit might take over a year to complete. The larger the estate, the larger the stakes and the more likely the challengers will persist with the lawsuit. Will contests lasting three years or more are not unheard of.

STRATEGY

Sometimes the intent of the challengers is not to get an outright victory in court, but to create such a problem that the executor decides the most efficient thing to do is compromise and pay off the challengers. If there are some grounds for challenge and the challengers have the financial resources to hire lawyers to handle their case, they could make life difficult for the executor and the persons named in the challenged will. The challengers can pressure those persons, who may tire of the inconvenience and stress. The lawsuit will also delay distributions from the estate for everyone. At some point the executor and the estate's lawyer(s) may decide that settling the lawsuit by paying off the challengers

will actually cost less than the legal costs of defending the will.

EXAMPLE Sara, the family matriarch, writes a new will two weeks before her death while she is in the hospital. In it, she disinherits two of her three children. The two disinherited children file a petition with the probate court to challenge the new will on the grounds that Sara was either not in her right mind, or that she was improperly influenced by other family members. Because the legal challenge to the will's validity will slow down the entire probate process, the executor and beneficiaries under the new will may be willing to negotiate with the disinherited family members rather than face a bitter court fight.

WHO PAYS THE LAWYERS?

In the United States each side of a will contest pays its own legal bills, win or lose. The estate will have to pay the costs of defending the will. If there is a prolonged legal battle, the attorney's fee can quickly diminish the estate's assets. In most cases, the lawsuit will ultimately reduce the "residue" of the estate—that part of the estate that is not a specific gift. Because this is often the surviving spouse's share, the surviving spouse may find that the amount he or she receives after the will contest is substantially reduced.

IN TERROREM CLAUSE

Some wills contain an *in terrorem* clause. Such clauses prohibit an heir from challenging the validity of a will. If an heir challenges the validity of the will but loses, the *in terrorem* clause operates so that the heir forfeits any provision in the will in his favor. In other words, the heir must decide if he wants to gamble: he can take a small guaranteed gift or he can challenge the will on an all-or-nothing basis. If he successfully challenges the will he may get a large gift, but if he loses, the will is enforced and gives him nothing at all.

Because this sort of clause can operate to perpetrate a fraud, some states will not enforce such clauses against good faith challengers. For example, if a disinherited child challenges a new will in good faith, alleging undue influence, then the *in terrorem* clause would not be allowed to penalize the challenger if he loses his suit.

GROUNDS FOR CHALLENGING A WILL

Wills are most commonly challenged by heirs and family members who have been disinherited by a more recent will. In most states the grounds for challenging a will are quite limited. Generally, challenges fit into four categories:

1. lack of formalities;
2. lack of testamentary capacity;
3. lack of true volition; and
4. promises to make a gift.

Remember that unfairness is an insufficient ground for challenging a will.

Lack of Formalities

The most straightforward basis for challenging a will is that it does not contain the requisite formalities. The law is quite strict about legal formalities and if a will is not properly signed and witnessed then the will cannot legally operate. Common defects would include lack of a signature or lack of proper witnesses.

Signatures

To be legally valid a testator must sign the will. Normally the will must be signed at the end of the document. Problems arise when the testator signs in the wrong place. In most cases this will not invalidate the will if the court finds that the testator still wanted the document to operate as his will. However, a misplaced signature may also show that the testator lacked the mental competence to make a will (see below).

Aiding a Signature

Testamentary capacity has more to do with mental capacity than physical abilities. But what happens if a testator is mentally capable of making a will but is physically unable to move his hands to sign his name to the will? Court cases have held that a frail testator may be "helped" if they really want to sign a document. Another individual can make the signature on the will if the impaired testator acknowledges it. This type of signature is obviously open to challenge.

EXAMPLE Kevin, who is 90 years old, is in the hospital suffering from a life-threatening illness. A few days before his death, Kevin "signs" a new will that is typed up by his daughter Hillary. The new will gives the bulk of Kevin's estate to Hillary, while her two sisters get modest gifts. Because Kevin was shaking so violently, Hillary helped him by holding his hand while he signed his name on the will. It was obvious to all present that Kevin could not have signed on his own. Although Kevin may have created a valid new will, the sisters may challenge the new will arguing that Hillary, not Kevin, signed the will. The court would have to resolve all of this by calling hospital personnel and any others who were present at the time the will was signed. Of course the best witness—Kevin—is unavailable to tell what he really intended.

Witnesses

Although sometimes taken for granted, proper witnessing of a will is essential. Some states require two witnesses and others three. At one time a person who received a gift in the will could not witness it. Today that rule has been changed in many states. Even if a witness must come forward to testify about the testator's legal capacity, that witness will be able to receive a gift in the will.

Witnesses themselves must have legal capacity at the time the will is signed. A person challenging the will may allege that one or both witnesses themselves lacked legal capacity to serve as a valid witness. If one of the two was incompetent then the entire will is invalidated.

In most states the witnesses must actually see the testator sign the will or acknowledge that the document is indeed her will. A challenger might allege that the testator's signature on the will is a forgery, or that witnesses signed the will after the testator's death.

Lack of Testamentary Capacity

Probably the most common ground for challenging a will is to question the testamentary capacity of the testator. Because many challenged wills are executed when the testator is elderly or is suffering from a last illness, the testator's mental capacity is called into question. Additionally, challengers sometimes allege that a testator who was under heavy medication did not have the testamentary capacity to make a new will. Legal capacity to make a will is discussed in more detail later in the chapter.

Lack of Volitional Consent

Challengers may also allege that the testator lacked volitional consent. In this type of will contest, the challenger alleges that the testator did not voluntarily execute the will, but was tricked or pressured into signing the document. Normally the challenger will argue that the will was a product of either fraud, undue influence, or a mistake.

Fraud

To prove fraud, a challenger must provide evidence that someone made a false representation to the testator with an intent to deceive him, and that the testator relied on the deception to the detriment of the challenger. In most states, fraud must be shown by "clear and convincing" evidence. Although this is a lighter burden than the "beyond a reasonable doubt" standard used in criminal trials, the "clear and convincing" standard is still a difficult one to meet. However, if the challenger can show fraud, then the will is set aside.

Two Types of Fraud

Legally, there are two types of fraud: fraud in the execution and fraud in the inducement. Fraud in the execution occurs when a party misrepresents the contents or character of a will to the testator. For example, if a testator is tricked into signing a will that he believes is some other sort of document, this is fraud in the execution. The testator signed willingly, but he did not understand the nature of the document, so it will be set aside.

EXAMPLE Ann visits her grandfather in the hospital. Ann shows him a legal document which she describes as a deed to his house. She tells him that by signing the "deed" the house will be put in joint names so she can care for it while he is in the hospital. Grandfather signs and two other persons present sign as witnesses. In reality, the document is not a deed, but a new will drafted by Ann. This document should not be treated as a will because Ann misrepresented the nature of the document that her grand-

father signed. This is an example of "fraud in the execution."

Fraud in the inducement involves a deception as to facts outside the will. For example, if a potential heir falsely convinces the testator that he needs money because he has a rare disease that will require expensive treatment, this would be fraud in the inducement, because the fraud involves a misrepresentation of facts outside the will.

Undue Influence

Will contests are often based on undue influence. To show undue influence, a party must demonstrate that there was overpersuasion or coercion used to overcome the testator's free will, and that but for the undue influence, the will would have been made differently. Most undue influence cases arise when the overreaching party has a confidential relationship or a relationship of trust with the testator and the testator is in a vulnerable condition because of illness or stress.

Close relatives may be accused of exerting undue influence. Will contests often pit one family member against another with the challenger maintaining that one heir pressured the testator to change a will in his or her favor. When an elderly parent disinherits sons and daughters in favor of a second spouse, the children might not be able to challenge the legal sufficiency of the will or the testator's legal competence, but they may be able to successfully allege undue influence if it appears that the spouse dominated the testator's free will.

Trusted advisors including attorneys, accountants, and members of the clergy are sometimes accused of undue influence after a deathbed change in a will. If a party has a confidential relationship with the testators and a provision is drawn in favor of that party, this creates a presumption of undue influence.

For example, if shortly before her client's death an attorney changes the client's will to provide her with a large gift, the attorney will have to rebut the inference that the gift was a result of her undue influence. In other words, the attorney will have the burden of showing that the deceased made the gift of his own free will. Without the deceased present, this will be extremely difficult for the attorney to actually prove.

Mistake

Alleging that the testator was mistaken or confused about certain facts does not generally render a will invalid, although a procedural mistake might be sufficient for a successful will challenge. For example, if the testator mistakenly believes that he needs no witness signatures on his will, the mistake can render the will invalid.

A mistaken belief does not invalidate a provision in a will unless the belief is a result of fraud. For example, if a relative mistakenly advises a testator that only close family members may be given property in a will, that misinformation is not enough to invalidate a will. If the testator's mistaken belief is the product of fraud, however, the will might be successfully challenged.

EXAMPLE Thinking his brother Fred is dead, David leaves his entire estate to his sister Ruth, his only other surviving relative. If Fred is alive, he might come and try to have the will set aside because of the mistake, arguing that David would have made a gift in his favor had he known the truth. Most courts will not declare David's will invalid, despite the obvious mistake. Some courts will try to correct the mistake if it is mentioned in the will: "Knowing my sister is my sole relative, I leave her my entire estate."

Sometimes a will is challenged because it contains a typographical mistake. Although testators are presumed to have read and know the contents of their wills, they do not always read their wills with extreme care. Wills have been challenged when the language of the will seems contrary to the plain intent of the testator. The challenger would have a very heavy burden of proof to have the will declared invalid, although some courts have effectively rewritten parts of wills in an attempt to carry out what they believe to have been a testator's intent.

OBSERVATION *Some situations have elements of both mistake and fraud. An adult child might fraudulently tell his elderly father that under state law, parents must leave all of their property to their children (which of course is not true in any state). If the father relies on the child's advice and makes a will leaving property only to his children, the father has made a mistake that was induced by the adult child's fraud. A probate court would probably analyze this as a fraud case.*

Promises to Make a Gift

Finally, a will may be challenged if the deceased promised to make a gift in a will but did not. Generally a promise to make a gift in the future is unenforceable. In other words, if the testator promised to leave property to someone in his will, although the testator may be under a moral obligation to do so, he is under no legal obligation. However, a person may also enter into a contract to make a will. For example, a prenuptial agreement that specifies that a spouse is to receive a certain sum of money on the testator's death would be an enforceable contract.

Not infrequently a testator will promise to make a gift in a will in return for the performance of services. For example, a father might promise one son that he will receive the family farm if the son agrees to live on the farm and help the father for a number of years. In some states this type of agreement is enforceable as a contract if the son provided the requested services. When an expected or contracted-for gift is not made in a will, the disappointed heir frequently challenges it, alleging a contract to make a will.

LEGAL CAPACITY TO MAKE A WILL

A basic legal requirement for a valid will is that the testator must be legally competent to make a will. Legal competence is generally required in most legal transactions. For example, to sign a lease or a contract you must be legally competent. However, legal competence becomes especially significant where wills are concerned because they are often made by the elderly, or by persons in their last illness. Not surprisingly, the rules are fairly well-established in this area with little variation state by state.

Age

In most states, a minor under the age of 18 has no legal capacity to make a will. Many states will not admit a will to probate if it was made by an individual under the age of 18.

General Legal Capacity Distinguished

Although the concept of legal capacity is used in a number of contexts, the test used to determine legal capacity to make a will is not as strict as the test for capacity to enter into a valid contract. In most states, the decedent must have a sound mind at the time the will is actually signed. It is not enough that the testator had a sound mind when the will was planned. In other words, the testator must be legally competent both at the time the will is signed and when the witnesses verify that the deceased acknowledged the document as his will. As a rule, all parties sign at the same time.

FOUR REQUIREMENTS FOR TESTAMENTARY CAPACITY

The following are the basic requirements for legal capacity to make a will:

1. the testator must understand the nature and extent of his or her property;
2. the testator must recognize the "natural objects of his or her bounty" (he must be able to remember who his family is);
3. the testator needs to understand the testamentary act; and
4. the testator must understand the relation of the first three elements to one another.

A person who is seriously ill may have diminished legal capacity and therefore be unable to make a legally valid will. Problems in this area can arise when an elderly person makes a will.

Understanding the Nature and Extent of Property

The first proof of testamentary capacity is the testator's understanding of the nature and extent of his property. To satisfy this requirement the testator needs to have a general knowledge of his property. For example, there is no need for the testator to know the names of the individual stock in his stock portfolio; it is only necessary that he knows that he owns some stock or investments. However, there

may be problems if the testator has little idea of how large his estate is.

Recognizing the "Natural Objects of His Bounty"

Second, the testator must recognize the natural objects of his bounty. In other words, he must understand who are the members of his family. In practice this may be difficult if the testator tends to be forgetful. Some older individuals may have excellent memories of their childhood, but may be unable to recall which of their children are currently alive. In such a case, the requirement would not be satisfied and the individual would not be legally competent to sign a will.

Understanding the Testamentary Act

The third requirement for legal competence is the testator's understanding of the nature of the testamentary act. In other words, the testator must understand that the will operates to dispose of her property at death.

Understanding the Relationship Between the First Three Elements

The fourth criterion of legal competence is the testator's understanding of the relationship of the first three criteria to one another. In other words, the testator must be able to understand the relationship between the family, the property, and the operation of the will.

Proof

Actually determining if an individual is legally competent can be troublesome. It can be hard to distinguish confusion from mental incompetence. This is especially so if the individual is ill and under medication. If the testator can recall both his family and property, but is too confused about the operation of the will, it is simply too late to make a will. The testator lacks the legal competence required by the law, and the will, even if signed, will be invalid if challenged.

Court Procedures

The persons challenging the will have the burden of proof in court. They must demonstrate to the court that the testator lacked one or more of the four elements of testamentary capacity. If they fail to make a case, then the will withstands challenge. Testamentary capacity must be measured at the exact moment when the will is made. It is not sufficient to show that the deceased lacked capacity at some later time. The court will give heavy weight to the testimony of witnesses who were present at the time the deceased signed the will.

However, other individuals can also give testimony. An attending doctor, nurse, or caregiver can be called as a witness. Because such individuals have more experience and knowledge in this area, and are unlikely to have an interest in the outcome of the case, their testimony will be given great weight by the court.

Mistaken Beliefs

A testator's mistaken belief of facts does not render a will invalid. Even an unreasonable and erroneous belief is not in itself enough to prove the incapacity of a testator. For example, if a testator erroneously and unreasonably believes that his son had plotted against him for years, this is no reason to question the legal competence of the father, nor to invalidate his will.

Insane Delusions

On the other hand, if it can be demonstrated that the testator had insane delusions, this might be evidence that a testator did not in fact have sufficient legal capacity to make a will. In most states, for an insane delusion to invalidate a will, the will itself must be a product of the delusion. In other words, one or more specific provisions must have been written because of the delusion.

....

OBSERVATION *The testimony of a psychiatrist could be used to establish or rebut the finding that the deceased had a serious mental illness that produced the insane delusion.*

....

CHAPTER 12 Understanding Trusts

INTRODUCTION

Trusts are frequently used in conjunction with a will to carry out the testator's wishes. Trusts are also created in a variety of circumstances to provide estate tax savings. It is very common for the executor of the will also to be named as the trustee of the decedent's trust. Accordingly, executors need a basic working knowledge of how trusts operate and about common situations in which trusts are appropriate in carrying out the beneficiaries' needs. Executors also need to be alert to certain problems that may arise with the use of trusts. This chapter provides an overview of trusts. The chapter will discuss the legal basics and will also describe several kinds of trusts that an executor may encounter. The chapter details many of the trustee's duties, and discusses problems that are sometimes encountered by trustees. Finally, the chapter contains a brief discussion of trust accounting and trust taxation. Chapter 15, "Avoiding Probate," provides a discussion of living trusts that operate as will substitutes.

WHAT IS A TRUST?

Most people are familiar with the term *trust fund*, a phrase often associated with the wealthy. However, a trust can also be a useful and cost-effective way for middle-income individuals to carry out their estate plans. In some cases, trusts can also be employed to reduce federal estate tax (see Chapter 13, "Estate and Gift Tax Basics"). It is increasingly common for people to have a trust that operates together with their will.

A trust is simply an "artificial" entity that holds property for the benefit of someone. A trust is similar to a corporation because it is a legal device that meets a certain need.

A trust represents a fiduciary relationship between the trustee, who holds legal title to the res (trust property) for the benefit of the beneficiary. While the trustee has legal title to the res, the beneficiary has an equitable title and equitable rights in the property. The party who establishes the trust is known as the grantor, trustor, or settlor. The trustee may either be an individual or an institution, such as a bank's trust department.

Although the law implies the creation of a trust in certain situations, the typical trust is an express trust, memorialized in a document that spells out the rights and duties of the parties.

Essentially, a testamentary trust, set forth in a will (effective upon the death of the grantor), allows a person to accomplish what he might have done himself had he lived. Property is put into a trust and administered by a trustee for the benefit of one or more beneficiaries.

EXAMPLE 1 Howard establishes a trust for his three young children. On his death the children will receive income earned by the trust property until they reach the age of 21. When the last child reaches age 21, the trustee will terminate the trust and distribute one-third of any remaining trust property to each of the three children.

EXAMPLE 2 Jane is caring for her elderly mother. Jane establishes a trust to benefit her mother in case she dies unexpectedly. In the event of Jane's death, the property in the trust will generate enough income to support the mother for the rest of her life.

PARTIES TO A TRUST

There are normally three distinct parties involved in a trust:

1. the grantor,
2. the beneficiary (or beneficiaries), and
3. the trustee.

The grantor (or settlor) is the person who puts property into the trust. The beneficiary or beneficiaries receive the property or income from the property. The trustee is the party who administers the trust for the benefit of the beneficiary or beneficiaries.

There can be one or more than one grantor. There can also be one or more beneficiaries.

EXAMPLE John and Mary, a married couple, wish to set up a trust to provide for their three children. They can establish the trust so that each child receives the same amount of income, or they can set up the trust so that the children each receive different amounts. They can even provide that the three children will receive their income or property at different times—when each attains age 25, for example. A trust provides maximum flexibility.

Beneficiaries

Beneficiaries under a trust are either income beneficiaries, who have a right to current income, or remainder beneficiaries, who have a "remainder interest" in the trust property after the income beneficiaries receive income for a period defined in the trust document.

The Trustee

A trust must have both property and a trustee. In selecting a trustee, a grantor has the option to select either an individual or an institution. A trusted advisor such as an attorney, CPA, or business associate would be a good choice as a trustee if she is familiar with the family. A family member is another obvious choice and he will often work without compensation. Trustees usually get a percentage of the trust's assets as a fee, and a trustee, other than perhaps a close family member, should not be expected to serve for free. An additional discussion of the trustee comes later in this chapter.

TYPES OF TRUSTS

Trusts can be classified in a number of different ways, including revocable or irrevocable trusts and testamentary or *inter vivos* trusts.

Revocable Versus Irrevocable Trusts

Trusts may be revocable or irrevocable. In other words, a trust can be created that can be terminated at any time, much like a will, but a trust can also be created so as to be unalterable, or irrevocable.

Individuals are sometimes reluctant to start a trust because they are not sure if the trust can be terminated. If a trust is revocable, then the grantor—the party who establishes the trust—can terminate the trust even if property has already flowed into it.

Testamentary Versus *Inter Vivos* Trusts

Trusts are also classified as either testamentary or *inter vivos*. A testamentary trust is a trust created in a will, not in any other document. The trust will be effective upon the grantor's death. An *inter vivos* trust (also called a *living trust*) is established during the grantor's life and becomes effective during the grantor's life.

EXAMPLE A married couple with minor children might set up a testamentary trust as part of their will. In the event both parents die, their property would drop into the trust for the benefit of their children.

An *inter vivos* trust is a trust that is established and operates during the grantor's lifetime. For this reason, this kind of trust is popularly called a living trust and is frequently used as a will substitute (see Chapter 15, "Avoiding Probate").

···

OBSERVATION *Although technically the term* inter vivos trust *or* living trust *is used to describe any trust that is established during the grantor's life, the term* living trust *is most commonly thought of as a trust used as a will substitute (in which property will pass to the heirs through the trust rather than passing through probate under the will).*

···

Other Types of Trusts

A deceased may have established one or more trusts during his life. The will itself may create one or more trusts. Following is a brief description of various types of trusts.

Support Trusts

As its name implies, a support trust is established to support one or more named individuals. This type of trust would be most appropriate if the beneficiary is a minor, or an elderly person unable or perhaps uneager to manage investment duties.

For example, a support trust would be appropriate for an elderly individual facing physical or mental disability to establish a trust for his own benefit. The elderly person may be unable to handle his affairs, or may simply want someone else to look after them. Some authorities suggest that a grantor utilize revocable rather than irrevocable trusts for this purpose. This allows the grantor (in this case also the beneficiary) to remove the trustee if friction arises. Note that the trust would become irrevocable upon the incompetency of the individual since he is no longer legally capable of handling his own affairs.

An irrevocable or revocable trust is not affected by a grantor's mental incompetency. Accordingly, it is a good vehicle for those with fading faculties.

Spendthrift Trust

A spendthrift trust is a trust that contains a spendthrift clause that prohibits voluntary or involuntary "alienation" of the beneficiary's right to income or *corpus* (property in the trust).

Sprinkling Trust

A sprinkling trust allows the trustee the discretion to "sprinkle" income among several beneficiaries, or to accumulate the income in the trust.

Totten Trust

Also called a *savings bank trust*, a Totten trust is an informal trust that is created when a party establishes a bank account "in trust" for another individual. The rules on Totten trusts vary state by state. Generally, a Totten trust can be revoked by the grantor. If the account is funded at the time of the grantor's death, a valid trust has been created. However, some state courts have held that no trust has been created—the money belongs to the depositor. New York has very specific rules concerning Totten trusts, and New Yorkers should examine the state laws thoroughly.

2503(c) Trust

This special trust can be created for minors under age 21; it is a trust that need not distribute its income annually. If the trust meets two conditions, then the entire amount of the trust will qualify as a present interest eligible for the annual $10,000 gift tax exclusion. The two conditions are:

1. Until the beneficiary attains age 21, the trustee may pay the income and/or corpus to the beneficiary; and
2. any income or corpus allocated to the beneficiary will pass to the beneficiary when he attains age 21. If the beneficiary dies before attaining age 21, the income and/or corpus must be paid to the beneficiary's estate or to a person the minor may appoint if the minor possesses a general power of appointment.

Medicaid Trust

Family members often wish to create a trust to provide limited support to a disabled relative who is receiving Medicaid. Although at one time such trusts were permissible, current rules greatly limit their availability. A "Medicaid trust" may be considered invalid and may be invaded by the government for reimbursement of the disabled party's expenses.

Charitable Trust

Wealthy individuals often establish a charitable trust for the benefit or betterment of the public at large, or for some specific community. For example, a trust could be created to support arts projects in a particular city.

REASONS FOR USING TRUSTS

Because of their flexibility, trusts have been used widely in estate planning. Trusts are particularly effective when combined with a valid will. Together, the two integrated documents can carry forward the deceased's wishes, and can even protect heirs from problems that the deceased had no reason to anticipate at the time of death. A few examples of problem-solving trusts will illustrate their many benefits.

Providing Support

Parents with minor children often set up a trust in their wills for their children's benefit. If the parents die, much of their property will flow into the trust for the support of the children. This is usually preferable to leaving the money to a close relative who promises to care for the children. By having the trust in place with an independent trustee, the parents can rest assured that the money will actually be used to support the children.

Similarly, a trust can be used to provide guaranteed support for a spouse, or adult children. It can also be useful in providing support for an ex-spouse or children from a prior marriage. Because of their flexibility, trusts can be fashioned to carry out the grantor's instructions, no matter how complex the family circumstances.

Delaying a Gift or Bequest

Although a grantor may want to make a gift to an heir, she may feel that the recipient is not ready to handle the money. A trust provides an effective way to postpone all or a portion of the gift. A trust allows for a good deal of flexibility because the grantor can give the trustee detailed instructions and conditions in advance. Experience has shown that individuals acquire maturity with age, and many trusts are written to take this into account.

A common condition for distributions of property from a trust is the attainment of a specific age. For example, a trust might provide that an heir is to receive $100,000. However, the money is to go to the trust and distributions of cash will be made by the trustee to the heir only when the heir reaches age 30 or 40.

Making Class Gifts

Trusts may also be set up for a class of heirs such as grandchildren. One type of trust is the so-called sprinkling trust which allows the trustee some discretion in making payments to members of a particular class. For example, if a grandparent leaves property in trust for five grandchildren, the trustee may be given the power to make discretionary payments. The ability to make discretionary payments would allow the trustee to use more of the trust's property to benefit a grandchild who had special needs such as an acute medical problem. A trust may be unrelated to the grantor's death, the grantor may create the trust to assist himself.

PLANNING TIP *Investment Goals* *Many individuals set up trusts to help them meet investment goals by providing for professional management. For example, an individual with substantial assets might put those investment assets in a trust and hire a professional trustee to manage them.*

PLANNING TIP *Dealing with Incapacity* *An individual may set up a trust to deal with his own incapacity—especially in his later years.*

EXAMPLE Ken, who is 80 and a childless widower, is diagnosed with Alzheimer's disease. In consultation with his attorney, he establishes a trust with an institutional trustee to manage his assets. The trust will provide income and care for Ken despite his incapacity.

Tax Savings

Trusts are frequently established to reduce transfer taxes—federal estate and gift taxes. Tax issues are discussed later in the chapter.

Asset Management and Distribution

Establishing a trust allows the grantor to carefully direct the trustee in both the management and distribution of the assets. In some cases the grantor may be comfortable giving the trustee broad discretion over management and distribution, with the intent of providing the trustee with maximum flexibility to meet changed conditions. On the other hand, the trust may be written to strictly limit the trustee's discretion. For example, if a grantor has an irresponsible heir, the trust document may give the trustee quite specific directions as to distributions to that individual. Such directions might be written so as to give the trustee broader discretion in making distributions to the heir for emergencies or other important expenses.

TRUST OPERATION
Importance of the Trust Document
Although the trustee is appointed by the grantor, the trustee does not work at the direction of the grantor but according to the terms of the trust. The trustee must follow state statutes when direction in the trust is absent. For example, if the trust directs the trustee to invest the trust property in a specified way, the trustee must follow the instructions. If the trust is silent on the point, the trustee must follow the requirements imposed by state law.

Note that the beneficiary need not know of the existence of the trustee or even of the trust.

THE TRUSTEE
Fiduciary Duty
A trustee has a fiduciary duty not to waste the assets of the trust. A fiduciary duty goes beyond mere honesty. The trustee must actively look out for the best interests of the beneficiary, even if that is adverse to his own best interest. The trustee has a number of specific duties, including the duty to safeguard and not waste the trust's assets; a duty not to commingle the trust's property with his own; a duty to make the trust assets "productive" (in other words, to earn a decent return); and a duty to diversify assets to lessen risk.

Duty to Distribute Income
The trustee's duty to distribute income is governed both by state law and by the trust instrument itself. In the unlikely event that the trust instrument is silent on the point, the trustee will make distributions in accordance with the "prudent person" standard. In most cases the trust instrument will provide some directions on distribution. At one extreme, the trust may give the trustee no discretion and will specify when and how distributions are to be made. At the other extreme, the trust instrument may give the trustee broad discretion in making distributions.

If the trustee has broad powers to distribute income, tax consequences are one factor that must be considered in arriving at an amount of income to distribute. Perhaps the most important consideration is the purpose of the trust. Frequently a trust is established to delay distributions of income to the beneficiary. When the purpose of the trust argues for making a distribution of income but the tax consequences argue against it, the trustee must make a professional judgment in discharging his fiduciary responsibility. In some cases a trustee may not be able to determine with any precision the income of a trust until after the close of the year.

Institutional Trustees
Many people feel more secure with an institutional trustee. Bank trust departments and trust companies provide trustee services for a fee. Institutions have trained professionals on staff who devote full time to administering trusts. Additionally, institutions can provide continuity: unlike an individual, an institution will usually be able to provide services for as long as needed. If an individual is no longer able to serve as trustee, the individual trustee must resign the position.

Because individuals can resign, and even institutions can disappear, it is always best to name a successor trustee in the trust. Although a court would name a successor if none is named in the trust's terms, it is far easier for all involved if the document names the backup trustee. Additionally, if the trustee is an individual, one should always name an institution as an ultimate successor in case none of the individuals are willing or able to serve. In some states only in-state banks and trust companies can act as corporate trustees. If the trust document attempts to name an out-of-state corporate trustee, the named trustee may be unqualified to serve and must be replaced.

TRUSTEE PROBLEMS
Although most trusts do not experience trustee problems, they are numerous enough to merit discussion.

Contingent Trustees

Normally the trust document will name a trustee and then a contingent trustee(s) if the primary trustee is unwilling or unable to serve. The most common reasons for inability to serve are death or old age. Accordingly, many attorneys will designate an institutional trustee as the backup. In the event the individual trustee is unable or unwilling to perform, the institutional trustee—a bank or trust company—will be able to substitute its services.

Unqualified Trustee

A named trustee may be unqualified for a variety of reasons. In the case of an individual trustee, the trustee may lack the required mental capacity to administer the trust. In such a case, the beneficiaries or another interested party must petition the court to replace the trustee. The court will ordinarily appoint the contingent trustee, or if no contingent trustee is specified, the court will appoint a qualified trustee. On occasion, trustee is also a beneficiary. Problems will arise if the trustee becomes the sole beneficiary, because this would effect a legal "merger," which would terminate the trust.

Removal of a Trustee

Friction between the trustee and the beneficiaries can develop. Typical conflicts arise over allegedly poor performance of trust investments that minimize income, and/or lack of discretionary distributions to beneficiaries. Less commonly, the beneficiaries may allege a direct conflict of interest.

It is hard to remove a trustee who has produced disappointing investment results or who has determined that discretionary payments should not be paid to beneficiaries. Absent evidence of fraud, negligence, or neglect of duties, most courts would be reluctant to remove a trustee, even if all the beneficiaries petition the court to do so.

Generally, a trustee can only be involuntarily removed from his position by a court. Although hard feelings between the trustee and the beneficiaries are not normally enough to warrant removal, friction that interferes with the administration of the trust may be sufficient cause for removal.

A trustee can be removed for other reasons. For example, if the trustee is unable to administer the trust because of substance abuse, mental incapacity, or lack of professional skill, the court may order removal. Similarly, if the trustee commits an act that is a violation of fiduciary duty, has a significant conflict of interest, or fails to segregate or diversify the trust assets as required, the trustee may face removal.

Resignation

A trustee who is unable or unwilling to perform may resign but must petition the appropriate court before doing so. Occasionally a trust document may give a trustee unilateral power to resign without court approval. On the other hand, if a named trustee has not accepted the appointment, she may disclaim the duties before performing without court approval.

TRUST TAX ISSUES

Trusts are often established to minimize taxes—especially federal transfer taxes. As a rule, there will be an important nontax reason to create the trust in addition to the tax-minimization motivation.

Transfer Taxes

Although most individuals are familiar with income taxes and sales taxes, the federal government also imposes three *transfer taxes:*

- gift tax
- estate tax
- generation-skipping tax

The gift tax is due when a *donor* transfers property to a *donee.* The tax is paid by the donor. The estate tax is paid by the estate of the deceased. The generation-skipping transfer tax is a special type of gift tax that applies when a transfer "skips" a generation, such as when a grandfather makes a gift to a granddaughter. Not all transfers are taxable. Individuals generally only to need to worry about these taxes once their transfers exceed $600,000. Estate and gift taxes are detailed in Chapter 13, "Estate and Gift Tax Basics."

TYPES OF TAX-ADVANTAGED TRUSTS

There are several techniques employing trusts that can reduce transfer taxes and preserve property for the family.

EXAMPLE An individual might establish a trust to maximize the use of the $10,000 annual gift tax exclusion. If the total amount of the trust is less than the *unified credit* amount (the credit allows $600,000 of the estate to escape taxation. The amount is scheduled to rise to $1,000,000), then no transfer taxes will be due. This type of trust would be a good vehicle to prevent asset appreciation from being subject to estate tax on the taxpayer's death.

The following are brief, and very incomplete, descriptions of some of these techniques.

Marital Deduction Trusts

Wills often contain trusts designed to maximize the unlimited marital deduction and reduce federal estate taxes. The surviving spouse would receive income from the trust during his lifetime, and the trust assets would pass to the children on the death of that surviving spouse. To qualify for the marital deduction, income to the surviving spouse must be mandatory. However, distributions of *corpus* (property in the trust) could either be limited or prohibited altogether.

QTIP Trusts

Qualified Terminable Interest Trusts (QTIPs) are also common in estate planning. These trusts allow a surviving spouse to use the income generated from property in a trust, but the spouse cannot reach the trust property itself. The trust property goes to the couple's children or to other beneficiaries of their choice on the death of the surviving spouse. This technique can produce impressive tax savings.

GRITs, GRATs, and GRUTs

Grantor retained income trusts (GRITs), grantor retained annuity trusts (GRATs), and grantor retained unitrusts (GRUTs) are all trust techniques that allow a taxpayer to maximize the value of the unified credit for transfer taxes. By using these trusts, a taxpayer is able to transfer appreciation out of an estate without making an outright gift of the property. These trusts can be a very effective way of maximizing the value of the unified credit.

Life Insurance Trusts

Life insurance is often referred to as a tax-free investment. However, life insurance owned by the testator at death will be included in the taxable estate and potentially exposed to federal estate tax rates between 37 and 55 percent. Life insurance in a properly drawn life insurance trust will not be subject to these estate taxes.

Crummey Trust

A Crummey trust also allows a grantor to benefit from the annual $10,000 gift tax exclusion. Unlike a section 2503(c) trust, the beneficiary can be of any age. A beneficiary of a Crummey trust must have a demand power that allows him to demand trust assets. The demand power makes the trust a present interest, which qualifies for the annual exclusion.

Generation-Skipping Trust

Grandparents who want to make gifts to grandchildren have to plan around the generation-skipping transfer tax. One strategy is to utilize a generation-skipping trust that is designed to make distributions to persons at least two generations removed from the grantor, such as grandchildren or great-grandchildren.

TAX ISSUES

Trusts are generally perceived as tax-saving devices. Historically, this reputation is well-deserved. Besides providing professional management of assets, protection from creditors, and delayed distribution of property, trusts have often provided relief from both income taxes and transfer taxes.

For the past 20 years the Congress and the Treasury Department have been gradually eliminating the traditional tax advantages of trusts. Although trusts still have the potential to reduce transfer taxes, their ability to reduce income taxes has been almost eliminated. Trusts are often created for the valid nontax reasons of delaying distribution of income to beneficiaries. However, the current income taxation of trust income creates strong disincentives for delaying distributions.

Income Taxation of Trusts

Generally trusts are taxed in a manner similar to individual taxpayers. While simple trusts get a $300 exemption, a complex trust's exemption is $600. Income retained by a trust in excess of $7,500 is currently taxed at a flat rate of 39.6 percent.

Tax Return Filing

The trust's trustee is required to file Form 1041, the U. S. Fiduciary Income Tax Return, no later than the fifteenth day of the fourth month following the end of the trust's taxable year. Trust returns must be filed with the IRS Service Center for the region in which the trustee resides or has his principal place of business.

PLANNING NOTE *Note that although an estate need not file a Form 1041 Fiduciary Income Tax Return unless the estate's taxable income exceeds $600, an income tax return must be filed for a trust if gross income exceeds $600 or if it has any amount of taxable trust income. If any beneficiary is a nonresident alien, a return must be filed. A sample of Form 1041 appears in Appendix E.*

Fiduciary Accounting Income

The trustee must calculate the trust's Fiduciary Accounting Income (FAI). Allocation of income and expense items is governed by state law, not the Internal Revenue Code. The accounting is done pursuant to the trust instrument and also local law. State law gives the grantor the right to allocate items of income and expense either to the income beneficiary or corpus. This allocation will be respected. If the trust document does not specify the allocation of the item, state law will control. Many states have adopted the Uniform Principal and Income Act, which prescribes the proper accounting of items to income and principal.

EXAMPLE The Brewer Family Trust has $10,000 of tax-exempt interest income, $7,000 of capital gain,

and a $5,000 trustee's fee. The trust instrument may allocate any of these items to income or corpus. If the trust document is silent, the tax exempt income would go to the income beneficiary, the capital gain to corpus, and the trustee's fee would be derived in equal shares from income and principal.

Income Taxation of Trust Beneficiaries

Generally, distributions from trusts are taxable to their recipients with two important exceptions:

1. distributions in excess of "distributable net income" are tax-free; and
2. specific bequests of money or property may also be tax-free.

Items of income retain their character when received by beneficiaries. Accordingly, an item may be capital or ordinary, active or passive, or an AMT (Alternative Minimum Tax) preference item. However, NOLs (net operating losses) and capital losses do not flow through to beneficiaries except in the year the trust terminates.

Tax Rules for Grantor Trusts

A grantor trust is one that operates as a legal trust under state law but not for federal income tax purposes. Accordingly, income is taxed to the grantor rather than to the trust. However, for nontax purposes the trust, not the grantor, has legal title to the property. For this treatment the grantor must not be able to control the property in the trust.

The tax code's grantor trust rules allow for trust income to be taxed to the grantor in situations in which the grantor has essentially retained too much control over the trust assets. When a grantor is "treated as owner," the income, deductions, and credits attributable to the trust are reported on the grantor's tax return rather than on the trust's return. A transfer to a revocable trust would cause the income to be taxed to the grantor under these rules.

TRUST ACCOUNTING RULES
Income and Principal

Trusts normally have an income interest and a principal interest (corpus). The income beneficiary receives current income while the remainderman—the person who will receive the remainder of the trust on the death of the beneficiary—receives the principal interest. All receipts and disbursements are classified as either income or principal. The trust instrument can allocate specific items of income and disbursements to either income or principal. If the instrument is silent, state law will control the classification.

Many states have adopted the Revised Uniform Principal and Income Act (RUPIA), although with modifications in some states. The act classifies income and disbursements as follows:

To Income

- rent
- interest
- dividends
- net business profits
- 72½ percent royalties
- property taxes
- interest expense
- property insurance
- ordinary repairs
- taxes on accounting income depreciation

To Principal

- gains on sale of property
- stock dividends
- 27½ percent royalties
- principal payments on debt
- capital improvements
- extraordinary repairs
- taxes on gains

Adverse Interests

It is not uncommon for the holder of an income interest to be in conflict with the holder of the principal interest. For example, assume that a trust provides that income from land be paid to a surviving spouse for life with a remainder to the children of the grantor. Whereas the surviving spouse, as income beneficiary, may desire to maximize the return from the land, the remainderman may desire that resources such as timber be preserved for their benefit. This could lead to a conflict with the mother wanting the timber cut for income, while her children want the trees left standing.

CHAPTER 13 Estate and Gift Tax Basics

INTRODUCTION

The federal government imposes an estate tax on estates that exceed $600,000 in value. The taxes are paid by either the estate or by the heirs, depending on the instructions in the will. The estate tax works together with the federal gift tax to impose a tax on the "transfer" of wealth. A few states also impose an inheritance tax at the time of death. An inheritance tax is normally paid by the heirs. Although the executor is not expected to be a tax expert or even expected to prepare the estate tax return, the executor needs to understand some of the basic concepts of the taxes that will be imposed on the estate. This chapter discusses a few basic requirements for filing Form 706, the Federal Estate Tax Return, and addresses common types of legal postmortem planning that can reduce estate taxes. Finally, the chapter briefly outlines income tax concerns as they relate to the estate tax.

NOTE *Form 706, the U.S. Estate Tax Return; Form 1041, the U.S. Income Tax Return for Estates and Trusts, and a completed Form 1040, U.S. Individual Tax Return for a deceased individual, are located in Appendix E.*

OBSERVATION *The $600,000 figure mentioned in this chapter is now scheduled to rise to $1,000,000 by the year 2006.*

ESTATE AND GIFT TAXES

The federal estate and gift taxes are a unified system. They are imposed at the same tax rate, and apply when there is a transfer of property from one person to another. Accordingly, both of these taxes are termed transfer taxes. Either tax only applies after $600,000 of property has been transferred. In other words, a person may transfer $600,000 before death, at death, or in a combination of both and still not be subject to tax. Once the $600,000 has been exceeded, however, the transfer will normally be taxable.

The $600,000 of assets pass tax-free by means of a *unified tax credit* rather than a deduction. In other words, instead of providing a $600,000 deduction, the tax is calculated and a credit is used to reduce the tax. If an estate was valued at exactly $600,000, the estate tax would be $192,800. However, the amount of the unified credit is also $192,800, so there is no tax due ($192,800 tax – $192,800 credit = $0 tax due).

The Estate Tax

If the deceased had a sizable estate, significant death taxes may be imposed by both the federal and state governments. The federal government imposes an estate tax which is a wealth tax. The tax operates similarly to the real estate tax on homes, and is imposed on the value of the property contained in the estate at the time of the owner's death.

The Gift Tax

The federal government also imposes a tax on gifts made during a person's lifetime. This tax is imposed at the same tax rate as the estate tax. The gift tax is paid by the *donor* when the donor makes a gift to a *donee*.

OBSERVATION *Although the estate tax and the gift tax are imposed using the same rate schedule, the estate tax is actually far higher. This occurs because the tax is imposed on all property owned at death. The money that the executor uses to pay the tax is itself taxed. Money that is used to pay gift tax is not subject to either the gift tax or the estate tax.*

Tax Rates

Estate and gift tax rates are extremely high. The federal transfer taxes generally will not apply at all unless transfers of $600,000 are made. If an estate contains less than $600,000 after payment of any expenses, no tax will normally be due. Once the estate is over $600,000, however, the excess over $600,000 will be subject to the federal estate tax, which will be imposed at rates between 37 and 55 percent. Compare this to the income tax rates, which range between 15 and 39.6 percent for individuals. On estates exceeding $2 million in value, the tax is imposed at 55 percent, which means that the government will be getting 55 cents of each dollar, while the heirs will be getting only 45 cents.

WARNING *The $600,000 amount will increase in the future.*

STATE INHERITANCE TAXES

A few states additionally impose an inheritance tax at death. An inheritance tax is imposed on the heirs and taxes the right to inherit property. Because the details of state inheritance taxes differ, this discussion will generally be confined to the federal estate tax.

WARNING *If the estate is believed to exceed $600,000 in assets, the executor should certainly get professional tax advice. Even if an individual prepares her own Form 1040, it's probably not a good idea for her to attempt to prepare Form 706. Although the estate's attorney will*

normally be able to handle the details, including filing the return, additional professionals may be needed. The executor is ultimately responsible for seeing that tax matters are handled properly. Details about the preparation and filing of the actual estate tax return are discussed later in this chapter.

TRANSFERS TO SURVIVING SPOUSES

Although most transfers of property are subject to either the federal estate or gift tax, a transfer to a spouse during life or at death also receives a deduction which eliminates any tax. For example, although a $100,000 lifetime transfer to a spouse is potentially subject to gift tax, it also qualifies for a $100,000 deduction, so no tax is due.

Transfers to a spouse can be made—without limit—during the donor's life or in a will without triggering estate or gift tax. If the deceased was married, his or her spouse may receive the entire estate intact, without any reduction for federal estate tax. The tax law allows an unlimited marital deduction. If all the property in the estate is left to the surviving spouse, then no federal estate tax will be due. This is sometimes termed the *first to die rule*. When spouses have wills leaving one another all of their property, there is no tax imposed on the first spouse to die. In practice, this approach may not be the wisest course of action. If the second spouse dies without getting remarried, the estate will get no marital deduction at death. Because the estate tax rates rise with the amount of property in an estate, taxing only one estate rather than two can actually result in a larger tax bill and less wealth for other family members.

TRANSFERS TO A CHARITY

Transfers made to a bona fide charity during the donor's life or in a will also escape estate and gift tax. Wealthy individuals often make such gifts to reduce their taxes and to benefit worthy organizations. From a tax standpoint, making a lifetime gift to a qualified nonprofit organization may provide a distinct advantage over leaving the money to the organization in a will. For taxpayers eligible to itemize deductions, any lifetime gifts will generate an income tax deduction. Such gifts will also reduce the size of their estate and will lower federal estate taxes that may be due, and may also reduce any probate fees based on the value of the estate.

Although gifts of money are the most common, other property—even a family home—may be given to a charity. Many individuals also leave stocks and bonds to charities. Nearly anything of value can make a meaningful contribution to a charity. An alternative to a bequest in a will is to designate the charity as beneficiary of a life insurance policy.

Charitable Remainder Trusts

A decedent may have established a trust to benefit a charity. This is often done in the form of an annuity trust that pays a surviving spouse an annuity during his or her life. Individuals who own appreciated investments such as stocks and bonds can find this strategy especially attractive. This arrangement combines tax savings for the family and a charitable gift after death. In return, the charity will provide the individual with a lifetime annuity. Because of the tax advantages provided by the charitable deduction, the grantor will be able to receive a better return on his money than if he sold the investments and reinvested the after-tax proceeds in an annuity or a bank account.

$10,000 ANNUAL GIFT EXCLUSION

Individuals sometimes want to avoid estate taxes by reducing the amount of their property so it does not exceed the $600,000 threshold. Gifting away property is one solution, but there is a federal gift tax that applies at the same rate as the estate tax. However, an individual can give away $10,000 per individual recipient per year without any gift tax due; married couples can give away $20,000 per individual per year (this is called a *split gift*). There is no requirement that the recipients of the gifts be family members and there is no lifetime limit. Ten gifts of $10,000 would reduce the estate $100,000 per year or by $1 million if the gifts were to continue for ten years.

OBSERVATION *The $10,000 exclusion will be increased to compensate for inflation beginning in 1998.*

TAX MINIMIZATION

The federal estate tax has been termed a *voluntary tax*. Because not many taxpayers consider themselves "volunteers," they sometimes try to avoid or greatly reduce the tax through careful estate planning. Accordingly, many estate plans contain complicated provisions designed to reduce estate taxes. However, if there was little planning done before death or if the deceased died without a will or trust, possible tax savings will probably not be realized. A good deal of hard-earned wealth will go to the federal government rather than staying in the family. There are some postmortem (after death) elections that can be made by the executor that can also reduce estate taxes. These will be discussed later in this chapter.

CALCULATING THE $600,000 TAX THRESHOLD

Although $600,000 sounds like a lot of money, a surprising number of people are potentially subject to the federal tax. In calculating the value of the estate, the executor must include everything owned at death, including five items that may push the deceased's holdings over the $600,000 threshold. (Recall that the $600,000 figure will be increased in the future.)

- family home and other real estate
- investments
- business interests
- retirement plans and pensions
- life insurance owned by the deceased

Because of the increase in real estate values and on pensions and other retirement plans, many middle-class people find themselves above the $600,000 threshold, which has not been raised for over a decade. Accordingly, estate planning is no longer reserved merely for the rich, but is something that all retired persons should consider carefully. It is not patriotic to overpay your taxes.

WARNING *Even though they are not included in the "probate estate" for state law purposes, some items may be deemed as part of an estate for federal estate tax purposes.*

Family Home and Other Real Estate

Although housing prices rise and fall in the short

run, many individuals have seen a substantial appreciation in the value of their family home and other real estate since 1970. While this appreciation looks attractive, it can also create an estate tax problem—especially in California and Hawaii, where even modest homes sell for hundreds of thousands of dollars. For many individuals, the family home is their primary asset and much of their estate planning may revolve around how to best transfer the home. Many individuals have established "residential GRITs," which essentially involves putting a home in trust while still retaining possession. Such trusts can significantly reduce estate taxes. An executor who encounters a GRIT should consult with the attorney about the estate tax consequences. If the family home has been transferred to the surviving spouse, the transfer will not generate estate taxes on the death of the first spouse. Real estate requires an accurate valuation.

Investments

Many people have seen their investment portfolios appreciate during the last decade as the result of a strong stock market. These appreciated portfolios also have the potential to generate a lot of estate tax. The valuation of listed securities is relatively straightforward, and can be achieved by locating the securities value in the *Wall Street Journal*.

Business Interests

Ownership interests in sole proprietorships, partnerships, S Corporations, and other corporations are includable in the taxable estate. These ownership interests are often very valuable and can also generate a lot of estate tax. In some cases, the executor may make certain elections that can significantly reduce the tax. These elections are discussed later in this chapter under the heading "Postmortem Planning." Proper valuation of a closely held business interest is very important. The executor is well-advised to engage a valuation specialist to help determine the proper value of the business interest as it should be reported on the estate tax return.

Retirement Plans and Pensions

In computing amounts in excess of $600,000, do not fail to include the value of pensions and other retirement arrangements. The value of retirement plans can be substantial and many individuals are unaware of the death-tax implications of such plans. Normally the retirement income will be subject to *both* income tax and estate tax. The amounts in a retirement plan are normally untaxed income, but income tax will have to be paid as the amounts are received. Additionally, the value of the retirement plan—often several hundreds of thousands of dollars—is includable in the deceased's taxable estate. Accordingly, the amount in retirement plans may be greatly reduced by taxes before the heirs actually receive any money. Valuation is available from the employer, insurer, or other entity that distributes the retirement income.

Life Insurance

As mentioned above, in calculating the threshold $600,000 amount, the government includes a number of items that are not included in the probate estate for state law purposes. For example, if at the time of death, the deceased owned a life insurance policy that has a cash value, the face value—not merely the cash value—of the policy will be counted in calculating the $600,000. This is true even though the deceased named someone else as beneficiary of the death benefit.

Large estates typically have a number of debts, including state death taxes; and administrative costs, including funeral expenses and probate fees and expenses. Having life insurance in place ensures that sufficient cash is available to pay these taxes and other expenses. In the case of a wealthy individual whose estate will be subject to federal estate tax, life insurance will provide needed liquidity to the estate. Generally, federal estate taxes are due within nine months after the date of death, although installment payments are sometimes available. Life insurance proceeds provide a quick and reliable source of money to pay the tax. Although a life insurance policy is purchased to provide liquidity for federal death taxes, the policy itself may generate additional tax if the deceased owned the policy or if the estate is named as beneficiary. This could be avoided if the policy is linked to a life insurance trust or payable to a beneficiary who agrees to lend funds to the estate to pay the tax. Valuation of policies can be obtained from the insurer.

Power of Appointment

A power of appointment is the right to control the disposition of property, and may be given by the decedent to another individual who will exercise the right. The power is similar to the power invested in the trustee of a trust. A power of appointment may either be general power or a special power (sometimes referred to as a limited power). A general power gives the holder the right to distribute the property as he sees fit. In contrast, a special power of appointment gives the holder only power to make a gift during a specific time period, or to make only limited gifts. For example, a special power could be drafted that allowed the holder to distribute assets, or to pass on the power itself among a certain defined class of beneficiaries, such as "grandchildren."

Powers of appointment have estate tax consequences. If the deceased holds a general power of appointment at the time of death, then the property subject to the power will be included in her estate.

EXAMPLE Mary establishes a revocable trust and retains the power during life to invade the trust to meet living expenses or to make gifts. Mary retains a general power of appointment and the property will be included in her taxable estate.

Under the tax code a special power of appointment is not included in the deceased's taxable estate. A special power of appointment gives the deceased the right to appoint the property but he may not distribute the property to himself, his estate, his creditors, or the estate's creditors.

Co-owned Property

As discussed in earlier chapters, individuals frequently put the title to property in joint names because co-ownership can be an effective way to avoid having the property pass through probate. The co-owner merely becomes the sole owner upon the death of the first owner. However, if the

deceased is a co-owner of property, his share of the property's value will be subject to federal estate tax even though the property passes outside his probate estate. This rule applies whether the property is co-owned or whether the decedent had a life estate and the remainder is owned by another.

EXAMPLE Sam and his son Kevin buy a home. Sam buys a life estate which allows him to live in the property for life, while his son buys the remainder, which gives Kevin sole ownership of the property after Sam's death. The value of Sam's life estate is included in his estate even though it lapses on his death. Under the tax code, the result would have been the same even if Sam had transferred legal ownership of the property to Kevin but continued to live in the house until his death.

Community Property

In the nine community property states (Arizona, California, Idaho, Louisiana, Nevada, New Mexico, Texas, Washington, and Wisconsin), married couples typically own community property. A decedent's estate includes all of the separate property owned individually by the deceased plus one-half of the couple's community property.

Although there are some state-by-state variations, separate property is property that was owned prior to marriage, and property received by one spouse as a gift, an inheritance, or proceeds of a life insurance policy. Community property is property that the couple has earned during their marriage. Salaries and business profits are typically considered community property. Unmarried people do not have community property.

WHO PAYS THE ESTATE TAX?

An often-overlooked area in estate tax planning is determining who will pay the estate tax. Although the estate normally pays, the determination is actually made in the will. It is up to the deceased to decide whose share of the estate should be used to pay any estate taxes that may be due. For example, if the estate is going to be reduced by estate taxes, one or more of the heirs' shares will be reduced to pay the tax. If the will does not provide whose share of the estate will be reduced to pay the taxes, state law will control. The law in some states provides that the tax will be paid from the residue of the estate. If the deceased had planned on his spouse getting the residue, this rule will result in the spouse's share being significantly reduced while other heirs get their full share of the estate tax-free.

....

WARNING *The executor and the attorney should carefully examine the will's tax apportionment clause to determine who should pay. If there is no answer then state law needs to be consulted.*

....

FILING THE ESTATE TAX RETURN (FORM 706)

The law requires that the executor files the Federal Estate Tax Return (Form 706) and pays any estate tax nine months after death, when the value of the net estate exceeds $600,000 (or the amount established by Congress in the future). Even for relatively simple estates, this short time frame can be difficult to meet in practice. Inventorying and valuing property can be extremely time-consuming. In some cases there may be valuable assets that generate a lot of estate tax but little cash to actually pay the tax. Luckily the tax code allows extensions and some relief measures are also available to the executor.

Extensions

Although the Federal Estate Tax Return is due nine months after death, an extension for a "reasonable amount of time" is available if the executor files IRS Form 4769, Application for Extension of Time to File a Return and/or Pay U.S. Estate (and Generation-Skipping Transfer) Taxes.

The application for the extension must detail why it is impossible or impracticable for the executor to file a reasonably complete return on or before the due date. The extension request needs to be filed before the nine-month period has expired.

Although the time alloted for extensions will generally not be greater than six months to a year, the IRS has discretion to extend time for payment up to ten years if reasonable cause is shown. Normally the executor would have to show some extreme hardship to have the time to pay extended from one year to ten. Heirs of small business owners may be

able to get a fifteen-year extension. This is discussed later in this chapter under "Postmortem Planning."

....

WARNING *Failure to file the Federal Estate Tax Return on time may result in a penalty equal to 5 percent of the amount of the tax due if the filing is less than one month late, with an additional 5 percent for each additional month, not to exceed 25 percent in the aggregate. If the failure to file is due to reasonable cause and not due to willful neglect, late penalties may be waived.*

....

WARNING *To avoid the penalty for failure to file, the executor must provide a written statement to the District Director or to the Director of the appropriate Internal Revenue Service Center, detailing the circumstances that would constitute reasonable cause for the failure to file. Reliance on an accountant or attorney is generally insufficient evidence to establish reasonable cause.*

....

COMPLETING THE ESTATE TAX RETURN

Preparation of the Federal Estate Tax Return is complex and time-consuming. Usually either the estate's attorney or a CPA will complete the form.

Contents of the Return

The return (a copy of which is found in Appendix E) includes numerous schedules on which the executor must detail all of the deceased's property, along with proper valuations. The schedules include:

Schedule A, Real Estate

Schedule A-1, Section 2032A Valuation ("special use valuation")

Schedule B, Stocks and Bonds

Schedule C, Mortgages, Notes, and Cash

Schedule D, Insurance on the Decedent's Life

Schedule E, Jointly Owned Property

Schedule F, Other Miscellaneous Property

Schedule G, Transfers During Decedent's Life (details gifts)

Schedule H, Powers of Appointment

Schedule I, Annuities

Schedule J, Funeral Expenses and Expenses Incurred in Administering Property Subject to Claims

Schedule K, Debts of the Decedent and Mortgages and Liens

Schedule L, Net Losses During Administration and Expenses Incurred in Administering Property Not Subject to Claims

Schedule M, Bequests, to Surviving Spouse (Marital Deduction)

Schedule N, (no current schedule)

Schedule O, Charitable, Public, and Similar Gifts and Bequests

Schedule P, Credit for Foreign Death Taxes

Schedule Q, Credit for Tax on Prior Transfers

Schedule R, Generation-Skipping Transfer Tax (GSTT)

Schedule S, Increased Estate Tax on Excess Retirement Accumulations

WARNING *The Federal Estate Tax Return requires a surprising amount of detail, and the amount of preparation time should not be underestimated. If information is missing or unavailable, the executor should consult with the estate's attorney to determine how to complete the return.*

Valuation of Property

The executor must place a value on each item of property listed in the return. In practice it can be difficult to value many items of property. Interests in small businesses are especially troublesome. The executor will normally hire one or more appraisers to help with valuation. These appraisals must be filed along with the Federal Estate Tax Return.

Alternate Valuation Date

The executor may be able to reduce federal estate tax by electing the alternate valuation date. If the executor so elects, all property still in the estate will be valued sixth months after the date of death. Assets no longer in the estate are valued as of their date of sale or distribution.

Additional Documents to Be Filed

When filing the Federal Estate Tax Return with the IRS, the executor will also have to include a copy of the following documents:

1. certified copy of the will
2. court order admitting the will to probate

3. Life Insurance Statement (Form 712) describing all policies
4. evidence of alternate valuations, if elected
5. appraisals
6. financial statements if decedent owned a small business
7. trust documents
8. powers of appointment
9. disclaimers
10. extension requests to file or pay tax

PAYING THE ESTATE TAX

Generally, the estate tax is due when the return is filed, nine months after death. The tax must be paid by the executor. If there is no executor appointed by the time the tax is due, any person possessing the decedent's property must pay the tax.

Discharge of Liability for Estate Tax

As a rule, the executor is liable for any unpaid estate tax. However, once the tax has been paid, the executor should apply to the IRS for a discharge from personal liability for tax. The executor should request the IRS to issue Form 7990, U.S. Estate Tax Certificate of Discharge From Personal Liability, after payment of the tax and any interest due.

WARNING *A discharge of the executor by the local probate court is not a release from the executor's tax liability.*

WARNING *An executor may be liable for estate tax even after resigning and being replaced by a new executor. If the payment of the estate tax is extended, and his successor fails to pay any of the remaining estate tax installments, the original executor remains liable for the estate tax.*

Transferee Liability

If the estate tax is not paid by the executor when due, the *transferees* of the estate become liable. A transferee is a party who has received property from the estate not only after the decedent's death but also from *inter vivos* (predeath) transfers required to be included in the decedent's gross estate.

WARNING *The IRS does not consider an extension to file the return to be an extension to pay the tax. The executor needs to ask for both.*

INCOME TAX ISSUES

Although this chapter is devoted to explaining the federal estate and gift tax, sometimes estate tax and income tax issues overlap. The executor is ultimately responsible for seeing that the Federal Estate Tax Return (Form 706) and the Fiduciary Income Tax Return (Form 1041) are filed. A final income tax return (Form 1040) will have to be filed for the deceased. When there is a surviving spouse, filing a joint return is usually advantageous. However, when filing a final tax return, the advantages of filing a separate tax return need to be weighed. If a final joint return has been filed and an executor reconsiders the advantages of filing separately, he may cancel the joint return and file a separate return for the decedent within one year from the due date of the return.

Unpaid medical expenses are deductible for federal estate tax purposes on the Federal Estate Tax Return, Form 706, or the executor can deduct such medical expenses on the decedent's final Form 1040. However, the medical expenses cannot be deducted on both forms. If no estate tax is due, then the expenses should be deducted on the deceased's Form 1040. Income tax issues are discussed in more detail in Chapter 8, "Paying Creditors and Taxes."

If the estate employs both an attorney and an accountant, each might assume the other will be preparing the returns. The executor should determine which professional will be preparing which return; the executor also needs to verify that the returns are filed on time.

How to Deduct Medical Expenses

Medical expenses of a decedent are deductible from either income tax or estate tax, but not both. For income tax purposes, medical expenses are only deductible to the extent they exceed 7½ percent of adjusted gross income (AGI). To maximize the benefit of the deduction, the executor should compare the decedent's personal income tax rate and the decedent's estate tax rate before making the election.

Because estate tax rates generally exceed income tax rates, it is generally better to claim the expenses on the Federal Estate Tax Return. Medical deductions are explained more fully in Chapter 8, "Paying Creditors and Taxes."

Income in Respect of a Decedent (IRD)

Executors also need to consider "income in respect of a decedent" issues. Income in respect of a decedent (IRD) is income that is accrued by a cash basis taxpayer before death but is not includable on the decedent's last Form 1040. IRD must be included in the decedent's estate. Typical IRD items include salary and commissions, investment income, and proceeds from the installment sales of property. Additionally, income from S Corporations and partnerships can also be deemed IRD income.

POSTMORTEM PLANNING

Postmortem means "after death." Although a will becomes final at the time of death, the executor and other family members can engage in a limited amount of postmortem planning, which can often reduce estate taxes and preserve more property for the heirs.

Postmortem planning essentially entails establishing devices that will allow another party to make dispositive and tax decisions after the deceased's death. Nontax techniques are generally established in a will or trust. The tax code provides the deceased's executor with several elections that can minimize both income taxes and transfer taxes. A few techniques, for example disclaimers, can further both nontax and tax goals.

REDEMPTION TO PAY DEATH TAXES FOR BUSINESS OWNERS

The tax law provides a special relief provision for small business owners, which is found in tax code section 303. An executor may redeem (buy) stock from the estate of a decedent or from beneficiaries of an estate to pay estate tax, state death taxes, and administrative expenses, if stock of a redeemed corporation makes up 35 percent of the estate and redemption occurs in a set period after death. Stock of two or more companies may be aggregated to meet the 35 percent test.

Essentially this allows the estate of a small business owner to sell its stock back to the corporation. Normally the proceeds are used by the executor to pay estate taxes. Although section 303 redemptions were originally envisioned to help pay death taxes, they can be undertaken to meet any liquidity needs of the estate.

OBSERVATION *Certain family-owned businesses are now also eligible for an estate tax exclusion of up to $1,300,000.*

ELECTION FOR DEFERRAL OF TAXES

Congress enacted another relief provision for heirs of a small business owner. In the past, families were sometimes forced to sell a family business because they lacked the cash to pay the estate tax. This relief provision, found in tax code section 6166, allows the executor to defer the payment of estate taxes attributable to the value of the deceased's business. This rule allows the estate to pay the estate taxes over a ten-year period and also allows up to a five-year deferral. During the five years after death, the estate merely pays interest on the tax. The estate then makes installment payments of the tax and interest payments over the next ten years. To qualify for this tax break, the value of the closely held business interest must exceed 35 percent of the adjusted gross value of the estate.

SPECIAL USE VALUATION FOR FARMERS

Congress likes family farmers and they have passed a relief provision to help keep farms in family hands. An executor may elect to value real property used in a farm trade at its business value rather than its fair market value. The maximum reduction in value is limited to $750,000. However, with an estate tax ranging between 37 and 55 percent, this benefit can save a family $250,000–350,000 in estate taxes.

To qualify, all property used in the farm must

1. comprise at least 50 percent of the adjusted value of the gross estate and,
2. the real property must comprise at least 25 percent of the adjusted value.

The property must pass to a "qualified heir" of the decedent. If the property is ultimately disposed of to a nonfamily member within ten years of the decedent's death, or if the qualified heir ceases to use the property for farm purposes, an additional estate tax is due.

OBSERVATION *The $750,000 amount will be indexed for inflation after 1998.*

DISCLAIMERS

Disclaimers can be used for both tax and nontax planning.

Generally, any party may refuse to receive a gift and heirs may also disclaim an inheritance under a will. Often disclaimers are used for estate tax savings when a party wishes to avoid receiving property in his own name.

A disclaimer is the right to reject a bequest made in a will or trust. The party can refuse to take the property. If an alternate beneficiary is mentioned, then the property skips the first beneficiary and passes to the second. For example, a father could disclaim property which could then pass to his child. If the will provides for no alternate beneficiary, the disclaimed property will pass to another party under the operation of local law. The estate's attorney can help determine exactly how a decedent's property will pass once it is disclaimed.

A disclaimer must generally comply with both state law and federal tax law if it is to provide any tax advantages. Starting with the basic premise that a person can refuse a gift, a potential heir can always refuse or disclaim property to be received whether under a will or through intestate distribution.

What Can Be Disclaimed

Almost any property can be disclaimed, including joint interests in bank accounts, real estate, or community property. The law also allows partial disclaimers.

EXAMPLE Andrew left the entire residue of his estate to his son Howard. Howard can disclaim all or perhaps 50 percent of the residue. Disclaiming would make sense if Howard does not need the property and wants to avoid estate tax problems himself. It would also allow Howard to move property to another person or persons—perhaps his own children if they are named as contingent beneficiaries in Andrew's will.

Similarly a disclaimer can be based on a formula. For example, a will might provide that a gift may be disclaimed under a formula in order to fund a trust to use up the unified credit.

Other situations in which a disclaimer can lead to tax savings include:

1. disclaiming powers of appointment
2. making sure "farm property" goes to a "qualified heir" so it qualifies for the special use valuation (discussed above)
3. preventing an inadvertent termination of an S Corporation when S Corporation stock is left to an ineligible shareholder, such as an ineligible trust
4. keeping property out of the hands of creditors
5. curing a defective tax clause in a will

Disclaimer by Surviving Spouse

A common use of qualified disclaimers is to increase or reduce the size of a surviving spouse's estate to maximize the use of the unified tax credit. Assume that John and Mary are well-to-do, and their estate planner has suggested that John plan to leave property to other family members or to charity, with a view toward minimizing Mary's estate tax burden on his death. John, like many husbands, finds this objectionable and wants a will that provides that all his property go to Mary. Additionally, over the years he has purchased significant amounts of life insurance naming Mary as beneficiary. This is a quite common occurrence. John is naturally reluctant to expose Mary to financial risk late in life. Although

there is no federal estate tax imposed on property left to a surviving spouse in a will, if John predeceases Mary, Mary will be left with a large potential estate comprised of her own property, the property left in John's will, and the insurance proceeds. The tax will be imposed not on John's estate but on Mary's. To the extent that she cannot gift away the property during her lifetime, the estate may be exposed to estate tax because it exceeds her unified estate tax credit (which shelters $600,000 of property) and less will be left for her heirs.

If, at John's death, Mary feels confident that her own property and the proceeds of John's life insurance will provide for her needs, she could use a qualified disclaimer to disclaim John's property in favor of other family members. The disclaimer will effectively transfer property to other family members without the need for costly trusts or a formal gifting program.

For tax purposes a disclaimer must be:

1. in writing,
2. made within nine months of the initial transfer, and
3. irrevocable.

Additionally, the disclaimant must not have previously accepted the bequest or benefited from it, and cannot direct who will receive the disclaimed property. Some older couples whose children are well-off financially make gifts to the children but provide that the children may disclaim in favor of a charity.

Although disclaimers are typically used by the surviving spouse to pass property to children, the reverse strategy may also be used. For example, a child could disclaim in favor of the surviving spouse if the parent needs the funds or to maximize the use of the marital deduction if the family wants to avoid paying estate taxes immediately.

CHAPTER 14

Streamlined Probate

INTRODUCTION

any states now provide a streamlined probate process for smaller estates. This procedure may be less expensive and time-consuming for both the executor and for those named as beneficiaries in the deceased's will. These are major advantages, so executors should carefully consider using the streamlined process if the estate qualifies. This chapter outlines how these procedures work.

OVERVIEW

Many states have two separate streamlined procedures, one of which involves the filing of an affidavit in place of the appointment of an executor. A number of states also offer a procedure called *summary probate*, which is somewhat more complicated than the affidavit procedure, but still far less complicated than standard probate. In most states, these procedures can be used if the deceased died with or without a will.

AFFIDAVIT PROCEDURES

About half the fifty states have a streamlined probate procedure that allows a person who will succeed to ownership of the deceased's property to file a form called an *affidavit* with the probate court to transfer ownership of the property. This process does away with most of the legal complications surrounding traditional probate.

Terminology

Some states refer to this type of proceeding as "Small Estate Probate." Others call it "Probate by Affidavit." The procedures also vary somewhat state by state. In all states that offer this procedure, the transfer of assets is based on the filing of an affidavit. A listing of states that permit Probate by Affidavit appears in Appendix B. This chapter describes how it is commonly accomplished.

Savings

In most cases there will be no need for a lawyer to settle an estate by the affidavit process. Legal fees to probate even a modest estate will usually exceed $1,000 and they can quickly escalate.

Time will also be saved. Using formal procedures, few estates can be closed in less than six months, with a twelve-month time frame being more typical in many states. Streamlined probate can often be completed in a month or two.

Qualifying Estates

The most important issue to determine is whether the estate qualifies. The requirements vary from state to state. Note that the filing requirements change from time to time, so be sure to check with your local probate court to confirm the figures.

Generally, an estate will qualify if there is a minimal amount of property in the estate. In most states you cannot use the process at all if the estate contains any real estate (which the legal system calls *real property*). In other states the presence of real estate does not necessarily preclude probate by affidavit, but the value of the real estate may.

....

OBSERVATION *In some states determining whether an estate qualifies can be difficult because the law defines the upper limit in a confusing way. Although most states merely provide dollar figure valuations for different kinds of property, a few states express the upper limit in terms such as "the sum of the spousal election, plus administrative costs and expenses of the last illness and funeral." Some probate courts will have a booklet or an information sheet to help determine eligibility.*

....

OBSERVATION *A few states will only allow this probate by affidavit if it is specifically authorized in the deceased's will. In other states, it is only available if all persons named in the will agree to use of the procedure. Frequently, they will agree because it will minimize delay in receiving property from the deceased. Most states allow the procedure if the deceased died without a will.*

....

Nonprobate Assets

Although it may seem that streamlined probate is unavailable because the deceased owned a home or other real estate, this is not always the case. It depends on how the home or property is legally titled. If the ownership of the real estate was placed in joint names on a deed, the real estate will pass outside probate and will not be part of the estate. In this situation, a family could still use the streamlined procedures even though the deceased owned a home or condominium.

EXAMPLE Before her death, Doris put ownership of her home, her car, and most of her bank accounts in joint names. At her death she owned a small checking account in her own name plus her clothes and household furnishings. The value of these items is

under $10,000. In about half of the fifty states, her family would be able to use the simpler probate process to avoid both lawyer's fees and delays.

For more detail on nonprobate assets and legal ownership, see Chapter 15, "Avoiding Probate."

Valuing the Property

Note that in determining whether the deceased's estate qualifies, you must use the "fair market value" of the property. This value is not what the deceased paid, but what a disinterested person would pay for it at the time of death. The value of any liens or mortgages on the property are not deducted in arriving at the fair market value.

EXAMPLE The state statute provides that probate by affidavit is available for estates under $30,000. The deceased owned a one-year-old car at death, which she purchased for $40,000. The Kelly *Blue Book* price of a one-year-old used car of that make is $35,000. There is a $10,000 outstanding car loan. The car is valued at its $35,000 fair market value with no reduction for the loan. Therefore the estate is ineligible because the value of the property exceeds the $30,000 limit.

Who May File?

In most states that offer the affidavit procedure, one or more of the deceased's *claiming successors* may file the affidavit. A claiming successor is simply someone who is named in the will, or someone who is an *heir at law* (someone who would take property in intestacy when there is no will).

Contents of the Affidavit

Although procedures differ from state to state, the affidavit must contain most, if not all, of the following information:

- name, age, domicile, address, and Social Security number of the deceased
- date and place of decedent's death
- fair market value and description of decedent's property
- statement that no other probate proceedings are under way

- information about whether deceased died testate (with a will) or intestate (without a will)
- list of deceased's heirs and their addresses (including heirs at law, those persons who would receive property in the absence of a will)
- list of names and addresses of persons who are named in the will
- statement that each heir and beneficiary will be mailed a copy of the deceased's will (if any)
- statement that reasonable efforts have been made to locate creditors of the estate
- list of expenses and claims against the estate remaining to be paid (including reimbursement of expenses incurred by the *affiant* (the person signing the affidavit)
- creditors' names and addresses who have a disputed claim with the estate
- copy of the death certificate and will (if any)

OBSERVATION *It is a good practice to get all of the claiming successors to sign the affidavit. This eliminates any concern that the affidavit might be challenged.*

Procedures

Once the affidavit has been duly filed, the affiant is empowered under the law to do the following:

1. take custody and control of the deceased's property;
2. pay claims (bills) on behalf of the deceased;
3. transfer or sell a motor vehicle owned by the deceased; and
4. sell other property.

Property Transfers

The affidavit procedure can be used to transfer ownership of property. However, in most states real estate cannot be transferred using this procedure. A person must present a copy of the affidavit to any person having possession or custody of the deceased's property.

EXAMPLE 1 Doris's will provides that all of her bank accounts and the property in her bank safe-deposit box are to go to her sister Bernice. Bernice needs to present a certified copy of the affidavit to the bank.

The bank will transfer the bank accounts and the box to Bernice.

EXAMPLE 2 Doris's will provides that all of her personal property will go to her sister Bernice, including her car and some IBM stock. Bernice can transfer ownership of Doris's car by presenting a certified copy of the affidavit to the Department of Motor Vehicles. She can transfer ownership of the stock in the same way by presenting it to IBM's official "transfer agent," listed on the shares themselves.

Treatment of Creditors

When an heir or a beneficiary named in the will files an affidavit, he must try to locate and pay all of the deceased's creditors. The law provides that if creditors are unhappy with their treatment and dispute the amount they are paid, they can go back to the probate court to contest the entire affidavit process.

A creditor of the deceased's estate may also file an affidavit for such claims and expenses as:
- funeral expenses;
- administrative expenses of the estate; and
- other debts of the deceased.

Affiant's Duties

The affiant's duties toward the estate's property and creditors are the same as those of an executor. The court demands absolute honesty toward people named in the will and creditors of the deceased.

Beneficiaries and Heirs

The affidavit procedure does not change or modify the laws concerning distribution of property. The normal rules governing distribution under a will or intestacy control (see Chapter 6, "Understanding Wills," and Chapter 10, "Intestacy—When There Is No Will"). Although the affidavit procedure seems very informal, the affiant must take care to follow these rules to the letter when distributing the property.

Conversion to Formal Probate

An interested person—a person named in the will, or a creditor—can always petition the court to force a formal probate proceeding if he is fearful of the streamlined process. A person may feel that his interests will be better protected if there is court supervision of the property and its distribution. He may also feel that he needs a judicial determination of the meaning of the will.

If a formal probate proceeding is commenced, the executor can take possession of all of the deceased's property. Even after all of the deceased's property has been distributed by affidavit procedure, a beneficiary under a will or a creditor can ask the probate court to look into the handling of the estate.

SUMMARY PROBATE

In addition to the affidavit procedure described above, some states have a second type of stream-lined probate process, frequently called *summary probate*. Estates that are too large for the affidavit procedure may be eligible for summary probate. In most states this procedure can be used to transfer ownership of real estate like the family home, whereas the affidavit procedure cannot usually transfer ownership of real estate.

Procedure

In most states an interested party—one who is named in a will or who is an "heir at law" and would inherit if there is no will—must petition the court. The petition must be accompanied by an inventory and appraisal of all of the deceased's property, the death certificate, and a copy of the will, if any. Notice of the proceeding must be given to all interested parties. The probate court will consider the petition and, if accepted, will issue an order specifying who will be given title to the property.

In states that have adopted the Uniform Probate Code, summary probate is available if there is a surviving spouse and minor children. The probate process is handled informally. If the value of the probate estate does not exceed the amount of the state's "family allowance," funeral expenses, expenses of the last illness, and costs of administration, the court will order immediate distribution of the estate without public notice or notice to creditors.

CHAPTER 15

Avoiding Probate

INTRODUCTION

A lthough this book is about probating an estate, certain property owned by the deceased may avoid probate either inadvertently or through advance planning. In some cases a deceased may have arranged his affairs by using a living trust in an attempt to entirely avoid probate. Sometimes this type of planning is effective, but sometimes there must be probate proceedings even when a living trust is created. This chapter describes the pros and cons of avoiding probate. It also describes a number of will substitutes—including putting property in joint names—that are frequently used to avoid probate. Finally, the chapter details the use of living trusts.*

WHY PEOPLE TRY TO AVOID PROBATE

Probate is about as popular as a root canal job. Even people who really know nothing about the process have a very negative image of it. Most adults have heard horror stories of endless court proceedings and large legal fees depleting the estate left to a poor widow. And in fact, probate procedures are often time-consuming and expensive.

High Probate Fees

Legal Fees

Legal fees to probate an estate can significantly diminish the amount received by beneficiaries.

The more time the attorney spends helping the executor, the higher the legal bills will be. The states have varying rules concerning attorney fees for handling probate matters. Some states have adopted a percentage system, whereby the attorney is paid a flat fee based on the value of the estate. The percentage paid to the attorney decreases as the value of the estate increases. In other states the attorney gets a "reasonable fee" based on the number of hours worked and the difficulty of the work.

Ancillary Administration

If an individual owns real estate in a state other than his residence, there will have to be additional ancillary administration in the state where the real estate is located. If property is owned in a number of states, there may have to be several such proceedings. Ancillary administration adds substantial costs to the probate bill, largely due to increases in legal fees.

---

* For more detailed information on methods of avoiding probate, see Berg, Adriane G. *Keys to Avoiding and Reducing Estate Taxes.* Hauppauge, New York: Barron's Educational Series, Inc., 1992. For advice on planning your estate, including how to avoid probate costs, see Shenkman, Martin. *Estate Planning: Step-by-Step.* Hauppauge, New York: Barron's Educational Series, Inc., 1997.

Other Professional Expenses

Legal fees and the executor's fee aren't the only expenses of probate. Property must be valued for the court, so appraisers often have to be hired. Tax returns must be filed for both the deceased and the estate, so accountants must be hired. If the decedent died owning over $600,000 of property, death taxes will be due. This type of tax work can be expensive, especially if the estate is audited by the IRS. In general, the larger the probate estate, the greater the costs and the longer the delays.

EXAMPLE Assume both Mr. Jones and Mr. Smith die owning $1 million of property in a state that calculates both legal fees and executor fees based on the value of the estate. Assume that the combined fee percentage is 8 percent of the estate's assets. Assume that all of Mr. Jones's estate will pass through probate, but $400,000 of Smith's real estate will pass outside probate. The fees on Jones's property will be $80,000 ($1 million × 8%) while the fees on Smith's will be only $48,000 ($600,000 × 8%). The $32,000 fee reduction is directly attributable to the fact that Smith arranged to keep the property out of the probate estate. Instead of going to the lawyers and executor, the $32,000 will go to the heirs.

OBSERVATION *An executor may not view a reduction in the executor's fee as an advantage. Most executors put in a lot of hard work and earn their fees.*

PLANNING TIP *If the surviving spouse is serving as executor and is to receive the bulk of the estate, it makes sense for him to serve without receiving a fee. If the funds are received as a fee, the amount must be declared as income on the individuals Form 1040 and taxes must be paid on it. If the surviving spouse receives the funds as an heir, however, the amount is received tax-free. On the other hand, an executor's fee is deductible in computing any federal estate tax. If the estate tax rate is higher than the surviving spouse's marginal income tax rate, it may be preferable to take the fee. Executors should check with their tax advisor before making this decision. The decision generally doesn't have to be made until the estate is being closed.*

Delay

In addition to the complaints about high fees, heirs frequently complain about delays in probate. In most states, it is difficult to close any estate in less than six months, and twelve months is more common for even uncomplicated estates.

Lawsuits

Occasionally estates and executors get involved in lawsuits. Someone may sue the estate over unresolved business dealings that he had with the deceased before death. The executor may have to finish up a lawsuit filed by the deceased or may have to file a lawsuit to recover property owned by the decedent but held by others. Whatever the case, civil lawsuits move slowly and will invariably slow down the probate process.

Will Contests

The cost and delay of probate will expand greatly if a will is contested by a disappointed heir. A will contest usually tries to set aside a will in favor of an earlier will. These types of complications are considered in Chapter 11, "Will Contests."

ASSETS PASSING OUTSIDE PROBATE

Finally, you should keep in mind that even when there is a probate procedure with an executor, some assets avoid probate by passing outside the estate, namely, property held in joint names, such as joint bank accounts; real property held in joint names; and property held in *inter vivos*, or living trusts. Such will substitutes will be discussed in more detail below.

USING WILL SUBSTITUTES

With advance planning, probate may be avoided altogether. In other cases this type of planning can at least reduce the cost and duration of the probate procedure.

Advantages of Will Substitutes

A *will substitute* is any transfer of property that occurs outside the state probate process—the property's title is transferred without falling into the probate estate. There are three primary advantages to this technique:

1. the transfer of title will be immediate upon the death of the decedent;

2. the transfer will go unpublicized; and

3. will substitutes reduce probate fees.

Prompt Transfer of Title

Using will substitutes insures that the transfer of title will be immediate upon the death of the decedent. Transfers from probate estates take many months and even years in extreme cases—justifiable cause for complaints by heirs. When will substitutes are used, title vests promptly and delay is avoided.

No Publicity

Another advantage to using will substitutes is that the transfer is a private transaction rather than a matter of public record. Because the transfer is not made in the will, it will be difficult and, in some cases, impossible for uninvolved parties to learn the details of the transfer.

If the deceased was well-known, the press may be interested in publicizing the contents of the will. The family may wish to keep potentially embarrassing bequests private. Even when there are no embarrassing facts, privacy is often desirable. Many individuals wish to keep their wealth a private matter.

Smaller Estates

If a person's estate is expected to be relatively small, it may be efficient to dispose of most of the decedent's property through the will substitute technique. In some states, the costs associated with probating an estate will be so high for even small estates that it is far more efficient to leave most of the property in will substitutes.

Joint Ownership

Joint ownership of property is a common form of will substitute, which allows one co-owner to leave property to the other. The property will automatically be owned by the co-owner on death, and so never pass through the probate estate. Spouses may jointly own homes and other property, and on the death of the first spouse, ownership of the property passes entirely to the other. Joint ownership is probably the most common type of will substitute.

Types of Co-ownership

There is more than one way to take co-ownership of property. Property ownership is a matter of state law. Nine states—Arizona, California, Idaho, Louisiana, Nevada, New Mexico, Texas, Washington, and Wisconsin—use the community property system which creates a special type of co-interest between spouses. Community property is described in detail in Chapter 7. The other states are known as *common law* states. These states generally do not focus on marital status in establishing co-ownership.

There are actually five common types of co-ownership:

1. joint tenancy

2. tenancy in common

3. tenancy by the entireties

4. community property

5. marital property

Joint Tenancy and Tenancy in Common

There is a legal distinction between *joint tenancy* and *tenancy in common*. During life they are quite similar, though not identical. On the death of a co-owner, the difference is quite extreme. Both joint tenancy and tenancy in common are forms of "concurrent" co-ownership. Two or more individuals may own property in the same or different percentages.

Survivorship Issues

A joint tenancy is usually defined as "Joint tenancy with right of survivorship." This means that when one of the joint tenants dies, the deceased's interest passes automatically to the surviving tenants.

EXAMPLE Three brothers each own a one-third interest in a parcel of land as joint tenants with right of survivorship. If one brother dies, his interest will pass to the other brothers. The two surviving brothers will then each own a one-half interest in the parcel. This would be true even if the deceased's will read: "I leave all of my property to my wife." The deceased's interest in the land ceased on his death and his wife will not have an interest in the parcel.

A tenancy in common is a form of ownership in which each owner has an undivided interest in the property. If co-owners take title as tenants in common the result is different than if they are joint tenants with right of survivorship. A tenancy in common can be sold, gifted, willed, or passed through the laws of intestacy.

EXAMPLE Suppose the same three brothers in the prior example own the same parcel of land, but as tenants in common. The deceased brother's interest would pass to his surviving spouse under the terms of his will. The two surviving brothers would continue to own a one-third interest, as would the surviving spouse. The result would probably be the same if the deceased brother died without a will and had no children.

Creation of the Legal Interest
If a party really wants to create a joint tenancy, title must be taken as joint owners with right of survivorship rather than as tenants in common. The legal designation on the title or deed, not the intent of the deceased, will control. Although joint tenants seem to have survivorship rights in one another's property, a joint tenant can "sever" the joint tenancy and create a tenancy in common.

EXAMPLE Three brothers take title to a parcel of land as joint tenants with right of survivorship. When one brother learns that his wife will not receive his interest at death, he severs the joint tenancy and becomes a tenant in common. He then will be able to leave the property to his wife—or anyone else—in his will.

Tenancy by the Entireties
A few states still recognize tenancy by the entirety. This form of ownership can only exist between a married couple, and ceases on the death of one spouse or divorce. The legal implications are essentially identical to joint ownership with right of survivorship, except that the tenancy cannot be converted to a tenancy in common unless the marriage is dissolved or both spouses consent to the conversion. This type of tenancy prevents one spouse from selling—and sometimes mortgaging—marital property without the other spouse's consent.

Community Property
Nine states have community property systems. Although the details of the state systems differ in some respects, the general scheme is similar. Community property only relates to married couples. In a community property state, the spouses typically own property that is community property and also property that each spouse owns individually. Each spouse has a one-half undivided interest in each item of community property. At death, a spouse can dispose of all his separate property, but only his one-half interest in the community property. In some states a spouse cannot make a lifetime gift of community property without the other spouse's consent.

The classification of property in community property states is detailed in Chapter 7.

PLANNING TIP *A competent local attorney should accurately classify each item of property as community property or separate property. An agreement between the spouses is recommended when classification is in doubt.*

Marital Property
Although there are some state-by-state variations, all nine community property states use the same basic scheme to determine if a surviving spouse has a legal interest in property acquired during marriage. The situation is far more complicated in the other states. In some noncommuntiy property states, legal title controls. In others, there is still a presumption that property acquired during marriage belongs solely to the husband. In still other states, a surviving spouse will have legal rights only in property that is owned by the spouses in joint tenancy with right of survivorship. Other states, however, recognize the concept of marital property, which gives the surviving spouse some rights in property acquired during marriage, recognizing that couples frequently don't give much thought to the legal implications of putting names on deeds and car titles.

Other Commonly Held Types of Property
Spouses and other family members commonly hold property in joint names, such as joint bank accounts with right of survivorship, bank account trusts, and U.S. savings bonds. There is no legal limitation on who may be a co-owner. Additionally, an individual may make a gift of a fractional interest in property. For example, a person could give someone a 20 percent interest in a piece of real estate, which would then become theirs on death.

Individuals should always get legal advice before placing property in joint ownership. State laws distinguish between tenancy in the entireties, tenancy in common, and joint tenancy with right of survivorship. The disposition of the property at the time of death depends on the technical designation of the co-ownership. Unfortunately, property is often titled without legal advice and property owners do not understand the implications for their heirs. If joint tenancy has been arranged, executors should anticipate that they may face some unpleasant moments with disappointed heirs.

Disadvantages of Joint Ownership

Creating joint interests in property is not always advisable, even between spouses. Property can be lost if one spouse files for bankruptcy—or worse, for divorce. The law of property varies state by state and can be tricky. Although beneficiary designations can be handled by laypersons, retitling property in joint names should only be done with the advice of an attorney.

Future Interests

Besides concurrent joint ownership, it is possible to give away so-called future interests in property either currently or in a will. A person who has a *future interest* has an ownership interest in property but with delayed possession. For example, Grey might want his son to have his farm after his death, but Grey wishes to live on the property for the remainder of his life. Grey could retain a life estate in the property and give his son a remainder interest. Both Grey and his son would be owners but only Grey would have current possession. Grey would have the right to use the property for his life, but it would automatically become his son's property on Grey's death. This type of ownership is also an effective will substitute and can avoid probate.

There are a number of different future interests that can be tailored to meet particular needs. As with other types of ownership, there may be federal estate tax implications even though the property passes outside the probate estate for state law purposes.

Transferring a joint interest in property may create a taxable gift. This sort of tax determination should be undertaken by an attorney. Similarly, although jointly held property may pass outside the

state probate estate, it may be included in the taxable estate for federal estate tax purposes. This sort of tax determination should be undertaken by an experienced estate planner. (See Chapter 13, "Estate and Gift Tax Basics.")

OTHER WILL SUBSTITUTES

Although joint ownership of property is the most common type of will substitute it is not the only one. An executor is likely to encounter one or more of these when probating an estate. Other types of will substitutes include:

- life insurance proceeds
- U.S. Savings Bonds with a payable-on-death designation
- annuities
- custodial accounts for minors
- trusts

Another type of will substitute is the living trust, which holds all of an individual's property. Living trusts have become increasingly popular because they avoid the delay and expense of probate. These will be discussed later in the chapter. Other types of trusts are discussed in Chapter 12, "Understanding Trusts."

All of these will substitutes have a beneficiary designation. When the owner dies, title to the property automatically vests in the beneficiary without going through probate. Because in many states both the executor's fee and fees for attorneys are based on the value of the property in the estate, the use of such will substitutes can effectively reduce probate fees.

LIVING TRUSTS

OBSERVATION *Technically, any trust that is established during a grantor's life is called an* inter vivos *or living trust. However, in popular usage,* living trust *frequently refers to an* inter vivos *trust intended to work as a will substitute. The trust is used in place of a will with the intent of avoiding probate.*

Generally, a living trust operates as a will substitute. Instead of using a will to distribute property at death, an individual will transfer legal title to his property to the living trust during his life. The grantor of a living trust gives control over the trust property to a trustee. The trust is therefore operative during the grantor's life. Eventually, when he dies, the trustee who administers the trust will distribute the property to those parties that the deceased designated.

Although such trusts may be irrevocable, trusts used as will substitutes are typically set up as revocable trusts so that may be easily changed or canceled.

Living trusts have become increasingly popular because they avoid the delay and expense of probate. However in some states, because probate costs are not as high as generally perceived, a living trust may provide little in the way of savings.

The biggest advantage of a living trust is the avoidance of state probate fees and delay. Because the legal title to the property has been transferred to the trust, the property will pass outside probate. Accordingly, there will be little delay in distributing the assets, and probate fees will largely be eliminated.

Disadvantages of Living Trusts

There are some disadvantages to living trusts that are not always noted. First, there are set-up costs and trustee's fees. In some states where probate fees are relatively low, the costs associated with the trust will be about the same as those that would arise in the probate of a will, assuming that the person's affairs are in good order.

Selecting a Trustee

Additionally, a person must select a trustee who will be absolutely honest. The person establishing the trust is free to select either an individual or an institution, such as a trust company or a bank, to serve as trustee. Although a trustee has a fiduciary duty to protect the trust assets, individuals have on occasion stolen trust assets. The grantor of the trust should monitor the trustee's activities with some degree of diligence.

Because the trustee of the living trust will be working closely with the family and other heirs during their bereavement, the trustee's personal qualities are important. If possible, the person establishing the trust should take the time to introduce his heirs to the trustee and make sure that they understand how the trust will work after his death.

Deciding Between a Will and a Living Trust

Setting up a living trust is not terribly complicated and, in fact, the terms of most living trusts closely parallel the provisions in a typical will. Attorneys who prepare wills also typically prepare living trusts for clients at their request.

The fee for establishing a trust will typically be higher than for preparing a will, and additional costs will be incurred related to transferring legal title to the assets. However, because the trust will be outside probate, the fees after death should be minimal.

APPENDIX A   Sample Will

his appendix contains a sample filled-in will and a sample filled-in durable power of attorney.

SAMPLE WILL

This sample will is included for illustrative purposes only. It would not necessarily be valid in all states.

LAST WILL OF

Robert Brown, Jr.

I, Robert Brown, Jr., of Sagebrush, Wyoming, do make, publish and declare this my last Will, hereby revoking all former wills and codicils.

ARTICLE I

FAMILY

I am the husband of Ellen L. Brown, and the father of three children: Mark A. Brown, Carol Brown, and Timothy J. Brown.

As used in this Will, "children" shall mean my children named above and any other children born to or adopted by me hereafter either before or after my death.

ARTICLE II

APPOINTMENT OF FIDUCIARIES

A. *Executors.* I nominate my wife, Ellen L. Brown, as Executor of my estate and of this my last Will. If my wife is unable or unwilling to serve, or to continue to serve, I nominate Mark A. Brown as my Executor.

B. *Waiver of Bond.* To the extent allowed by law, I direct that any of the fiduciaries named above, or their alternates or successors, shall be entitled to serve without bond or other undertaking and without reporting or accounting to any court.

ARTICLE III

PAYMENT OF DEBTS AND EXPENSES

I direct the payment out of my estate of all my just debts allowed in the course of administration, the expenses of my last illness and funeral and the expenses of the administration of my estate.

1

ARTICLE IV

HOUSEHOLD FURNISHINGS AND
OTHER PERSONAL PROPERTY

A. If my wife survives me, I give to my wife, Ellen L. Brown, all my interest in household furniture and furnishings, books, apparel, art objects, collections, jewelry and similar personal effects; sporting and recreational equipment; all other tangible property for personal use; all other like contents of my home and any vacation property that I may own or reside in on the date of my death; all animals; any motor vehicles that I may own on the date of my death; and any unexpired insurance on all such property.

B. If my wife, Ellen L. Brown, does not survive me, I give the property described in this Article to my children who survive me, to be divided among them in equal shares. My Executor shall determine the division, and that determination shall be conclusive.

ARTICLE V

RESIDUE OF ESTATE

A. If my wife, Ellen L. Brown, survives me, I give to my wife all the residue of my estate.

B. If my wife, Ellen L. Brown, does not survive me, I give the residue of my estate in equal shares to my three children. My Executor shall determine the division, and that determination shall be conclusive.

ARTICLE VI

SURVIVORSHIP

If any beneficiary named or described in this Will dies within four (4) months after my death, all the provisions in this Will for the benefit of such deceased beneficiary shall lapse, and this Will shall be construed as though the fact were that he or she predeceased me.

ARTICLE VII

TAXES

All estate, inheritance, succession, transfer and other taxes, including any interest and penalties thereon, (death taxes) that become payable by reason of my death with respect to property passing under this Will shall be paid out of the residue of my estate, without reimbursement from the recipients of such property and without apportionment. All death taxes attributable to property not passing under this Will shall be apportioned in the manner provided by law.

ARTICLE VIII

FIDUCIARY POWERS

A. I give to my Executor all the powers conferred upon an executor by the laws of Wyoming, whether or not such powers are exercised in the State of Wyoming.

B. In addition to such powers, but without limitation thereof, I give to my Executor full power and authority:

1. *Division of Estate.* To make any distribution in cash or in specific property and to cause any share to be composed of property different in kind from any other share and to make pro rata or non pro rata distributions, without regard to any difference in the tax basis of the property and without the requirement of making any adjustment among the beneficiaries. Any such distributions, allocations or valuations shall be binding and conclusive on all parties.

2. *Tax Elections/Discretions.* My Executor shall have sole discretion to: (1) claim deductions available to me or to my estate on estate tax returns or on state or federal income tax returns; (2) use date-of-death values or alternate valuation date values for estate tax purposes; and (3) make any other election or decision available under any federal or state tax laws. Any such election or decision may be made regardless of the effect thereof on any beneficiary or on any interest passing under this Will or otherwise, and without adjustment between income and principal or among beneficiaries.

3. *Distributions to Minors.* To distribute any interest in my estate to which a minor beneficiary is entitled to the individual selected by my Executor as Custodian under the Wyoming Uniform Transfers to Minors Act or under any other comparable law of the state where the minor beneficiary is domiciled.

3

ARTICLE IX

MISCELLANEOUS

A. *Table of Contents, Titles, Captions.* The table of contents, titles and captions used in this instrument are for convenience of reference only and shall not be construed to have any legal effect.

B. *Statutory References.* All statutory references in this instrument shall be construed to refer to that statutory section mentioned, related successor sections and corresponding provisions of any subsequent law, including all amendments.

IN WITNESS WHEREOF, I have signed this my last will

this   day of   , 1998.

x

Robert Brown, Jr.

Social Security No. 078-00-0000

x   Residing at   , Wyoming

x   Residing at   , Wyoming

STATE OF Wyoming   )

) ss.

County of Jackson   )

4

We, the undersigned, being sworn, each say:

We are the attesting witnesses to the Will executed by Robert Brown, Jr., dated   1998, consisting of five typewritten pages, including this page. The Will was executed in our presence and in the presence of the testator who declared the instrument to be his Will and requested us to sign our names as witnesses, which we did. To the best of our knowledge and belief, at the time of executing the Will the testator was of legal age, of sound mind, and not acting under any restraint, undue influence, duress or fraudulent misrepresentation.

x   x

(signature)   (print name)   date

x   x

(signature)   (print name)   date

SUBSCRIBED AND SWORN to by each of the affiants above named on

this   day of   , 1998.

_____

Notary Public for Wyoming

My Commission expires: _____

5

SAMPLE DURABLE POWER OF ATTORNEY

This sample power of attorney is included for illustrative purposes only. It would not necessarily be valid in all states.

DURABLE GENERAL POWER OF ATTORNEY

I, Robert Brown, Jr., do hereby make, constitute and appoint Ellen L. Brown, my wife, my Agent and attorney in fact (hereinafter called Agent), with power and authority:

1. *Support.* To make expenditures for my care, maintenance, support and general welfare, and to distribute such sums as are necessary for the care, maintenance, education and support of members of my immediate family who are or become dependent upon me for support;

2. *Management.* To take possession of, manage, administer, operate, maintain, improve and control all my property, real and personal; to insure and keep the same insured; and to pay any and all taxes, charges and assessments that may be levied or imposed upon any thereof;

3. *Collections.* To collect and receive any money, property, debts or claims whatsoever, now or hereafter due, owing and payable or belonging to me; and to forgive debts; and to give receipts, acquittance or other sufficient discharges for any of the same;

4. *Checks and Notes.* To sign, endorse, sell, discount, deliver and/or deposit checks, drafts, notes and negotiable or nonnegotiable instruments, including any payments to me drawn on the Treasury of the United States or the State of Wyoming or any other state or governmental entity, and to accept drafts;

5. *Investments.* To retain any property in the hands of the Agent in the form in which it was received; and to make investments and changes of investments in such securities, including common and preferred stocks of corporations or other property, real or personal, as my Agent may deem prudent;

6. *Debts.* To pay my debts and other obligations;

7. *Litigation.* To sue upon, defend, compromise, submit to arbitration or adjust any controversies in which I may be interested; and to act in my name in any complaints, proceedings or suits with all the powers I would possess if personally present and under no legal disability;

1

8. *Acquisition.* To bargain for, buy and deal in property and goods of every description;

9. *Disposition.* To sell, convey, grant, exchange, transfer, option, convert, mortgage, pledge, consign, lease and otherwise dispose of any of my property, whether real or personal;

10. *Borrowing.* To advance or loan the Agent's own funds on my behalf; and to borrow any sums of money on such terms and at such rate of interest as my Agent may deem proper and to give security for the repayment of the same;

11. *Agreements.* To make and deliver any deeds, conveyances, contracts, covenants and other instruments, undertakings or agreements, either orally or in writing, which my Agent may deem proper;

12. *Voting.* To appear and vote for me in person or by proxy at any corporate or other meeting;

13. *Safe-Deposit Box.* To have access to any safe-deposit box which has been rented in my name or in the name of myself and any other person or persons;

14. *Withdrawal of Funds.* To withdraw any monies deposited with any bank, mutual savings bank, credit union, savings and loan association, mutual fund, money market account, investment advisor or broker in my name or in the name of myself and any other person or persons and generally to do any business with any such financial institution or agency on my behalf;

15. *Tax Returns.* To sign and file on my behalf all city, county, state, federal and other governmental or quasi-governmental tax returns or reports, including income, gift, sales, business, and property tax returns or reports of every kind whatsoever; to execute waivers, extension agreements, settlement agreements and closing agreements with respect to those returns and to appear for me, in person or by attorney, and represent me before the United States Treasury Department or the Wyoming Department of Revenue or the taxing authority of any other state or governmental entity;

16. *Government Benefits.* To do and perform every act necessary or desirable and to serve as representative payee with respect to rights and entitlements for my benefit and the benefit of my spouse from Social Security, Medicare and military service;

2

17. *Treasury Bonds.* To purchase U.S. Treasury bonds or other instruments redeemable at par in payment of federal estate taxes;

18. *Additions to Trust.* To add any or all of my assets to a trust created by me alone or in conjunction with one or more other persons and already in existence at the time of the creation of this power if the trust provides that the income and principal shall be paid to me or applied for my benefit during my lifetime;

19. *Business Interests.* To continue as a going concern any business interest owned by me, either individually or as a co-partner;

20. *Substitution and Delegation.* To appoint and substitute for my said Agent any Agents, nominees or attorneys to exercise any or all of the powers herein and to revoke their authority at pleasure.

General Authority. I authorize my Agent for me in my name generally to do and perform all and every act and thing necessary or desirable to conduct, manage and control all my business and my property, wheresoever situated, and whether now owned or hereafter acquired, as my Agent may deem for my best interests and to execute and acknowledge any and all instruments necessary or proper to carry out the foregoing powers, hereby releasing all third persons from responsibility for my Agent's acts and omissions and I empower my Agent to indemnify all such persons against loss, expense and liability.

Third Party Reliance. Third persons may conclusively rely upon the continued validity of this Power of Attorney until receiving actual knowledge of its revocation. Third persons may conclusively rely on a copy of this instrument in its entirety or any portion thereof certified as such by my Agent.

Durability. These powers of attorney shall be exercisable by my Agent on my behalf notwithstanding that I may become legally disabled or incompetent.

Governing Law. All questions pertaining to validity, interpretation and administration of this power shall be determined in accordance with the laws of Wyoming.

3

IN WITNESS WHEREOF, I have hereunto set my hand and seal this _____ day of _____ , 1998.

_____

STATE OF Wyoming)   _____ , 19___ .

) ss.

County of Jackson)

Personally appeared _____ and acknowledged the foregoing instrument to be his/her voluntary act and deed.

IN TESTIMONY WHEREOF, I have hereunto set my hand and affixed my official seal the day and year last above written.

_____

Notary Public for Wyoming

My Commission expires: _____

4

APPENDIX B   State Laws

his appendix contains tables illustrating the differences in the
various state probate laws.

State	Name of Probate Court	Holographic Wills Recognized?	Will Revoked by Divorce or Annulment?*
Alabama	Probate Court	no	yes
Alaska	Superior Court	yes	yes
Arizona	Superior Court	yes	yes
Arkansas	Probate Court	yes (3 witnesses required)	yes
California	Superior Court	yes (date required in some cases)	no
Colorado	District Court	no	yes
Connecticut	Probate Court	no	no
Delaware	Court of Chancery	no	yes
District of Columbia	Superior Court, Probate Division	no	no
Florida	Circuit Court	no	divorce, yes annulment, no
Georgia	Probate Court	no	no
Hawaii	Circuit Court	no	yes
Idaho	District Court	yes	yes
Illinois	Circuit Court	no	yes
Indiana	Probate Court	no	yes
Iowa	District Court	no	yes
Kansas	District Court	no	yes
Kentucky	District Court	yes	no
Louisiana	District Court	yes (if dated with 2 witnesses)	no
Maine	Probate Court	yes	yes
Maryland	Orphan's Court	yes (if in military)	no
Massachusetts	Probate and Family Court	no	no
Michigan	Probate Court	yes (if dated)	yes
Minnesota	Probate Court	no	yes
Mississippi	Chancery Court	yes	no
Missouri	Circuit Court	no	divorce, yes annulment, no
Montana	District Court	yes	yes
Nebraska	County Court	yes (if dated in in some cases)	yes
Nevada	District Court	yes (if dated)	no
New Hampshire	Probate Court	no	no
New Jersey	Surrogate's Court	yes	yes (unless will provides otherwise)
New Mexico	Probate Court	no	yes
New York	Surrogate's Court	yes (if in military)	no
North Carolina	Superior Court	yes (3 witnesses may be needed to establish)	yes
North Dakota	County Court	yes	yes
Ohio	Court of Common Pleas	no	yes
Oklahoma	District Court	yes (if dated)	yes
Oregon	Circuit Court	no	yes

State	Name of Probate Court	Holographic Wills Recognized?	Will Revoked by Divorce or Annulment?*
Pennsylvania	Orphan's Court	yes	divorce, yes annulment, no
Rhode Island	Probate Court	no	no
South Carolina	Probate Court	no	divorce, yes annulment, no
South Dakota	Circuit Court	yes (if dated)	no
Tennessee	Probate Court	***	yes
Texas	Probate Court	yes (2 witnesses may be needed to establish)	yes
Utah	District Court	yes	yes
Vermont	Probate Court	no	no
Virginia	Circuit Court	yes (2 witnesses necessary)	divorce, yes annulment, no
Washington	Superior Court	no	divorce, yes annulment, no
West Virginia	County Commission	yes	no
Wisconsin	Circuit Court	no	yes
Wyoming	District Court	yes	no

*Note: Remarriage to former spouse may revive rights in many states.

State	Streamlined Summary Probate Available?	Transfer of Small Estate by Affidavit?	State Inheritance Tax?
Alabama	yes	no	no
Alaska	yes	yes	no
Arizona	yes	yes	no
Arkansas	yes	yes	no
California	yes	yes	no
Colorado	yes	yes	no
Connecticut	no	yes	yes
Delaware	no	yes	yes
District of Columbia	yes	no	no
Florida	yes	no	no
Georgia	no	no	no
Hawaii	yes	yes	no
Idaho	yes	yes	no
Illinois	yes	yes	no
Indiana	yes	yes	yes
Iowa	yes	no	yes
Kansas	yes	no	yes
Kentucky	yes	no	yes
Louisiana	no	yes	yes
Maine	yes	yes	no
Maryland	yes	no	yes
Massachusetts	yes	yes	no
Michigan	yes	no	yes
Minnesota	yes	yes	no
Mississippi	no	yes	no
Missouri	yes	yes	no
Montana	yes	yes	yes
Nebraska	yes	yes	yes
Nevada	yes	yes	no
New Hampshire	yes	yes	yes
New Jersey	no	yes	yes
New Mexico	yes	yes	no
New York	yes	yes	yes
North Carolina	no	yes	yes
North Dakota	yes	yes	no
Ohio	yes	yes	no
Oklahoma	yes	no	no
Oregon	yes	yes	no
Pennsylvania	yes	no	yes
Rhode Island	no	yes	no
South Carolina	yes	yes	no

State	Streamlined Summary Probate Available?	Transfer of Small Estate by Affidavit?	State Inheritance Tax?
South Dakota	yes	yes	yes
Tennessee	yes	yes	yes
Texas	yes	no	no
Utah	yes	yes	no
Vermont	yes	no	no
Virginia	yes	yes	no
Washington	no	yes	no
West Virginia	yes	yes	no
Wisconsin	yes	yes	no
Wyoming	yes	yes	no

State	Inventory Deadline After Executor Appointment*	Spousal Elective Share/Amount
Alabama	3	yes; 1/3
Alaska	3	yes; 1/3
Arizona	3	no; community property state
Arkansas	2	yes; state-specific-scheme
California	4	no; community property state
Colorado	3	yes; 1/2
Connecticut	2	yes; lifetime use of 1/3
Delaware	3	yes; 1/3
District of Columbia	3	yes; 1/2 or 1/3 of real property and 1/3 of other property
Florida	60 days	yes; 30% of Florida property
Georgia	4	no
Hawaii	30 days	yes; 1/3
Idaho	3	yes; 1/2 of property acquired during the marriage if acquired outside Idaho, plus 1/2 of community property
Illinois	60 days	yes; 1/2 (or 1/3 if children)
Indiana	2	yes; 1/2
Iowa	90 days	yes; 1/3
Kansas	30 days	yes; 1/3
Kentucky	2	yes; 1/2
Louisiana	only if requested by heir	no; community property state
Maine	3	yes; 1/3
Maryland	3	yes; 1/2 (1/3 if children)
Massachusetts	3	yes; 1/3
Michigan	60 days	yes; 1/2 lifetime or 1/3 real estate
Minnesota	6	yes; 1/3
Mississippi	90 days	yes; 1/3
Missouri	30 days	yes; 1/2 (1/3 if children)
Montana	3	yes; 1/3
Nebraska	2	yes; 1/2
Nevada	60 days	no; community property state
New Hampshire	3	yes; 1/3 (special rules if no children
New Jersey	none required	yes; 1/3
New Mexico	3	no; community property state
New York	6	yes; 1/3 to 1/2
North Carolina	3	yes; varies
North Dakota	6	yes; 1/3
Ohio	1	yes; 1/3 to 1/2
Oklahoma	2	yes; 1/2 of property acquired during marriage
Oregon	60 days	yes; 1/4
Pennsylvania	4	yes; 1/3

State	Inventory Deadline After Executor Appointment*	Spousal Elective Share/Amount
Rhode Island	30 days	yes; use of real estate for lifetime
South Carolina	60 days	yes; 1/3
South Dakota	9 after death	yes; greater of $100,000 or 1/3
Tennessee	60 days	yes; 1/3
Texas	90 days	no; community property state
Utah	3	yes; 1/3
Vermont	30 days	yes; 1/3 to 1/2
Virginia	4	yes; 1/2 (1/3 if children)
Washington	3	no; community property state
West Virginia	14	yes; 1/3
Wisconsin	6	no; community property state
Wyoming	120 days	yes; 1/4 to 1/2

*In number of months, unless otherwise indicated.

Frequently Asked Questions

Q: WHAT EXACTLY IS PROBATE?

A: Probate is the court-supervised distribution of assets after a person's death. Today many states allow "unsupervised" probate—the executor is allowed to carry out the estate's business without appearing in court for the most part. Probate exists to protect the deceased's property for both creditors and heirs.

Q: WHO APPOINTS THE EXECUTOR OF THE ESTATE?

A: A will normally appoints an executor, but the choice must be approved by the probate court. In most states the surviving spouse has a legal right to act as executor if she so desires.

Q: A WILL HAS NOMINATED ME AS EXECUTOR. DO I HAVE TO SERVE?

A: No. An individual has a right to decline appointment as an executor.

Q: WHAT IS THE DIFFERENCE BETWEEN AN "EXECUTOR" AND A "PERSONAL REPRESENTATIVE"?

A: These are different names for the same person. Some states use the older term, "executor" while other states use the newer term, "personal representative."

Q: THE DECEASED OWNED TWO HOMES, ONE IN NEW YORK AND ONE IN FLORIDA. WHERE SHOULD THE ESTATE BE PROBATED?

A: The estate should be probated in the state where the deceased had "domicile"—essentially the place of legal residence. In some cases this can be unclear. The place of death is not conclusive.

Q: DOES THE EXECUTOR GET PAID?

A: Yes. An executor normally gets paid although the executor can decline any compensation. The compensation varies state by state. In some states it is linked to the value of the estate.

Q: WHAT IS "ANCILLARY PROBATE"?

A: Ancillary probate is a probate proceeding that takes place in a second state where the deceased owned property.

Q: ARE THERE ANY ADVANTAGES TO AN EXECUTOR'S DECLINING COMPENSATION?

A: Yes. A surviving spouse who will receive all the property in the estate is normally better off declining compensation. The executor's fee is subject to income tax, but property received from the estate is not. Accordingly, by taking the fee, the surviving spouse would increase his or her income taxes.

Q: WHAT HAPPENS TO A PERSON'S PROPERTY IF HE DIES WITHOUT A WILL?

A: If an individual dies without a will, his property will be distributed to his nearest relatives by operation of the law in his state of domicile. If an individual has no close relatives, the property may go to the state.

Q: IS A PRENUPTIAL AGREEMENT ENFORCEABLE IF THE WILL DIFFERS FROM THE AGREEMENT?

A: Yes. A prenuptial agreement may be enforceable and may limit the amount a surviving spouse will take from the deceased's estate. In most states a prenuptial agreement will be enforced if there was full disclosure of facts at the time the agreement was made and the signer was represented by an attorney.

Q: A PERSON DIED WITH A WILL. THE WILL WAS WRITTEN YEARS AGO WHILE THE DECEASED WAS MARRIED; THE DECEASED WAS DIVORCED TWO YEARS AGO. DOES THE EX-SPOUSE GET ALL THE GIFTS LISTED IN THE WILL?

A: Probably not. In most states a divorce will either revoke all or parts of a will. In many states the ex-spouse will not get the gifts listed in the will. You will need to check with a local attorney on this point.

Q: AN INDIVIDUAL DIED LEAVING ONLY AN UNWITNESSED HAND-WRITTEN WILL. IS IT VALID?

A: In most states an unwitnessed handwritten will (called a "holographic will") is not valid.

Q: CAN A PERSON LEGALLY DISINHERIT HIS SPOUSE?

A: No. All states have statutory protection for a surviving spouse that allows the spouse to receive part of the estate even if the will attempts to leave the spouse nothing.

Q: CAN A PERSON LEGALLY DISINHERIT HIS CHILD?

A: Yes. If the will names the child and provides that he or she gets nothing. If the will fails to name the child, the child may receive property in most states.

Q: AN INDIVIDUAL DIED WITH SUBSTANTIAL DEBTS. WHO IS RESPONSIBLE FOR PAYING THEM?

A: The executor is responsible for paying the deceased's debts from the property in the estate.

Q: HAVE DEATH TAXES BEEN ABOLISHED?

A: No. Both the state and the federal governments still impose death taxes. State death taxes are called inheritance taxes and the federal tax is called the estate tax. Smaller estates are not subject to these taxes.

Q: IS A FEDERAL INCOME TAX RETURN DUE FOR THE YEAR IN WHICH THE DECEASED DIED?

A: Yes. A federal income tax return, Form 1040, must be filed for the deceased, and a Form 1041 must be filed for the estate. The executor must see that these forms are prepared and filed.

Q: A LIVING TRUST WAS CREATED BY THE DECEASED. WILL THERE BE ANY PROBATE PROCEEDINGS?

A: It depends. A living trust can be used as a "will substitute." The trust, rather than a will, distributes the property at death. If all the deceased's property was legally transferred into the trust, probate may be avoided. On the other hand, if certain property was not in the trust the estate may still have to be probated.

Q: WHAT DOES THE PHRASE "ELECTING AGAINST THE WILL" MEAN?

A: A surviving spouse who has been disinherited in a will can seek a forced share of the deceased's estate. Normally the surviving spouse will receive one-third of the estate by operation of state law.

Q: A WILL LEFT ALL OF A PERSON'S PROPERTY TO HIS BROTHER. THE PERSON ALSO OWNED A LIFE INSURANCE POLICY NAMING HIS CHURCH AS BENEFICIARY. DOES THE WILL CONTROL THE LIFE INSURANCE BENEFICIARY DESIGNATION?

A: No. Beneficiary designations on life insurance policies, savings bonds, annuities, and pensions are not controlled by the will. In this case, the church will receive the life insurance proceeds despite the language of the will.

Q: ALTHOUGH THE WILL LISTS MANY GIFTS TO A NUMBER OF RELATIVES AND CHARITIES, THE DECEASED DIED WITH VERY LITTLE PROPERTY. WHAT HAPPENS TO THE GIFTS MADE IN THE ESTATE?

A: The will can only give away property the deceased owned at death. If the estate has few assets, the heirs may get nothing.

Q: THE DECEASED LEFT HIS BUICK TO HIS BROTHER, BUT THE AUTO IS SUBJECT TO A CAR LOAN. SHOULD THE ESTATE PAY OFF THE LOAN?

A: No. The brother receives the Buick subject to the car loan.

Q: THE DECEASED OWNED A BUSINESS AND VARIOUS INVESTMENT PROPERTIES. WHAT HAPPENS TO THESE PROPERTIES AT DEATH?

A: The executor is responsible for managing the deceased's business and investment properties. The will should control their ultimate disposition.

Q: THE DECEASED'S WILL PROVIDES THAT MUCH OF HIS PROPERTY IS TO GO TO HIS THREE CHILDREN WHO ARE NAMED IN THE WILL. THE DECEASED REMARRIED AND HAD A YOUNG CHILD SINCE THE WILL WAS WRITTEN. DOES THE YOUNGEST CHILD RECEIVE ANYTHING UNDER THE WILL?

A: All states have laws dealing with children who are omitted from wills. The child will receive property from the estate according to local law.

Q: HOW AND WHY ARE WILLS CONTESTED?

A: Wills are typically contested by disappointed heirs. To contest a will, the parties must show that the deceased was not legally competent at the time the will was made or that the will was a product of fraud, duress, or undue influence.

Glossary

BEQUEST A bequest is a gift of personal property in a will.

CLASS GIFT A gift to a number of parties, usually family members. For example, if you make a class gift to your grandchildren, all of your grandchildren will share in the gift.

CODICIL A short addition to a will that updates or changes a will.

CONTINGENT BENEFICIARY An alternate beneficiary who will receive your property if the first beneficiary predeceases you.

DEATH TAXES Federal estate taxes are imposed on sizable estates at death. Some states also impose inheritance taxes on heirs.

DEVISE A devise is a gift of land or real estate.

DISINHERITANCE Cutting out a person, usually a relative, from an inheritance. Usually, anyone except a spouse can be disinherited.

DURESS The use of improper threats inducing a person to make a will. Wills can be challenged by showing duress.

ELECTION AGAINST THE WILL see Forced Share

ESCHEAT The process whereby property is turned over to the state government after death. If a person dies without a will or close relatives, the property may escheat to the state government.

ESTATE Legal entity that holds your property after death. Your estate is administered by an executor on behalf of your heirs and creditors.

EXECUTOR The party who administers the deceased's estate. The executor is typically named in the will, but the court will appoint one if none is named or the named party declines to serve.

FORCED SHARE Spouse's right to take a fixed percent of an estate in lieu of the amount received in a will.

FRAUD The use of trickery to induce a person to make a will. Wills can be challenged by showing fraud.

HOLOGRAPHIC WILLS Handwritten but unwitnessed will that is valid in a minority of states.

INTESTACY Dying without a will.

JOINT WILLS Two wills with reciprocal provisions contained in one legal document, generally written by spouses.

LAPSE A gift to a predeceased heir is considered to have lapsed. In many states an anti-lapse statute awards the gift to the family of the predeceased heir.

LEGACY A legacy is a gift of money.

LEGAL CAPACITY Legal ability to write a valid will, which requires four elements: a knowledge of 1) one's family, 2) one's property, 3) the nature of making a will, and 4) the relation of each element to the other.

LEGAL TITLE Legal ownership of property evidenced by deed or title rather than mere use or possession.

MUTUAL WILLS Separate will documents with reciprocal provisions, usually prepared by spouses.

PERSONAL REPRESENTATIVE see Executor

PRETERMITTED HEIR A child omitted from a will. In most states the omission is presumed inadvertent and the omitted child will receive a share of the parent's estate.

PROBATE The process of collecting the property of the decedent, paying debts, and distributing the remainder of the estate to the heirs according to the terms of the will.

RESIDUARY The part of the estate that is not specifically designated to go to a particular heir.

REVOCATION Cancelling a will by writing a later will, or physically destroying the old will.

SPENDTHRIFT TRUST A trust that cannot be reached by creditors of the beneficiary.

UNDUE INFLUENCE The use of overpersuasion by a trusted party to induce a person to make a will. Wills can be challenged by showing undue influence.

WILL CONTEST Legal challenge to a will. Wills can be challenged by showing lack of legal capacity, fraud, duress, or undue influence.

Federal Tax Forms

T his appendix contains blank tax forms and instructions used in
preparing and filing a federal income tax return for the estate
and a federal estate tax return for the deceased for the tax year 1996.
Current forms are available at your local public library and post office
or by calling the Internal Revenue Service toll-free at 1-800-829-3676.

Department of the Treasury
Internal Revenue Service

Instructions for the Requester of Form W-9

(March 1994)

Request for Taxpayer Identification Number and Certification

Section references are to the Internal Revenue Code, unless otherwise noted.

These instructions supplement the instructions on the Form W-9, for the requester. The payee may also need these instructions.

Substitute Form W-9

You may use a substitute Form W-9 (your own version) as long as it is substantially similar to the official Form W-9 and conforms to Temporary Regulations section 35a.9999-1, Q/A-36. You may not use a substitute form to require the payee, by signing, to agree to provisions unrelated to TIN certification.

TIN Applied For

If the payee returns the Form W-9 with "Applied For" written in Part I, the payee must provide you with a TIN within 60 days. During this 60-day period, you have two options for withholding on reportable interest or dividend payments. For other reportable payments, if you do not receive the payee's TIN within the 60 days you must backup withhold, until the payee furnishes you with his or her TIN.

Option 1.—You must backup withhold on any withdrawals the payee makes from the account after 7 business days after you receive the Form W-9.

Option 2.—You must backup withhold on any reportable interest or dividend payments made to the payee's account, regardless of whether the payee makes any withdrawals. Backup withholding under this option must begin no later than 7 business days after you receive the Form W-9. Under this option, you must refund the amounts withheld if you receive the payee's certified TIN within the 60-day period and the payee was not otherwise subject to backup withholding during the period.

Payees and Payments Exempt From Backup Withholding

The following is a list of payees exempt from backup withholding and for which no information reporting is required. For interest and dividends, all listed payees are exempt except item **(9)**. For broker transactions, payees listed in items **(1)** through **(13)** and a person registered under the Investment Advisers Act of 1940 who regularly acts as a broker are exempt. Payments subject to reporting under sections 6041 and 6041A are generally exempt from backup withholding only if made to payees described in items **(1)** through **(7)**, except a corporation that provides medical and health care services or bills and collects payments for such services is not exempt from backup withholding or information reporting. Only payees described in items **(2)** through **(6)** are exempt from backup withholding for barter exchange transactions, patronage dividends, and payments by certain fishing boat operators.

(1) A corporation.

(2) An organization exempt from tax under section 501(a), or an IRA, or a custodial account under section 403(b)(7).

(3) The United States or any of its agencies or instrumentalities.

(4) A state, the District of Columbia, a possession of the United States, or any of their political subdivisions or instrumentalities.

(5) A foreign government or any of its political subdivisions, agencies, or instrumentalities.

(6) An international organization or any of its agencies or instrumentalities.

(7) A foreign central bank of issue.

(8) A dealer in securities or commodities required to register in the United States or a possession of the United States.

(9) A futures commission merchant registered with the Commodity Futures Trading Commission.

(10) A real estate investment trust.

(11) An entity registered at all times during the tax year under the Investment Company Act of 1940.

(12) A common trust fund operated by a bank under section 584(a).

(13) A financial institution.

(14) A middleman known in the investment community as a nominee or listed in the most recent publication of the American Society of Corporate Secretaries, Inc., Nominee List.

(15) A trust exempt from tax under section 664 or described in section 4947.

Payments of **dividends and patronage dividends** generally not subject to backup withholding include the following:

● Payments to nonresident aliens subject to withholding under section 1441.

● Payments to partnerships not engaged in a trade or business in the United States and that have at least one nonresident partner.

● Payments of patronage dividends not paid in money.

- Payments made by certain foreign organizations.

Payments of **interest** generally not subject to backup withholding include the following:

- Payments of interest on obligations issued by individuals.

Note: *The payee may be subject to backup withholding if this interest is $600 or more and is paid in the course of your trade or business and the payee has not provided his or her correct TIN to you.*

- Payments of tax-exempt interest (including exempt-interest dividends under section 852).
- Payments described in section 6049(b)(5) to nonresident aliens.
- Payments on tax-free covenant bonds under section 1451.
- Payments made by certain foreign organizations.
- Mortgage interest paid to you.

Payments that are not subject to information reporting are also not subject to backup withholding. For details, see sections 6041, 6041A(a), 6042, 6044, 6045, 6049, 6050A, and 6050N, and their regulations.

For more information on backup withholding and your requirements, get **Pub. 1679,** A Guide to Backup Withholding, and **Pub. 1281,** Backup Withholding on Missing and Incorrect TINs.

Names and TINs To Use for Information Reporting

Show the full name and address as provided on the Form W-9 on the appropriate information return. If payments have been made to more than one recipient or the account is in more than one name, enter ONLY on the first name line the name of the recipient whose TIN is shown on the information return. Show the names of any other individual recipients in the area below the first name line, if desired.

For sole proprietors, show the individual's name on the first name line. On the second name line, you may enter the business name if provided. You may not enter only the business name. For the TIN, enter either the individual's SSN or the EIN of the business (sole proprietorship).

Notices From the IRS About Your Payees

We will send you a notice if the payee's name and TIN on the information return you filed do not match our records. You may need tc send a "B" Notice to the payee to solicit his or her TIN. See Pub. 1679 and Pub. 1281 for copies of the two different "B" Notices.

 Printed on recycled paper

*U.S. Government Printing Office: 1994 — 301-628/00119

Form **W-9**

(Rev. December 1996)

Department of the Treasury
Internal Revenue Service

Request for Taxpayer
Identification Number and Certification

Give form to the requester. Do NOT send to the IRS.

Please print or type

Name (If a joint account or you changed your name, see **Specific Instructions** on page 2.)

Business name, if different from above. (See **Specific Instructions** on page 2.)

Check appropriate box: ☐ Individual/Sole proprietor ☐ Corporation ☐ Partnership ☐ Other ▶ ....

Address (number, street, and apt. or suite no.)

Requester's name and address (optional)

City, state, and ZIP code

Part I — Taxpayer Identification Number (TIN)

Enter your TIN in the appropriate box. For individuals, this is your social security number (SSN). However, if you are a resident alien OR a sole proprietor, see the instructions on page 2. For other entities, it is your employer identification number (EIN). If you do not have a number, see **How To Get a TIN** on page 2.

Note: *If the account is in more than one name, see the chart on page 2 for guidelines on whose number to enter.*

Social security number

OR

Employer identification number

List account number(s) here (optional)

Part II — For Payees Exempt From Backup Withholding (See the instructions on page 2.)

▶

Part III — Certification

Under penalties of perjury, I certify that:

1. The number shown on this form is my correct taxpayer identification number (or I am waiting for a number to be issued to me), **and**

2. I am not subject to backup withholding because: **(a)** I am exempt from backup withholding, or **(b)** I have not been notified by the Internal Revenue Service (IRS) that I am subject to backup withholding as a result of a failure to report all interest or dividends, or **(c)** the IRS has notified me that I am no longer subject to backup withholding.

Certification Instructions.—You must cross out item **2** above if you have been notified by the IRS that you are currently subject to backup withholding because you have failed to report all interest and dividends on your tax return. For real estate transactions, item **2** does not apply. For mortgage interest paid, acquisition or abandonment of secured property, cancellation of debt, contributions to an individual retirement arrangement (IRA), and generally, payments other than interest and dividends, you are not required to sign the Certification, but you must provide your correct TIN. (See the instructions on page 2.)

Sign Here | Signature ▶ | Date ▶

Purpose of Form.—A person who is required to file an information return with the IRS must get your correct taxpayer identification number (TIN) to report, for example, income paid to you, real estate transactions, mortgage interest you paid, acquisition or abandonment of secured property, cancellation of debt, or contributions you made to an IRA.

Use Form W-9 to give your correct TIN to the person requesting it (the requester) and, when applicable, to:

1. Certify the TIN you are giving is correct (or you are waiting for a number to be issued),

2. Certify you are not subject to backup withholding, or

3. Claim exemption from backup withholding if you are an exempt payee.

Note: *If a requester gives you a form other than a W-9 to request your TIN, you must use the requester's form if it is substantially similar to this Form W-9.*

What Is Backup Withholding?—Persons making certain payments to you must withhold and pay to the IRS 31% of such payments under certain conditions. This is called "backup withholding." Payments that may be subject to backup withholding

include interest, dividends, broker and barter exchange transactions, rents, royalties, nonemployee pay, and certain payments from fishing boat operators. Real estate transactions are not subject to backup withholding.

If you give the requester your correct TIN, make the proper certifications, and report all your taxable interest and dividends on your tax return, payments you receive will not be subject to backup withholding. Payments you receive **will** be subject to backup withholding if:

1. You do not furnish your TIN to the requester, or

2. The IRS tells the requester that you furnished an incorrect TIN, or

3. The IRS tells you that you are subject to backup withholding because you did not report all your interest and dividends on your tax return (for reportable interest and dividends only), or

4. You do not certify to the requester that you are not subject to backup withholding under 3 above (for reportable interest and dividend accounts opened after 1983 only), or

5. You do not certify your TIN when required. See the Part III instructions on page 2 for details.

Certain payees and payments are exempt from backup withholding. See the Part II instructions and the separate **Instructions for the Requester of Form W-9.**

Penalties

Failure To Furnish TIN.—If you fail to furnish your correct TIN to a requester, you are subject to a penalty of $50 for each such failure unless your failure is due to reasonable cause and not to willful neglect.

Civil Penalty for False Information With Respect to Withholding.—If you make a false statement with no reasonable basis that results in no backup withholding, you are subject to a $500 penalty.

Criminal Penalty for Falsifying Information.— Willfully falsifying certifications or affirmations may subject you to criminal penalties including fines and/or imprisonment.

Misuse of TINs.—If the requester discloses or uses TINs in violation of Federal law, the requester may be subject to civil and criminal penalties.

Form **W-9** (Rev. 12-96)

Specific Instructions

Name.—If you are an individual, you must generally enter the name shown on your social security card. However, if you have changed your last name, for instance, due to marriage, without informing the Social Security Administration of the name change, enter your first name, the last name shown on your social security card, and your new last name.

If the account is in joint names, list first and then circle the name of the person or entity whose number you enter in Part I of the form.

Sole Proprietor.—You must enter your **individual** name as shown on your social security card. You may enter your business, trade, or "doing business as" name on the business name line.

Other Entities.—Enter the business name as shown on required Federal tax documents. This name should match the name shown on the charter or other legal document creating the entity. You may enter any business, trade, or "doing business as" name on the business name line.

Part I—Taxpayer Identification Number (TIN)

You must enter your TIN in the appropriate box. If you are a resident alien and you do not have and are not eligible to get an SSN, your TIN is your IRS individual taxpayer identification number (ITIN). Enter it in the social security number box. If you do not have an ITIN, see **How To Get a TIN** below.

If you are a sole proprietor and you have an EIN, you may enter either your SSN or EIN. However, using your EIN may result in unnecessary notices to the requester.

Note: *See the chart on this page for further clarification of name and TIN combinations.*

How To Get a TIN.—If you do not have a TIN, apply for one immediately. To apply for an SSN, get **Form SS-5** from your local Social Security Administration office. Get **Form W-7** to apply for an ITIN or **Form SS-4** to apply for an EIN. You can get Forms W-7 and SS-4 from the IRS by calling 1-800-TAX-FORM (1-800-829-3676).

If you do not have a TIN, write "Applied For" in the space for the TIN, sign and date the form, and give it to the requester. For interest and dividend payments, and certain payments made with respect to readily tradable instruments, you will generally have 60 days to get a TIN and give it to the requester. Other payments are subject to backup withholding.

Note: *Writing "Applied For" means that you have already applied for a TIN OR that you intend to apply for one soon.*

Part II—For Payees Exempt From Backup Withholding

Individuals (including sole proprietors) are **not** exempt from backup withholding. Corporations are exempt from backup withholding for certain payments, such as interest and dividends. For more information on exempt payees, see the separate Instructions for the Requester of Form W-9.

If you are exempt from backup withholding, you should still complete this form to avoid possible erroneous backup withholding. Enter your correct TIN in Part I, write "Exempt" in Part II, and sign and date the form.

If you are a nonresident alien or a foreign entity not subject to backup withholding, give the requester a completed **Form W-8**, Certificate of Foreign Status.

Part III—Certification

For a joint account, only the person whose TIN is shown in Part I should sign (when required).

1. Interest, Dividend, and Barter Exchange Accounts Opened Before 1984 and Broker Accounts Considered Active During 1983. You must give your correct TIN, but you do not have to sign the certification.

2. Interest, Dividend, Broker, and Barter Exchange Accounts Opened After 1983 and Broker Accounts Considered Inactive During 1983. You must sign the certification or backup withholding will apply. If you are subject to backup withholding and you are merely providing your correct TIN to the requester, you must cross out item **2** in the certification before signing the form.

3. Real Estate Transactions. You must sign the certification. You may cross out item **2** of the certification.

4. Other Payments. You must give your correct TIN, but you do not have to sign the certification unless you have been notified that you have previously given an incorrect TIN. "Other payments" include payments made in the course of the requester's trade or business for rents, royalties, goods (other than bills for merchandise), medical and health care services (including payments to corporations), payments to a nonemployee for services (including attorney and accounting fees), and payments to certain fishing boat crew members.

5. Mortgage Interest Paid by You, Acquisition or Abandonment of Secured Property, Cancellation of Debt, or IRA Contributions. You must give your correct TIN, but you do not have to sign the certification.

Privacy Act Notice

Section 6109 of the Internal Revenue Code requires you to give your correct TIN to persons who must file information returns with the IRS to report interest, dividends, and certain other income paid to you, mortgage interest you paid, the acquisition or abandonment of secured property, cancellation of debt, or contributions you made to an IRA. The IRS uses the numbers for identification purposes and to help verify the accuracy of your tax return. The IRS may also provide this information to the Department of Justice for civil and criminal litigation and to cities, states, and the District of Columbia to carry out their tax laws.

You must provide your TIN whether or not you are required to file a tax return. Payers must generally withhold 31% of taxable interest, dividend, and certain other payments to a payee who does not give a TIN to a payer. Certain penalties may also apply.

What Name and Number To Give the Requester

For this type of account:	Give name and SSN of:
1. Individual	The individual
2. Two or more individuals (joint account)	The actual owner of the account or, if combined funds, the first individual on the account [1]
3. Custodian account of a minor (Uniform Gift to Minors Act)	The minor [2]
4. a. The usual revocable savings trust (grantor is also trustee)	The grantor-trustee [1]
b. So-called trust account that is not a legal or valid trust under state law	The actual owner [1]
5. Sole proprietorship	The owner [3]

For this type of account:	Give name and EIN of:
6. Sole proprietorship	The owner [3]
7. A valid trust, estate, or pension trust	Legal entity [4]
8. Corporate	The corporation
9. Association, club, religious, charitable, educational, or other tax-exempt organization	The organization
10. Partnership	The partnership
11. A broker or registered nominee	The broker or nominee
12. Account with the Department of Agriculture in the name of a public entity (such as a state or local government, school district, or prison) that receives agricultural program payments	The public entity

[1] List first and circle the name of the person whose number you furnish. If only one person on a joint account has an SSN, that person's number must be furnished.

[2] Circle the minor's name and furnish the minor's SSN.

[3] You must show your individual name, but you may also enter your business or "doing business as" name. You may use either your SSN or EIN (if you have one).

[4] List first and circle the name of the legal trust, estate, or pension trust. (Do not furnish the TIN of the personal representative or trustee unless the legal entity itself is not designated in the account title.)

Note: *If no name is circled when more than one name is listed, the number will be considered to be that of the first name listed.*

Department of the Treasury
Internal Revenue Service

Instructions for Form 706
(Revised August 1993)
United States Estate (and Generation-Skipping Transfer) Tax Return
For decedents dying after October 8, 1990.
Section references are to the Internal Revenue Code unless otherwise noted.

Paperwork Reduction Act Notice.—We ask for the information on this form to carry out the Internal Revenue laws of the United States. You are required to give us the information. We need it to ensure that you are complying with these laws and to allow us to figure and collect the right amount of tax.

The time needed to complete and file this form and related schedules will vary depending on individual circumstances. The estimated average times are:

Form	Recordkeeping	Learning about the law or the form	Preparing the form	Copying, assembling, and sending the form to the IRS
706	2 hr., 11 min.	1 hr., 9 min.	3 hr., 26 min.	49 min.
Sch. A	20 min.	16 min.	10 min.	20 min.
A-1	46 min.	25 min.	59 min.	49 min.
B	20 min.	10 min.	11 min.	20 min.
C	13 min.	2 min.	8 min.	20 min.
D	7 min.	6 min.	8 min.	20 min.
E	40 min.	7 min.	24 min.	20 min.
F	33 min.	6 min.	21 min.	20 min.
G	26 min.	18 min.	11 min.	14 min.
H	26 min.	6 min.	10 min.	14 min.
I	26 min.	25 min.	11 min.	20 min.
J	26 min.	5 min.	16 min.	20 min.
K	26 min.	9 min.	10 min.	20 min.
L	13 min.	5 min.	10 min.	20 min.
M	13 min.	31 min.	24 min.	20 min.
O	20 min.	9 min.	18 min.	17 min
P	7 min.	14 min.	18 min.	14 min.
Q	7 min.	10 min.	11 min.	14 min.
Q Wksht.	7 min.	10 min.	59 min.	20 min.
R	20 min.	34 min.	1 hr., 1 min.	49 min.
R-1	7 min.	29 min.	24 min.	20 min.
S	26 min.	22 min.	37 min.	25 min.
Contin.	20 min.	3 min.	7 min.	20 min.

If you have comments concerning the accuracy of these time estimates or suggestions for making this form more simple, we would be happy to hear from you. You can write to both the **Internal Revenue Service**, Attention: Reports Clearance Officer, T:FP, Washington, DC 20224; and the **Office of Management and Budget,** Paperwork Reduction Project (1545-0015), Washington, DC 20503. **DO NOT** send the tax form to either of these offices. Instead, see **Where To File** on page 2.

Change To Note

● The Omnibus Budget Reconciliation Act of 1993 increased the maximum estate tax rate to 53% for taxable estates in excess of $2.5 million and 55% for taxable estates in excess of $3 million. This increase is permanent and applies to the estates of decedents dying after December 31, 1992. Because the February 1993 revision of Form 706 is based on a maximum estate tax rate of 50%, it should not be used.

	For Decedents Dying			Use Revision of
After	and	**Before**		**Form 706 Dated**
--------------------		January 1, 1982		November, 1981
December 31, 1981		October 23, 1986		November, 1987
October 22, 1986		January 1, 1990		October, 1988
December 31, 1989		October 9, 1990		July, 1990
October 8, 1990		January 1, 1993		October, 1991
October 8, 1990		--------------------		August, 1993

General Instructions

Purpose of Form

The executor of a decedent's estate uses Form 706 to figure the estate tax imposed by Chapter 11 of the Internal Revenue Code. This tax is levied on the entire taxable estate, not just on the share received by a particular beneficiary. Form 706 is also used to compute the generation-skipping transfer (GST) tax imposed by Chapter 13 on direct skips (transfers to skip persons of interests in property included in the decedent's gross estate).

Which Estates Must File

Form 706 must be filed by the executor for the estate of every U.S. citizen or resident whose gross estate, plus adjusted taxable gifts and specific exemption, is more than certain limits.

To determine whether you must file a return for the estate, add:

1. The adjusted taxable gifts (under section 2001(b)) made by the decedent after December 31, 1976;

2. The total specific exemption allowed under section 2521 (as in effect before its repeal by the Tax Reform Act of 1976) for gifts made by the decedent after September 8, 1976; and

3. The decedent's gross estate **valued at the date of death.**

You must file a return for the estate if the total of 1, 2, and 3 above is more than $600,000 for decedents dying after 1986. For filing requirements for decedents dying after 1981 and before 1986, see the November 1987 Revision of Form 706.

Gross Estate

The gross estate includes all property in which the decedent had an interest (including real property outside the United States). It also includes:

● Certain transfers made during the decedent's life without an adequate and full consideration in money or money's worth;

● Annuities;

● Joint estates with right of survivorship;

● Tenancies by the entirety;

● Life insurance proceeds (even though payable to beneficiaries other than the estate);

● Property over which the decedent possessed a general power of appointment;

● Dower or curtesy (or statutory estate) of the surviving spouse;

● Community property to the extent of the decedent's interest as defined by applicable law.

For more specific information, see the instructions for Schedules A through I.

U.S. Citizens or Residents; Nonresident Noncitizens

File Form 706 for the estates of decedents who were either U.S. citizens or U.S. residents at the time of death. File **Form 706-NA,** United States Estate (and Generation-Skipping Transfer) Tax Return, Estate of nonresident not a citizen of the United States, for the estates of nonresident alien decedents (decedents who were neither U.S. citizens nor residents at the time of death).

Residents of U.S. Possessions

All references to citizens of the United States are subject to the provisions of sections 2208 and 2209, relating to decedents who were U.S. citizens and residents of a U.S. possession on the date of death. If such a decedent became a U.S. citizen only because of his or her connection with a possession, then the decedent is considered a nonresident alien decedent for estate tax purposes, and you should file Form 706-NA. If such a decedent became a U.S. citizen wholly independently of his or her connection with a possession, then the decedent is considered a U.S. citizen for estate tax purposes, and you should file Form 706.

Executor

The term "executor" means the executor, personal representative, or administrator of the decedent's estate. If none of these is appointed, qualified, and acting in the United States, every person in actual or constructive possession of any property of the decedent is considered an executor and must file a return.

When To File

You must file Form 706 to report estate and/or generation-skipping transfer tax within 9 months after the date of the decedent's death unless you receive an extension of time to file. Use **Form 4768,** Application for Extension of Time To File a Return and/or Pay U.S. Estate (and Generation-Skipping Transfer) Taxes, to apply for an extension of time. If you received an extension, attach a copy of it to Form 706.

Where To File

Unless the return is hand carried to the office of the District Director, please mail it to the Internal Revenue Service Center indicated below for the state where the **decedent was domiciled** at the time of death. If you are filing a return for the estate of a nonresident U.S. citizen, mail it to the Internal Revenue Service Center, Philadelphia, PA 19255, USA.

Where To File.—

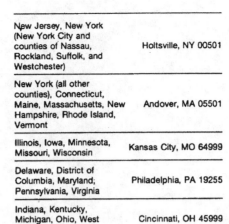

New Jersey, New York (New York City and counties of Nassau, Rockland, Suffolk, and Westchester)	Holtsville, NY 00501
New York (all other counties), Connecticut, Maine, Massachusetts, New Hampshire, Rhode Island, Vermont	Andover, MA 05501
Illinois, Iowa, Minnesota, Missouri, Wisconsin	Kansas City, MO 64999
Delaware, District of Columbia, Maryland, Pennsylvania, Virginia	Philadelphia, PA 19255
Indiana, Kentucky, Michigan, Ohio, West Virginia	Cincinnati, OH 45999
Kansas, New Mexico, Oklahoma, Texas	Austin, TX 73301
Alaska, Arizona, California (counties of Alpine, Amador, Butte, Calaveras, Colusa, Contra Costa, Del Norte, El Dorado, Glenn, Humboldt, Lake, Lassen, Marin, Mendocino, Modoc, Napa, Nevada, Placer, Plumas, Sacramento, San Joaquin, Shasta, Sierra, Siskiyou, Solano, Sonoma, Sutter, Tehama, Trinity, Yolo, and Yuba), Colorado, Idaho, Montana, Nebraska, Nevada, North Dakota, Oregon, South Dakota, Utah, Washington, Wyoming	Ogden, UT 84201
California (all other counties), Hawaii	Fresno, CA 93888
Alabama, Arkansas, Louisiana, Mississippi, North Carolina, Tennessee	Memphis, TN 37501

Paying the Tax

The estate and GST taxes are due within 9 months after the date of the decedent's death unless an extension of time for payment has been granted, or unless you have properly elected under section 6166 to pay in installments, or under section 6163 to postpone the part of the tax attributable to a reversionary or remainder interest. These elections are made by checking lines 3 and 4 (respectively) of Part 3, Elections by the Executor, and attaching the required statements.

If the tax paid with the return is different from the balance due as figured on the return, explain the difference in an attached statement. If you have made prior payments to IRS or redeemed certain marketable United States Treasury bonds to pay the estate tax (see the last paragraph of the instructions to Schedule B), attach a statement to Form 706 including these facts. If an extension of time to pay has been granted, attach a copy of the approved Form 4768 to Form 706.

Make the check payable to the Internal Revenue Service. Please write the decedent's name, social security number, and "Form 706" on the check to assist us in posting it to the proper account.

Signature and Verification

If there is more than one executor, all listed executors must verify and sign the return. All executors are responsible for the return as filed and are liable for penalties provided for erroneous or false returns.

If two or more persons are liable for filing the return, they should all join together in filing one complete return. However, if they are unable to join in making one complete return, each is required to file a return disclosing all the information the person has in the case, including the name of every person holding an interest in the property and a full description of the property. If the appointed, qualified, and acting executor is unable to make a complete return, then every person holding an interest in the property must, on notice from the IRS, make a return regarding that interest.

The executor who files the return must, in every case, sign the declaration on page 1 under penalties of perjury. If the return is prepared by someone other than the person who is filing the return, the preparer must also sign at the bottom of page 1.

Part 1

Line 2

Enter the social security number assigned specifically to the decedent. You cannot use the social security number assigned to the decedent's spouse. If the decedent did not have a social security number, the executor should obtain one for the decedent by filing **Form SS-5** with a local Social Security Administration office.

Line 6a—Name of Executor

If there is more than one executor, enter the name of the executor to be contacted by the IRS. List the other executors' names, addresses, and SSNs (if applicable) on an attached sheet.

Line 6b—Executor's Address

Use **Form 8822,** Change of Address, to report a change of the executor's address.

Line 6c—Executor's Social Security Number

Only individual executors should complete this line. If there is more than one individual executor, all should list their social security numbers on an attached sheet.

Supplemental Documents

You must attach the death certificate to the return.

If the decedent was a citizen or resident and died testate, attach a certified copy of the will to the return. Other supplemental documents may be required as explained below. Examples include Forms 712, 709, 709-A, and 706CE, trust and power of appointment instruments, death certificate, and state certification of payment of death taxes. If you do not file these documents

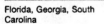

Florida, Georgia, South Carolina   Atlanta, GA 39901

with the return, the processing of the return will be delayed.

If the decedent was a U.S. citizen but not a resident of the United States, you must attach the following documents to the return: (1) a copy of the inventory of property and the schedule of liabilities, claims against the estate, and expenses of administration filed with the foreign court of probate jurisdiction, certified by a proper official of the court; (2) a copy of the return filed under the foreign inheritance, estate, legacy, succession tax, or other death tax act, certified by a proper official of the foreign tax department, if the estate is subject to such a foreign tax; and (3) if the decedent died testate, a certified copy of the will.

Rounding Off to Whole Dollars

You may show the money items on the return and accompanying schedules as whole-dollar amounts. To do so, drop any amount less than 50 cents and increase any amount from 50 cents through 99 cents to the next higher dollar.

Penalties

Section 6651 provides for penalties for both late filing and for late payment unless there is reasonable cause for the delay. The law also provides for penalties for willful attempts to evade payment of tax. The late filing penalty will not be imposed if the taxpayer can show that the failure to file a timely return is due to reasonable cause. Executors filing late (after the due date, including extensions) should attach an explanation to the return to show reasonable cause.

Section 6662 provides a penalty for the underpayment of estate tax of $5,000 or more when the underpayment is attributable to valuation understatements. A valuation understatement occurs when the value of property reported on Form 706 is 50 percent or less of the actual value of the property.

These penalties also apply to late filing, late payment, and underpayment of GST taxes.

Publication 448

Additional information may be found in Pub. 448, Federal Estate and Gift Taxes.

Specific Instructions

You must file the first three pages of Form 706 and all required schedules. Schedules A through I must be filed, as appropriate, to support the entries in items 1 through 9 of the Recapitulation.

If you enter zero on any item of the Recapitulation, you need not file the schedule (except for Schedule F) referred to on that item.

If you claim any deductions on items 11 through 19 of the Recapitulation, you must complete and attach the appropriate

Schedule(s) to support the claimed deductions.

If you claim the credits for foreign death taxes or tax on prior transfers, you must complete and attach Schedule P or Q.

Form 706 has 41 numbered pages. The pages are perforated so that you can remove them for copying and filing. When you complete the return, staple all the required pages together in the proper order.

Number the items you list on each schedule, beginning with 1 each time. Total the items listed on the schedule and its attachments, Continuation Schedules, etc. Enter the total of all attachments, Continuation Schedules, etc., at the bottom of the printed schedule, but do not carry the totals forward from one schedule to the next. Enter the total or totals for each schedule on the Recapitulation, page 3, Form 706.

Do not complete the "Alternate valuation date" or "Alternate value" columns of any schedule unless you elected alternate valuation on line 1 of Part 3, Elections by the Executor.

If there is not enough space on a schedule to list all the items, attach a Continuation Schedule (or additional sheets of the same size) to the back of the schedule. The Continuation Schedule is located at the end of the Form 706 package. You should photocopy the blank schedule before completing it if you will need more than one copy.

Instructions for Part 3.— Elections by the Executor

Line 1—Alternate Valuation

Unless you elect at the time you file the return to adopt alternate valuation as authorized by section 2032, you must value all property included in the gross estate on the date of the decedent's death. Alternate valuation cannot be applied to only a part of the property. You may elect special use valuation (line 2) in addition to alternate valuation.

You may not elect alternate valuation unless the election will decrease both the value of the gross estate and the total net estate and GST taxes due after application of all allowable credits.

Alternate valuation is elected by checking "Yes" on line 1 and filing Form 706. Once made, the election may not be revoked. The election may be made on a late filed Form 706 provided it is not filed later than 1 year after the due date (including extensions).

If you elect alternate valuation, value the property that is included in the gross estate as of the applicable dates as follows:

1. Any property distributed, sold, exchanged, or otherwise disposed of or separated or passed from the gross estate by any method within 6 months after the decedent's death is valued on the date of distribution, sale, exchange, or other disposition, whichever occurs first. Value

this property on the date it ceases to form a part of the gross estate, that is, on the date the title passes as the result of its sale, exchange, or other disposition.

2. Any property not distributed, sold, exchanged, or otherwise disposed of within the 6-month period is valued on the date 6 months after the date of the decedent's death.

3. Any property, interest, or estate that is "affected by mere lapse of time" is valued as of the date of decedent's death or on the date of its distribution, sale, exchange, or other disposition, whichever occurs first. However, you may change the date of death value to account for any change in value that is not due to a "mere lapse of time" on the date of its distribution, sale, exchange, or other disposition.

The property included in the alternate valuation and valued as of 6 months after the date of the decedent's death, or as of some intermediate date (as described above) is the property included in the gross estate on the date of the decedent's death. Therefore, you must first determine what property constituted the gross estate at the decedent's death.

Interest accrued to the date of the decedent's death on bonds, notes, and other interest-bearing obligations is property of the gross estate on the date of death and is included in the alternate valuation. Rent accrued to the date of the decedent's death on leased real or personal property is property of the gross estate on the date of death and is included in the alternate valuation.

Outstanding dividends that were declared to stockholders of record on or before the date of the decedent's death are considered property of the gross estate on the date of death, and are included in the alternate valuation. Ordinary dividends declared to stockholders of record after the date of the decedent's death are not property of the gross estate on the date of death and are not included in the alternate valuation. However, if dividends are declared to stockholders of record after the date of the decedent's death so that the shares of stock at the later valuation date do not reasonably represent the same property at the date of the decedent's death, include those dividends (except dividends paid from earnings of the corporation after the date of the decedent's death) in the alternate valuation.

As part of each Schedule A through I, you must show: (1) what property is included in the gross estate on the date of the decedent's death; (2) what property was distributed, sold, exchanged, or otherwise disposed of within the 6-month period after the decedent's death, and the dates of these distributions, etc. These two items should be entered in the "Description" column of each schedule. Briefly explain the status or disposition governing the alternate valuation date, such as: "Not disposed of within 6 months following death," "Distributed," "Sold," "Bond paid on maturity," etc. In this same column, describe each item of principal

and includible income; **(3)** the date of death value, entered in the appropriate value column with items of principal and includible income shown separately; and **(4)** the alternate value, entered in the appropriate value column with items of principal and includible income shown separately. In the case of any interest or estate, the value of which is affected by lapse of time, such as patents, leaseholds, estates for the life of another, or remainder interests, the value shown under the heading "Alternate value" must be the adjusted value (i.e., value as of the date of death with an adjustment reflecting any difference in its value as of the later date not due to lapse of time).

Distributions, sales, exchanges, and other dispositions of the property within the 6-month period after the decedent's death must be supported by evidence. If the court issued an order of distribution during that period, you must submit a certified copy of the order as part of the evidence. The District Director may require you to submit additional evidence if necessary.

Line 2—Special Use Valuation of Section 2032A

Under section 2032A, you may elect to value certain farm and closely held business real property at its farm or business use value rather than its fair market value. You may elect both special use valuation and alternate valuation. To elect this valuation you must check "Yes" to line 2 and complete and attach Schedule A-1 and its required additional statements. **You must file Schedule A-1 and its required attachments with Form 706 for this election to be valid.** You may make the election on a late filed return so long as it is the first return filed.

The total value of the property valued under section 2032A may not be decreased from fair market value by more than $750,000.

Real property may qualify for the section 2032A election if:

1. The decedent was a U.S. citizen or resident at the time of death;

2. The real property is located in the United States;

3. At the decedent's death the real property was used by the decedent or a family member for farming or in a trade or business or is rented for such use by the surviving spouse to a family member on a net cash basis;

4. The real property was acquired from or passed from the decedent to a qualified heir of the decedent;

5. The real property was owned and used in a qualified manner by the decedent or a member of the decedent's family during 5 of the 8 years before the decedent's death;

6. There was material participation by the decedent or a member of the decedent's family during 5 of the 8 years before the decedent's death; and

7. The qualified property is the percentage of the decedent's gross estate specified in section 2032A.

For definitions and additional information, see section 2032A and the related regulations.

Include the words "section 2032A valuation" in the "Description" column of any Form 706 schedule if section 2032A property is included in the decedent's gross estate.

An election under section 2032A need not include all the property in an estate that is eligible for special use valuation, but sufficient property to satisfy the threshold requirements of section 2032A(b)(1)(B) must be specially valued under the election.

If joint or undivided interests (e.g., interests as joint tenants or tenants in common) in the same property are received from a decedent by qualified heirs, an election with respect to one heir's joint or undivided interest need not include any other heir's interest in the same property if the electing heir's interest plus other property to be specially valued satisfies the requirements of section 2032A(b)(1)(B).

If successive interests (e.g., life estates and remainder interests) are created by a decedent in otherwise qualified property, an election under section 2032A is available only with respect to that property (or part) in which qualified heirs of the decedent receive all of the successive interests, and such an election must include the interests of all of those heirs.

For example, if a surviving spouse receives a life estate in otherwise qualified property and the spouse's brother receives a remainder interest in fee, no part of the property may be valued pursuant to an election under section 2032A.

Where successive interests in specially valued property are created, remainder interests are treated as being received by qualified heirs only if the remainder interests are not contingent on surviving a nonfamily member or are not subject to divestment in favor of a nonfamily member.

Protective Election.—You may make a protective election to specially value qualified real property. Under this election, whether or not you may ultimately use special use valuation depends upon values as finally determined (or agreed to following examination of the return) meeting the requirements of section 2032A.

To make a protective election, check "Yes" to line 2 and complete Schedule A-1 according to its instructions for "Protective Election."

If you make a protective election, you should complete this Form 706 by valuing all property at its fair market value. Do not use special use valuation. Usually, this will result in higher estate and GST tax liabilities than will be ultimately determined if special use valuation is allowed. **The protective election does not extend the time to pay the taxes shown on the return.** If you wish to extend the time to

pay the taxes, you should file Form 4768 in adequate time *before* the return due date.

If it is found that the estate qualifies for special use valuation based on the values as finally determined (or agreed to following examination of the return), you must file an amended Form 706 (with a complete section 2032A election) within 60 days after the date of this determination. Complete the amended return using special use values under the rules of section 2032A, and complete Schedule A-1 and attach *all* of the required statements.

Line 3—Installment Payments

If you check this line to make a protective election, you should attach a notice of protective election as described in Regulations section 20.6166-1(d). If you check this line to make a final election, you should attach the notice of election described in Regulations section 20.6166-1(b).

In computing the adjusted gross estate under section 6166(b)(6) to determine whether an election may be made under section 6166, the net amount of any real estate in a closely held business must be used.

You may also elect to pay GST taxes in installments. See section 6166(i).

Line 4—Reversionary or Remainder Interests

For the details of this election, see section 6163 and the related regulations.

Instructions for Part 4.— General Information (pages 2 and 3)

Power of Attorney

Completing the authorization on page 2 of Form 706 will authorize one attorney, accountant, or enrolled agent to represent the estate and receive confidential tax information, but will not authorize the representative to enter into closing agreements for the estate. **If you wish to represent the estate, you must complete and sign the authorization.**

If you wish to authorize persons other than attorneys, accountants, and enrolled agents, or if you wish to authorize more than one person, to receive confidential information or represent the estate, you must complete and attach **Form 2848,** Power of Attorney and Declaration of Representative.

You must also complete and attach Form 2848 if you wish to authorize someone to enter into closing agreements for the estate.

If you wish only to authorize someone to inspect and/or receive confidential tax information (but not to represent you before the IRS), you must complete and file **Form 8821,** Tax Information Authorization.

Line 4

Complete line 4 whether or not there is a surviving spouse and whether or not the surviving spouse received any benefits from the estate. If there was no surviving spouse on the date of decedent's death, enter "None" in line 4a and leave lines 4b and 4c blank. The value entered in line 4c need not be exact. See the instructions for "Amount," under line 5, below.

Line 5

Name.—Enter the name of each individual, trust, or estate who received (or will receive) benefits of $5,000 or more from the estate directly as an heir, next-of-kin, devisee, or legatee; or indirectly (for example, as beneficiary of an annuity or insurance policy, shareholder of a corporation, or partner of a partnership that is an heir, etc.).

Identifying Number.—Enter the social security number of each individual beneficiary listed. If the number is unknown, or the individual has no number, please indicate "unknown" or "none." For trusts and other estates, enter the employer identification number.

Relationship.—For each individual beneficiary enter the relationship (if known) to the decedent by reason of blood, marriage, or adoption. For trust or estate beneficiaries, indicate TRUST or ESTATE.

Amount.—Enter the amount actually distributed (or to be distributed) to each beneficiary including transfers during the decedent's life from Schedule G required to be included in the gross estate. The value to be entered need not be exact. A reasonable estimate is sufficient. For example, where precise values cannot readily be determined, as with certain future interests, a reasonable approximation should be entered. The total of these distributions should approximate the amount of gross estate reduced by funeral and administrative expenses, debts and mortgages, bequests to surviving spouse, charitable bequests, and any Federal and state estate and GST taxes paid (or payable) relating to the benefits received by the beneficiaries listed on lines 4 and 5.

All distributions of less than $5,000 to specific beneficiaries may be included with distributions to unascertainable beneficiaries on the line provided.

Line 6—Section 2044 Property

If you answered "Yes," these assets must be shown on Schedule F.

Section 2044 property is property for which a previous section 2056(b)(7) election (QTIP election) has been made, or for which a similar gift tax election (section 2523) has been made. For more details see Pub. 448.

Line 8—Insurance Not Included in the Gross Estate

If you checked "Yes" for either 8a or 8b, you must complete and attach Schedule D and attach a **Form 712**, Life Insurance

Statement, for each policy and an explanation of why the policy or its proceeds are not includible in the gross estate.

Line 10—Partnership Interests and Stock in Close Corporations

If you answered "Yes" to line 10, you must include full details for partnerships and unincorporated businesses on Schedule F (Schedule E if the partnership interest is jointly owned). You must include full details for the stock of inactive or close corporations on Schedule B.

Value these interests using the rules of Regulations section 20.2031-2 (stocks) or 20.2031-3 (other business interests).

A "close corporation" is a corporation whose shares are owned by a limited number of shareholders. Often, one family holds the entire stock issue. As a result, little, if any, trading of the stock takes place. There is, therefore, no established market for the stock, and those sales that do occur are at irregular intervals and seldom reflect all the elements of a representative transaction as defined by the term "fair market value."

Line 12—Trusts

If you answered "Yes" to either 12a or 12b, you must attach a copy of the trust instrument for each trust.

You must complete Schedule G if you answered "Yes" to 12a and Schedule F if you answered "Yes" to 12b.

Line 14—Transitional Marital Deduction Computation

You must check "Yes" if property passes to the surviving spouse under a maximum marital deduction formula provision that meets the requirements of section 403(e)(3) of the Economic Recovery Tax Act of 1981 (P. L. 97-34; 95 Stat. 305).

If you check "Yes" to line 14, you must compute the marital deduction under the rules that were in effect before the Economic Recovery Tax Act of 1981.

For a format for this computation, you should obtain the November 1981 revision of Form 706 and its instructions. The computation is items 19 through 26 of the Recapitulation. You should also apply the rules of Rev. Rul. 80-148, 1980-1 C.B. 207, if there is property that passes to the surviving spouse outside of the maximum marital deduction formula provision.

Line 16—Excess Retirement Accumulation

If the decedent did not have any interest in a qualified employer plan or individual retirement plan (defined in section 7701(a)(37)), check "No" to this question.

Note: *The tax on excess retirement accumulations will not apply to most decedents because the present value of the hypothetical annuity is usually so large that very few decedents will have a larger total interest in qualified plans and individual retirement plans. The rules below are a general description of the section*

4980A(d) excess retirement accumulation. If it appears, after reading these rules, that there is the possibility of such an excess, see the instructions for Schedule S on page 20 for more information.

A "qualified plan" means any:

1. Qualified pension, profit-sharing, or stock bonus plan described in section 401(a) that includes a trust exempt from tax under section 501(a);

2. Annuity plan described in section 403(a);

3. Annuity contract, custodial account, or retirement income account described in section 403(b)(1), 403(b)(7), or 403(b)(9);

4. Qualified bond purchase plan described in section 405(a) prior to that section's repeal by section 491(a) of the Tax Reform Act of 1984.

To determine if the decedent had an excess retirement accumulation, you must first total all of the decedent's interests (as of the date of death) in qualified plans and individual retirement plans. Then determine the present (date of death or alternate valuation date) value of a hypothetical life annuity for the decedent. This hypothetical life annuity must pay the decedent the greater of $150,000 (unindexed) or $112,500 (indexed) per year, times the multiplier described in the instructions for line 3, Part III, of Schedule S. Those instructions are on page 21.

If the decedent's total interest in the plans is greater than the value of this hypothetical annuity, then there is an excess retirement accumulation, and you should check "Yes" to question 16 and attach Schedule S to your return.

Instructions for Part 5.— Recapitulation (Page 3 of Form 706)

Gross Estate

Items 1 through 9.—You must make an entry in each of items 1 through 9. If the gross estate does not contain any assets of the type specified by a given item, enter zero for that item. Entering zero for any of items 1 through 9 is a statement by the executor, made under penalties of perjury, that the gross estate does not contain any includible assets covered by that item. Do not enter any amounts in the "Alternate value" column unless you elected alternate valuation on line 1 of Elections by the Executor on page 2.

Which Schedules To Attach for Items 1 Through 9.—You must attach Schedule F to the return and answer its questions even if you report no assets on it.

You must attach Schedules A, B, and C if the gross estate includes any Real Estate; Stocks and Bonds; or Mortgages, Notes, and Cash, respectively. You must attach Schedule D if the gross estate includes any Life Insurance or if you answered "Yes" to question 8a. You must attach Schedule E if the gross estate contains any Jointly Owned Property or if you answered "Yes" to question 9. You must attach Schedule G if the decedent

made any of the lifetime transfers to be listed on that schedule or if you answered "Yes" to question 11 or 12a. You must attach Schedule H if you answered "Yes" to question 13. You must attach Schedule I if you answered "Yes" to question 15.

Deductions

Items 11 Through 19.—You must attach the appropriate schedules for the deductions you claim.

Item 15.—If item 14 is less than or equal to the value (at the time of the decedent's death) of the property subject to claims, enter the amount from item 14 on item 15.

If the amount on item 14 is more than the value of the property subject to claims, enter the greater of (a) the value of the property subject to claims, or (b) the amount actually paid at the time the return is filed.

In no event should you enter more on item 15 than the amount on item 14. See section 2053 and the related regulations for more information.

Instructions for Part 2.—Tax Computation (Page 1 of Form 706)

In general, the estate tax is figured by applying the unified rates shown in Table A to the total of transfers both during life and at death, and then subtracting the gift taxes. **You must complete the Tax Computation.**

Line 1

If you elected alternate valuation on line 1, Part 3, **Elections by the Executor,** enter the amount you entered in the "Alternate value" column of item 10 of Part 5, Recapitulation. Otherwise, enter the amount from the "Value at date of death" column.

Lines 4 and 9

Three worksheets are provided to help you compute the entries for these lines. You need not file these worksheets with your return but should keep them for your records. Worksheet TG allows you to reconcile the decedent's lifetime taxable gifts to compute totals that will be used for the line 4 and line 9 worksheets. You must get all of the decedent's gift tax returns (**Form 709,** United States Gift (and Generation-Skipping Transfer) Tax Return) before you complete Worksheet TG. The amounts you will enter on Worksheet TG can usually be derived from these returns as filed. However, if any of the returns were audited by the IRS, you should use the amounts that were finally determined as a result of the audits.

Special Treatment of Split Gifts.—These special rules apply only if:

1. The decedent's spouse predeceased the decedent;

2. The decedent's spouse made gifts that were "split" with the decedent under the rules of section 2513;

3. The decedent was the "consenting spouse" for those split gifts, as that term is used on Form 709; and

4. The split gifts were included in the decedent's spouse's gross estate under section 2035.

If all four conditions above are met, *do not include* these gifts on line 4 of the Tax Computation and *do not include* the gift taxes payable on these gifts on line 9 of the Tax Computation. These adjustments are incorporated into the worksheets.

Line 7

Lines 7a–c are used to calculate the phaseout of the unified credit and graduated rates. The phaseout applies only to estates in which the amount the tentative tax is computed on exceeds $10 million.

Line 12

If the decedent made gifts (including gifts made by the decedent's spouse and treated as made by the decedent by reason of gift splitting) after September 8, 1976, and before January 1, 1977, for which the decedent claimed a specific exemption, the unified credit on this estate tax return must be reduced. The reduction is figured by entering 20% of the specific exemption claimed for these gifts. (**Note:**

The specific exemption was allowed by section 2521 for gifts made before January 1, 1977.)

If the decedent did not make any gifts between September 8, 1976, and January 1, 1977, or if the decedent made gifts during that period but did not claim the specific exemption, enter zero.

Line 15

You may take a credit on line 15 for estate, inheritance, legacy, or succession taxes paid as the result of the decedent's death to any state or the District of Columbia. However, see section 2053(d) and the related regulations for exceptions and limits if you elected to deduct the taxes from the value of the gross estate.

If you make a section 6166 election to pay the Federal estate tax in installments and make a similar election to pay the state death tax in installments, see Rev. Rul. 86-38, 1986-1 C.B. 296, for the method of computing the credit allowed with this Form 706.

The credit may not be more than the amount figured by using Table B on page 9, based on the value of the adjusted taxable estate. The adjusted taxable estate is the amount of the Federal taxable estate (line 3 of the Tax Computation) reduced by $60,000. You may claim an anticipated amount of credit and figure the Federal estate tax on the return before the state death taxes have been paid. However, the credit cannot be finally allowed unless you pay the state death taxes and claim the credit within 4 years after the return is filed (or later as provided by the Code if a petition is filed with the Tax Court of the United States, or if you have an extension of time to pay) and submit evidence that the tax has been paid. If you claim the credit for any state death tax that is later recovered, see Regulations section 20.2016-1 for the notice you are required to give the IRS within 30 days.

If you transfer property other than cash to the state in payment of state inheritance taxes, the amount you may claim as credit is the lesser of the state inheritance tax liability discharged or the fair market value of the property on the date of the transfer.

Worksheet TG   Taxable Gifts Reconciliation
To be used for lines 4 and 9 of the Tax Computation

	a. Calendar year or calendar quarter	b. Total taxable gifts reported on Form 709 for period (see Note)	Note: *For the definition of a taxable gift see section 2503. Ignore the old specific exemption. Follow Form 709. That is, include only the decedent's one-half of split gifts, whether the gifts were made by the decedent or the decedent's spouse.*			
Gifts made after June 6, 1932, and before 1977			c. Taxable amount included in col. b for gifts included in the gross estate	d. Taxable amount included in col. b for gifts that qualify for "special treatment of split gifts" described above	e. Gift tax paid by decedent on gifts in col. d	f. Gift tax paid by decedent's spouse on gifts in col. c
	1. Total taxable gifts made before 1977					
Gifts made after 1976						
	2. Totals for gifts made after 1976					

Line 4 Worksheet   Adjusted Taxable Gifts Made After 1976

1. Taxable gifts made after 1976. Enter the amount from line 2, column b, Worksheet TG . . . . . .
2. Taxable gifts made after 1976 reportable on Schedule G. Enter the amount from line 2, column c, Worksheet TG . . . .
3. Taxable gifts made after 1976 that qualify for "special treatment." Enter the amount from line 2, column d, Worksheet TG . . . .
4. Add lines 2 and 3 . . . .
5. Adjusted taxable gifts. Subtract line 4 from line 1. Enter here and on line 4 of the Tax Computation of Form 706 . . . .

Line 9 Worksheet Gift Tax on Gifts Made After 1976

a. Calendar year or calendar quarter Total pre-1977 taxable gifts. Enter the amount from line 1, Worksheet TG	b. Total taxable gifts for prior periods (from Form 709, Tax Computation, line 2)	c. Taxable gifts for this period (from Form 709, Tax Computation, line 1)	d. Tax payable using Table A (on page 9)	e. Unused unified credit for this period (see below)	f. Tax payable for this period (subtract col. e from col. d)

1. Total gift taxes payable on gifts made after 1976 (combine the amounts in column f) . . . . . .

2. Gift taxes paid by the decedent on gifts that qualify for "special treatment." Enter the amount from line 2, column e, Worksheet TG on page 7 . . . .

3. Subtract line 2 from line 1 . . . .

4. Gift tax paid by decedent's spouse on split gifts included on Schedule G. Enter the amount from line 2, column f, Worksheet TG on page 7 . . . .

5. Add lines 3 and 4. Enter here and on line 9 of the Tax Computation of Form 706 . . . .

Column d: To figure the "tax payable" for this column, you must use Table A in these instructions, *as it applies to the year of the decedent's death rather than to the year the gifts were actually made.* To compute the entry for col. d, you should figure the "tax payable" on the amount in col. b and subtract it from the "tax payable" on the amounts in cols. b and c added together. Enter the difference in col. d.

If the amount in columns b and c combined exceeds $10 million *for any given calendar year,* then you must calculate the tax in column d for that year using the Form 709 revision in effect for the *year of the decedent's death.*

To calculate the tax, enter the amount for the appropriate year from column c of the worksheet on line 1 of the Tax Computation of the Form 709. Enter the amount from column b on line 2 of the Tax Computation. Complete the Tax Computation through the tax due before any reduction for the unified credit and enter that amount in column d, above.

Column e: To figure the unused unified credit, use the unified credit in effect for the year the gift was made. This amount should be on line 12 of the Tax Computation of the Form 709 filed for the gift.

For more details, see Rev. Rul. 86-117, 1986-2 C.B. 157.

You should send the following evidence to the IRS:

1. Certificate of the proper officer of the taxing state, or the District of Columbia, showing: (a) the total amount of tax imposed (before adding interest and penalties and before allowing discount); (b) the amount of discount allowed; (c) the amount of penalties and interest imposed or charged; (d) the total amount actually paid in cash; and (e) the date of payment.

2. Any additional proof the IRS specifically requests.

You should file the evidence requested above with the return if possible. Otherwise, send it as soon after you file the return as possible.

Line 17

You may take a credit for Federal gift taxes imposed by Chapter 12 of the Code, and the corresponding provisions of prior laws, on certain transfers the decedent made before January 1, 1977, that are included in the gross estate. The credit cannot be more than the amount figured by the following formula:

$$\frac{\text{Gross estate tax minus (the sum of the state death taxes and unified credit)}}{\text{Value of gross estate minus (the sum of the deductions for charitable, public, and similar gifts and bequests and marital deduction)}} \times \text{Value of included gift}$$

For more information, see the regulations under section 2012. This computation may be made using **Form 4808,** Computation of Credit for Gift Tax. Attach a copy of a completed Form 4808 or the computation of the credit. Also attach all available copies of Forms 709 filed by the decedent to help verify the amounts entered on lines 4, 9, and 17.

Line 23

If you answered "Yes" to question 16 of General Information, you must complete Schedule S. Enter the tax due from line 17 of Schedule S on line 23. This increased estate tax may not be offset by any of the estate tax credits on lines 11–19.

Line 26

You may not use these bonds to pay the GST tax. You may use these bonds to pay the increased estate tax shown on line 23.

Instructions for Schedule A.—Real Estate

See the reverse side of Schedule A on Form 706.

Instructions for Schedule B.—Stocks and Bonds

General

If the total gross estate contains any stocks or bonds, you must complete Schedule B and file it with the return.

On Schedule B list the stocks and bonds included in the decedent's gross estate. Number each item in the left-hand column. **Bonds that are exempt from Federal income taxes are not exempt from estate taxes unless specifically exempted by an estate tax provision of the Code.** Therefore, you should list these bonds on Schedule B.

Public housing bonds includible in the gross estate must be included at their full value.

If you paid any estate, inheritance, legacy, or succession tax to a foreign country on any stocks or bonds included

(continued on page 10)

Table A—Unified Rate Schedule

Column A — Taxable amount over	Column B — Taxable amount not over	Column C — Tax on amount in column A	Column D — Rate of tax on excess over amount in column A
			(Percent)
0	$10,000	0	18
$10,000	20,000	$1,800	20
20,000	40,000	3,800	22
40,000	60,000	8,200	24
60,000	80,000	13,000	26
80,000	100,000	18,200	28
100,000	150,000	23,800	30
150,000	250,000	38,800	32
250,000	500,000	70,800	34
500,000	750,000	155,800	37
750,000	1,000,000	248,300	39
1,000,000	1,250,000	345,800	41
1,250,000	1,500,000	448,300	43
1,500,000	2,000,000	555,800	45
2,000,000	2,500,000	780,800	49
2,500,000	3,000,000	1,025,800	53
3,000,000	----------	1,290,800	55

Table B Worksheet

Federal Adjusted Taxable Estate

1	Federal taxable estate (from Tax Computation, Form 706, line 3)	$_____
2	Adjustment	60,000
3	Federal adjusted taxable estate. Subtract line 2 from line 1. Use this amount to compute maximum credit for state death taxes in Table B.	_____

Table B

Computation of Maximum Credit for State Death Taxes
(Based on Federal adjusted taxable estate computed using the worksheet above.)

(1) Adjusted taxable estate equal to or more than—	(2) Adjusted taxable estate less than—	(3) Credit on amount in column (1)	(4) Rate of credit on excess over amount in column (1)	(1) Adjusted taxable estate equal to or more than—	(2) Adjusted taxable estate less than—	(3) Credit on amount in column (1)	(4) Rate of credit on excess over amount in column (1)
			(Percent)				(Percent)
0	$40,000	0	None	2,040,000	2,540,000	106,800	8.0
$40,000	90,000	0	0.8	2,540,000	3,040,000	146,800	8.8
90,000	140,000	$400	1.6	3,040,000	3,540,000	190,800	9.6
140,000	240,000	1,200	2.4	3,540,000	4,040,000	238,800	10.4
240,000	440,000	3,600	3.2	4,040,000	5,040,000	290,800	11.2
440,000	640,000	10,000	4.0	5,040,000	6,040,000	402,800	12.0
640,000	840,000	18,000	4.8	6,040,000	7,040,000	522,800	12.8
840,000	1,040,000	27,600	5.6	7,040,000	8,040,000	650,800	13.6
1,040,000	1,540,000	38,800	6.4	8,040,000	9,040,000	786,800	14.4
1,540,000	2,040,000	70,800	7.2	9,040,000	10,040,000	930,800	15.2
				10,040,000	----------	1,082,800	16.0

Examples showing use of Schedule B
Example where the alternate valuation is not adopted; date of death, January 1, 1993

Item number	Description including face amount of bonds or number of shares and par value where needed for identification. Give CUSIP number if available.	Unit value	Alternate valuation date	Alternate value	Value at date of death
1	$60,000-Arkansas Railroad Co. first mortgage 4%, 20-year bonds, due 1995. Interest payable quarterly on Feb. 1, May 1, Aug. 1 and Nov. 1; N.Y. Exchange, CUSIP No. XXXXXXXXX	100	----------	----------	60,000
	Interest coupons attached to bonds, item 1, due and payable on Nov. 1, 1992, but not cashed at date of death	----------	----------	----------	600
	Interest accrued on item 1, from Nov. 1, 1992, to Jan. 1, 1993 . .	----------	----------	----------	400
2	500 shares Public Service Corp., common; N.Y. Exchange, CUSIP No. XXXXXXXXX	110	----------	----------	55,000
	Dividend on item 2 of $2 per share declared Dec. 10, 1992, payable on Jan. 10, 1993, to holders of record on Dec. 30, 1992	----------	----------	----------	1,000

Example where the alternate valuation is adopted; date of death, January 1, 1993

Item number	Description including face amount of bonds or number of shares and par value where needed for identification. Give CUSIP number if available.	Unit value	Alternate valuation date	Alternate value	Value at date of death
1	$60,000-Arkansas Railroad Co. first mortgage 4%, 20-year bonds, due 1995. Interest payable quarterly on Feb. 1, May 1, Aug. 1 and Nov. 1; N.Y. Exchange, CUSIP No. XXXXXXXXX	100	....	....	60,000
	$30,000 of item 1 distributed to legatees on Apr. 1, 1993 . . .	99	4/1/93	29,700	....
	$30,000 of item 1 sold by executor on May 2, 1993	98	5/2/93	29,400	....
	Interest coupons attached to bonds, item 1, due and payable on Nov. 1, 1992, but not cashed at date of death. Cashed by executor on Feb. 1, 1993	....	2/1/93	600	600
	Interest accrued on item 1, from Nov. 1, 1992, to Jan. 1, 1993. Cashed by executor on Feb. 1, 1993	....	2/1/93	400	400
2	500 shares of Public Service Corp., common; N.Y. Exchange, CUSIP No. XXXXXXXXX	110	....	....	55,000
	Not disposed of within 6 months following death	90	7/1/93	45,000	....
	Dividend on item 2 of $2 per share declared Dec. 10, 1992, and paid on Jan. 10, 1993, to holders of record on Dec. 30, 1992	....	1/10/93	1,000	1,000

(Continued from page 8)

in this schedule, group those stocks and bonds together and label them "Subjected to Foreign Death Taxes."

List interest and dividends on each stock or bond separately. Indicate as a separate item dividends that have not been collected at death, but which are payable to the decedent or the estate because the decedent was a stockholder of record on the date of death. However, if the stock is being traded on an exchange and is selling ex-dividend on the date of the decedent's death, do not include the amount of the dividend as a separate item. Instead, add it to the ex-dividend quotation in determining the fair market value of the stock on the date of the decedent's death. Dividends declared on shares of stock before the death of the decedent but payable to stockholders of record on a date after the decedent's death are not includible in the gross estate for Federal estate tax purposes.

Description

For stocks indicate:
- Number of shares
- Whether common or preferred
- Issue
- Par value where needed for identification
- Price per share
- Exact name of corporation
- Principal exchange upon which sold, if listed on an exchange
- CUSIP number, if available

For bonds indicate:
- Quantity and denomination
- Name of obligor
- Date of maturity
- Interest rate
- Interest due date
- Principal exchange, if listed on an exchange
- CUSIP number, if available

If the stock or bond is unlisted, show the company's principal business office.

The CUSIP (Committee on Uniform Security Identification Procedure) number is a nine-digit number that is assigned to all stocks and bonds traded on major exchanges and many unlisted securities. Usually, the CUSIP number is printed on the face of the stock certificate. If the CUSIP number is not printed on the certificate, it may be obtained through the company's transfer agent.

Valuation

List the fair market value of the stocks or bonds. The fair market value of a stock or bond (whether listed or unlisted) is the mean between the highest and lowest selling prices quoted on the valuation date. If only the closing selling prices are available, then the fair market value is the mean between the quoted closing selling price on the valuation date and on the trading day before the valuation date. To figure the fair market value if there were no sales on the valuation date:

1. Find the mean between the highest and lowest selling prices on the nearest trading date before and the nearest trading date after the valuation date. Both trading dates must be reasonably close to the valuation date.

2. Prorate the difference between the mean prices to the valuation date.

3. Add or subtract (whichever applies) the prorated part of the difference to or from the mean price figured for the nearest trading date before the valuation date.

If no actual sales were made reasonably close to the valuation date, make the same computation using the mean between the bona fide bid and asked prices instead of sales prices. If actual sales prices or bona fide bid and asked prices are available within a reasonable period of time before the valuation date but not after the valuation date, or vice versa, use the mean between the highest and lowest sales

prices or bid and asked prices as the fair market value.

For example, assume that sales of stock nearest the valuation date (June 15) occurred 2 trading days before (June 13) and 3 trading days after (June 18). On those days the mean sale prices per share were $10 and $15, respectively. Therefore, the price of $12 is considered the fair market value of a share of stock on the valuation date. If, however, on June 13 and 18, the mean sale prices per share were $15 and $10, respectively, the fair market value of a share of stock on the valuation date is $13.

If only closing prices for bonds are available, see Regulations section 20.2031-2(b).

Apply the rules in the section 2031 regulations to determine the value of inactive stock and stock in close corporations. Send with the schedule complete financial and other data used to determine value, including balance sheets (particularly the one nearest the valuation date) and statements of the net earnings or operating results and dividends paid for each of the 5 years immediately before the valuation date.

Securities reported as of no value, nominal value, or obsolete should be listed last. Include the address of the company and the state and date of the incorporation. Attach copies of correspondence or statements used to determine the "no value."

If the security was listed on more than one stock exchange, use either the records of the exchange where the security is principally traded or the composite listing of combined exchanges, if available, in a publication of general circulation. In valuing listed stocks and bonds, you should carefully check accurate records to obtain values for the applicable valuation date.

If you get quotations from brokers, or evidence of the sale of securities from the officers of the issuing companies, attach to the schedule copies of the letters

furnishing these quotations or evidence of sale.

See Rev. Rul. 69-489, 1969-2 C.B. 172, for the special valuation rules for certain marketable U.S. Treasury Bonds (issued before March 4, 1971). These bonds, commonly called "flower bonds," may be redeemed at par plus accrued interest in payment of the tax at any Federal Reserve bank, the office of the Treasurer of the United States, or the Bureau of the Public Debt, as explained in Rev. Proc. 69-18, 1969-2 C.B. 300.

Instructions for Schedule D.—Insurance on the Decedent's Life

See the reverse side of Schedule D on Form 706.

Instructions for Schedule E.—Jointly Owned Property

See the reverse side of Schedule E on Form 706.

Instructions for Schedule F.—Other Miscellaneous Property

See the reverse side of Schedule F on Form 706.

Instructions for Schedule G.—Transfers During Decedent's Life

You must complete Schedule G and file it with the return if the decedent made any of the transfers described below in **1** through **5** or if you answered "Yes" on line 11 or 12a of Part 4, General Information.

Five types of transfers should be reported on this schedule:

1. *Certain gift taxes.—Section 2035(c).* Enter at item A of the Schedule the total value of the gift taxes that were paid by the decedent or the estate on gifts made by the decedent or the decedent's spouse within 3 years before death.

The date of the gift, not the date of payment of the gift tax, determines whether a gift tax paid is included in the gross estate under this rule. Therefore, you should carefully examine the Forms 709 filed by the decedent and the decedent's spouse to determine what part of the total gift taxes reported on them was attributable to gifts made within 3 years before death. For example, if the decedent died on July 10, 1993, you should examine gift tax returns for 1993, 1992, 1991, and 1990. However, the gift taxes on the 1990 returns that are attributable to gifts made before July 10, 1990, are not included in the gross estate.

Attach an explanation of how you computed the includible gift taxes if you do not include in the gross estate the entire gift taxes shown on any Form 709 filed within 3 years of death. Also attach copies

of any pertinent gift tax returns filed by the decedent's spouse within 3 years of death.

2. *Other transfers within 3 years before death.—Section 2035(a).* These transfers include *only* the following:

● Any transfer by the decedent with respect to a life insurance policy within 3 years before death.

● Any transfer within 3 years before death of a retained section 2036 life estate, section 2037 reversionary interest, or section 2038 power to revoke, etc., if the property subject to the life estate, interest, or power would have been included in the gross estate had the decedent continued to possess the life estate, interest, or power until death.

These transfers are reported on Schedule G regardless of whether a gift tax return was required to be filed for them when they were made. However, the amount includible and the information required to be shown for the transfers are determined:

● For insurance on the life of the decedent using the instructions to Schedule D. (Attach Form(s) 712.)

● For insurance on the life of another using the instructions to Schedule F. (Attach Form(s) 712.)

● For sections 2036, 2037, and 2038 transfers, using paragraphs *3, 4,* and *5* of these instructions.

3. *Transfers with retained life estate (section 2036).—*These are transfers in which the decedent retained the income from the transferred property or the right to designate the person or persons who will possess or enjoy the transferred property, or the income from the transferred property if the transfer was made:

(a) Between March 4, 1931, and June 6, 1932, inclusive, and the decedent alone retained the right to so designate for life, or for any period that did not in fact end before the decedent's death; or

(b) After June 6, 1932, and the decedent retained the right to so designate, either alone or with any person, for life, for any period that must be ascertained by reference to the decedent's death, or for any period that did not in fact end before the decedent's death.

Retained Voting Rights. Transfers with a retained life estate also include transfers of stock in a "controlled corporation" after June 22, 1976, if the decedent retained or acquired voting rights in the stock. If the decedent retained direct or indirect voting rights in a controlled corporation, the decedent is considered to have retained enjoyment of the transferred property. A corporation is a "controlled corporation" if the decedent owned (actually or constructively) or had the right (either alone or with any other person) to vote at least 20% of the total combined voting power of all classes of stock. See section 2036(b). If these voting rights ceased or were relinquished within 3 years before the decedent's death, the corporate interests are included in the gross estate as if the decedent had actually retained the voting rights until death.

4. *Transfers taking effect at death (section 2037).—*These are transfers made on or after September 8, 1916, that took effect at the decedent's death. A transfer that takes effect at the decedent's death is one under which possession or enjoyment can be obtained only by surviving the decedent. A transfer is not treated as one that takes effect at the decedent's death unless the decedent retained a reversionary interest in the property that immediately before the decedent's death had a value of more than 5% of the value of the transferred property. If the transfer was made before October 8, 1949, the reversionary interest must have arisen by the express terms of the instrument of transfer.

5. *Revocable transfers (section 2038).—*These are transfers in which the enjoyment of the transferred property was subject at decedent's death to any change through the exercise of a power to alter, amend, revoke, or terminate, as follows:

● If the transfer was made before 4:01 p.m., eastern standard time, June 2, 1924, and the power was reserved at the time of the transfer and was exercisable by the decedent alone or with a person who had no substantial adverse interest in the transferred property.

● If the transfer was made on or after 4:01 p.m., eastern standard time, June 2, 1924, and before June 23, 1936, and the power was reserved at the time of the transfer and was exercisable by the decedent alone or with any person (regardless of whether that person had a substantial adverse interest in the transferred property), or

● If the transfer was made after June 22, 1936, regardless of whether the power was reserved at the time of the transfer or later created or conferred, regardless of the source from which the power was acquired, regardless of whether the power was exercisable by the decedent alone or with any person, and regardless of whether that person had a substantial adverse interest in the transferred property.

● If the decedent relinquished within 3 years before death any of the includible powers described above, you should determine the gross estate as if the decedent had actually retained the powers until death.

For more detailed information on which transfers are includible in the gross estate, see the Estate Tax Regulations.

Special Valuation Rules for Certain Lifetime Transfers

Note: *Code sections 2701–2704 were enacted by the Omnibus Budget Reconciliation Act of 1990. These sections provide rules for valuing certain transfers to family members and are generally effective for transfers occurring after October 8, 1990.*

Section 2701 deals with the transfer of an interest in a corporation or partnership while retaining certain distribution rights, or a liquidation, put, call, or conversion right.

Section 2702 deals with the transfer of an interest in a trust while retaining any interest other than a qualified interest. In general, a qualified interest is a right to receive certain distributions from the trust at least annually, or a noncontingent remainder interest if all of the other interests in the trust are distribution rights specified in section 2702.

Section 2703 provides rules for the valuation of property transferred to a family member but subject to an option, agreement, or other right to acquire or use the property at less than fair market value. It also applies to transfers subject to restrictions on the right to sell or use the property.

Finally, section 2704 provides that in certain cases the lapse of a voting or liquidation right in a family-owned corporation or partnership will result in a deemed transfer.

These rules have potential consequenses for the valuation of property in an estate. If the decedent (or any member of his or her family) was involved in any such transactions, see Code sections 2701–2704 for additional details.

How To Complete Schedule G

All transfers (other than outright transfers not in trust and bona fide sales) made by the decedent at any time during life must be reported on the Schedule regardless of whether you believe the transfers are subject to tax. If the decedent made any transfers not described in the instructions on page 11, the transfers should not be shown on Schedule G. Instead, attach a statement describing these transfers: list the date of the transfer, the amount or value, and the type of transfer.

Complete the schedule for each transfer that is included in the gross estate under sections 2035(a), 2036, 2037, and 2038 as described on page 11.

In the "Item number" column, number each transfer consecutively beginning with 1. In the "Description" column, list the name of the transferee, the date of the transfer, and give a complete description of the property. Transfers included in the gross estate should be valued on the date of the decedent's death or, if the alternate valuation is adopted, according to section 2032.

If only part of the property transferred meets the terms of section 2035(a), 2036, 2037, or 2038, then only a corresponding part of the value of the property should be included in the value of the gross estate. If the transferee makes additions or improvements to the property, the increased value of the property at the valuation date should not be included on Schedule G. However, if only a part of the value of the property is included, enter the value of the whole under the column headed "Description" and explain what part was included.

Attachments.—If a transfer, by trust or otherwise, was made by a written instrument, attach a copy of the instrument

to the Schedule. If of public record, the copy should be certified; if not of record, the copy should be verified.

Instructions for Schedule H.—Powers of Appointment

You must complete Schedule H and file it with the return if you answered "Yes" to line 13 of Part 4, General Information.

On Schedule H include in the gross estate:

1. The value of property for which the decedent possessed a general power of appointment on the date of his or her death; and

2. The value of property for which the decedent possessed a general power of appointment which he or she exercised or released before death by disposing of it in such a way that if it were a transfer of property owned by the decedent, the property would be includible in the decedent's gross estate. (See section 2041 and Pub. 448 for more details.)

Powers of Appointment

A power of appointment includes all powers which are in substance and effect powers of appointment regardless of how they are identified and regardless of local property laws. For example, if a settlor transfers property in trust for the life of his wife, with a power in the wife to appropriate or consume the principal of the trust, the wife has a power of appointment.

General Power of Appointment.—A general power of appointment is a power that is exercisable in favor of the decedent, the decedent's estate, the decedent's creditors, or the creditors of the decedent's estate, except:

1. A power to consume, invade, or appropriate property for the benefit of the decedent that is limited by an ascertainable standard relating to health, education, support, or maintenance of the decedent.

2. A power created on or before October 21, 1942, that is exercisable by the decedent only in conjunction with another person.

3. A power created after October 21, 1942, exercisable by the decedent only in conjunction with (a) the creator of the power, or (b) a person who has a substantial interest in the property subject to the power, which is adverse to the exercise of the power in favor of the decedent.

A part of a power created after October 21, 1942, is considered a general power of appointment if the power:

1. May only be exercised by the decedent in conjunction with another person; and

2. Is also exercisable in favor of the other person (in addition to being exercisable in favor of the decedent, the decedent's creditors, the decedent's estate, or the creditors of the decedent's estate).

The part to include in the gross estate as a general power of appointment is figured by dividing the value of the property by the number of persons (including the decedent) in favor of whom the power is exercisable.

Date Power Was Created.—Generally, a power of appointment created by will is considered created on the date of the testator's death. However, a power of appointment created by a will executed on or before October 21, 1942, is considered a power created on or before that date if the person executing the will died before July 1, 1949, without having republished the will, by codicil or otherwise, after October 21, 1942.

A power of appointment created by an inter vivos instrument is considered created on the date the instrument takes effect. If the holder of a power exercises it by creating a second power, the second power is considered as created at the time of the exercise of the first.

Attachments

If the decedent ever possessed a power of appointment, attach a certified or verified copy of the instrument granting the power and a certified or verified copy of any instrument by which the power was exercised or released. You must file these copies even if you contend that the power was not a general power of appointment, and that the property is not otherwise includible in the gross estate.

Instructions for Schedule I.—Annuities

You must complete Schedule I and file it with the return if you answered "Yes" to question 15 of Part 4, General Information. Enter on Schedule I every annuity that meets all of conditions 1–4 under **General,** below, and every annuity described in paragraphs **a–h** of **Annuities Under Approved Plans,** even if the annuities are wholly or partially excluded from the gross estate.

See the instructions for line 3 of Schedule M for a discussion regarding the QTIP treatment of certain joint and survivor annuities.

General

Except as otherwise provided under **Annuities Under Approved Plans** on page 13, include in the gross estate on this schedule all or part of the value of an annuity receivable by any beneficiary following the death of the decedent under a contract or agreement that satisfies all four conditions below:

1. The contract or agreement is not a policy of insurance on the life of the decedent;

2. The contract or agreement was entered into after March 3, 1931;

3. The annuity is receivable by the beneficiary because he or she survived the decedent; and

4. Under the contract or agreement, an annuity was payable to the decedent (or

the decedent possessed the right to receive the annuity) either alone or in conjunction with another, for the decedent's life or for any period not ascertainable without reference to the decedent's death or for any period that did not in fact end before the decedent's death.

Part Includible.—If the decedent contributed only part of the purchase price of the contract or agreement, include in the gross estate only that part of the value of the annuity receivable by the surviving beneficiary that the decedent's contribution to the purchase price of the annuity or agreement bears to the total purchase price. For example, if the value of the survivor's annuity was $20,000 and the decedent had contributed three-fourths of the purchase price of the contract, the amount includible is $15,000 (¾ × $20,000). Except as provided under **Annuities Under Approved Plans,** contributions made by the decedent's employer to the purchase price of the contract or agreement are considered made by the decedent if they were made by the employer because of the decedent's employment. For more information, see section 2039.

"Annuity" Defined.—The term "annuity" includes one or more payments extending over any period of time. The payments may be equal or unequal, conditional or unconditional, periodic or sporadic. The following are examples of contracts (but not necessarily the only forms of contracts) for annuities that must be included in the gross estate:

1. A contract under which the decedent immediately before death was receiving or was entitled to receive, for the duration of life, an annuity with payments to continue after death to a designated beneficiary, if surviving the decedent;

2. A contract under which the decedent immediately before death was receiving or was entitled to receive, together with another person, an annuity payable to the decedent and the other person for their joint lives, with payments to continue to the survivor following the death of either;

3. A contract or agreement entered into by the decedent and employer under which the decedent immediately before death and following retirement was receiving, or was entitled to receive, an annuity payable to the decedent for life and after the decedent's death to a designated beneficiary, if surviving the decedent, whether the payments after the decedent's death are fixed by the contract or subject to an option or election exercised or exercisable by the decedent. However, see **Annuities Under Approved Plans,** below;

4. A contract or agreement entered into by the decedent and employer under which at the decedent's death, before retirement or before the expiration of a stated period of time, an annuity was payable to a designated beneficiary, if surviving the decedent. However, see **Annuities Under Approved Plans,** below;

5. A contract or agreement under which the decedent immediately before death was receiving, or was entitled to receive, an annuity for a stated period of time, with the annuity to continue to a designated beneficiary, surviving the decedent, upon the decedent's death before the expiration of that period of time;

6. An annuity contract or other arrangement providing for a series of substantially equal periodic payments to be made to a beneficiary for life or over a period of at least 36 months after the date of the decedent's death under an individual retirement account, annuity, or bond as described in section 2039(e) (before its repeal by P.L. 98-369).

Annuities Under Approved Plans.—The statute allowing an exclusion for annuities under approved plans has been repealed. However, under the special rules provided for the annuities described in a–h below, it may be possible to exclude part or all of the value of these annuities from the gross estate.

No exclusion is allowed for annuities under approved plans unless either condition **1** or **2** below is met:

1. On December 31, 1984, the decedent was both a participant in the plan and in pay status (i.e., had received at least one benefit payment on or before December 31, 1984), and the decedent irrevocably elected the form of the benefit before July 18, 1984; or

2. The decedent separated from service before January 1, 1985, and did not change the form of benefit before death.

If either of the above conditions is met, an exclusion is allowed. The exclusion may not exceed $100,000 unless either of the two additional conditions below is met:

1. On December 31, 1982, the decedent was both a participant in the plan and in pay status (i.e., had received at least one benefit payment on or before December 31, 1982), and the decedent irrevocably elected the form of the benefit before January 1, 1983; or

2. The decedent separated from service before January 1, 1983, and did not change the form of benefit before death.

If either of the above conditions is met, the exclusion is not subject to the $100,000 limitation.

Approved Plans:

a. An employees' trust (or under a contract purchased by an employees' trust) forming part of a pension, stock bonus, or profit-sharing plan that met all the requirements of section 401(a), either at the time of the decedent's separation from employment (whether by death or otherwise) or at the time of the termination of the plan (if earlier);

b. A retirement annuity contract purchased by the employer (but not by an employees' trust) under a plan that, at the time of the decedent's separation from employment (by death or otherwise), or at the time of the termination of the plan (if earlier), was a plan described in section 403(a);

c. A retirement annuity contract purchased for an employee by an employer that is an organization referred to in section 170(b)(1)(A)(ii) or (vi), or that is a religious organization (other than a trust), and that is exempt from tax under section 501(a);

d. Chapter 73 of Title 10 of the United States Code;

e. A bond purchase plan described in section 405 (before its repeal by P.L. 98-369, effective for obligations issued after December 31, 1983.)

If an annuity under an "approved plan" described in **a–e** above is receivable by a beneficiary other than the executor and the decedent made no contributions under the plan toward the cost, no part of the value of the annuity, subject to the $100,000 limitation (if applicable), is includible in the gross estate. If the decedent made a contribution under a plan described in **a–e** above toward the cost, include in the gross estate on this schedule that proportion of the value of the annuity which the amount of the decedent's contribution under the plan bears to the total amount of all contributions under the plan. The remaining value of the annuity is excludable from the gross estate subject to the $100,000 limitation (if applicable). For the rules to determine whether the decedent made contributions to the plan, see Pub. 448.

Note: *The accounts, annuities, and bonds described in f–h, below, are "approved plans" only if they provide for a series of substantially equal periodic payments to be made to a beneficiary for life, or over a period of at least 36 months after the date of the decedent's death.*

f. An individual retirement account described in section 408(a);

g. An individual retirement annuity described in section 408(b);

h. A retirement bond described in section 409(a)(before its repeal by P.L. 98-369).

Subject to the $100,000 limitation, if applicable, if an annuity under a "plan" described in **f–h** above is receivable by a beneficiary other than the executor, the entire value of the annuity is excludable from the gross estate even if the decedent made a contribution under the plan. However, if any payment to or for an account or annuity described in paragraph **f, g,** or **h** above was not allowable as an income tax deduction under section 219 (and was not a rollover contribution as described in section 2039(e) before its repeal by P.L. 98-369), include in the gross estate on this schedule that proportion of the value of the annuity which the amount not allowable as a deduction under section 219 and not a rollover contribution bears to the total amount paid to or for such account or annuity. For more information, see Regulations section 20.2039-5.

If any part of an annuity under a "plan" described in **a–h** above is receivable by the executor, it is generally includible in the gross estate on this schedule to the extent that it is receivable by the executor in that

capacity. In general, the annuity is receivable by the executor if it is to be paid to the executor or if there is an agreement (expressed or implied) that it will be applied by the beneficiary for the benefit of the estate (such as in discharge of the estate's liability for death taxes or debts of the decedent, etc.) or that its distribution will be governed to any extent by the terms of the decedent's will or the laws of descent and distribution.

If data available to you does not indicate whether the plan satisfies the requirements of section 401(a), 403(a), 408(a), 408(b), or 409(a), you may obtain that information from the District Director of Internal Revenue for the district where the employer's principal place of business is located.

Line A—Lump Sum Distribution Election

The election pertaining to the lump sum distribution from qualified plans (approved plans) excludes from the gross estate all or part of the lump sum distribution that would otherwise be includible. When the recipient makes the election to take a lump sum distribution and include it in his or her income tax, the amount excluded from the gross estate is the portion attributable to the employer contributions. The portion, if any, attributable to the employee-decedent's contributions is always includible. The actual election is made by the recipient of the distribution by taking the lump sum distribution and by treating it as taxable on his or her income tax return as described in Regulations section 20.2039-4(d). The election is irrevocable. However, you may not compute the gross estate in accordance with this election unless you check "Yes" to line A and attach the name, address, and identifying number of the recipients of the lump sum distributions. See Regulations section 20.2039-4.

How To Complete the Schedule

In describing an annuity, give the name and address of the grantor of the annuity. Specify if the annuity is under an approved plan. If it is under an approved plan, you must state the ratio of the decedent's contribution to the total purchase price of the annuity. If the decedent was employed at the time of death and an annuity as described in paragraph 4 of **Annuity Defined,** on page 13, became payable to any beneficiary because the beneficiary survived the decedent, you must state the ratio of the decedent's contribution to the total purchase price of the annuity. If an annuity under an individual retirement account or annuity became payable to any beneficiary because that beneficiary survived the decedent and is payable to the beneficiary for life or for at least 36 months following the decedent's death, you must state the ratio of the amount paid for the individual retirement account or annuity that was not allowable as an income tax deduction under section 219 (other than a rollover contribution) to the total amount paid for the account or annuity. If the annuity is payable out of a

trust or other fund, the description should be sufficiently complete to fully identify it. If the annuity is payable for a term of years, include the duration of the term and the date on which it began, and if payable for the life of a person other than the decedent, include the date of birth of that person. If the annuity is wholly or partially excluded from the gross estate, enter the amount excluded under "Description" and explain how you computed the exclusion.

Instructions for Schedule J.—Funeral Expenses and Expenses Incurred in Administering Property Subject to Claims

See the reverse side of Schedule J on Form 706.

Instructions for Schedule K.—Debts of the Decedent and Mortgages and Liens

You must complete and attach Schedule K if you claimed deductions on either item 12 or item 13 of Part 5, Recapitulation.

Debts of the Decedent

List under "Debts of the Decedent" only valid debts the decedent owed at the time of death. List any indebtedness secured by a mortgage or other lien on property of the gross estate under the heading "Mortgages and Liens." If the amount of the debt is disputed or the subject of litigation, deduct only the amount the estate concedes to be a valid claim. Enter the amount in contest in the column provided.

Generally, if the claim against the estate is based on a promise or agreement, the deduction is limited to the extent that the liability was contracted bona fide and for an adequate and full consideration in money or money's worth. However, any enforceable claim based on a promise or agreement of the decedent to make a contribution or gift (such as a pledge or a subscription) to or for the use of a charitable, public, religious, etc., organization is deductible to the extent that the deduction would be allowed as a bequest under the statute that applies.

Certain claims of a former spouse against the estate based on the relinquishment of marital rights are deductible on Schedule K. For these claims to be deductible, all of the following conditions must be met:

● The decedent and the decedent's spouse must have entered into a written agreement relative to their marital and property rights.

● The decedent and the spouse must have been divorced before the decedent's death and the divorce must have occurred within the 3-year period beginning on the date 1 year before the agreement was entered into. It is not required that the agreement be approved by the divorce decree.

● The property or interest transferred under the agreement must be transferred

to the decedent's spouse in settlement of the spouse's marital rights.

You may not deduct a claim made against the estate by a remainderman relating to section 2044 property. Section 2044 property is described in the instructions to line 6 of Part 4, General Information.

Include in this schedule notes unsecured by mortgage or other lien and give full details, including name of payee, face and unpaid balance, date and term of note, interest rate, and date to which interest was paid before death. Include the exact nature of the claim as well as the name of the creditor. If the claim is for services performed over a period of time, state the period covered by the claim. Example: Edison Electric Illuminating Co., for electric service during December 1992, $150.

If the amount of the claim is the unpaid balance due on a contract for the purchase of any property included in the gross estate, indicate the schedule and item number where you reported the property. If the claim represents a joint and separate liability, give full facts and explain the financial responsibility of the co-obligor.

Property and Income Taxes.—The deduction for property taxes is limited to the taxes accrued before the date of the decedent's death. Federal taxes on income received during the decedent's lifetime are deductible, but taxes on income received after death are not deductible.

Keep all vouchers or original records for inspection by the Internal Revenue Service.

Allowable Death Taxes.—If you elect to take a deduction under section 2053(d) rather than a credit under section 2011 or section 2014, the deduction is subject to the limitations described in section 2053(d) and its regulations. If you have difficulty figuring the deduction, you may request a computation of it. Send your request within a reasonable amount of time before the due date of the return to the Commissioner of Internal Revenue, Washington, DC 20224. Attach to your request a copy of the will and relevant documents, a statement showing the distribution of the estate under the decedent's will, and a computation of the state or foreign death tax showing the amount payable by charity.

Mortgages and Liens

List under "Mortgages and Liens" only obligations secured by mortgages or other liens on property that you included in the gross estate at its full value or at a value that was undiminished by the amount of the mortgage or lien. If the debt is enforceable against other property of the estate not subject to the mortgage or lien, or if the decedent was personally liable for the debt, you must include the full value of the property subject to the mortgage or lien in the gross estate under the appropriate schedule and may deduct the mortgage or lien on the property on this schedule. However, if the decedent's estate is not liable, include in the gross estate only the value of the equity of

redemption (or the value of the property less the amount of the debt), and do not deduct any portion of the indebtedness on this schedule.

Notes and other obligations secured by the deposit of collateral, such as stocks, bonds, etc., also should be listed under "Mortgages and Liens."

Description

Include under the "Description" column the particular schedule and item number where the property subject to the mortgage or lien is reported in the gross estate.

Include the name and address of the mortgagee, payee, or obligee, and the date and term of the mortgage, note, or other agreement by which the debt was established. Also include the face amount, the unpaid balance, the rate of interest, and date to which the interest was paid before the decedent's death.

Instructions for Schedule L.—Net Losses During Administration and Expenses Incurred in Administering Property Not Subject to Claims

You must complete Schedule L and file it with the return if you claim deductions on either item 16 or item 17 of Part 5, Recapitulation.

Net Losses During Administration

You may deduct only those losses from thefts, fires, storms, shipwrecks, or other casualties that occurred during the settlement of the estate. You may deduct only the amount not reimbursed by insurance or otherwise.

Describe in detail the loss sustained and the cause. If you received insurance or other compensation for the loss, state the amount collected. Identify the property for which you are claiming the loss by indicating the particular schedule and item number where the property is included in the gross estate.

If you elect alternate valuation, do not deduct the amount by which you reduced the value of an item to include it in the gross estate.

Do not deduct losses claimed as a deduction on a Federal income tax return or depreciation in the value of securities or other property.

Expenses Incurred in Administering Property Not Subject to Claims

You may deduct expenses incurred in administering property that is included in the gross estate but that is not subject to claims. You may only deduct these expenses if they were paid before the section 6501 period of limitations for assessment expired.

The expenses deductible on the schedule are usually expenses incurred in the administration of a trust established by the decedent before death. They may also be incurred in the collection of other assets or the transfer or clearance of title to other property included in the decedent's gross estate for estate tax purposes, but not included in the decedent's probate estate. The expenses deductible on this schedule are limited to those that are the result of settling the decedent's interest in the property or of vesting good title to the property in the beneficiaries. Expenses incurred on behalf of the transferees (except those described above) are not deductible. Examples of deductible and nondeductible expenses are provided in Regulations section 20.2053-8.

List the names and addresses of the persons to whom each expense was payable and the nature of the expense. Identify the property for which the expense was incurred by indicating the schedule and item number where the property is included in the gross estate. If you do not know the exact amount of the expense, you may deduct an estimate, provided that the amount may be verified with reasonable certainty and will be paid before the period of limitations for assessment (referred to above) expires. Keep all vouchers and receipts for inspection by the Internal Revenue Service.

Instructions for Schedule M.—Bequests, etc. to Surviving Spouse (Marital Deduction)

See pages 28 through 30 of Form 706 for these instructions.

Instructions for Schedule O.—Charitable, Public, and Similar Gifts and Bequests

General

You must complete Schedule O and file it with the return if you claim a deduction on item 19 of the Recapitulation.

You can claim the charitable deduction allowed under section 2055 for the value of property in the decedent's estate that was transferred by the decedent during life or by will to a charitable institution as explained in Pub. 448.

The deduction is limited to the amount actually available for charitable uses. Therefore, if under the terms of a will or the provisions of local law, or for any other reason, the Federal estate tax, the Federal GST tax, or any other estate, GST, succession, legacy, or inheritance tax is payable in whole or in part out of any bequest, legacy, or devise that would otherwise be allowed as a charitable deduction, the amount you may deduct is the amount of the bequest, legacy, or devise reduced by the total amount of the taxes.

For split-interest trusts (or pooled income funds) enter in the "Amount" column the amount treated as passing to the charity. Do not enter the entire amount that passes to the trust (fund).

If you are deducting the value of the residue or a part of the residue passing to charity under the decedent's will, attach a copy of the computation showing how you determined the value, including any reduction for the taxes described above.

Also include:

1. A statement that shows the values of all specific and general legacies or devises for both charitable and noncharitable uses. For each legacy or devise, indicate the paragraph or section of the decedent's will or codicil that applies. (If legacies are made to each member of a class (e.g., $1,000 to each of the decedent's employees), show only the number of each class and the total value of property they received.)

2. The date of birth of all life tenants or annuitants, the length of whose lives may affect the value of the interest passing to charity under the decedent's will.

3. A statement showing the value of all property that is included in the decedent's gross estate but does not pass under the will, such as transfers, jointly owned property that passed to the survivor on decedent's death, and insurance payable to specific beneficiaries.

4. Any other important information such as that relating to any claim, not arising under the will, to any part of the estate (e.g., a spouse claiming dower or curtesy, or similar rights).

Line 2

The charitable deduction is allowed for amounts that are transferred to charitable organizations as a result of a qualified disclaimer. To be a qualified disclaimer, a refusal to accept an interest in property must meet the conditions of section 2518. These are explained in Pub. 448 and Regulations sections 25.2518-1 through 25.2518-3. If property passes to a charitable beneficiary as the result of a qualified disclaimer, check the "Yes" box on line 2 and attach a copy of the written disclaimer required by section 2518(b).

Attachments

If the charitable transfer was made by will, attach a certified copy of the order admitting the will to probate, in addition to the copy of the will. If the charitable transfer was made by any other written instrument, attach a copy. If the instrument is of record, the copy should be certified; if not, the copy should be verified.

Value

The valuation dates used in determining the value of the gross estate apply also on Schedule O.

Instructions for Schedule P.—Credit for Foreign Death Taxes

General

If you claim a credit on line 18 of Part 2, Tax Computation, you must complete Schedule P and file it with the return. **You must attach Form(s) 706CE, Certificate of Payment of Foreign Death Tax, to support any credit you claim.**

The credit for foreign death taxes is allowable only if the decedent was a citizen or resident of the United States. However, see section 2053(d) and the related regulations for exceptions and limitations if the executor has elected, in certain cases, to deduct these taxes from the value of the gross estate. For a resident, not a citizen, who was a citizen or subject of a foreign country for which the President has issued a proclamation under section 2014(h), the credit is allowable only if the country of which the decedent was a national allows a similar credit to decedents who were U.S. citizens residing in that country.

The credit is authorized either by statute or by treaty. If a credit is authorized by a treaty, whichever of the following is the most beneficial to the estate is allowed: **(a)** the credit computed under the treaty; **(b)** the credit computed under the statute; or **(c)** the credit computed under the treaty, plus the credit computed under the statute for death taxes paid to each political subdivision or possession of the treaty country that are not directly or indirectly creditable under the treaty. Under the statute, the credit is authorized for all death taxes (national and local) imposed in the foreign country. Whether local taxes are the basis for a credit under a treaty depends upon the provisions of the particular treaty.

If a credit for death taxes paid in more than one foreign country is allowable, a separate computation of the credit must be made for each foreign country. The copies of Schedule P on which the additional computations are made should be attached to the copy of Schedule P provided in the return.

The total credit allowable in respect to any property, whether subjected to tax by one or more than one foreign country, is limited to the amount of the Federal estate tax attributable to the property. The anticipated amount of the credit may be computed on the return, but the credit cannot finally be allowed until the foreign tax has been paid and a Form 706CE evidencing payment is filed. Section 2014(g) provides that for credits for foreign death taxes, each U.S. possession is deemed a foreign country.

If a credit is claimed for any foreign death tax that is later recovered, see Regulations section 20.2016-1 for the notice required within 30 days.

Credit Under the Statute

For the credit allowed by the statute, the question of whether particular property is situated in the foreign country imposing the tax is determined by the same principles that would apply in determining whether similar property of a nonresident not a U.S. citizen is situated within the United States for purposes of the Federal estate tax. See the instructions for Form 706-NA.

Computation of Credit Under the Statute

Item 1.—Enter the amount of the estate, inheritance, legacy, and succession taxes paid to the foreign country and its possessions or political subdivisions, attributable to property that is **(a)** situated in that country, **(b)** subjected to these taxes, and **(c)** included in the gross estate. The amount entered at item 1 should not include any tax paid to the foreign country with respect to property not situated in that country and should not include any tax paid to the foreign country with respect to property not included in the gross estate. If only a part of the property subjected to foreign taxes is both situated in the foreign country and included in the gross estate, it will be necessary to determine the portion of the taxes attributable to that part of the property. Also attach the computation of the amount entered at item 1.

Item 2.—Enter the value of the gross estate less the total of the deductions on items 18 and 19 of Part 5, Recapitulation.

Item 3.—Enter the value of the property situated in the foreign country that is subjected to the foreign taxes and included in the gross estate, less those portions of the deductions taken on Schedules M and O that are attributable to the property.

Item 4.—Subtract line 17, Part 2, Form 706 from line 16, Part 2, Form 706, and enter the balance at item 4 of Schedule P.

Credit Under Treaties

If you are reporting any items on this return based on the provisions of a death tax treaty, you may have to attach a statement to this return disclosing the return position that is treaty based. See Regulations section 301.6114-1 for details.

In General.—If the provisions of a treaty apply to the estate of a U.S. citizen or resident, a credit is authorized for payment of the foreign death tax or taxes specified in the treaty. Death tax conventions are in effect with the following countries: Australia, Austria, Denmark, Germany, Finland, France, Greece, Ireland, Italy, Japan, Netherlands, Norway, Republic of South Africa, Sweden, Switzerland, and the United Kingdom.

A credit claimed under a treaty is in general computed on Schedule P in the same manner as the credit is computed under the statute with the following principal exceptions: **(a)** the situs rules contained in the treaty apply in determining whether property was situated in the foreign country; **(b)** the credit may be allowed only for payment of the death tax or taxes specified in the treaty (but see the instructions above for credit under the statute for death taxes paid to each political subdivision or possession of the treaty country that are not directly or indirectly creditable under the treaty); **(c)** if specifically provided, the credit is proportionately shared for the tax applicable to property situated outside both countries, or that was deemed in some instances situated within both countries; and **(d)** the amount entered at item 4 of Schedule P is the amount shown on line 16 of Part 2, Tax Computation, less the total of the amounts on lines 17 and 19 of the Tax Computation. (If a credit is claimed for tax on prior transfers, it will be necessary to complete Schedule Q before completing Schedule P.) For examples of computation of credits under the treaties, see the applicable regulations.

Computation of Credit in Cases Where Property Is Situated Outside Both Countries or Deemed Situated Within Both Countries.—See the appropriate treaty for details.

Instructions for Schedule Q.—Credit for Tax on Prior Transfers

General

You must complete Schedule Q and file it with the return if you claim a credit on line 19 of Part 2, Tax Computation.

The term "transferee" means the decedent for whose estate this return is filed. If the transferee received property from a transferor who died within 10 years before, or 2 years after, the transferee, a credit is allowable on this return for all or part of the Federal estate tax paid by the transferor's estate with respect to the transfer. There is no requirement that the property be identified in the estate of the transferee or that it exist on the date of the transferee's death. It is sufficient for the allowance of the credit that the transfer of the property was subjected to Federal estate tax in the estate of the transferor and that the specified period of time has not elapsed. A credit may be allowed with respect to property received as the result of the exercise or nonexercise of a power of appointment when the property is included in the gross estate of the donee of the power.

If the transferee was the transferor's surviving spouse, no credit is allowed for property received from the transferor to the extent that a marital deduction was allowed to the transferor's estate for the property. There is no credit for tax on prior transfers for Federal gift taxes paid in connection with the transfer of the property to the transferee.

If you are claiming a credit for tax on prior transfers on Form 706-NA, you should first complete and attach the Recapitulation from Form 706 before computing the credit on Schedule Q from Form 706.

Section 2056(d)(3) contains specific rules for allowing a credit for certain transfers to a spouse who was not a U.S. citizen where

the property passed outright to the spouse, or to a "qualified domestic trust."

Property

The term "property" includes any interest (legal or equitable) of which the transferee received the beneficial ownership. The transferee is considered the beneficial owner of property over which the transferee received a general power of appointment. Property does not include interests to which the transferee received only a bare legal title, such as that of a trustee. Neither does it include an interest in property over which the transferee received a power of appointment that is not a general power of appointment. In addition to interests in which the transferee received the complete ownership, the credit may be allowed for annuities, life estates, terms for years, remainder interests (whether contingent or vested), and any other interest that is less than the complete ownership of the property, to the extent that the transferee became the beneficial owner of the interest.

Maximum Amount of the Credit

The maximum amount of the credit is the smaller of:

1. The amount of the estate tax of the transferor's estate attributable to the transferred property, or

2. The amount by which **(a)** an estate tax on the transferee's estate determined without the credit for tax on prior transfers, exceeds **(b)** an estate tax on the transferee's estate determined by excluding from the gross estate the net value of the transfer. If credit for a particular foreign death tax may be taken under either the statute or a death duty convention, and on this return the credit actually is taken under the convention, then no credit for that foreign death tax may be taken into consideration in computing estate tax **(a)** or estate tax **(b)**.

Percent Allowable

Where Transferee Predeceased the Transferor.—If not more than 2 years elapsed between the dates of death, the credit allowed is 100% of the maximum amount. If more than 2 years elapsed between the dates of death, no credit is allowed.

Where Transferor Predeceased the Transferee.—The percent of the maximum amount that is allowed as a credit depends on the number of years that elapsed between dates of death. It is determined using the following table:

Period of Time Exceeding	Not Exceeding	Percent Allowable
- - - - -	2 years	100
2 years	4 years	80
4 years	6 years	60
6 years	8 years	40
8 years	10 years	20
10 years	- - - - -	none

How To Compute the Credit

A worksheet is provided on the last page of these instructions to allow you to compute the limits before completing Schedule Q. Transfer the appropriate amounts from the worksheet to Schedule Q as indicated on the schedule. You do not need to file the worksheet with your Form 706, but should keep it for your records.

Cases Involving Transfers From Two or More Transferors.—Part I of the worksheet and Schedule Q enable you to compute the credit for as many as three transferors. The number of transferors is irrelevant to Part II of the worksheet. If you are computing the credit for more than three transferors, use more than one worksheet and Schedule Q, Part I, and combine the totals for the appropriate lines.

Section 2032A Additional Tax.—If the *transferor's* estate elected special use valuation and the additional estate tax of section 2032A(c) was imposed at any time up to 2 years after the death of the *decedent for whom you are filing this return,* check the box on Schedule Q. On lines 1 and 9 of the worksheet, include the property subject to the additional estate tax at its fair market value rather than its special use value. On line 10 of the worksheet, include the additional estate tax paid as a Federal estate tax paid.

How To Complete the Worksheet

Most of the information to complete Part I of the worksheet should be obtained from the transferor's Form 706.

Line 5.—Enter on line 5 the applicable marital deduction claimed for the transferor's estate (from the transferor's Form 706).

Lines 10-18.—Enter on these lines the appropriate taxes paid by the transferor's estate.

If the transferor's estate elected to pay the Federal estate tax in installments, enter on line 10 only the total of the installments that have actually been paid at the time you file this Form 706. See Rev. Rul. 83-15, 1983-1 C.B. 224, for more details. Do not include as estate tax any tax attributable to section 4980A.

Line 21.—Add lines 13, 15, 17, and 18 of Part 2, Tax Computation, of this Form 706 and subtract this total from line 10 of the Tax Computation. Enter the result on line 21 of the worksheet.

Line 26.—If you computed the marital deduction on this Form 706 using the rules that were in effect before the Economic Recovery Tax Act of 1981 (as described in the instructions to line 14 of Part 4 of General Information), enter on line 26 the lesser of: the marital deduction you claimed on line 18 of Part 5 of the Recapitulation; or 50% of the "reduced adjusted gross estate." If you computed the marital deduction using the unlimited marital deduction in effect for decedents dying after 1981, for purposes of determining the marital deduction for the reduced gross estate, see Rev. Rul. 90-2,

1990-1 C.B. 170. To determine the "reduced adjusted gross estate," subtract the amount on line 25 of the Schedule Q worksheet from the amount on line 24 of the worksheet. If community property is included in the amount on line 24 of the worksheet, compute the reduced adjusted gross estate using the rules of Regulations section 20.2056(c)-2 and Rev. Rul. 76-311, 1976-2 C.B. 261.

Instructions for Schedules R and R-1.— Generation-Skipping Transfer Tax

Introduction and Overview

Schedule R is used to compute the generation-skipping transfer (GST) tax that is payable by the estate. Schedule R-1 (Form 706) is used to compute the GST tax that is payable by certain trusts that are includible in the gross estate.

The GST tax that is to be reported on Form 706 is imposed only on "direct skips occurring at death." Unlike the estate tax, which is imposed on the value of the entire taxable estate regardless of whom it is distributed to, the GST tax is imposed only on the value of interests in property, wherever located, that actually pass to certain transferees, who are referred to as "skip persons."

For purposes of Form 706, the property interests transferred must be includible in the gross estate before they are subject to the GST tax. Therefore, the first step in computing the GST tax liability is to determine the property interests includible in the gross estate by completing Schedules A–I of Form 706.

The second step is to determine who the "skip persons" are. To do this, assign each transferee to a generation and determine whether each transferee is a "natural person" or a "trust" for GST purposes.

The third step is to determine which skip persons are transferees of "interests in property." If the skip person is a "natural person," anything transferred is an "interest in property." If the skip person is a "trust," make this determination using the rules under **Interest in Property,** on page 18. These first three steps are described in detail under the heading **Determining Which Transfers Are Direct Skips.**

The fourth step is to determine whether to enter the transfer on Schedule R or on Schedule R-1. See the rules under the heading **Dividing Direct Skips Between Schedules R and R-1.**

The fifth step is to complete Schedules R and R-1 using the **How To Complete** instructions on page 19, for each schedule.

Determining Which Transfers Are Direct Skips

Effective Dates.—The rules below apply only for the purpose of determining if a transfer is a direct skip that should be reported on Schedule R or R-1 of Form 706.

In General.—The GST tax is effective for the estates of decedents dying after October 22, 1986.

Wills and revocable trusts.—For the estates of decedents dying before January 1, 1987, the GST tax will not apply to transfers under wills and revocable trusts executed before October 22, 1986.

Irrevocable trusts.—The GST tax will not apply to any transfer under a trust that was irrevocable on September 25, 1985, but only to the extent that the transfer was not made out of corpus added to the trust after September 25, 1985. An addition to the corpus after that date will cause a proportionate part of future income and appreciation to be subject to the GST tax. For more information, see Temporary Regulations section 26.2601-1(b)(1)(ii).

Mental disability.—If the decedent was, on October 22, 1986, under a mental disability to change the disposition of his or her property and did not regain the competence to dispose of property before death, the GST tax will not apply to any property included in the gross estate (other than property transferred on behalf of the decedent during life and after October 21, 1986). The GST tax will also not apply to any transfer under a trust to the extent that the trust consists of property included in the gross estate (other than property transferred on behalf of the decedent during life and after October 21, 1986).

The term "mental disability" means the decedent's mental incompetence to execute an instrument governing the disposition of his or her property, whether or not there has been an adjudication of incompetence and whether or not there has been an appointment of any other person charged with the care of the person or property of the transferor.

If the decedent had been adjudged mentally incompetent, a copy of the judgment or decree must be filed with this return.

If the decedent had not been adjudged mentally incompetent, the executor must file with the return a certification from a qualified physician stating that in his opinion the decedent had been mentally incompetent at all times on and after October 22, 1986, and that the decedent had not regained the competence to modify or revoke the terms of the trust or will prior to his death or a statement as to why no such certification may be obtained from a physician.

Direct Skip.—The GST tax reported on Form 706 and Schedule R-1 (Form 706) is imposed only on direct skips. For purposes of Form 706, a direct skip is a transfer that is: **(1)** subject to the estate tax, **(2)** of an interest in property, and **(3)** to a skip person. All three requirements must be met before the transfer is subject to the GST tax. A transfer is "subject to the estate tax" if you are required to list it on any of Schedules A–I of Form 706. To determine if a transfer is of an "interest in property" and to a "skip person," you must first determine if the transferee is a "natural person" or a "trust" as defined below.

Trust.—For purposes of the GST tax, a "trust" includes not only an explicit trust (as defined in **Special Rule for Trusts Other than Explicit Trusts** on page 19), but also any other arrangement (other than an estate) which, although not explicitly a trust, has substantially the same effect as a trust. For example, "trust" includes life estates with remainders, terms for years, and insurance and annuity contracts.

Substantially separate and independent shares of different beneficiaries in a trust are treated as separate trusts.

Interest in Property.—If a transfer is made to a "natural person," it is always considered a transfer of an interest in property for purposes of the GST tax.

If a transfer is made to a "trust," a person will have an interest in the property transferred to the trust if that person either has a present right to receive income or corpus from the trust (such as an income interest for life) or is a permissible current recipient of income or corpus from the trust (e.g., may receive income or corpus at the discretion of the trustee).

Skip Person.—A transferee who is a "natural person" is a "skip person" if that transferee is assigned to a generation that is two or more generations below the generation assignment of the decedent. See **Determining the Generation of a Transferee,** below.

A transferee who is a "trust" is a "skip person" if all the "interests in the property" (as defined above) transferred to the trust are held by skip persons. Thus, whenever a non-skip person has an interest in a trust, the trust will not be a skip person even though a skip person also has an interest in the trust.

A trust will also be a "skip person" if there are no "interests in the property" transferred to the trust held by any person, and future distributions or terminations from the trust can be made only to skip persons.

Non-Skip Person.—A non-skip person is any transferee who is not a skip person.

Determining the Generation of a Transferee.—Generally, a generation is determined along family lines as follows:

1. Where the beneficiary is a lineal descendant of a grandparent of the decedent (for example, the decedent's cousin, niece, nephew, etc.), the number of generations between the decedent and the beneficiary is determined by subtracting the number of generations between the grandparent and the decedent from the number of generations between the grandparent and the beneficiary.

2. Where the beneficiary is a lineal descendant of a grandparent of a spouse (or former spouse) of the decedent, the number of generations between the decedent and the beneficiary is determined by subtracting the number of generations between the grandparent and the spouse (or former spouse) from the number of generations between the grandparent and the beneficiary.

3. A person who at any time was married to a person described in **1** or **2**

above is assigned to the generation of that person. A person who at any time was married to the decedent is assigned to the decedent's generation.

4. A relationship by adoption or half-blood is treated as a relationship by whole-blood.

5. A person who is not assigned to a generation according to **1, 2, 3,** or **4** above is assigned to a generation based on his or her birth date, as follows:

a. A person who was born not more than 12½ years after the decedent is in the decedent's generation.

b. A person born more than 12½ years, but not more than 37½ years, after the decedent is in the first generation younger than the decedent.

c. A similar rule applies for a new generation every 25 years.

If more than one of the rules for assigning generations applies to a transferee, that transferee is generally assigned to the youngest of the generations that would apply.

If an estate, trust, partnership, corporation, or other entity (other than certain charitable organizations and trusts described in sections 511(a)(2) and 511(b)(2)) is a transferee, then each person who indirectly receives the property interests through the entity is treated as a transferee and is assigned to a generation as explained in the above rules. However, this look-thru rule does not apply for the purpose of determining whether a transfer to a trust is a direct skip.

Generation Assignment Where Intervening Parent Is Dead.—If property is transferred to the decedent's grandchild, and at the date of death, the grandchild's parent (who is the decedent's or the decedent's spouse's or the decedent's former spouse's child) is dead, then for purposes of generation assignment the grandchild will be considered to be the decedent's child rather than the decedent's grandchild. Thus, the transfer of the property will not be a direct skip. The grandchild's children will be treated as the decedent's grandchildren rather than the decedent's great-grandchildren.

This rule is also applied to the decedent's lineal descendants below the level of grandchild. For example, if the decedent's grandchild is dead, the decedent's great-grandchildren who are lineal descendants of the dead grandchild are considered the decedent's grandchildren for purposes of the GST tax.

If any transfer of property to a trust would have been a direct skip except for this generation assignment rule, then the rule also applies to transfers from the trust attributable to such property.

Charitable Organizations.—Charitable organizations and trusts described in sections 511(a)(2) and 511(b)(2) are assigned to the decedent's generation. Transfers to such organizations are therefore not subject to the GST tax.

Charitable Remainder Trusts.—Transfers to or in the form of charitable remainder

annuity trusts, charitable remainder unitrusts, and pooled income funds are not considered made to skip persons and, therefore, are not direct skips even if all of the life beneficiaries are skip persons.

Estate Tax Value.—Estate tax value is the value shown on Schedules A–I of this Form 706.

Examples.—The rules above can be illustrated by the following examples:

Example 1.—Under the will, the decedent's house is transferred to the decedent's daughter for her life with the remainder passing to her children. This transfer is made to a "trust" even though there is no explicit trust instrument. The interest in the property transferred (the present right to use the house) is transferred to a nonskip person (the decedent's daughter). Therefore, the trust is not a skip person because there is an interest in the transferred property that is held by a nonskip person. The transfer is not a direct skip.

Example 2.—The will bequeaths $100,000 to the decedent's grandchild. This transfer is a direct skip that is not made in trust and should be shown on Schedule R.

Example 3.—The will establishes a trust that is required to accumulate income for 10 years and then pay its income to the decedent's grandchildren for the rest of their lives and, upon their deaths, distribute the corpus to the decedent's great-grandchildren. Because the trust has no current beneficiaries, there are no present interests in the property transferred to the trust. All of the persons to whom the trust can make future distributions (including distributions upon the termination of interests in property held in trust) are skip persons (i.e., the decedent's grandchildren and great-grandchildren). Therefore, the trust itself is a skip person and you should show the transfer on Schedule R.

Example 4.—The will establishes a trust that is to pay all of its income to the decedent's grandchildren for 10 years. At the end of 10 years, the corpus is to be distributed to the decedent's children. All of the interests in this trust are held by skip persons. Therefore, the trust is a skip person and you should show this transfer on Schedule R. You should show the estate tax value of all the property transferred to the trust even though the trust has some ultimate beneficiaries who are nonskip persons.

Dividing Direct Skips Between Schedules R and R-1

Report all generation-skipping transfers on Schedule R unless the rules below specifically provide that they are to be reported on Schedule R-1.

Under section 2603(a)(2), the GST tax on direct skips from a trust (as defined for GST tax purposes on page 18) is to be paid by the trustee and not by the estate. Schedule R-1 serves as a notification from the executor to the trustee that a GST tax is due.

For a direct skip to be reportable on Schedule R-1, the trust must be includible in the decedent's gross estate.

If the decedent was the surviving spouse life beneficiary of a marital deduction power of appointment (or QTIP) trust created by the decedent's spouse, then transfers caused by reason of the decedent's death from that trust to skip persons are direct skips required to be reported on Schedule R-1.

If a direct skip is made "from a trust" under these rules, it is reportable on Schedule R-1 even if it is also made "to a trust" rather than to an individual.

Similarly, if property in a trust (as defined for GST tax purposes on page 18) is included in the decedent's gross estate under section 2035, 2036, 2037, 2038, 2039, 2041, or 2042 and such property is, by reason of the decedent's death, transferred to skip persons, the transfers are direct skips required to be reported on Schedule R-1.

Special Rule For Trusts Other Than Explicit Trusts.—An **explicit trust** is a trust as defined in Regulations section 301.7701-4(a) as "an arrangement created by a will or by an inter vivos declaration whereby trustees take title to property for the purpose of protecting or conserving it for the beneficiaries under the ordinary rules applied in chancery or probate courts." Direct skips from explicit trusts are required to be reported on Schedule R-1 regardless of their size unless the executor is also a trustee (see below).

Direct skips from trusts that are trusts for GST tax purposes but are not explicit trusts are to be shown on Schedule R-1 only if the total of all tentative maximum direct skips from the entity is more than $100,000. If this total is $100,000 or less, the skips should be shown on Schedule R. For purposes of the $100,000 limit, "tentative maximum direct skips" is the amount you would enter on line 5 of Schedule R-1 if you were to file that schedule.

A liquidating trust (such as a bankruptcy trust) under Regulations section 301.7701-4(d) is not treated as an explicit trust for the purposes of this special rule.

If the proceeds of a life insurance policy are includible in the gross estate and are payable to a beneficiary who is a skip person, the transfer is a direct skip from a trust that is not an explicit trust. It should be reported on Schedule R-1 if the total of all the tentative maximum direct skips from the company is more than $100,000. Otherwise, it should be reported on Schedule R.

Similarly, if an annuity is includible on Schedule I and its survivor benefits are payable to a beneficiary who is a skip person, then the estate tax value of the annuity should be reported as a direct skip on Schedule R-1 if the total tentative maximum direct skips from the entity paying the annuity is more than $100,000.

Executor as Trustee.—If any of the executors of the decedent's estate are trustees of the trust, then all direct skips

with respect to that trust must be shown on Schedule R and not on Schedule R-1 even if they would otherwise have been required to be shown on Schedule R-1. This rule applies even if the trust has other trustees who are not executors of the decedent's estate.

How To Complete Schedules R and R-1

Valuation.—Enter on Schedules R and R-1 the estate tax value of the property interests subject to the direct skips. If you elected alternate valuation (section 2032) and/or special use valuation (section 2032A), you must use the alternate and/or special values on Schedules R and R-1.

How To Complete Schedule R

Part 1—GST Exemption Reconciliation.— Part 1, line 6 of both Parts 2 and 3, and line 4 of Schedule R-1 are used to allocate the decedent's $1 million GST exemption. This allocation is made by filing Form 706. Once made, the allocation is irrevocable. You are not required to allocate all of the decedent's GST exemption. However, the portion of the exemption that you do not allocate will be allocated by IRS under the deemed allocation at death rules of section 2632(c).

Special QTIP election.—In the case of property for which a marital deduction is allowed to the decedent's estate under section 2056(b)(7) (QTIP election), section 2652(a)(3) allows you to treat such property for purposes of the GST tax as if the election to be treated as qualified terminable interest property had not been made.

The 2652(a)(3) election must include the value of all property in the trust for which a QTIP election was allowed under section 2056(b)(7).

If a section 2652(a)(3) election is made, then the decedent will for GST tax purposes be treated as the transferor of all the property in the trust for which a marital deduction was allowed to the decedent's estate under section 2056(b)(7). In this case, the executor of the decedent's estate may allocate part or all of the decedent's GST exemption to the property.

Line 2.—These allocations will have been made either on Forms 709 filed by the decedent or on Notices of Allocation made by the decedent for inter vivos transfers that were not direct skips but to which the decedent allocated the GST exemption. These allocations by the decedent are irrevocable.

Line 3.—Make an entry on this line if you are filing Form(s) 709 for the decedent and wish to allocate any exemption.

Lines 4, 5, and 6.—These lines represent your allocation of the GST exemption to direct skips made by reason of the decedent's death. Complete Parts 2 and 3 and Schedule R-1 before completing these lines.

Line 9.—Line 9 is used to allocate the remaining unused GST exemption (from line 8) and to help you compute the trust's inclusion ratio. Line 9 is a Notice of

Allocation for allocating the GST exemption to trusts as to which the decedent is the transferor and from which a generation-skipping transfer could occur after the decedent's death. If line 9 is not completed, the deemed allocation at death rules will apply to allocate the decedent's remaining unused GST exemption, first to property that is the subject of a direct skip occurring at the decedent's death, and, then to trusts as to which the decedent is the transferor. If you wish to avoid the application of the deemed allocation rules, you should enter on line 9 every trust (except certain trusts entered on Schedule R-1, as described below) to which you wish to allocate any part of the decedent's GST exemption. Unless you enter a trust on line 9, the unused GST exemption will be allocated to it under the deemed allocation rules.

If a trust is entered on Schedule R-1, the amount you entered on line 4 of Schedule R-1 serves as a Notice of Allocation and you need not enter the trust on line 9 unless you wish to allocate more than the Schedule R-1, line 4 amount to the trust. However, you must enter the trust on line 9 if you wish to allocate any of the unused GST exemption amount to it. Such an additional allocation would not ordinarily be appropriate in the case of a trust entered on Schedule R-1 when the trust property passes outright (rather than to another trust) at the decedent's death. However, where section 2032A property is involved it may be appropriate to allocate additional exemption amounts to the property. See the instructions for line 10.

Note: *To avoid application of the deemed allocation rules, Form 706 and Schedule R should be filed to allocate the exemption to trusts that may later have taxable terminations or distributions under section 2612 even if the form is not required to be filed to report estate or GST tax.*

Line 9, Column C.—Enter the GST exemption included on lines 2–6, above, that was allocated to the trust.

Line 9, Column D.—The line 8 amount is to be allocated in column D of line 9. This amount may be allocated to transfers into trusts that are not otherwise reported on Form 706. For example, the line 8 amount may be allocated to an inter vivos trust established by the decedent during his or her lifetime and not included in the gross estate. This allocation is made by identifying the trust on line 9 and making an allocation to it using column D. If the trust is not included in the gross estate, value the trust as of the date of death. You should inform the trustee of each trust listed on line 9 of the total GST exemption you allocated to the trust. The trustee will need this information to compute the GST tax on future distributions and terminations.

Line 9, Column E.—*Trust's Inclusion Ratio.*—The trustee must know the trust's inclusion ratio to figure the trust's GST tax for future distributions and terminations. You are not required to inform the trustee of the inclusion ratio and may not have enough information to compute it. Therefore, you are not required to make an

entry in column E. However, column E and the worksheet below are provided to assist you in computing the inclusion ratio for the trustee if you wish to do so.

You should inform the trustee of the amount of the GST exemption you allocated to the trust. Line 9, columns C and D may be used to compute this amount for each trust.

This worksheet will compute an accurate inclusion ratio only if the decedent was the only settlor of the trust. You should use a separate worksheet for each trust (or separate share of a trust that is treated as a separate trust).

1	Total estate and gift tax value of all of the property interests that passed to the trust . . . . _____
2	Estate taxes, state death taxes, and other charges actually recovered from the trust . . . . _____
3	GST taxes imposed on direct skips to skip persons other than this trust and borne by the property transferred to this trust . . . . _____
4	GST taxes actually recovered from this trust (from Schedule R, Part 2, line 8 or Schedule R-1, line 6) . . . . _____
5	Add lines 2–4 . . . . _____
6	Subtract line 5 from line 1 . . . _____
7	Add columns C and D of line 9 . . _____
8	Divide line 7 by line 6 . . . . . _____
9	Trust's inclusion ratio. Subtract line 8 from 1.000 . . . . _____

Line 10.—*Special Use Allocation.*—For skip persons who receive an interest in section 2032A special use property, you may allocate more GST exemption than the direct skip amount to reduce the additional GST tax that would be due when the interest is later disposed of or qualified use ceases. See Schedule A-1 of this Form 706 for more details about this additional GST tax.

Enter on line 10 the total additional GST exemption you are allocating to all skip persons who received any interest in section 2032A property. Attach a special use allocation schedule listing each such skip person and the amount of the GST exemption allocated to that person.

If you do not allocate the GST exemption, it will be automatically allocated under the deemed allocation at death rules. To the extent any amount is not so allocated it will be automatically allocated (under regulations to be published) to the earliest disposition or cessation that is subject to the GST tax. Under certain circumstances, post-death events may cause the decedent to be treated as a transferor for purposes of Chapter 13.

Line 10 may be used to set aside an exemption amount for such an event. You must attach a schedule listing each such event and the amount of exemption allocated to that event.

Parts 2 and 3.—Part 2 is used to compute the GST tax on transfers in which the property interests transferred are to bear the GST tax on the transfers. Part 3 is to be used to report the GST tax on transfers

in which the property interests transferred do not bear the GST tax on the transfers.

Section 2603(b) requires that unless the governing instrument provides otherwise, the GST tax is to be charged to the property constituting the transfer. Therefore, you will usually enter all of the direct skips on Part 2.

You may enter a transfer on Part 3 only if the will or trust instrument directs, by specific reference, that the GST tax is not to be paid from the transferred property interests.

Part 2—Line 3.—Enter -0- on this line unless the will or trust instrument specifies that the GST taxes will be paid by property other than that constituting the transfer (as described above). Enter on line 3 the total of the GST taxes shown on Part 3 and Schedule(s) R-1 that are payable out of the property interests shown on Part 2, line 1.

Part 2—Line 6.—Do not enter more than the amount on line 5. Additional allocations may be made using Part 1.

Part 3—Line 3.—See the instructions to Part 2, line 3, above. Enter only the total of the GST taxes shown on Schedule(s) R-1 that are payable out of the property interests shown on Part 3, line 1.

Part 3—Line 6.—See the instructions to Part 2, line 6, above.

How To Complete Schedule R-1

Filing Due Date.—Enter the due date of Schedule R, Form 706. You must send the copies of Schedule R-1 to the fiduciary by this date.

Line 4.—Do not enter more than the amount on line 3. If you wish to allocate an additional GST exemption, you must use Schedule R, Part 1. Making an entry in line 4 constitutes a Notice of Allocation of the decedent's GST exemption to the trust.

Line 6.—If the property interests entered on line 1 will not bear the GST tax, multiply line 6 by 55% (.55).

Signature.—The executor(s) must sign Schedule R-1 in the same manner as Form 706. See **Signature and Verification** on page 2.

Filing Schedule R-1.—Attach one copy of each Schedule R-1 that you prepare to Form 706. Send two copies of each Schedule R-1 to the fiduciary.

Instructions for Schedule S.—Increased Estate Tax on Excess Retirement Accumulations

The executor uses Schedule S to figure the increased estate tax imposed by section 4980A(d) on excess accumulations in qualified employer plans (plans) and individual retirement plans (IRAs). Schedule S may be filed only as an attachment to Form 706.

Which Estates Must File

All estates must file Schedule S if the estate has any excess accumulation (as calculated on line 16 of the Tax

Computation of Schedule S). Schedule S must be filed regardless of the size of the gross estate and regardless of whether the estate is otherwise required to file Form 706.

The section 4980A(d) tax also applies to the estates of nonresident alien decedents whether or not they are otherwise required to file Form 706-NA. In these instructions, references to Form 706 should be construed as references to Form 706-NA if the decedent was a nonresident alien.

When To File

Schedule S is considered an integral part of Form 706 and you must file it with the estate's Form 706. Therefore, the due date is determined by the due date, with extensions, of the estate's Form 706.

Where To File

Schedule S must be attached to and filed with the Form 706.

Paying the Tax

The increased estate tax shown on Schedule S is due at the same time as the estate tax (if any) shown on the Form 706.

You may not make a section 6166 or 6163 election to defer the payment of the increased estate tax.

Part I.—Tax Computation

Line 1.—Spousal Election.—Section 4980A(d)(5) provides that if a surviving spouse is the beneficiary of all of the decedent's retirement accumulations (subject to a de minimis exception), then the spouse may elect not to have the excess accumulation rules apply to the decedent but to have section 4980A apply to such interests and any distributions attributable to such interests as if they were the surviving spouse's.

To make the election, the spouse must attach a statement to the decedent's Form 706. The statement must be signed by the spouse and must indicate clearly that the spouse is making the election provided for in section 4980A(d)(5).

If the spouse makes the election, check the box on line 1 and complete lines 2–12 of Part I, Schedule S.

Line 2.—List each plan and IRA in which the decedent had any interest at the time of death. If you need more space, list the additional plans and IRAs on an attached sheet. Also list any plans in which the decedent was an alternate payee if payments to the decedent would have been includible in the decedent's gross income under a qualified domestic relations order within the meaning of section 414(p).

If an IRA does not have an EIN, enter "None" in the EIN column.

*Rollover IRAs.—*If the decedent was a surviving spouse who rolled over a distribution from a plan or IRA of the predeceased spouse into an IRA established in the surviving spouse's own

name, do not list the IRA on line 2 unless contributions or transfers other than the rollover amount were made to the IRA. If such other contributions or transfers were made, then you must list the IRA on line 2 and include the entire value of the decedent's interest in the IRA on line 3.

If the decedent was a surviving spouse who elected to treat an inherited IRA (described in section 408(d)(3)(C)(ii) as his or her own IRA and made no further contributions to it, do not list the IRA on line 2.

If the decedent (whether or not a surviving spouse) elected to treat an IRA as subject to the distribution requirements of section 408(a)(6) (before its amendment by section 521(b) of the Tax Reform Act of 1984), under Regulations section 1.408-2(b)(7)(ii), do not list the IRA on line 2 if it meets those distribution requirements.

Lines 3–10.—Consolidate all of the decedent's IRAs in column D. If there are more than three plans, compute their value on an attached sheet following the same format as lines 3–10.

Line 3.—Value of Decedent's Interest.—Value the decedent's interest in the plan or IRA using the estate tax valuation rules, including the alternate valuation election under section 2032. See page 3 for details on making this election. Do not reduce this value by any of the credits, deductions, exclusions, etc., that otherwise apply for estate tax purposes. Do not apply community property rules to reduce the value of the decedent's interest.

You should include in the value all amounts payable to beneficiaries of the decedent under the plan or IRA (including amounts payable to a surviving spouse under a qualified joint and survivor annuity or qualified preretirement survivor annuity), whether or not these amounts are otherwise included in valuing the decedent's gross estate.

Exclude from the value the excess (if any) of interests payable immediately after death over the value of the same interests immediately before death.

Line 4.—Post-Death Rollovers.—Enter on this line any amounts that: **(1)** were distributed from the plan or account within 60 days before the decedent's death, and **(2)** were rolled over into an IRA after the date of death and within 60 days after the distribution. Value the rolled over amounts as of the date they were received by the IRA.

Line 6.—Alternate Payees.—Enter on this line the amount of any portion of the decedent's interest in the plan that is payable to an alternate payee and is included in the payee's gross income under a qualified domestic relations order (within the meaning of section 414(p)).

Line 8.—Excess Life Insurance Amounts.—If the plan held a life insurance policy on the decedent's life, enter here the amount excludable from the beneficiary's income under section 101(a). This is the amount by which the death

benefit payable under the policy exceeds the cash surrender value of the policy immediately before the decedent's death. Do not enter on this line amounts that are excludable from gross income under section 101(b) (employee death benefits).

Line 9.—Decedent's Interest as a Beneficiary.—Enter on this line the amount of the decedent's interest in a plan or IRA by reason of the death of another individual.

Do not enter on this line any plans or IRAs that are reported on line 2 of Part I as a result of the decedent having made a spousal election under section 4980A(d)(5).

Line 17.—Increased Estate Tax.—The tax shown on line 17 may not be reduced or offset by any of the estate tax credits. Enter the line 17 amount on line 23 of the Tax Computation on page 1 of Form 706. (If you are filing Schedule S with Form 706-NA, enter the line 17 amount on line 16 of the Tax Computation of Form 706-NA.)

Part II.—Grandfather Election

Line 1.—If you checked "Yes," attach the **Form 5329,** Return for Additional Taxes Attributable to Qualified Retirement Plans (Including IRAs), Annuities, and Modified Endowment Contracts, on which the election was made.

Line 2.—Initial Grandfather Amount.—If you checked "Yes" on line 1, enter the initial grandfather amount shown on the Form 5329 on which the grandfather election was made.

Line 3.—Previously Recovered Amounts.—Enter the total of the amounts treated as recoveries of the grandfather amount from previously filed Forms 5329.

Part III.—Computation of Hypothetical Life Annuity

Line 1.—Decedent's Attained Age.—Enter the decedent's attained age in whole years on the date of death. For example, if the decedent was 60 years and 11 months old on the date of death, enter "60" on line 1.

Line 2.—Annual Annuity Amount.—If you did not check "Yes" to line 1 of Part II, enter the greater of $150,000 or $112,500 indexed for inflation as described in Temp. Regs. section 54.4981A-1T(a-9).

If you checked "Yes" to line 1 of Part II, enter $112,500 indexed for inflation as described in Temp. Regs. section 54.4981A-1T(a-9).

Line 3.—Present Value Multipliers.—Section 5031 of the Technical and Miscellaneous Revenue Act of 1988 required the IRS to issue new present value tables using revised mortality figures. Also, to determine the present value multiplier under the new procedure, you must use an interest rate that is revised monthly. The IRS will announce the applicable rate in a news release and will publish it in a revenue ruling in the Internal Revenue Bulletin.

The IRS has published new present value tables for some interest rates in Notice 89-60, 1989-1 C.B. 700. The complete tables have been printed in **Pub. 1457,** Actuarial Values—Alpha Volume, which can be purchased from the Superintendent of Documents, U.S. Government Printing Office, Washington, DC 20402.

To calculate the present value of an annuity if the tables are not available, and for additional information on the new rules, see Notice 89-60 as noted above, and Notice 89-24, 1989-1 C.B. 660.

Worksheet for Schedule Q—Credit for Tax on Prior Transfers

Part I Transferor's tax on prior transfers

Item	Transferor (From Schedule Q)			Total for all transfers (line 8 only)
	A	B	C	
1. Gross value of prior transfer to this transferee				
2. Death taxes payable from prior transfer				
3. Encumbrances allocable to prior transfer				
4. Obligations allocable to prior transfer .				
5. Marital deduction applicable to line 1 above, as shown on transferor's Form 706 . .				
6. **Total** (Add lines 2, 3, 4, and 5) .				
7. **Net value of transfers** (Subtract line 6 from line 1)				
8. **Net value of transfers** (Add columns A, B, and C of line 7)				
9. Transferor's taxable estate				
10. Federal estate tax paid				
11. State death taxes paid				
12. Foreign death taxes paid				
13. Other death taxes paid				
14. **Total taxes paid** (Add lines 10, 11, 12, and 13)				
15. **Value of transferor's estate** (Subtract line 14 from line 9)				
16. Net Federal estate tax paid on transferor's estate				
17. Credit for gift tax paid on transferor's estate				
18. Credit allowed transferor's estate for tax on prior transfers from prior transferor(s) who died within 10 years before death of decedent . . .				
19. **Tax on transferor's estate** (Add lines 16, 17, and 18)				
20. Transferor's tax on prior transfers ((Line 7 ÷ line 15) × line 19 of respective estates) .				

Part II Transferee's tax on prior transfers

Item	Amount
21. Transferee's actual tax before allowance of credit for prior transfers (see instructions)	
22. Total gross estate of transferee (from line 1 of the Tax Computation, page 1, Form 706)	
23. Net value of all transfers (from line 8 of this worksheet)	
24. Transferee's reduced gross estate (subtract line 23 from line 22)	
25. Total debts and deductions (not including marital and charitable deductions) (items 15, 16, and 17 of the Recapitulation, page 3, Form 706)	
26. Marital deduction (from item 18, Recapitulation, page 3, Form 706) (see instructions) .	
27. Charitable bequests (from item 19, Recapitulation, page 3, Form 706)	
28. Charitable deduction proportion ([line 23 ÷ (line 22–line 25)] × line 27)	
29. Reduced charitable deduction (subtract line 28 from line 27)	
30. Transferee's deduction as adjusted (add lines 25, 26, and 29)	
31. (a) Transferee's reduced taxable estate (subtract line 30 from line 24)	
(b) Adjusted taxable gifts	
(c) Total reduced taxable estate (add lines 31(a) and 31(b))	
32. Tentative tax on reduced taxable estate	
33. (a) Post-1976 gift taxes paid	
(b) Unified credit	
(c) Section 2011 state death tax credit	
(d) Section 2012 gift tax credit	
(e) Section 2014 foreign death tax credit	
(f) Total credits (add lines 33(a) through 33(e))	
34. Net tax on reduced taxable estate (subtract line 33(f) from line 32)	
35. Transferee's tax on prior transfers (subtract line 34 from line 21)	

*U.S. Government Printing Office: 1996 — 417-702/64175

Form **706**

(Rev. August 1993)

Department of the Treasury
Internal Revenue Service

United States Estate (and Generation-Skipping Transfer) Tax Return

Estate of a citizen or resident of the United States (see separate instructions). To be filed for decedents dying after October 8, 1990. For Paperwork Reduction Act Notice, see page 1 of the instructions.

OMB No. 1545-0015
Expires 12-31-95

Part 1.—Decedent and Executor

1a Decedent's first name and middle initial (and maiden name, if any)	**1b** Decedent's last name	**2** Decedent's social security no.
3a Domicile at time of death (county and state, or foreign country)	**3b** Year domicile established **4** Date of birth **5** Date of death	
6a Name of executor (see instructions)	**6b** Executor's address (number and street including apartment or suite no. or rural route; city, town, or post office; state; and ZIP code)	
6c Executor's social security number (see instructions)		
7a Name and location of court where will was probated or estate administered		**7b** Case number

8 If decedent died testate, check here ▶ ☐ and attach a certified copy of the will.   **9** If Form 4768 is attached, check here ▶ ☐

10 If Schedule R-1 is attached, check here ▶ ☐

Part 2.—Tax Computation

1 Total gross estate (from Part 5, Recapitulation, page 3, item 10)	**1**	
2 Total allowable deductions (from Part 5, Recapitulation, page 3, item 20)	**2**	
3 Taxable estate (subtract line 2 from line 1)	**3**	
4 Adjusted taxable gifts (total taxable gifts (within the meaning of section 2503) made by the decedent after December 31, 1976, other than gifts that are includible in decedent's gross estate (section 2001(b))	**4**	
5 Add lines 3 and 4	**5**	
6 Tentative tax on the amount on line 5 from Table A in the instructions	**6**	
7a If line 5 exceeds $10,000,000, enter the lesser of line 5 or $21,040,000. If line 5 is $10,000,000 or less, skip lines 7a and 7b and enter -0- on line 7c . **7a**		
b Subtract $10,000,000 from line 7a **7b**		
c Enter 5% (.05) of line 7b	**7c**	
8 Total tentative tax (add lines 6 and 7c)	**8**	
9 Total gift tax payable with respect to gifts made by the decedent after December 31, 1976. Include gift taxes by the decedent's spouse for such spouse's share of split gifts (section 2513) only if the decedent was the donor of these gifts and they are includible in the decedent's gross estate (see instructions)	**9**	
10 Gross estate tax (subtract line 9 from line 8)	**10**	
11 Maximum unified credit against estate tax **11** 192,800 00		
12 Adjustment to unified credit. (This adjustment may not exceed $6,000. See page 6 of the instructions.) **12**		
13 Allowable unified credit (subtract line 12 from line 11)	**13**	
14 Subtract line 13 from line 10 (but do not enter less than zero)	**14**	
15 Credit for state death taxes. Do not enter more than line 14. Compute the credit by using the amount on line 3 less $60,000. See Table B in the instructions and **attach credit evidence** (see instructions)	**15**	
16 Subtract line 15 from line 14	**16**	
17 Credit for Federal gift taxes on pre-1977 gifts (section 2012) (attach computation) **17**		
18 Credit for foreign death taxes (from Schedule(s) P). (Attach Form(s) 706CE) **18**		
19 Credit for tax on prior transfers (from Schedule Q) **19**		
20 Total (add lines 17, 18, and 19)	**20**	
21 Net estate tax (subtract line 20 from line 16)	**21**	
22 Generation-skipping transfer taxes (from Schedule R, Part 2, line 10)	**22**	
23 Section 4980A increased estate tax (from Schedule S, Part I, line 17) (see instructions)	**23**	
24 Total transfer taxes (add lines 21, 22, and 23)	**24**	
25 Prior payments. Explain in an attached statement **25**		
26 United States Treasury bonds redeemed in payment of estate tax . . **26**		
27 Total (add lines 25 and 26)	**27**	
28 Balance due (or overpayment) (subtract line 27 from line 24)	**28**	

Under penalties of perjury, I declare that I have examined this return, including accompanying schedules and statements, and to the best of my knowledge and belief, it is true, correct, and complete. Declaration of preparer other than the executor is based on all information of which preparer has any knowledge.

Signature(s) of executor(s)   Date

Signature of preparer other than executor   Address (and ZIP code)   Date

Cat. No. 20548R

Form 706 (Rev. 8-93)

Estate of:

Part 3.—Elections by the Executor

Please check the "Yes" or "No" box for each question.

		Yes	No
1	Do you elect alternate valuation?		
2	Do you elect special use valuation? If "Yes," you must complete and attach Schedule A–1		
3	Do you elect to pay the taxes in installments as described in section 6166? If "Yes," you must attach the additional information described in the instructions.		
4	Do you elect to postpone the part of the taxes attributable to a reversionary or remainder interest as described in section 6163?		

Part 4.—General Information (Note: *Please attach the necessary supplemental documents.* **You must attach the death certificate.**)

Authorization to receive confidential tax information under Regulations section 601.504(b)(2)(i), to act as the estate's representative before the Internal Revenue Service, and to make written or oral presentations on behalf of the estate if return prepared by an attorney, accountant, or enrolled agent for the executor:

Name of representative (print or type)	State	Address (number, street, and room or suite no., city, state, and ZIP code)

I declare that I am the ☐ attorney/ ☐ certified public accountant/ ☐ enrolled agent (you must check the applicable box) for the executor and prepared this return for the executor. I am not under suspension or disbarment from practice before the Internal Revenue Service and am qualified to practice in the state shown above.

Signature	CAF number	Date	Telephone number

1 Death certificate number and issuing authority (attach a copy of the death certificate to this return).

2 Decedent's business or occupation. If retired, check here ▶ ☐ and state decedent's former business or occupation.

3 Marital status of the decedent at time of death:
☐ Married
☐ Widow or widower—Name, SSN, and date of death of deceased spouse ▶
☐ Single
☐ Legally separated
☐ Divorced—Date divorce decree became final ▶

4a Surviving spouse's name	**4b** Social security number	**4c** Amount received (see instructions)

5 Individuals (other than the surviving spouse), trusts, or other estates who receive benefits from the estate (do not include charitable beneficiaries shown in Schedule O) (see instructions). For Privacy Act Notice (applicable to individual beneficiaries only), see the Instructions for Form 1040.

Name of individual, trust, or estate receiving $5,000 or more	Identifying number	Relationship to decedent	Amount (see instructions)

All unascertainable beneficiaries and those who receive less than $5,000 ▶

Total

(Continued on next page)

Page 2

Part 4.—General Information (continued)

		Yes	No
Please check the "Yes" or "No" box for each question.			
6	Does the gross estate contain any section 2044 property (qualified terminable interest property (QTIP) from a prior gift or estate) (see page 5 of the instructions)?		
7a	Have Federal gift tax returns ever been filed? . . . . •.		
	If "Yes," please attach copies of the returns, if available, and furnish the following information:		

7b Period(s) covered	**7c** Internal Revenue office(s) where filed

If you answer "Yes" to any of questions 8–16, you must attach additional information as described in the instructions.

		Yes	No
8a	Was there any insurance on the decedent's life that is not included on the return as part of the gross estate?		
b	Did the decedent own any insurance on the life of another that is not included in the gross estate?		
9	Did the decedent at the time of death own any property as a joint tenant with right of survivorship in which (a) one or more of the other joint tenants was someone other than the decedent's spouse, and (b) less than the full value of the property is included on the return as part of the gross estate? If "Yes," you must complete and attach Schedule E		
10	Did the decedent, at the time of death, own any interest in a partnership or unincorporated business or any stock in an inactive or closely held corporation?		
11	Did the decedent make any transfer described in section 2035, 2036, 2037, or 2038 (see the instructions for Schedule G)? If "Yes," you must complete and attach Schedule G		
12	Were there in existence at the time of the decedent's death:		
a	Any trusts created by the decedent during his or her lifetime?		
b	Any trusts not created by the decedent under which the decedent possessed any power, beneficial interest, or trusteeship?		
13	Did the decedent ever possess, exercise, or release any general power of appointment? If "Yes," you must complete and attach Schedule H		
14	Was the marital deduction computed under the transitional rule of Public Law 97-34, section 403(e)(3) (Economic Recovery Tax Act of 1981)? If "Yes," attach a separate computation of the marital deduction, enter the amount on item 18 of the Recapitulation, and note on item 18 "computation attached."		
15	Was the decedent, immediately before death, receiving an annuity described in the "General" paragraph of the instructions for Schedule I? If "Yes," you must complete and attach Schedule I		
16	Did the decedent have a total "excess retirement accumulation" (as defined in section 4980A(d)) in qualified employer plans and individual retirement plans? If "Yes," you must complete and attach Schedule S		

Part 5.—Recapitulation

Item number	Gross estate	Alternate value	Value at date of death
1	Schedule A—Real Estate		
2	Schedule B—Stocks and Bonds.		
3	Schedule C—Mortgages, Notes, and Cash		
4	Schedule D—Insurance on the Decedent's Life (attach Form(s) 712)		
5	Schedule E—Jointly Owned Property (attach Form(s) 712 for life insurance) . . .		
6	Schedule F—Other Miscellaneous Property (attach Form(s) 712 for life insurance) .		
7	Schedule G—Transfers During Decedent's Life (attach Form(s) 712 for life insurance)		
8	Schedule H—Powers of Appointment		
9	Schedule I—Annuities		
10	Total gross estate (add items 1 through 9). Enter here and on line 1 of the Tax Computation		

Item number	Deductions	Amount
11	Schedule J—Funeral Expenses and Expenses Incurred in Administering Property Subject to Claims . . .	
12	Schedule K—Debts of the Decedent	
13	Schedule K—Mortgages and Liens	
14	Total of items 11 through 13	
15	Allowable amount of deductions from item 14 (see the instructions for item 15 of the Recapitulation) . . .	
16	Schedule L—Net Losses During Administration	
17	Schedule L—Expenses Incurred in Administering Property Not Subject to Claims	
18	Schedule M—Bequests, etc., to Surviving Spouse	
19	Schedule O—Charitable, Public, and Similar Gifts and Bequests	
20	Total allowable deductions (add items 15 through 19). Enter here and on line 2 of the Tax Computation . . .	

Estate of:

SCHEDULE A—Real Estate

(For jointly owned property that must be disclosed on Schedule E, see the instructions for Schedule E.)

(Real estate that is part of a sole proprietorship should be shown on Schedule F. Real estate that is included in the gross estate under section 2035, 2036, 2037, or 2038 should be shown on Schedule G. Real estate that is included in the gross estate under section 2041 should be shown on Schedule H.)

(If you elect section 2032A valuation, you must complete Schedule A and Schedule A-1.)

Item number	Description	Alternate valuation date	Alternate value	Value at date of death
1				
	Total from continuation schedule(s) (or additional sheet(s)) attached to this schedule . .			
	TOTAL. (Also enter on Part 5, Recapitulation, page 3, at item 1.)			

(If more space is needed, attach the continuation schedule from the end of this package or additional sheets of the same size.)

(See the instructions on the reverse side.)

Schedule A—Page 4

Instructions for Schedule A—Real Estate

If the total gross estate contains any real estate, you must complete Schedule A and file it with the return. On Schedule A list real estate the decedent owned or had contracted to purchase. Number each parcel in the left-hand column.

Describe the real estate in enough detail so that the IRS can easily locate it for inspection and valuation. For each parcel of real estate, report the area and, if the parcel is improved, describe the improvements. For city or town property, report the street and number, ward, subdivision, block and lot, etc. For rural property, report the township, range, landmarks, etc.

If any item of real estate is subject to a mortgage for which the decedent's estate is liable, that is, if the indebtedness may be charged against other property of the estate that is not subject to that mortgage, or if the decedent was personally liable for that mortgage, you must report the full value of the property in the value column.

Enter the amount of the mortgage under "Description" on this schedule. The unpaid amount of the mortgage may be deducted on Schedule K. If the decedent's estate is NOT liable for the amount of the mortgage, report only the value of the equity of redemption (or value of the property less the indebtedness) in the value column as part of the gross estate. Do not enter any amount less than zero. Do not deduct the amount of indebtedness on Schedule K.

Also list on Schedule A real property the decedent contracted to purchase. Report the full value of the property and not the equity in the value column. Deduct the unpaid part of the purchase price on Schedule K.

Report the value of real estate without reducing it for homestead or other exemption, or the value of dower, curtesy, or a statutory estate created instead of dower or curtesy.

Explain how the reported values were determined and attach copies of any appraisals.

Schedule A Examples

In this example, the alternate valuation is not adopted; the date of death is January 1, 1993.

Item number	Description	Alternate valuation date	Alternate value	Value at date of death
1	House and lot, 1921 William Street NW, Washington, DC (lot 6, square 481). Rent of $2,700 due at end of each quarter, February 1, May 1, August 1, and November 1. Value based on appraisal, copy of which is attached			108,000
	Rent due on item 1 for quarter ending November 1, 1992, but not collected at date of death			2,700
	Rent accrued on item 1 for November and December 1992			1,800
2	House and lot, 304 Jefferson Street, Alexandria, VA (lot 18, square 40). Rent of $600 payable monthly. Value based on appraisal, copy of which is attached			96,000
	Rent due on item 2 for December 1992, but not collected at date of death . . .			600

In this example, alternate valuation is adopted; the date of death is January 1, 1993.

Item number	Description	Alternate valuation date	Alternate value	Value at date of death
1	House and lot, 1921 William Street NW, Washington, DC (lot 6, square 481). Rent of $2,700 due at end of each quarter, February 1, May 1, August 1, and November 1. Value based on appraisal, copy of which is attached. Not disposed of within 6 months following death	7/1/93	90,000	108,000
	Rent due on item 1 for quarter ending November 1, 1992, but not collected until February 1, 1993	2/1/93	2,700	2,700
	Rent accrued on item 1 for November and December 1992, collected on February 1, 1993	2/1/93	1,800	1,800
2	House and lot, 304 Jefferson Street, Alexandria, VA (lot 18, square 40). Rent of $600 payable monthly. Value based on appraisal, copy of which is attached. Property exchanged for farm on May 1, 1993	5/1/93	90,000	96,000
	Rent due on item 2 for December 1992, but not collected until February 1, 1993 .	2/1/93	600	600

Instructions for Schedule A-1.—Section 2032A Valuation

The election to value certain farm and closely held business property at its special use value is made by checking "Yes" to line 2 of Part 3, Elections by the Executor, Form 706. Schedule A-1 is used to report the additional information that must be submitted to support this election. In order to make a valid election, you must complete Schedule A-1 and attach all of the required statements and appraisals.

For definitions and additional information concerning special use valuation, see section 2032A and the related regulations.

Part 1.—Type of Election

Estate and GST Tax Elections.—If you elect special use valuation for the estate tax, you must also elect special use valuation for the GST tax and vice versa.

You must value each specific property interest at the same value for GST tax purposes that you value it at for estate tax purposes.

Protective Election.—To make the protective election described in the separate instructions for line 2 of Part 3, Elections by the Executor, you must check this box, enter the decedent's name and social security number in the spaces provided at the top of Schedule A-1, and complete line 1 and column A of lines 3 and 4 of Part 2. For purposes of the protective election, list on line 3 all of the real property that passes to the qualified heirs even though some of the property will be shown on line 2 when the additional notice of election is subsequently filed. You need not complete columns B–D of lines 3 and 4. You need not complete any other line entries on Schedule A-1. Completing Schedule A-1 as described above constitutes a Notice of Protective Election as described in Regulations section 20.2032A-8(b).

Part 2.—Notice of Election

Line 10.—Because the special use valuation election creates a potential tax liability for the recapture tax of section 2032A(c), you must list each person who receives an interest in the specially valued property on Schedule A-1. If there are more than eight persons who receive interests, use an additional sheet that follows the format of line 10. In the columns "Fair market value" and "Special use value," you should enter the total respective values of all the specially valued property interests received by each person.

GST Tax Savings

To compute the additional GST tax due upon disposition (or cessation of qualified use) of the property, each "skip person" (as defined in the instructions to Schedule R) who receives an interest in the specially valued property must know the total GST tax savings on all of the interests in specially valued property received. This GST tax savings is the difference between the total GST tax that was imposed on all of the interests in specially valued property received by the skip person valued at their special use value and the total GST tax that would have been imposed on the same interests received by the skip person had they been valued at their fair market value.

Because the GST tax depends on the executor's allocation of the GST exemption and the grandchild exclusion, the skip person who receives the interests is unable to compute this GST tax savings. Therefore, for each skip person who receives an interest in specially valued property, you must attach worksheets showing the total GST tax savings attributable to all of that person's interests in specially valued property.

How To Compute the GST Tax Savings.—Before computing each skip person's GST tax savings, you must complete Schedules R and R-1 for the entire estate (using the special use values).

For each skip person, you must complete two Schedules R (Parts 2 and 3 only) as worksheets, one showing the interests in specially valued property received by the skip person at their special use value and one showing the same interests at their fair market value.

If the skip person received interests in specially valued property that were shown on Schedule R-1, show these interests on the Schedule R, Parts 2 and 3 worksheets, as appropriate. Do not use Schedule R-1 as a worksheet.

Completing the Special Use Value Worksheets.—On lines 2–4 and 6, enter -0-.

Completing the Fair Market Value Worksheets.—*Lines 2 and 3, fixed taxes and other charges.*—If valuing the interests at their fair market value (instead of special use value) causes any of these taxes and charges to increase, enter the increased amount (only) on these lines and attach an explanation of the increase. Otherwise, enter -0-.

Line 6—GST exemption.—If you completed line 10 of Schedule R, Part 1, enter on line 6 the amount shown for the skip person on the *line 10 special use allocation schedule* you attached to Schedule R. If you did not complete line 10 of Schedule R, Part 1, enter -0- on line 6.

Total GST Tax Savings.—For each skip person, subtract the tax amount on line 10, Part 2 of the special use value worksheet from the tax amount on line 10, Part 2 of the fair market value worksheet. This difference is the skip person's total GST tax savings.

Part 3.—Agreement to Special Valuation Under Section 2032A

The agreement to special valuation by persons with an interest in property is required under section 2032A(a)(1)(B) and (d)(2) and must be signed by all parties who have any interest in the property being valued based on its qualified use as of the date of the decedent's death.

An interest in property is an interest that, as of the date of the decedent's death, can be asserted under applicable local law so as to affect the disposition of the specially valued property by the estate. Any person who at the decedent's death has any such interest in the property, whether present or future, or vested or contingent, must enter into the agreement. Included are owners of remainder and executory interests; the holders of general or special powers of appointment; beneficiaries of a gift over in default of exercise of any such power; joint tenants and holders of similar undivided interests when the decedent held only a joint or undivided interest in the property or when only an undivided interest is specially valued; and trustees of trusts and representatives of other entities holding title to, or holding any interests in the property. An heir who has the power under local law to caveat (challenge) a will and thereby affect disposition of the property is not, however, considered to be a person with an interest in property under section 2032A solely by reason of that right. Likewise, creditors of an estate are not such persons solely by reason of their status as creditors.

If any person required to enter into the agreement either desires that an agent act for him or her or cannot legally bind himself or herself due to infancy or other incompetency, or due to death before the election under section 2032A is timely exercised, a representative authorized by local law to bind the person in an agreement of this nature may sign the agreement on his or her behalf.

The Internal Revenue Service will contact the agent designated in the agreement on all matters relating to continued qualification under section 2032A of the specially valued real property and on all matters relating to the special lien arising under section 6324B. It is the duty of the agent as attorney-in-fact for the parties with interests in the specially valued property to furnish the IRS with any requested information and to notify the IRS of any disposition or cessation of qualified use of any part of the property.

Checklist for Section 2032A Election—*If you are going to make the special use valuation election on Schedule A-1, please use this checklist to ensure that you are providing everything necessary to make a valid election.*

To have a valid special use valuation election under section 2032A, you must file, in addition to the Federal estate tax return, **(a)** a notice of election (Schedule A-1, Part 2), and **(b)** a fully executed agreement (Schedule A-1, Part 3). You must include certain information in the notice of election. To ensure that the notice of election includes all of the information required for a valid election, use the following checklist. The checklist is for your use only. Do not file it with the return.

1. Does the notice of election include the decedent's name and social security number as they appear on the estate tax return?

2. Does the notice of election include the relevant qualified use of the property to be specially valued?

3. Does the notice of election describe the items of real property shown on the estate tax return that are to be specially valued and identify the property by the Form 706 schedule and item number?

4. Does the notice of election include the fair market value of the real property to be specially valued and also include its value based on the qualified use (determined without the adjustments provided in section 2032A(b)(3)(B))?

5. Does the notice of election include the adjusted value (as defined in section 2032A(b)(3)(B)) of **(a)** all real property that both passes from the decedent and is used in a qualified use, without regard to whether it is to be specially valued, and **(b)** all real property to be specially valued?

6. Does the notice of election include **(a)** the items of personal property shown on the estate tax return that pass from the decedent to a qualified heir and that are used in qualified use and **(b)** the total value of such personal property adjusted under section 2032A(b)(3)(B)?

7. Does the notice of election include the adjusted value of the gross estate? (See section 2032A(b)(3)(A).)

8. Does the notice of election include the method used to determine the special use value?

9. Does the notice of election include copies of written appraisals of the fair market value of the real property?

10. Does the notice of election include a statement that the decedent and/or a member of his or her family has owned all of the specially valued property for at least 5 years of the 8 years immediately preceding the date of the decedent's death?

11. Does the notice of election include a statement as to whether there were any periods during the 8-year period preceding the decedent's date of death during which the decedent or a member of his or her family **(a)** did not own the property to be specially valued, **(b)** use it in a qualified use, or **(c)** materially participate in the operation of the farm or other business? (See section 2032A(e)(6).)

12. Does the notice of election include, for each item of specially valued property, the name of every person taking an interest in that item of specially valued property and the following information about each such person: **(a)** the person's address, **(b)** the person's taxpayer identification number, **(c)** the person's relationship to the decedent, and **(d)** the value of the property interest passing to that person based on both fair market value and qualified use?

13. Does the notice of election include affidavits describing the activities constituting material participation and the identity of the material participants?

14. Does the notice of election include a legal description of each item of specially valued property?

(In the case of an election made for qualified woodlands, the information included in the notice of election must include the reason for entitlement to the woodlands election.)

Any election made under section 2032A will not be valid unless a properly executed agreement (Schedule A-1, Part 3) is filed with the estate tax return. To ensure that the agreement satisfies the requirements for a valid election, use the following checklist.

1. Has the agreement been signed by each and every qualified heir having an interest in the property being specially valued?

2. Has every qualified heir expressed consent to personal liability under section 2032A(c) in the event of an early disposition or early cessation of qualified use?

3. Is the agreement that is actually signed by the qualified heirs in a form that is binding on all of the qualified heirs having an interest in the specially valued property?

4. Does the agreement designate an agent to act for the parties to the agreement in all dealings with the IRS on matters arising under section 2032A?

5. Has the agreement been signed by the designated agent and does it give the address of the agent?

	Decedent's Social Security Number
Estate of:	

SCHEDULE A-1—Section 2032A Valuation

Part 1.—Type of Election (Before making an election, see the checklist on page 7.):

☐ **Protective election (Regulations section 20.2032A-8(b)).**—Complete Part 2, line 1, and column A of lines 3 and 4. (See instructions.)

☐ **Regular election.**—Complete all of Part 2 (including line 11, if applicable) and Part 3. (See instructions.)

Before completing Schedule A-1, see the checklist on page 7 for the information and documents that must be included to make a valid election.

The election is not valid unless the agreement (i.e., Part 3-Agreement to Special Valuation Under Section 2032A)—

- Is signed by each and every qualified heir with an interest in the specially valued property, and
- Is attached to this return when it is filed.

Part 2.—Notice of Election (Regulations section 20.2032A-8(a)(3))

Note: *All real property entered on lines 2 and 3 must also be entered on Schedules A, E, F, G, or H, as applicable.*

1 Qualified use—check one ▶ ☐ Farm used for farming, or

  ▶ ☐ Trade or business other than farming

2 Real property used in a qualified use, passing to qualified heirs, and to be specially valued on this Form 706.

A Schedule and item number from Form 706	B Full value (without section 2032A(b)(3)(B) adjustment)	C Adjusted value (with section 2032A(b)(3)(B) adjustment)	D Value based on qualified use (without section 2032A(b)(3)(B) adjustment)

Totals . . . .

Attach a legal description of all property listed on line 2.

Attach copies of appraisals showing the column B values for all property listed on line 2.

3 Real property used in a qualified use, passing to qualified heirs, but not specially valued on this Form 706.

A Schedule and item number from Form 706	B Full value (without section 2032A(b)(3)(B) adjustment)	C Adjusted value (with section 2032A(b)(3)(B) adjustment)	D Value based on qualified use (without section 2032A(b)(3)(B) adjustment)

Totals . . . .

If you checked "Regular election," you must attach copies of appraisals showing the column B values for all property listed on line 3.

(Continued on next page)

4 Personal property used in a qualified use and passing to qualified heirs.

A Schedule and item number from Form 706	B Adjusted value (with section 2032A(b)(3)(B) adjustment)	A (continued) Schedule and item number from Form 706	B (continued) Adjusted value (with section 2032A(b)(3)(B) adjustment)
		"Subtotal" from Col. B, below left	

Subtotal . . . .   **Total adjusted value** . . .

5 Enter the value of the total gross estate as adjusted under section 2032A(b)(3)(A). ▶ _____

6 **Attach a description of the method used to determine the special value based on qualified use.**

7 Did the decedent and/or a member of his or her family own all property listed on line 2 for at least 5 of the 8 years immediately preceding the date of the decedent's death? . . . . ☐ **Yes** ☐ **No**

8 Were there any periods during the 8-year period preceding the date of the decedent's death during which the decedent or a member of his or her family:

	Yes	No
a Did not own the property listed on line 2 above?		
b Did not use the property listed on line 2 above in a qualified use?		
c Did not materially participate in the operation of the farm or other business within the meaning of section 2032A(e)(6)?		

If "Yes" to any of the above, you must attach a statement listing the periods. If applicable, describe whether the exceptions of sections 2032A(b)(4) or (5) are met.

9 **Attach affidavits describing the activities constituting material participation and the identity and relationship to the decedent of the material participants.**

10 Persons holding interests. Enter the requested information for each party who received any interest in the specially valued property. **(Each of the qualified heirs receiving an interest in the property must sign the agreement, and the agreement must be filed with this return.)**

	Name	Address
A		
B		
C		
D		
E		
F		
G		
H		

	Identifying number	Relationship to decedent	Fair market value	Special use value
A				
B				
C				
D				
E				
F				
G				
H				

You must attach a computation of the GST tax savings attributable to direct skips for each person listed above who is a skip person. (See instructions.)

11 **Woodlands election.**—Check here ▶ ☐ if you wish to make a woodlands election as described in section 2032A(e)(13). Enter the Schedule and item numbers from Form 706 of the property for which you are making this election ▶ _____ You must attach a statement explaining why you are entitled to make this election. The IRS may issue regulations that require more information to substantiate this election. You will be notified by the IRS if you must supply further information.

Schedule A-1—Page 9

Part 3.—Agreement to Special Valuation Under Section 2032A

Estate of:	Date of Death	Decedent's Social Security Number

There cannot be a valid election unless:

- The agreement is executed by each and every one of the qualified heirs, and
- The agreement is included with the estate tax return when the estate tax return is filed.

We (list all qualified heirs and other persons having an interest in the property required to sign this agreement)

_____

_____ ,

being all the qualified heirs and _____

_____ ,

being all other parties having interests in the property which is qualified real property and which is valued under section 2032A of the
Internal Revenue Code, do hereby approve of the election made by _____ ,
Executor/Administrator of the estate of _____ ,
pursuant to section 2032A to value said property on the basis of the qualified use to which the property is devoted and do hereby enter
into this agreement pursuant to section 2032A(d).

The undersigned agree and consent to the application of subsection (c) of section 2032A of the Code with respect to all the property
described on line 2 of Part 2 of Schedule A-1 of Form 706, attached to this agreement. More specifically, the undersigned heirs expressly
agree and consent to personal liability under subsection (c) of 2032A for the additional estate and GST taxes imposed by that subsection
with respect to their respective interests in the above-described property in the event of certain early dispositions of the property or early
cessation of the qualified use of the property. It is understood that if a qualified heir disposes of any interest in qualified real property to
any member of his or her family, such member may thereafter be treated as the qualified heir with respect to such interest upon filing a
Form 706-A and a new agreement.

The undersigned interested parties who are not qualified heirs consent to the collection of any additional estate and GST taxes imposed
under section 2032A(c) of the Code from the specially valued property.

If there is a disposition of any interest which passes or has passed to him or her or if there is a cessation of the qualified use of any
specially valued property which passes or passed to him or her, each of the undersigned heirs agrees to file a **Form 706-A,** United States
Additional Estate Tax Return, and pay any additional estate and GST taxes due within 6 months of the disposition or cessation.

It is understood by all interested parties that this agreement is a condition precedent to the election of special use valuation under section
2032A of the Code and must be executed by every interested party even though that person may not have received the estate (or GST)
tax benefits or be in possession of such property.

Each of the undersigned understands that by making this election, a lien will be created and recorded pursuant to section 6324B of the
Code on the property referred to in this agreement for the adjusted tax differences with respect to the estate as defined in section
2032A(c)(2)(C).

As the interested parties, the undersigned designate the following individual as their agent for all dealings with the Internal Revenue Service
concerning the continued qualification of the specially valued property under section 2032A of the Code and on all issues regarding the
special lien under section 6324B. The agent is authorized to act for the parties with respect to all dealings with the Service on matters
affecting the qualified real property described earlier. This authority includes the following:

- To receive confidential information on all matters relating to continued qualification under section 2032A of the specially valued
  real property and on all matters relating to the special lien arising under section 6324B.

- To furnish the Service with any requested information concerning the property.

- To notify the Service of any disposition or cessation of qualified use of any part of the property.

- To receive, but not to endorse and collect, checks in payment of any refund of Internal Revenue taxes, penalties, or interest.

- To execute waivers (including offers of waivers) of restrictions on assessment or collection of deficiencies in tax and waivers of
  notice of disallowance of a claim for credit or refund.

- To execute closing agreements under section 7121.

(continued on next page)

Part 3.—Agreement to Special Valuation Under Section 2032A *(Continued)*

Estate of:	Date of Death	Decedent's Social Security Number

- Other acts (specify) ▶ _____

By signing this agreement, the agent agrees to provide the Service with any requested information concerning this property and to notify the Service of any disposition or cessation of the qualified use of any part of this property.

Name of Agent	Signature	Address

The property to which this agreement relates is listed in Form 706, United States Estate (and Generation-Skipping Transfer) Tax Return, and in the Notice of Election, along with its fair market value according to section 2031 of the Code and its special use value according to section 2032A. The name, address, social security number, and interest (including the value) of each of the undersigned in this property are as set forth in the attached Notice of Election.

IN WITNESS WHEREOF, the undersigned have hereunto set their hands at _____

this _____ day of _____ .

SIGNATURES OF EACH OF THE QUALIFIED HEIRS:

Signature of qualified heir	Signature of qualified heir
Signature of qualified heir	Signature of qualified heir
Signature of qualified heir	Signature of qualified heir
Signature of qualified heir	Signature of qualified heir
Signature of qualified heir	Signature of qualified heir
Signature of qualified heir	Signature of qualified heir

Signatures of other interested parties

Signatures of other interested parties

Schedule A-1—Page 11

Estate of:

SCHEDULE B—Stocks and Bonds

(For jointly owned property that must be disclosed on Schedule E, see the instructions for Schedule E.)

Item number	Description including face amount of bonds or number of shares and par value where needed for identification. Give CUSIP number if available.	Unit value	Alternate valuation date	Alternate value	Value at date of death
1					
	Total from continuation schedule(s) (or additional sheet(s)) attached to this schedule . .				
	TOTAL. (Also enter on Part 5, Recapitulation, page 3, at item 2.)				

(If more space is needed, attach the continuation schedule from the end of this package or additional sheets of the same size.)

(The instructions to Schedule B are in the separate instructions.)

Schedule B—Page 12

Estate of:

SCHEDULE C—Mortgages, Notes, and Cash
(For jointly owned property that must be disclosed on Schedule E, see the instructions for Schedule E.)

Item number	Description	Alternate valuation date	Alternate value	Value at date of death
1				
	Total from continuation schedule(s) (or additional sheet(s)) attached to this schedule .			
	TOTAL. (Also enter on Part 5, Recapitulation, page 3, at item 3.)			

(If more space is needed, attach the continuation schedule from the end of this package or additional sheets of the same size.)
(See the instructions on the reverse side.)

Instructions for Schedule C.— Mortgages, Notes, and Cash

If the total gross estate contains any mortgages, notes, or cash, you must complete Schedule C and file it with the return.

On Schedule C list mortgages and notes *payable to* the decedent at the time of death. (Mortgages and notes *payable by* the decedent should be listed (if deductible) on Schedule K.) Also list on Schedule C cash the decedent had at the date of death.

Group the items in the following categories and list the categories in the following order:

1. Mortgages.—List: (a) the face value and unpaid balance; (b) date of mortgage; (c) date of maturity; (d) name of maker; (e) property mortgaged; and (f) interest dates and rate of interest. For example: bond and mortgage of $50,000, unpaid balance $24,000; dated January 1, 1980; John Doe to Richard Roe; premises 22 Clinton Street, Newark, NJ; due January 1, 1993, interest payable at 10% a year January 1 and July 1.

2. Promissory notes.—Describe in the same way as mortgages.

3. Contract by the decedent to sell land.—List: (a) the name of the purchaser; (b) date of contract; (c) description of property; (d) sale price; (e) initial payment; (f) amounts of installment payment; (g) unpaid balance of principal; and (h) interest rate.

4. Cash in possession.—List separately from bank deposits.

5. Cash in banks, savings and loan associations, and other types of financial organizations.—List: (a) the name and address of each financial organization; (b) amount in each account; (c) serial number; and (d) nature of account, indicating whether checking, savings, time deposit, etc. If you obtain statements from the financial organizations, keep them for IRS inspection.

Estate of:

SCHEDULE D—Insurance on the Decedent's Life

You must list **all** policies on the life of the decedent and attach a Form 712 for each policy.

Item number	Description	Alternate valuation date	Alternate value	Value at date of death
1				
	Total from continuation schedule(s) (or additional sheet(s)) attached to this schedule .			
	TOTAL. (Also enter on Part 5, Recapitulation, page 3, at item 4.)			

(If more space is needed, attach the continuation schedule from the end of this package or additional sheets of the same size.)

(See the instructions on the reverse side.)

Instructions for Schedule D.—Insurance on the Decedent's Life

If there was any insurance on the decedent's life, whether or not included in the gross estate, you must complete Schedule D and file it with the return.

Insurance you must include on Schedule D.—Under section 2042 you must include in the gross estate:

- Insurance on the decedent's life receivable by or for the benefit of the estate; and
- Insurance on the decedent's life receivable by beneficiaries other than the estate, as described below.

The term "insurance" refers to life insurance of every description, including death benefits paid by fraternal beneficiary societies operating under the lodge system, and death benefits paid under no-fault automobile insurance policies if the no-fault insurer was unconditionally bound to pay the benefit in the event of the insured's death.

Insurance in favor of the estate.—Include on Schedule D the full amount of the proceeds of insurance on the life of the decedent receivable by the executor or otherwise payable to or for the benefit of the estate. Insurance in favor of the estate includes insurance used to pay the estate tax, and any other taxes, debts, or charges that are enforceable against the estate. The manner in which the policy is drawn is immaterial as long as there is an obligation, legally binding on the beneficiary, to use the proceeds to pay taxes, debts, or charges. You must include the full amount even though the premiums or other consideration may have been paid by a person other than the decedent.

Insurance receivable by beneficiaries other than the estate.—Include on Schedule D the proceeds of all insurance on the life of the decedent not receivable by or for the benefit of the decedent's estate if the decedent possessed at death any of the incidents of ownership, exercisable either alone or in conjunction with any person.

Incidents of ownership in a policy include:

- The right of the insured or estate to its economic benefits;
- The power to change the beneficiary;
- The power to surrender or cancel the policy;
- The power to assign the policy or to revoke an assignment;
- The power to pledge the policy for a loan;
- The power to obtain from the insurer a loan against the surrender value of the policy;
- A reversionary interest if the value of the reversionary interest was more than 5% of the value of the policy immediately before the decedent died. (An interest in an insurance policy is considered a reversionary interest if, for example, the proceeds become payable to the insured's estate or payable as the insured directs if the beneficiary dies before the insured.)

Life insurance not includible in the gross estate under section 2042 may be includible under some other section of the Code. For example, a life insurance policy could be transferred by the decedent in such a way that it would be includible in the gross estate under section 2036, 2037, or 2038. (See the instructions to Schedule G for a description of these sections.)

Completing the Schedule

You must list every policy of insurance on the life of the decedent, whether or not it is included in the gross estate.

Under "Description" list:

- Name of the insurance company and
- Number of the policy.

For every policy of life insurance listed on the schedule, you must request a statement on **Form 712,** Life Insurance Statement, from the company that issued the policy. Attach the Form 712 to the back of Schedule D.

If the policy proceeds are paid in one sum, enter the net proceeds received (from Form 712, line 24) in the value (and alternate value) columns of Schedule D. If the policy proceeds are not paid in one sum, enter the value of the proceeds as of the date of the decedent's death (from Form 712, line 25).

If part or all of the policy proceeds are not included in the gross estate, you must explain why they were not included.

Estate of:

SCHEDULE E—Jointly Owned Property
(If you elect section 2032A valuation, you must complete Schedule E and Schedule A-1.)

PART 1.—Qualified Joint Interests—Interests Held by the Decedent and His or Her Spouse as the Only Joint Tenants (Section 2040(b)(2))

Item number	Description For securities, give CUSIP number, if available.	Alternate valuation date	Alternate value	Value at date of death
	Total from continuation schedule(s) (or additional sheet(s)) attached to this schedule.			
1a	Totals			
1b	Amounts included in gross estate (one-half of line 1a)			

PART 2.—All Other Joint Interests

2a State the name and address of each surviving co-tenant. If there are more than three surviving co-tenants, list the additional co-tenants on an attached sheet.

Name	Address (number and street, city, state, and ZIP code)
A.	
B.	
C.	

Item number	Enter letter for co-tenant	Description (including alternate valuation date if any) For securities, give CUSIP number, if available.	Percentage includible	Includible alternate value	Includible value at date of death
		Total from continuation schedule(s) (or additional sheet(s)) attached to this schedule.			
2b		Total other joint interests			
3		**Total includible joint interests** (add lines 1b and 2b). Also enter on Part 5, Recapitulation, page 3, at item 5			

(If more space is needed, attach the continuation schedule from the end of this package or additional sheets of the same size.)
(See the instructions on the reverse side.)

Schedule E—Page 17

Instructions for Schedule E.—Jointly Owned Property

You must complete Schedule E and file it with the return if the decedent owned any joint property at the time of death, whether or not the decedent's interest is includible in the gross estate.

Enter on this schedule all property of whatever kind or character, whether real estate, personal property, or bank accounts, in which the decedent held at the time of death an interest either as a joint tenant with right to survivorship or as a tenant by the entirety.

Do not list on this schedule property that the decedent held as a tenant in common, but report the value of the interest on Schedule A if real estate, or on the appropriate schedule if personal property. Similarly, community property held by the decedent and spouse should be reported on the appropriate Schedules A through I. The decedent's interest in a partnership should not be entered on this schedule unless the partnership interest itself is jointly owned. Solely owned partnership interests should be reported on Schedule F, "Other Miscellaneous Property."

Part 1.—Qualified joint interests held by decedent and spouse.—Under section 2040(b)(2), a joint interest is a qualified joint interest if the decedent and the surviving spouse held the interest as:

- Tenants by the entirety, or
- Joint tenants with right of survivorship if the decedent and the decedent's spouse are the only joint tenants.

Interests that meet either of the two requirements above should be entered in Part 1. Joint interests that do not meet either of the two requirements above should be entered in Part 2.

Under "Description," describe the property as required in the instructions for Schedules A, B, C, and F for the type of property involved. For example, jointly held stocks and bonds should be described using the rules given in the instructions to Schedule B.

Under "Alternate value" and "Value at date of death," enter the full value of the property.

Note: *You cannot claim the special treatment under section 2040(b) for property held jointly by a decedent and a surviving spouse who is not a U.S. citizen. You must report these joint interests on Part 2 of Schedule E, not Part 1.*

Part 2.—Other joint interests.—All joint interests that were not entered in Part 1 must be entered in Part 2.

For each item of property, enter the appropriate letter A, B, C, etc., from line 2a to indicate the name and address of the surviving co-tenant.

Under "Description," describe the property as required in the instructions for Schedules A, B, C, and F for the type of property involved.

In the "Percentage includible" column, enter the percentage of the total value of the property that you intend to include in the gross estate.

Generally, you must include the full value of the jointly owned property in the gross estate. However, the full value should not be included if you can show that a part of the property originally belonged to the other tenant or tenants and was never received or acquired by the other tenant or tenants from the decedent for less than adequate and full consideration in money or money's worth, or unless you can show that any part of the property was acquired with consideration originally belonging to the surviving joint tenant or tenants. In this case, you may exclude from the value of the property an amount proportionate to the consideration furnished by the other tenant or tenants. Relinquishing or promising to relinquish dower, curtesy, or statutory estate created instead of dower or curtesy, or other marital rights in the decedent's property or estate is not consideration in money or money's worth. See the Schedule A instructions for the value to show for real property that is subject to a mortgage.

If the property was acquired by the decedent and another person or persons by gift, bequest, devise, or inheritance as joint tenants, and their interests are not otherwise specified by law, include only that part of the value of the property that is figured by dividing the full value of the property by the number of joint tenants.

If you believe that less than the full value of the entire property is includible in the gross estate for tax purposes, you must establish the right to include the smaller value by attaching proof of the extent, origin, and nature of the decedent's interest and the interest(s) of the decedent's co-tenant or co-tenants.

In the "Includible alternate value" and "Includible value at date of death" columns, you should enter only the values that you believe are includible in the gross estate.

Estate of:

SCHEDULE F—Other Miscellaneous Property Not Reportable Under Any Other Schedule

(For jointly owned property that must be disclosed on Schedule E, see the instructions for Schedule E.)
(If you elect section 2032A valuation, you must complete Schedule F and Schedule A-1.)

		Yes	No
1	Did the decedent at the time of death own any articles of artistic or collectible value in excess of $3,000 or any collections whose artistic or collectible value combined at date of death exceeded $10,000? . . . . If "Yes," submit full details on this schedule and attach appraisals.		
2	Has the decedent's estate, spouse, or any other person, received (or will receive) any bonus or award as a result of the decedent's employment or death? . . . . If "Yes," submit full details on this schedule.		
3	Did the decedent at the time of death have, or have access to, a safe deposit box? . . . . If "Yes," state location, and if held in joint names of decedent and another, state name and relationship of joint depositor.		

If any of the contents of the safe deposit box are omitted from the schedules in this return, explain fully why omitted.

Item number	Description For securities, give CUSIP number, if available.	Alternate valuation date	Alternate value	Value at date of death
1				
	Total from continuation schedule(s) (or additional sheet(s)) attached to this schedule. .			
	TOTAL. (Also enter on Part 5, Recapitulation, page 3, at item 6.)			

(If more space is needed, attach the continuation schedule from the end of this package or additional sheets of the same size.)
(See the instructions on the reverse side.)

Instructions for Schedule F.—Other Miscellaneous Property

You must complete Schedule F and file it with the return.

On Schedule F list all items that must be included in the gross estate that are not reported on any other schedule, including:

- Debts due the decedent (other than notes and mortgages included on Schedule C)
- Interests in business
- Insurance on the life of another (obtain and attach **Form 712,** Life Insurance Statement, for each policy)

Note for single premium or paid-up policies: *In certain situations, for example where the surrender value of the policy exceeds its replacement cost, the true economic value of the policy will be greater than the amount shown on line 56 of Form 712. In these situations, you should report the full economic value of the policy on Schedule F. See Rev. Rul. 78-137, 1978-1 C.B. 280 for details.*

- Section 2044 property
- Claims (including the value of the decedent's interest in a claim for refund of income taxes or the amount of the refund actually received)
- Rights
- Royalties
- Leaseholds
- Judgments
- Reversionary or remainder interests
- Shares in trust funds (attach a copy of the trust instrument)

- Household goods and personal effects, including wearing apparel
- Farm products and growing crops
- Livestock
- Farm machinery
- Automobiles

If the decedent owned any interest in a partnership or unincorporated business, attach a statement of assets and liabilities for the valuation date and for the 5 years before the valuation date. Also attach statements of the net earnings for the same 5 years. You must account for goodwill in the valuation. In general, furnish the same information and follow the methods used to value close corporations. See the instructions for Schedule B.

All partnership interests should be reported on Schedule F unless the partnership interest, itself, is jointly owned. Jointly owned partnership interests should be reported on Schedule E.

If real estate is owned by the sole proprietorship, it should be reported on Schedule F and not on Schedule A. Describe the real estate with the same detail required for Schedule A.

Line 1.—If the decedent owned at the date of death articles with artistic or intrinsic value (e.g., jewelry, furs, silverware, books, statuary, vases, oriental rugs, coin or stamp collections), check the "Yes" box on line 1 and provide full details. If any one article is valued at more than $3,000, or any collection of similar articles is valued at more than $10,000, attach an appraisal by an expert under oath and the required statement regarding the appraiser's qualifications (see Regulations section 20.2031-6(b)).

Form 706 (Rev. 8-93)

Estate of:

SCHEDULE G—Transfers During Decedent's Life
(If you elect section 2032A valuation, you must complete Schedule G and Schedule A-1.)

Item number	Description For securities, give CUSIP number, if available.	Alternate valuation date	Alternate value	Value at date of death
A.	Gift tax paid by the decedent or the estate for all gifts made by the decedent or his or her spouse within 3 years before the decedent's death (section 2035(c))	X X X X X		
B.	Transfers includible under section 2035(a), 2036, 2037, or 2038:			
1				
	Total from continuation schedule(s) (or additional sheet(s)) attached to this schedule .			
	TOTAL. (Also enter on Part 5, Recapitulation, page 3, at item 7.).			

SCHEDULE H—Powers of Appointment
(Include "5 and 5 lapsing" powers (section 2041(b)(2)) held by the decedent.)
(If you elect section 2032A valuation, you must complete Schedule H and Schedule A-1.)

Item number	Description	Alternate valuation date	Alternate value	Value at date of death
1				
	Total from continuation schedule(s) (or additional sheet(s)) attached to this schedule .			
	TOTAL. (Also enter on Part 5, Recapitulation, page 3, at item 8.).			

(If more space is needed, attach the continuation schedule from the end of this package or additional sheets of the same size.)
(The instructions to Schedules G and H are in the separate instructions.)

Schedules G and H—Page 21

Form 706 (Rev. 8-93)

Estate of:

SCHEDULE I—Annuities

Note: *Generally, no exclusion is allowed for the estates of decedents dying after December 31, 1984 (see instructions).*

A Are you excluding from the decedent's gross estate the value of a lump-sum distribution described in section 2039(f)(2)? . . . .

If "Yes," you must attach the information required by the instructions.

Item number	Description Show the entire value of the annuity before any exclusions.	Alternate valuation date	Includible alternate value	Includible value at date of death
1				

Total from continuation schedule(s) (or additional sheet(s)) attached to this schedule .

TOTAL (Also enter on Part 5, Recapitulation, page 3, at item 9.) . . . .

(If more space is needed, attach the continuation schedule from the end of this package or additional sheets of the same size.)

(The instructions to Schedule I are in the separate instructions.)

Schedule I—Page 22

Estate of:

SCHEDULE J—Funeral Expenses and Expenses Incurred in Administering Property Subject to Claims

Note: *Do not list on this schedule expenses of administering property not subject to claims. For those expenses, see the instructions for Schedule L.*

If executors' commissions, attorney fees, etc., are claimed and allowed as a deduction for estate tax purposes, they are not allowable as a deduction in computing the taxable income of the estate for Federal income tax purposes. They are allowable as an income tax deduction on Form 1041 if a waiver is filed to waive the deduction on Form 706 (see the Form 1041 instructions).

Item number	Description	Expense amount	Total Amount
1	**A. Funeral expenses:**		
	Total funeral expenses		
	B. Administration expenses:		
1	Executors' commissions—amount estimated/agreed upon/paid. (Strike out the words that do not apply.)		
2	Attorney fees—amount estimated/agreed upon/paid. (Strike out the words that do not apply.) . . .		
3	Accountant fees—amount estimated/agreed upon/paid. (Strike out the words that do not apply.) . .		
4	Miscellaneous expenses:	Expense amount	
	Total miscellaneous expenses from continuation schedule(s) (or additional sheet(s)) attached to this schedule		
	Total miscellaneous expenses		
	TOTAL. (Also enter on Part 5, Recapitulation, page 3, at item 11.)		

(If more space is needed, attach the continuation schedule from the end of this package or additional sheets of the same size.)
(See the instructions on the reverse side.)

Instructions for Schedule J.—
Funeral Expenses and Expenses Incurred in Administering Property Subject to Claims

General.—You must complete and file Schedule J if you claim a deduction on item 11 of Part 5, Recapitulation.

On Schedule J, itemize funeral expenses and expenses incurred in administering property subject to claims. List the names and addresses of persons to whom the expenses are payable and describe the nature of the expense. **Do not list expenses incurred in administering property not subject to claims on this schedule. List them on Schedule L instead.**

Funeral Expenses.—Itemize funeral expenses on line A. Deduct from the expenses any amounts that were reimbursed, such as death benefits payable by the Social Security Administration and the Veterans Administration.

Executors' Commissions.—When you file the return, you may deduct commissions that have actually been paid to you or that you expect will be paid. You may not deduct commissions if none will be collected. If the amount of the commissions has not been fixed by decree of the proper court, the deduction will be allowed on the final examination of the return, provided that:

- The District Director is reasonably satisfied that the commissions claimed will be paid;
- The amount entered as a deduction is within the amount allowable by the laws of the jurisdiction where the estate is being administered;
- It is in accordance with the usually accepted practice in that jurisdiction for estates of similar size and character.

If you have not been paid the commissions claimed at the time of the final examination of the return, you must support the amount you deducted with an affidavit or statement signed under the penalties of perjury that the amount has been agreed upon and will be paid.

You may not deduct a bequest or devise made to you instead of commissions. If, however, the decedent fixed by will the compensation payable to you for services to be rendered in the administration of the estate, you may deduct this amount to the extent it is not more than the compensation allowable by the local law or practice.

Do not deduct on this schedule amounts paid as trustees' commissions whether received by you acting in the capacity of a trustee or by a separate trustee. If such amounts were paid in administering property not subject to claims, deduct them on Schedule L.

Note: *Executors' commissions are taxable income to the executors. Therefore, be sure to include them as income on your individual income tax return.*

Attorney Fees.—Enter the amount of attorney fees that have actually been paid or that you reasonably expect to be paid. If on the final examination of the return the fees claimed have not been awarded by the proper court and paid, the deduction will be allowed provided the District Director is reasonably satisfied that the amount claimed will be paid and that it does not exceed a reasonable payment for the services performed, taking into account the size and character of the estate and the local law and practice. If the fees claimed have not been paid at the time of final examination of the return, the amount deducted must be supported by an affidavit, or statement signed under the penalties of perjury, by the executor or the attorney stating that the amount has been agreed upon and will be paid.

Do not deduct attorney fees incidental to litigation incurred by the beneficiaries. These expenses are charged against the beneficiaries personally and are not administration expenses authorized by the Code.

Miscellaneous Expenses.—Miscellaneous administration expenses necessarily incurred in preserving and distributing the estate are deductible. These expenses include appraiser's and accountant's fees, certain court costs, and costs of storing or maintaining assets of the estate.

The expenses of selling assets are deductible only if the sale is necessary to pay the decedent's debts, the expenses of administration, or taxes, or to preserve the estate or carry out distribution.

Estate of:

SCHEDULE K—Debts of the Decedent, and Mortgages and Liens

Item number	Debts of the Decedent—Creditor and nature of claim, and allowable death taxes	Amount unpaid to date	Amount in contest	Amount claimed as a deduction
1				
	Total from continuation schedule(s) (or additional sheet(s)) attached to this schedule			
	TOTAL. (Also enter on Part 5, Recapitulation, page 3, at item 12.)			

Item number	Mortgages and Liens—Description	Amount
1		
	Total from continuation schedule(s) (or additional sheet(s)) attached to this schedule	
	TOTAL. (Also enter on Part 5, Recapitulation, page 3, at item 13.)	

(If more space is needed, attach the continuation schedule from the end of this package or additional sheets of the same size.)
(The instructions to Schedule K are in the separate instructions.)

Estate of:

SCHEDULE L—Net Losses During Administration and
Expenses Incurred in Administering Property Not Subject to Claims

Item number	Net losses during administration (Note: *Do not deduct losses claimed on a Federal income tax return.*)	Amount
1		
	Total from continuation schedule(s) (or additional sheet(s)) attached to this schedule	
	TOTAL. (Also enter on Part 5, Recapitulation, page 3, at item 16.)	

Item number	Expenses incurred in administering property not subject to claims (Indicate whether estimated, agreed upon, or paid.)	Amount
1		
	Total from continuation schedule(s) (or additional sheet(s)) attached to this schedule	
	TOTAL. (Also enter on Part 5, Recapitulation, page 3, at item 17.)	

(If more space is needed, attach the continuation schedule from the end of this package or additional sheets of the same size.)

Schedule L —Page 26   (The instructions to Schedule L are in the separate instructions.)

Estate of:

SCHEDULE M—Bequests, etc., to Surviving Spouse

Election To Deduct Qualified Terminable Interest Property Under Section 2056(b)(7).—If a trust (or other property) meets the requirements of qualified terminable interest property under section 2056(b)(7), and

  a. The trust or other property is listed on Schedule M, and

  b. The value of the trust (or other property) is entered in whole or in part as a deduction on Schedule M,

then unless the executor specifically identifies the trust (all or a fractional portion or percentage) or other property to be excluded from the election the executor shall be deemed to have made an election to have such trust (or other property) treated as qualified terminable interest property under section 2056(b)(7).

  If less than the entire value of the trust (or other property) that the executor has included in the gross estate is entered as a deduction on Schedule M, the executor shall be considered to have made an election only as to a fraction of the trust (or other property). The numerator of this fraction is equal to the amount of the trust (or other property) deducted on Schedule M. The denominator is equal to the total value of the trust (or other property).

Election To Deduct Qualified Domestic Trust Property Under Section 2056A.—If a trust meets the requirements of a qualified domestic trust under section 2056A(a) and this return is filed no later than 1 year after the time prescribed by law (including extensions) for filing the return, and

  a. The entire value of a trust or trust property is listed on Schedule M, and

  b. The entire value of the trust or trust property is entered as a deduction on Schedule M,

then unless the executor specifically identifies the trust to be excluded from the election, the executor shall be deemed to have made an election to have the entire trust treated as qualified domestic trust property.

		Yes	No
1	Did any property pass to the surviving spouse as a result of a qualified disclaimer?		
	If "Yes," attach a copy of the written disclaimer required by section 2518(b).		
2a	In what country was the surviving spouse born? _____		
b	What is the surviving spouse's date of birth? _____		
c	Is the surviving spouse a U.S. citizen?		
d	If the surviving spouse is a naturalized citizen, when did the surviving spouse acquire citizenship? _____		
e	If the surviving spouse is not a U.S. citizen, of what country is the surviving spouse a citizen? _____		
3	**Election out of QTIP Treatment of Annuities.**—Do you elect under section 2056(b)(7)(C)(ii) **not** to treat as qualified terminable interest property any joint and survivor annuities that are included in the gross estate and would otherwise be treated as qualified terminable interest property under section 2056(b)(7)(C)? (see instructions)		

Item number	Description of property interests passing to surviving spouse	Amount
1		
	Total from continuation schedule(s) (or additional sheet(s)) attached to this schedule	
4	**Total** amount of property interests listed on Schedule M	**4**
5a	Federal estate taxes (including section 4980A taxes) payable out of property interests listed on Schedule M	**5a**
b	Other death taxes payable out of property interests listed on Schedule M . . .	**5b**
c	Federal and state GST taxes payable out of property interests listed on Schedule M	**5c**
d	Add items a, b, and c	**5d**
6	Net amount of property interests listed on Schedule M (subtract 5d from 4). Also enter on Part 5, Recapitulation, page 3, at item 18	**6**

(If more space is needed, attach the continuation schedule from the end of this package or additional sheets of the same size.)

(See the instructions on the reverse side.)

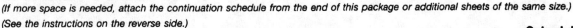

Examples of Listing of Property Interests on Schedule M

Item number	Description of property interests passing to surviving spouse	Amount
1	One-half the value of a house and lot, 256 South West Street, held by decedent and surviving spouse as joint tenants with right of survivorship under deed dated July 15, 1957 (Schedule E, Part I, item 1)	$ 32,500
2	Proceeds of Gibraltar Life Insurance Company policy No. 104729, payable in one sum to surviving spouse (Schedule D, item 3)	20,000
3	Cash bequest under Paragraph Six of will	100,000

Instructions for Schedule M.—Bequests, etc., to Surviving Spouse (Marital Deduction)

General

You must complete Schedule M and file it with the return if you claim a deduction on item 18 of Part 5, Recapitulation.

The marital deduction is authorized by section 2056 for certain property interests that pass from the decedent to the surviving spouse. You may claim the deduction only for property interests that are included in the decedent's gross estate (Schedules A through I).

Note: *The marital deduction is generally not allowed if the surviving spouse is **not** a U.S. citizen. The marital deduction is allowed for property passing to such a surviving spouse in a "qualified domestic trust" or if such property is transferred or irrevocably assigned to such a trust before the estate tax return is filed. The executor must elect qualified domestic trust status on this return. See the instructions on pages 27, 29, and 30 for details on the election.*

Property Interests That You May List on Schedule M

Generally, you may list on Schedule M all property interests that pass from the decedent to the surviving spouse and are included in the gross estate. However, you should not list any "Nondeductible terminable interests" (described below) on Schedule M unless you are making a QTIP election. The property for which you make this election must be included on Schedule M. See "Qualified Terminable Interest Property" on the following page.

For the rules on common disaster and survival for a limited period, see section 2056(b)(3).

You may list on Schedule M only those interests that the surviving spouse takes:

1. As the decedent's legatee, devisee, heir, or donee;

2. As the decedent's surviving tenant by the entirety or joint tenant;

3. As an appointee under the decedent's exercise of a power or as a taker in default at the decedent's nonexercise of a power;

4. As a beneficiary of insurance on the decedent's life;

5. As the surviving spouse taking under dower or curtesy (or similar statutory interest); and

6. As a transferee of a transfer made by the decedent at any time.

Property Interests That You May Not List on Schedule M

You should not list on Schedule M:

1. The value of any property that does not pass from the decedent to the surviving spouse.

2. Property interests that are not included in the decedent's gross estate.

3. The full value of a property interest for which a deduction was claimed on Schedules J through L. The value of the property interest should be reduced by the deductions claimed with respect to it.

4. The full value of a property interest that passes to the surviving spouse subject to a mortgage or other encumbrance or an obligation of the surviving spouse. Include on Schedule M only the net value of the interest after reducing it by the amount of the mortgage or other debt.

5. Nondeductible terminable interests (described below).

6. Any property interest disclaimed by the surviving spouse.

Terminable Interests

Certain interests in property passing from a decedent to a surviving spouse are referred to as *terminable interests.* These are interests that will terminate or fail after the passage of time, or on the occurrence or nonoccurrence of some contingency. Examples are: life estates, annuities, estates for terms of years, and patents.

The ownership of a bond, note, or other contractual obligation, which when discharged would not have the effect of an annuity for life or for a term, is not considered a terminable interest.

Nondeductible terminable interests.— A terminable interest is *nondeductible,* and should not be entered on Schedule M (unless you are making a QTIP election) if:

1. Another interest in the same property passed from the decedent to some other person for less than adequate and full consideration in money or money's worth; and

2. By reason of its passing, the other person or that person's heirs may enjoy part of the property after the termination of the surviving spouse's interest.

This rule applies even though the interest that passes from the decedent to a person other than the surviving spouse is not included in the gross estate, and regardless of when the interest passes. The rule also applies regardless of whether the surviving spouse's interest and the other person's interest pass from the decedent at the same time. Property interests that are considered to pass to a person other than the surviving spouse are any property interest that: **(a)** passes under a decedent's will or intestacy; **(b)** was transferred by a decedent during life; or **(c)** is held by or passed on to any person as a decedent's joint tenant, as appointee under a decedent's exercise of a power, as taker in default at a decedent's release or nonexercise of a power, or as a beneficiary of insurance in the decedent's life.

For example, a decedent devised real property to his wife for life, with remainder to his children. The life interest that passed to the wife does not qualify for the marital deduction because it will terminate at her death and the children will thereafter possess or enjoy the property.

However, if the decedent purchased a joint and survivor annuity for himself and his wife who survived him, the value of the survivor's annuity, to the extent that it is included in the gross estate, qualifies for the marital deduction because even though the interest will terminate on the wife's death, no one else will possess or enjoy any part of the property.

The marital deduction is not allowed for an interest that the decedent directed the executor or a trustee to convert, after death, into a terminable interest for the surviving spouse. The marital deduction is not allowed for such an interest even if there was no interest

in the property passing to another person and even if the terminable interest would otherwise have been deductible under the exceptions described below for life estate and life insurance and annuity payments with powers of appointment. For more information, see Regulations sections 20.2056(b)-1(f) and 20.2056(b)-1(g), Example (7).

If any property interest passing from the decedent to the surviving spouse may be paid or otherwise satisfied out of any of a group of assets, the value of the property interest is, for the entry on Schedule M, reduced by the value of any asset or assets that, if passing from the decedent to the surviving spouse, would be nondeductible terminable interests. Examples of property interests that may be paid or otherwise satisfied out of any of a group of assets are a bequest of the residue of the decedent's estate, or of a share of the residue, and a cash legacy payable out of the general estate.

Example: A decedent bequeathed $100,000 to the surviving spouse. The general estate includes a term for years (valued at $10,000 in determining the value of the gross estate) in an office building, which interest was retained by the decedent under a deed of the building by gift to a son. Accordingly, the value of the specific bequest entered on Schedule M is $90,000.

Life Estate With Power of Appointment in the Surviving Spouse.—A property interest, whether or not in trust, will be treated as passing to the surviving spouse, and will not be treated as a nondeductible terminable interest if: **(a)** the surviving spouse is entitled for life to all of the income from the entire interest; **(b)** the income is payable annually or at more frequent intervals; **(c)** the surviving spouse has the power, exercisable in favor of the surviving spouse or the estate of the surviving spouse, to appoint the entire interest; **(d)** the power is exercisable by the surviving spouse alone and (whether exercisable by will or during life) is exercisable by the surviving spouse in all events; and **(e)** no part of the entire interest is subject to a power in any other person to appoint any part to any person other than the surviving spouse (or the surviving spouse's legal representative or relative if the surviving spouse is disabled. See Rev. Rul. 85-35 1985-1 C.B. 328). If these five conditions are satisfied only for a specific portion of the entire interest, see the section 2056(b) regulations to determine the amount of the marital deduction.

Life Insurance, Endowment, or Annuity Payments, With Power of Appointment in Surviving Spouse.—A property interest consisting of the entire proceeds under a life insurance, endowment, or

annuity contract is treated as passing from the decedent to the surviving spouse, and will not be treated as a nondeductible terminable interest if: **(a)** the surviving spouse is entitled to receive the proceeds in installments, or is entitled to interest on them, with all amounts payable during the life of the spouse, payable only to the surviving spouse; **(b)** the installment or interest payments are payable annually, or more frequently, beginning not later than 13 months after the decedent's death; **(c)** the surviving spouse has the power, exercisable in favor of the surviving spouse or of the estate of the surviving spouse, to appoint all amounts payable under the contract; **(d)** the power is exercisable by the surviving spouse alone and (whether exercisable by will or during life) is exercisable by the surviving spouse in all events; and **(e)** no part of the amount payable under the contract is subject to a power in any other person to appoint any part to any person other than the surviving spouse. If these five conditions are satisfied only for a specific portion of the proceeds, see the section 2056(b) regulations to determine the amount of the marital deduction.

Charitable Remainder Trusts.—An interest in a charitable remainder trust will **not** be treated as a nondeductible terminable interest if:

1. The interest in the trust passes from the decedent to the surviving spouse; and

2. The surviving spouse is the only beneficiary of the trust other than charitable organizations described in section 170(c).

A "charitable remainder trust" is either a charitable remainder annuity trust or a charitable remainder unitrust. (See section 664 for descriptions of these trusts.)

Election To Deduct Qualified Terminable Interests (QTIP)

You may elect to claim a marital deduction for qualified terminable interest property or property interests. You make the QTIP election simply by listing the qualified terminable interest property on Schedule M and deducting its value. You are presumed to have made the QTIP election if you list the property and deduct its value on Schedule M. If you make this election, the surviving spouse's gross estate will include the value of the "qualified terminable interest property." See the instructions for line 6 of General Information for more details. **The election is irrevocable.**

If you file a Form 706 in which you do not make this election, you may not file an amended return to make the election

unless you file the amended return on or before the due date for filing the original Form 706.

The effect of the election is that the property (interest) will be treated as passing to the surviving spouse and will not be treated as a nondeductible terminable interest. All of the other marital deduction requirements must still be satisfied before you may make this election. For example, you may not make this election for property or property interests that are not included in the decedent's gross estate.

Qualified Terminable Interest Property is property (a) that passes from the decedent, and (b) in which the surviving spouse has a qualifying income interest for life.

The surviving spouse has a *qualifying income interest for life* if the surviving spouse is entitled to all of the income from the property payable annually or at more frequent intervals, or has a usufruct interest for life in the property, and during the surviving spouse's lifetime no person has a power to appoint any part of the property to any person other than the surviving spouse. An annuity is treated as an income interest regardless of whether the property from which the annuity is payable can be separately identified.

The QTIP election may be made for all or any part of a qualified terminable interest property. A partial election must relate to a fractional or percentile share of the property so that the elective part will reflect its proportionate share of the increase or decline in the whole of the property when applying sections 2044 or 2519. Thus, if the interest of the surviving spouse in a trust (or other property in which the spouse has a qualified life estate) is qualified terminable interest property, you may make an election for a part of the trust (or other property) only if the election relates to a defined fraction or percentage of the entire trust (or other property). The fraction or percentage may be defined by means of a formula.

Qualified Domestic Trust Election (QDOT)

The marital deduction is allowed for transfers to a surviving spouse who is not a U.S. citizen only if the property passes to the surviving spouse in a "qualified domestic trust" (QDOT) or if such property is transferred or irrevocably assigned to a QDOT before the decedent's estate tax return is filed.

A QDOT is any trust:

1. That requires at least one trustee to be either an individual who is a citizen of the United States or a domestic corporation;

2. That requires that no distribution of corpus from the trust can be made unless such a trustee has the right to withhold from the distribution the tax imposed on the QDOT;

3. That meets the requirements of any applicable regulations; and

4. For which the executor has made an election on the estate tax return of the decedent.

You make the QDOT election simply by listing the qualified domestic trust or the **entire value** of the trust property on Schedule M and deducting its value. You are presumed to have made the QDOT election if you list the trust or trust property and deduct its value on Schedule M. **Once made, the election is irrevocable.**

If an election is made to deduct qualified domestic trust property under section 2056A(d), the following information should be provided for each qualified domestic trust on an attachment to this schedule:

1. The name and address of every trustee;

2. A description of each transfer passing from the decedent that is the source of the property to be placed in trust; and

3. The employer identification number for the trust.

The election must be made for an entire QDOT trust. In listing a trust for which you are making a QDOT election, unless you specifically identify the trust as not subject to the election, the election will be considered made for the entire trust.

The determination of whether a trust qualifies as a QDOT will be made as of the date the decedent's Form 706 is filed. If, however, judicial proceedings are brought before the Form 706's due date (including extensions) to have the trust revised to meet the QDOT requirements, then the determination will not be made until the court-ordered changes to the trust are made.

Line 1

If property passes to the surviving spouse as the result of a qualified disclaimer, check "Yes" and attach a copy of the written disclaimer required by section 2518(b).

Line 3

Section 2056(b)(7) creates an automatic QTIP election for certain joint and survivor annuities that are includible in the estate under section 2039. To qualify, only the surviving spouse can have the right to receive payments before the death of the surviving spouse.

The executor can elect out of QTIP treatment, however, by checking the "Yes" box on line 3. Once made, the election is irrevocable. If there is more than one such joint and survivor annuity, you are not required to make the election for all of them.

If you make the election out of QTIP treatment by checking "Yes" on line 3, you cannot deduct the amount of the annuity on Schedule M. If you do not make the election out, you must list the joint and survivor annuities on Schedule M.

Listing Property Interest on Schedule M

List each property interest included in the gross estate that passes from the decedent to the surviving spouse and for which a marital deduction is claimed. This includes otherwise nondeductible terminable interest property for which you are making a QTIP election. Number each item in sequence and describe each item in detail. Describe the instrument (including any clause or paragraph number) or provision of law under which each item passed to the surviving spouse. If possible, show where each item appears (number and schedule) on Schedules A through I.

In listing otherwise nondeductible property for which you are making a QTIP election, unless you specifically identify a fractional portion of the trust or other property as not subject to the election, the election will be considered made for all of the trust or other property.

Enter the value of each interest before taking into account the Federal estate tax or any other death tax. The valuation dates used in determining the value of the gross estate apply also on Schedule M.

If Schedule M includes a bequest of the residue or a part of the residue of the decedent's estate, attach a copy of the computation showing how the value of the residue was determined. Include a statement showing:

● The value of all property that is included in the decedent's gross estate (Schedules A through I) but is not a part of the decedent's probate estate, such as lifetime transfers, jointly owned property that passed to the survivor on decedent's death, and the insurance payable to specific beneficiaries.

● The values of all specific and general legacies or devises, with reference to the applicable clause or paragraph of the decedent's will or codicil. (If legacies are made to each member of a class, for example, $1,000 to each of decedent's employees, only the number in each class and the total value of property received by them need be furnished.)

● The date of birth of all persons, the length of whose lives may affect the value of the residuary interest passing to the surviving spouse.

● Any other important information such as that relating to any claim to any part of the estate not arising under the will.

Lines 5a, b, and c.—The total of the values listed on Schedule M must be reduced by the amount of the Federal estate tax, the Federal GST tax, and the amount of state or other death and GST taxes paid out of the property interest involved. If you enter an amount for state or other death or GST taxes on lines 5b or 5c, identify the taxes and attach your computation of them. For additional information, see **Pub. 904**, Interrelated Computations for Estate and Gift Taxes.

Attachments.—If you list property interests passing by the decedent's will on Schedule M, attach a certified copy of the order admitting the will to probate. If, when you file the return, the court of probate jurisdiction has entered any decree interpreting the will or any of its provisions affecting any of the interests listed on Schedule M, or has entered any order of distribution, attach a copy of the decree or order. In addition, the District Director may request other evidence to support the marital deduction claimed.

Form 706 (Rev. 8-93)

Estate of:

SCHEDULE O—Charitable, Public, and Similar Gifts and Bequests

	Yes	No
1a If the transfer was made by will, has any action been instituted to have interpreted or to contest the will or any of its provisions affecting the charitable deductions claimed in this schedule? . . . . If "Yes," full details must be submitted with this schedule.		
b According to the information and belief of the person or persons filing this return, is any such action planned? If "Yes," full details must be submitted with this schedule.		
2 Did any property pass to charity as the result of a qualified disclaimer? . . . . If "Yes," attach a copy of the written disclaimer required by section 2518(b).		

Item number	Name and address of beneficiary	Character of institution	Amount
1			

Total from continuation schedule(s) (or additional sheet(s)) attached to this schedule . . . .

3	Total		**3**	
4a	Federal estate tax (including section 4980A taxes) payable out of property interests listed above	**4a**		
b	Other death taxes payable out of property interests listed above	**4b**		
c	Federal and state GST taxes payable out of property interests listed above	**4c**		
d	Add items a, b, and c		**4d**	
5	Net value of property interests listed above (subtract 4d from 3). Also enter on Part 5, Recapitulation, page 3, at item 19		**5**	

(If more space is needed, attach the continuation schedule from the end of this package or additional sheets of the same size.)
(The instructions to Schedule O are in the separate instructions.)

Schedule O—Page 31

Estate of: _____

SCHEDULE P—Credit for Foreign Death Taxes

List all foreign countries to which death taxes have been paid and for which a credit is claimed on this return.

....

If a credit is claimed for death taxes paid to more than one foreign country, compute the credit for taxes paid to one country on this sheet and attach a separate copy of Schedule P for each of the other countries.

The credit computed on this sheet is for the ....
(Name of death tax or taxes)

.... imposed in ....
(Name of country)

Credit is computed under the ....
(Insert title of treaty or "statute")

Citizenship (nationality) of decedent at time of death

(All amounts and values must be entered in United States money)

1 Total of estate, inheritance, legacy, and succession taxes imposed in the country named above attributable to property situated in that country, subjected to these taxes, and included in the gross estate (as defined by statute)	
2 Value of the gross estate (adjusted, if necessary, according to the instructions for item 2)	
3 Value of property situated in that country, subjected to death taxes imposed in that country, and included in the gross estate (adjusted, if necessary, according to the instructions for item 3)	
4 Tax imposed by section 2001 reduced by the total credits claimed under sections 2010, 2011, and 2012 (see instructions)	
5 Amount of Federal estate tax attributable to property specified at item 3. (Divide item 3 by item 2 and multiply the result by item 4.)	
6 Credit for death taxes imposed in the country named above (the smaller of item 1 or item 5). Also enter on line 18 of Part 2, Tax Computation	

SCHEDULE Q—Credit for Tax on Prior Transfers

Part 1.—Transferor Information

	Name of transferor	Social security number	IRS office where estate tax return was filed	Date of death
A				
B				
C				

Check here ▶ ☐ if section 2013(f) (special valuation of farm, etc., real property) adjustments to the computation of the credit were made (see instructions).

Part 2.—Computation of Credit (see instructions)

Item	Transferor			Total A, B, & C
	A	B	C	
1 Transferee's tax as apportioned (from worksheet, (line 7 ÷ line 8) × line 35 for each column) . .				
2 Transferor's tax (from each column of worksheet, line 20)				
3 Maximum amount before percentage requirement (for each column, enter amount from line 1 or 2, whichever is smaller)				
4 Percentage allowed (each column) (see instructions)	%	%	%	
5 Credit allowable (line 3 × line 4 for each column)				
6 TOTAL credit allowable (add columns A, B, and C of line 5). Enter here and on line 19 of Part 2, Tax Computation				

(The instructions to Schedules P and Q are in the separate instructions.)

SCHEDULE R—Generation-Skipping Transfer Tax

Note: *To avoid application of the deemed allocation rules, Form 706 and Schedule R should be filed to allocate the GST exemption to trusts that may later have taxable terminations or distributions under section 2612 even if the form is not required to be filed to report estate or GST tax.*

*The GST tax is imposed on taxable transfers of interests in property located **outside the United States** as well as property located inside the United States.*

Part 1.—GST Exemption Reconciliation (Section 2631) and Section 2652(a)(3) (Special QTIP) Election

Check box ▶ ☐ if you are making a section 2652(a)(3) (special QTIP) election (see instructions)

1	Maximum allowable GST exemption	**1** $1,000,000
2	Total GST exemption allocated by the decedent against decedent's lifetime transfers	**2**
3	Total GST exemption allocated by the executor, using Form 709, against decedent's lifetime transfers	**3**
4	GST exemption allocated on line 6 of Schedule R, Part 2	**4**
5	GST exemption allocated on line 6 of Schedule R, Part 3	**5**
6	Total GST exemption allocated on line 4 of Schedule(s) R-1	**6**
7	Total GST exemption allocated to intervivos transfers and direct skips (add lines 2–6)	**7**
8	GST exemption available to allocate to trusts and section 2032A interests (subtract line 7 from line 1)	**8**

9 Allocation of GST exemption to trusts (as defined for GST tax purposes):

A Name of trust	B Trust's EIN (if any)	C GST exemption allocated on lines 2–6, above (see instructions)	D Additional GST exemption allocated (see instructions)	E Trust's inclusion ratio (optional—see instructions)

9D Total. May not exceed line 8, above . . . . | **9D** |

10	GST exemption available to allocate to section 2032A interests received by individual beneficiaries (subtract line 9D from line 8). You must attach special use allocation schedule (see instructions)	**10**

(The instructions to Schedule R are in the separate instructions.)

Estate of:

Part 2.—Direct Skips Where the Property Interests Transferred Bear the GST Tax on the Direct Skips

Name of skip person	Description of property interest transferred	Estate tax value

1 Total estate tax values of all property interests listed above	**1**	
2 Estate taxes, state death taxes, and other charges borne by the property interests listed above.	**2**	
3 GST taxes borne by the property interests listed above but imposed on direct skips other than those shown on this Part 2. (See instructions.)	**3**	
4 Total fixed taxes and other charges. (Add lines 2 and 3.)	**4**	
5 Total tentative maximum direct skips. (Subtract line 4 from line 1.)	**5**	
6 GST exemption allocated	**6**	
7 Subtract line 6 from line 5	**7**	
8 GST tax due. (Divide line 7 by 2.818182)	**8**	
9 Enter the amount from line 8 of Schedule R, Part 3.	**9**	
10 **Total GST taxes payable by the estate.** (Add lines 8 and 9.) Enter here and on line 22 of the Tax Computation on page 1	**10**	

Schedule R—Page 34

Estate of:

Part 3.—Direct Skips Where the Property Interests Transferred Do Not Bear the GST Tax on the Direct Skips

Name of skip person	Description of property interest transferred	Estate tax value

1 Total estate tax values of all property interests listed above	**1**	
2 Estate taxes, state death taxes, and other charges borne by the property interests listed above .	**2**	
3 GST taxes borne by the property interests listed above but imposed on direct skips other than those shown on this Part 3. (See instructions.)	**3**	
4 Total fixed taxes and other charges. (Add lines 2 and 3.)	**4**	
5 Total tentative maximum direct skips. (Subtract line 4 from line 1.)	**5**	
6 GST exemption allocated	**6**	
7 Subtract line 6 from line 5	**7**	
8 GST tax due (multiply line 7 by .55). Enter here and on Schedule R, Part 2, line 9	**8**	

Schedule R—Page 35

Generation-Skipping Transfer Tax

Direct Skips From a Trust

Payment Voucher

OMB No. 1545-0015
Expires 12-31-95

Executor: File one copy with Form 706 and send two copies to the fiduciary. Do not pay the tax shown. See the separate instructions.
Fiduciary: See instructions on following page. Pay the tax shown on line 6.

Name of trust	Trust's EIN

Name and title of fiduciary	Name of decedent	

Address of fiduciary (number and street)	Decedent's SSN	Service Center where Form 706 was filed

City, state, and ZIP code	Name of executor	

Address of executor (number and street)	City, state, and ZIP code	

Date of decedent's death	Filing due date of Schedule R, Form 706 (with extensions)	

Part 1.—Computation of the GST Tax on the Direct Skip

Description of property interests subject to the direct skip	Estate tax value

1 Total estate tax value of all property interests listed above	**1**	
2 Estate taxes, state death taxes, and other charges borne by the property interests listed above.	**2**	
3 Tentative maximum direct skip from trust. (Subtract line 2 from line 1.)	**3**	
4 GST exemption allocated	**4**	
5 Subtract line 4 from line 3	**5**	
6 **GST tax due from fiduciary.** (Divide line 5 by 2.818182) **(See instructions if property will not bear the GST tax.)**	**6**	

Under penalties of perjury, I declare that I have examined this return, including accompanying schedules and statements, and to the best of my knowledge and belief, it is true, correct, and complete.

Signature(s) of executor(s)   Date

                                                                                  Date

Signature of fiduciary or officer representing fiduciary   Date

Instructions for Fiduciary

Purpose of Schedule R-1

Code section 2603(a)(2) provides that the Generation-Skipping Transfer (GST) tax imposed on a direct skip from a trust is to be paid by the trustee. Schedule R-1 (Form 706) serves as a payment voucher for the trustee to remit the GST tax to the IRS. See the instructions for Form 706 as to when a direct skip is from a trust.

How To Pay the GST Tax

The executor will compute the GST tax, complete Schedule R-1, and give you two copies. You should pay the GST tax using one copy and keep the other copy for your records.

The GST tax due is the amount shown on line 6. Make your check or money order for this amount payable to "Internal Revenue Service," write "GST tax" and the trust's EIN on it, and send it and one copy of the completed Schedule R-1 to the IRS Service Center where the Form 706 was filed, as shown on the front of the Schedule R-1.

When To Pay the GST Tax

The GST tax is due and payable 9 months after the decedent's date of death (entered by the executor on Schedule R-1). Interest will be charged on any GST taxes unpaid as of that date. However, you have an automatic extension of time to file Schedule R-1 and pay the GST tax due until 2 months after the due date (with extensions) for filing the decedent's Schedule R, Form 706. This Schedule R, Form 706 due date is entered by the executor on Schedule R-1. Thus, while interest will be due on unpaid GST taxes, no penalties will be charged if you file Schedule R-1 by this extended due date.

Signature

You, as fiduciary, must sign the Schedule R-1 in the space provided.

Form 706 (Rev. 8-93)

Estate of:

SCHEDULE S—Increased Estate Tax on Excess Retirement Accumulations
(Under section 4980A(d) of the Internal Revenue Code)

Part I **Tax Computation**

1 Check this box if a section 4980A(d)(5) spousal election is being made. . . . . ▶ ☐
You must attach the statement described in the instructions.

2 Enter the name and employer identification number (EIN) of each qualified employer plan and individual retirement account in which the decedent had an interest at the time of death:

Name	EIN
Plan #1	
Plan #2	
Plan #3	
IRA #1	
IRA #2	
IRA #3	

	A Plan #1	B Plan #2	C Plan #3	D All IRAs
3 Value of decedent's interest				
4 Amounts rolled over after death	/////	/////	/////	
5 Total value (add lines 3 and 4)				
6 Amounts payable to certain alternate payees (see instructions)				/////
7 Decedent's investment in the contract under section 72(f)				/////
8 Excess life insurance amount				
9 Decedent's interest as a beneficiary				
10 Total reductions in value (add lines 6, 7, 8, and 9)				
11 Net value of decedent's interest (subtract line 10 from line 5)				

12 Decedent's aggregate interest in all plans and IRAs (add columns A–D of line 11) . . . . . . ▶ **12**

13 Present value of hypothetical life annuity (from Part III, line 4) **13**

14 Remaining unused grandfather amount (from Part II, line 4) **14**

15 Enter the greater of line 13 or line 14 . . . . **15**

16 Excess retirement accumulation (subtract line 15 from line 12) **16**

17 Increased estate tax (multiply line 16 by 15%). Enter here and on line 23 of the Tax Computation on page 1 . . . . . **17**

(The instructions to Schedule S are in the separate instructions.)

Part II	**Grandfather Election**		
1	Was a grandfather election made on a previously filed Form 5329? . . . . ▶ ☐ Yes ☐ No		
	If "Yes," complete lines 2–4 below. **You may not make or revoke the grandfather election after the due date (with extensions) for filing the decedent's 1988 income tax return.** If "No," enter -0- on line 4 and skip to Part III.		
2	Initial grandfather amount	**2**	
3	Total amount previously recovered	**3**	
4	Remaining unused grandfather amount (subtract line 3 from line 2). Enter here and on Part I, line 14, on page 38	**4**	

Part III	**Computation of Hypothetical Life Annuity**		
1	Decedent's attained age at date of death (in whole years, rounded down)	**1**	
2	Applicable annual annuity amount (see instructions)	**2**	
3	Present value multiplier (see instructions)	**3**	
4	Present value of hypothetical life annuity (multiply line 2 by line 3). Enter here and on Part I, line 13, on page 38	**4**	

(Make copies of this schedule before completing it if you will need more than one schedule.)

Estate of:

CONTINUATION SCHEDULE

Continuation of Schedule _____
(Enter letter of schedule you are continuing.)

Item number	Description For securities, give CUSIP number, if available.	Unit value (Sch B, E, or G only)	Alternate valuation date	Alternate value	Value at date of death or amount deductible

TOTAL. (Carry forward to main schedule.) . . . .

Instructions for Continuation Schedule

The Continuation Schedule on page 40 provides a uniform format for listing additional assets from Schedules A, B, C, D, E, F, G, H, and I and additional deductions from Schedules J, K, L, M, and O. Use the Continuation Schedule when you need to list more assets or deductions than you have room for on one of the main schedules.

Use a separate Continuation Schedule for each main schedule you are continuing. For each schedule of Form 706, you may use as many Continuation Schedules as needed to list all the assets or deductions to be reported. Do not combine assets or deductions from different schedules on one Continuation Schedule. Because there is only one Continuation Schedule in this package, you should make copies of the schedule before completing it if you expect to need more than one.

Enter the letter of the schedule you are continuing in the space provided at the top of the Continuation Schedule. Complete the rest of the Continuation Schedule as explained in the instructions for the schedule you are continuing. Use the *Unit value* column only if you are continuing Schedules B, E, or G. For all other schedules, you may use the space under the *Unit value* column to continue your description.

To continue Schedule E, Part 2, you should enter the *Percentage includible* in the *Alternate valuation date* column of the Continuation Schedule.

To continue Schedule K, you should use the *Alternate valuation date* and *Alternate value* columns of the Continuation Schedule as *Amount unpaid to date* and *Amount in contest* columns, respectively.

To continue Schedules J, L, and M, you should use the *Alternate valuation date* and *Alternate value* columns of the Continuation Schedule to continue your description of the deductions. You should enter the amount of each deduction in the *amount deductible* column of the Continuation Schedule.

To continue Schedule O, you should use the space under the *Alternate valuation date* and *Alternate value* columns of the Continuation Schedule to provide the *Character of institution* information required on Schedule O. You should enter the amount of each deduction in the *amount deductible* column of the Continuation Schedule.

Carry the total from the Continuation Schedule(s) forward to the appropriate line of the main schedule.

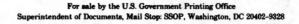

For sale by the U.S. Government Printing Office
Superintendent of Documents, Mail Stop: SSOP, Washington, DC 20402-9328

1996

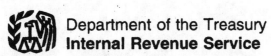

**Department of the Treasury
Internal Revenue Service**

Instructions for Form 1041 and Schedules A, B, D, G, I, J, and K-1

U.S. Income Tax Return for Estates and Trusts

Section references are to the Internal Revenue Code unless otherwise noted.

Paperwork Reduction Act Notice

We ask for the information on this form to carry out the Internal Revenue laws of the United States. You are required to give us the information. We need it to ensure that you are complying with these laws and to allow us to figure and collect the right amount of tax.

You are not required to provide the information requested on a form that is subject to the Paperwork Reduction Act unless the form displays a valid OMB control number. Books or records relating to a form or its instructions must be retained as long as their contents may become material in the administration of any Internal Revenue law. Generally, tax returns and return information are confidential, as required by Code section 6103.

The time needed to complete and file this form and related schedules will vary depending on individual circumstances. The estimated average times are:

	Form 1041	Schedule D	Schedule J	Schedule K-1
Recordkeeping	40 hr., 53 min.	16 hr., 1 min.	39 hr., 28 min.	8 hr., 22 min.
Learning about the law or the form	18 hr., 37 min.	1 hr., 47 min.	1 hr., 5 min.	1 hr., 12 min.
Preparing the form	34 hr., 58 min.	2 hr., 8 min.	1 hr., 47 min.	1 hr., 23 min.
Copying, assembling, and sending the form to the IRS	4 hr., 17 min.			

If you have comments concerning the accuracy of these time estimates or suggestions for making this form and related schedules simpler, we would be happy to hear from you. You can write to the Tax Forms Committee, Western Area Distribution Center, Rancho Cordova, CA 95743-0001. **DO NOT** send the tax form to this address. Instead, see **Where To File** on page 3.

Changes To Note

• Three new optional filing methods for certain grantor type trusts are available for tax years beginning after 1995. The optional methods are alternatives to the filing of Form 1041 for these trusts. If the trustee elects an optional method, he or she generally must file a final Form 1041 for the tax year that immediately precedes the first tax year for which the trustee elects to report under one of the optional methods. For details, see page 7.

• For tax years beginning in 1996, the requirement to file a return for a bankruptcy estate applies only if gross income is at least $5,900.

Unresolved Tax Problems

The Problem Resolution Program is for taxpayers that have been unable to resolve their problems with the IRS. If the estate or trust has a tax problem it cannot clear up through normal channels, write to the estate's or trust's local IRS District Director, or call the local IRS office and ask for Problem Resolution assistance. Persons who have access to TTY/TDD equipment may call 1-800-829-4059 to ask for help from Problem Resolution. This office cannot change the tax law or technical decisions. But it can help clear up problems that resulted from previous contacts.

How To Get Forms and Publications

By personal computer.— If you subscribe to an on-line service, ask if IRS information is available and, if so, how to access it. You can get information through IRIS, the Internal Revenue Information Services, on FedWorld, a government

bulletin board. Tax forms, instructions, publications, and other IRS information are available through IRIS.

IRIS is accessible directly using your modem by calling 703-321-8020. On the Internet, telnet to iris.irs.ustreas.gov or, for file transfer protocol services, connect to ftp.irs.ustreas.gov. If you are using the World Wide Web, connect to http://www.irs.ustreas.gov. FedWorld's help desk offers technical assistance on accessing IRIS (not tax help) during regular business hours at 703-487-4608. The IRIS menus offer information on available file formats and software needed to read and print files. You must print the forms to use them; they are not designed to be filled in on-screen.

Tax forms, instructions, and publications are also available on CD-ROM, including prior-year forms starting with the 1991 tax year. For ordering information and software requirements, contact the Government Printing Office's Superintendent of Documents (202-512-1800) or Federal Bulletin Board (202-512-1387).

By phone and in person.— To order forms and publications, call 1–800–TAX-FORM (1–800–829–3676). You can also get most forms and publications at your local IRS office.

General Instructions

Purpose of Form

The fiduciary of a domestic decedent's estate, trust, or bankruptcy estate uses Form 1041 to report: **(a)** the income, deductions, gains, losses, etc. of the estate or trust; **(b)** the income that is either accumulated or held for future distribution or distributed currently to the beneficiaries; **(c)** any income tax liability of the estate or trust; and **(d)** employment taxes on wages paid to household employees.

Income Taxation of Trusts and Decedents' Estates

A trust (except a grantor type trust) or a decedent's estate is a separate legal entity for Federal tax purposes. A decedent's estate comes into existence at the time of death of an individual. A trust may be created during an individual's life (inter vivos) or at the time of his or her death under a will (testamentary). If the trust instrument contains certain provisions, then the person creating the trust (the grantor) is treated as the owner of the trust's assets. Such a trust is a grantor type trust.

A trust or decedent's estate figures its gross income in much the same manner as an individual. Most deductions and credits allowed to individuals are also allowed to estates and trusts. However, there is one major distinction. A trust or decedent's estate is allowed an income distribution deduction for distributions to

beneficiaries. To figure this deduction, the fiduciary must complete Schedule B. The income distribution deduction determines the amount of the distribution that is taxed to the beneficiaries.

For this reason, a trust or decedent's estate sometimes is referred to as a "pass-through" entity. The beneficiary, and not the trust or decedent's estate, pays income tax on his or her distributive share of income. Schedule K-1 (Form 1041) is used to notify the beneficiaries of the amounts to be included on their income tax returns.

Before preparing Form 1041, the fiduciary must figure the accounting income of the estate or trust under the will or trust instrument and applicable local law to determine the amount, if any, of income that is required to be distributed because the income distribution deduction is based, in part, on that amount.

Definitions

Beneficiary

A beneficiary is an heir, a legatee, or a devisee.

Distributable Net Income (DNI)

The income distribution deduction allowable to estates and trusts for amounts paid, credited, or required to be distributed to beneficiaries is limited to distributable net income (DNI). This amount, which is figured on Schedule B, line 9, is also used to determine how much of an amount paid, credited, or required to be distributed to a beneficiary will be includible in his or her gross income.

Income and Deductions in Respect of a Decedent

When completing Form 1041, you must take into account any items that are income in respect of a decedent (IRD).

In general, income in respect of a decedent is income that a decedent was entitled to receive but that was not properly includible in the decedent's final Form 1040 under the decedent's method of accounting.

IRD includes: **(a)** all accrued income of a decedent who reported his or her income on a cash method of accounting; **(b)** income accrued solely because of the decedent's death in the case of a decedent who reported his or her income on the accrual method of accounting; and **(c)** income to which the decedent had a contingent claim at the time of his or her death.

Some examples of IRD of a decedent who kept his or her books on a cash method are:
• Deferred salary payments that are payable to the decedent's estate.
• Uncollected interest on U.S. savings bonds.
• Proceeds from the completed sale of farm produce.

• The portion of a lump sum distribution to the beneficiary of a decedent's IRA that equals the balance in the IRA at the time of the owner's death. This includes unrealized appreciation and income accrued to that date, less the aggregate amount of the owner's nondeductible contributions to the IRA. Such amounts are included in the beneficiary's gross income in the tax year that the distribution is received.

The IRD has the same character it would have had if the decedent lived and received such amount.

The following deductions and credits, when paid by the decedent's estate, are allowed on Form 1041 even though they were not allowable on the decedent's final Form 1040:
• Business expenses deductible under section 162.
• Interest deductible under section 163.
• Taxes deductible under section 164.
• Investment expenses described in section 212 (in excess of 2% of AGI).
• Percentage depletion allowed under section 611.
• Foreign tax credit.

For more information, see section 691.

Income Required To Be Distributed Currently

Income required to be distributed currently is income that is required to be distributed in the year it is received. The fiduciary must be under a duty to distribute the income currently, even if the actual distribution is not made until after the close of the trust's tax year. See Regulations section 1.651(a)-2.

Fiduciary

A fiduciary is a trustee of a trust; or an executor, executrix, administrator, administratrix, personal representative, or person in possession of property of a decedent's estate.

Note: *Any reference in these instructions to "you" means the fiduciary of the estate or trust.*

Trust

A trust is an arrangement created either by a will or by an inter vivos declaration by which trustees take title to property for the purpose of protecting or conserving it for the beneficiaries under the ordinary rules applied in chancery or probate courts.

Who Must File

Decedent's Estate

The fiduciary (or one of the joint fiduciaries) must file Form 1041 for the estate of a domestic decedent that has:

1. Gross income for the tax year of $600 or more, or

2. A beneficiary who is a nonresident alien.

Trust

The fiduciary (or one of the joint fiduciaries) must file Form 1041 for a domestic trust taxable under section 641 that has:

1. Any taxable income for the tax year, or

2. Gross income of $600 or more (regardless of taxable income), or

3. A beneficiary who is a nonresident alien.

Two or more trusts are treated as one trust if such trusts have substantially the same grantor(s) and substantially the same primary beneficiary(ies), and a principal purpose of such trusts is avoidance of tax. This provision applies only to that portion of the trust that is attributable to contributions to corpus made after March 1, 1984.

If you are a fiduciary of a nonresident alien estate or foreign trust with U.S. source income, file **Form 1040NR,** U.S. Nonresident Alien Income Tax Return.

Bankruptcy Estate

The bankruptcy trustee or debtor-in-possession must file Form 1041 for the estate of an individual involved in bankruptcy proceedings under chapter 7 or 11 of title 11 of the United States Code if the estate has gross income for the tax year of $5,900 or more. See **Of Special Interest To Bankruptcy Trustees and Debtors-in-Possession** on page 5 for other details.

Qualified Settlement Funds

The trustee of a designated or qualified settlement fund must file **Form 1120-SF,** U.S. Income Tax Return for Settlement Funds, rather than Form 1041. See Regulations section 1.468B-5.

Electronic and Magnetic Media Filing

Qualified fiduciaries or transmitters may be able to file Form 1041 and related schedules electronically or on magnetic media. Tax return data may be filed electronically using telephone lines or on magnetic media using magnetic tape or floppy diskette.

If you wish to do this, **Form 9041,** Application for Electronic/Magnetic Media Filing of Business and Employee Benefit Plan Returns, must be filed. If Form 1041 is filed electronically or on magnetic media, **Form 8453-F,** U.S. Estate or Trust Income Tax Declaration and Signature for Electronic and Magnetic Media Filing, must also be filed. For more details, get **Pub. 1437,** Procedures for Electronic and Magnetic Media Filing of U.S. Income Tax Returns for Estates and Trusts, Form 1041, and **Pub. 1438,** File Specifications, Validation Criteria, and Record Layouts for Electronic and Magnetic Media Filing of Estate and Trust Returns, Form 1041. To order these forms and publications, or

for more information on electronic and magnetic media filing of Form 1041, call the Magnetic Media Unit at the Philadelphia Service Center at (215) 516-7533 (not a toll-free number), or write to:

Internal Revenue Service Center
Attention: Magnetic Media Unit–DP 115
11601 Roosevelt Blvd.
Philadelphia, PA 19154

When To File

For calendar year estates and trusts, file Form 1041 and Schedules K-1 on or before April 15, 1997. For fiscal year estates and trusts, file Form 1041 by the 15th day of the 4th month following the close of the tax year. If the due date falls on a Saturday, Sunday, or legal holiday, file on the next business day. For example, an estate that has a tax year that ends on June 30, 1996, must file Form 1041 by October 15, 1997.

Extension of Time To File

Estates.— Use **Form 2758,** Application for Extension of Time To File Certain Excise, Income, Information, and Other Returns, to apply for an extension of time to file.

Trusts.— Use **Form 8736,** Application for Automatic Extension of Time To File U.S. Return for a Partnership, REMIC, or for Certain Trusts, to request an automatic 3-month extension of time to file.

If more time is needed, file **Form 8800,** Application for Additional Extension of Time To File U.S. Return for a Partnership, REMIC, or for Certain Trusts, for an additional extension of up to 3 months. To obtain this additional extension of time to file, you must show reasonable cause for the additional time you are requesting. Form 8800 must be filed by the extended due date for Form 1041.

Period Covered

File the 1996 return for calendar year 1996 and fiscal years beginning in 1996 and ending in 1997. If the return is for a fiscal year or a short tax year, fill in the tax year space at the top of the form.

The 1996 Form 1041 may also be used for a tax year beginning in 1997 if:

1. The estate or trust has a tax year of less than 12 months that begins and ends in 1997; and

2. The 1997 Form 1041 is not available by the time the estate or trust is required to file its tax return. However, the estate or trust must show its 1997 tax year on the 1996 Form 1041 and incorporate any tax law changes that are effective for tax years beginning after December 31, 1996.

Where To File

For all estates and trusts, except charitable and split-interest trusts and pooled income funds:

If you are located in	Please mail to the following Internal Revenue Service Center
New Jersey, New York (New York City and counties of Nassau, Rockland, Suffolk, and Westchester)	Holtsville, NY 00501
New York (all other counties), Connecticut, Maine, Massachusetts, New Hampshire, Rhode Island, Vermont	Andover, MA 05501
Florida, Georgia, South Carolina	Atlanta, GA 39901
Indiana, Kentucky, Michigan, Ohio, West Virginia	Cincinnati, OH 45999
Kansas, New Mexico, Oklahoma, Texas	Austin, TX 73301
Alaska, Arizona, California (counties of Alpine, Amador, Butte, Calaveras, Colusa, Contra Costa, Del Norte, El Dorado, Glenn, Humboldt, Lake, Lassen, Marin, Mendocino, Modoc, Napa, Nevada, Placer, Plumas, Sacramento, San Joaquin, Shasta, Sierra, Siskiyou, Solano, Sonoma, Sutter, Tehama, Trinity, Yolo, and Yuba), Colorado, Idaho, Montana, Nebraska, Nevada, North Dakota, Oregon, South Dakota, Utah, Washington, Wyoming	Ogden, UT 84201
California (all other counties), Hawaii	Fresno, CA 93888
Illinois, Iowa, Minnesota, Missouri, Wisconsin	Kansas City, MO 64999
Alabama, Arkansas, Louisiana, Mississippi, North Carolina, Tennessee	Memphis, TN 37501
Delaware, District of Columbia, Maryland, Pennsylvania, Virginia, any U.S. possession, or foreign country	Philadelphia, PA 19255

For a charitable or split-interest trust described in section 4947(a) and a pooled income fund defined in section 642(c)(5):

If you are located in	Please mail to the following Internal Revenue Service Center
Alabama, Arkansas, Florida, Georgia, Louisiana, Mississippi, North Carolina, South Carolina, Tennessee	Atlanta, GA 39901
Arizona, Colorado, Kansas, New Mexico, Oklahoma, Texas, Utah, Wyoming	Austin, TX 73301
Indiana, Kentucky, Michigan, Ohio, West Virginia	Cincinnati, OH 45999
Alaska, California, Hawaii, Idaho, Nevada, Oregon, Washington	Fresno, CA 93888
Connecticut, Maine, Massachusetts, New Hampshire, New York, Rhode Island, Vermont	Holtsville, NY 00501
Illinois, Iowa, Minnesota, Missouri, Montana, Nebraska, North Dakota, South Dakota, Wisconsin	Kansas City, MO 64999

Who Must Sign

The fiduciary, or an authorized representative, must sign Form 1041.

A financial institution that submitted estimated tax payments for trusts for which it is the trustee must enter its EIN in the space provided for the EIN of the fiduciary. Do not enter the EIN of the trust. For this purpose, a financial institution is one that maintains a Treasury Tax and Loan account. If you are an attorney or other individual functioning in a fiduciary capacity, leave this space blank. DO NOT enter your individual social security number (SSN).

If you, as fiduciary, fill in Form 1041, leave the Paid Preparer's space blank. If someone prepares this return and does not charge you, that person should not sign the return.

Generally, anyone who is paid to prepare a tax return must sign the return and fill in the other blanks in the Paid Preparer's Use Only area of the return.

The person required to sign the return must complete the required preparer information and:

● Sign it in the space provided for the preparer's signature. A facsimile signature is acceptable if certain conditions are met. See Regulations section 1.6695-1(b)(4)(iv) for details.

● Give you a copy of the return in addition to the copy to be filed with the IRS.

Accounting Methods

Figure taxable income using the method of accounting regularly used in keeping the estate's or trust's books and records. Generally, permissible methods include the cash method, the accrual method, or any other method authorized by the Internal Revenue Code. In all cases, the method used must clearly reflect income.

Generally, the estate or trust may change its accounting method (for income as a whole or for any material item) only by getting consent on **Form 3115,** Application for Change in Accounting Method. For more information, get **Pub. 538,** Accounting Periods and Methods.

Accounting Periods

For a decedent's estate, the moment of death determines the end of the decedent's tax year and the beginning of the estate's tax year. As executor or administrator, you choose the estate's tax period when you file its first income tax return. The estate's first tax year may be any period of 12 months or less that ends on the last day of a month. If you select the last day of any month other than December, you are adopting a fiscal tax year.

To change the accounting period of an estate, get **Form 1128,** Application To Adopt, Change, or Retain a Tax Year.

Generally, a trust must adopt a calendar year. The following trusts are exempt from this requirement:

● A trust that is exempt from tax under section 501(a);

● A charitable trust described in section 4947(a)(1); and

● A trust that is treated as wholly owned by a grantor under the rules of sections 671 through 679.

Rounding Off to Whole Dollars

You may show the money items on the return and accompanying schedules as whole-dollar amounts. To do so, drop amounts less than 50 cents and increase any amounts from 50 to 99 cents to the next dollar.

Estimated Tax

Generally, an estate or trust must pay estimated income tax for 1997 if it expects to owe, after subtracting any withholding and credits, at least $500 in tax, and it expects the withholding and credits to be less than the smaller of:

1. 90% of the tax shown on the 1997 tax return, or

2. 100% of the tax shown on the 1996 tax return (110% of that amount if the estate's or trust's adjusted gross income on that return is more than $150,000, and less than ⅔ of gross income for 1996 or 1997 is from farming or fishing).

However, if a return was not filed for 1996 or that return did not cover a full 12 months, item **2** does not apply.

Exceptions

Estimated tax payments are not required from:

1. An estate of a domestic decedent or a domestic trust that had no tax liability for the full 12-month 1996 tax year;

2. A decedent's estate for any tax year ending before the date that is 2 years after the decedent's death; or

3. A trust that was treated as owned by the decedent if the trust will receive the residue of the decedent's estate under the will (or if no will is admitted to probate, the trust primarily responsible for paying debts, taxes, and expenses of administration) for any tax year ending before the date that is 2 years after the decedent's death.

For more information, get **Form 1041-ES,** Estimated Income Tax for Estates and Trusts.

Section 643(g) Election

Fiduciaries of trusts that pay estimated tax may elect under section 643(g) to have any portion of their estimated tax payments allocated to any of the beneficiaries.

The fiduciary of a decedent's estate may make a section 643(g) election only for the final year of the estate.

See the instructions for line 24b for more details.

Interest and Penalties

Interest

Interest is charged on taxes not paid by the due date, even if an extension of time to file is granted.

Interest is also charged on the failure-to-file penalty, the accuracy-related penalty, and the fraud penalty. The interest charge is figured at a rate determined under section 6621.

Late Filing of Return

The law provides a penalty of 5% a month, or part of a month, up to a maximum of 25%, for each month the return is not filed. The penalty is imposed on the net amount due. If the return is more than 60 days late, the minimum penalty is the smaller of $100 or the tax due. The penalty will not be imposed if you can show that the failure to file on time was due to reasonable cause. If the failure is due to reasonable cause, attach an explanation to the return.

Late Payment of Tax

Generally, the penalty for not paying tax when due is ½ of 1% of the unpaid amount for each month or part of a month it remains unpaid. The maximum penalty is 25% of the unpaid amount. The penalty is imposed on the net amount due. Any penalty is in addition to interest charges on late payments.

Note: If you include interest or either of these penalties with your payment, identify and enter these amounts in the bottom margin of Form 1041, page 1. Do not include the interest or penalty amount in the balance of tax due on line 27.

Failure To Supply Schedule K-1

The fiduciary must provide Schedule K-1 (Form 1041) to each beneficiary who receives a distribution of property or an allocation of an item of the estate. A penalty of $50 (not to exceed $100,000 for any calendar year) will be imposed on the fiduciary for each failure to furnish Schedule K-1 to each beneficiary unless reasonable cause for each failure is established.

Underpaid Estimated Tax

If the fiduciary underpaid estimated tax, get **Form 2210,** Underpayment of Estimated Tax by Individuals, Estates, and Trusts, to figure any penalty. Enter the amount of any penalty on line 26, Form 1041.

Trust Fund Recovery Penalty

This penalty may apply if certain excise, income, social security, and Medicare taxes that must be collected or withheld are not collected or withheld, or these

taxes are not paid to the IRS. These taxes are generally reported on Forms 720, 941, 943, or 945. The trust fund recovery penalty may be imposed on all persons who are determined by the IRS to have been **responsible** for collecting, accounting for, and paying over these taxes, and who acted willfully in not doing so. The penalty is equal to the unpaid trust fund tax. See the instructions for Form 720, **Pub. 15 (Circular E)**, Employer's Tax Guide, or **Pub. 51 (Circular A)**, Agricultural Employer's Tax Guide, for more details, including the definition of responsible persons.

Other Penalties

Other penalties can be imposed for negligence, substantial underpayment of tax, and fraud. Get **Pub. 17**, Your Federal Income Tax, for details on these penalties.

Other Forms That May Be Required

Forms W-2 and **W-3**, Wage and Tax Statement; and Transmittal of Wage and Tax Statements.

Form 56, Notice Concerning Fiduciary Relationship.

Form 706, United States Estate (and Generation-Skipping Transfer) Tax Return; or **Form 706-NA**, United States Estate (and Generation-Skipping Transfer) Tax Return, Estate of nonresident not a citizen of the United States.

Form 706-GS(D), Generation-Skipping Transfer Tax Return For Distributions.

Form 706-GS(D-1), Notification of Distribution From a Generation-Skipping Trust.

Form 706-GS(T), Generation-Skipping Transfer Tax Return for Terminations.

Form 720, Quarterly Federal Excise Tax Return. Use Form 720 to report environmental excise taxes, communications and air transportation taxes, fuel taxes, luxury tax on passenger vehicles, manufacturers' taxes, ship passenger tax, and certain other excise taxes.

Caution: *See Trust Fund Recovery Penalty* on page 4.

Form 940 or **Form 940-EZ**, Employer's Annual Federal Unemployment (FUTA) Tax Return. The estate or trust may be liable for FUTA tax and may have to file Form 940 or 940-EZ if it paid wages of $1,500 or more in any calendar quarter during the calendar year (or the preceding calendar year) or one or more employees worked for the estate or trust for some part of a day in any 20 different weeks during the calendar year.

Form 941, Employer's Quarterly Federal Tax Return. Employers must file this form quarterly to report income tax withheld on wages and employer and employee social security and Medicare taxes. Agricultural employers must file **Form 943**, Employer's Annual Tax Return for

Agricultural Employees, instead of Form 941, to report income tax withheld and employer and employee social security and Medicare taxes on farmworkers.

Caution: *See Trust Fund Recovery Penalty* on page 4.

Form 945, Annual Return of Withheld Federal Income Tax. Use this form to report income tax withheld from nonpayroll payments, including pensions, annuities, IRAs, gambling winnings, and backup withholding.

Caution: *See Trust Fund Recovery Penalty* on page 4.

Form 1040, U.S. Individual Income Tax Return.

Form 1040NR, U.S. Nonresident Alien Income Tax Return.

Form 1041-A, U.S. Information Return— Trust Accumulation of Charitable Amounts.

Forms 1042 and **1042-S**, Annual Withholding Tax Return for U.S. Source Income of Foreign Persons; and Foreign Person's U.S. Source Income Subject to Withholding. Use these forms to report and transmit withheld tax on payments or distributions made to nonresident alien individuals, foreign partnerships, or foreign corporations to the extent such payments or distributions constitute gross income from sources within the United States that is not effectively connected with a U.S. trade or business. For more information, see sections 1441 and 1442, and **Pub. 515**, Withholding of Tax on Nonresident Aliens and Foreign Corporations.

Forms 1099-A, B, INT, MISC, OID, R, and S.—You may have to file these information returns to report abandonments, acquisitions through foreclosure, proceeds from broker and barter exchange transactions, interest payments, medical and dental health care payments, miscellaneous income, original issue discount, distributions from pensions, annuities, retirement or profit-sharing plans, individual retirement arrangements, insurance contracts, and proceeds from real estate transactions.

Also, use these returns to report amounts received as a nominee on behalf of another person, except amounts reported to beneficiaries on Schedule K-1 (Form 1041).

Form 8275, Disclosure Statement. File Form 8275 to disclose items or positions, except those contrary to a regulation, that are not otherwise adequately disclosed on a tax return. The disclosure is made to avoid parts of the accuracy-related penalty imposed for disregard of rules or substantial understatement of tax. Form 8275 is also used for disclosures relating to preparer penalties for understatements due to unrealistic positions or disregard of rules.

Form 8275-R, Regulation Disclosure Statement, is used to disclose any item on a tax return for which a position has been taken that is contrary to Treasury regulations.

Forms 8288 and **8288-A**, U.S. Withholding Tax Return for Dispositions by Foreign Persons of U.S. Real Property Interests; and Statement of Withholding on Dispositions by Foreign Persons of U.S. Real Property Interests. Use these forms to report and transmit withheld tax on the sale of U.S. real property by a foreign person. Also, use these forms to report and transmit tax withheld from amounts distributed to a foreign beneficiary from a "U.S. real property interest account" that a domestic estate or trust is required to establish under Regulations section 1.1445-5(c)(1)(iii).

Form 8300, Report of Cash Payments Over $10,000 Received in a Trade or Business. Generally, this form is used to report the receipt of more than $10,000 in cash or foreign currency in one transaction (or a series of related transactions).

Attachments

If you need more space on the forms or schedules, attach separate sheets. Use the same size and format as on the printed forms. **But show the totals on the printed forms.**

Attach these separate sheets after all the schedules and forms. Enter the estate's or trust's employer identification number on each sheet.

Do not file a copy of the decedent's will or the trust instrument unless the IRS requests it.

Additional Information

The following publications may assist you in preparing Form 1041.

Pub. 550, Investment Income and Expenses; and

Pub. 559, Survivors, Executors, and Administrators.

Of Special Interest to Bankruptcy Trustees and Debtors-in-Possession

Taxation of Bankruptcy Estates of an Individual

A bankruptcy estate is a separate taxable entity created when an individual debtor files a petition under either chapter 7 or 11 of title 11 of the U.S. Code. The estate is administered by a trustee or a debtor-in-possession. If the case is later dismissed by the bankruptcy court, the debtor is treated as if the bankruptcy petition had never been filed. This provision does NOT apply to partnerships or corporations.

Who Must File

Every trustee (or debtor-in-possession) for an individual's bankruptcy estate under chapter 7 or 11 of title 11 of the U.S. Code must file a return if the bankruptcy estate has gross income of $5,900 or more for tax years beginning in 1996.

Failure to do so may result in an estimated Request for Administrative Expenses being filed by the IRS in the bankruptcy proceeding or a motion to compel filing of the return.

Note: *The filing of a tax return for the bankruptcy estate does not relieve the individual debtor of his or her (or their) individual tax obligations.*

Employer Identification Number

Every bankruptcy estate of an individual required to file a return must have its own employer identification number (EIN). You may apply for one on **Form SS-4,** Application for Employer Identification Number. The social security number (SSN) of the individual debtor cannot be used as the EIN for the bankruptcy estate.

Accounting Period

A bankruptcy estate is allowed to have a fiscal year. The period can be no longer than 12 months.

When To File

File Form 1041 on or before the 15th day of the 4th month following the close of the tax year. Use Form 2758 to apply for an extension of time to file.

Disclosure of Return Information

Under section 6103(e)(5), tax returns of individual debtors who have filed for bankruptcy under chapters 7 or 11 of title 11 are, upon written request, open to inspection by or disclosure to the trustee.

The returns subject to disclosure to the trustee are those for the year the bankruptcy begins and prior years. Use **Form 4506,** Request for Copy or Transcript of Tax Form, to request copies of the individual debtor's tax returns.

If the bankruptcy case was not voluntary, disclosure cannot be made before the bankruptcy court has entered an order for relief, unless the court rules that the disclosure is needed for determining whether relief should be ordered.

Transfer of Tax Attributes From the Individual Debtor to the Bankruptcy Estate

The bankruptcy estate succeeds to the following tax attributes of the individual debtor:

1. Net operating loss (NOL) carryovers;
2. Charitable contributions carryovers;
3. Recovery of tax benefit items;
4. Credit carryovers;
5. Capital loss carryovers;
6. Basis, holding period, and character of assets;
7. Method of accounting;
8. Unused passive activity losses;
9. Unused passive activity credits; and
10. Unused section 465 losses.

Income, Deductions, and Credits

Under section 1398(c), the taxable income of the bankruptcy estate generally is figured in the same manner as an individual. The gross income of the bankruptcy estate includes any income included in property of the estate as defined in Bankruptcy Code section 541. Also included is gain from the sale of property. To figure gain, the trustee or debtor-in-possession must determine the correct basis of the property.

To determine whether any amount paid or incurred by the bankruptcy estate is allowable as a deduction or credit, or is treated as wages for employment tax purposes, treat the amount as if it were paid or incurred by the individual debtor in the same trade or business or other activity the debtor engaged in before the bankruptcy proceedings began.

Administrative expenses.— The bankruptcy estate is allowed a deduction for any administrative expense allowed under section 503 of title 11 of the U.S. Code, and any fee or charge assessed under chapter 123 of title 28 of the U.S. Code, to the extent not disallowed under an Internal Revenue Code provision (e.g., section 263, 265, or 275).

Administrative expense loss.— When figuring a net operating loss, nonbusiness deductions (including administrative expenses) are limited under section 172(d)(4) to the bankruptcy estate's nonbusiness income. The excess nonbusiness deductions are an administrative expense loss that may be carried back to each of the 3 preceding tax years and forward to each of the 7 succeeding tax years of the bankruptcy estate. The amount of an administrative expense loss that may be carried to any tax year is determined after the net operating loss deductions allowed for that year. An administrative expense loss is allowed only to the bankruptcy estate and cannot be carried to any tax year of the individual debtor.

Carryback of net operating losses and credits.— If the bankruptcy estate itself incurs a net operating loss (apart from losses carried forward to the estate from the individual debtor), it can carry back its net operating losses not only to previous tax years of the bankruptcy estate, but also to tax years of the individual debtor prior to the year in which the bankruptcy proceedings began. Excess credits, such as the foreign tax credit, also may be carried back to pre-bankruptcy years of the individual debtor.

Exemption.— For tax years beginning in 1996, a bankruptcy estate is allowed a personal exemption of $2,550.

Standard deduction.— For tax years beginning in 1996, a bankruptcy estate that does not itemize deductions is allowed a standard deduction of $3,350.

Discharge of indebtedness.— In a title 11 case, gross income does not include amounts that normally would be included in gross income resulting from the

discharge of indebtedness. However, any amounts excluded from gross income must be applied to reduce certain tax attributes in a certain order. Attach **Form 982,** Reduction of Tax Attributes Due to Discharge of Indebtedness, to show the reduction of tax attributes.

Tax Rate Schedule

Figure the tax for the bankruptcy estate using the tax rate schedule shown below. Enter the tax on Form 1040, line 38.

If taxable income is:

Over—	But not over—	The tax is:	Of the amount over—
$0	$20,050	15%	$0
20,050	48,450	$3,007.50 + 28%	20,050
48,450	73,850	10,959.50 + 31%	48,450
73,850	131,875	18,833.50 + 36%	73,850
131,875	------	39,722.50 + 39.6%	131,875

Prompt Determination of Tax Liability

To request a prompt determination of the tax liability of the bankruptcy estate, the trustee or debtor-in-possession must file a written application for the determination with the IRS District Director for the district in which the bankruptcy case is pending. The application must be submitted in duplicate and executed under the penalties of perjury. The trustee or debtor-in-possession must submit with the application an **exact copy** of the return (or returns) filed by the trustee with the IRS for a completed tax period, and a statement of the name and location of the office where the return was filed. The envelope should be marked, "Personal Attention of the Special Procedures Function (Bankruptcy Section). DO NOT OPEN IN MAILROOM."

The IRS will notify the trustee or debtor-in-possession within 60 days from receipt of the application whether the return filed by the trustee or debtor-in-possession has been selected for examination or has been accepted as filed. If the return is selected for examination, it will be examined as soon as possible. The IRS will notify the trustee or debtor-in-possession of any tax due within 180 days from receipt of the application or within any additional time permitted by the bankruptcy court.

See Rev. Proc. 81-17, 1981-1 C.B. 688.

Special Filing Instructions for Bankruptcy Estates

Use Form 1041 only as a transmittal for Form 1040. In the top margin of Form 1040 write "Attachment to Form 1041. DO NOT DETACH." Attach Form 1040 to Form 1041. Complete only the identification area at the top of Form 1041. Enter the name of the individual debtor in the following format: "John Q. Public Bankruptcy Estate." Beneath, enter the name of the trustee in the following format: "Avery Snow, Trustee." In item D, enter the date the petition was filed or the date of conversion to a chapter 7 or 11

case. Enter on Form 1041, line 23, any tax due from line 51 of Form 1040. Complete lines 24 through 29 of Form 1041, and sign and date it.

Specific Instructions

Name of Estate or Trust

Copy the exact name of the estate or trust from the **Form SS-4,** Application for Employer Identification Number, that you used to apply for the employer identification number (EIN).

If a grantor type trust (discussed below), write the name, identification number, and address of the grantor(s) or other person(s) in parentheses after the name of the trust.

Address

Include the suite, room, or other unit number after the street address.

If the Post Office does not deliver mail to the street address and the fiduciary has a P.O. box, show the box number instead of the street address.

If you change your address after filing Form 1041, use **Form 8822,** Change of Address, to notify the IRS.

A. Type of Entity

Check the appropriate box that describes the entity for which you are filing the return.

Note: *There are special filing requirements for grantor type trusts and bankruptcy estates (discussed below).*

Decedent's Estate

An estate of a deceased person is a taxable entity separate from the decedent. It generally continues to exist until the final distribution of the assets of the estate is made to the heirs and other beneficiaries. The income earned from the property of the estate during the period of administration or settlement must be accounted for and reported by the estate.

Simple Trust

A trust may qualify as a simple trust if:

1. The trust instrument requires that all income must be distributed currently;

2. The trust instrument does not provide that any amounts are to be paid, permanently set aside, or used for charitable purposes; and

3. The trust does not distribute amounts allocated to the corpus of the trust.

Complex Trust

A complex trust is any trust that does not qualify as a simple trust as explained above.

Grantor Type Trust

A grantor type trust is a legal trust under applicable state law that is not recognized as a separate taxable entity for income tax purposes because the grantor or other substantial owners have not relinquished complete dominion and control over the trust.

Generally, for transfers made in trust after March 1, 1986, the grantor is treated as the owner of any portion of a trust in which he or she has a reversionary interest in either the income or corpus therefrom, if, as of the inception of that portion of the trust, the value of that interest is more than 5% of the value of that portion. Also, the grantor is treated as holding any power or interest that was held by either the grantor's spouse at the time that the power or interest was created or who became the grantor's spouse after the creation of that power or interest.

Report on Form 1041 the part of the income that is taxable to the trust. Do not report on Form 1041 the income that is taxable to the grantor or another person. Instead, attach a separate sheet to report the following:

● The income of the trust that is taxable to the grantor or another person under sections 671 through 678;

● The name, identifying number, and address of the person(s) to whom the income is taxable; and

● Any deductions or credits applied to this income.

The income taxable to the grantor or another person under sections 671 through 678 and the deductions and credits applied to the income must be reported on the income tax return that person files.

Family estate trust.— A family estate trust is also known as a family, family estate, pure, equity, equity pure, prime, or constitutional trust.

In most cases, the grantor transfers property to the trust or assigns to the trust the income for services the grantor performs. The trust instrument usually provides:

● Evidence of ownership, such as certificates of beneficial interest in the trust.

● That the grantor is a trustee and executive officer.

● That the trust pays the living expenses for the grantor and the grantor's family.

● That the corpus and undistributed income are distributed to the owners after the trust is terminated.

Generally, a family estate trust is treated as a grantor type trust. For more information, see Rev. Rul. 75-257, 1975-2 C.B. 251.

Mortgage pools.— The trustee of a mortgage pool, such as the Federal National Mortgage Association, collects principal and interest payments on each mortgage and makes distributions to the certificate holders. Each pool is

considered a grantor type trust, and each certificate holder is treated as the owner of an undivided interest in the entire trust under the grantor trust rules. Certificate holders must report their proportionate share of the mortgage interest and other items of income on their individual tax returns.

Pre-need funeral trusts.— The purchasers of pre-need funeral services are the grantors and the owners of pre-need funeral trusts established under state laws. See Rev. Rul. 87-127, 1987-2 C.B. 156.

Nonqualified deferred compensation plans.— Taxpayers may adopt and maintain grantor trusts in connection with nonqualified deferred compensation plans (sometimes referred to as "rabbi trusts"). Rev. Proc. 92-64, 1992-2 C.B. 422, provides a "model grantor trust" for use in rabbi trust arrangements. The procedure also provides guidance for requesting rulings on the plans that use these trusts.

Optional filing methods for certain grantor type trusts.— Generally, for a trust all of which is treated as owned by one or more grantors or other persons, the trustee may use one of the following 3 optional methods to report instead of filing Form 1041:

Method 1. For a trust treated as owned by one grantor or by one other person, the trustee must give all payers of income during the tax year the name and taxpayer identification number (TIN) of the grantor or other person treated as the owner of the trust and the address of the trust. This method may be used only if the owner of the trust provides the trustee with a signed **Form W-9,** Request for Taxpayer Identification Number and Certification. In addition, unless the grantor or other person treated as owner of the trust is the trustee or a co-trustee of the trust, the trustee must give the grantor or other person treated as owner of the trust a statement that **(a)** shows all items of income, deduction, and credit of the trust; **(b)** identifies the payer of each item of income; **(c)** explains how the grantor or other person treated as owner of the trust takes those items into account when figuring the grantor's or other person's taxable income or tax; and **(d)** informs the grantor or other person treated as the owner of the trust that those items must be included when figuring taxable income and credits on his or her income tax return.

Method 2. For a trust treated as owned by one grantor or by one other person, the trustee must give all payers of income during the tax year the name, address, and TIN of the trust. The trustee also must file with the IRS the appropriate Forms 1099 to report the income or gross proceeds paid to the trust during the tax year that shows the trust as the payer and the grantor or other person treated as owner as the payee. The trustee must report each type of income in the aggregate and each item of gross proceeds separately. In addition, unless

the grantor or other person treated as owner of the trust is the trustee or a co-trustee of the trust, the trustee must give the grantor or other person treated as owner of the trust a statement that (a) shows all items of income, deduction, and credit of the trust; (b) explains how the grantor or other person treated as owner of the trust takes those items into account when figuring the grantor's or other person's taxable income or tax; and (c) informs the grantor or other person treated as the owner of the trust that those items must be included when figuring taxable income and credits on his or her income tax return. This statement satisfies the requirement to give the recipient copies of the Forms 1099 filed by the trustee.

Method 3. For a trust treated as owned by two or more grantors or other persons, the trustee must give all payers of income during the tax year the name, address, and TIN of the trust. The trustee also must file with the IRS the appropriate Forms 1099 to report the income or gross proceeds paid to the trust by all payers during the tax year attributable to the part of the trust treated as owned by each grantor or other person, showing the trust as the payer and each grantor or other person treated as owner of the trust as the payee. The trustee must report each type of income in the aggregate and each item of gross proceeds separately. In addition, the trustee must give each grantor or other person treated as owner of the trust a statement that (a) shows all items of income, deduction, and credit of the trust attributable to the part of the trust treated as owned by the grantor or other person; (b) explains how the grantor or other person treated as owner of the trust takes those items into account when figuring the grantor's or other person's taxable income or tax; and (c) informs the grantor or other person treated as owner of the trust that those items must be included when figuring taxable income and credits on his or her income tax return. This statement satisfies the requirement to give the recipient copies of the Forms 1099 filed by the trustee.

Exceptions.—The following trusts cannot report using the optional filing methods:

1. A common trust fund (as defined in section 584(a)).

2. A foreign trust or a trust that has any of its assets located outside the United States.

3. A qualified subchapter S trust (as defined in section 1361(d)(3)).

4. A trust all of which is treated as owned by one grantor or one other person whose tax year is other than a calendar year.

5. A trust all of which is treated as owned by one or more grantors or other persons, one of which is not a U.S. person.

6. A trust all of which is treated as owned by one or more grantors or other

persons if at least one grantor or other person is an exempt recipient for information reporting purposes, unless at least one grantor or other person is not an exempt recipient and the trustee reports without treating any of the grantors or other persons as exempt recipients.

A trustee who previously had filed Form 1041 for any tax year ending before January 1, 1996 (and who previously had not filed a final Form 1041 under the simplified filing rule in effect prior to January 1, 1996), or who files a Form 1041 for any later tax year, can change to one of the optional methods by filing a final Form 1041 for the tax year that immediately precedes the first tax year for which the trustee elects to report under one of the optional methods. On the front of the final Form 1041, the trustee must write "Pursuant to section 1.671–4(g), this is the final Form 1041 for this grantor trust," and check the "Final return" box in item F. For more details on changing reporting methods, including changes from one optional method to another, see Regulations section 1.671–4(g).

Backup withholding.— Generally, a grantor trust is considered a payor of reportable payments received by the trust for purposes of backup withholding. If the trust has 10 or fewer grantors, a reportable payment made to the trust is treated as a reportable payment of the same kind made to the grantors on the date the trust received the payment. If the trust has more than 10 grantors, a reportable payment made to the trust is treated as a payment of the same kind made by the trust to each grantor in an amount equal to the distribution made to each grantor on the date the grantor is paid or credited. The trustee must withhold 31% of reportable payments made to any grantor who is subject to backup withholding. For more information, see section 3406 and Temporary Regulations section 35a.9999-2, Q&A 20.

Bankruptcy Estate

A chapter 7 or 11 bankruptcy estate is a separate and distinct taxable entity from the individual debtor for Federal income tax purposes. See **Of Special Interest to Bankruptcy Trustees and Debtors-in-Possession** on page 5.

For more information, see section 1398 and **Pub. 908,** Bankruptcy Tax Guide.

Pooled Income Fund

A pooled income fund is a split-interest trust with a remainder interest for a public charity and a life income interest retained by the donor or for another person. The property is held in a pool with other pooled income fund property and does not include any tax-exempt securities. The income for a retained life interest is figured using the yearly rate of return earned by the trust. See section 642(c) and the related regulations for more information.

If you are filing for a pooled income fund, attach a statement to support the following:

• The calculation of the yearly rate of return.

• The computation of the deduction for distributions to the beneficiaries.

• The computation of any charitable deduction.

You do not have to complete Schedules A or B of Form 1041.

If the fund has accumulations of income, file Form 1041-A unless the fund is required to distribute all of its net income to beneficiaries currently.

You must also file **Form 5227,** Split-Interest Trust Information Return, for the pooled income fund.

B. Number of Schedules K-1 Attached

Every trust or decedent's estate claiming an income distribution deduction on page 1, line 18, must enter the number of Schedules K-1 (Form 1041) that are attached to Form 1041.

C. Employer Identification Number

Every estate or trust must have an EIN. To apply for one, use Form SS-4. You may get this form from the IRS or the Social Security Administration. See **Pub. 583,** Starting a Business and Keeping Records, for more information.

If you are filing a return for a mortgage pool, such as one created under the mortgage-backed security programs administered by the Federal National Mortgage Association ("Fannie Mae") or the Government National Mortgage Association ("Ginnie Mae"), the EIN stays with the pool if that pool is traded from one financial institution to another.

D. Date Entity Created

Enter the date the trust was created, or, if a decedent's estate, the date of the decedent's death.

E. Nonexempt Charitable and Split-Interest Trusts

Section 4947(a)(1) Trust

Check this box if the trust is a nonexempt charitable trust within the meaning of section 4947(a)(1). A nonexempt charitable trust is a trust that is not exempt from tax under section 501(a); all of the unexpired interests are devoted to one or more charitable purposes described in section 170(c)(2)(B); and for which a deduction was allowed under section 170 (for individual taxpayers) or similar Code section for personal holding companies, foreign personal holding companies, or estates or trusts (including a deduction for estate or gift tax purposes).

Not a Private Foundation

Check this box if the charitable trust is not treated as a private foundation under section 509. For more information, see Regulations section 53.4947-1.

If a nonexempt charitable trust is not treated as though it were a private foundation, the fiduciary must file **Form 990 (or Form 990-EZ),** Return of Organization Exempt From Income Tax, and **Schedule A (Form 990),** Organization Exempt Under Section 501(c)(3), in addition to Form 1041 if the trust's gross receipts are normally more than $25,000.

If a nonexempt charitable trust is not treated as though it were a private foundation, and it has no taxable income under Subtitle A, it can file either Form 990 or Form 990-EZ instead of Form 1041 to meet its section 6012 filing requirement.

Section 4947(a)(2) Trust

Check this box if the trust is a split-interest trust described in section 4947(a)(2). A split-interest trust is a trust that is not exempt from tax under section 501(a); has some unexpired interests that are devoted to purposes other than religious, charitable, or similar purposes described in section 170(c)(2)(B); and has amounts transferred in trust after May 26, 1969, for which a deduction was allowed under section 170 (for individual taxpayers) or similar Code section for personal holding companies, foreign personal holding companies, or estates or trusts (including a deduction for estate or gift tax purposes).

The fiduciary of a split-interest trust must also file Form 5227 (for amounts transferred in trust after May 26, 1969); and Form 1041-A if the trust's governing instrument does not require that all of the trust's income be distributed currently.

If a split-interest trust has any unrelated business taxable income, however, it must file Form 1041 to report all of its income and to pay any tax due.

Nonexempt Charitable Trust Treated as a Private Foundation

If a nonexempt charitable trust is treated as though it were a private foundation under section 509, then the fiduciary must file **Form 990-PF,** Return of Private Foundation, in addition to Form 1041.

If a nonexempt charitable trust is subject to any of the private foundation excise taxes, then it must also file **Form 4720,** Return of Certain Excise Taxes on Charities and Other Persons Under Chapters 41 and 42 of the Internal Revenue Code. Any private foundation taxes paid by the trust cannot be taken as a deduction on Form 1041.

If a nonexempt charitable trust is treated as though it were a private foundation, and it has no taxable income under Subtitle A, it may file Form 990-PF

instead of Form 1041 to meet its section 6012 filing requirement.

F. Initial Return, Amended Return, Final Return; or Change in Fiduciary's Name or Address

Amended Return

If you are filing an amended Form 1041, check the "Amended return" box. Complete the entire return, correct the appropriate lines with the new information, and refigure the estate's or trust's tax liability. If the total tax on line 23 is larger on the amended return than on the original return, you generally should pay the difference with the amended return. However, you should adjust this amount if there is any increase or decrease in the total payments shown on line 25. On an attached sheet explain the reason for the amendments and identify the lines and amounts being changed on the amended return.

If the amended return results in a change to income, or a change in distribution of any income or other information provided to a beneficiary, an amended Schedule K-1 (Form 1041) must also be filed with the amended Form 1041 and given to each beneficiary. Check the "Amended K-1" box at the top of the amended Schedule K-1.

Final Return

Check this box if this is a final return because the estate or trust has terminated. Also, check the "Final K-1" box at the top of Schedule K-1.

If, on the final return, there are excess deductions, an unused capital loss carryover, or a net operating loss carryover, see the discussion in the Schedule K-1 instructions on page 27. Figure the deductions on an attached sheet.

G. Pooled Mortgage Account

If you bought a pooled mortgage account during the year, and still have that pool at the end of the tax year, check the "Bought" box and enter the date of purchase. If you sold a pooled mortgage account that was purchased during this, or a previous, tax year, check the "Sold" box and enter the date of sale. If you neither bought nor sold a pooled mortgage account, skip this item.

Income

Special Rule for Blind Trust

If you are reporting income from a qualified blind trust (under the Ethics in Government Act of 1978), do not identify the payer of any income to the trust but complete the rest of the return as provided in the instructions. Also write "Blind Trust" at the top of page 1.

Line 1—Interest Income

Report the estate's or trust's share of all taxable interest income that was received during the tax year. Examples of taxable interest include interest from:

● Accounts (including certificates of deposit and money market accounts) with banks, credit unions, and thrifts.

● Notes, loans and mortgages.

● U.S. Treasury bills, notes, and bonds.

● U.S. savings bonds.

● Original issue discount.

● Income received as a regular interest holder of a real estate mortgage investment conduit (REMIC).

For taxable bonds acquired after 1987, amortizable bond premium is treated as an offset to the interest income instead of as a separate interest deduction. See Pub. 550.

For the year of the decedent's death, Forms 1099-INT issued in the decedent's name may include interest income earned after the date of death that should be reported on the income tax return of the decedent's estate. When preparing the decedent's final income tax return, report on line 1 of Schedule B (Form 1040) or Schedule 1 (Form 1040A) the total interest shown on Form 1099-INT. Under the last entry on line 1, subtotal all the interest reported on line 1. Below the subtotal, write "Form 1041" and the name and address shown on Form 1041 for the decedent's estate. Also, show the part of the interest reported on Form 1041 and subtract it from the subtotal.

Line 2—Dividends

Report the estate's or trust's share of all ordinary dividends received during the tax year.

For the year of the decedent's death, Forms 1099-DIV issued in the decedent's name may include dividends earned after the date of death that should be reported on the income tax return of the decedent's estate. When preparing the decedent's final income tax return, report on line 5 of Schedule B (Form 1040) or Schedule 1 (Form 1040A) the total dividends shown on Form 1099-DIV. Under the last entry on line 5, subtotal all the dividends reported on line 5. Below the subtotal, write "Form 1041" and the name and address shown on Form 1041 for the decedent's estate. Also, show the part of the dividends reported on Form 1041 and subtract it from the subtotal.

Note: Report capital gain distributions on Schedule D (Form 1041), line 10.

Line 3—Business Income or (Loss)

If the estate or trust operated a business, report the income and expenses on **Schedule C (Form 1040),** Profit or Loss From Business (or **Schedule C-EZ (Form 1040),** Net Profit From Business). Enter the net profit or (loss) from Schedule C (or Schedule C-EZ) on line 3.

Line 4—Capital Gain or (Loss)

Enter the gain from Schedule D (Form 1041), Part III, line 17, column (c); or the loss from Part IV, line 18.

Note: *Do not substitute Schedule D (Form 1040) for Schedule D (Form 1041).*

Line 5—Rents, Royalties, Partnerships, Other Estates and Trusts, etc.

Use **Schedule E (Form 1040),** Supplemental Income and Loss, to report the estate's or trust's share of income or (losses) from rents, royalties, partnerships, S corporations, other estates and trusts, and REMICs. Enter the net profit or (loss) from Schedule E on line 5. See the instructions for Schedule E (Form 1040) for reporting requirements.

If the estate or trust received a Schedule K-1 from a partnership, S corporation, or other flow-through entity, use the corresponding lines on Form 1041 to report the interest, dividends, capital gains, etc., from the flow-through entity.

Line 6—Farm Income or (Loss)

If the estate or trust operated a farm, use **Schedule F (Form 1040),** Profit or Loss From Farming, to report farm income and expenses. Enter the net profit or (loss) from Schedule F on line 6.

Line 7—Ordinary Gain or (Loss)

Enter from line 20, **Form 4797,** Sales of Business Property, the ordinary gain or loss from the sale or exchange of property other than capital assets and also from involuntary conversions (other than casualty or theft).

Line 8—Other Income

Enter other items of income not included on lines 1 through 7. List the type and amount on an attached schedule if the estate or trust has more than one item.

Items to be reported on line 8 include:

• Unpaid compensation received by the decedent's estate that is income in respect of a decedent.

• Any part of a total distribution shown on **Form 1099-R,** Distributions From Pensions, Annuities, Retirement or Profit-Sharing Plans, IRAs, Insurance Contracts, etc., that is treated as ordinary income. For more information, see the separate instructions for **Form 4972,** Tax on Lump-Sum Distributions.

Deductions

Amortization, Depletion, and Depreciation

A trust or decedent's estate is allowed a deduction for amortization, depletion, and depreciation only to the extent the deductions are not apportioned to the beneficiaries.

For a decedent's estate, the depreciation deduction is apportioned between the estate and the heirs,

legatees, and devisees on the basis of the estate's income allocable to each.

For a trust, the depreciation deduction is apportioned between the income beneficiaries and the trust on the basis of the trust income allocable to each, unless the governing instrument (or local law) requires or permits the trustee to maintain a depreciation reserve. If the trustee is required to maintain a reserve, the deduction is first allocated to the trust, up to the amount of the reserve. Any excess is allocated among the beneficiaries in the same manner as the trust's accounting income. See Regulations section 1.167(h)-1(b).

For mineral or timber property held by a decedent's estate, the depletion deduction is apportioned between the estate and the heirs, legatees, and devisees on the basis of the estate's income from such property allocable to each.

For mineral or timber property held in trust, the depletion deduction is apportioned between the income beneficiaries and the trust based on the trust income from such property allocable to each, unless the governing instrument (or local law) requires or permits the trustee to maintain a reserve for depletion. If the trustee is required to maintain a reserve, the deduction is first allocated to the trust, up to the amount of the reserve. Any excess is allocated among the beneficiaries in the same manner as the trust's accounting income. See Regulations section 1.611-1(c)(4).

The deduction for amortization is apportioned between an estate or trust and its beneficiaries under the same principles for apportioning the deductions for depreciation and depletion.

An estate or trust is not allowed to make an election under section 179 to expense certain tangible property.

The deduction for the amortization of reforestation expenditures under section 194 is allowed only to an estate.

The estate's or trust's share of amortization, depletion, and depreciation should be reported on the appropriate lines of Schedule C (or C-EZ), E, or F (Form 1040), the net income or loss from which is shown on line 3, 5, or 6 of Form 1041. If the deduction is not related to a specific business or activity, then report it on line 15a.

Allocation of Deductions for Tax-Exempt Income

Generally, no deduction that would otherwise be allowable is allowed for any expense (whether for business or for the production of income) that is allocable to tax-exempt income. Examples of tax-exempt income include:

• Certain death benefits (section 101);

• Interest on state or local bonds (section 103);

• Compensation for injuries or sickness (section 104); and

• Income from discharge of indebtedness in a title 11 case (section 108).

Exception. State income taxes and business expenses that are allocable to tax-exempt interest are deductible.

Expenses that are directly allocable to tax-exempt income are allocated only to tax-exempt income. A reasonable proportion of expenses indirectly allocable to both tax-exempt income and other income must be allocated to each class of income.

Deductions That May Be Allowable for Estate Tax Purposes

Administration expenses and casualty and theft losses deductible on Form 706 may be deducted, to the extent otherwise deductible for income tax purposes, on Form 1041 if the fiduciary files a statement waiving the right to deduct the expenses and losses on Form 706. The statement must be filed before the expiration of the statutory period of limitations for the tax year the deduction is claimed. See Pub. 559 for more information.

Accrued Expenses

Generally, an accrual basis taxpayer can deduct accrued expenses in the tax year that: **(a)** all events have occurred that determine the liability; and **(b)** the amount of the liability can be figured with reasonable accuracy. However, all the events that establish liability are treated as occurring only when economic performance takes place. There are exceptions for recurring items. See section 461(h).

Limitations on Deductions

At-Risk Loss Limitations

Generally, the amount the estate or trust has "at risk" limits the loss it can deduct for any tax year. Use **Form 6198,** At-Risk Limitations, to figure the deductible loss for the year and file it with Form 1041. For more information, get **Pub. 925,** Passive Activity and At-Risk Rules.

Passive Activity Loss and Credit Limitations

Section 469 and the regulations thereunder generally limit losses from passive activities to the amount of income derived from all passive activities. Similarly, credits from passive activities are generally limited to the tax attributable to such activities. These limitations are first applied at the estate or trust level.

Generally, an activity is a passive activity if it involves the conduct of any trade or business, and the taxpayer does not materially participate in the activity. Passive activities do not include working interests in oil and gas properties. See section 469(c)(3).

For a grantor trust, material participation is determined at the grantor level.

Generally, rental activities are passive activities, whether or not the taxpayer materially participates. However, certain taxpayers who materially participate in real property trades or businesses are not subject to the passive activity limitations on losses from rental real estate activities in which they materially participate. For more details, see section 469(c)(7).

Note: *Material participation standards for estates and trusts had not been established by regulations at the time these instructions went to print.*

For tax years of an estate ending less than 2 years after the decedent's date of death, up to $25,000 of deductions and deduction equivalents of credits from rental real estate activities in which the decedent actively participated is allowed. Any excess losses and/or credits are suspended for the year and carried forward.

If the estate or trust distributes an interest in a passive activity, the basis of the property immediately before the distribution is increased by the passive activity losses allocable to the interest, and such losses cannot be deducted. See section 469(j)(12).

Note: *Losses from passive activities are first subject to the at-risk rules. When the losses are deductible under the at-risk rules, the passive activity rules then apply.*

Portfolio income is not treated as income from a passive activity, and passive losses and credits generally may not be applied to offset it. Portfolio income generally includes interest, dividends, royalties, and income from annuities. Portfolio income of an estate or trust must be accounted for separately.

See **Form 8582,** Passive Activity Loss Limitations, to figure the amount of losses allowed from passive activities. See **Form 8582-CR,** Passive Activity Credit Limitations, to figure the amount of credit allowed for the current year.

Transactions Between Related Taxpayers

Under section 267, a trust that uses the accrual method of accounting may only deduct business expenses and interest owed to a related party in the year the payment is included in the income of the related party. For this purpose, a related party includes:

1. A grantor and a fiduciary of any trust;

2. A fiduciary of a trust and a fiduciary of another trust, if the same person is a grantor of both trusts;

3. A fiduciary of a trust and a beneficiary of such trust;

4. A fiduciary of a trust and a beneficiary of another trust, if the same person is a grantor of both trusts; and

5. A fiduciary of a trust and a corporation more than 50% in value of the outstanding stock of which is owned, directly or indirectly, by or for the trust or by or for a person who is a grantor of the trust.

Line 10—Interest

Enter the amount of interest (subject to limitations) paid or incurred by the estate or trust on amounts borrowed by the estate or trust, or on debt acquired by the estate or trust (e.g., outstanding obligations from the decedent) that is not claimed elsewhere on the return.

If the proceeds of a loan were used for more than one purpose (e.g., to purchase a portfolio investment and to acquire an interest in a passive activity), the fiduciary must make an interest allocation according to the rules in Temporary Regulations section 1.163-8T.

Do not include interest paid on indebtedness incurred or continued to purchase or carry obligations on which the interest is wholly exempt from income tax.

Personal interest is not deductible. Examples of personal interest include interest paid on:
● Revolving charge accounts.
● Personal notes for money borrowed from a bank, credit union, or other person.
● Installment loans on personal use property.
● Underpayments of Federal, state, or local income taxes.

Interest that is paid or incurred on indebtedness allocable to a trade or business (including a rental activity) should be deducted on the appropriate line of Schedule C (or C-EZ), E, or F (Form 1040), the net income or loss from which is shown on line 3, 5, or 6 of Form 1041.

Types of interest to include on line 10 are:

1. Any investment interest (subject to limitations);

2. Any qualified residence interest; and

3. Any interest payable under section 6601 on any unpaid portion of the estate tax attributable to the value of a reversionary or remainder interest in property, or an interest in a closely held business for the period during which an extension of time for payment of such tax is in effect.

Investment interest.— Generally, investment interest is interest (including amortizable bond premium on taxable bonds acquired after October 22, 1986, but before January 1, 1988) that is paid or incurred on indebtedness that is properly allocable to property held for investment. Investment interest does not include any qualified residence interest, or interest that is taken into account under section 469 in figuring income or loss from a passive activity.

Generally, net investment income is the excess of investment income over investment expenses. Investment expenses are those expenses (other than interest) allowable after application of the 2% floor on miscellaneous itemized deductions.

The amount of the investment interest deduction may be limited. Use **Form 4952,** Investment Interest Expense

Deduction, to figure the allowable investment interest deduction.

If you must complete Form 4952, check the box on line 10 and attach Form 4952. Then, add the deductible investment interest to the other types of deductible interest and enter the total on line 10.

Qualified residence interest.— Interest paid or incurred by an estate or trust on indebtedness secured by a qualified residence of a beneficiary of an estate or trust is treated as qualified residence interest if the residence would be a qualified residence (i.e., the principal residence or the second residence selected by the beneficiary) if owned by the beneficiary. The beneficiary must have a present interest in the estate or trust or an interest in the residuary of the estate or trust. See **Pub. 936,** Home Mortgage Interest Deduction, for an explanation of the general rules for deducting home mortgage interest.

See section 163(h)(3) for a definition of qualified residence interest and for limitations on indebtedness.

Line 11—Taxes

Enter any deductible taxes paid or incurred during the tax year that are not deductible elsewhere on Form 1041.

Deductible taxes include:
● State and local income or real property taxes.
● The generation-skipping transfer (GST) tax imposed on income distributions.

Do not deduct:
● Federal income taxes.
● Estate, inheritance, legacy, succession, and gift taxes.
● Federal duties and excise taxes.
● State and local sales taxes. Instead, treat these taxes as part of the cost of the property.

Line 12—Fiduciary Fees

Enter the deductible fees paid or incurred to the fiduciary for administering the estate or trust during the tax year.

Note: *Fiduciary fees deducted on Form 706 cannot be deducted on Form 1041.*

Line 15a—Other Deductions NOT Subject to the 2% Floor

Attach your own schedule, listing by type and amount, all allowable deductions that are not deductible elsewhere on Form 1041.

Do not include any losses on worthless bonds and similar obligations and nonbusiness bad debts. Report these losses on Schedule D (Form 1041).

Do not deduct medical or funeral expenses on Form 1041. Medical expenses of the decedent paid by the estate may be deductible on the decedent's income tax return for the year incurred. See section 213(c). Funeral expenses are deductible ONLY on Form 706.

The following are examples of deductions that are reported on line 15a.

Bond premium(s).— For taxable bonds acquired before October 23, 1986, if the fiduciary elected to amortize the premium, report the amortization on this line. For tax-exempt bonds, the amortization cannot be deducted. In all cases where the fiduciary has made an election to amortize the premium, the basis must be reduced by the amount of amortization.

For more information, see section 171 and Pub. 550.

If you claim a bond premium deduction for the estate or trust, figure the deduction on a separate sheet and attach it to Form 1041.

Casualty and theft losses.— Use **Form 4684,** Casualties and Thefts, to figure any deductible casualty and theft losses.

Deduction for clean-fuel vehicles.— Section 179A allows a deduction for part of the cost of qualified clean-fuel vehicle property. Get **Pub. 535,** Business Expenses, for more details.

Net operating loss deduction (NOLD).— An estate or trust is allowed the net operating loss deduction (NOLD) under section 172.

If you claim an NOLD for the estate or trust, figure the deduction on a separate sheet and attach it to this return.

Estate's or trust's share of amortization, depreciation, and depletion not claimed elsewhere.— If you cannot deduct the amortization, depreciation, and depletion as rent or royalty expenses on Schedule E (Form 1040), or as business or farm expenses on Schedule C, C-EZ, or F (Form 1040), itemize the fiduciary's share of the deductions on an attached sheet and include them on line 15a. Itemize each beneficiary's share of the deductions and report them on the appropriate line of Schedule K-1 (Form 1041).

Line 15b—Allowable Miscellaneous Itemized Deductions Subject to the 2% Floor

Miscellaneous itemized deductions are deductible only to the extent that the aggregate amount of such deductions exceeds 2% of adjusted gross income (AGI).

Miscellaneous itemized deductions do not include deductions for:
● Interest under section 163.
● Taxes under section 164.
● The amortization of bond premium under section 171.
● Estate taxes attributable to income in respect of a decedent under section 691(c).

For other exceptions, see section 67(b).

For estates and trusts, the AGI is figured by subtracting the following from total income on line 9 of page 1:

1. The administration costs of the estate or trust (the total of lines 12, 14, and 15a to the extent they are costs incurred in the administration of the estate

or trust) that would not have been incurred if the property were NOT held by the estate or trust;

2. The income distribution deduction (line 18);

3. The amount of the exemption (line 20);

4. The deduction for clean-fuel vehicles claimed on line 15a; and

5. The net operating loss deduction claimed on line 15a.

For those estates and trusts whose income distribution deduction is limited to the actual distribution, and NOT the DNI (i.e., the income distribution is less than the DNI), when computing the AGI, use the amount of the actual distribution.

For those estates and trusts whose income distribution deduction is limited to the DNI (i.e., the actual distribution exceeds the DNI), the DNI must be figured taking into account the allowable miscellaneous itemized deductions (AMID) after application of the 2% floor. In this situation there are two unknown amounts: **(a)** the AMID; and **(b)** the DNI.

The following example illustrates how an algebraic equation can be used to solve for these unknown amounts:

The Malcolm Smith Trust, a complex trust, earned $20,000 of dividend income, $20,000 of capital gains, and a fully deductible $5,000 loss from XYZ partnership (chargeable to corpus) in 1996. The trust instrument provides that capital gains are added to corpus. 50% of the fiduciary fees are allocated to income and 50% to corpus. The trust claimed a $2,000 deduction on line 12 of Form 1041. The trust incurred $1,500 of miscellaneous itemized deductions (chargeable to income), which are subject to the 2% floor. There are no other deductions. The trustee made a discretionary distribution of the accounting income of $17,500 to the trust's sole beneficiary.

Because the actual distribution can reasonably be expected to exceed the DNI, the trust must figure the DNI, taking into account the allowable miscellaneous itemized deductions, to determine the amount to enter on line 15b.

The trust also claims an exemption of $100 on line 20.

To compute line 15b, use the equation below:

AMID = total miscellaneous itemized deductions − (.02(AGI))

In the above example:

AMID = 1,500 − (.02(AGI))

In all situations, use the following equation to compute the AGI:

AGI = (line 9) − (the total of lines 12, 14, and 15a to the extent they are costs incurred in the administration of the estate or trust that would not have been incurred if the property were NOT held by the estate or trust) − (line 18) − (line 20).

Note: *There are no other deductions claimed by the trust on line 15a that are deductible in arriving at AGI.*

In the above example:

AGI = 35,000 − 2,000 − DNI − 100

Since the value of line 18 is not known because it is limited to the DNI, you are left with the following:

AGI = 32,900 − DNI

Substitute the value of AGI in the equation:

AMID = 1,500 − (.02(32,900 − DNI))

The equation cannot be solved until the value of DNI is known. The DNI can be expressed in terms of the AMID. To do this, compute the DNI using the known values. In this example, the DNI is equal to the total income of the trust (less any capital gains allocated to corpus; or plus any capital loss from line 4); less total deductions from line 16 (excluding any miscellaneous itemized deductions); less the AMID.

Thus, DNI = (line 9) − (line 17, column (b) of Schedule D (Form 1041)) − (line 16) − (AMID)

Substitute the known values:

DNI = 35,000 − 20,000 − 2,000 − AMID

DNI = 13,000 − AMID

Substitute the value of DNI in the equation to solve for AMID:

AMID = 1,500 − (.02(32,900 − (13,000 − AMID)))

AMID = 1,500 − (.02(32,900 − 13,000 + AMID))

AMID = 1,500 − (658 − 260 + .02 AMID)

AMID = 1,102 − .02AMID

1.02AMID = 1,102

AMID = 1,080

DNI = 11,920 (i.e., 13,000 − 1,080)

AGI = 20,980 (i.e., 32,900 − 11,920)

Note: *The income distribution deduction is equal to the smaller of the distribution ($17,500) or the DNI ($11,920).*

Enter the value of AMID on line 15b (the DNI should equal line 9 of Schedule B) and complete the rest of Form 1041 according to the instructions.

If the 2% floor is more than the deductions subject to the 2% floor, no deductions are allowed.

Line 18—Income Distribution Deduction

If the estate or trust was required to distribute income currently or if it paid, credited, or was required to distribute any other amounts to beneficiaries during the tax year, complete Schedule B to determine the estate's or trust's income distribution deduction. However, if you are filing for a pooled income fund, do not complete Schedule B. Instead, attach a statement to support the computation of the income distribution deduction. If the estate or trust claims an income distribution deduction, complete and attach:
● Parts I and II of Schedule I to refigure the deduction on a minimum tax basis; AND
● Schedule K-1 (Form 1041) for each beneficiary to which a distribution was made or required to be made.

Cemetery perpetual care fund.— On line 18, deduct the amount, not more than $5 per gravesite, paid for maintenance of cemetery property. To the right of the entry space for line 18, enter the number of gravesites. Also write "Section 642(i) trust" in parentheses after the trust's name at the top of Form 1041. You do not have to complete Schedules B of Form 1041 and K-1 (Form 1041).

Line 19—Estate Tax Deduction (Including Certain Generation-Skipping Transfer Taxes)

If the estate or trust includes income in respect of a decedent (IRD) in its gross income, and such amount was included in the decedent's gross estate for estate tax purposes, the estate or trust is allowed to deduct in the same tax year that portion of the estate tax imposed on the decedent's estate that is attributable to the inclusion of the IRD in the decedent's estate. For an example of the computation, see Regulations section 1.691(c)-1 and Pub. 559.

If any amount properly paid, credited, or required to be distributed by an estate or trust to a beneficiary consists of IRD received by the estate or trust, do not include such amounts in determining the estate tax deduction for the estate or trust. Figure the deduction on a separate sheet. Attach the sheet to your return. Also, a deduction is allowed for the GST tax imposed as a result of a taxable termination, or a direct skip occurring as a result of the death of the transferor. See section 691(c)(3). Enter the estate's or trust's share of these deductions on line 19.

Line 20—Exemption

Decedents' estates.— A decedent's estate is allowed a $600 exemption.

Trusts.— A trust whose governing instrument requires that all income be distributed currently is allowed a $300 exemption, even if it distributed amounts other than income during the tax year. All other trusts are allowed a $100 exemption. See Regulations section 1.642(b)-1.

Tax and Payments

Line 22—Taxable Income

Net operating loss.— If line 22 is a loss, the estate or trust may have a net operating loss (NOL). Do not include the deductions claimed on lines 13, 18, and 20 when figuring the amount of the NOL. An NOL generally may be carried back to the 3 prior tax years and forward to the following 15 tax years. Complete Schedule A of **Form 1045,** Application for Tentative Refund, to figure the amount of the NOL that is available for carryback or carryover. Use Form 1045 or file an amended return to apply for a refund based on an NOL carryback. For more information, get **Pub. 536,** Net Operating Losses.

On the termination of the estate or trust, any unused NOL carryover that would be allowable to the estate or trust in a later tax year, but for the termination, is allowed to the beneficiaries succeeding to the property of the estate or trust. See the instructions for Schedule K-1, lines 12d and 12e.

Excess deductions on termination.— If the estate or trust has for its final year deductions (excluding the charitable deduction and exemption) in excess of its gross income, the excess is allowed as an itemized deduction to the beneficiaries succeeding to the property of the estate or trust. However, an unused NOL carryover that is allowed to beneficiaries (as explained in the above paragraph) cannot also be treated as an excess deduction. If the final year of the estate or trust is also the last year of the NOL carryover period, the NOL carryover not absorbed in that tax year by the estate or trust is included as an excess deduction. See the instructions for Schedule K-1, line 12a.

Line 24a—1996 Estimated Tax Payments and Amount Applied From 1995 Return

Enter the amount of any estimated tax payment you made with Form 1041-ES for 1996 plus the amount of any overpayment from the 1995 return that was applied to the 1996 estimated tax.

If the estate or trust is the beneficiary of another trust, and received a payment of estimated tax that was credited to the trust (as reflected on the Schedule K-1 issued to the trust), then report this amount separately with the notation "section 643(g)" in the space next to line 24a.

Note: *Do not include on Form 1041 estimated tax paid by an individual before death. Instead, include the payments on the decedent's final Form 1040.*

Line 24b—Estimated Tax Payments Allocated to Beneficiaries

The trustee (or executor, for the final year of the estate) may elect under section 643(g) to have any portion of its estimated tax treated as a payment of estimated tax made by a beneficiary or beneficiaries. The election is made on **Form 1041-T,** Allocation of Estimated Tax Payments to Beneficiaries, which must be filed by the 65th day after the close of the trust's tax year. Form 1041-T shows the amounts to be allocated to each beneficiary. This amount is reported on the beneficiary's Schedule K-1, line 13a.

Failure to file Form 1041-T by the due date (March 6, 1997, for calendar year estates and trusts) will result in an invalid election. An invalid election will require the filing of amended Schedules K-1 for each beneficiary who was allocated a payment of estimated tax. Attach Form 1041-T to your return ONLY if you have

not yet filed it. If you have already filed Form 1041-T, do not attach a copy to your return.

Line 24d—Tax Paid With Extension of Time To File

If you filed either Form 2758 (for estates only), Form 8736, or Form 8800 to request an extension of time to file Form 1041, enter the amount that you paid with the extension request and check the appropriate box(es).

Line 24e—Federal Income Tax Withheld

Use line 24e to claim a credit for any Federal income tax withheld (and not repaid) by: (a) an employer on wages and salaries of a decedent received by the decedent's estate; (b) a payer of certain gambling winnings (e.g., state lottery winnings); or (c) a payer of distributions from pensions, annuities, retirement or profit-sharing plans, IRAs, insurance contracts, etc., received by a decedent's estate or trust. Attach a copy of **Form W-2, Form W-2G,** or **Form 1099-R.**

Backup withholding.— If the estate or trust received a 1996 Form 1099 showing Federal income tax withheld (i.e., backup withholding) on interest income, dividends, or other income, check the box and include the amount withheld on income retained by the estate or trust in the total for line 24e.

Report on Schedule K-1 (Form 1041), line 13, any credit for backup withholding on income distributed to the beneficiary.

Line 24f—Credit From Regulated Investment Companies

Attach copy B of **Form 2439,** Notice to Shareholder of Undistributed Long-Term Capital Gains.

Line 24g—Credit for Federal Tax on Fuels

Include any credit for Federal excise taxes paid on fuels that are ultimately used for nontaxable purposes (e.g., an off-highway business use) and any credit for a diesel-powered car, van, or light truck purchased before August 21, 1996. Attach **Form 4136,** Credit for Federal Tax Paid on Fuels. Get **Pub. 378,** Fuel Tax Credits and Refunds, for more information.

Line 26—Underpayment of Estimated Tax

If line 27 is at least $500 and more than 10% of the tax shown on Form 1041, or the estate or trust underpaid its 1996 estimated tax liability for any payment period, it may owe a penalty. See Form 2210 to determine whether the estate or trust owes a penalty and to figure the amount of the penalty.

Note: *The penalty may be waived under certain conditions. Get Pub. 505, Tax Withholding and Estimated Tax, for details.*

Line 27—Tax Due

You must pay the tax in full when the return is filed. Make the check or money order payable to "Internal Revenue Service." Write the EIN and "1996 Form 1041" on the payment. Enclose, but do not attach, the payment with Form 1041.

Line 29a—Credit to 1997 Estimated Tax

Enter the amount from line 28 that you want applied to the estate's or trust's 1997 estimated tax.

Schedule A—Charitable Deduction

General Instructions

Generally, any part of the gross income of an estate or trust (other than a simple trust) that, under the terms of the will or governing instrument, is paid (or treated as paid) during the tax year for a charitable purpose specified in section 170(c) is allowed as a deduction to the estate or trust. It is not necessary that the charitable organization be created or organized in the United States.

Trusts that claim a charitable deduction must also file Form 1041-A. See Form 1041-A for exceptions.

A pooled income fund, nonexempt private foundation, or trust with unrelated business income should attach a separate sheet to Form 1041 instead of using Schedule A of Form 1041 to figure the charitable deduction.

Election to treat contributions as paid in the prior tax year.— The fiduciary of an estate or trust may elect to treat as paid during the tax year any amount of gross income received during that tax year or any prior tax year that was paid in the next tax year for a charitable purpose.

To make the election, the fiduciary must file a statement with Form 1041 for the tax year in which the contribution is treated as paid. This statement must include:

1. The name and address of the fiduciary;

2. The name of the estate or trust;

3. An indication that the fiduciary is making an election under section 642(c)(1) for contributions treated as paid during such tax year;

4. The name and address of each organization to which any such contribution is paid; and

5. The amount of each contribution and date of actual payment or, if applicable, the total amount of contributions paid to each organization during the next tax year, to be treated as paid in the prior tax year.

The election must be filed by the due date (including extensions) for Form 1041 for the next tax year.

For more information about the charitable deduction, see section 642(c) and related regulations.

Specific Instructions

Line 1—Amounts Paid for Charitable Purposes From Gross Income

Enter amounts that were paid for a charitable purpose out of the estate's or trust's gross income, including any capital gains that are attributable to income under the governing instrument or local law. Include amounts paid during the tax year from gross income received in a prior tax year, but only if no deduction was allowed for any prior tax year for these amounts. Do not include any capital gains for the tax year allocated to corpus and paid or permanently set aside for charitable purposes. Instead, enter these amounts on line 6.

Line 2—Amounts Permanently Set Aside for Charitable Purposes From Gross Income

Estates, and certain trusts, may claim a deduction for amounts permanently set aside for a charitable purpose from gross income. Such amounts must be permanently set aside during the tax year or be used exclusively for religious, charitable, scientific, literary, or educational purposes, or for the prevention of cruelty to children or animals, or for the establishment, acquisition, maintenance, or operation of a public cemetery not operated for profit.

For a trust to qualify, the trust may not be a simple trust, and the set aside amounts must be required by the terms of a trust instrument that was created on or before October 9, 1969.

Further, the trust instrument must provide for an irrevocable remainder interest to be transferred to or for the use of an organization described in section 170(c); OR the trust must have been created by a grantor who was at all times after October 9, 1969, under a mental disability to change the terms of the trust.

Also, certain testamentary trusts that were established by a will that was executed on or before October 9, 1969, may qualify. See Regulations section 1.642(c)-2(b).

Do not include any capital gains for the tax year allocated to corpus and paid or permanently set aside for charitable purposes. Instead, enter these amounts on line 6.

Line 4—Tax-Exempt Income Allocable to Charitable Contributions

Any estate or trust that pays or sets aside any part of its income for a charitable purpose must reduce the deduction by the portion allocable to any tax-exempt income. If the governing instrument specifically provides as to the source from which amounts are paid, permanently set aside, or to be used for charitable purposes, the specific provisions control. In all other cases, determine the amount of tax-exempt income allocable to charitable contributions by multiplying line 3 by a fraction, the numerator of which is

the total tax-exempt income of the estate or trust, and the denominator of which is the gross income of the estate or trust. Do not include in the denominator any losses allocated to corpus.

Line 6—Capital Gains for the Tax Year Allocated to Corpus and Paid or Permanently Set Aside for Charitable Purposes

Enter the total of all capital gains for the tax year that are:

- Allocated to corpus; and
- Paid or permanently set aside for charitable purposes.

Schedule B—Income Distribution Deduction

General Instructions

If the estate or trust was required to distribute income currently or if it paid, credited, or was required to distribute any other amounts to beneficiaries during the tax year, complete Schedule B to determine the estate's or trust's income distribution deduction. However, if you are filing for a pooled income fund, do not complete Schedule B. Instead, attach a statement to support the computation of the income distribution deduction.

Note: *Use Schedule I to compute the DNI and income distribution deduction on a minimum tax basis.*

Separate share rule.— If a single trust has more than one beneficiary, and if different beneficiaries have substantially separate and independent shares, their shares are treated as separate trusts for the sole purpose of determining the DNI allocable to the respective beneficiaries. If the separate share rule applies, figure the DNI allocable to each beneficiary on a separate sheet and attach the sheet to this return. Any deduction or loss that is applicable solely to one separate share of the trust is not available to any other share of the same trust. For more information, see section 663(c) and related regulations.

Specific Instructions

Line 1—Adjusted Total Income

If the amount on line 17 of page 1 is a loss that is attributable wholly or in part to the capital loss limitation rules under section 1211(b) (line 4), then enter as a negative amount on line 1, Schedule B, the smaller of the loss from line 17 on page 1, or the loss from line 4 on page 1. If the line 17 loss is not attributable to the capital loss on line 4, enter zero.

If you are filing for a simple trust, subtract from adjusted total income any extraordinary dividends or taxable stock dividends included on page 1, line 2, and determined under the governing instrument and applicable local law to be allocable to corpus.

Line 2—Adjusted Tax-Exempt Interest

To figure the adjusted tax-exempt interest:

Step 1. Add tax-exempt interest income on line 4 of Schedule A, any expenses allowable under section 212 allocable to tax-exempt interest, and any interest expense allocable to tax-exempt interest.

Step 2. Subtract the Step 1 total from the amount of tax-exempt interest (including exempt-interest dividends) received.

Section 212 expenses that are directly allocable to tax-exempt interest are allocated only to tax-exempt interest. A reasonable proportion of section 212 expenses that are indirectly allocable to both tax-exempt interest and other income must be allocated to each class of income.

Figure the interest expense allocable to tax-exempt interest according to the guidelines in Rev. Proc. 72-18, 1972-1 C.B. 740.

See Regulations sections 1.643(a)-5 and 1.265-1 for more information.

Line 3

Include all capital gains, whether or not distributed, that are attributable to income under the governing instrument or local law. For example, if the trustee distributed 50% of the current year's capital gains to the income beneficiaries (and reflects this amount in column (a), line 17 of Schedule D (Form 1041)), but under the governing instrument all capital gains are attributable to income, then include 100% of the capital gains on line 3. If the amount on Schedule D (Form 1041), line 17, column (a) is a net loss, enter zero.

Line 5

In figuring the amount of long-term capital gain for the tax year included on Schedule A, line 3, the specific provisions of the governing instrument control if the instrument specifically provides as to the source from which amounts are paid, permanently set aside, or to be used for charitable purposes. In all other cases, determine the amount to enter by multiplying line 3 of Schedule A by a fraction, the numerator of which is the amount of long-term capital gains that are included in the accounting income of the estate or trust (i.e., not allocated to corpus) AND are distributed to charities, and the denominator of which is all items of income (including the amount of such long-term capital gains) included in the DNI.

Line 6

Figure line 6 in a similar manner as line 5.

Line 10—Accounting Income

If you are filing for a decedent's estate or a simple trust, skip this line. If you are filing for a complex trust, enter the income for the tax year determined under the terms of the governing instrument and

applicable local law. Do not include extraordinary dividends or taxable stock dividends determined under the governing instrument and applicable local law to be allocable to corpus.

Lines 11 and 12

Do not include any:
- Amounts deducted on prior year's return that were required to be distributed in the prior year.
- Amount that is properly paid or credited as a gift or bequest of a specific amount of money or specific property. (To qualify as a gift or bequest, the amount must be paid in three or fewer installments.) An amount that can be paid or credited only from income is not considered a gift or bequest.
- Amount paid or permanently set aside for charitable purposes or otherwise qualifying for the charitable deduction.

Line 11—Income Required To Be Distributed Currently

Line 11 is to be completed by all simple trusts as well as complex trusts, and decedent's estates, that are required to distribute income currently, whether it is distributed or not. The determination of whether trust income is required to be distributed currently depends on the terms of the governing instrument and the applicable local law.

The line 11 distributions are referred to as first tier distributions and are deductible by the estate or trust to the extent of the DNI. The beneficiary includes such amounts in his or her income to the extent of his or her proportionate share of the DNI.

Line 12—Other Amounts Paid, Credited, or Otherwise Required To Be Distributed

Line 12 is to be completed ONLY by a decedent's estate or complex trust. These distributions consist of any other amounts paid, credited, or required to be distributed and are referred to as second tier distributions. Such amounts include annuities to the extent not paid out of income, discretionary distributions of corpus, and distributions of property in kind.

If Form 1041-T was filed to elect to treat estimated tax payments as made by a beneficiary, the payments are treated as paid or credited to the beneficiary on the last day of the tax year and must be included on line 12.

Unless a section 643(e)(3) election is made, the value of all noncash property actually paid, credited, or required to be distributed to any beneficiaries is the smaller of:

1. The estate's or trust's adjusted basis in the property immediately before distribution, plus any gain or minus any loss recognized by the estate or trust on the distribution (basis of beneficiary), or

2. The fair market value (FMV) of such property.

If a section 643(e)(3) election is made by the fiduciary, then the amount entered on line 12 will be the FMV of the property.

A fiduciary of a complex trust may elect to treat any amount paid or credited to a beneficiary within 65 days following the close of the tax year as being paid or credited on the last day of that tax year. To make this election, see the instructions for Question 6 on page 17.

The beneficiary includes the amounts on line 12 in his or her income only to the extent of his or her proportionate share of the DNI.

Complex trusts.— If the second tier distributions exceed the DNI allocable to the second tier, the trust may have an accumulation distribution. See the line 13 instructions below.

Line 13—Total Distributions

If line 13 is more than line 10 and you are filing for a complex trust, complete **Schedule J (Form 1041)** and file it with Form 1041 unless the trust has no previously accumulated income.

Line 14—Adjustment for Tax-Exempt Income

In figuring the income distribution deduction, the estate or trust is not allowed a deduction for any item of the DNI that is not included in the gross income of the estate or trust. Thus, for purposes of figuring the allowable income distribution deduction, the DNI (line 9) is figured without regard to any tax-exempt interest.

If tax-exempt interest is the only tax-exempt income included in the total distributions (line 13), and the DNI (line 9) is less than or equal to line 13, then enter on line 14 the amount from line 2.

If tax-exempt interest is the only tax-exempt income included in the total distributions (line 13), and the DNI is more than line 13 (i.e., the estate or trust made a distribution that is less than the DNI), then figure the adjustment by multiplying line 2 by a fraction, the numerator of which is the total distributions (line 13), and the denominator of which is the DNI (line 9). Enter the result on line 14.

If line 13 includes tax-exempt income other than tax-exempt interest, figure line 14 by subtracting the total of the following from tax-exempt income included on line 13:

1. The charitable contribution deduction allocable to such tax-exempt income, and

2. Expenses allocable to tax-exempt income.

Expenses that are directly allocable to tax-exempt income are allocated only to tax-exempt income. A reasonable proportion of expenses indirectly allocable to both tax-exempt income and other income must be allocated to each class of income.

Line 17—Income Distribution Deduction

The income distribution deduction determines the amount of income that will

be taxed to the beneficiaries. The total amount of income for regular tax purposes that is reflected on line 7 of the individual beneficiaries' Schedules K-1 should equal the amount claimed on line 17.

Schedule G—Tax Computation

Line 1a

Tax rate schedule.— For tax years beginning in 1996, figure the tax using the Tax Rate Schedule below. Enter the tax on line 1a and check the "Tax rate schedule" box.

1996 Tax Rate Schedule

If taxable income is:			
Over—	But not over—	Its tax is:	Of the amount over—
$0	$1,600	15%	$0
1,600	3,800	$240.00 + 28%	1,600
3,800	5,800	856.00 + 31%	3,800
5,800	7,900	1,476.00 + 36%	5,800
7,900	-----	2,232.00 + 39.6%	7,900

Schedule D.— If the estate or trust had a net capital gain and taxable income of more than $3,800, complete Part VI of Schedule D (Form 1041), enter the tax from line 45 of Schedule D, and check the "Schedule D" box.

Line 1b—Other Taxes

Include any additional tax from the following:

- **Form 4972**, Tax on Lump-Sum Distributions.
- Section 644 tax on trusts.

Section 644 tax.— If the trust sells or exchanges property at a gain within 2 years after receiving it from a transferor, a section 644 tax may be due. The tax may be due if both **1** and **2** below apply:

1. There is an includible gain (defined below) recognized by the trust; and

2. At the time the trust received the property, the property had an FMV higher than its adjusted basis.

The trustee is authorized by section 6103(e)(1)(A)(ii) to inspect the transferor's income tax return to the extent necessary to figure the section 644 tax if the transferor refuses to make a disclosure to the trustee.

Includible gain is the smaller of **1** or **2** below:

1. The gain recognized by the trust on the sale or exchange of the property; or

2. The amount by which the FMV of the property at the time of the initial transfer to the trust exceeds the adjusted basis of the property immediately after the transfer.

Figure the tax on the includible gain by subtracting the transferor's actual tax for the tax year of the sale or exchange from the transferor's tax for the year of the sale

or exchange refigured to include the includible gain minus any deductions allocable to the gain.

See section 644 for additional information, including character rules, special rules, exceptions, installment sale rules, and the interest due on the tax if the transferor and the trust have different tax years.

If the section 644 tax is the only tax due on line 1b, enter the amount of the tax on line 1b and write "Section 644 tax" to the left of the amount column on line 1b. If there is more than one tax, include the amount of the section 644 tax in the total tax entered on line 1b.

Attach the section 644 tax computation to the return. When figuring the trust's taxable income, exclude the amount of any includible gain minus any deductions allocable to the gain.

Line 2a—Foreign Tax Credit

Attach **Form 1116**, Foreign Tax Credit (Individual, Estate, Trust, or Nonresident Alien Individual), if you elect to claim credit for income or profits taxes paid or accrued to a foreign country or a U.S. possession. The estate or trust may claim credit for that part of the foreign taxes not allocable to the beneficiaries (including charitable beneficiaries). Enter the estate's or trust's share of the credit on line 2a. See **Pub. 514**, Foreign Tax Credit for Individuals, for details.

Line 2b

Nonconventional Source Fuel Credit

If the estate or trust can claim any section 29 credit for producing fuel from a nonconventional source, figure the credit on a separate sheet and attach it to the return. Include the credit on line 2b.

Qualified Electric Vehicle Credit

Use **Form 8834**, Qualified Electric Vehicle Credit, if the estate or trust can claim a credit for the purchase of a new qualified electric vehicle. Include the credit on line 2b.

Line 2c—General Business Credit

Complete this line if the estate or trust is claiming any of the credits listed below. Use the appropriate credit form to figure the credit. If the estate or trust is claiming only one credit, enter the form number and the amount of the credit in the space provided.

If the estate or trust is claiming more than one credit (not including the empowerment zone employment credit), a credit from a passive activity (other than the low-income housing credit or the empowerment zone employment credit), or a credit carryforward, also complete **Form 3800**, General Business Credit, to figure the total credit and enter the amount from Form 3800 on line 2c. Also, be sure to check the box for Form 3800.

Do not include any amounts that are allocated to a beneficiary. Credits that are allocated between the estate or trust and

the beneficiaries are listed in the instructions for Schedule K-1, line 13, on page 27. Generally, these credits are apportioned on the basis of the income allocable to the estate or trust and the beneficiaries.

- Investment credit (Form 3468).
- Work opportunity credit (Form 5884).
- Credit for alcohol used as fuel (Form 6478).
- Credit for increasing research activities (Form 6765).
- Low-income housing credit (Form 8586).
- Enhanced oil recovery credit (Form 8830).
- Disabled access credit (Form 8826).
- Renewable electricity production credit (Form 8835).
- Empowerment zone employment credit (Form 8844).
- Indian employment credit (Form 8845).
- Credit for employer social security and Medicare taxes paid on certain employee tips (Form 8846).
- Orphan drug credit (Form 8820).
- Credit for contributions to selected community development corporations (Form 8847).

Line 2d—Credit for Prior Year Minimum Tax

An estate or trust that paid alternative minimum tax in a previous year may be eligible for a minimum tax credit in 1996. See **Form 8801**, Credit for Prior Year Minimum Tax—Individuals, Estates, and Trusts.

Line 5—Recapture Taxes

Recapture of investment credit.— If the estate or trust disposed of investment credit property or changed its use before the end of its useful life or recovery period, get **Form 4255**, Recapture of Investment Credit, to figure the recapture tax allocable to the estate or trust.

Recapture of low-income housing credit.— If the estate or trust disposed of property (or there was a reduction in the qualified basis of the property) on which the low-income housing credit was claimed, get **Form 8611**, Recapture of Low-Income Housing Credit, to figure any recapture tax allocable to the estate or trust.

Recapture of qualified electric vehicle credit.— If the estate or trust claimed the qualified electric vehicle credit in a prior tax year for a vehicle that ceased to qualify for the credit, part or all of the credit may have to be recaptured. See Pub. 535 for details. If the estate or trust owes any recapture tax, include it on line 5 and write "QEV" on the dotted line to the left of the entry space.

Recapture of the Indian employment credit.— Generally, if the estate or trust terminates a qualified employee less than 1 year after the date of initial employment, any Indian employment credit allowed for a prior tax year by reason of wages paid

or incurred to that employee must be recaptured. See Form 8845 for details. If the estate or trust owes any recapture tax, include it on line 5 and write "45A" on the dotted line to the left of the entry space.

Line 7—Household Employment Taxes

If **any** of the following apply, get **Schedule H (Form 1040)**, Household Employment Taxes, and its instructions, to see if the estate or trust owes these taxes.

1. The estate or trust paid **any one** household employee cash wages of $1,000 or more in 1996. When figuring the amount of cash wages paid, combine cash wages paid by the estate or trust with cash wages paid to the household employee in the same calendar year by the household of the decedent or beneficiary for whom the administrator, executor, or trustee of the estate or trust is acting.

2. The estate or trust withheld Federal income tax during 1996 at the request of any household employee.

3. The estate or trust paid **total** cash wages of $1,000 or more in **any** calendar **quarter** of 1995 or 1996 to household employees.

Line 8—Total Tax

Interest on tax deferred under the installment method for certain nondealer real property installment obligations.— If an obligation arising from the disposition of real property to which section 453A applies is outstanding at the close of the year, the estate or trust must include the interest due under section 453A(c) in the amount to be entered on line 8 of Schedule G, Form 1041, with the notation "Section 453A(c) interest." Attach a schedule showing the computation.

Form 4970, Tax on Accumulation Distribution of Trusts.— Include on this line any tax due on an accumulation distribution from a trust. To the left of the entry space, write "From Form 4970" and the amount of the tax.

Form 8697, Interest Computation Under the Look-Back Method for Completed Long-Term Contracts.— Include the interest due under the look-back method of section 460(b)(2). To the left of the entry space, write "From Form 8697" and the amount of interest due.

Form 5329, Additional Taxes Attributable to Qualified Retirement Plans (Including IRAs), Annuities, and Modified Endowment Contracts.— If the estate or trust fails to receive the minimum distribution under section 4974, use Form 5329 to pay the excise tax. To the left of the entry space, write "From Form 5329" and the amount of the tax.

Other Information

Question 1

If the estate or trust received tax-exempt income, figure the allocation of expenses between tax-exempt and taxable income on a separate sheet and attach it to the return. Enter only the deductible amounts on the return. Do not figure the allocation on the return itself. For more information, see the instructions for **Allocation of Deductions for Tax-Exempt Income** on page 10.

Report the amount of tax-exempt interest income received or accrued in the space provided below Question 1.

Also, include any exempt-interest dividends the estate or trust received as a shareholder in a mutual fund or other regulated investment company.

Question 2

All salaries, wages, and other compensation for personal services must be included on the return of the person who earned the income, even if the income was irrevocably assigned to a trust by a contract assignment or similar arrangement.

The grantor or person creating the trust is considered the owner if he or she keeps "beneficial enjoyment" of or substantial control over the trust property. The trust's income, deductions, and credits are allocable to the owner.

If you checked "Yes" for Question 2, see the **Grantor Type Trust** instructions on page 7.

Question 3

Check the "Yes" box and enter the name of the foreign country if either **1** or **2** below applies.

1. At any time during the year the estate or trust had an interest in or signature or other authority over a bank, securities, or other financial account in a foreign country.

Exception. Check "No" if either of the following applies to the estate or trust:
● The combined value of the accounts was $10,000 or less during the whole year; OR
● The accounts were with a U.S. military banking facility operated by a U.S. financial institution.

2. The estate or trust owns more than 50% of the stock in any corporation that owns one or more foreign bank accounts.

Get **Form TD F 90-22.1,** Report of Foreign Bank and Financial Accounts, to see if the estate or trust is considered to have an interest in or signature or other authority over a bank, securities, or other financial account in a foreign country.

If you checked "Yes" for Question 3, file Form TD F 90-22.1 by June 30, 1997, with the Department of the Treasury at the address shown on the form.
Form TD F 90-22.1 is not a tax return, so do not file it with Form 1041.

You may order Form TD F 90-22.1 by calling 1-800-829-3676 (1-800-TAX-FORM).

Question 4

If the estate or trust received a distribution from a foreign trust after August 20, 1996, it must provide additional information. For this purpose, a loan of cash or marketable securities generally is considered to be a distribution. See **Pub. 553,** Highlights of 1996 Tax Changes, for details.

If the estate or trust was the grantor of, or the transferor to, a foreign trust that existed during the tax year, it may have to file **Form 3520,** Creation of or Transfers to Certain Foreign Trusts, **Form 3520-A,** Annual Return of Foreign Trust With U.S. Beneficiaries, or **Form 926,** Return by a U.S. Transferor of Property to a Foreign Corporation, Foreign Estate or Trust, or Foreign Partnership.

Question 5

An estate or trust claiming an interest deduction for qualified residence interest (as defined in section 163(h)(3)) on seller-provided financing, must include on an attachment to the 1996 Form 1041 the name, address, and taxpayer identifying number of the person to whom the interest was paid or accrued (i.e., the seller).

If the estate or trust received or accrued such interest, it must provide identical information on the person liable for such interest (i.e., the buyer). This information does not need to be reported if it duplicates information already reported on Form 1098.

Question 6

To make the section 663(b) election for a complex trust to treat any amount paid or credited to a beneficiary within 65 days following the close of the tax year as being paid or credited on the last day of that tax year, check the box. For the election to be valid, you must file Form 1041 by the due date (including extensions). Once made, the election is irrevocable.

Question 7

To make the section 643(e)(3) election to recognize gain on property distributed in kind, check the box and see the instructions for Schedule D (Form 1041).

Question 8

If the decedent's estate has been open for more than 2 years, check the box and attach an explanation for the delay in closing the estate.

Schedule I—Alternative Minimum Tax

General Instructions

Use Schedule I to compute:

1. The estate's or trust's alternative minimum taxable income;

2. The income distribution deduction on a minimum tax basis; and

3. The estate's or trust's alternative minimum tax (AMT).

Who Must Complete

• Complete Schedule I, Parts I and II, if the decedent's estate or trust is required to complete Schedule B.

• Complete Schedule I, Parts I and III, if the decedent's estate's or trust's share of alternative minimum taxable income (Part I, line 12) exceeds $22,500.

Recordkeeping

Schedule I contains adjustments and tax preference items that are treated differently for regular tax and AMT purposes. If you, as fiduciary for the estate or trust, completed a form to figure an item for regular tax purposes, you may have to complete it a second time for AMT purposes. Generally, the difference between the amounts on the two forms is the AMT adjustment or tax preference item to enter on Schedule I. Except for Form 1116, any additional form completed for AMT purposes does not have to be filed with Form 1041.

For regular tax purposes, some deductions and credits may result in carrybacks or carryforwards to other tax years. Examples are: investment interest expense; a net operating loss deduction; a capital loss; and the foreign tax credit. Because these items may be refigured for the AMT, the carryback or carryforward amount may be different for regular and AMT purposes. Therefore, you should keep records of these different carryforward and carryback amounts for the AMT and regular tax. The AMT carryforward will be important in completing Schedule I for 1997.

Credit for Prior Year Minimum Tax

Estates and trusts that paid alternative minimum tax in 1995, or had a minimum tax credit carryforward, may be eligible for a minimum tax credit in 1996. See Form 8801.

Partners, Shareholders, etc.

An estate or trust that is a partner in a partnership or a shareholder in an S corporation must take into account its share of items of income and deductions that enter into the computation of its adjustments and tax preference items.

Allocation of Deductions to Beneficiaries

The distributable net alternative minimum taxable income (DNAMTI) of the estate or trust does not include amounts of depreciation, depletion, and amortization that are allocated to the beneficiaries, just as the distributable net income (DNI) of the estate or trust does not include these items for regular tax purposes.

Report separately on line 11 of Schedule K-1 (Form 1041) any adjustments or tax preference items attributable to depreciation, depletion, and amortization that were allocated to the beneficiaries.

Optional Write-Off Period Under Section 59(e)

The estate or trust may elect under section 59(e) to use an optional 10-year (60-month for intangible drilling and development expenditures and 3-year for circulation expenditures) write-off period for certain expenditures. If this election is made, the optional write-off period is used for regular tax purposes and there is no AMT adjustment. This election can be made for the following items:

• Circulation expenditures (section 173).

• Research and experimental expenditures (section 174).

• Intangible drilling and development expenditures (section 263(c)).

• Development expenditures for mines and natural deposits (section 616).

• Mining exploration expenditures (section 617(a)).

The election must be made in the year the expenditure was made and may be revoked only with IRS consent. See section 59(e) for more details.

Specific Instructions

Part I—Estate's or Trust's Share of Alternative Minimum Taxable Income

Line 1—Adjusted Total Income or (Loss)

Enter the amount from line 17 of page 1. If the adjusted total income includes the amount of the alcohol fuel credit as required under section 87, reduce the adjusted total income by the credit included in income.

Line 2—Net Operating Loss Deduction

Enter any net operating loss deduction (NOLD) from line 15a of page 1 as a positive amount.

Line 4a—Interest

In determining the alternative minimum taxable income, qualified residence interest (other than qualified housing interest defined in section 56(e)) is not allowed.

If you completed Form 4952 for regular tax purposes, you may have an adjustment on this line. Refigure your investment interest expense on another Form 4952 as follows:

Step 1. On line 1 of Form 4952, add any interest expense allocable to specified private activity bonds issued after August 7, 1986, to the other interest expense. For a definition of "specified private activity bonds," see the instructions for line 4p.

Step 2. On line 2, enter the AMT disallowed investment interest expense from 1995.

Step 3. When completing Part II of Form 4952, refigure gross income from property held for investment, any net gain from the disposition of property held for investment, and any investment expenses, taking into account all AMT adjustments and tax preference items that apply. Include any interest income and investment expenses from private activity bonds issued after August 7, 1986.

To figure the adjustment for line 4a, subtract the total interest allowable for AMT purposes from the interest deduction claimed on line 10 of page 1. If the total interest expense allowed for AMT purposes is more than that allowed for regular tax purposes, enter the difference as a negative amount on line 4a.

Line 4b—Taxes

Enter any state, local, or foreign real property taxes; state or local personal property taxes; and state, local, or foreign income taxes that were included on line 11 of page 1.

Line 4d—Refund of Taxes

Enter any refunds received in 1996 of taxes described for line 4b above that were deducted in a tax year after 1986.

Line 4e—Depreciation of Property Placed in Service After 1986

Caution: *Do not include on this line any depreciation adjustment from:* (a) *an activity for which you are not at risk;* (b) *a partnership or an S corporation if the basis limitations under section 704(d) or 1366(d) apply;* (c) *a tax shelter farm activity;* or (d) *a passive activity.* Instead, take these depreciation adjustments into account when figuring the adjustments on line 4l, 4m, or 4n, whichever applies.

For AMT purposes, the depreciation deduction for tangible property placed in service after 1986 (or after July 31, 1986, if an election was made) must be refigured under the alternative depreciation system (ADS) described in section 168(g).

For property, other than residential rental and nonresidential real property, use the 150% declining balance method (switching to the straight line method in the first tax year when that method gives a better result). However, use the straight line method if that method was used for regular tax purposes. Generally, ADS depreciation is figured over the class life of the property. For tangible personal property not assigned a class life, use 12 years. See Pub. 946, How To Depreciate Property, for a discussion of class lives.

For residential rental and nonresidential real property, use the straight line method over 40 years.

Use the same convention that was used for regular tax purposes.

See Rev. Proc. 87-57, 1987-2 C.B. 687, or Pub. 946 for the optional tables for the alternative minimum tax, using the 150% declining balance method.

Do not make an adjustment for motion picture films, videotapes, sound recordings, or property depreciated under the unit-of-production method or any other method not expressed in a term of years. (See section 168(f)(1), (2), (3), or (4).)

When refiguring the depreciation deduction, be sure to report any adjustment from depreciation that was allocated to the beneficiary for regular tax purposes separately on line 11 of Schedule K-1 (Form 1041).

To figure the adjustment, subtract the depreciation for AMT purposes from the depreciation for regular tax purposes.

If the depreciation figured for AMT purposes exceeds the depreciation allowed for regular tax purposes, enter the adjustment as a negative amount.

Line 4f—Circulation and Research and Experimental Expenditures

Caution: *Do not make this adjustment for expenditures for which you elected the optional 3-year write-off period (10-year for research and experimental expenditures) under section 59(e) for regular tax purposes.*

Circulation expenditures.— Circulation expenditures deducted under section 173(a) for regular tax purposes must be amortized for AMT purposes over 3 years beginning with the year the expenditures were paid or incurred.

Research and experimental expenditures.— Research and experimental expenditures deducted under section 174(a) for regular tax purposes generally must be amortized for AMT purposes over 10 years beginning with the year the expenditures were paid or incurred. However, do not make an adjustment for expenditures paid or incurred in connection with an activity in which the estate or trust materially participated under the passive activity rules.

Enter the difference between the amount allowed for AMT purposes and the amount allowed for regular tax purposes. If the amount for AMT purposes exceeds the amount allowed for regular tax purposes, enter the difference as a negative amount.

See section 56(b)(2)(B) for a discussion of the rules for losses on properties for which a deduction was allowed under section 173(a) or 174(a).

Line 4g—Mining Exploration and Development Costs

Caution: *Do not make this adjustment for costs for which you elected the optional 10-year write-off period under section 59(e) for regular tax purposes.*

Expenditures for the development or exploration of a mine or certain other mineral deposits (other than an oil, gas, or geothermal well) deducted under

sections 616(a) and 617(a) for regular tax purposes must be amortized for AMT purposes over 10 years beginning with the year the expenditures were paid or incurred.

Enter the difference between the amount allowed for AMT purposes and the amount allowed for regular tax purposes. If the amount allowed for AMT purposes exceeds the amount deducted for regular tax purposes, enter the difference as a negative amount.

See section 56(a)(2)(B) for a discussion of the rules for losses sustained on properties for which a deduction was allowed under section 616(a) or 617(a).

Line 4h—Long-Term Contracts Entered Into After February 28, 1986

For AMT purposes, the percentage of completion method of accounting described in section 460(b) generally must be used. This rule generally does not apply to home construction contracts (as defined in section 460(e)(6)).

Note: *Contracts described in section 460(e)(1) are subject to the simplified method of cost allocation of section 460(b)(4).*

Enter the difference between the amount reported for regular tax purposes and the AMT amount. If the AMT amount is less than the amount figured for regular tax purposes, enter the difference as a negative amount.

Line 4i—Amortization of Pollution Control Facilities

The amortization deduction under section 169 is not allowed for AMT purposes. Instead, the deduction is determined under the ADS described in section 168(g) using the Asset Depreciation Range class life for the facility under the straight line method.

To figure the adjustment, subtract the amortization deduction taken for regular tax purposes from the depreciation deduction determined under the ADS.

If the deduction allowed for AMT purposes is more than the amount allowed for regular tax purposes, enter the difference as a negative amount.

Line 4j—Installment Sales of Certain Property

For either of the following kinds of dispositions in which the estate or trust used the installment method for regular tax purposes, refigure the income for AMT purposes without regard to the installment method:

1. Any disposition after March 1, 1986, of property used or produced in a farming business that was held primarily for sale to customers.

2. Any nondealer disposition of property that occurred after August 16, 1986, but before the first day of your tax year that began in 1987, if an obligation that arose from the disposition was an installment obligation to which the proportionate disallowance rule applied.

Enter the difference between the income that was reported for regular tax purposes and the income for AMT purposes. If the AMT amount is less than that reported for the regular tax, enter the difference as a negative amount.

Line 4k—Adjusted Gain or Loss (Including Incentive Stock Options)

Adjusted gain or loss.— If the estate or trust sold or exchanged property during the year, or had a casualty gain or loss to business or income-producing property, it may have an adjustment. The gain or loss on the disposition of certain assets is refigured for AMT purposes. Use this line if the estate or trust reported a gain or loss on Form 4797, Schedule D (Form 1041), or Form 4684 (Section B). When figuring the adjusted basis for those forms, take into account any AMT adjustments made this year, or in previous years, for items related to lines 4e, 4f, 4g, and 4i of Schedule I. For example, to figure the adjusted basis for AMT purposes, reduce the cost of an asset only by the depreciation allowed for AMT purposes.

Enter the difference between the gain or loss reported for regular tax purposes, and that figured for AMT purposes. If the AMT gain is less than the gain reported for regular tax purposes, enter the adjustment as a negative amount. If the AMT loss is more than the loss allowed for regular tax purposes, enter the adjustment as a negative amount.

Incentive stock options (ISOs).— For regular tax purposes, no income is recognized when an incentive stock option (as defined in section 422(b)) is granted or exercised. However, this rule does not apply for AMT purposes. Instead, the estate or trust must generally include the excess, if any, of:

1. The fair market value of the option (determined without regard to any lapse restriction) at the first time its rights in the option become transferable or when these rights are no longer subject to a substantial risk of forfeiture, over

2. The amount paid for the option.

Increase the AMT basis of any stock acquired through the exercise of an incentive stock option by the amount of the adjustment.

If the estate or trust acquired stock by exercising an incentive stock option and disposed of that stock in the same year, the tax treatment for regular and AMT purposes is the same.

See section 83 for more details.

Line 4l—Certain Loss Limitations

Caution: *If the loss is from a passive activity, use line 4n instead. If the loss is from a tax shelter farm activity (that is not passive), use line 4m.*

Refigure your allowable losses for AMT purposes from activities for which you are not at risk and basis limitations applicable to interests in partnerships and stock in S corporations, by taking into account your AMT adjustments and tax preference

items. See sections 59(h), 465, 704(d), and 1366(d).

Enter the difference between the loss reported for regular tax purposes and the AMT loss. If the AMT loss is more than the loss reported for regular tax purposes, enter the adjustment as a negative amount.

Line 4m—Tax Shelter Farm Activities

Note: *Use this line only if the tax shelter farm activity is not a passive activity. Otherwise, use line 4n.*

For AMT purposes, no loss is allowed from any tax shelter farm activity as defined in section 58(a)(2).

An excess farm loss from one farm activity cannot be netted against income from another farm activity. Any disallowed loss (for AMT purposes) is carried forward until offset by income from the same activity or when the entire activity is sold.

Include any other adjustment or tax preference item and your prior year AMT unallowed loss when refiguring the farm loss. For example, if depreciation must be refigured for AMT purposes, include the adjustment on this line. DO NOT include it again on line 4e, 4r, or 4s.

Determine your tax shelter farm activity gain or loss for AMT purposes using the same rules you used for regular tax purposes except that any AMT loss is allowed only to the extent that a taxpayer is insolvent (see section 58(c)(1)). An AMT loss may not be used in the current tax year to offset gains from other tax shelter farm activities. Instead, it must be suspended and carried forward indefinitely until either you have a gain in a subsequent tax year from that same tax shelter farm activity or the activity is disposed of.

Line 4n—Passive Activities

For AMT purposes, the rules described in section 469 apply, except that in applying the limitations, minimum tax rules apply.

Refigure passive activity gains and losses on an AMT basis. Refigure a passive activity gain or loss by taking into account all AMT adjustments or tax preference items that pertain to that activity.

You may complete a second Form 8582 to determine the passive activity losses allowed for AMT purposes, but do not send this AMT Form 8582 to the IRS.

Note: *The amount of any passive activity loss that is not deductible (and is therefore carried forward) for AMT purposes is likely to differ from the amount (if any) that is carried forward for regular tax purposes. Therefore, it is essential that you retain adequate records for both AMT and regular tax purposes.*

Enter the difference between the loss reported on page 1, and the AMT loss, if any.

Caution: *Do not enter again elsewhere on this schedule any AMT adjustment or tax preference item included on this line.*

Publicly traded partnerships (PTPs).— If the estate or trust had a loss from a PTP, refigure the loss using any AMT adjustments and tax preference items.

Line 4o—Beneficiaries of Other Trusts or Decedent's Estates

If the estate or trust is the beneficiary of another estate or trust, enter the adjustment for minimum tax purposes from line 8, Schedule K-1 (Form 1041).

Line 4p—Tax-Exempt Interest From Specified Private Activity Bonds

Enter the interest earned from specified private activity bonds reduced (but not below zero) by any deduction that would have been allowable if the interest were includible in gross income for regular tax purposes. Specified private activity bonds are any qualified bonds (as defined in section 141) issued after August 7, 1986. See section 57(a)(5) for more information.

Exempt-interest dividends paid by a regulated investment company are treated as interest from specified private activity bonds to the extent the dividends are attributable to interest received by the company on the bonds, minus an allocable share of the expenses paid or incurred by the company in earning the interest.

Line 4q—Depletion

Refigure the depletion deduction for AMT purposes by using only the income and deductions allowed for the AMT when refiguring the limit based on taxable income from the property under section 613(a) and the limit based on taxable income, with certain adjustments, under section 613A(d)(1). Also, the depletion deduction for mines, wells, and other natural deposits under section 611 is limited to the property's adjusted basis at the end of the year, as refigured for the AMT, unless the estate or trust is an independent producer or royalty owner claiming percentage depletion for oil and gas wells. Figure this limit separately for each property. When refiguring the property's adjusted basis, take into account any AMT adjustments made this year or in previous years that affect basis (other than the current year's depletion).

Enter on line 4q the difference between the regular tax and AMT deduction. If the AMT deduction is more than the regular tax deduction, enter the difference as a negative amount.

Line 4r—Accelerated Depreciation of Real Property Placed in Service Before 1987

For AMT purposes, use the straight line method to figure depreciation. Use a recovery period of 19 years for 19-year real property and 15 years for low-income housing. Enter the excess of depreciation claimed for regular tax purposes over depreciation refigured using the straight line method. Figure this amount separately for each property and include on line 4r only positive amounts.

Line 4s—Accelerated Depreciation of Leased Personal Property Placed in Service Before 1987

For leased personal property other than recovery property, enter the amount by which the regular tax depreciation using the pre-1987 rules exceeds the depreciation allowable using the straight line method

For leased 10-year recovery property and leased 15-year public utility property, enter the amount by which the depreciation deduction determined for regular tax purposes is more than the deduction allowable using the straight line method with a half-year convention, no salvage value, and the following recovery period:

10-year property .... 15 years
15-year public utility property .... 22 years

Figure this amount separately for each property and include on line 4s only positive amounts.

Line 4t—Intangible Drilling Costs

Caution: *Do not make this adjustment for costs for which you elected the optional 60-month write-off under section 59(e) for regular tax purposes.*

Except as provided below, intangible drilling costs (IDCs) from oil, gas, and geothermal wells are a tax preference item to the extent that the excess IDCs exceed 65% of the net income from the wells. Figure the tax preference item for all geothermal properties separately from the preference for all oil and gas properties.

Excess IDCs are figured by taking the amount of your IDCs allowed for regular tax purposes under section 263(c) (not including any section 263(c) deduction for nonproductive wells) minus the amount that would have been allowed if that amount had been amortized over a 120-month period starting with the month the well was placed in production.

Note: *Cost depletion can be substituted for the amount allowed using amortization over 120 months.*

Net income is determined by taking the gross income from all oil, gas, and geothermal wells reduced by the deductions allocable to those properties (determined without regard to excess IDCs). When figuring net income, use only income and deductions allowed for the AMT.

Exception. The preference for IDCs from oil and gas wells does not apply to taxpayers who are independent producers (i.e., not integrated oil companies as defined in section 291(b)(4)). However, this benefit may be limited. First, figure the IDC preference as if this exception did not apply. Then, for purposes of this exception, complete Schedule I through line 6, including the IDC preference. If the amount of the IDC preference exceeds 40% of the amount figured for line 6, enter the excess on line 4t (the benefit of this exception is limited). If the amount of the

IDC preference is equal to or less than 40% of the amount figured for line 6, do not enter an amount on line 4t (the benefit of this exception is not limited).

Line 4u—Other Adjustments

Include on this line:

- **Patron's adjustment.**—Distributions the estate or trust received from a cooperative may be includible in income. Unless the distributions are nontaxable, include on line 4u the total AMT patronage dividend adjustment reported to the estate or trust from the cooperative.

- **Related adjustments.**—AMT adjustments and tax preference items may affect deductions that are based on an income limit other than AGI or modified AGI (e.g., farm conservation expenses). Refigure these deductions using the income limit as modified for the AMT. Include the difference between the regular tax and AMT deduction on line 4u. If the AMT tax deduction is more than the regular tax deduction, include the difference as a negative amount.

Note: *Do not make an adjustment on line 4u for an item you refigured on another line of Schedule I (e.g., line 4q).*

Line 7—Alternative Tax Net Operating Loss Deduction (ATNOLD)

For tax years beginning after 1986, the net operating loss (NOL) under section 172(c) is modified for alternative tax purposes by (a) adding the adjustments made under sections 56 and 58 (subtracting if the adjustments are negative); and (b) reducing the NOL by any item of tax preference under section 57 (except the appreciated charitable contribution preference item).

When figuring an NOL from a loss year prior to 1987, the rules in effect before enactment of the Tax Reform Act (TRA) of 1986 apply. The NOL under section 172(c) is reduced by the amount of the tax preference items that were taken into account in figuring the NOL. In addition, the NOL is figured by taking into account only itemized deductions that were alternative tax itemized deductions for the tax year and that were a modification to the NOL under section 172(d). See sections 55(d) and 172 as in effect before the TRA of 1986.

If this estate or trust is the beneficiary of another estate or trust that terminated in 1996, include any AMT NOL carryover that was reported on line 12e of Schedule K-1 (Form 1041).

The ATNOLD may be limited. To figure the ATNOLD limitation, first figure AMTI without regard to the ATNOLD. For this purpose, figure a tentative amount for line 4q of Schedule I by treating line 7 as if it were zero. Then, figure a tentative amount for line 6 of Schedule I. The ATNOLD limitation is 90% of the tentative line 6 amount. Enter on line 7 the smaller of the ATNOLD or the ATNOLD limitation. Any alternative tax NOL not used because of the ATNOLD limitation can be carried

back or forward. See section 172(b) for details. The treatment of alternative tax NOLs does not affect your regular tax NOL.

Note: *If you elected under section 172(b)(3) to forego the carryback period for regular tax purposes, the election will also apply for the AMT.*

Part II—Income Distribution Deduction on a Minimum Tax Basis

Line 13—Adjusted Alternative Minimum Taxable Income

If the amount on line 8 of Schedule I is less than zero, and the negative number is attributable wholly or in part to the capital loss limitation rules under section 1211(b), then enter as a negative number the smaller of (a) the loss from line 8; or (b) the loss from line 4 on page 1.

Line 14—Adjusted Tax-Exempt Interest

To figure the adjusted tax-exempt interest (including exempt-interest dividends received as a shareholder in a mutual fund or other regulated investment company), subtract the total of (a) any tax-exempt interest from line 4 of Schedule A of Form 1041 figured for AMT purposes; and (b) any section 212 expenses allowable for AMT purposes allocable to tax-exempt interest from the amount of tax-exempt interest received. DO NOT subtract any deductions reported on lines 4a through 4c. Section 212 expenses that are directly allocable to tax-exempt interest are allocated only to tax-exempt interest. A reasonable proportion of section 212 expenses that are indirectly allocable to both tax-exempt interest and other income must be allocated to each class of income.

Line 17

Enter any capital gains that were paid or permanently set aside for charitable purposes from the current year's income included on line 3 of Schedule A.

Lines 18 and 19

Capital gains and losses must take into account any basis adjustments from line 4k, Part I.

Line 24—Adjustment for Tax-Exempt Income

In figuring the income distribution deduction on a minimum tax basis, the estate or trust is not allowed a deduction for any item of DNAMTI (line 20) that is not included in the gross income of the estate or trust figured on an AMT basis. Thus, for purposes of figuring the allowable income distribution deduction on a minimum tax basis, the DNAMTI is figured without regard to any tax-exempt interest (except for amounts from line 4p).

If tax-exempt interest is the only tax-exempt income included in the total distributions (line 23), and the DNAMTI (line 20) is less than or equal to line 23, then enter on line 24 the amount from line 14.

If tax-exempt interest is the only tax-exempt income included in the total distributions (line 23), and the DNAMTI is more than line 23 (i.e., the estate or trust made a distribution that is less than the DNAMTI), then figure the adjustment by multiplying line 14 by a fraction, the numerator of which is the total distributions (line 23), and the denominator of which is the DNAMTI (line 20). Enter the result on line 24.

If line 23 includes tax-exempt income other than tax-exempt interest (except for amounts from line 4p), figure line 24 by subtracting the total expenses allocable to tax-exempt income that are allowable for AMT purposes from tax-exempt income included on line 23.

Expenses that are directly allocable to tax-exempt income are allocated only to tax-exempt income. A reasonable proportion of expenses indirectly allocable to both tax-exempt income and other income must be allocated to each class of income.

Line 27—Income Distribution Deduction on a Minimum Tax Basis

Allocate the income distribution deduction figured on a minimum tax basis among the beneficiaries in the same manner as income was allocated for regular tax purposes. Report each beneficiary's share on line 6 of Schedule K-1 (Form 1041).

Part III—Alternative Minimum Tax Computation

Line 36—Alternative Minimum Foreign Tax Credit

To figure the AMT foreign tax credit:

1. Complete and attach Form 1116, with the notation at the top, "Alt Min Tax" for each type of income specified at the top of Form 1116.

2. Complete Part I, entering income, deductions, etc., attributable to sources outside the United States computed on a minimum tax basis.

3. Complete Part III. On line 9, do not enter any taxes taken into account in a tax year beginning after 1986 that are treated under section 904(c) as paid or accrued in a tax year beginning before 1987. On line 10 of Form 1116, enter the alternative minimum tax foreign tax credit carryover, and on line 17 of Form 1116, enter the alternative minimum taxable income from line 12 of Schedule I. On line 19 of Form 1116, enter the amount from line 35 of Schedule I.

Complete Part IV. The foreign tax credit from line 32 of the AMT Form 1116 is limited to the tax on line 35 of Schedule I, less 10% of what would have been the tax on line 35 of Schedule I, if line 7 of Schedule I had been zero and the exception for intangible drilling costs does not apply (see the instructions for line 4t on page 20). If Schedule I, line 7, is zero or blank, and the estate or trust has no intangible drilling costs (or the exception does not apply), enter on Schedule I, line 36, the smaller of Form 1116, line 32; or

90% of Schedule I, line 35. If line 7 has an entry (other than zero), or the exception for intangible drilling costs applies, for purposes of this line refigure what the tax would have been on Schedule I, line 35, if line 7 were zero and the exception did not apply. Multiply that amount by 10% and subtract the result from line 35. Enter on Schedule I, line 36, the smaller of that amount or the amount from Form 1116, line 32.

If the AMT foreign tax credit is limited, any unused amount can be carried back or forward in accordance with section 904(c).

Note: *The election to forego the carryback period for regular tax purposes also applies for the AMT.*

Line 38—Regular Tax Before Credits

Enter the tax from line 1a of Schedule G, reduced by the amount of any foreign tax credit entered on line 2a of Schedule G. DO NOT deduct any foreign tax credit that was allocated to the beneficiaries.

Schedule D (Form 1041)— Capital Gains and Losses

General Instructions

Use Schedule D (Form 1041) to report gains and losses from the sale or exchange of capital assets by an estate or trust.

To report sales or exchanges of property other than capital assets, including the sale or exchange of property used in a trade or business and involuntary conversions (other than casualties and thefts), see Form 4797 and related instructions.

If property is involuntarily converted because of a casualty or theft, use Form 4684.

Capital Asset

Each item of property held by the estate or trust (whether or not connected with its trade or business) is a capital asset except:

- Inventoriable assets or property held primarily for sale to customers;
- Depreciable or real property used in a trade or business;
- Certain copyrights, literary, musical, or artistic compositions, letters or memoranda, or similar property;
- Accounts or notes receivable acquired in the ordinary course of a trade or business for services rendered or from the sale of inventoriable assets or property held primarily for sale to customers; and
- Certain U.S. Government publications not purchased at the public sale price.

You may find additional helpful information in the following publications:
- **Pub. 544,** Sales and Other Dispositions of Assets; and
- **Pub. 551,** Basis of Assets.

Short-Term or Long-Term

Separate the capital gains and losses according to how long the estate or trust held or owned the property. The holding period for short-term capital gains and losses is 1 year or less. The holding period for long-term capital gains and losses is more than 1 year. Property acquired by a decedent's estate from the decedent is considered as held for more than 1 year.

When you figure the length of the period the estate or trust held property, begin counting on the day after the estate or trust acquired the property and include the day the estate or trust disposed of it. Use the trade dates for the date of acquisition and sale of stocks and bonds traded on an exchange or over-the-counter market.

Section 643(e)(3) Election

For noncash property distributions, a fiduciary may elect to have the estate or trust recognize gain or loss in the same manner as if the distributed property had been sold to the beneficiary at its fair market value (FMV). The distribution deduction is the property's FMV. This election applies to all distributions made by the estate or trust during the tax year and, once made, may be revoked only with the consent of the IRS.

Note that section 267 does not allow a deduction for any loss from the sale of property on which a trust makes a section 643(e)(3) election. In addition, when a trust distributes depreciable property, section 1239 applies to deny capital gains treatment on the gain to the trust if the trust makes a section 643(e)(3) election.

Section 644 Tax on Trusts

If a trust sells or exchanges property at a gain within 2 years after receiving it from a transferor, a special tax may be due. **Do not report includible gains under section 644 on Schedule D.** The tax on these gains is reported separately on Form 1041. For more information, see the instructions for Schedule G, line 1b, on page 16.

Related Persons

A trust cannot deduct a loss from the sale or exchange of property directly or indirectly between any of the following:
- A grantor and a fiduciary of a trust;
- A fiduciary and a fiduciary or beneficiary of another trust created by the same grantor;
- A fiduciary and a beneficiary of the same trust; or
- A trust fiduciary and a corporation of which more than 50% in value of the outstanding stock is owned directly or indirectly by or for the trust or by or for the grantor of the trust.

Items for Special Treatment

The following items may require special treatment:

- Exchange of "like-kind" property.
- Wash sales of stock or securities (including contracts or options to acquire or sell stock or securities) (section 1091).
- Gain or loss on options to buy or sell (section 1234).
- Certain real estate subdivided for sale that may be considered a capital asset (section 1237).
- Gain on disposition of stock in an Interest Charge Domestic International Sales Corporation (section 995(c)).
- Gain on the sale or exchange of stock in certain foreign corporations (section 1248).
- Sales of stock received under a qualified public utility dividend reinvestment plan. See Pub. 550 for details.
- Transfer of appreciated property to a political organization (section 84).
- Distributions received from an employee pension, profit sharing, or stock bonus plan. See Form 4972.
- Disposition of market discount bonds (section 1276).
- Section 1256 contracts and straddles are reported on **Form 6781,** Gains and Losses From Section 1256 Contracts and Straddles.

Specific Instructions

Lines 1 and 7

Short-term and long-term capital gains and losses.— Enter all sales of stocks, bonds, etc.

Redemption of stock to pay death taxes.— If stock is redeemed under the provisions of section 303, list and identify it on line 7 and give the name of the decedent and the IRS office where the estate tax or generation-skipping transfer tax return was filed.

If you are reporting capital gain from a lump-sum distribution, see the instructions for Form 4972 for information about the death benefit exclusion and the Federal estate tax.

Column (d)—Sales Price

Enter either the gross sales price or the net sales price from the sale. On sales of stocks and bonds, report the gross amount as reported to the estate or trust on Form 1099-B or similar statement. However, if the estate or trust was advised that gross proceeds less commissions and option premiums were reported to the IRS, enter that net amount in column (d).

Column (e)—Cost or Other Basis

Basis of trust property.— Generally, the basis of property acquired by gift is the same as the basis in the hands of the donor. If the fair market value (FMV) of the property at the time it was transferred to the trust is less than the transferor's basis, then the FMV is used for determining any loss on disposition.

If the property was transferred to the trust after 1976, and a gift tax was paid under Chapter 12, then increase the donor's basis as follows:

Multiply the amount of the gift tax paid by a fraction, the numerator of which is the net appreciation in value of the gift (discussed below), and the denominator of which is the amount of the gift. For this purpose, the **net appreciation in value of the gift** is the amount by which the FMV of the gift exceeds the donor's adjusted basis.

Basis of decedent's estate property.— Generally, the basis of property acquired by a decedent's estate is the FMV of the property at the date of the decedent's death, or the alternate valuation date if the executor elected to use an alternate valuation under section 2032.

See Pub. 551 for a discussion of the valuation of qualified real property under section 2032A.

Basis of property for bankruptcy estates.— Generally, the basis of property held by the bankruptcy estate is the same as the basis in the hands of the individual debtor.

Adjustments to basis.— Before figuring any gain or loss on the sale, exchange, or other disposition of property owned by the estate or trust, adjustments to the property's basis may be required.

Some items that may increase the basis include:

1. Broker's fees and commissions.

2. Reinvested dividends that were previously reported as income.

3. Reinvested capital gains that were previously reported as income.

4. Costs that were capitalized.

5. Original issue discount that has been previously included in income.

Some items that may decrease the basis include:

1. Nontaxable distributions that consist of return of capital.

2. Deductions previously allowed or allowable for depreciation.

3. Casualty or theft loss deductions.

See Pub. 551 for additional information.

See section 852(f) for treatment of load charges incurred in acquiring stock in a regulated investment company.

Carryover basis.— Carryover basis determined under repealed section 1023 applies to property acquired from a decedent who died after December 31, 1976, and before November 7, 1978, only if the executor elected it on a **Form 5970-A,** Election of Carryover Basis, that was filed on time.

Lines 2 and 8

Installment sales.— If the estate or trust sold property at a gain during the tax year, and will receive a payment in a later tax year, report the sale on the installment method and file **Form 6252,** Installment Sale Income, unless you elect not to do so.

Also, use Form 6252 to report any payment received in 1996 from a sale made in an earlier tax year that was reported on the installment method.

To elect out of the installment method, report the full amount of the gain on a timely filed return (including extensions).

Exchange of "like-kind" property.— Generally, no gain or loss is recognized when property held for productive use in a trade or business or for investment is exchanged solely for property of a like-kind to be held either for productive use in a trade or business or for investment. However, if a trust exchanges like-kind property with a related person (see **Related Persons** on page 22), and before 2 years after the date of the last transfer that was part of the exchange the related person disposes of the property, or the trust disposes of the property received in exchange from the related person, then the original exchange will not qualify for nonrecognition. See section 1031(f) for exceptions.

Complete and attach **Form 8824,** Like-Kind Exchanges, to Form 1041 for each exchange.

Line 10—Capital Gain Distributions

Enter as a long-term capital gain on line 10, capital gain distributions paid during the year, regardless of how long the estate or trust held its investment. Also enter any amounts shown on Form 2439 that represent the estate's or trust's share of the undistributed capital gains of a regulated investment company. Include on Form 1041, line 24f, the tax paid by the company as shown on Form 2439. Add to the basis of the stock the excess of the amount included in income over the credit if the amount is not distributed.

Line 15, Column (a)—Beneficiaries' Net Short-Term Capital Gain or Loss

Enter the amount of net short-term capital gain or loss allocable to the beneficiary or beneficiaries. Except in the final year, include only those short-term capital losses that are taken into account in determining the amount of gain from the sale or exchange of capital assets that is paid, credited, or required to be distributed to any beneficiary during the tax year. See Regulations section 1.643(a)-3 for more information about allocation of capital gains and losses.

Except in the final year, if the losses from the sale or exchange of capital assets are more than the gains, all of the losses are allocated to the estate or trust and none are allocated to the beneficiaries.

Line 15, Column (b)—Estate's or Trust's Net Short-Term Capital Gain or Loss

Enter the amount of the net short-term capital gain or loss allocable to the estate or trust. Include any capital gain paid or permanently set aside for a charitable purpose specified in section 642(c).

Line 15, Column (c)—Total

Enter the total of the amounts entered in columns (a) and (b). The amount in column (c) should be the same as the amount on line 6.

Line 16—Net Long-Term Capital Gain or Loss

Allocate the net long-term capital gain or loss on line 16 in the same manner as the net short-term capital gain or loss on line 15.

Part IV—Capital Loss Limitation

If the sum of all the capital losses is more than the sum of all the capital gains, then these capital losses are allowed as a deduction only to the extent of the smaller of the net loss or $3,000.

Part V—Capital Loss Carryovers From 1996 to 1997

For any year (including the final year) in which capital losses exceed capital gains, complete Part V to figure the capital loss carryover. A capital loss carryover may be carried forward indefinitely. Capital losses keep their character as either short-term or long-term when carried over to the following year.

Part VI—Tax Computation Using Maximum Capital Gains Rate

Line 37c

If the estate or trust received capital gains that were derived from income in respect of a decedent, and a section 691(c)(4) deduction was claimed, then line 37c must be reduced by the portion of the section 691(c)(4) deduction claimed on Form 1041, page 1, line 19.

Line 44

To figure the regular tax, use the 1996 Tax Rate Schedule on page 16.

Line 45

If the tax using the maximum capital gains rate (line 43) is less than the regular tax (line 44), enter the amount from line 45 on line 1a of Schedule G, Form 1041, and check the "Schedule D" box.

Schedule J (Form 1041)— Accumulation Distribution for a Complex Trust

General Instructions

Use Schedule J (Form 1041) to report an accumulation distribution for a complex trust. An accumulation distribution is the excess of amounts properly paid, credited, or required to be distributed (other than income required to be distributed currently) over the DNI of the trust reduced by income required to be distributed currently. To have an accumulation distribution, the distribution must exceed the accounting income of the trust.

Specific Instructions

Part I—Accumulation Distribution in 1996

Line 1—Distribution Under Section 661(a)(2)

Enter the amount from Schedule B of Form 1041, line 12, for 1996. This is the amount properly paid, credited, or required to be distributed other than the amount of income for the current tax year required to be distributed currently.

Line 2—Distributable Net Income

Enter the amount from Schedule B of Form 1041, line 9, for 1996. This is the amount of distributable net income (DNI) for the current tax year determined under section 643(a).

Line 3—Distribution Under Section 661(a)(1)

Enter the amount from Schedule B of Form 1041, line 11, for 1996. This is the amount of income for the current tax year required to be distributed currently.

Line 5—Accumulation Distribution

If line 13, Schedule B of Form 1041 is more than line 10, Schedule B of Form 1041, complete the rest of Schedule J and file it with Form 1041, unless the trust has no previously accumulated income.

Generally, amounts accumulated before a beneficiary reaches age 21 may be excluded by the beneficiary. See sections 665 and 667(c) for exceptions relating to multiple trusts. The trustee reports to the IRS the total amount of the accumulation distribution before any reduction for income accumulated before the beneficiary reaches age 21. If the multiple trust rules do not apply, the beneficiary claims the exclusion when filing **Form 4970**, Tax on Accumulation Distribution of Trusts, as you may not be aware that the beneficiary may be a beneficiary of other trusts with other trustees.

For examples of accumulation distributions that include payments from one trust to another trust, and amounts distributed for a dependent's support, see Regulations section 1.665(b)-1A(b).

Part II—Ordinary Income Accumulation Distribution

Line 6—Distributable Net Income for Earlier Years

Enter the applicable amounts as follows:

Throwback year(s)	Amount from line
1969–1977	Schedule C, Form 1041, line 5
1978–1979	Form 1041, line 61
1980	Form 1041, line 60
1981–1982	Form 1041, line 58
1983–1995	Schedule B, Form 1041, line 9

For information about throwback years, see the instructions for line 13. For purposes of line 6, in figuring the DNI of the trust for a throwback year, subtract any estate tax deduction for income in respect of a decedent if the income is includible in figuring the DNI of the trust for that year.

Line 7—Distributions Made During Earlier Years

Enter the applicable amounts as follows:

Throwback year(s)	Amount from line
1969–1977	Schedule C, Form 1041, line 8
1978	Form 1041, line 64
1979	Form 1041, line 65
1980	Form 1041, line 64
1981–1982	Form 1041, line 62
1983–1995	Schedule B, Form 1041, line 13

Line 11—Prior Accumulation Distribution Thrown Back to any Throwback Year

Enter the amount of prior accumulation distributions thrown back to the throwback years. Do not enter distributions excluded under section 663(a)(1) for gifts, bequests, etc.

Line 13—Throwback Years

Allocate the amount on line 5 that is an accumulation distribution to the earliest applicable year first, but do not allocate more than the amount on line 12 for any throwback year. An accumulation distribution is thrown back first to the earliest preceding tax year in which there is undistributed net income (UNI). Then, it is thrown back beginning with the next earliest year to any remaining preceding tax years of the trust. The portion of the accumulation distribution allocated to the earliest preceding tax year is the amount of the UNI for that year. The portion of the accumulation distribution allocated to any remaining preceding tax year is the amount by which the accumulation distribution is larger than the total of the UNI for all earlier preceding tax years.

A tax year of a trust during which the trust was a simple trust for the entire year is not a preceding tax year unless (a) during that year the trust received outside income or (b) the trustee did not distribute all of the trust's income that was required to be distributed currently for that year. In this case, UNI for that year must not be more than the greater of the outside income or income not distributed during that year.

The term "outside income" means amounts that are included in the DNI of the trust for that year but that are not "income" of the trust as defined in Regulations section 1.643(b)-1. Some examples of outside income are: (a) income taxable to the trust under section 691; (b) unrealized accounts receivable that were assigned to the trust; and (c) distributions from another trust that include the DNI or UNI of the other trust. Enter the applicable year at the top of each column for each throwback year.

Line 16—Tax-Exempt Interest Included on Line 13

For each throwback year, divide line 15 by line 6 and multiply the result by the following:

Throwback year(s)	Amount from line
1969–1977	Schedule C, Form 1041, line 2(a)
1978–1979	Form 1041, line 58(a)
1980	Form 1041, line 57(a)
1981–1982	Form 1041, line 55(a)
1983–1995	Schedule B, Form 1041, line 2

Part III—Taxes Imposed on Undistributed Net Income

For the regular tax computation, if there is a capital gain, complete lines 18 through 25 for each throwback year. If the trustee elected the alternative tax on capital gains, complete lines 26 through 31 instead of lines 18 through 25 for each applicable year. If there is no capital gain for any year, or there is a capital loss for every year, enter on line 9 the amount of the tax for each year identified in the instruction for line 18 and do not complete Part III. If the trust received an accumulation distribution from another trust, see Regulations section 1.665(b)-1A.

Note: *The alternative tax on capital gains was repealed for tax years beginning after December 31, 1978. The maximum rate on net capital gain for 1981, 1987, and 1991 through 1995 is not an alternative tax for this purpose.*

Line 18—Regular Tax

Enter the applicable amounts as follows:

Throwback year(s)	Amount from line
1969–1976	Form 1041, page 1, line 24
1977	Form 1041, page 1, line 26
1978–1979	Form 1041, line 27
1980–1984	Form 1041, line 26c
1985–1986	Form 1041, line 25c
1987	Form 1041, line 22c
1988–1995	Schedule G, Form 1041, line 1a

Line 19—Trust's Share of Net Short-Term Gain

For each throwback year, enter the smaller of the capital gain from the two lines indicated. If there is a capital loss or a zero on either or both of the two lines indicated, enter zero on line 19.

Throwback year(s)	Amount from line
1969–1970	Schedule D, Line 10, column 2, or Schedule D, line 12, column 2.
1971–1978	Schedule D, line 14, column 2, or Schedule D, line 16, column 2.
1979	Schedule D, line 18, column (b), or Schedule D, line 20, column (b).
1980–1981	Schedule D, line 14, column (b), or Schedule D, line 16, column (b).
1982	Schedule D, line 16, column (b),or Schedule D, line 18, column (b).
1983–1995	Schedule D, line 15, column (b), or Schedule D, line 17, column (b).

Line 20—Trust's Share of Net Long-Term Gain

Enter the applicable amounts as follows:

Throwback year(s)	Amount from line
1969–1970	50% of Schedule D, line 13(e)
1971–1977	50% of Schedule D, line 17(e)
1978	Schedule D, line 17(e), or line 31, whichever is applicable, less Form 1041, line 23.
1979	Schedule D, line 25 or line 27, whichever is applicable, less Form 1041, line 23.
1980–1981	Schedule D, line 21, less Schedule D, line 22
1982	Schedule D, line 23, less Schedule D, line 24.
1983–1986	Schedule D, line 22, less Schedule D, line 23.
1987–1995	Schedule D, the smaller of any gain on line 16 or line 17, column (b).

Line 22—Taxable Income

Enter the applicable amounts as follows:

Throwback year(s)	Amount from line
1969–1976	Form 1041, page 1, line 23
1977	Form 1041, page 1, line 25
1978–1979	Form 1041, line 26
1980–1984	Form 1041, line 25
1985–1986	Form 1041, line 24
1987	Form 1041, line 21
1988–1995	Form 1041, line 22

Line 26—Tax on Income Other Than Long-Term Capital Gain

Enter the applicable amounts as follows:

Throwback year(s)	Amount from line
1969	Schedule D, line 20
1970	Schedule D, line 19
1971	Schedule D, line 50
1972–1975	Schedule D, line 48
1976–1978	Schedule D, line 27

Line 27—Trust's Share of Net Short-Term Gain

If there is a loss on any of the following lines, enter zero on line 27 for the applicable throwback year. Otherwise, enter the applicable amounts as follows:

Throwback year(s)	Amount from line
1969–1970	Schedule D, line 10, column 2
1971–1978	Schedule D, line 14, column 2

Line 28—Trust's Share of Taxable Income Less Section 1202 Deduction

Enter the applicable amounts as follows:

Throwback year(s)	Amount from line
1969	Schedule D, line 19
1970	Schedule D, line 18
1971	Schedule D, line 38
1972–1975	Schedule D, line 39
1976–1978	Schedule D, line 21

Part IV—Allocation to Beneficiary

Complete Part IV for each beneficiary. If the accumulation distribution is allocated to more than one beneficiary, attach an additional copy of Schedule J with Part IV completed for each additional beneficiary. Give each beneficiary a copy of his or her respective Part IV information. If more than 5 throwback years are involved, use another Schedule J, completing Parts II and III for each additional throwback year.

If the beneficiary is a nonresident alien individual or a foreign corporation, see section 667(e) about retaining the character of the amounts distributed to determine the amount of the U.S. withholding tax.

The beneficiary uses Form 4970 to figure the tax on the distribution. The beneficiary also uses Form 4970 for the section 667(b)(6) tax adjustment if an accumulation distribution is subject to estate or generation-skipping transfer tax. This is because the trustee may not be the estate or generation-skipping transfer tax return filer.

Schedule K-1 (Form 1041)—Beneficiary's Share of Income, Deductions, Credits, etc.

General Instructions

Use Schedule K-1 (Form 1041) to report the beneficiary's share of income, deductions, and credits from a trust or a decedent's estate.

Who Must File

The fiduciary (or one of the joint fiduciaries) must file Schedule K-1. A copy of each beneficiary's Schedule K-1 is attached to the Form 1041 filed with the IRS and each beneficiary is given a copy of his or her respective Schedule K-1. One copy of each Schedule K-1 must be retained for the fiduciary's records.

Beneficiary's Identifying Number

As a payer of income, you are required under section 6109 to request and provide a proper identifying number for each recipient of income. Enter the beneficiary's number on the respective Schedules K-1 when you file Form 1041. Individuals and business recipients are responsible for giving you their taxpayer identification numbers upon request. You may use **Form W-9**, Request for Taxpayer Identification Number and Certification, to request the beneficiary's identifying number.

Penalty.— Under section 6723, the payer is charged a $50 penalty for each failure to provide a required taxpayer identification number, unless reasonable cause is established for not providing it. Explain any reasonable cause in a signed affidavit and attach it to this return.

Tax Shelter's Identification Number

If the estate or trust is a tax shelter, is involved in a tax shelter, or is considered to be the organizer of a tax shelter, there are reporting requirements under section 6111 for both the fiduciaries and the beneficiaries.

See **Form 8264**, Application for Registration of a Tax Shelter, and **Form 8271**, Investor Reporting of Tax Shelter Registration Number, and their related instructions for information regarding the fiduciary's reporting requirements.

Substitute Forms

You do not need prior IRS approval for a substitute Schedule K-1 (Form 1041) that follows the specifications for filing substitute Schedules K-1 in **Pub. 1167**, Substitute Printed, Computer-Prepared, and Computer-Generated Tax Forms and Schedules, or is an exact copy of an IRS Schedule K-1. You must request IRS approval to use other substitute Schedules K-1. To request approval, write to: Internal Revenue Service, Attention: Substitute Forms Program Coordinator, T:FP:S, 1111 Constitution Avenue, N.W., Washington, DC 20224.

Inclusion of Amounts in Beneficiaries' Income

Simple trust.— The beneficiary of a simple trust must include in his or her gross income the amount of the income required to be distributed currently, whether or not distributed, or if the income required to be distributed currently to all beneficiaries exceeds the distributable net income (DNI), his or her proportionate share of the DNI. The determination of whether trust income is required to be distributed currently depends on the terms of the trust instrument and applicable local law. See Regulations section 1.652(c)-4 for a comprehensive example.

Estates and complex trusts.— The beneficiary of a decedent's estate or complex trust must include in his or her gross income the sum of:

1. The amount of the income required to be distributed currently, or if the income required to be distributed currently to all beneficiaries exceeds the DNI (figured without taking into account the charitable deduction), his or her proportionate share of the DNI (as so figured); and

2. All other amounts properly paid, credited, or required to be distributed, or if the sum of the income required to be distributed currently and other amounts properly paid, credited, or required to be distributed to all beneficiaries exceeds the DNI, his or her proportionate share of the excess of DNI over the income required to be distributed currently.

See Regulations section 1.662(c)-4 for a comprehensive example.

For complex trusts that have more than one beneficiary, and if different beneficiaries have substantially separate and independent shares, their shares are treated as separate trusts for the sole purpose of determining the amount of DNI allocable to the respective beneficiaries. For examples of the application of the separate share rule, see the regulations under section 663(c).

Character of Income.— The beneficiary's income is considered to have the same proportion of each class of items entering into the computation of DNI that the total of each class has to the DNI (e.g., half dividends and half interest

if the income of the estate or trust is half dividends and half interest).

Allocation of deductions.— Generally, items of deduction that enter into the computation of DNI are allocated among the items of income to the extent such allocation is not inconsistent with the rules set out in section 469 and its regulations, relating to passive activity loss limitations, in the following order.

First, all deductions directly attributable to a specific class of income are deducted from that income. For example, rental expenses, to the extent allowable, are deducted from rental income.

Second, deductions that are not directly attributable to a specific class of income generally may be allocated to any class of income, as long as a reasonable portion is allocated to any tax-exempt income. Deductions considered not directly attributable to a specific class of income under this rule include fiduciary fees, safe deposit box rental charges, and state income and personal property taxes. The charitable deduction, however, must be ratably apportioned among each class of income included in DNI.

Finally, any excess deductions that are directly attributable to a class of income may be allocated to another class of income. In no case can excess deductions from a passive activity be allocated to income from a nonpassive activity, or to portfolio income earned by the estate or trust. Excess deductions attributable to tax-exempt income cannot offset any other class of income.

In no case can deductions be allocated to an item of income that is not included in the computation of DNI, or attributable to corpus.

Except for the final year, and for depreciation or depletion allocations in excess of income (see Rev. Rul. 74-530, 1974-2 C.B. 188), you may not show any negative amounts for any class of income because the beneficiary generally may not claim losses or deductions from the estate or trust.

Gifts and bequests.— Do not include in the beneficiary's income any gifts or bequests of a specific sum of money or of specific property under the terms of the governing instrument that are paid or credited in three installments or less.

Amounts that can be paid or credited only from income of the estate or trust do not qualify as a gift or bequest of a specific sum of money.

Past years.— Do not include in the beneficiary's income any amounts deducted on Form 1041 for an earlier year that were credited or required to be distributed in that earlier year.

Beneficiary's Tax Year

The beneficiary's income from the estate or trust must be included in the beneficiary's tax year during which the tax year of the estate or trust ends. See Pub. 559 for more information, including the

effect of the death of a beneficiary during the tax year of the estate or trust.

Specific Instructions

Line 1—Interest

Enter the beneficiary's share of the taxable interest income minus allocable deductions.

Line 2—Dividends

Enter the beneficiary's share of dividend income minus allocable deductions.

Line 3a—Net Short-Term Capital Gain

Enter the beneficiary's share of the net short-term capital gain from line 15, column (a), Schedule D (Form 1041), minus allocable deductions. Do not enter a loss on line 3a. If, for the final year of the estate or trust, there is a capital loss carryover, enter on line 12b the beneficiary's share of short-term capital loss carryover as a loss in parentheses. However, if the beneficiary is a corporation, enter on line 12b the beneficiary's share of all short- and long-term capital loss carryovers as a single item in parentheses. See section 642(h) and related regulations for more information.

Line 3b—Net Long-Term Capital Gain

Enter the beneficiary's share of the net long-term capital gain from line 16, column (a), Schedule D (Form 1041), minus allocable deductions. Do not enter a loss on line 3b. If, for the final year of the estate or trust, there is a capital loss carryover, enter on line 12c the beneficiary's share of the long-term capital loss carryover as a loss in parentheses. (If the beneficiary is a corporation, see the instructions for line 3a.) See section 642(h) and related regulations for more information.

Gains, or losses, from the complete, or partial, disposition of a rental, rental real estate, or trade or business activity that is a passive activity, must be shown on an attachment to Schedule K-1.

Line 4a—Annuities, Royalties, and Other Nonpassive Income

Enter the beneficiary's share of annuities, royalties, or any other income, minus allocable deductions (other than directly apportionable deductions), that is NOT subject to any passive activity loss limitation rules at the beneficiary level. Use line 5a to report income items subject to the passive activity rules at the beneficiary's level.

Lines 4b and 5b—Depreciation

Enter the beneficiary's share of the depreciation deductions attributable to each activity reported on lines 4a and 5a. See the instructions on page 10 for a discussion of how the depreciation deduction is apportioned between the beneficiaries and the estate or trust. Report any AMT adjustment or tax preference item attributable to depreciation separately on line 11a.

Note: *An estate or trust cannot make an election under section 179 to expense certain tangible property.*

Lines 4c and 5c—Depletion

Enter the beneficiary's share of the depletion deduction under section 611 attributable to each activity reported on lines 4a and 5a. See the instructions on page 10 for a discussion of how the depletion deduction is apportioned between the beneficiaries and the estate or trust. Report any tax preference item attributable to depletion separately on line 11b.

Lines 4d and 5d—Amortization

Itemize the beneficiary's share of the amortization deductions attributable to each activity reported on lines 4a and 5a. Apportion the amortization deductions between the estate or trust and the beneficiaries in the same way that the depreciation and depletion deductions are divided. Report any AMT adjustment attributable to amortization separately on line 11c.

Line 5a—Trade or Business, Rental Real Estate, and Other Rental Income

Enter the beneficiary's share of trade or business, rental real estate, and other rental income, minus allocable deductions (other than directly apportionable deductions). To assist the beneficiary in figuring any applicable passive activity loss limitations, also attach a separate schedule showing the beneficiary's share of income derived from each trade or business, rental real estate, and other rental activity.

Lines 5b Through 5d

Caution: *The limitations on passive activity losses and credits under section 469 apply to estates and trusts. Estates and trusts that distribute income to beneficiaries are allowed to apportion depreciation, depletion, and amortization deductions to the beneficiaries. These deductions are referred to as "directly apportionable deductions."*

Rules for treating a beneficiary's income and directly apportionable deductions from an estate or trust and other rules for applying the passive loss and credit limitations to beneficiaries of estates and trusts have not yet been issued.

Any directly apportionable deduction, such as depreciation, is treated by the beneficiary as having been incurred in the same activity as incurred by the estate or trust. However, the character of such deduction may be determined as if the beneficiary incurred the deduction directly.

To assist the beneficiary in figuring any applicable passive activity loss limitations, also attach a separate schedule showing the beneficiary's share of directly apportionable deductions derived from each trade or business, rental real estate, and other rental activity.

Line 6—Income for Minimum Tax Purposes

Enter the beneficiary's share of the income distribution deduction figured on a minimum tax basis from line 27 of Schedule I.

Line 7—Income for Regular Tax Purposes

Enter the beneficiary's share of the income distribution deduction figured on line 17 of Schedule B. This amount should equal the sum of lines 1 through 3b, 4a, and 5a.

Line 9—Estate Tax Deduction (Including Generation-Skipping Transfer Taxes)

If the distribution deduction consists of any income in respect of a decedent, and the estate or trust was allowed a deduction under section 691(c) for the estate tax paid attributable to such income (see the line 19 instructions on page 13), then the beneficiary is allowed an estate tax deduction in proportion to his or her share of the distribution that consists of such income. For an example of the computation, see Regulations section 1.691(c)-2. Figure the computation on a separate sheet and attach it to the return.

Line 10—Foreign Taxes

List on a separate sheet the beneficiary's share of the applicable foreign taxes paid or accrued and the various foreign source figures needed to figure the beneficiary's foreign tax credit. See Pub. 514 and section 901(b)(5) for special rules about foreign taxes.

Lines 11a through 11c

Enter any adjustments or tax preference items attributable to depreciation, depletion, or amortization that were allocated to the beneficiary. For property placed in service before 1987, report separately the accelerated depreciation of real and leased personal property.

Line 11d—Exclusion Items

Enter the beneficiary's share of the adjustment for minimum tax purposes from Schedule K-1, line 8, that is attributable to exclusion items (Schedule I, lines 4a through 4d, 4p, and 4q).

Line 12a—Excess Deductions on Termination

If this is the final return and there are excess deductions on termination (see the instructions for line 22 on page 13), enter the beneficiary's share of the excess deductions on line 12a. Figure the deductions on a separate sheet and attach it to the return.

Excess deductions on termination occur only during the last tax year of the trust or decedent's estate when the total deductions (excluding the charitable deduction and exemption) are greater than the gross income during that tax year. Generally, a deduction based on an NOL carryover is not available to a beneficiary as an excess deduction. However, if the last tax year of the estate or trust is also the last year in which an NOL carryover may be taken (see section 172(b)), the NOL carryover is considered an excess deduction on the termination of the estate or trust to the extent it is not absorbed by the estate or trust during its final tax year. For more information, see Regulations section 1.642(h)-4 for a discussion of the allocation of the carryover among the beneficiaries.

Only the beneficiary of an estate or trust that succeeds to its property is allowed to deduct that entity's excess deductions on termination. A beneficiary who does not have enough income in that year to absorb the entire deduction may not carry the balance over to any succeeding year. An individual beneficiary must be able to itemize deductions in order to claim the excess deductions in determining taxable income.

Lines 12b and 12c—Unused Capital Loss Carryover

Upon termination of the trust or decedent's estate, the beneficiary succeeding to the property is allowed as a deduction any unused capital loss carryover under section 1212. If the estate or trust incurs capital losses in the final year, use Part V of Schedule D (Form 1041) to figure the amount of capital loss carryover to be allocated to the beneficiary.

Lines 12d and 12e—Net Operating Loss (NOL) Carryover

Upon termination of a trust or decedent's estate, a beneficiary succeeding to its property is allowed to deduct any unused NOL (and any AMT NOL) carryover for regular and AMT purposes if the carryover would be allowable to the estate or trust in a later tax year but for the termination. Enter on lines 12d and 12e the unused carryover amounts.

Line 13—Other

Itemize on line 13, or on a separate sheet if more space is needed, the beneficiary's tax information not entered elsewhere on Schedule K-1. This includes the allocable share, if any, of:
- Payment of estimated tax to be credited to the beneficiary (section 643(g));
- Tax-exempt interest income received or accrued by the trust (including exempt-interest dividends from a mutual fund or other regulated investment company);
- Investment income (section 163(d));
- Gross farming and fishing income;
- Credit for backup withholding (section 3406);
- The information a beneficiary will need to figure any investment credit;
- The work opportunity credit;
- The alcohol fuel credit;
- The credit for increasing research activities;
- The low-income housing credit;
- The renewable electricity production credit;
- The empowerment zone employment credit;
- The Indian employment credit;
- The orphan drug credit; and
- The information a beneficiary will need to figure any recapture taxes.

Note: *Upon termination of an estate or trust, any suspended passive activity losses (PALs) relating to an interest in a passive activity cannot be allocated to the beneficiary. Instead, the basis in such activity is increased by the amount of any PALs allocable to the interest, and no losses are allowed as a deduction on the estate's or trust's final Form 1041.*

Form **1041**

Department of the Treasury—Internal Revenue Service

U.S. Income Tax Return for Estates and Trusts

1996

For calendar year 1996 or fiscal year beginning   , 1996, and ending   , 19

OMB No. 1545-0092

A Type of entity:

- [ ] Decedent's estate
- [ ] Simple trust
- [ ] Complex trust
- [ ] Grantor type trust
- [ ] Bankruptcy estate–Ch. 7
- [ ] Bankruptcy estate–Ch. 11
- [ ] Pooled income fund

Name of estate or trust (If a grantor type trust, see page 7 of the instructions.)

Name and title of fiduciary

Number, street, and room or suite no. (If a P.O. box, see page 7 of the instructions.)

City or town, state, and ZIP code

C Employer identification number

D Date entity created

E Nonexempt charitable and split-interest trusts, check applicable boxes (see page 8 of the instructions):
- [ ] Described in section 4947(a)(1)
- [ ] Not a private foundation
- [ ] Described in section 4947(a)(2)

B Number of Schedules K-1 attached (see instructions) ▶

F Check applicable boxes:
- [ ] Initial return
- [ ] Final return
- [ ] Amended return
- [ ] Change in fiduciary's name
- [ ] Change in fiduciary's address

G Pooled mortgage account (see page 9 of the instructions):
- [ ] Bought
- [ ] Sold
- Date:

Income

1	Interest income	1
2	Dividends	2
3	Business income or (loss) (attach Schedule C or C-EZ (Form 1040))	3
4	Capital gain or (loss) (attach Schedule D (Form 1041))	4
5	Rents, royalties, partnerships, other estates and trusts, etc. (attach Schedule E (Form 1040))	5
6	Farm income or (loss) (attach Schedule F (Form 1040))	6
7	Ordinary gain or (loss) (attach Form 4797)	7
8	Other income. List type and amount	8
9	**Total income.** Combine lines 1 through 8 ▶	9

Deductions

10	Interest. Check if Form 4952 is attached ▶ ☐	10
11	Taxes	11
12	Fiduciary fees	12
13	Charitable deduction (from Schedule A, line 7)	13
14	Attorney, accountant, and return preparer fees	14
15a	Other deductions NOT subject to the 2% floor (attach schedule)	15a
b	Allowable miscellaneous itemized deductions subject to the 2% floor	15b
16	**Total.** Add lines 10 through 15b	16
17	Adjusted total income or (loss). Subtract line 16 from line 9. Enter here and on Schedule B, line 1 ▶	17
18	Income distribution deduction (from Schedule B, line 17) (attach Schedules K-1 (Form 1041))	18
19	Estate tax deduction (including certain generation-skipping taxes) (attach computation)	19
20	Exemption	20
21	**Total deductions.** Add lines 18 through 20 ▶	21

Tax and Payments

22	Taxable income. Subtract line 21 from line 17. If a loss, see page 13 of the instructions	22
23	**Total tax** (from Schedule G, line 8)	23
24	**Payments: a** 1996 estimated tax payments and amount applied from 1995 return	24a
b	Estimated tax payments allocated to beneficiaries (from Form 1041-T)	24b
c	Subtract line 24b from line 24a	24c
d	Tax paid with extension of time to file: ☐ Form 2758 ☐ Form 8736 ☐ Form 8800	24d
e	Federal income tax withheld. If any is from Form(s) 1099, check ▶ ☐	24e
	Other payments: **f** Form 2439 _____ ; **g** Form 4136 _____ ; Total ▶	24h
25	**Total payments.** Add lines 24c through 24e, and 24h	25
26	Estimated tax penalty (see page 13 of the instructions)	26
27	**Tax due.** If line 25 is smaller than the total of lines 23 and 26, enter amount owed	27
28	**Overpayment.** If line 25 is larger than the total of lines 23 and 26, enter amount overpaid	28
29	Amount of line 28 to be: **a** Credited to 1997 estimated tax ▶ ; **b** Refunded ▶	29

Please Sign Here

Under penalties of perjury, I declare that I have examined this return, including accompanying schedules and statements, and to the best of my knowledge and belief, it is true, correct, and complete. Declaration of preparer (other than fiduciary) is based on all information of which preparer has any knowledge.

▶ Signature of fiduciary or officer representing fiduciary   Date

EIN of fiduciary if a financial institution (see page 4 of the instructions)

Paid Preparer's Use Only

Preparer's signature ▶	Date	Check if self-employed ▶ ☐ Preparer's social security no.
Firm's name (or yours if self-employed) and address ▶		EIN ▶ ZIP code ▶

For Paperwork Reduction Act Notice, see page 1 of the separate instructions.   Cat. No. 11370H   Form **1041** (1996)

Schedule A	Charitable Deduction. Do not complete for a simple trust or a pooled income fund.		
1	Amounts paid for charitable purposes from gross income	1	
2	Amounts permanently set aside for charitable purposes from gross income	2	
3	Add lines 1 and 2	3	
4	Tax-exempt income allocable to charitable contributions (see page 14 of the instructions) . .	4	
5	Subtract line 4 from line 3	5	
6	Capital gains for the tax year allocated to corpus and paid or permanently set aside for charitable purposes	6	
7	**Charitable deduction.** Add lines 5 and 6. Enter here and on page 1, line 13	7	

Schedule B	Income Distribution Deduction		
1	Adjusted total income (from page 1, line 17) (see page 14 of the instructions)	1	
2	Adjusted tax-exempt interest	2	
3	Total net gain from Schedule D (Form 1041), line 17, column (a) (see page 15 of the instructions)	3	
4	Enter amount from Schedule A, line 6	4	
5	Long-term capital gain for the tax year included on Schedule A, line 3	5	
6	Short-term capital gain for the tax year included on Schedule A, line 3	6	
7	If the amount on page 1, line 4, is a capital loss, enter here as a positive figure	7	
8	If the amount on page 1, line 4, is a capital gain, enter here as a negative figure	8	
9	**Distributable net income (DNI).** Combine lines 1 through 8. If zero or less, enter -0-	9	
10	If a complex trust, enter accounting income for the tax year as determined under the governing instrument and applicable local law **10**		
11	Income required to be distributed currently	11	
12	Other amounts paid, credited, or otherwise required to be distributed	12	
13	Total distributions. Add lines 11 and 12. If greater than line 10, see page 15 of the instructions	13	
14	Enter the amount of tax-exempt income included on line 13	14	
15	Tentative income distribution deduction. Subtract line 14 from line 13	15	
16	Tentative income distribution deduction. Subtract line 2 from line 9. If zero or less, enter -0-	16	
17	**Income distribution deduction.** Enter the smaller of line 15 or line 16 here and on page 1, line 18	17	

Schedule G	Tax Computation (see page 16 of the instructions)		
1	**Tax: a** ☐ Tax rate schedule or ☐ Schedule D (Form 1041) . .	**1a**	
	b Other taxes	**1b**	
	c Total. Add lines 1a and 1b . . . . ▶	**1c**	
2a	Foreign tax credit (attach Form 1116)	**2a**	
b	Check: ☐ Nonconventional source fuel credit ☐ Form 8834 . . .	**2b**	
c	General business credit. Enter here and check which forms are attached:		
	☐ Form 3800 or ☐ Forms (specify) ▶	**2c**	
d	Credit for prior year minimum tax (attach Form 8801)	**2d**	
3	**Total credits.** Add lines 2a through 2d . . . . ▶	3	
4	Subtract line 3 from line 1c	4	
5	Recapture taxes. Check if from: ☐ Form 4255 ☐ Form 8611	5	
6	Alternative minimum tax (from Schedule I, line 41)	6	
7	Household employment taxes. Attach Schedule H (Form 1040)	7	
8	**Total tax.** Add lines 4 through 7. Enter here and on page 1, line 23 . . . . . . ▶	8	

Other Information

		Yes	No
1	Did the estate or trust receive tax-exempt income? If "Yes," attach a computation of the allocation of expenses. Enter the amount of tax-exempt interest income and exempt-interest dividends ▶ $		
2	Did the estate or trust receive all or any part of the earnings (salary, wages, and other compensation) of any individual by reason of a contract assignment or similar arrangement?		
3	At any time during calendar year 1996, did the estate or trust have an interest in or a signature or other authority over a bank, securities, or other financial account in a foreign country? See page 17 of the instructions for exceptions and filing requirements for Form TD F 90-22.1. If "Yes," enter the name of the foreign country ▶		
4	During the tax year, did the estate or trust receive a distribution from, or was it the grantor of, or transferor to, a foreign trust? If "Yes," see page 17 of the instructions for other forms the estate or trust may have to file . . .		
5	Did the estate or trust receive, or pay, any seller-financed mortgage interest? If "Yes," see page 17 of the instructions for required attachment		
6	If this is a complex trust making the section 663(b) election, check here (see page 17 of the instructions) ▶ ☐		
7	To make a section 643(e)(3) election, attach Schedule D (Form 1041), and check here (see page 17) . ▶ ☐		
8	If the decedent's estate has been open for more than 2 years, check here . . . . ▶ ☐		

Schedule I	Alternative Minimum Tax (see pages 18 through 22 of the instructions)

Part I—Estate's or Trust's Share of Alternative Minimum Taxable Income

1	Adjusted total income or (loss) (from page 1, line 17)	**1**	
2	Net operating loss deduction. Enter as a positive amount	**2**	
3	Add lines 1 and 2	**3**	
4	**Adjustments and tax preference items:**		
a	Interest	4a	
b	Taxes	4b	
c	Miscellaneous itemized deductions (from page 1, line 15b)	4c	
d	Refund of taxes	4d (	)
e	Depreciation of property placed in service after 1986	4e	
f	Circulation and research and experimental expenditures	4f	
g	Mining exploration and development costs	4g	
h	Long-term contracts entered into after February 28, 1986	4h	
i	Amortization of pollution control facilities	4i	
j	Installment sales of certain property	4j	
k	Adjusted gain or loss (including incentive stock options)	4k	
l	Certain loss limitations	4l	
m	Tax shelter farm activities	4m	
n	Passive activities	4n	
o	Beneficiaries of other trusts or decedent's estates	4o	
p	Tax-exempt interest from specified private activity bonds	4p	
q	Depletion	4q	
r	Accelerated depreciation of real property placed in service before 1987	4r	
s	Accelerated depreciation of leased personal property placed in service before 1987	4s	
t	Intangible drilling costs	4t	
u	Other adjustments	4u	
5	Combine lines 4a through 4u	**5**	
6	Add lines 3 and 5	**6**	
7	Alternative tax net operating loss deduction (see page 21 of the instructions for limitations) . .	**7**	
8	Adjusted alternative minimum taxable income. Subtract line 7 from line 6. Enter here and on line 13	**8**	
	Note: *Complete Part II before going to line 9.*		
9	Income distribution deduction from line 27	9	
10	Estate tax deduction (from page 1, line 19)	10	
11	Add lines 9 and 10	**11**	
12	Estate's or trust's share of alternative minimum taxable income. Subtract line 11 from line 8 .	**12**	

12 ...If line 12 is:

● $22,500 or less, stop here and enter -0- on Schedule G, line 6. The estate or trust is not liable for the alternative minimum tax.

● Over $22,500, but less than $165,000, go to line 28.

● $165,000 or more, enter the amount from line 12 on line 34 and go to line 35.

(continued on page 4)

Part II—Income Distribution Deduction on a Minimum Tax Basis

13	Adjusted alternative minimum taxable income (from line 8)	**13**	
14	Adjusted tax-exempt interest (other than amounts included on line 4p)	**14**	
15	Total net gain from Schedule D (Form 1041), line 17, column (a). If a loss, enter -0-	**15**	
16	Capital gains for the tax year allocated to corpus and paid or permanently set aside for charitable purposes (from Schedule A, line 6)	**16**	
17	Capital gains paid or permanently set aside for charitable purposes from current year's income (see page 21 of the instructions).	**17**	
18	Capital gains computed on a minimum tax basis included on line 8	**18**	( )
19	Capital losses computed on a minimum tax basis included on line 8. Enter as a positive amount	**19**	
20	Distributable net alternative minimum taxable income (DNAMTI). Combine lines 13 through 19 .	**20**	
21	Income required to be distributed currently (from Schedule B, line 11)	**21**	
22	Other amounts paid, credited, or otherwise required to be distributed (from Schedule B, line 12)	**22**	
23	Total distributions. Add lines 21 and 22	**23**	
24	Tax-exempt income included on line 23 (other than amounts included on line 4p)	**24**	
25	Tentative income distribution deduction on a minimum tax basis. Subtract line 24 from line 23 .	**25**	
26	Tentative income distribution deduction on a minimum tax basis. Subtract line 14 from line 20 .	**26**	
27	**Income distribution deduction on a minimum tax basis.** Enter the smaller of line 25 or line 26. Enter here and on line 9	**27**	

Part III—Alternative Minimum Tax

28	Exemption amount			**28**	$22,500
29	Enter the amount from line 12	**29**			
30	Phase-out of exemption amount	**30**	$75,000		
31	Subtract line 30 from line 29. If zero or less, enter -0-	**31**			
32	Multiply line 31 by 25% (.25)			**32**	
33	Subtract line 32 from line 28. If zero or less, enter -0-			**33**	
34	Subtract line 33 from line 29			**34**	
35	If line 34 is:				
	• $175,000 or less, multiply line 34 by 26% (.26).				
	• Over $175,000, multiply line 34 by 28% (.28) and subtract $3,500 from the result			**35**	
36	Alternative minimum foreign tax credit (see page 21 of instructions)			**36**	
37	Tentative minimum tax. Subtract line 36 from line 35			**37**	
38	Regular tax before credits (see page 22 of instructions)	**38**			
39	Section 644 tax included on Schedule G, line 1b	**39**			
40	Add lines 38 and 39			**40**	
41	**Alternative minimum tax.** Subtract line 40 from line 37. If zero or less, enter -0-. Enter here and on Schedule G, line 6			**41**	

 Printed on recycled paper

SCHEDULE D
(Form 1041)

Department of the Treasury
Internal Revenue Service

Capital Gains and Losses

▶ Attach to Form 1041 (or Form 5227). See the separate instructions for Form 1041 (or Form 5227).

OMB No. 1545-0092

1996

Name of estate or trust	Employer identification number

Note: *Form 5227 filers need to complete ONLY Parts I and II.*

Part I Short-Term Capital Gains and Losses—Assets Held One Year or Less

(a) Description of property (Example, 100 shares 7% preferred of "Z" Co.)	(b) Date acquired (mo., day, yr.)	(c) Date sold (mo., day, yr.)	(d) Sales price	(e) Cost or other basis (see instructions)	(f) Gain or (loss) (col. (d) less col. (e))
1					

2 Short-term capital gain or (loss) from Forms 4684, 6252, 6781, and 8824	2	
3 Net short-term gain or (loss) from partnerships, S corporations, and other estates or trusts	3	
4 Net gain or (loss). Combine lines 1 through 3	4	
5 Short-term capital loss carryover from 1995 Schedule D, line 28	5 ( )	
6 Net short-term gain or (loss). Combine lines 4 and 5. Enter here and on line 15 below . . . ▶	6	

Part II Long-Term Capital Gains and Losses—Assets Held More Than One Year

7					

8 Long-term capital gain or (loss) from Forms 2439, 4684, 6252, 6781, and 8824	8	
9 Net long-term gain or (loss) from partnerships, S corporations, and other estates or trusts . . .	9	
10 Capital gain distributions	10	
11 Gain from Form 4797	11	
12 Net gain or (loss). Combine lines 7 through 11	12	
13 Long-term capital loss carryover from 1995 Schedule D, line 35	13 ( )	
14 Net long-term gain or (loss). Combine lines 12 and 13. Enter here and on line 16 below . . . ▶	14	

Part III Summary of Parts I and II

		(a) Beneficiaries' (see instructions)	(b) Estate's or trust's	(c) Total
15 Net short-term gain or (loss) from line 6, above.	15			
16 Net long-term gain or (loss) from line 14, above	16			
17 Total net gain or (loss). Combine lines 15 and 16 . . . ▶	17			

Note: *If line 17, column (c), is a net gain, enter the gain on Form 1041, line 4. If lines 16 and 17, column (b) are net gains, go to Part VI, and DO NOT complete Parts IV and V. If line 17, column (c), is a net loss, complete Parts IV and V, as necessary.*

For Paperwork Reduction Act Notice, see page 1 of the Instructions for Form 1041.   Cat. No. 11376V   **Schedule D (Form 1041) 1996**

Part IV	**Capital Loss Limitation**		

18	Enter here and enter as a (loss) on Form 1041, line 4, the smaller of: **a** The loss on line 17, column (c); **or** **b** $3,000	**18** (	)

If the loss on line 17, column (c) is more than $3,000, OR if Form 1041, page 1, line 22, is a loss, complete Part V to determine your capital loss carryover.

Part V	**Capital Loss Carryovers From 1996 to 1997**		

Section A.—Carryover Limit

19	Enter taxable income or (loss) from Form 1041, line 22	**19**	
20	Enter loss from line 18 as a positive amount	**20**	
21	Enter amount from Form 1041, line 20	**21**	
22	Adjusted taxable income. Combine lines 19, 20, and 21, but do not enter less than zero . . .	**22**	
23	Enter the smaller of line 20 or line 22	**23**	

Section B.—Short-Term Capital Loss Carryover
(Complete this part only if there is a loss on line 6 and line 17, column (c).)

24	Enter loss from line 6 as a positive amount	**24**	
25	Enter gain, if any, from line 14. If that line is blank or shows a loss, enter -0- **25**		
26	Enter amount from line 23 . . . . **26**		
27	Add lines 25 and 26	**27**	
28	**Short-term capital loss carryover to 1997.** Subtract line 27 from line 24. If zero or less, enter -0-. If this is the final return of the trust or decedent's estate, also enter on Schedule K-1 (Form 1041), line 12b	**28**	

Section C.—Long-Term Capital Loss Carryover
(Complete this part only if there is a loss on line 14 and line 17, column (c).)

29	Enter loss from line 14 as a positive amount	**29**	
30	Enter gain, if any, from line 6. If that line is blank or shows a loss, enter -0-	**30**	
31	Enter amount from line 23 . . . . **31**		
32	Enter amount, if any, from line 24 . . . . **32**		
33	Subtract line 32 from line 31. If zero or less, enter -0-	**33**	
34	Add lines 30 and 33	**34**	
35	**Long-term capital loss carryover to 1997.** Subtract line 34 from line 29. If zero or less, enter -0-. If this is the final return of the trust or decedent's estate, also enter on Schedule K-1 (Form 1041), line 12c	**35**	

Part VI	**Tax Computation Using Maximum Capital Gains Rate** (Complete this part only if both lines 16 and 17, column (b) are gains, and Form 1041, line 22 is more than $3,800.)		

36	Enter taxable income from Form 1041, line 22	**36**	
37a	**Net capital gain.** Enter the smaller of line 16 or 17, column (b) **37a**		
b	If you are filing Form 4952, enter the amount from Form 4952, line 4e . . **37b**		
c	Subtract line 37b from line 37a. If zero or less, stop here; you cannot use Part VI to figure the tax for the estate or trust. Instead, use the 1996 Tax Rate Schedule	**37c**	
38	Subtract line 37c from line 36. If zero or less, enter -0-	**38**	
39	Enter the greater of line 38 or $1,600	**39**	
40	Tax on amount on line 39 from the 1996 Tax Rate Schedule. If line 39 is $1,600, enter $240.00 .	**40**	
41	Subtract line 39 from line 36. If zero or less, enter -0-	**41**	
42	Multiply line 41 by 28% (.28)	**42**	
43	Maximum capital gains tax. Add lines 40 and 42	**43**	
44	Tax on amount on line 36 from the 1996 Tax Rate Schedule	**44**	
45	**Tax.** Enter the smaller of line 43 or line 44 here and on line 1a of Schedule G, Form 1041 . .	**45**	

SCHEDULE K-1 (Form 1041)	Beneficiary's Share of Income, Deductions, Credits, etc.	OMB No. 1545-0092

SCHEDULE K-1
(Form 1041)

Department of the Treasury
Internal Revenue Service

Beneficiary's Share of Income, Deductions, Credits, etc.

for the calendar year 1996, or fiscal year

beginning .... , 1996, ending .... , 19 ....

► Complete a separate Schedule K-1 for each beneficiary.

OMB No. 1545-0092

1996

Name of trust or decedent's estate

☐ Amended K-1
☐ Final K-1

Beneficiary's identifying number ►

Estate's or trust's EIN ►

Beneficiary's name, address, and ZIP code

Fiduciary's name, address, and ZIP code

(a) Allocable share item		(b) Amount	(c) Calendar year 1996 Form 1040 filers enter the amounts in column (b) on:
1 Interest.	1		Schedule B, Part I, line 1
2 Dividends	2		Schedule B, Part II, line 5
3a Net short-term capital gain	3a		Schedule D, line 5, column (g)
b Net long-term capital gain	3b		Schedule D, line 13, column (g)
4a Annuities, royalties, and other nonpassive income before directly apportioned deductions	4a		Schedule E, Part III, column (f)
b Depreciation	4b		⎫ Include on the applicable line of the appropriate tax form
c Depletion	4c		
d Amortization	4d		⎭
5a Trade or business, rental real estate, and other rental income before directly apportioned deductions (see instructions) .	5a		Schedule E, Part III
b Depreciation	5b		⎫ Include on the applicable line of the appropriate tax form
c Depletion	5c		
d Amortization	5d		⎭
6 Income for minimum tax purposes	6		
7 Income for regular tax purposes (add lines 1 through 3b, 4a, and 5a)	7		
8 Adjustment for minimum tax purposes (subtract line 7 from line 6).	8		Form 6251, line 12
9 Estate tax deduction (including certain generation-skipping transfer taxes)	9		Schedule A, line 27
10 Foreign taxes.	10		Form 1116 or Schedule A (Form 1040), line 8
11 Adjustments and tax preference items (itemize):			
a Accelerated depreciation	11a		⎫ Include on the applicable line of Form 6251
b Depletion	11b		
c Amortization	11c		⎭
d Exclusion items	11d		1997 Form 8801
12 Deductions in the final year of trust or decedent's estate:			
a Excess deductions on termination (see instructions)	12a		Schedule A, line 22
b Short-term capital loss carryover	12b		Schedule D, line 5, column (f)
c Long-term capital loss carryover	12c		Schedule D, line 13, column (f)
d Net operating loss (NOL) carryover for regular tax purposes	12d		Form 1040, line 21
e NOL carryover for minimum tax purposes	12e		See the instructions for Form 6251, line 20
f	12f		⎫ Include on the applicable line
g	12g		⎭ of the appropriate tax form
13 Other (itemize):			
a Payments of estimated taxes credited to you . .	13a		Form 1040, line 53
b Tax-exempt interest	13b		Form 1040, line 8b
c	13c		⎫
d	13d		
e	13e		⎬ Include on the applicable line
f	13f		of the appropriate tax form
g	13g		
h	13h		⎭

For Paperwork Reduction Act Notice, see page 1 of the Instructions for Form 1041.   Cat. No. 11380D   **Schedule K-1 (Form 1041) 1996**

Instructions for Beneficiary Filing Form 1040

Note: *The fiduciary's instructions for completing Schedule K-1 are in the Instructions for Form 1041.*

General Instructions

Purpose of Form

The fiduciary of a trust or decedent's estate uses Schedule K-1 to report your share of the trust's or estate's income, credits, deductions, etc. **Keep it for your records. Do not file it with your tax return.** A copy has been filed with the IRS.

Tax Shelters

If you receive a copy of **Form 8271,** Investor Reporting of Tax Shelter Registration Number, see the instructions for Form 8271 to determine your reporting requirements.

Errors

If you think the fiduciary has made an error on your Schedule K-1, notify the fiduciary and ask for an amended or a corrected Schedule K-1. Do not change any items on your copy. Be sure that the fiduciary sends a copy of the amended Schedule K-1 to the IRS.

Beneficiaries of Generation-Skipping Trusts

If you received **Form 706-GS(D-1),** Notification of Distribution From a Generation-Skipping Trust, and paid a generation-skipping transfer (GST) tax on **Form 706-GS(D),** Generation-Skipping Transfer Tax Return for Distributions, you can deduct the GST tax paid on income distributions on Schedule A (Form 1040), line 8. To figure the deduction, see the instructions for Form 706-GS(D).

Specific Instructions

Lines 3a and 3b

If there is an attachment to this Schedule K-1 reporting a disposition of a passive activity, see the instructions for **Form 8582,** Passive Activity Loss Limitations, for information on the treatment of dispositions of interests in a passive activity.

Lines 5b through 5d

The deductions on lines 5b through 5d may be subject to the passive loss limitations of Internal Revenue Code section 469, which generally limits deductions from passive activities to the income from those activities. The rules for applying these limitations to beneficiaries have not yet been issued. For more details, see **Pub. 925,** Passive Activity and At-Risk Rules.

Line 11d

If you pay alternative minimum tax in 1996, the amount on line 11d will help you figure any minimum tax credit for 1997. See the 1997 **Form 8801,** Credit for Prior Year Minimum Tax—Individuals, Estates, and Trusts, for more information.

Line 13a

To figure any underpayment and penalty on **Form 2210,** Underpayment of Estimated Tax by Individuals, Estates, and Trusts, treat the amount entered on line 13a as an estimated tax payment made on January 15, 1997.

Lines 13c through 13h

The amount of gross farming and fishing income is included on line 5a. This income is also separately stated on line 13 to help you determine if you are subject to a penalty for underpayment of estimated tax. Report the amount of gross farming and fishing income on Schedule E (Form 1040), line 41.

Table A. Checklist of Forms and Due Dates —For Executor, Administrator, or Personal Representative

Form No.	Title	Due Date
SS-4	Application for Employer Identification Number	As soon as possible. The identification number must be included in returns, statements, and other documents.
56	Notice Concerning Fiduciary Relationship	As soon as all of the necessary information is available.*
706	United States Estate (and Generation-Skipping Transfer) Tax Return	9 months after date of decedent's death.
706-A	United States Additional Estate Tax Return	6 months after cessation or disposition of special-use valuation property.
706-CE	Certificate of Payment of Foreign Death Tax	9 months after decedent's death. To be filed with Form 706.
706-GS(D)	Generation-Skipping Transfer Tax Return for Distributions	See form instructions.
706-GS(D-1)	Notification of Distribution From A Generation-Skipping Trust	See form instructions.
706-GS(T)	Generation-Skipping Transfer Tax Return for Terminations	See form instructions.
706-NA	United States Estate (and Generation-Skipping Transfer) Tax Return, Estate of nonresident not a citizen of the United States	9 months after date of decedent's death.
712	Life Insurance Statement	Part I to be filed with estate tax return.
1040	U.S. Individual Income Tax Return	Generally, April 15th of the year after death.
1040NR	U.S. Nonresident Alien Income Tax Return	See form instructions.
1041	U.S. Income Tax Return for Estates and Trusts	15th day of 4th month after end of estate's tax year.
1041-A	U.S. Information Return—Trust Accumulation of Charitable Amounts	April 15th.
1041-T	Allocation of Estimated Tax Payments to Beneficiaries	March 6th.
1041-ES	Estimated Income Tax for Estates and Trusts	Generally, April 15, June 15, Sept. 15, and Jan. 15 for calendar-year filers.
1042	Annual Withholding Tax Return for U.S. Source Income of Foreign Persons	March 15th.
1042-S	Foreign Person's U.S. Source Income Subject to Withholding	March 15th.
1310	Statement of Person Claiming Refund Due a Deceased Taxpayer	To be filed with Form 1040, Form 1040A, Form 1040EZ, or Form 1040NR if refund is due.
2758	Application for Extension of Time To File Certain Excise, Income, Information, and Other Returns	Sufficiently early to permit IRS to consider the application and reply before the due date of Form 1041.
4768	Application for Extension of Time To File a Return and/or Pay U.S. Estate (and Generation-Skipping Transfer) Taxes	Sufficiently early to permit IRS to consider the application and reply before the estate tax due date.
4810	Request for Prompt Assessment Under Internal Revenue Code Section 6501(d)	As soon as possible after filing Form 1040 or Form 1041.
8300	Report of Cash Payments Over $10,000 Received in a Trade or Business	15th day after the date of the transaction.
8822	Change of Address	As soon as the address is changed.

* A personal representative must report the termination of the estate, in writing, to the Internal Revenue Service. Form 56 may be used for this purpose.

Table B. Worksheet to Reconcile Amounts Reported in Name of Decedent on Information Forms (Forms W-2, 1099-INT, 1099-DIV, Etc.) (Please Keep This for Your Records)

Name of Decedent	Date of Death	Decedent's Social Security Number		

Name of Personal Representative, Executor, or Administrator		Estate's Employer Identfication Number (If Any)		

Source (list each payer)	A Enter total amount shown on information form	B Enter part of amount in Column A reportable on decedent's final return	C Amount reportable on estate's or beneficiary's income tax return (Column A minus Column B)	D Portion of Column C that is "income in respect of a decedent"
1. Wages				
2. Interest income				
3. Dividends				
4. State income tax refund				
5. Capital gains				
6. Pension income				
7. Rents, royalties				
8. Taxes withheld*				
9. Other items, such as: social security, business and farm income or loss, unemployment compensation, etc.				

* List each withholding agent (employer, etc.)

Form **1041**	Department of the Treasury—Internal Revenue Service **U.S. Income Tax Return for Estates and Trusts**		**1996**	

For calendar year 1996 or fiscal year beginning _____ , 1996, and ending _____ , 19___ | OMB No. 1545-0092

A Type of entity:
- [✓] Decedent's estate
- [ ] Simple trust
- [ ] Complex trust
- [ ] Grantor type trust
- [ ] Bankruptcy estate-Ch. 7
- [ ] Bankruptcy estate-Ch. 11
- [ ] Pooled income fund

B Number of Schedules K-1 attached (see instructions) ▶ *1*

Name of estate or trust (If a grantor type trust, see page 7 of the instructions.)

Estate of John R. Smith

Name and title of fiduciary
Charles R. Smith, Executor

Number, street, and room or suite no. (If a P.O. box, see page 7 of the instructions.)
6406 Mayflower St.

City or town, state, and ZIP code
Juneville, ME 00000

C Employer identification number
10 : 0123456

D Date entity created
4-9-96

E Nonexempt charitable and split-interest trusts, check applicable boxes (see page 8 of the instructions):
- [ ] Described in section 4947(a)(1)
- [ ] Not a private foundation
- [ ] Described in section 4947(a)(2)

F Check applicable boxes:
- [✓] Initial return
- [ ] Final return
- [ ] Amended return
- [ ] Change in fiduciary's name
- [ ] Change in fiduciary's address

G Pooled mortgage account (see page 9 of the instructions):
- [ ] Bought [ ] Sold. Date:

Income

1	Interest income	1	2,250
2	Dividends	2	750
3	Business income or (loss) (attach Schedule C or C-EZ (Form 1040))	3	
4	Capital gain or (loss) (attach Schedule D (Form 1041))	4	200
5	Rents, royalties, partnerships, other estates and trusts, etc. (attach Schedule E (Form 1040))	5	
6	Farm income or (loss) (attach Schedule F (Form 1040))	6	
7	Ordinary gain or (loss) (attach Form 4797)	7	
8	Other income. List type and amount ...... *Salary and vacation pay*	8	12,000
9	Total income. Combine lines 1 through 8 ▶	9	15,200

Deductions

10	Interest. Check if Form 4952 is attached ▶ [ ]	10	
11	Taxes	11	2,250
12	Fiduciary fees	12	
13	Charitable deduction (from Schedule A, line 7)	13	
14	Attorney, accountant, and return preparer fees	14	325
15a	Other deductions NOT subject to the 2% floor (attach schedule)	15a	
b	Allowable miscellaneous itemized deductions subject to the 2% floor	15b	
16	Total. Add lines 10 through 15b	16	2,575
17	Adjusted total income or (loss). Subtract line 16 from line 9. Enter here and on Schedule B, line 1 ▶	17	12,625
18	Income distribution deduction (from Schedule B, line 17) (attach Schedules K-1 (Form 1041))	18	2,000
19	Estate tax deduction (including certain generation-skipping taxes) (attach computation)	19	
20	Exemption	20	600
21	Total deductions. Add lines 18 through 20 ▶	21	2,600

Tax and Payments

22	Taxable income. Subtract line 21 from line 17. If a loss, see page 13 of the instructions	22	10,025
23	Total tax (from Schedule G, line 8)	23	3,050
24	Payments: a 1996 estimated tax payments and amount applied from 1995 return	24a	
b	Estimated tax payments allocated to beneficiaries (from Form 1041-T)	24b	
c	Subtract line 24b from line 24a	24c	
d	Tax paid with extension of time to file: [ ] Form 2758 [ ] Form 8736 [ ] Form 8800	24d	
e	Federal income tax withheld. If any is from Form(s) 1099, check ▶ [ ]	24e	
	Other payments: f Form 2439 _____ ; g Form 4136 _____ ; Total ▶	24h	
25	Total payments. Add lines 24c through 24e, and 24h ▶	25	
26	Estimated tax penalty (see page 13 of the instructions)	26	
27	Tax due. If line 25 is smaller than the total of lines 23 and 26, enter amount owed	27	3,050
28	Overpayment. If line 25 is larger than the total of lines 23 and 26, enter amount overpaid	28	
29	Amount of line 28 to be: a Credited to 1997 estimated tax ▶ ; b Refunded ▶	29	

Please Sign Here

Under penalties of perjury, I declare that I have examined this return, including accompanying schedules and statements, and to the best of my knowledge and belief, it is true, correct, and complete. Declaration of preparer (other than fiduciary) is based on all information of which preparer has any knowledge.

▶ *Charles R. Smith, Executor* | *3-24-97* | ▶
Signature of fiduciary or officer representing fiduciary | Date | EIN of fiduciary if a financial institution (see page 4 of the instructions)

Paid Preparer's Use Only

Preparer's signature ▶	Date	Check if self-employed ▶ [ ]	Preparer's social security no.
Firm's name (or yours if self-employed) and address ▶		EIN ▶	
		ZIP code ▶	

For Paperwork Reduction Act Notice, see page 1 of the separate instructions. | Cat. No. 11370H | Form **1041** (1996)

Form 1041 (1996) Page **2**

Schedule A — Charitable Deduction. Do not complete for a simple trust or a pooled income fund.

1	Amounts paid for charitable purposes from gross income	1	
2	Amounts permanently set aside for charitable purposes from gross income	2	
3	Add lines 1 and 2	3	
4	Tax-exempt income allocable to charitable contributions (see page 14 of the instructions)	4	
5	Subtract line 4 from line 3	5	
6	Capital gains for the tax year allocated to corpus and paid or permanently set aside for charitable purposes	6	
7	**Charitable deduction.** Add lines 5 and 6. Enter here and on page 1, line 13	7	

Schedule B — Income Distribution Deduction

1	Adjusted total income (from page 1, line 17) (see page 14 of the instructions)	1	12,625
2	Adjusted tax-exempt interest	2	
3	Total net gain from Schedule D (Form 1041), line 17, column (a) (see page 15 of the instructions)	3	
4	Enter amount from Schedule A, line 6	4	
5	Long-term capital gain for the tax year included on Schedule A, line 3	5	
6	Short-term capital gain for the tax year included on Schedule A, line 3	6	
7	If the amount on page 1, line 4, is a capital loss, enter here as a positive figure	7	
8	If the amount on page 1, line 4, is a capital gain, enter here as a negative figure	8	(200)
9	**Distributable net income (DNI).** Combine lines 1 through 8. If zero or less, enter -0-	9	12,425
10	If a complex trust, enter accounting income for the tax year as determined under the governing instrument and applicable local law [10]		
11	Income required to be distributed currently	11	
12	Other amounts paid, credited, or otherwise required to be distributed	12	2,000
13	Total distributions. Add lines 11 and 12. If greater than line 10, see page 15 of the instructions	13	2,000
14	Enter the amount of tax-exempt income included on line 13	14	
15	Tentative income distribution deduction. Subtract line 14 from line 13	15	2,000
16	Tentative income distribution deduction. Subtract line 2 from line 9. If zero or less, enter -0-	16	12,425
17	**Income distribution deduction.** Enter the smaller of line 15 or line 16 here and on page 1, line 18	17	2,000

Schedule G — Tax Computation (see page 16 of the instructions)

1	**Tax:** a ☐ Tax rate schedule or ☐ Schedule D (Form 1041)	1a	3,050	
	b Other taxes	1b		
	c Total. Add lines 1a and 1b			1c 3,050
2a	Foreign tax credit (attach Form 1116)	2a		
b	Check: ☐ Nonconventional source fuel credit ☐ Form 8834	2b		
c	General business credit. Enter here and check which forms are attached: ☐ Form 3800 or ☐ Forms (specify) ▶	2c		
d	Credit for prior year minimum tax (attach Form 8801)	2d		
3	**Total credits.** Add lines 2a through 2d			3
4	Subtract line 3 from line 1c			4 3,050
5	Recapture taxes. Check if from: ☐ Form 4255 ☐ Form 8611			5
6	Alternative minimum tax (from Schedule I, line 41)			6 -0-
7	Household employment taxes. Attach Schedule H (Form 1040)			7
8	**Total tax.** Add lines 4 through 7. Enter here and on page 1, line 23			8 3,050

Other Information

		Yes	No
1	Did the estate or trust receive tax-exempt income? If "Yes," attach a computation of the allocation of expenses. Enter the amount of tax-exempt interest income and exempt-interest dividends ▶ $		✓
2	Did the estate or trust receive all or any part of the earnings (salary, wages, and other compensation) of any individual by reason of a contract assignment or similar arrangement?		✓
3	At any time during calendar year 1996, did the estate or trust have an interest in or a signature or other authority over a bank, securities, or other financial account in a foreign country? See page 17 of the instructions for exceptions and filing requirements for Form TD F 90-22.1. If "Yes," enter the name of the foreign country ▶		✓
4	During the tax year, did the estate or trust receive a distribution from, or was it the grantor of, or transferor to, a foreign trust? If "Yes," see page 17 of the instructions for other forms the estate or trust may have to file		✓
5	Did the estate or trust receive, or pay, any seller-financed mortgage interest? If "Yes," see page 17 of the instructions for required attachment		✓
6	If this is a complex trust making the section 663(b) election, check here (see page 17 of the instructions) ▶ ☐		
7	To make a section 643(e)(3) election, attach Schedule D (Form 1041), and check here (see page 17). ▶ ☐		
8	If the decedent's estate has been open for more than 2 years, check here ▶ ☐		

Page 32

Form 1041 (1996)   Page **3**

| Schedule I | Alternative Minimum Tax (see pages 18 through 22 of the instructions) |

Part I—Estate's or Trust's Share of Alternative Minimum Taxable Income

1	Adjusted total income or (loss) (from page 1, line 17)	**1**	*12,625*
2	Net operating loss deduction. Enter as a positive amount	**2**	
3	Add lines 1 and 2	**3**	*12,625*
4	**Adjustments and tax preference items:**		

a	Interest	**4a**	
b	Taxes	**4b**	*2,250*
c	Miscellaneous itemized deductions (from page 1, line 15b) . . .	**4c**	
d	Refund of taxes	**4d**	( )
e	Depreciation of property placed in service after 1986	**4e**	
f	Circulation and research and experimental expenditures	**4f**	
g	Mining exploration and development costs	**4g**	
h	Long-term contracts entered into after February 28, 1986	**4h**	
i	Amortization of pollution control facilities	**4i**	
j	Installment sales of certain property	**4j**	
k	Adjusted gain or loss (including incentive stock options)	**4k**	
l	Certain loss limitations	**4l**	
m	Tax shelter farm activities	**4m**	
n	Passive activities	**4n**	
o	Beneficiaries of other trusts or decedent's estates	**4o**	
p	Tax-exempt interest from specified private activity bonds	**4p**	
q	Depletion	**4q**	
r	Accelerated depreciation of real property placed in service before 1987	**4r**	
s	Accelerated depreciation of leased personal property placed in service before 1987	**4s**	
t	Intangible drilling costs	**4t**	
u	Other adjustments	**4u**	

5	Combine lines 4a through 4u	**5**	*2,250*
6	Add lines 3 and 5	**6**	*14,875*
7	Alternative tax net operating loss deduction (see page 21 of the instructions for limitations) . .	**7**	
8	Adjusted alternative minimum taxable income. Subtract line 7 from line 6. Enter here and on line 13	**8**	*14,875*
	Note: *Complete Part II before going to line 9.*		
9	Income distribution deduction from line 27	**9**	
10	Estate tax deduction (from page 1, line 19)	**10**	
11	Add lines 9 and 10	**11**	*2,000*
12	Estate's or trust's share of alternative minimum taxable income. Subtract line 11 from line 8 .	**12**	*12,875*

If line 12 is:
* $22,500 or less, stop here and enter -0- on Schedule G, line 6. The estate or trust is not liable for the alternative minimum tax.
* Over $22,500, but less than $165,000, go to line 28.
* $165,000 or more, enter the amount from line 12 on line 34 and go to line 35.

(continued on page 4)

Form 1041 (1996)   Page **4**

Part II—Income Distribution Deduction on a Minimum Tax Basis

13	Adjusted alternative minimum taxable income (from line 8)	13	*14,875*
14	Adjusted tax-exempt interest (other than amounts included on line 4p)	14	
15	Total net gain from Schedule D (Form 1041), line 17, column (a). If a loss, enter -0-	15	
16	Capital gains for the tax year allocated to corpus and paid or permanently set aside for charitable purposes (from Schedule A, line 6)	16	
17	Capital gains paid or permanently set aside for charitable purposes from current year's income (see page 21 of the instructions).	17	
18	Capital gains computed on a minimum tax basis included on line 8	18	(*200*)
19	Capital losses computed on a minimum tax basis included on line 8. Enter as a positive amount	19	
20	Distributable net alternative minimum taxable income (DNAMTI). Combine lines 13 through 19.	20	*14,675*
21	Income required to be distributed currently (from Schedule B, line 11)	21	
22	Other amounts paid, credited, or otherwise required to be distributed (from Schedule B, line 12)	22	*2,000*
23	Total distributions. Add lines 21 and 22	23	*2,000*
24	Tax-exempt income included on line 23 (other than amounts included on line 4p)	24	
25	Tentative income distribution deduction on a minimum tax basis. Subtract line 24 from line 23.	25	*2,000*
26	Tentative income distribution deduction on a minimum tax basis. Subtract line 14 from line 20.	26	*14,675*
27	**Income distribution deduction on a minimum tax basis.** Enter the smaller of line 25 or line 26. Enter here and on line 9	27	*2,000*

Part III—Alternative Minimum Tax

28	Exemption amount		28	$22,500
29	Enter the amount from line 12	29		
30	Phase-out of exemption amount	30	$75,000	
31	Subtract line 30 from line 29. If zero or less, enter -0-	31		
32	Multiply line 31 by 25% (.25)		32	
33	Subtract line 32 from line 28. If zero or less, enter -0- . . . . . . :		33	
34	Subtract line 33 from line 29		34	
35	If line 34 is:			
	• $175,000 or less, multiply line 34 by 26% (.26).			
	• Over $175,000, multiply line 34 by 28% (.28) and subtract $3,500 from the result		35	
36	Alternative minimum foreign tax credit (see page 21 of instructions).		36	
37	Tentative minimum tax. Subtract line 36 from line 35		37	
38	Regular tax before credits (see page 22 of instructions)	38		
39	Section 644 tax included on Schedule G, line 1b	39		
40	Add lines 38 and 39.		40	
41	**Alternative minimum tax.** Subtract line 40 from line 37. If zero or less, enter -0-. Enter here and on Schedule G, line 6		41	

♲ *Printed on recycled paper*

Page 34

SCHEDULE D (Form 1041) Department of the Treasury Internal Revenue Service	Capital Gains and Losses ▶ Attach to Form 1041 (or Form 5227). See the separate instructions for Form 1041 (or Form 5227).	OMB No. 1545-0092 1996

Name of estate or trust	Employer identification number
Estate of John R. Smith	10 : 0123456

Note: *Form 5227 filers need to complete ONLY Parts I and II.*

Part I — Short-Term Capital Gains and Losses—Assets Held One Year or Less

(a) Description of property (Example, 100 shares 7% preferred of "Z" Co.)	(b) Date acquired (mo., day, yr.)	(c) Date sold (mo., day, yr.)	(d) Sales price	(e) Cost or other basis (see instructions)	(f) Gain or (loss) (col. (d) less col. (e))
1					

2 Short-term capital gain or (loss) from Forms 4684, 6252, 6781, and 8824	**2**	
3 Net short-term gain or (loss) from partnerships, S corporations, and other estates or trusts . . .	**3**	
4 Net gain or (loss). Combine lines 1 through 3	**4**	
5 Short-term capital loss carryover from 1995 Schedule D, line 28	**5**	( )
6 Net short-term gain or (loss). Combine lines 4 and 5. Enter here and on line 15 below . . . ▶	**6**	

Part II — Long-Term Capital Gains and Losses—Assets Held More Than One Year

7 *Coin Collection*	*4-9-96*	*9-21-96*	*3,000*	*2,800*	*200*

8 Long-term capital gain or (loss) from Forms 2439, 4684, 6252, 6781, and 8824	**8**	
9 Net long-term gain or (loss) from partnerships, S corporations, and other estates or trusts . . .	**9**	
10 Capital gain distributions	**10**	
11 Gain from Form 4797	**11**	
12 Net gain or (loss). Combine lines 7 through 11	**12**	*200*
13 Long-term capital loss carryover from 1995 Schedule D, line 35	**13**	( )
14 Net long-term gain or (loss). Combine lines 12 and 13. Enter here and on line 16 below . . . ▶	**14**	*200*

Part III — Summary of Parts I and II

		(a) Beneficiaries' (see instructions)	(b) Estate's or trust's	(c) Total
15 Net short-term gain or (loss) from line 6, above	**15**			
16 Net long-term gain or (loss) from line 14, above	**16**		*200*	*200*
17 Total net gain or (loss). Combine lines 15 and 16 . . . ▶	**17**		*200*	*200*

Note: *If line 17, column (c), is a net gain, enter the gain on Form 1041, line 4. If lines 16 and 17, column (b) are net gains, go to Part VI, and DO NOT complete Parts IV and V. If line 17, column (c), is a net loss, complete Parts IV and V, as necessary.*

For Paperwork Reduction Act Notice, see page 1 of the Instructions for Form 1041.　　Cat. No. 11376V　　Schedule D (Form 1041) 1996

Schedule D (Form 1041) 1996

Page **2**

Part IV   Capital Loss Limitation.

18   Enter here and enter as a (loss) on Form 1041, line 4, the smaller of:
   a   The loss on line 17, column (c); or
   b $3,000 . . . .   **18** (   )

If the loss on line 17, column (c) is more than $3,000, OR if Form 1041, page 1, line 22, is a loss, complete Part V to determine your capital loss carryover.

Part V   Capital Loss Carryovers From 1996 to 1997

Section A.—Carryover Limit

19	Enter taxable income or (loss) from Form 1041, line 22.	**19**	
20	Enter loss from line 18 as a positive amount	**20**	
21	Enter amount from Form 1041, line 20	**21**	
22	Adjusted taxable income. Combine lines 19, 20, and 21, but do not enter less than zero	**22**	
23	Enter the smaller of line 20 or line 22.	**23**	

Section B.—Short-Term Capital Loss Carryover
(Complete this part only if there is a loss on line 6 and line 17, column (c).)

24	Enter loss from line 6 as a positive amount	**24**	
25	Enter gain, if any, from line 14. If that line is blank or shows a loss, enter -0- **25**		
26	Enter amount from line 23 . . . . **26**		
27	Add lines 25 and 26	**27**	
28	**Short-term capital loss carryover to 1997.** Subtract line 27 from line 24. If zero or less, enter -0-. If this is the final return of the trust or decedent's estate, also enter on Schedule K-1 (Form 1041), line 12b	**28**	

Section C.—Long-Term Capital Loss Carryover
(Complete this part only if there is a loss on line 14 and line 17, column (c).)

29	Enter loss from line 14 as a positive amount	**29**	
30	Enter gain, if any, from line 6. If that line is blank or shows a loss, enter -0-. . . .	**30**	
31	Enter amount from line 23 . . . . **31**		
32	Enter amount, if any, from line 24 . . . . **32**		
33	Subtract line 32 from line 31. If zero or less, enter -0-	**33**	
34	Add lines 30 and 33	**34**	
35	**Long-term capital loss carryover to 1997.** Subtract line 34 from line 29. If zero or less, enter -0-. If this is the final return of the trust or decedent's estate, also enter on Schedule K-1 (Form 1041), line 12c.	**35**	

Part VI   Tax Computation Using Maximum Capital Gains Rate (Complete this part only if both lines 16 and 17, column (b) are gains, and Form 1041, line 22 is more than $3,800.)

36	Enter taxable income from Form 1041, line 22.	**36**	10,025
37a	Net capital gain. Enter the smaller of line 16 or 17, column (b) **37a** 200		
b	If you are filing Form 4952, enter the amount from Form 4952, line 4e . **37b**		
c	Subtract line 37b from line 37a. If zero or less, stop here; you cannot use Part VI to figure the tax for the estate or trust. Instead, use the 1996 Tax Rate Schedule	**37c**	200
38	Subtract line 37c from line 36. If zero or less, enter -0-.	**38**	9,825
39	Enter the greater of line 38 or $1,600	**39**	9,825
40	Tax on amount on line 39 from the 1996 Tax Rate Schedule. If line 39 is $1,600, enter $240.00 .	**40**	2,994
41	Subtract line 39 from line 36. If zero or less, enter -0-	**41**	200
42	Multiply line 41 by 28% (.28)	**42**	56
43	Maximum capital gains tax. Add lines 40 and 42	**43**	3,050
44	Tax on amount on line 36 from the 1996 Tax Rate Schedule	**44**	3,074
45	**Tax.** Enter the smaller of line 43 or line 44 here and on line 1a of Schedule G, Form 1041 . .	**45**	3,050

Printed on recycled paper

| SCHEDULE K-1
(Form 1041)

Department of the Treasury
Internal Revenue Service | Beneficiary's Share of Income, Deductions, Credits, etc.
for the calendar year 1996, or fiscal year
beginning ...., 1996, ending ...., 19 ....
▶ Complete a separate Schedule K-1 for each beneficiary. | OMB No. 1545-0092

19**96** |

Name of trust or decedent's estate

Estate of John R. Smith

☐ Amended K-1
☐ Final K-1

| Beneficiary's identifying number ▶ *123-00-6789* | Estate's or trust's EIN ▶ *10 0123456* |

Beneficiary's name, address, and ZIP code	Fiduciary's name, address, and ZIP code
James Smith *6407 Mayflower Street,* *Juneville, ME 00000*	*Charles R. Smith, Executor* *6406 Mayflower Street* *Juneville, ME 00000*

(a) Allocable share item		(b) Amount	(c) Calendar year 1996 Form 1040 filers enter the amounts in column (b) on:
1 Interest.	1	*300*	Schedule B, Part I, line 1
2 Dividends	2	*100*	Schedule B, Part II, line 5
3a Net short-term capital gain	3a		Schedule D, line 5, column (g)
b Net long-term capital gain	3b		Schedule D, line 13, column (g)
4a Annuities, royalties, and other nonpassive income before directly apportioned deductions	4a	*1,600*	Schedule E, Part III, column (f)
b Depreciation	4b		Include on the applicable line of the appropriate tax form
c Depletion	4c		
d Amortization	4d		
5a Trade or business, rental real estate, and other rental income before directly apportioned deductions (see instructions)	5a		Schedule E, Part III
b Depreciation	5b		Include on the applicable line of the appropriate tax form
c Depletion	5c		
d Amortization	5d		
6 Income for minimum tax purposes	6	*2,000*	
7 Income for regular tax purposes (add lines 1 through 3b, 4a, and 5a)	7	*2,000*	
8 Adjustment for minimum tax purposes (subtract line 7 from line 6)	8		Form 6251, line 12
9 Estate tax deduction (including certain generation-skipping transfer taxes)	9		Schedule A, line 27
10 Foreign taxes	10		Form 1116 or Schedule A (Form 1040), line 8
11 Adjustments and tax preference items (itemize):			
a Accelerated depreciation	11a		Include on the applicable line of Form 6251
b Depletion	11b		
c Amortization	11c		
d Exclusion items	11d		1997 Form 8801
12 Deductions in the final year of trust or decedent's estate:			
a Excess deductions on termination (see instructions)	12a		Schedule A, line 22
b Short-term capital loss carryover	12b		Schedule D, line 5, column (f)
c Long-term capital loss carryover	12c		Schedule D, line 13, column (f)
d Net operating loss (NOL) carryover for regular tax purposes	12d		Form 1040, line 21
e NOL carryover for minimum tax purposes	12e		See the instructions for Form 6251, line 20
f	12f		Include on the applicable line of the appropriate tax form
g	12g		
13 Other (itemize):			
a Payments of estimated taxes credited to you	13a		Form 1040, line 53
b Tax-exempt interest	13b		Form 1040, line 8b
c	13c		Include on the applicable line of the appropriate tax form
d	13d		
e	13e		
f	13f		
g	13g		
h	13h		

For Paperwork Reduction Act Notice, see page 1 of the instructions for Form 1041.   Cat. No. 11380D   **Schedule K-1 (Form 1041) 1996**

Page 37

DECEASED   John R. Smith - April 9, 1996

Form **1040**   Department of the Treasury—Internal Revenue Service
U.S. Individual Income Tax Return **1996**   (99)   IRS Use Only—Do not write or staple in this space.

For the year Jan. 1–Dec. 31, 1996, or other tax year beginning ____, 1996, ending ____, 19___   OMB No. 1545-0074

Label
(See page 11.)

Use the IRS label. Otherwise, please print or type.

Your first name and initial: John R.	Last name: Smith
If a joint return, spouse's first name and initial: Mary L.	Last name: Smith

Your social security number: 234 00 7890
Spouse's social security number: 567 00 0123

Home address (number and street). If you have a P.O. box, see page 11.   Apt. no.
6406 Mayflower St.

City, town or post office, state, and ZIP code. If you have a foreign address, see page 11.
Juneville, ME   00000

For help finding line instructions, see pages 2 and 3 in the booklet.

Presidential Election Campaign
(See page 11.)

Do you want $3 to go to this fund? . . . .   Yes ✓ No
If a joint return, does your spouse want $3 to go to this fund? . . . . . .   Yes ✓ No

Note: Checking "Yes" will not change your tax or reduce your refund.

Filing Status
Check only one box.

1. ☐ Single
2. ✓ Married filing joint return (even if only one had income)
3. ☐ Married filing separate return. Enter spouse's social security no. above and full name here. ▶ _____
4. ☐ Head of household (with qualifying person). (See instructions.) If the qualifying person is a child but not your dependent, enter this child's name here. ▶ _____
5. ☐ Qualifying widow(er) with dependent child (year spouse died ▶ 19___). (See instructions.)

Exemptions

6a ✓ Yourself. If your parent (or someone else) can claim you as a dependent on his or her tax return, do not check box 6a . . . .

b ✓ Spouse . . . .

No. of boxes checked on lines 6a and 6b: 2

c Dependents:

(1) First name Last name	(2) Dependent's social security number. If born in Dec. 1996, see inst.	(3) Dependent's relationship to you	(4) No. of months lived in your home in 1996

No. of your children on line 6c who:
• lived with you
• did not live with you due to divorce or separation (see instructions)

Dependents on 6c not entered above

If more than six dependents, see the instructions for line 6c.

Add numbers entered on lines above ▶ 2

d Total number of exemptions claimed . . . .

Income

Attach Copy B of your Forms W-2, W-2G, and 1099-R here.

If you did not get a W-2, see the instructions for line 7.

Enclose, but do not attach, any payment. Also, please enclose Form 1040-V (see the instructions for line 62).

7	Wages, salaries, tips, etc. Attach Form(s) W-2	7	9,000
8a	Taxable interest. Attach Schedule B if over $400 . . .	8a	2,740
b	Tax-exempt interest. DO NOT include on line 8a . . 8b		
9	Dividend income. Attach Schedule B if over $400 . .	9	
10	Taxable refunds, credits, or offsets of state and local income taxes (see instructions) .	10	
11	Alimony received	11	
12	Business income or (loss). Attach Schedule C or C-EZ .	12	
13	Capital gain or (loss). If required, attach Schedule D .	13	
14	Other gains or (losses). Attach Form 4797	14	
15a	Total IRA distributions . . 15a	b Taxable amount (see inst.)	15b	
16a	Total pensions and annuities 16a	b Taxable amount (see inst.)	16b	
17	Rental real estate, royalties, partnerships, S corporations, trusts, etc. Attach Schedule E	17	4,008
18	Farm income or (loss). Attach Schedule F	18	
19	Unemployment compensation	19	
20a	Social security benefits 20a	b Taxable amount (see inst.)	20b	
21	Other income. List type and amount—see instructions	21	
22	Add the amounts in the far right column for lines 7 through 21. This is your total income ▶	22	15,748

Adjusted Gross Income

If line 31 is under $28,495 (under $9,500 if a child did not live with you), see the instructions for line 54.

23a	Your IRA deduction (see instructions) 23a	
b	Spouse's IRA deduction (see instructions) 23b	
24	Moving expenses. Attach Form 3903 or 3903-F . . 24	
25	One-half of self-employment tax. Attach Schedule SE 25	
26	Self-employed health insurance deduction (see inst.) . 26	
27	Keogh & self-employed SEP plans. If SEP, check ▶ ☐ 27	
28	Penalty on early withdrawal of savings 28	
29	Alimony paid. Recipient's SSN ▶ _____ 29	
30	Add lines 23a through 29	30	
31	Subtract line 30 from line 22. This is your adjusted gross income ▶	31	15,748

For Privacy Act and Paperwork Reduction Act Notice, see page 7.   Cat. No. 11320B   Form **1040** (1996)

Form 1040 (1996)   Page **2**

Tax Computation	32	Amount from line 31 (adjusted gross income)	32	15,748

33a Check if: ☐ **You** were 65 or older, ☐ Blind; ☐ **Spouse** was 65 or older, ☐ Blind.
Add the number of boxes checked above and enter the total here ► 33a

b If you are married filing separately and your spouse itemizes deductions or you were a dual-status alien, see instructions and check here ► 33b ☐

34 Enter the larger of your:
Itemized deductions from Schedule A, line 28, OR
Standard deduction shown below for your filing status. **But see the** instructions if you checked any box on line 33a or b or someone can claim you as a dependent.
- Single—$4,000 • Married filing jointly or Qualifying widow(er)—$6,700
- Head of household—$5,900 • Married filing separately—$3,350
| 34 | 7,071 |

35 Subtract line 34 from line 32 | 35 | 8,677 |

If you want the IRS to figure your tax, see the instructions for line 37.

36 If line 32 is $88,475 or less, multiply $2,550 by the total number of exemptions claimed on line 6d. If line 32 is over $88,475, see the worksheet in the inst. for the amount to enter. | 36 | 5,100 |

37 **Taxable income.** Subtract line 36 from line 35. If line 36 is more than line 35, enter -0- | 37 | 3,577 |

38 **Tax.** See instructions. Check if total includes any tax from a ☐ Form(s) 8814 b ☐ Form 4972 ► | 38 | 536 |

Credits
39 Credit for child and dependent care expenses. Attach Form 2441 | 39 |
40 Credit for the elderly or the disabled. Attach Schedule R | 40 |
41 Foreign tax credit. Attach Form 1116 | 41 |
42 Other. Check if from a ☐ Form 3800 b ☐ Form 8396 c ☐ Form 8801 d ☐ Form (specify) | 42 |
43 Add lines 39 through 42 | 43 |
44 Subtract line 43 from line 38. If line 43 is more than line 38, enter -0- ► | 44 | 536 |

Other Taxes
45 Self-employment tax. Attach Schedule SE | 45 |
46 Alternative minimum tax. Attach Form 6251 | 46 |
47 Social security and Medicare tax on tip income not reported to employer. Attach Form 4137 | 47 |
48 Tax on qualified retirement plans, including IRAs. If required, attach Form 5329 | 48 |
49 Advance earned income credit payments from Form(s) W-2 | 49 |
50 Household employment taxes. Attach Schedule H | 50 |
51 Add lines 44 through 50. This is your **total tax** ► | 51 | 536 |

Payments
Attach Forms W-2, W-2G, and 1099-R on the front.
52 Federal income tax withheld from Forms W-2 and 1099 | 52 | 2,305 |
53 1996 estimated tax payments and amount applied from 1995 return | 53 |
54 **Earned income credit.** Attach Schedule EIC if you have a qualifying child. Nontaxable earned income: amount ► and type ► | 54 |
55 Amount paid with Form 4868 (request for extension) | 55 |
56 Excess social security and RRTA tax withheld (see inst.) | 56 |
57 Other payments. Check if from a ☐ Form 2439 b ☐ Form 4136 | 57 |
58 Add lines 52 through 57. These are your **total payments** ► | 58 | 2,305 |

Refund
Have it sent directly to your bank account! See inst. and fill in 60b, c, and d.
59 If line 58 is more than line 51, subtract line 51 from line 58. This is the amount you **OVERPAID** ► | 59 | 1,769 |
60a Amount of line 59 you want **REFUNDED TO YOU.** ► | 60a | 1,769 |
b Routing number ___ c Type: ☐ Checking ☐ Savings
d Account number ___
61 Amount of line 59 you want **APPLIED TO YOUR 1997 ESTIMATED TAX** ► | 61 |

Amount You Owe
62 If line 51 is more than line 58, subtract line 58 from line 51. This is the **AMOUNT YOU OWE.** For details on how to pay and use **Form 1040-V**, see instructions ► | 62 |
63 Estimated tax penalty. Also include on line 62 | 63 |

Sign Here
Keep a copy of this return for your records.
Under penalties of perjury, I declare that I have examined this return and accompanying schedules and statements, and to the best of my knowledge and belief, they are true, correct, and complete. Declaration of preparer (other than taxpayer) is based on all information of which preparer has any knowledge.

Your signature: *Charles R. Smith, Executor* Date 3-25-97 Your occupation
Spouse's signature. If a joint return, BOTH must sign. *Mary L. Smith* Date 3-25-97 Spouse's occupation *Homemaker*

Paid Preparer's Use Only
Preparer's signature | Date | Check if self-employed ☐ | Preparer's social security no.
Firm's name (or yours if self-employed) and address | EIN | ZIP code

SCHEDULES A&B
(Form 1040)

Department of the Treasury
Internal Revenue Service (99)

Schedule A—Itemized Deductions

(Schedule B is on back)

▶ Attach to Form 1040. ▶ See Instructions for Schedules A and B (Form 1040).

OMB No. 1545-0074

1996

Attachment Sequence No. **07**

Name(s) shown on Form 1040

John R. (Deceased) & Mary L. Smith

Your social security number

234 00 7890

Medical and Dental Expenses		Caution: *Do not include expenses reimbursed or paid by others.*			
	1	Medical and dental expenses (see page A-1)	1	2,561	
	2	Enter amount from Form 1040, line 32.	2	15,748	
	3	Multiply line 2 above by 7.5% (.075)	3	1,181	
	4	Subtract line 3 from line 1. If line 3 is more than line 1, enter -0-			4 1,380
Taxes You Paid (See page A-1.)	5	State and local income taxes	5	791	
	6	Real estate taxes (see page A-2)	6	1,100	
	7	Personal property taxes	7		
	8	Other taxes. List type and amount ▶	8		
	9	Add lines 5 through 8			9 1,891
Interest You Paid (See page A-2.) **Note:** Personal interest is not deductible.	10	Home mortgage interest and points reported to you on Form 1098	10		
	11	Home mortgage interest not reported to you on Form 1098. If paid to the person from whom you bought the home, see page A-2 and show that person's name, identifying no., and address ▶	11		
	12	Points not reported to you on Form 1098. See page A-3 for special rules	12		
	13	Investment interest. If required, attach Form 4952. (See page A-3.)	13		
	14	Add lines 10 through 13			14
Gifts to Charity If you made a gift and got a benefit for it, see page A-3.	15	Gifts by cash or check. If you made any gift of $250 or more, see page A-3	15	3,800	
	16	Other than by cash or check. If any gift of $250 or more, see page A-3. If over $500, you **MUST** attach Form 8283	16		
	17	Carryover from prior year	17		
	18	Add lines 15 through 17			18 3,800
Casualty and Theft Losses	19	Casualty or theft loss(es). Attach Form 4684. (See page A-4.)			19
Job Expenses and Most Other Miscellaneous Deductions (See page A-4 for expenses to deduct here.)	20	Unreimbursed employee expenses—job travel, union dues, job education, etc. If required, you **MUST** attach Form 2106 or 2106-EZ. (See page A-4.) ▶	20		
	21	Tax preparation fees	21		
	22	Other expenses—investment, safe deposit box, etc. List type and amount ▶	22		
	23	Add lines 20 through 22	23		
	24	Enter amount from Form 1040, line 32.	24		
	25	Multiply line 24 above by 2% (.02)	25		
	26	Subtract line 25 from line 23. If line 25 is more than line 23, enter -0-			26
Other Miscellaneous Deductions	27	Other—from list on page A-4. List type and amount ▶			27
Total Itemized Deductions	28	Is Form 1040, line 32, over $117,950 (over $58,975 if married filing separately)? **NO.** Your deduction is not limited. Add the amounts in the far right column for lines 4 through 27. Also, enter on Form 1040, line 34, the **larger of** this amount or your standard deduction. **YES.** Your deduction may be limited. See page A-5 for the amount to enter.		▶	28 7,071

For Paperwork Reduction Act Notice, see Form 1040 instructions. Cat. No. 11330X Schedule A (Form 1040) 1996

Schedules A&B (Form 1040) 1996   OMB No. 1545-0074   Page **2**

Name(s) shown on Form 1040. Do not enter name and social security number if shown on other side. | Your social security number

Schedule B—Interest and Dividend Income

Attachment Sequence No. **08**

Part I Interest Income (See page B-1.)

Note: If you had over $400 in taxable interest income, you must also complete Part III.

		Amount
1	List name of payer. If any interest is from a seller-financed mortgage and the buyer used the property as a personal residence, see page B-1 and list this interest first. Also, show that buyer's social security number and address ▶	
	First S&L of Jumeville	1,900
	Series EE U.S. Savings Bonds – Interest Includible Before Decedent's Death	840

Note: If you received a Form 1099-INT, Form 1099-OID, or substitute statement from a brokerage firm, list the firm's name as the payer and enter the total interest shown on that form.

2	Add the amounts on line 1	2,740
3	Excludable interest on series EE U.S. savings bonds issued after 1989 from Form 8815, line 14. You MUST attach Form 8815 to Form 1040	-0-
4	Subtract line 3 from line 2. Enter the result here and on Form 1040, line 8a ▶	2,740

Part II Dividend Income (See page B-1.)

Note: If you had over $400 in gross dividends and/or other distributions on stock, you must also complete Part III.

		Amount
5	List name of payer. Include gross dividends and/or other distributions on stock here. Any capital gain distributions and nontaxable distributions will be deducted on lines 7 and 8 ▶	

Note: If you received a Form 1099-DIV or substitute statement from a brokerage firm, list the firm's name as the payer and enter the total dividends shown on that form.

6	Add the amounts on line 5	
7	Capital gain distributions. Enter here and on Schedule D*	
8	Nontaxable distributions. (See the inst. for Form 1040, line 9.)	
9	Add lines 7 and 8	
10	Subtract line 9 from line 6. Enter the result here and on Form 1040, line 9 ▶	

*If you do not need Schedule D to report any other gains or losses, see the instructions for Form 1040, line 13.

Part III Foreign Accounts and Trusts (See page B-1.)

You must complete this part if you (a) had over $400 of interest or dividends; (b) had a foreign account; or (c) received a distribution from, or were a grantor of, or a transferor to, a foreign trust.

		Yes	No
11a	At any time during 1996, did you have an interest in or a signature or other authority over a financial account in a foreign country, such as a bank account, securities account, or other financial account? See page B-1 for exceptions and filing requirements for Form TD F 90-22.1		✓
b	If "Yes," enter the name of the foreign country ▶		
12	During 1996, did you receive a distribution from, or were you the grantor of, or transferor to, a foreign trust? If "Yes," see page B-2 for other forms you may have to file		✓

For Paperwork Reduction Act Notice, see Form 1040 instructions.   Schedule B (Form 1040) 1996

SCHEDULE E
(Form 1040)

Department of the Treasury
Internal Revenue Service   (99)

Supplemental Income and Loss

(From rental real estate, royalties, partnerships,
S corporations, estates, trusts, REMICs, etc.)

▶ Attach to Form 1040 or Form 1041.   ▶ See Instructions for Schedule E (Form 1040).

OMB No. 1545-0074

1996

Attachment
Sequence No. **13**

Name(s) shown on return: *John R. (Deceased) & Mary L. Smith*

Your social security number: *234 00 7890*

Part I Income or Loss From Rental Real Estate and Royalties Note: *Report income and expenses from your business of renting personal property on Schedule C or C-EZ (see page E-1). Report farm rental income or loss from Form 4835 on page 2, line 39.*

1 Show the kind and location of each rental real estate property:

A *House., 137 Main Street, Juneville, ME. 00000*
B
C

2 For each rental real estate property listed on line 1, did you or your family use it for personal purposes for more than the greater of 14 days or 10% of the total days rented at fair rental value during the tax year? (See page E-1.)

	Yes	No
A		✓
B		
C		

Income:

		A	B	C		Totals (Add columns A, B, and C.)
3	Rents received	8,400			3	
4	Royalties received				4	

Expenses:

		A	B	C		
5	Advertising					
6	Auto and travel (see page E-2)					
7	Cleaning and maintenance					
8	Commissions					
9	Insurance	260				
10	Legal and other professional fees					
11	Management fees					
12	Mortgage interest paid to banks, etc. (see page E-2)	410			12	
13	Other interest					
14	Repairs	350				
15	Supplies					
16	Taxes	700				
17	Utilities					
18	Other (list) ▶					
19	Add lines 5 through 18	1,720			19	
20	Depreciation expense or depletion (see page E-2)	2,672			20	
21	Total expenses. Add lines 19 and 20	4,392				
22	Income or (loss) from rental real estate or royalty properties. Subtract line 21 from line 3 (rents) or line 4 (royalties). If the result is a (loss), see page E-2 to find out if you must file **Form 6198**	4,008				
23	Deductible rental real estate loss. **Caution:** *Your rental real estate loss on line 22 may be limited. See page E-3 to find out if you must file* **Form 8582.** *Real estate professionals must complete line 42 on page 2*	(	)(	)(	)	

24 **Income.** Add positive amounts shown on line 22. **Do not** include any losses . . . . | 24 | 4,008

25 **Losses.** Add royalty losses from line 22 and rental real estate losses from line 23. Enter the total losses here . | 25 | ( )

26 Total rental real estate and royalty income or (loss). Combine lines 24 and 25. Enter the result here. If Parts II, III, IV, and line 39 on page 2 do not apply to you, also enter this amount on Form 1040, line 17. Otherwise, include this amount in the total on line 40 on page 2 . . . . | 26 | 4,008

For Paperwork Reduction Act Notice, see Form 1040 Instructions.   Cat. No. 11344L   Schedule E (Form 1040) 1996

Form 4562

Department of the Treasury
Internal Revenue Service (99)

Depreciation and Amortization
(Including Information on Listed Property)

▶ See separate instructions. ▶ Attach this form to your return.

OMB No. 1545-0172

1996

Attachment
Sequence No. **67**

Name(s) shown on return	Business or activity to which this form relates	Identifying number
John R. (Deceased) & Mary L. Smith		234-00-7890

Part I — Election To Expense Certain Tangible Property (Section 179) (Note: *If you have any "listed property," complete Part V before you complete Part I.*)

1	Maximum dollar limitation. If an enterprise zone business, see page 2 of the instructions . .	1	$17,500
2	Total cost of section 179 property placed in service. See page 2 of the instructions	2	
3	Threshold cost of section 179 property before reduction in limitation	3	$200,000
4	Reduction in limitation. Subtract line 3 from line 2. If zero or less, enter -0-	4	
5	Dollar limitation for tax year. Subtract line 4 from line 1. If zero or less, enter -0-. If married filing separately, see page 2 of the instructions	5	

(a) Description of property	(b) Cost (business use only)	(c) Elected cost
6		

7	Listed property. Enter amount from line 27	7	
8	Total elected cost of section 179 property. Add amounts in column (c), lines 6 and 7 . . .	8	
9	Tentative deduction. Enter the smaller of line 5 or line 8	9	
10	Carryover of disallowed deduction from 1995. See page 2 of the instructions	10	
11	Business income limitation. Enter the smaller of business income (not less than zero) or line 5 (see instructions)	11	
12	Section 179 expense deduction. Add lines 9 and 10, but do not enter more than line 11 . .	12	
13	Carryover of disallowed deduction to 1997. Add lines 9 and 10, less line 12 ▶	13	

Note: *Do not use Part II or Part III below for listed property (automobiles, certain other vehicles, cellular telephones, certain computers, or property used for entertainment, recreation, or amusement). Instead, use Part V for listed property.*

Part II — MACRS Depreciation For Assets Placed in Service ONLY During Your 1996 Tax Year (Do Not Include Listed Property.)

Section A—General Asset Account Election

14	If you are making the election under section 168(i)(4) to group any assets placed in service during the tax year into one or more general asset accounts, check this box. See page 2 of the instructions . . . . ▶	☐

Section B—General Depreciation System (GDS) (See page 3 of the instructions.)

(a) Classification of property	(b) Month and year placed in service	(c) Basis for depreciation (business/investment use only—see instructions)	(d) Recovery period	(e) Convention	(f) Method	(g) Depreciation deduction
15a 3-year property						
b 5-year property						
c 7-year property						
d 10-year property						
e 15-year property						
f 20-year property						
g 25-year property			25 yrs.		S/L	
h Residential rental property			27.5 yrs.	MM	S/L	
			27.5 yrs.	MM	S/L	
i Nonresidential real property			39 yrs.	MM	S/L	
				MM	S/L	

Section C—Alternative Depreciation System (ADS) (See page 4 of the instructions.)

16a Class life					S/L	
b 12-year			12 yrs.		S/L	
c 40-year	4-96	45,000	40 yrs.	MM	S/L	797

Part III — Other Depreciation (Do Not Include Listed Property.) (See page 4 of the instructions.)

17	GDS and ADS deductions for assets placed in service in tax years beginning before 1996	17	
18	Property subject to section 168(f)(1) election	18	
19	ACRS and other depreciation	19	1,875

Part IV — Summary (See page 4 of the instructions.)

20	Listed property. Enter amount from line 26	20	
21	Total. Add deductions on line 12, lines 15 and 16 in column (g), and lines 17 through 20. Enter here and on the appropriate lines of your return. Partnerships and S corporations—see instructions . .	21	2,672
22	For assets shown above and placed in service during the current year, enter the portion of the basis attributable to section 263A costs	22	

For Paperwork Reduction Act Notice, see page 1 of the separate instructions.　　Cat. No. 12906N　　Form **4562** (1996)

Page 30

**Department
of the
Treasury**

**Internal
Revenue
Service**

Publication 559
Cat. No. 15107U

Survivors, Executors, and Administrators

For use in preparing

1996 Returns

Get forms and other information faster and easier by:
COMPUTER
- World Wide Web▶ http://www.irs.ustreas.gov
- FTP▶ ftp.irs.ustreas.gov
- IRIS at FedWorld▶ (703) 321-8020

FAX
- From your FAX machine, dial▶(703) 487-4160.

See *How To Get More Information* in this publication.

Contents

Important Changes

Individual taxpayer identification number (ITIN). The IRS will issue an ITIN to a nonresident or resident alien who does not have and is not eligible to get a social security number (SSN). To apply for an ITIN, file Form W-7 with the IRS. It usually takes 30 days to get it. The ITIN is entered wherever an SSN is requested on a tax return.

An ITIN is for tax use only. It does not entitle the holder to social security benefits or change the holder's employment or immigration status under U.S. law.

Death benefit exclusion repealed. The death benefit exclusion does not apply with respect to employees dying after August 20, 1996.

Basis of inherited S corporation stock. The basis of inherited S corporation stock must be reduced if there is income in respect of a decedent attributable to that stock. This provision is effective with respect to decedents dying after August 20, 1996.

Introduction

This publication is designed to help those in charge of the property (estate) of an individual who has died. It shows them how to complete and file federal income tax returns and points out their responsibility to pay any taxes due.

A comprehensive example, using tax forms, is included near the end of this publication. Also included at the end of this publication are:

1) A checklist of the forms you may need and their due dates, and

2) A worksheet to reconcile amounts reported in the decedent's name on information Forms W-2, 1099-INT, 1099-DIV, etc. The worksheet will help you correctly determine the income to report on the decedent's final return and on the returns for either the estate or a beneficiary.

Useful Items

You may want to see:

Publication

☐ **950** Introduction to Estate and Gift Taxes

Form (and Instructions)

☐ **1040** U.S. Individual Income Tax Return

☐ **1041** U.S. Income Tax Return for Estates and Trusts

☐ **706** United States Estate (and Generation-Skipping Transfer) Tax Return

See *How To Get More Information,* near the end of this publication for information about getting these publications and forms.

Personal Representatives

A *personal representative* of an estate is an executor, administrator, or anyone who is in charge of the decedent's property. Generally, an *executor* (or executrix) is named in a decedent's will to administer the estate and distribute properties as the decedent has directed. An *administrator* (or administratrix) is usually appointed by the court if no will exists, if no executor was named in the will, or if the named executor cannot or will not serve.

In general, an executor and an administrator perform the same duties and have the same responsibilities.

For estate tax purposes, if there is no executor or administrator appointed, qualified, and acting within the United States, the term "executor" includes anyone in actual or constructive possession of any property of the decedent. It includes, among others, the decedent's agents and representatives; safe-deposit companies, warehouse companies, and other custodians of property in this country; brokers holding securities of the decedent as collateral; and the debtors of the decedent who are in this country.

Because a personal representative for a decedent's estate can be an executor, administrator, or anyone in charge of the decedent's property, the term "personal representative" will be used throughout this publication.

Duties

The primary duties of a personal representative are to collect all the decedent's assets, pay the creditors, and distribute the remaining assets to the heirs or other beneficiaries.

The personal representative also must:

1) File any income tax return and the estate tax return when due, and

2) Pay the tax determined up to the date of discharge from duties.

Other duties of the personal representative in federal tax matters are discussed in other sections of this publication. If any beneficiary is a nonresident alien, get Publication 515, *Withholding of Tax on Nonresident Aliens and Foreign Corporations,* for information on the personal representative's duties as a withholding agent.

Penalty. There is a penalty for failure to file a tax return when due unless the failure is due to reasonable cause. Relying on an agent (attorney, accountant, etc.) is not reasonable cause for late filing. It is the personal representative's duty to file the returns for the decedent and the estate when due.

Identification number. The first action you should take if you are the personal representative for the decedent is to apply for an *employer identification number* for the estate. You should apply for this number as soon as possible because you need to enter it on returns, statements, and other documents that you file concerning the estate. You must also give the number to payers of interest and dividends and other payers who must file a return concerning the estate. You must apply for the number on *Form SS-4, Application for Employer Identification Number,* available from IRS and Social Security Administration offices.

Payers of interest and dividends report amounts on Forms 1099 using the identification number of the person to whom the account is payable. After a decedent's death, the Forms 1099 must reflect the identification number of the estate or beneficiary to whom the amounts are payable. As the personal representative handling the estate you must furnish this identification number to the payer. For example, if interest is payable to the estate, the estate's identification number must be provided to the payer and used to report the interest on Form 1099-INT, *Interest Income.* If the interest is payable to a surviving joint owner, the survivor's identification number must be provided to the payer and used to report the interest.

The deceased individual's identifying number must not be used to file an individual tax return after the decedent's final tax return. It also must not be used to make estimated tax payments for a tax year after the year of death.

Penalty. If you do not include the employer identification number on any return, statement, or other document, you are liable for a penalty for each failure, unless you can show reasonable cause. You are also liable for a penalty if you do not give the employer identification number to another person, or if you do not include the taxpayer identification number of another person on a return, statement, or other document.

Notice of fiduciary relationship. The term "fiduciary" means any person acting for another person. It applies to persons who have positions of trust on behalf of others. A personal representative for a decedent's estate is a fiduciary.

If you are appointed to act in any fiduciary capacity for another, you must file a written notice with the IRS stating this. *Form 56, Notice Concerning Fiduciary Relationship,* can be used for this purpose. The instructions and other requirements are given on the back of the form.

Filing the notice. File the written notice (or Form 56) with the IRS service center where the returns are filed for the person (or estate) for whom you are acting. You should file this notice as soon as all of the necessary information (including the employer identification number) is available. It notifies the IRS that, as the fiduciary, you are assuming the powers, rights, duties, and privileges of the decedent, and allows the IRS to mail to you all tax notices concerning the person (or estate) you represent. The notice remains in effect until you notify the appropriate IRS office that your relationship to the estate has terminated.

Termination notice. When you are relieved of your responsibilities as personal representative, you must advise the IRS office where you filed the written notice (or Form 56) either that the estate has been terminated or that your successor has been appointed. If the estate is terminated, you must furnish satisfactory evidence of the termination of the estate. Use Form 56 for the termination notice by completing the appropriate part on the form and attaching the required evidence. If another has been appointed to succeed you as the personal representative, you should give the name and address of your successor.

Request for prompt assessment (charge) of tax. The IRS ordinarily has 3 years from the date an income tax return is filed, or its due date, whichever is later, to charge any additional tax that is due. However, as a personal representative you may request a prompt assessment of tax after the return has been filed. This reduces the time for making the assessment to 18 months from the date the written request for prompt assessment was received. This request can be made for any income tax return of the decedent and for the income tax return of the decedent's estate. This may permit a quicker settlement of the tax liability of the estate and an earlier final distribution of the assets to the beneficiaries.

Form 4810. Form 4810, *Request for Prompt Assessment Under Internal Revenue Code Section 6501(d)*, can be used for making this request. It must be filed separately from any other document. The request should be filed with the IRS office where the return was filed. If Form 4810 is not used, you must clearly indicate that it is a request for prompt assessment under section 6501(d) of the Internal Revenue Code.

As the personal representative for the decedent's estate, you are responsible for any additional taxes that may be due. You can request prompt assessment of any taxes (other than federal estate taxes) for any open years for the decedent, even though the returns were filed before the decedent's death.

Failure to report income. If you or the decedent failed to report substantial amounts of gross income (more than 25% of the gross income reported on the return) or filed a false or fraudulent return, your request for prompt assessment will not shorten the period during which the IRS may assess the additional tax. However, such a request may relieve you of personal liability for the tax if you did not have knowledge of the unpaid tax.

Insolvent estate. If a decedent's estate is insufficient to pay all the decedent's debts, the debts due the United States must be paid first. Both the decedent's federal income tax liabilities at the time of death and the estate's income tax liability are debts due the United States. The personal representative of an insolvent estate is personally responsible for any tax liability of the decedent or of the estate if he or she had notice of such tax obligations or had failed to exercise due care in determining if such obligations existed before distribution of the estate's assets and before being discharged from duties. The extent of such personal responsibility is the amount of any other payments made before paying the debts due the United States. The income tax liabilities need not be formally assessed for the personal representative to be liable if he or she

was aware or should have been aware of their existence.

Fees Received by Personal Representatives

All personal representatives must include in their gross incomes fees paid to them from an estate. If paid to a professional executor or administrator, self-employment tax also applies to such fees. For a nonprofessional executor or administrator (a person serving in such capacity in an isolated instance, such as a friend or relative of the decedent), self-employment tax only applies if a trade or business is included in the estate's assets, the executor actively participates in the business, and the fees are related to operation of the business.

Final Return for Decedent

The personal representative (defined earlier) must file the final income tax return of the decedent for the year of death and any returns not filed for preceding years. A surviving spouse, under certain circumstances, may have to file the returns for the decedent. See *Joint Return*, below.

Return for preceding year. If an individual died after the close of the tax year, but before the return for that year was filed, the return for the year just closed will not be the final return. The return for that year will be a regular return and the personal representative must file it.

Example. Samantha Smith died on March 21, 1996, before filing her 1995 tax return. Her personal representative must file her 1995 return by April 15, 1996. Her final tax return is due April 15, 1997.

Filing Requirements

The income, age, and filing status of a decedent generally determine the filing requirements. In general, filing status depends on whether the decedent was considered single or married at the time of death. Gross income usually means money, goods, and property an individual received on which he or she must pay tax. It includes gross receipts from self-employment minus any cost of goods sold. It does not include nontaxable income. See Publication 501, *Exemptions, Standard Deduction, and Filing Information*.

Refund

A return should be filed to obtain a refund if tax was withheld from salaries, wages, pensions, or annuities, or if estimated tax was paid, even if a return is not required to be filed. Also, the decedent may be entitled to other credits that result in a refund. These advance payments of tax and credits are discussed later under *Credits, Other Taxes, and Payments*.

Form 1310. Generally, a person who is filing a return for a decedent and claiming a refund must file a Form 1310, *Statement of Person*

Claiming Refund Due a Deceased Taxpayer, with the return. However, if the person claiming the refund is a surviving spouse filing a joint return with the decedent, or a court-appointed or certified personal representative filing an original return for the decedent, Form 1310 is not needed. The personal representative must attach to the return a copy of the court certificate showing that he or she was appointed the personal representative.

Example. Assume that Mr. Green died on January 4, 1996, before filing his tax return. On April 3 of the same year, you were appointed the personal representative for Mr. Green's estate, and you filed his Form 1040 showing a refund due. You do not need Form 1310 to claim the refund if you attach a copy of the court certificate showing you were appointed the personal representative.

Nonresident Alien

If the decedent was a nonresident alien who would have had to file Form 1040NR, *U.S. Nonresident Alien Income Tax Return*, you must file that form for the decedent's final tax year. See the instructions for Form 1040NR for the filing requirements, due date, and where to file.

Joint Return

Generally, the personal representative and the surviving spouse can file a joint return for the decedent and the surviving spouse. However, the surviving spouse alone can file the joint return if no personal representative has been appointed before the due date for filing the final joint return for the year of death. This also applies to the return for the preceding year if the decedent died after the close of the preceding tax year and before the due date for filing that return. The income of the decedent that was includible on his or her return for the year up to the date of death (see *Income To Include*, later) and the income of the surviving spouse for the entire year must be included in the final joint return.

A final joint return with the deceased spouse cannot be filed if the surviving spouse remarried before the end of the year of the decedent's death. The filing status of the deceased spouse in this instance is "married filing separate return."

For information about tax benefits a surviving spouse may be entitled to, see *Tax Benefits for Survivors*, later under *Other Tax Information*.

Personal representative may revoke joint return election. A court-appointed personal representative may revoke an election to file a joint return that was previously made by the surviving spouse alone. This is done by filing a separate return for the decedent within one year from the due date of the return (including any extensions). The joint return made by the surviving spouse will then be regarded as the separate return of that spouse by excluding the decedent's items and refiguring the tax liability.

Page 3

Income To Include

The decedent's income includible on the final return is generally determined as if the person were still alive except that the taxable period is usually shorter because it ends on the date of death. The method of accounting regularly used by the decedent before death also determines the income includible on the final return. This section explains how some types of income are reported on the final return.

For more information about accounting methods, get Publication 538, *Accounting Periods and Methods.*

Under the Cash Method

If the decedent accounted for income under the cash method, only those items actually or constructively received before death are accounted for in the final return.

Constructive receipt of income. Interest from coupons on the decedent's bonds was constructively received by the decedent if the coupons matured in the decedent's final tax year, but had not been cashed. Include the interest in the final return.

Generally, a dividend was constructively received if it was available for use by the decedent without restriction. If the corporation customarily mailed its dividend checks, the dividend was includible when received. If the individual died between the time the dividend was declared and the time it was received in the mail, the decedent did not constructively receive it before death. Do not include the dividend in the final return.

Under an Accrual Method

Generally, under an accrual method of accounting, income is reported when earned.

If the decedent used an accrual method, only the income items normally accrued before death are to be included in the final return.

Partnership Income

The death of a partner generally does not close the partnership's tax year before it normally ends. It continues for both the remaining partners and the deceased partner. Even if the partnership has only two partners, the death of one does not terminate the partnership or close its tax year, provided the deceased partner's estate or successor continues to share in the partnership's profits or losses. If the surviving partner terminates the partnership by discontinuing its business operations, the partnership tax year closes as of the date of termination. If the deceased partner's estate or successor sells, exchanges, or liquidates its entire interest in the partnership, the partnership's tax year for the estate or successor will close as of the date of the sale or exchange or the date the liquidation is completed.

On the decedent's final return include the decedent's distributive share of partnership income for the partnership's tax year ending within or with the decedent's last tax year (the year ending on the date of death).

Do not include on the final return the distributive share of partnership income for a partnership's tax year ending after the decedent's death. In this case, partnership income earned up to and including the date of death is income in respect of the decedent, discussed later. Income earned after the date of death to the end of the partnership's tax year is income to the estate or successor in interest.

Example. Mary Smith was a partner in XYZ partnership and reported her income on a tax year ending December 31. The partnership uses a tax year ending June 30. Mary died August 31, 1996, and her estate established its tax year ending August 31.

The distributive share of taxable income from the partnership based on the decedent's partnership interest is reported as follows:

1) Final Return for the Decedent — January 1 through August 31, 1996, includes income from the XYZ partnership year ending June 30, 1996.

2) Income Tax Return of the Estate — September 1, 1996, through August 31, 1997, includes income from the XYZ partnership year ending June 30, 1997. The portion of income from the partnership for the period July 1, 1996, through August 31, 1996, is income in respect of a decedent.

S Corporation Income

If the decedent was a shareholder in an S corporation, you must include on the final return the decedent's share of S corporation income for the corporation's tax year that ends within or with the decedent's last tax year (year ending on the date of death). The final return must also include the decedent's pro rata share of the S corporation's income for the period between the end of the corporation's last tax year and the date of death.

The income for the part of the S corporation's tax year after the shareholder's death is income to the estate or other person who has acquired the stock in the S corporation.

Self-Employment Income

Include self-employment income actually or constructively received or accrued, depending on the decedent's accounting method. For self-employment tax purposes only, the decedent's self-employment income will include the decedent's distributive share of a partnership's income or loss through the end of the month in which death occurred. For this purpose only, the partnership's income or loss is considered to be earned ratably over the partnership's tax year.

Community Income

If the decedent was married and was domiciled in a community property state, half of the income received and half of the expenses paid during the decedent's tax year by either the decedent or spouse may be considered to be the income and expense of the other. For more information, get Publication 555, *Community Property.*

Interest and Dividend Income (Forms 1099)

A Form 1099 should be received for the decedent reporting interest and dividends that were includible on his or her return before death. A separate Form 1099 should be received showing the interest and dividends includible on the returns of the estate or other recipient after the date of death and payable to the estate or other recipient. You can request corrected Forms 1099, if these forms do not properly reflect the right recipient or amounts.

The amount reported on Form 1099-INT or Form 1099-DIV, *Dividends and Distributions,* may not necessarily be the correct amount that should be properly reported on each income tax return. For example, a Form 1099-INT reporting interest payable to a decedent may include income that should be reported on the final income tax return of the decedent, as well as income that the estate or other recipient should report, either as income earned after death or as income in respect of the decedent (discussed later). For income earned after death, you should ask the payer for a Form 1099 that properly identifies the recipient (by name and identification number) and the proper amount. If that is not possible, or if the form includes an amount that represents income in respect of the decedent, include an explanation, such as that shown under *How to report,* next, describing the amounts that are properly reported on the decedent's final return.

How to report. If you are preparing the decedent's final return and you have received a Form 1099-INT or a Form 1099-DIV for the decedent that includes amounts belonging to the decedent and to another recipient (the decedent's estate or another beneficiary), report the total interest shown on Form 1099-INT on Schedule 1 (Form 1040A) or on Schedule B (Form 1040). Next, enter a "subtotal" of the interest shown on Forms 1099, and the interest reportable from other sources for which you did not receive Forms 1099. Show any interest (including any interest you receive as a nominee) belonging to another recipient separately and subtract it from the subtotal. Identify the amount of this adjustment as "Nominee Distribution" or other appropriate designation. Report dividend income on the appropriate schedule using the same procedure.

Note. If the decedent received amounts as a nominee, you must give the actual owner a Form 1099, unless the owner is the decedent's spouse.

Exemptions and Deductions

Generally, the rules for exemptions and deductions allowed to an individual also apply to the decedent's final income tax return. Show on the final return deductible items the decedent paid before death (or accrued, if the decedent reported deductions on an accrual method). This section contains a detailed discussion of medical expenses because, under certain conditions, the tax treatment can be different for the medical expenses of the decedent. See *Medical Expenses*, below.

Exemptions

You can claim the personal exemption in full on a final income tax return. If the decedent was another person's dependent (i.e., a parent's), you cannot claim the personal exemption on the decedent's final return.

Standard Deduction

If you do not itemize deductions on the final return, the full amount of the appropriate standard deduction is allowed regardless of the date of death. For information on the appropriate standard deduction, get Publication 501, *Exemptions, Standard Deduction, and Filing Information*.

Medical Expenses

Medical expenses paid before death by the decedent are deductible on the final income tax return if deductions are itemized. This includes expenses for the decedent as well as for the decedent's spouse and dependents.

Election for decedent's expenses. Medical expenses that are not deductible on the final income tax return are liabilities of the estate and are shown on the federal estate tax return (Form 706). However, if medical expenses for the decedent are paid out of the estate during the 1–year period beginning with the day after death, you can elect to treat all or part of the expenses as paid by the decedent at the time they were incurred.

If you make the election, you can claim all or part of the expenses on the decedent's income tax return rather than on the federal estate tax return (Form 706). You can deduct expenses incurred in the year of death on the final income tax return. You should file an amended return (Form 1040X) for medical expenses incurred in an earlier year, unless the statutory period for filing a claim for that year has expired.

Making the election. You make the election by filing with the decedent's income tax return, or amended return, a statement in duplicate that you have not claimed the amount as an estate tax deduction, and that the estate waives the right to claim the amount as a deduction. This election applies only to expenses incurred for the decedent, not to expenses incurred to provide medical care for dependents.

Deduction. The amount you can deduct on the income tax return is the amount above 7.5% of adjusted gross income. The amounts not deductible because of this percentage cannot be claimed on the federal estate tax return.

Example. Richard Brown used the cash method of accounting and filed his income tax return on a calendar year basis. Mr. Brown died on June 1, 1996, after incurring $800 in medical expenses. Of that amount, $500 was incurred in 1995 and $300 was incurred in 1996. Richard filed his 1995 income tax return

before April 15, 1996. The personal representative of the estate paid the entire $800 liability in August 1996.

The personal representative may then file an amended return (Form 1040X) for 1995 claiming the $500 medical expense as a deduction. The $300 of expenses incurred in 1996 can be deducted on the final income tax return, although it was paid after Richard's death. The personal representative must file a statement in duplicate with each return stating that these amounts have not been claimed on the federal estate tax return (Form 706), and waiving the right to claim such a deduction on Form 706 in the future.

Medical expenses not paid by estate. Medical expenses for the care of the decedent paid by a survivor who can claim the decedent as a dependent are deductible on the survivor's income tax return for the tax year in which paid, whether or not they are paid before or after the decedent's death. If the decedent was a child of divorced or separated parents, the medical expenses are usually deductible by both the custodial and noncustodial parent to the extent paid by each parent during the year. See Publication 502, *Medical and Dental Expenses*, for more information.

Insurance reimbursements. Insurance reimbursements of previously deducted medical expenses due a decedent at the time of death and later received by the decedent's estate are includible in the income tax return of the estate (Form 1041) for the year the reimbursements are received. The reimbursements are also includible in the decedent's gross estate.

Deduction for Losses

You can deduct a decedent's net operating loss from prior-year business operations and any capital losses (capital losses include capital loss carryovers) only on the decedent's final income tax return. You cannot deduct any unused net operating loss or capital loss on the estate's income tax return. However, a net operating loss carryback resulting from a net business loss on the decedent's final income tax return can be carried back to prior years.

At-risk loss limits. Special at-risk rules apply to most activities that are engaged in as a trade or business or for the production of income.

These rules limit the amount of deductible loss to the amount for which the decedent was considered at risk in the activity. A decedent generally will be considered at risk to the extent of the cash and the adjusted basis of property that he or she contributed to the activity and any amounts the decedent borrowed for use in the activity. However, a decedent will be considered at risk for amounts borrowed only if he or she was personally liable for the repayment or if the amounts borrowed were secured by property other than that used in the activity. The decedent is not considered at risk for borrowed amounts if the lender has an interest in the activity or if the lender is related to the decedent. For more information,

get Publication 925, *Passive Activity and At-Risk Rules*.

Passive activity rules. A passive activity is any trade or business activity in which the taxpayer does not materially participate. To determine material participation, get Publication 925. Rental activities are also passive activities regardless of the taxpayer's participation, unless the taxpayer meets certain eligibility requirements.

Individuals, estates, and trusts can offset passive activity losses only against passive activity income. Passive activity losses or credits that are not allowed in one tax year can be carried forward to the next year.

In general, if a passive activity interest is transferred because of the death of a taxpayer, the accumulated unused passive activity losses are allowed as a deduction against the decedent's income in the year of death. Losses are allowed only to the extent they are greater than the excess of the transferee's (recipient of the interest transferred) basis in the property over the decedent's adjusted basis in the property immediately before death. The portion of the losses that is equal to the excess is not allowed as a deduction for any tax year.

Use Form 8582, *Passive Activity Loss Limitations*, to summarize losses and income from passive activities and to figure the amounts allowed. For more information, get Publication 925.

Credits, Other Taxes, and Payments

This section includes brief discussions of some of the tax credits, types of taxes that may be owed, income tax withheld, and estimated tax payments that are reported on the final return of a decedent.

Credits

You can claim on the final income tax return any tax credits that applied to the decedent before death.

Earned income credit. You can claim the refundable earned income credit on the decedent's final return even though the return covers less than 12 months. If the allowable credit is more than the tax liability for the year, the excess is refunded.

For more information, get Publication 596, *Earned Income Credit*.

Credit for the elderly or the disabled. This credit is allowable on a decedent's final income tax return if the decedent was age 65 or older or had retired before the end of the year on permanent and total disability.

For more information, get Publication 524, *Credit for the Elderly or the Disabled*.

Business tax credit. The general business credit available to a taxpayer is limited. Any unused credit generally is carried back 3 years and then carried forward for up to 15 years. After the 15–year period, a deduction may be allowed for any unused business credit. If the taxpayer dies before the end of the 15–year period, the deduction generally is allowed in the year of death.

For more information, get Publication 334, *Tax Guide for Small Business (For Individuals Who Use Schedule C or C–EZ).*

Other Taxes

Taxes other than income tax that may be owed on the final return of a decedent include self-employment tax and alternative minimum tax, which are reported in the *Other Taxes* section of Form 1040.

Self-employment tax. If the decedent had net earnings from self-employment of $400 or more in the year of death, self-employment tax may be owed on the final return.

Alternative minimum tax (AMT). The tax laws give special treatment to some kinds of income and allow special deductions and credits for some kinds of expenses. So that taxpayers who benefit from these laws will pay at least a minimum amount of tax, a special tax has been enacted—the "alternative minimum tax" (AMT). In general, the AMT is the excess of the tentative minimum tax over the regular tax shown on the return.

Form 6251. Use Form 6251, *Alternative Minimum Tax—Individuals,* to figure this tax on the decedent's final income tax return. See the form instructions for information on when you must attach the form to the tax return.

Payments of Tax

The income tax withheld from the decedent's salary, wages, pensions, or annuities, and the amount paid as estimated tax, for example, are credits (advance payments of tax) that you must claim on the final return.

If you need information on claiming the tax withheld or estimated tax paid, get Publication 505, *Tax Withholding and Estimated Tax.*

Maximum Tax Rate on Capital Gains

The highest tax rate on taxable income is 39.6%. However, the highest tax rate on a net capital gain is 28%. A net capital gain is the excess of net long-term capital gains over net short-term capital losses. The maximum 28% rate applies if a long-term capital gain is shown on line 17, Schedule D (Form 1040), and a net gain is shown on line 18, Schedule D (Form 1040). See the *Capital Gain Tax Worksheet* in the Form 1040 instructions for line 38.

Name, Address, and Signature

The word "DECEASED," the decedent's name, and the date of death should be written across the top of the tax return. In the name and address space you should write the name and address of the decedent and the surviving spouse. If a joint return is not being filed, the decedent's name should be written in the name space and the personal representative's name and address should be written in the remaining space.

Signature. If a personal representative has been appointed, that person must sign the return. If it is a joint return, the surviving spouse must also sign it. If no personal representative has been appointed, the surviving spouse (on a joint return) should sign the return and write in the signature area "Filing as surviving spouse." If no personal representative has been appointed and if there is no surviving spouse, the person in charge of the decedent's property must file and sign the return as "personal representative."

When and Where To File

The final individual income tax return is due at the same time the decedent's return would have been due had death not occurred. A final return for a decedent who was a calendar year taxpayer is generally due on April 15 following the year of death, regardless of when during the year death occurred. However, when the due date falls on a Saturday, Sunday, or legal holiday, you can file on the next business day.

The tax return must be prepared on a form for the year of death regardless of when during the year death occurred.

You can mail the final income tax return of the decedent to the Internal Revenue Service center for the place where you live. You also may handcarry the return to any office of the district director within your district.

Tax Forgiveness for Deaths Due to Military or Terrorist Actions

If the decedent was a member of the Armed Forces or a civilian employee of the United States, the decedent's income tax liability may be forgiven if his or her death was due to service in a combat zone or to military or terrorist actions.

Combat Zone

If a member of the Armed Forces of the United States dies while in active service in a combat zone or from wounds, disease, or injury incurred in a combat zone, the decedent's income tax liability is abated (forgiven) for the entire year in which death occurred and for any prior tax year beginning with the year before the wounds, disease, or injury occurred. The tax liability is also forgiven for any earlier year in which the decedent served at least 1 day in a combat zone.

If the tax (including interest, additions to the tax, and additional amounts) for these years has been assessed, the assessment will be forgiven. If the tax has been collected (regardless of the date of collection), that tax will be credited or refunded.

Any of the decedent's income tax for tax years before those mentioned above that remains unpaid as of the actual (or presumptive) date of death will not be assessed. If any unpaid tax (including interest, additions to the tax, and additional amounts) has been assessed, this assessment will be forgiven. Also, if any tax was collected after the date of death, that amount will be credited or refunded.

The date of death of a member of the Armed Forces reported as missing in action or as a prisoner of war is the date his or her name is removed from missing status for military pay purposes. This is true even if death actually occurred earlier.

Military or Terrorist Actions

The decedent's income tax liability is forgiven if, at death, he or she was a military or civilian employee of the United States who died because of wounds or injury incurred:

1) While a U.S. employee, and

2) In a military or terrorist action outside the United States.

The forgiveness applies to the tax year in which death occurred and for any prior tax year in the period beginning with the year before the year in which the wounds or injury occurred.

Example. The income tax liability of a civilian employee of the United States who died in 1996 because of wounds incurred while a U.S. employee outside the United States in a terrorist attack that occurred in 1987 will be forgiven for 1996 and for all prior tax years in the period 1986–1995. Refunds are allowed for the tax years for which the period for filing a claim for refund has not ended.

Military or terrorist action defined. Military or terrorist action means:

1) Any terrorist activity that most of the evidence indicates was directed against the United States or any of its allies, and

2) Any military action involving the U.S. Armed Forces and resulting from violence or aggression against the United States or any of its allies, or the threat of such violence or aggression.

Military action does not include training exercises. Any multinational force in which the United States is participating is treated as an ally of the United States.

Claim for Credit or Refund

If any of these tax-forgiveness situations applies to a prior year tax, any tax paid for which the period for filing a claim has not ended will be credited or refunded; if any tax is still due, it will be canceled. The normal period for filing a claim for credit or refund is 3 years after the return was filed or 2 years after the tax was paid, whichever is later.

Special rules. Some of the rules for filing a claim for credit or refund differ depending on:

1) Whether the decedent's death was due to service in a combat zone or to military or terrorist action, and

2) Whether a joint return was filed.

Combat zone death. If death occurred in a combat zone, the period for filing the claim is extended by:

1) The amount of time served in the combat zone (including any period in which the individual was in missing status); plus

2) The period of continuous qualified hospitalization for injury from service in the combat zone, if any; plus

3) The next 180 days.

Qualified hospitalization means any hospitalization outside the United States, and any hospitalization in the United States of not more than 5 years.

You can get the refund by filing Form 1040X, *Amended U.S. Individual Income Tax Return.*

Joint returns. If a joint return was filed, you must determine the part of the joint income tax liability that is for the decedent and eligible for the refund. Determine the decedent's tax liability as follows:

1) Figure the income tax for which the decedent would have been liable if a separate return had been filed.

2) Figure the income tax for which the spouse would have been liable if a separate return had been filed.

3) Multiply the joint tax liability by a fraction. The numerator (top number) of the fraction is the amount in (1), above. The denominator (bottom number) of the fraction is the total of (1) and (2).

The amount in (3) above is the decedent's tax liability that is eligible for the refund.

Military or terrorist action death. If the earlier discussion under *Military or Terrorist Actions* applies to a decedent, you must do the following:

1) If a U.S. individual income tax return (Form 1040, 1040A, or 1040EZ) has not been filed, you should make a claim for refund of any withheld income tax or estimated tax payments by filing Form 1040, 1040A, or 1040EZ. Form W–2, *Wage and Tax Statement,* must accompany all returns.

2) If a U.S. individual income tax return has been filed, you should make a claim for refund by filing Form 1040X. You must file a separate Form 1040X for each year in question.

You must file these returns and claims with the Internal Revenue Service, Management Support Branch, P.O. Box 267, Covington, KY 41019, Attn: KITA Coordinator, Stop 28.

Identify all returns and claims for refund by writing "KITA"in bold letters on the top of page 1 of the return or claim. On the Form 1040 or Form 1040A write the phrase"KITA—see attached " on the line for "Total tax" ("Tax" on Form 1040EZ). On the Form 1040X, write the phrase on the line for "Total tax liability."

The attachment should include a computation of the decedent's tax liability (before figuring any amount to be forgiven) and a computation of the amount that is to be forgiven. On joint returns reporting taxable income of the surviving spouse, you must make an allocation

of the tax as described earlier under *Joint returns.* If you cannot make a proper allocation, you should attach a statement of all income and deductions allocable to each spouse and the IRS will make the proper allocation.

The following *necessary documents* must accompany all of these returns and claims for refund under these procedures:

1) Form 1310, *Statement of Person Claiming Refund Due a Deceased Taxpayer.*

2) A certification from the Department of Defense or the Department of State that the death was due to military or terrorist action outside the United States. For military employees and civilian employees of the Department of Defense, certification must be made by that department on Form DOD 1300. For civilian employees of all other agencies, certification must be a letter signed by the Director General of the Foreign Service, Department of State, or his/her delegate. The certification must include the individual's name and social security number, the date of injury, the date of death, and a statement that the individual died as the result of a military or terrorist action outside the United States and was an employee of the United States at the date of injury and at the date of death.

If the certification has been received, but you do not have enough tax information to file a timely claim for refund, you can suspend the period for filing a claim by filing Form 1040X, attaching Form 1310 and a statement that an amended claim will be filed as soon as you have the required tax information.

Filing Reminders

To minimize the time needed to process the decedent's final return and issue any refund, be sure to follow these procedures:

• Write "DECEASED," the decedent's name, and the date of death across the top of the tax return.

• If a personal representative has been appointed, the personal representative must sign the return.

• If you are the decedent's spouse filing a joint return with the decedent, write "Filing as surviving spouse" in the area where you sign the return. If a personal representative has been appointed, the personal representative must also sign the return.

• To claim a refund for the decedent:

   If you are the decedent's spouse filing a joint return with the decedent, file only the tax return to claim the refund.

   If you are the personal representative and the return is not a joint return filed with the decedent's surviving spouse, file the return and attach a copy of the certificate that shows your appointment by the court. (A power of attorney or a copy of the decedent's will is not acceptable evidence of your appointment as

the personal representative). If you are filing an amended return, attach Form 1310 and a copy of the certificate of appointment (or, if you have already sent the certificate of appointment to IRS, write "Certificate Previously Filed" at the bottom of Form 1310).

If you are not filing a joint return as the surviving spouse and a personal representative has not been appointed, file the return and attach Form 1310 and proof of death (generally, a copy of the death certificate).

Other Tax Information

This section contains information about the effect of an individual's death on the income tax liability of the survivors (including widows and widowers), the beneficiaries, and the estate.

Your Federal Income Tax (Publication 17), published by the IRS, contains comprehensive information to help individual taxpayers prepare their own income tax returns. Also, there are many other taxpayer information publications on specific topics. You can get single copies of these publications free from the IRS Forms Distribution Center. See *How To Get More Information* near the end of this publication.

Tax Benefits for Survivors

Survivors can qualify for certain benefits when filing their own income tax returns.

Joint return by surviving spouse. A surviving spouse can file a joint return for the year of death and may qualify for special tax rates for the following 2 years, as explained under *Qualifying widows and widowers,* below.

Decedent as your dependent. If the decedent qualified as your dependent for the part of the year before death, you can claim the full exemption amount for the dependent on your tax return, regardless of when death occurred during the year.

Qualifying widows and widowers. If your spouse died within the 2 tax years preceding the year for which your return is being filed, you may be eligible to claim the filing status of qualifying widow(er) with dependent child and qualify to use the *Married filing jointly* tax rates.

Requirements. Generally, you qualify for this special benefit if you meet all of the following requirements:

1) You were entitled to file a joint return with your spouse for the year of death—whether or not you actually filed jointly;

2) You did not remarry before the end of the current tax year;

3) You have a child, stepchild, or foster child who qualifies as your dependent for the tax year; and

4) You provide more than half the cost of maintaining your home, which is the principal residence of that child for the entire year except for temporary absences.

Example. William Burns's wife died in 1994. Mr. Burns has not remarried and continued throughout 1995 and 1996 to maintain a home for himself and his dependent child. For 1994 he was entitled to file a joint return for himself and his deceased wife. For 1995 and 1996, he qualifies to file as a "Qualifying widow(er) with dependent child." For later years, he may qualify to file as a head of household.

Figuring your tax. Include only your own income, exemptions, and deductions in figuring your tax, but check the box on line 5 (Form 1040 or 1040A) under filing status on your tax return and enter the year of death in the parentheses. Use the Tax Rate Schedule or the column in the Tax Table for *Married filing jointly*, which gives you the split-income benefits.

The last year you can file jointly with, or claim an exemption for, your deceased spouse is the year of death.

Joint return filing rules. If you are the surviving spouse and a personal representative is handling the estate for the decedent, you should coordinate filing your return for the year of death with this personal representative. See the filing requirements for a joint return earlier under *Final Return for Decedent.*

Income in Respect of the Decedent

All gross income that the decedent would have received had death not occurred, that was not properly includible on the final return, discussed earlier, is income in respect of the decedent.

How To Report

Income in respect of a decedent must be included in the gross income of:

1) The decedent's estate, if the estate receives it, or

2) The beneficiary, if the right to income is passed directly to the beneficiary and the beneficiary receives it, or

3) Any person to whom the estate properly distributes the right to receive it.

Example 1. Frank Johnson owned and operated an apple orchard. He used the cash method of accounting. He sold and delivered 1,000 bushels of apples to a canning factory for $2,000, but did not receive payment before his death. When the estate was settled, payment had not been made and the estate transferred the right to the payment to his widow. When Frank's widow collects the $2,000, she must include that amount in her return. It is not to be reported on the final return of the decedent nor on the return of the estate.

Example 2. Assume Frank Johnson used the accrual method of accounting in Example 1. The amount accrued from the sale of the apples would be included on his final return.

Neither the estate nor the widow will realize income in respect of the decedent when the money is later paid.

Example 3. On February 1, George High, a cash method taxpayer, sold his tractor for $3,000, payable March 1 of the same year. His adjusted basis in the tractor was $2,000. Mr. High died on February 15, before receiving payment. The gain to be reported as income in respect of the decedent is the $1,000 difference between the decedent's basis in the property and the sale proceeds. In other words, the income in respect of the decedent is the gain the decedent would have realized had he lived.

Example 4. Cathy O'Neil was entitled to a large salary payment at the date of her death. The amount was to be paid in five annual installments. The estate, after collecting two installments, distributed the right to the remaining installments to you, the beneficiary. None of the payments would be included in Cathy's final return. The estate must include in its gross income the two installments it received, and you must include in your gross income each of the three installments as you receive them.

Example 5. You inherited the right to receive renewal commissions on life insurance sold by your father before his death. You inherited the right from your mother, who acquired it by bequest from your father. Your mother died before she received all the commissions she had the right to receive, so you received the rest. None of these commissions were included in your father's final return. But the commissions received by your mother were included in her gross income. The commissions you received are not includible in your mother's gross income, even on her final return. You must include them in your income.

Character of income. The character of the income you receive in respect of a decedent is the same as it would have been to the decedent if he or she were alive. If the income would have been a capital gain to the decedent, it will be a capital gain to you.

Transfer of right to income. If you transfer your right to income in respect of a decedent, you must include in your income the greater of:

1) The amount you receive for the right, or

2) The fair market value of the right you transfer.

If you make a gift of such a right, you must include in your gross income the fair market value of the right at the time of the gift.

If the right to income from an installment obligation is transferred, the amount you must include in income is reduced by the basis of the obligation. See *Installment obligations,* below.

Transfer defined. A transfer for this purpose includes a sale, exchange, or other disposition, the satisfaction of an installment obligation at other than face value, or the cancellation of an installment obligation.

Installment obligations. If the decedent had sold property using the installment method and you collect payments on an installment obligation you acquired from the decedent, use the same gross profit percentage the decedent used to figure the part of each payment that represents profit. Include in your income the same profit the decedent would have included had death not occurred. Get Publication 537, *Installment Sales.*

If you dispose of an installment obligation acquired from a decedent (other than by transfer to the obligor), the rules explained in Publication 537 for figuring gain or loss on the disposition apply to you.

Transfer to obligor. A transfer of a right to income has occurred if the decedent (seller) had sold property using the installment method and the installment obligation is transferred to the obligor (buyer or person legally obligated to pay the installments). A transfer also occurs if the obligation is canceled either at death or by the estate or person receiving the obligation from the decedent. An obligation that becomes unenforceable is treated as having been canceled. (Such cancellation amounts to a transfer as defined earlier under *Transfer of right to income.*

If such a transfer occurs, the amount included in the income of the transferor (the estate or beneficiary) is the greater of the amount received or the fair market value of the installment obligation at the time of transfer, reduced by the basis of the obligation. The basis of the obligation is the decedent's basis, adjusted for all installment payments received after the decedent's death and before the transfer.

If the decedent and obligor were related persons, the fair market value of the obligation cannot be less than its face value.

Specific Types of Income in Respect of a Decedent

This section explains and provides examples of some specific types of income in respect of a decedent.

Wages. The entire amount of wages or other employee compensation earned by the decedent but unpaid at the time of death is income in respect of the decedent. The income is not reduced by any amounts withheld by the employer when paid to the estate or other beneficiary. If the income is $600 or more, the employer should report it in box 3 of Form 1099–MISC and give the recipient a copy of the form or a similar statement.

Wages paid as income in respect of a decedent are not subject to federal income tax withholding. However, if paid during the calendar year of death, they are subject to withholding for social security and Medicare taxes. These taxes should be included on the decedent's Form W–2 with the taxes withheld before death. Wages paid as income in respect of a decedent after the year of death generally are not subject to withholding for any federal taxes.

Farm income from crops, crop shares, and livestock. A farmer's growing crops and livestock at the date of death would not normally give rise to income in respect of a decedent or income to be included in the final return. However, when a cash method farmer receives rent in the form of crop shares or livestock and owns the crop shares or livestock at the time of death, the rent is income in respect of a decedent and is reported in the year in which the crop shares or livestock are sold or otherwise disposed of. The same treatment applies to crop shares or livestock the decedent had a right to receive as rent at the time of death for economic activities that occurred before death.

If the individual died during a rent period, only the portion of the proceeds from the portion of the rent period ending with death is income in respect of a decedent. The proceeds from the portion of the rent period from the day after death to the end of the rent period are income to the estate. Cash rent or crop shares and livestock received as rent and reduced to cash by the decedent are includible in the final return even though the rent period did not end until after death.

Example. Alonzo Roberts, who used the cash method of accounting, leased part of his farm for a 1–year period beginning March 1. The rental was one-third of the crop, payable in cash when the crop share is sold at the direction of Roberts. Roberts died on June 30 and was alive during 122 days of the rental period. Seven months later, Roberts' personal representative ordered the crop to be sold and was paid $1,500. Of the $1,500, 122/365, or $501, is income in respect of a decedent. The balance of the $1,500 received by the estate, $999, is income to the estate.

Partnership income. Any part of a distributive share of partnership income of the estate or other successor in interest of a deceased partner that is for the period ending with the date of the decedent's death is income in respect of a decedent. Any partnership income for the period after the decedent's death is income of the estate or other successor in interest. These rules apply to the partnership's tax year that ends after the date of the decedent's death. See *Partnership Income* under *Income To Include*, earlier in the section titled *Final Return for Decedent*.

If the partner who died had been receiving payments representing a distributive share or guaranteed payment in liquidation of the partner's interest in a partnership, the remaining payments made to the estate or other successor interest are income in respect of the decedent. The estate or the successor receiving the payments will have to include them in gross income when received. Similarly, the estate or other successor in interest receives income in respect of a decedent if amounts are paid by a third person in exchange for the successor's right to the future payments.

For a complete discussion of partnership rules, get Publication 541, *Partnerships*.

U.S. Savings Bonds acquired from decedent. If Series E or EE U.S. Savings Bonds that were owned by a cash method individual who had chosen to report the interest each year (or by an accrual method individual) are transferred because of death, the increase in value of the bonds (interest earned) in the year of death up to the date of death must be reported on the decedent's final return. The transferee (estate or beneficiary) reports on its return only the interest earned after the date of death.

The redemption values of U.S. Savings Bonds generally are available from local banks or savings and loan institutions. You also can get such information from your nearest Federal Reserve Bank; or you can purchase the *Tables of Redemption Values for U.S. Savings Bonds* from the Superintendent of Documents, U.S. Government Printing Office, Washington, D.C. 20402–9325.

If the bonds transferred because of death were owned by a cash method individual who had not chosen to report the interest each year and had purchased the bonds entirely with personal funds, interest earned before death must be reported in one of the following ways:

1) The person (executor, administrator, etc.) who must file the final income tax return of the decedent can *elect* to include in it all of the interest earned on the bonds before the decedent's death. The transferee (estate or beneficiary) then includes in its return only the interest earned after the date of death; or

2) If the election in (1), above, was not made, the interest earned to the date of death is income in respect of the decedent and is not included in the decedent's final return. In this case, all of the interest earned before and after the decedent's death is income to the transferee (estate or beneficiary). A transferee who uses the cash method of accounting and who has not chosen to report the interest annually may defer reporting any of it until the bonds are cashed or the date of maturity, whichever is earlier. In the year the interest is reported, the transferee may claim a deduction for any federal estate tax paid that arose because of the part of interest (if any) included in the decedent's estate.

Example 1. Your uncle, a cash method taxpayer, died and left you a $1,000 Series EE Bond. He had bought the bond for $500 and had not chosen to report the increase in value each year. At the date of death, interest of $94 had accrued on the bond, and its value of $594 at date of death was included in your uncle's estate. Your uncle's personal representative did not choose to include the $94 accrued interest in the decedent's final income tax return. You are a cash method taxpayer and do not choose to report the increase in value each year as it is earned. Assuming you cash it when it reaches maturity value of $1,000, you would report $500 interest income (the difference between maturity value of $1,000 and the original cost of $500) in that year. You also are entitled to claim, in that year, a deduction for any federal estate tax resulting from the inclusion in your uncle's estate of the $94 increase in value.

Example 2. If, in Example 1, the personal representative had chosen to include the $94 interest earned on the bond before death in the final income tax return of your uncle, you would report only $406 ($500 minus $94) as interest when you cashed the bond at maturity. Since this $406 represents the interest earned after your uncle's death and was not included in his estate, no deduction for federal estate tax is allowable for this amount.

Example 3. Your uncle died owning Series H Bonds that he acquired in exchange for Series E Bonds. You were the beneficiary on these bonds. The decedent used the cash method of accounting and had not chosen to report the increase in redemption price of the Series E Bonds each year as it accrued. Your uncle's personal representative made no election to include any interest earned before death in the decedent's final return. Your income in respect of the decedent is the sum of the unreported increase in value of the Series E Bonds, which constituted part of the amount paid for Series H Bonds, and the interest, if any, payable on the Series H Bonds but not received as of the date of the decedent's death.

Specific dollar amount legacy satisfied by transfer of bonds. If you receive Series E or EE Bonds from an estate in satisfaction of a specific dollar amount legacy and the decedent was a cash method taxpayer who did not elect to report interest each year, only the interest earned after you receive the bonds is your income. The interest earned to the date of death plus any further interest earned to the date of distribution is income to (and reportable by) the estate.

Cashing U.S. Savings Bonds. When you cash a U.S. Savings Bond that you acquired from a decedent, the bank or other payer that redeems it must give you a Form 1099–INT, *Interest Income,* if the interest part of the payment you receive is $10 or more. Your Form 1099–INT should show the difference between the amount received and the cost of the bond. The interest shown on your Form 1099–INT will not be reduced by any interest reported by the decedent before death, or, if elected, by the personal representative on the final income tax return of the decedent, or by the estate on the estate's income tax return. Your Form 1099–INT may show more interest than you must include in your income.

You must make an adjustment on your tax return to report the correct amount of interest. Get Publication 550, *Investment Income and Expenses,* for information about the correct reporting of this interest.

Interest accrued on U.S. Treasury bonds. The interest accrued on U.S. Treasury bonds owned by a cash method taxpayer and redeemable for the payment of federal estate taxes that was not received as of the date of the individual's death is income in respect of the decedent. This interest is not included in the decedent's final income tax return. The estate will treat such interest as taxable income in the tax year received if it chooses to redeem the U.S. Treasury bonds to pay federal estate taxes. If the person entitled to the bonds by bequest, devise, or inheritance, or because of the death of the individual (owner) receives them, that person will treat the accrued interest as taxable income in the year the interest is received. Interest that accrues on the U.S. Treasury bonds after the owner's death does not represent income in respect of the decedent. The interest, however, is taxable income and must be included in the gross income of the respective recipients.

Interest accrued on savings certificates. The interest accrued on savings certificates (redeemable after death without forfeiture of interest) that is for the period from the date of the last interest payment and ending with the date of the decedent's death, but not received as of that date, is income in respect of a decedent. Interest for a period after the decedent's death that becomes payable on the certificates after death is not income in respect of a decedent, but is taxable income includible in the gross income of the respective recipients.

Inherited IRAs. If a beneficiary receives a lump-sum distribution from an IRA he or she inherited, all or some of it may be taxable. The distribution is taxable in the year received as income in respect of a decedent up to the decedent's taxable IRA balance. This is the decedent's balance at the time of death, including unrealized appreciation and income accrued to date of death, minus any nontaxable basis (nondeductible contributions). Amounts distributed that are more than the decedent's entire IRA balance (includes taxable and nontaxable amounts) at the time of death are the income of the beneficiary.

If the beneficiary is the decedent's surviving spouse and that spouse properly rolls over the distribution into another IRA, the distribution is not currently taxed.

For the special rules on inherited IRAs, see Publication 590, *Individual Retirement Arrangements (IRAs)*.

Deductions in Respect of the Decedent

Items such as business expenses, income-producing expenses, interest, and taxes, for which the decedent was liable but which are not properly allowable as deductions on the decedent's final income tax return, will be allowed when paid:

1) As a deduction to the estate; or

2) If the estate was not liable for them, as a deduction to the person who acquired an interest in the decedent's property (subject to such obligations) because of death.

Similar treatment is given to the foreign tax credit. A beneficiary who must pay a foreign tax on income in respect of a decedent will be entitled to claim the foreign tax credit.

Depletion. The deduction for percentage depletion is allowable only to the person (estate or beneficiary) who receives the income in respect of the decedent to which the deduction relates, whether or not that person receives the property from which the income is derived. An heir who (because of the decedent's death) receives income as a result of the sale of units of mineral by the decedent (who used the cash method) will be entitled to the depletion allowance for that income. If the decedent had not figured the deduction on the basis of percentage depletion, any depletion deduction to which the decedent was entitled at the time of death would be allowable on the decedent's final return, and no depletion deduction in respect of the decedent would be allowed anyone else.

For more information about depletion, get Publication 535, *Business Expenses*.

Estate Tax Deduction

Income that a decedent had a right to receive is included in the decedent's gross estate and is subject to estate tax. This income in respect of a decedent is also taxed when received by the recipient (estate or beneficiary). However, an income tax deduction is allowed to the recipient for the estate tax paid on the income.

The deduction for estate tax can be claimed only for the same tax year in which the income in respect of the decedent must be included in the recipient's gross income. (This also is true for income in respect of a prior decedent.)

Individuals can claim this deduction only as an itemized deduction, provided they are otherwise eligible to itemize deductions. This deduction is *not* subject to the 2% limit on miscellaneous itemized deductions. Estates can claim the deduction on the line provided for the deduction on Form 1041. For the alternative minimum tax computation, the deduction is not included in the itemized deductions that are an adjustment to taxable income.

If the income in respect of the decedent is capital gain income, for figuring the maximum tax on net capital gain (or any net capital loss limits), the gain must be reduced, but not below zero, by any deduction for estate tax paid on such gain.

Computation. To figure a recipient's estate tax deduction, determine—

1) The estate tax that qualifies for the deduction, and

2) The recipient's part of the deductible tax.

Deductible estate tax. The estate tax is the tax on the taxable estate, reduced by any credits allowed. The estate tax qualifying for the deduction is the part for the net value of all the items in the estate that represent income in respect of the decedent. *Net value* is the excess of the items of income in respect of the decedent over the items of expenses in respect of the decedent. The deductible estate tax is the difference between the actual estate tax and the estate tax determined without including net value.

Example 1. Jack Sage, an attorney who used the cash method of accounting, died in 1996. At the time of his death, he was entitled to receive $12,000 from clients for his services and he had accrued bond interest of $8,000, for a total income in respect of the decedent of $20,000. He also owed $5,000 for business expenses for which his estate was liable. The income and expenses were reported on Jack's estate tax return.

The tax on Jack's estate was $9,460 after credits. The net value of the items included as income in respect of the decedent is $15,000 ($20,000 minus $5,000). The estate tax determined without including the $15,000 in the taxable estate is $4,840, after credits. The estate tax that qualifies for the deduction is $4,620 ($9,460 minus $4,840).

Recipient's deductible part. Figure the recipient's part of the deductible estate tax by dividing the estate tax value of the items of income in respect of the decedent included in the recipient's gross income (the numerator) by the total value of all items included in the estate that represents income in respect of the decedent (the denominator). If the amount included in the recipient's gross income is less than the estate tax value of the item, use the lesser amount in the numerator.

Example 2. As the beneficiary of Jack's estate (Example 1, above), you collect the $12,000 accounts receivable from the clients during 1996. You will include this amount in your gross income for 1996. If you itemize your deductions for 1996, you can claim an estate tax deduction of $2,772 figured as follows:

$$\frac{\text{Value included in your income}}{\text{Total value of income in respect of decedent}} \times \frac{\text{Estate tax qualifying for deduction}}{}$$

$$\frac{\$12,000}{\$20,000} \times \$4,620 = \$2,772$$

If the amount you collected for the accounts receivable was more than $12,000, you would still claim $2,772 as an estate tax deduction because only the $12,000 actually reported on the estate tax return can be used in the above computation. However, if you collected less than the $12,000 reported on the estate tax return, use the smaller amount to figure the estate tax deduction.

Estates. The estate tax deduction allowed an estate is figured in the same manner as just discussed. However, any income in respect of a decedent received by the estate during the tax year is reduced by any such income that is properly paid, credited, or required to be distributed by the estate to a beneficiary. The beneficiary would include such distributed income in respect of a decedent for figuring the beneficiary's deduction.

Surviving annuitants. For the estate tax deduction, an annuity received by a surviving annuitant under a joint and survivor annuity contract is considered income in respect of a decedent. The deceased annuitant must have died after the annuity starting date. You must make a special computation to figure the estate tax deduction for the surviving annuitant.

See the Income Tax Regulations under Section 1.691(d)–1.

Gifts, Insurance, and Inheritances

Property received as a gift, bequest, or inheritance is not included in your income. But if property you receive in this manner later produces income, such as interest, dividends, or rentals, that income is taxable to you. The income from property donated to a trust that is paid, credited, or distributed to you is taxable income to you. If the gift, bequest, or inheritance is the income from property, that income is taxable to you.

If you receive property from a decedent's estate in satisfaction of your right to the income of the estate, it is treated as a bequest or inheritance of income from property. See *Distributions to Beneficiaries From an Estate*, later.

Insurance

The proceeds from a decedent's life insurance policy paid by reason of his or her death generally are excluded from income. The exclusion applies to any beneficiary, whether a family member or other individual, a corporation, or a partnership.

Life insurance proceeds. Life insurance proceeds paid because of the death of the insured (or because the insured is a member of the U.S. uniformed services who is missing in action) are not taxable unless the policy was transferred to you for a valuable consideration. This rule also applies to benefits that are paid because of the death of the insured under accident, health, and variable life insurance policies and endowment contracts. However, if the proceeds are received in installments, see the discussion under *Insurance received in installments*, below.

Veterans' insurance proceeds. Veterans' insurance proceeds and dividends are not taxable either to the veteran or to the beneficiaries.

Interest on dividends left on deposit with the Department of Veterans Affairs is not taxable.

Insurance received in installments. If, because of the death of the insured, you will receive life insurance proceeds in installments, you can exclude a part of each installment from your income.

The part of each installment you can exclude is the amount held by the insurance company (generally, the total lump sum payable at the insured's death) divided by the number of periods in which the installments are to be paid. Amounts you receive that are more than the excludable part must be included in your income as interest income.

Specified number of installments. If you will receive a specified number of installments under the insurance contract, figure the part of each installment you can exclude by dividing the amount held by the insurance company by the number of installments to which

you are entitled. A secondary beneficiary, in case you die before you receive all of the installments, is entitled to the same exclusion.

Example. As beneficiary, you choose to receive $40,000 of life insurance proceeds in 10 annual installments of $6,000. Each year, you can exclude from your gross income $4,000 ($40,000 ÷ 10) as a return of principal. The balance of the installment, $2,000, is taxable as interest income.

Specified amount payable. If each installment you receive under the insurance contract is a specific amount based on a guaranteed rate of interest, but the number of installments you will receive is uncertain, the part of each installment that you can exclude from income is the amount held by the insurance company divided by the number of installments necessary to use up the principal and guaranteed interest in the contract.

Example. The face amount of the policy is $150,000, and as beneficiary you choose to receive monthly installments of $1,250. The insurer's settlement option guarantees you this payment for 240 months based on a guaranteed rate of interest. It also provides that interest that is more than the guarantee may be credited to the principal balance according to the insurer's earnings. The excludable part of each guaranteed installment is $625 ($150,000 ÷ 240), or $7,500 for an entire year. The balance of each guaranteed installment, $625 (or $7,500 for a year), is income to you. The full amount of any additional payment for interest is income to you.

Installments for life. If, as the beneficiary under an insurance contract, you will receive the proceeds in installments for the rest of your life without a refund or certain guaranteed period, the part of each annual installment that you can exclude from income is the amount held by the insurance company, divided by your life expectancy. If the contract provides for a refund or guaranteed payments, the amount held by the insurance company for this calculation is reduced by the actuarial value of the refund or the guaranteed payments.

Example. As beneficiary, you choose to receive the $50,000 proceeds from a life insurance contract under a "life-income-with-cash-refund option." You are guaranteed $2,700 a year for the rest of your life (which is estimated by use of mortality tables to be 25 years from the insured's death). The actuarial value of the refund feature is $9,000. The amount held by the insurance company, reduced by the value of the guarantee, is $41,000 ($50,000 minus $9,000) and the excludable part of each installment representing a return of principal is $1,640 ($41,000 ÷ 25). The remaining $1,060 ($2,700 minus $1,640) is interest income to you. If you should die before receiving the entire $50,000, the refund payable to the refund beneficiary is not taxable.

Interest option on insurance. If death proceeds of life insurance are left on deposit with an insurance company under an agreement to

pay interest only, the interest paid or credited to the beneficiary is taxable to the beneficiary.

Flexible premium contracts. A life insurance contract (including any qualified additional benefits) is a flexible premium life insurance contract if it provides for the payment of one or more premiums that are not fixed by the insurer as to both timing and amount. For contracts issued before January 1, 1985, the proceeds paid because of the death of the insured under a flexible premium contract will be excluded from the recipient's gross income only if the contracts meet the requirements explained under section 101(f) of the Internal Revenue Code.

Basis of Inherited Property

Your basis for property inherited from (or passing from) a decedent is generally one of the following:

1) The fair market value of the property at the date of the individual's death;

2) The fair market value on the alternate valuation date (discussed in the instructions for Form 706), if so elected by the personal representative for the estate; or

3) The value under the special-use valuation method for real property used in farming or other closely held business (see *Special-use valuation*, later), if so elected by the personal representative.

Exception for appreciated property. If you or your spouse gave *appreciated property* to an individual during the 1–year period ending on the date of that individual's death and you (or your spouse) later acquired the same property from the decedent, your basis in the property is the same as the decedent's adjusted basis immediately before death.

Appreciated property. Appreciated property is property with a fair market value greater than its adjusted basis on the day it was transferred to the decedent.

Special-use valuation. If you are a *qualified heir* and you receive a *farm or other closely held business real property* from the estate for which the personal representative elected special-use valuation, your basis is the value of the property on the basis of its actual use rather than its fair market value.

If you are a qualified heir and you buy special-use valuation property from the estate, your basis is the estate's basis (determined under the special-use valuation method) immediately before your purchase.

You are a *qualified heir* if you are an ancestor (parent, grandparent, etc.), the spouse, or a lineal descendant (child, grandchild, etc.) of the decedent, a lineal descendant of the decedent's parent or spouse, or the spouse of any of these lineal descendants.

Increased basis for special-use valuation property. Under certain conditions, some or all of the estate tax benefits obtained by using special-use valuation will be subject to recapture. If you must pay any additional estate (recapture) tax, you can elect to increase your basis in the special-use valuation property to its fair market value on the date of the decedent's death (or on the alternate valuation date, if the personal representative so elected).

If you elect to increase your basis, you must pay interest on the recapture tax for the period from the date 9 months after the decedent's death until the date you pay the recapture tax.

For more information on special-use valuation and the recapture tax, get Form 706 & 706–A and instructions.

Adjusted basis for S corporation stock. The basis of inherited S corporation stock must be reduced if there is income in respect of a decedent attributable to that stock. This provision is effective with respect to decedents dying after August 20, 1996.

Joint interest. Figure the surviving tenant's new basis of property jointly owned (joint tenancy or tenancy by the entirety) by adding the surviving tenant's original basis in the property to the value of the part of the property (one of the three values described earlier) included in the decedent's estate. Subtract from the sum any deductions for wear and tear, such as depreciation or depletion, allowed to the surviving tenant on that property.

Example. Fred and Anne Maple (brother and sister) owned, as joint tenants with right of survivorship, rental property they purchased for $60,000. Anne paid $15,000 of the purchase price and Fred paid $45,000. Under local law, each had a half interest in the income from the property. When Fred died, the fair market value of the property was $100,000. Depreciation deductions allowed before Fred's death were $20,000. Anne's basis in the property is $80,000 figured as follows:

Anne's original basis		$15,000
Interest acquired from Fred (¾ of $100,000)	75,000	$90,000
Minus: ½ of $20,000 depreciation		10,000
Anne's basis		$80,000

Qualified joint interest. One-half of the value of property (one of the three values described earlier) owned by a decedent and spouse as tenants by the entirety, or as joint tenants with right of survivorship if the decedent and spouse are the only joint tenants, is included in the decedent's gross estate. This is true regardless of how much each contributed toward the purchase price.

Figure the basis for a surviving spouse by adding one-half of the property's cost basis to the value included in the gross estate. Subtract from this sum any deductions for wear and tear, such as depreciation or depletion, allowed on that property to the surviving spouse.

Example. Dan and Diane Gilbert owned, as tenants by the entirety, rental property they purchased for $60,000. Dan paid $15,000 of the purchase price and Diane paid $45,000. Under local law, each had a half interest in the income from the property. When Diane died,

the fair market value of the property was $100,000. Depreciation deductions allowed before Diane's death were $20,000. Dan's basis in the property is $70,000 figured as follows:

One-half of cost basis (½ of $60,000)		$30,000
Interest acquired from Diane (½ of $100,000)	50,000	$80,000
Minus: ½ of $20,000 depreciation		10,000
Dan's basis		$70,000

For more information about determining basis and adjusted basis in property, get Publication 551, *Basis of Assets.*

Community property state. If you and your spouse lived in a community property state, get Publication 551 for a discussion about figuring the basis of your community property after your spouse's death.

Depreciation. If you can depreciate property you inherited, you generally must use the modified accelerated cost recovery system (MACRS) to determine depreciation.

For joint interests and qualified joint interests, you must make two computations to figure depreciation: one for your original basis in the property and another for the inherited part of the property. Continue depreciating your original basis under the same method you had used in previous years. Depreciate the inherited part using MACRS.

For more information get Publication 946, *How To Depreciate Property.*

Substantial valuation misstatement. If the value or adjusted basis of any property claimed on an income tax return is 200% or more of the amount determined to be the correct amount, there is a substantial valuation misstatement. If this misstatement results in an underpayment of tax of more than $5,000, an addition to tax of 20% of the underpayment can apply. The penalty increases to 40% if the value or adjusted basis is 400% or more of the amount determined to be the correct amount. If the value shown on the estate tax return is overstated and you use that value as your basis in the inherited property, you could be liable for the addition to tax.

The IRS may waive all or part of the addition to tax if you have a reasonable basis for the claimed value. The fact that the adjusted basis on your income tax return is the same as the value on the estate tax return is not enough to show that you had a reasonable basis to claim the valuation.

Holding period. If you inherited property that is a capital asset and sell or dispose of it within 1 year after the decedent's death, you are considered to have held it for more than 1 year. You would have a long-term capital gain or loss.

Property distributed in kind. Your basis in property distributed in kind by a decedent's estate is the same as the estate's basis immediately before the distribution plus any gain, or

minus any loss, recognized by the estate. Property is distributed in kind if it satisfies your right to receive another property or amount, such as the income of the estate or a specific dollar amount. Property distributed in kind generally includes any noncash property you receive from the estate other than:

1) A specific bequest (unless it must be distributed in more than three installments), or

2) Real property, the title to which passes directly to you under local law.

For information on an estate's recognized gain or loss on distributions in kind, see *Income To Include* under *Income Tax Return of an Estate—Form 1041*, later.

Death Benefit Exclusion

Beneficiaries (or the estate) of a deceased employee may qualify for the death benefit exclusion on employers' payments made because of an employee's (or, in some cases, a former employee's) death. The term "employee" includes a self-employed individual if the amounts are paid by a qualified trust or under a qualified plan.

 The death benefit exclusion does not apply with respect to employees dying after August 20, 1996.

The amount excluded from income with respect to any deceased employee cannot exceed $5,000 regardless of the number of employers or the number of beneficiaries. The exclusion applies whether there are one or more payments.

Example. Samuel Wilson was an officer in a corporation at the time of his death in January. The board of directors voted to pay Sam's salary for the rest of the year to his widow in consideration of his past services. During the year, the corporation paid Mrs. Wilson a total of $38,000. The first $5,000 she received is excludable from her income, but she must include the balance of $33,000 on line 21, Form 1040.

If an annuity is paid. If an annuity is paid, add the death benefit exclusion amount to the cost of the annuity at the annuity starting date. You recover the cost tax free from the annuity payments using the *General Rule* or the *Simplified General Rule*. For more information, get Publication 575, *Pension and Annuity Income (Including Simplified General Rule)* and Publication 939, *Pension General Rule (Nonsimplified Method).*

If you are the surviving annuitant under a joint and survivor annuity, you will not qualify for the death benefit exclusion if the deceased employee had retired and received any annuity payments or was entitled to such payments but died before receiving them. However, if you are the survivor of a disability retiree, you may qualify for the exclusion. Get Publication 575.

Death benefit for public safety officers.
The death benefit payable to surviving dependents of public safety officers (law enforcement officers or firefighters) who die as a result of injuries sustained in the line of duty is not included in either the beneficiaries' income or the decedent's gross estate. It is not subject to the $5,000 exclusion limit for other death benefits. The benefit is administered through the Bureau of Justice Assistance (BJA).

The BJA can pay the surviving dependents an interim benefit up to $3,000 if it determines that a public safety officer's death is one for which a benefit will probably be paid. If there is no final payment, the recipient of the interim benefit is liable for repayment. However, the BJA may waive all or part of the repayment if it will cause a hardship. If all or part of the repayment is waived, that amount is not included in gross income.

Other Items of Income

Some other items of income that you, as a survivor or beneficiary, may receive are discussed below. Lump-sum payments you receive as the surviving spouse or beneficiary of a deceased employee may represent accrued salary payments; distributions from employee profit-sharing, pension, annuity, and stock bonus plans; or other items that should be treated separately for tax purposes. The treatment of these lump-sum payments depends on what the payments represent.

Salary or wages. Salary or wages paid after the employee's death are usually taxable income to the beneficiary. See *Wages,* earlier, under *Specific Types of Income in Respect of a Decedent.*

Lump-sum distributions. You may be able to choose optional methods to figure the tax on lump-sum distributions from qualified employee retirement plans. For more information, get Publication 575.

Pensions and annuities. For beneficiaries of deceased employees who receive pensions and annuities, get Publication 575. For beneficiaries of federal Civil Service employees, get Publication 721, *Tax Guide to U.S. Civil Service Retirement Benefits.*

Inherited IRAs. If a person other than the decedent's spouse inherits an IRA, that person cannot treat the IRA as one established on his or her behalf. If an IRA distribution is from contributions that were deducted or from earnings and gains in the IRA, it is fully taxable income. If there were nondeductible contributions, an allocation between taxable and nontaxable income must be made. (See *Inherited IRAs,* under *Income in Respect of the Decedent,* earlier, and Publication 590, *Individual Retirement Arrangements (IRAs)).* The IRA cannot be rolled over into, or receive a rollover from, another IRA. No deduction is allowed for amounts paid into that inherited IRA. For more information about IRAs, get Publication 590.

Estate income. Estates may have to pay federal income tax. Beneficiaries may have to pay tax on their share of estate income. However, there is never a double tax. See *Distributions to Beneficiaries From an Estate,* later.

Income Tax Return of an Estate– Form 1041

An estate is a taxable entity separate from the decedent and comes into being with the death of the individual. It exists until the final distribution of its assets to the heirs and other beneficiaries. The income earned by the assets during this period must be reported by the estate under the conditions described in this publication. The tax generally is figured in the same manner and on the same basis as for individuals, with certain differences in the computation of deductions and credits, as explained later.

The estate's income, like an individual's income, must be reported annually on either a calendar or fiscal year basis. As the personal representative, you choose the estate's accounting period when you file its first Form 1041, *U.S. Income Tax Return for Estates and Trusts.* The estate's first tax year can be any period that ends on the last day of a month and does not exceed 12 months.

Once you choose the tax year, you cannot change it without the permission of the IRS. Also, on the first income tax return, you must choose the accounting method (cash, accrual, or other) you will use to report the estate's income. Once you have used a method, you ordinarily cannot change it without the consent of the IRS. For a more complete discussion of accounting periods and methods, get Publication 538, *Accounting Periods and Methods.*

Filing Requirements

Every domestic estate with gross income of $600 or more during a tax year must file a Form 1041. If one or more of the beneficiaries of the domestic estate are nonresident alien individuals, the personal representative must file Form 1041, even if the gross income of the estate is less than $600.

A fiduciary for a nonresident alien estate with U.S. source income, including any income that is effectively connected with the conduct of a trade or business in the United States, must file *Form 1040NR, U.S. Nonresident Alien Income Tax Return,* as the income tax return of the estate.

A nonresident alien who was a *resident of* Puerto Rico, Guam, American Samoa, or the Commonwealth of the Northern Mariana Islands for the entire tax year will, for this purpose, be treated as a resident alien of the United States.

Schedule K–1 (Form 1041)

As personal representative, you must file a separate Schedule K–1 (Form 1041), or an acceptable substitute (described below), for each beneficiary. File these schedules with Form 1041. You must show each beneficiary's

taxpayer identification number. A $50 penalty is charged for each failure to provide the identifying number of each beneficiary unless reasonable cause is established for not providing it. When you assume your duties as the personal representative, you must ask each beneficiary to give you a taxpayer identification number. However, it is not required of a nonresident alien beneficiary who is not engaged in a trade or business within the United States or of an executor or administrator of the estate unless that person is also a beneficiary.

As personal representative, you must also furnish a Schedule K–1 (Form 1041), or a substitute, to the beneficiary by the date on which the Form 1041 is filed. Failure to provide this payee statement can result in a penalty of $50 for each failure. This penalty also applies if you omit information or include incorrect information on the payee statement.

You do not need prior approval for a *substitute* Schedule K–1 (Form 1041) that is an exact copy of the official schedule or that follows the specifications in Publication 1167, *Substitute Printed, Computer-Prepared, and Computer-Generated Tax Forms and Schedules.* You must have prior approval for any other substitute Schedule K–1 (Form 1041).

Beneficiaries. The personal representative has a fiduciary responsibility to the ultimate recipients of the income and the property of the estate. While the courts use a number of names to designate specific types of beneficiaries or the recipients of various types of property, it is sufficient in this publication to call all of them beneficiaries.

Liability of the beneficiary. The income tax liability of an estate attaches to the assets of the estate. If the income is distributed or must be distributed during the current tax year, it is reportable by each beneficiary on his or her individual income tax return. If the income does not have to be distributed, and is not distributed but is retained by the estate, the income tax on the income is payable by the estate. If the income is distributed later without the payment of the taxes due, the beneficiary can be liable for tax due and unpaid, to the extent of the value of the estate assets received.

Income of the estate is taxed to either the estate or the beneficiary, but not to both.

Nonresident alien beneficiary. As a resident or domestic fiduciary, in addition to filing Form 1041, you must file the return and pay the tax that may be due from a nonresident alien beneficiary. Depending upon a number of factors, you may or may not have to file Form 1040NR. For more information, get Publication 519, *U.S. Tax Guide for Aliens.*

You do not have to file the nonresident alien's return and pay the tax if that beneficiary has appointed an agent in the United States to file a federal income tax return. However, you must attach to the estate's return (Form 1041) a copy of the document that appoints the beneficiary's agent. You also must file Form 1042, *Annual Withholding Tax Return for U.S. Source Income of Foreign Persons,* in connection with income tax to be paid at the source on certain payments to nonresident aliens.

Page 13

Amended Return

If you have to file an amended Form 1041, use a copy of the form for the appropriate year and check the "Amended return" box. Complete the entire return, correct the appropriate lines with the new information, and refigure the tax liability. On an attached sheet, explain the reason for the changes and identify the lines and amounts being changed.

If the amended return results in a change to income, or a change in distribution of any income or other information provided to a beneficiary, you must file an amended Schedule K-1 (Form 1041) and give a copy to each beneficiary. Check the "Amended K-1" box at the top of Schedule K-1.

Information Returns

Even though you may not have to file an income tax return for the estate, you may have to file Form 1099-DIV, *Dividends and Distributions,* Form 1099-INT, *Interest Income,* or Form 1099-MISC, *Miscellaneous Income,* if you receive the income as a nominee or middleman for another person. For more information on filing information returns see the *Instructions for Forms 1099, 1098, 5498, and W-2G.*

You will not have to file information returns for the estate if the estate is the record owner and you file an income tax return for the estate on Form 1041 giving the name, address, and identifying number of each actual owner and furnish a completed Schedule K-1 (Form 1041) to each actual owner.

Penalty. A penalty of up to $50 can be charged for each failure to file or failure to include correct information on an information return. (Failure to include correct information includes failure to include all the information required and inclusion of incorrect information.) If it is shown that such failure is due to intentional disregard of the filing requirement, the penalty amount increases.

See the *Instructions for Forms 1099, 1098, 5498, and W-2G* for more information.

Two or More Personal Representatives

If property is located outside the state in which the decedent's home was located, more than one personal representative may be designated by the will or appointed by the court. The person designated or appointed to administer the estate in the state of the decedent's permanent home is called the *domiciliary representative.* The person designated or appointed to administer property in a state other than that of the decedent's permanent home is called an *ancillary representative.*

Separate Forms 1041. Each representative must file a separate Form 1041. The domiciliary representative must include the estate's entire income in the return. The ancillary representative files with the appropriate IRS office for the ancillary's location. The ancillary representative should provide the following information on the return:

1) The name and address of the domiciliary representative;

2) The amount of gross income received by the ancillary representative; and

3) The deductions claimed against that income (including any income properly paid or credited by the ancillary representative to a beneficiary).

Estate of a nonresident alien. If the estate of a nonresident alien has a nonresident alien domiciliary representative and an ancillary representative who is a citizen or resident of the United States, the ancillary representative, in addition to filing a Form 1040NR to provide the information described in the preceding paragraph, must also file the return that the domiciliary representative otherwise would have to file.

Copy of the Will

You do not have to file a copy of the decedent's will unless requested by the IRS. If requested, you must attach a statement to it indicating how much of the estate's income is taxable to the estate or to the beneficiaries. You should also attach a statement signed by you under penalties of perjury that the will is a true and complete copy.

Income To Include

The estate's taxable income generally is figured the same way as an individual's income, except as explained in the following discussions.

Gross income of an estate consists of all items of income received or accrued during the tax year. It includes dividends, interest, rents, royalties, gain from the sale of property, and income from business, partnerships, trusts, and any other sources. For a discussion of income from dividends, interest, and other investment income and also gains and losses from the sale of investment property, get Publication 550. For a discussion of gains and losses from the sale of other property, including business property, get Publication 544, *Sales and Other Dispositions of Assets.*

If, as the personal representative, your duties include the operation of the decedent's business, get Publication 334, *Tax Guide for Small Business (For Individuals Who Use Schedule C or C-EZ).* This publication explains the income, excise, and employment tax laws that apply to a sole proprietorship.

Income in respect of the decedent. As the personal representative of the estate, you may receive income that the decedent would have reported had death not occurred. For an explanation of this income, see *Income in Respect of the Decedent* under *Other Tax Information,* earlier. An estate may qualify to claim a deduction for estate taxes if the estate must include in gross income for any tax year an amount of income in respect of a decedent. See *Estate Tax Deduction,* earlier under *Other Tax Information* and its discussion *Deductions in Respect of the Decedent.*

Gain (or loss) from sale of property. During the administration of the estate, you may find it necessary or desirable to sell all or part of the estate's assets to pay debts and expenses of administration, or to make proper distributions of the assets to the beneficiaries. While you may have the legal authority to dispose of the property, title to it may be vested (given a legal interest in the property) in one or more of the beneficiaries. This is usually true of real property. To determine whether any gain or loss must be reported by the estate or by the beneficiaries, consult local law to determine the legal owner.

Redemption of stock to pay death taxes. Under certain conditions, a distribution to a shareholder (including the estate) in redemption of stock that was included in the decedent's gross estate may be allowed capital gain (or loss) treatment.

Character of asset. The character of an asset in the hands of an estate determines whether gain or loss on its sale or other disposition is capital or ordinary. The asset's character depends on how the estate holds or uses it. If it was a capital asset to the decedent, it generally will be a capital asset to the estate. If it was land or depreciable property used in the decedent's business and the estate continues the business, it generally will have the same character to the estate that it had in the decedent's hands. If it was held by the decedent for sale to customers, it generally will be considered to be held for sale to customers by the estate if the decedent's business continues to operate during the administration of the estate.

Holding period. An estate (or other recipient) that acquires a capital asset from a decedent and sells or otherwise disposes of it within 1 year of the decedent's death is considered to have held that asset for the required long-term holding period of more than 1 year.

Basis of asset. The basis used to figure gain or loss for property the estate receives from the decedent usually is its fair market value at the date of death, or at the alternate valuation date, if elected. Also see *Special-use valuation* under *Basis of Inherited Property* in the *Other Tax Information* section, earlier.

If the estate purchases property after the decedent's death, the basis generally will be its cost.

The basis of certain appreciated property the estate receives from the decedent will be the decedent's adjusted basis in the property immediately before death. This applies if the property was acquired by the decedent as a gift during the 1-year period before death, the property's fair market value on the date of the gift was greater than the donor's adjusted basis, and the proceeds of the sale of the property are distributed to the donor (or the donor's spouse).

Schedule D (Form 1041). To report gains (and losses) from the sale or exchange of capital assets by the estate, file Schedule D (Form 1041) with Form 1041. For additional information about the treatment of capital gains and losses, get the instructions for Schedule D.

Installment obligations. If an installment obligation owned by the decedent is transferred by the estate to the obligor (buyer or person obligated to pay) or is canceled at death, include the income from that event in the gross income of the estate. See *Installment obligations* under *Income in Respect of the Decedent* in the *Other Tax Information* section, earlier. Get Publication 537 for information about installment sales.

Gain from sale of special-use valuation property. If you elected special-use valuation for farm or other closely held business real property and that property is sold to a *qualified heir*, the estate will recognize gain on the sale if the fair market value on the date of the sale exceeds the fair market value on the date of the decedent's death (or on the alternate valuation date if it was elected).

Qualified heirs. Qualified heirs include the decedent's ancestors (parents, grandparents, etc.) and spouse, the decedent's lineal descendants (children, grandchildren, etc.) and their spouses, and lineal descendants (and their spouses) of the decedent's parents or spouse.

For more information about special-use valuation, get Form 706 and its instructions.

Gain from transfer of property to a political organization. Appreciated property that is transferred to a political organization is treated as sold by the estate. Appreciated property is property that has a fair market value (on the date of the transfer) greater than the estate's basis. The gain recognized is the difference between the estate's basis and the fair market value on the date transferred.

A political organization is any party, committee, association, fund, or other organization formed and operated to accept contributions or make expenditures for influencing the nomination, election, or appointment of an individual to any federal, state, or local public office.

Gain or loss on distributions in kind. An estate recognizes gain or loss on a distribution of property in kind to a beneficiary only in the following situations:

1) The distribution satisfies the beneficiary's right to receive either—

   a) A specific dollar amount (whether payable in cash, in unspecified property, or in both), or

   b) A specific property other than the property distributed.

2) You choose to recognize the gain or loss on the estate's income tax return.

The gain or loss is usually the difference between the fair market value of the property when distributed and the estate's basis in the property. But see *Gain from sale of special-use valuation property,* earlier, for a limit on the gain recognized on a transfer of such property to a qualified heir.

If you choose to recognize gain or loss, the choice applies to all noncash distributions during the tax year except charitable distributions

and specific bequests. To make the choice, report the gain or loss on a Schedule D (Form 1041) attached to the estate's Form 1041 and check the box on line 7 in the *Other Information* section of Form 1041. You must make the choice by the due date (including extensions) of the estate's income tax return for the year of distribution. You must get the consent of the IRS to revoke the choice.

For more information, see *Property distributed in kind* under *Distributions Deduction,* later.

Exemption and Deductions

In figuring taxable income, an estate is generally allowed the same deductions as an individual. Special rules, however, apply to some deductions for an estate. This section includes discussions of those deductions affected by the special rules.

Exemption Deduction

An estate is allowed an exemption deduction of $600 in figuring its taxable income. No exemption for dependents is allowed to an estate. Even though the first return of an estate may be for a period of less than 12 months, the exemption is $600. If, however, the estate was given permission to change its accounting period, the exemption is $50 for each month of the short year.

Contributions

An estate qualifies for a deduction for amounts of gross income paid or permanently set aside for qualified charitable organizations. The adjusted gross income limits for individuals do not apply. However, to be deductible by an estate, the contribution must be specifically provided for in the decedent's will. If there is no will, or if the will makes no provision for the payment to a charitable organization, then a deduction will not be allowed even though all of the beneficiaries may agree to the gift.

You cannot deduct any contribution from income that is not included in the estate's gross income. If the will specifically provides that the contributions are to be paid out of the estate's gross income, the contributions are fully deductible. However, if the will contains no specific provisions, the contributions are considered to have been paid and are deductible in the same proportion as the gross income bears to the total of all classes of income.

For more information about contributions, get Publication 526, *Charitable Contributions,* and Publication 561, *Determining the Value of Donated Property.*

Losses

Generally, an estate can claim a deduction for a loss that it sustains on the sale of property. If an estate has a loss from the sale of property (other than stock) to a personal representative or beneficiary of such estate, it also can claim a loss deduction. For a discussion of an estate's recognized loss on a distribution of

property in kind to a beneficiary, see *Income To Include,* earlier.

Net operating loss deduction. An estate can claim a net operating loss deduction, figured in the same way as an individual's, except that it cannot deduct any distributions to beneficiaries (discussed later) or the deduction for charitable contributions in figuring the loss or the loss carryover. For a discussion of the carryover of an unused net operating loss to a beneficiary upon termination of the estate, see *Termination of Estate,* later, and get Publication 536, *Net Operating Losses.*

Casualty and theft losses. Losses incurred for casualty and theft during the administration of the estate can be deducted only if they have not been claimed on the federal estate tax return (Form 706). You must file a statement with the estate's income tax return waiving the deduction for estate tax purposes. See *Administration Expenses,* below.

The same rules that apply to individuals apply to the estate, except that in figuring the adjusted gross income of the estate used to figure the deductible loss, you deduct any administration expenses claimed. Get Form 4684, *Casualties and Thefts,* and its instructions to figure any loss deduction.

Carryover losses. Carryover losses resulting from net operating losses or capital losses sustained by the decedent *before death* cannot be deducted on the estate's income tax return.

Administration Expenses

Expenses of administering an estate can be deducted either from the gross estate in figuring the federal estate tax on Form 706 or from the estate's gross income in figuring the estate's income tax on Form 1041. However, these expenses cannot be claimed for *both* estate tax and income tax purposes. In most cases, this rule also applies to expenses incurred in the sale of property by an estate (not as a dealer).

To prevent a double deduction, amounts otherwise allowable in figuring the decedent's taxable estate for federal estate tax on Form 706 will not be allowed as a deduction in figuring the income tax of the estate or of any other person unless the personal representative files a statement, in duplicate, that the items of expense, as listed in the statement, have not been claimed as deductions for federal estate tax purposes and that all rights to claim such deductions are *waived.* One deduction or part of a deduction can be claimed for income tax purposes if the appropriate statement is filed, while another deduction or part is claimed for estate tax purposes. Claiming a deduction in figuring the estate income tax is not prevented when the same deduction is claimed on the estate tax return, so long as the estate tax deduction is not finally allowed and the preceding statement is filed. The statement can be filed at any time before the expiration of the statute of limitations that applies to the tax year for which the deduction is sought. This waiver procedure also applies to casualty losses incurred during administration of the estate.

Accrued expenses. The rules preventing double deductions do not apply to deductions for taxes, interest, business expenses, and other items accrued at the date of death. These expenses are allowable as a deduction for estate tax purposes as claims against the estate and also are allowable as deductions in respect of a decedent for income tax purposes. Deductions for interest, business expenses, and other items not accrued at the date of the decedent's death are allowable only as a deduction for administration expenses for both estate and income tax purposes and do not qualify for a double deduction.

Expenses allocable to tax-exempt income. When figuring the estate's taxable income on Form 1041, you cannot deduct administration expenses allocable to any of the estate's tax-exempt income. However, you can deduct these administration expenses when figuring the taxable estate for federal estate tax purposes on Form 706.

Depreciation and Depletion

The allowable deductions for depreciation and depletion that accrue after the decedent's death must be apportioned between the estate and the beneficiaries, depending on the income of the estate that is allocable to each.

Example. In 1996 the decedent's estate realized $3,000 of business income during the administration of the estate. The personal representative distributed $1,000 of the income to the decedent's son Ned and $2,000 to another son, Bill. The allowable depreciation on the business property is $300. Ned can take a deduction of $100 (($1,000 ÷ $3,000) × $300), and Bill can take a deduction of $200 (($2,000 ÷ $3,000) × $300).

Distributions Deduction

An estate is allowed a deduction for the tax year for any income that must be distributed currently and for other amounts that are properly paid or credited, or that must be distributed to beneficiaries. The deduction is limited to the **distributable net income** of the estate.

For special rules that apply in figuring the estate's distribution deduction, see *Special Rules for Distributions* under *Distributions to Beneficiaries From an Estate,* later.

Distributable net income. Distributable net income (determined on Schedule B of Form 1041) is the estate's income available for distribution. It is the estate's taxable income, with the following modifications:

Distributions to beneficiaries. Distributions to beneficiaries are not deducted.

Estate tax deduction. The deduction for estate tax on income in respect of the decedent is not allowed.

Personal exemption. No personal exemption deduction is allowed.

Capital gains. Capital gains ordinarily are not included in distributable net income. However, you include them in distributable net income if:

1) The gain is allocated to income in the accounts of the estate or by notice to the beneficiaries under the terms of the will or by local law;

2) The gain is allocated to the corpus or principal of the estate and is actually distributed to the beneficiaries during the tax year;

3) The gain is used, under either the terms of the will or the practice of the personal representative, to determine the amount that is distributed or must be distributed; or

4) Charitable contributions are made out of capital gains.

Capital losses. Capital losses are excluded in figuring distributable net income unless they enter into the computation of any capital gain that is distributed or must be distributed during the year.

Tax-exempt interest. Tax-exempt interest, including exempt-interest dividends, though excluded from the estate's gross income, is included in the distributable net income, but is reduced by:

1) The expenses that were not allowed in computing the estate's taxable income because they were attributable to tax-exempt interest (see *Expenses allocable to tax-exempt income* under *Administration Expenses,* earlier); and

2) The part of the tax-exempt interest deemed to have been used to make a charitable contribution. See *Contributions,* earlier.

The total tax-exempt interest earned by an estate must be shown in the *Other Information* section of the Form 1041. The beneficiary's part of the tax-exempt interest is shown on the Schedule K–1, Form 1041.

Income that must be distributed currently. The distributions deduction includes any amount of income that, under the terms of the decedent's will or by reason of local law, must be distributed currently. This includes an amount that may be paid out of income or corpus (such as an annuity) to the extent it is paid out of income for the tax year. The deduction is allowed to the estate even if the personal representative does not make the distribution until a later year or makes no distribution until the final settlement and termination of the estate.

Support allowances. The distribution deduction includes any support allowance that, under a court order or decree or local law, the estate must pay the decedent's surviving spouse or other dependent for a limited period during administration of the estate. The allowance is deductible as income that must be distributed currently or as any other amount paid, credited, or required to be distributed, as discussed next.

Any other amount paid, credited, or required to be distributed. Any other amount paid, credited, or required to be distributed is allowed as a deduction to the estate only in the year actually paid, credited, or distributed. If there is no specific requirement by local law or by the terms of the will that income earned by the estate during administration be distributed currently, a deduction for distributions to the beneficiaries will be allowed to the estate, but only for the actual distributions during the tax year.

If the personal representative has discretion as to when the income is distributed, the deduction is allowed only in the year of distribution.

Alimony and separate maintenance. Alimony and separate maintenance payments that must be included in the spouse's or former spouse's income may be deducted as income that must be distributed currently if they are paid, credited, or distributed out of the income of the estate for the tax year. That spouse or former spouse is treated as a beneficiary.

Payment of beneficiary's obligations. Any payment made by the estate to satisfy a legal obligation of any person is deductible as income that must be distributed currently or as any other amount paid, credited, or required to be distributed. This includes a payment made to satisfy the person's obligation under local law to support another person, such as the person's minor child. The person whose obligation is satisfied is treated as a beneficiary of the estate.

This does not apply to a payment made to satisfy a person's obligation to pay alimony or separate maintenance.

The value of an interest in real estate. The value of an interest in real estate owned by a decedent, title to which passes directly to the beneficiaries under local law, is not included as any other amount paid, credited, or required to be distributed.

Property distributed in kind. If an estate distributes property in kind, the estate's deduction ordinarily is the lesser of its basis in the property or the property's fair market value when distributed. However, the deduction is the property's fair market value if the estate recognizes gain on the distribution. See *Gain or loss on distributions in kind* under *Income To Include,* earlier.

Property is distributed in kind if it satisfies the beneficiary's right to receive another property or amount, such as the income of the estate or a specific dollar amount. It generally includes any noncash distribution other than:

1) A specific bequest (unless it must be distributed in more than three installments), or

2) Real property, the title to which passes directly to the beneficiary under local law.

Character of amounts distributed. If the decedent's will or local law does not provide for the allocation of different classes of income, you must treat the amount deductible for distributions to beneficiaries as consisting of the same proportion of each class of items entering into the computation of distributable net income as the total of each class bears to the total distributable net income. For more information about the character of distributions, see *Character of Distributions* under *Distributions to Beneficiaries From an Estate,* later.

Example. An estate has distributable net income of $2,000, consisting of $1,000 of taxable interest and $1,000 of rental income. Distributions to the beneficiary total $1,500. The distribution deduction consists of $750 of taxable interest and $750 of rental income, unless the will or local law provides a different allocation.

Limit on deduction for distributions. You cannot deduct any amount of distributable net income not included in the estate's gross income.

Example. An estate has distributable net income of $2,000, consisting of $1,000 of dividends and $1,000 of tax-exempt interest. Distributions to the beneficiaries are $1,500. Except for this rule, the distribution deduction would be $1,500 ($750 of dividends and $750 of tax-exempt interest). However, as the result of this rule, the distribution deduction is limited to $750, because no deduction is allowed for the tax-exempt interest distributed.

Funeral and Medical Expenses

No deduction can be taken for funeral expenses or medical and dental expenses on the estate's income tax return, Form 1041.

Funeral expenses. Funeral expenses paid by the estate are not deductible in figuring the estate's taxable income on Form 1041. They are deductible only for determining the taxable estate for federal estate tax purposes on Form 706.

Medical and dental expenses of a decedent. The medical and dental expenses of a decedent paid by the estate are not deductible in figuring the estate's taxable income on Form 1041. You can deduct them in figuring the taxable estate for federal estate tax purposes on Form 706. If these expenses are paid within the 1½-year period beginning with the day after the decedent's death, you can elect to deduct them on the decedent's income tax return (Form 1040) for the year in which they were incurred. See *Exemptions and Deductions* under *Final Return for Decedent,* earlier.

Credits, Tax, and Payments

This section includes brief discussions of some of the tax credits, types of taxes that may be owed, and estimated tax payments

that are reported on the income tax return of the estate, Form 1041.

Credits

Estates generally are allowed the same tax credits that are allowed to individuals. The credits generally are allocated between the estate and the beneficiaries. However, estates are not allowed the credit for the elderly or the disabled or the earned income credit discussed earlier under *Final Return for Decedent.*

Foreign tax credit. Foreign tax credit is discussed in Publication 514, *Foreign Tax Credit for Individuals.*

General business credit. The general business credit is available to an estate that is involved in a business. The credit is limited to the estate's regular tax liability with certain adjustments minus the greater of:

1) The tentative minimum tax for the year, or

2) 25% of tax liability that is more than $25,000. The $25,000 must be reduced to an amount that bears the same ratio to $25,000 as the income that is not allocated to beneficiaries bears to the total income of the estate.

Tax

An estate cannot use the Tax Table that applies to individuals. The tax rate schedule to use is in the instructions for Form 1041.

Maximum tax rate on capital gains. The maximum 28% rate on net capital gains is figured in Part VI of Schedule D (Form 1041). Complete Part VI if both lines 16 and 17, column (b), are net gains and the estate's taxable income (line 22, Form 1041) is more than $3,800.

Alternative minimum tax (AMT). An estate may be liable for the alternative minimum tax. To figure the alternative minimum tax, use Schedule I (Form 1041), *Alternative Minimum Tax.* Certain credits may be limited by any "tentative minimum tax" figured on line 37, Part III of Schedule I (Form 1041), even if there is no alternative minimum tax liability.

If the estate takes a deduction for distributions to beneficiaries, complete Part I and Part II of Schedule I even if the estate does not owe alternative minimum tax. Allocate the income distribution deduction figured on a minimum tax basis among the beneficiaries and report each beneficiary's share on Schedule K–1 (Form 1041). Also show each beneficiary's share of any adjustments or tax preference items for depreciation, depletion, and amortization.

For more information, get the instructions to Form 1041.

Payments

The estate's income tax liability must be paid in full when the return is filed. You may have to pay estimated tax, however, as explained next.

Estimated tax. Estates with tax years ending 2 or more years after the date of the decedent's death must pay estimated tax in the same manner as individuals.

If you must make estimated tax payments for 1997, use *Form 1041–ES, Estimated Income Tax for Estates and Trusts,* to determine the estimated tax to be paid.

Generally, you must pay estimated tax if the estate is expected to owe, after subtracting any withholding and credits, at least $500 in tax for 1997. You will not, however, have to pay estimated tax if you expect the withholding and credits to be at least:

1) 90% of the tax to be shown on the 1997 return, or

2) 100% of the tax shown on the 1996 return (assuming the return covered all 12 months).

The percentage in (2) above is 110% if the estate's 1996 adjusted gross income (AGI) was $150,000 or more. To figure the estate's AGI, see the instructions for line 15b, Form 1041.

The general rule is that you must make your first estimated tax payment by April 15, 1997. You can either pay all of your estimated tax at that time or pay it in four equal amounts that are due by April 15, 1997; June 16, 1997; September 15, 1997; and January 15, 1998. For exceptions to the general rule, get the instructions for Form 1041–ES and Publication 505.

If your return is on a fiscal year basis, your due dates are the 15th day of the 4th, 6th, and 9th months of your fiscal year and the 1st month of the following fiscal year.

If any of these dates fall on a Saturday, Sunday, or legal holiday, use the next business day.

You may be charged a penalty for not paying enough estimated tax or for not making the payment on time in the required amount (even if you have an overpayment on your tax return). Get Form 2210, *Underpayment of Estimated Tax by Individuals, Estates and Trusts,* to figure any penalty.

For more information, get the instructions for Form 1041–ES and Publication 505.

Name, Address, and Signature

In the top space of the name and address area of Form 1041, enter the exact name of the estate from the Form SS–4 used to apply for the estate's employer identification number. In the remaining spaces, enter the name and address of the personal representative (fiduciary) of the estate.

Signature. The personal representative (or its authorized officer if the personal representative is not an individual) must sign the return. An individual who prepares the return for pay must manually sign the return as preparer. Signature stamps or labels are not acceptable. For additional information about the requirements for preparers of returns, see the instructions for Form 1041.

When and Where To File

When you file Form 1041 (or Form 1040NR if it applies) depends on whether you choose a calendar year or a fiscal year as the estate's accounting period. Where you file Form 1041 depends on where you, as the personal representative, live or have your principal office.

When to file. If you choose the calendar year as the estate's accounting period, the Form 1041 for 1996 is due by April 15 (June 16, 1997, in the case of Form 1040NR for a non-resident alien estate that does not have an office in the United States). If you choose a fiscal year, the Form 1041 is due by the 15th day of the 4th month (6th month in the case of Form 1040NR) after the end of the tax year. If the due date is a Saturday, Sunday, or legal holiday, the return is due on the next business day.

Extension of time to file. An extension of time to file Form 1041 may be granted if you have clearly described the reasons that will cause your delay in filing the return. Use Form 2758, *Application for Extension of Time To File Certain Excise, Income, Information, and Other Returns,* to request an extension. The extension is not automatic, so you should request it early enough for the IRS to act on the application before the regular due date of Form 1041. You should file Form 2758 in duplicate with the IRS office where you must file Form 1041.

If you have not yet established an accounting period, filing Form 2758 will serve to establish the accounting period stated on that form. Changing to another accounting period requires prior approval of the IRS.

Generally, an extension of time to file a return *does not extend the time for payment of tax due.* You must pay the total income tax estimated to be due on Form 1041 in full by the regular due date of the return. For additional information, see the instructions for Form 2758.

Where to file. As the personal representative of an estate, file the estate's income tax return (Form 1041) with the Internal Revenue Service center for the state where you live or have your principal place of business. A list of the states and addresses that apply is in the instructions for Form 1041.

You must send Form 1040NR to the Internal Revenue Service Center, Philadelphia, PA 19255.

Electronic filing. Form 1041 can be filed electronically or on magnetic tape. See the instructions for Form 1041 for more information.

Distributions to Beneficiaries From an Estate

If you are the beneficiary of an estate that must distribute all its income currently, you must report your share of the distributable net income whether or not you have actually received it.

If you are the beneficiary of an estate that does not have to distribute all its income currently, you must report all income that must be distributed to you (whether or not actually distributed) plus all other amounts paid, credited, or required to be distributed to you, up to your share of distributable net income. Distributable net income (figured without the charitable deduction) is the income of the estate available for distribution. As explained earlier in *Distributions Deduction* under *Income Tax Return of an Estate–Form 1041* and its discussion, *Exemption and Deductions,* for an amount to be currently distributable income, there must be a specific requirement for current distribution either under local law or by the terms of the decedent's will. If there is no such requirement, the income is reportable only when distributed.

Income That Must Be Distributed Currently

Beneficiaries who are entitled to receive currently distributable income generally must include in gross income the entire amount due them. However, if the currently distributable income is more than the estate's distributable net income figured without deducting charitable contributions, each beneficiary must include in gross income a ratable part of the distributable net income.

Example. Under the terms of the will of Gerald Peters, $5,000 a year is to be paid to his widow and $2,500 a year is to be paid to his daughter out of the estate's income during the period of administration. There are no charitable contributions. For the year, the estate's distributable net income is only $6,000. Since the distributable net income is less than the currently distributable income, the widow must include in her gross income only $4,000 ([5,000 ÷ 7,500] × $6,000), and the daughter must include in her gross income only $2,000 ([2,500 ÷ 7,500] × $6,000).

Annuity payable out of income or corpus. Income that must be distributed currently includes any amount that must be paid out of income or corpus (principal of the estate) to the extent the amount is satisfied out of income for the tax year. An annuity that must be paid in all events (either out of income or corpus) would qualify as income that must be distributed currently to the extent there is income of the estate not paid, credited, or required to be distributed to other beneficiaries for the tax year.

Example 1. Henry Frank's will provides that $500 be paid to the local Community Chest out of the income each year. It also provides that $2,000 a year is currently distributable out of income to his brother, Fred, and an annuity of $3,000 is to be paid to his sister, Sharon, out of income or corpus. Capital gains are allocable to corpus, but all expenses are to be charged against income. Last year, the estate had income of $6,000 and expenses of $3,000. The personal representative paid the $500 to the Community Chest and made the distributions to Fred and Sharon as required by the will.

The estate's distributable net income (figured before the charitable contribution) is $3,000. The currently distributable income totals $2,500 ($2,000 to Fred and $500 to Sharon). The income available for Sharon's annuity is only $500 because the will requires that the charitable contribution be paid out of current income. Because the $2,500 treated as distributed currently is less than the $3,000 distributable net income (before the contribution), Fred must include $2,000 in his gross income, and Sharon must include $500 in her gross income.

Example 2. Assume the same facts as in Example 1 except that the estate has an additional $1,000 of administration expenses, commissions, etc., that are chargeable to corpus. The estate's distributable net income (figured before the charitable contribution) is now $2,000 ($3,000 minus $1,000 additional expense). The amount treated as currently distributable income is still $2,500 ($2,000 to Fred and $500 to Sharon). Because the $2,500, treated as distributed currently, is more than the $2,000 distributable net income, Fred has to include only $1,600 ([2,000 ÷ 2,500] × $2,000) in his gross income and Sharon has to include only $400 ([500 ÷ 2,500] × $2,000) in her gross income. Because Fred and Sharon are beneficiaries of amounts that must be distributed currently, they do not benefit from the reduction of distributable net income by the charitable contribution deduction.

Other Amounts Distributed

Any other amount paid, credited, or required to be distributed to the beneficiary for the tax year also must be included in the beneficiary's gross income. Such an amount is in addition to those amounts that must be distributed currently, as discussed earlier. It does not include gifts or bequests of specific sums of money or specific property if such sums are paid in three or fewer installments. However, amounts that can be paid only out of income are not excluded under this rule. If the sum of the income that must be distributed currently and other amounts paid, credited, or required to be distributed exceeds distributable net income, these other amounts are included in the beneficiary's gross income only to the extent distributable net income exceeds the income that must be distributed currently. If there is more than one beneficiary, each will include in gross income only a pro rata share of such amounts.

Examples of other amounts paid are:

1) Distributions made at the discretion of the personal representative;

2) Distributions required by the terms of the will upon the happening of a specific event;

3) Annuities that must be paid in any event, but only out of corpus (principal);

4) Distributions of property in kind as defined earlier in *Distributions Deduction* under *Income Tax Return of an Estate—Form 1041* and its discussion, *Exemption and Deductions;* and

5) Distributions required for the support of the decedent's surviving spouse or other dependent for a limited period, but only out of corpus (principal).

If an estate distributes property in kind, the amount of the distribution ordinarily is the lesser of the estate's basis in the property or the property's fair market value when distributed. However, the amount of the distribution is the property's fair market value if the estate recognizes gain on the distribution. See *Gain or loss on distributions in kind* in the discussion *Income To Include* under *Income Tax Return of an Estate—Form 1041,* earlier.

Example. The terms of Michael Scott's will require the distribution of $2,500 of income annually to his wife, Susan. If any income remains, it may be accumulated or distributed to his two children, Joe and Alice, in amounts at the discretion of the personal representative. The personal representative also may invade the corpus (principal) for the benefit of Scott's wife and children.

Last year, the estate had income of $6,000 after deduction of all expenses. Its distributable net income is also $6,000. The personal representative distributed the required $2,500 of income to Susan. In addition, the personal representative distributed $1,500 each to Joe and Alice and an additional $2,000 to Susan.

Susan includes in her gross income the $2,500 of currently distributable income. The other amounts distributed totaled $5,000 ($1,500 + $1,500 + $2,000) and are includible in the income of Susan, Joe, and Alice to the extent of $3,500 (distributable net income of $6,000 minus currently distributable income to Susan of $2,500). Susan will include an additional $1,400 ([2,000 ÷5,000] × $3,500) in her gross income. Joe and Alice each will include $1,050 ([1,500 ÷ 5,000] × $3,500) in their gross incomes.

Discharge of a Legal Obligation

If an estate, under the terms of a will, discharges a legal obligation of a beneficiary, the discharge is included in that beneficiary's income as either currently distributable income or other amount paid. This does not apply to the discharge of a beneficiary's obligation to pay alimony or separate maintenance.

The beneficiary's legal obligations include a legal obligation of support, for example, of a minor child. Local law determines a legal obligation of support.

Character of Distributions

An amount distributed to a beneficiary for inclusion in gross income retains the same character for the beneficiary that it had for the estate.

No charitable contributions are made. If no charitable contributions are made during the tax year, you must treat the distributions as consisting of the same proportion of each class of items entering into the computation of distributable net income as the total of each class bears to the total distributable net income. Distributable net income was defined earlier in *Distributions Deduction* under *Income Tax Return of an Estate—Form 1041* and its discussion, *Exemption and Deductions.* However, if the will or local law specifically provides or requires a different allocation, you must use that allocation.

Example 1. An estate has distributable net income of $3,000, consisting of $1,800 in rents and $1,200 in taxable interest. There is no provision in the will or local law for the allocation of income. The personal representative distributes $1,500 each to Jim and Ted, beneficiaries under their father's will. Each will be treated as having received $900 in rents and $600 of taxable interest.

Example 2. Assume in Example 1 that the will provides for the payment of the taxable interest to Jim and the rental income to Ted and that the personal representative distributed the income under those provisions. Jim is treated as having received $1,200 in taxable interest and Ted is treated as having received $1,800 of rental income.

If a charitable contribution is made. If a charitable contribution is made by an estate and the terms of the will or local law provide for the contribution to be paid from specified sources, that provision governs. If no provision or requirement exists, the charitable contribution deduction must be allocated among the classes of income entering into the computation of the income of the estate before allocation of other deductions among the items of distributable net income. In allocating items of income and deductions to beneficiaries to whom income must be distributed currently, the charitable contribution deduction is not taken into account to the extent that it exceeds income for the year reduced by currently distributable income.

Example. The will of Harry Thomas requires a current distribution out of income of $3,000 a year to his wife, Betty, during the administration of the estate. The will also provides that the personal representative, using discretion, may distribute the balance of the current earnings either to Harry's son, Tim, or to one or more of certain designated charities. Last year, the estate's income consisted of $4,000 of taxable interest and $1,000 of tax-exempt interest. There were no deductible expenses. The personal representative distributed the $3,000 to Betty, made a contribution of $2,500 to the local heart association, and paid $1,500 to Tim.

The distributable net income for determining the character of the distribution to Betty is $3,000. The charitable contribution deduction to be taken into account for this computation is $2,000 (the estate's income ($5,000) minus the currently distributable income ($3,000)). The $2,000 charitable contribution deduction must be allocated: $1,600 ([4,000 ÷ 5,000] × $2,000) to taxable interest and $400 ([1,000 ÷ 5,000] × $2,000) to tax-exempt interest. Betty is considered to have received $2,400 ($4,000 minus $1,600) of taxable interest and $600 ($1,000 minus $400) of tax-exempt interest. She must include the $2,400 in her gross income. She must report the $600 of tax-exempt interest, but it is not taxable.

To determine the amount to be included in the gross income of Tim, however, take into account the entire charitable contribution deduction. Since the currently distributable income is greater than the estate's income after taking into account the charitable contribution deduction, none of the amount paid to Tim must be included in his gross income for the year.

How and When To Report

How you report your income from the estate depends on the character of the income in the hands of the estate. When you report the income depends on whether it represents amounts credited or required to be distributed to you or other amounts.

How to report estate income. Each item of income keeps the same character in your hands as it had in the hands of the estate. If the items of income distributed or considered to be distributed to you include dividends, tax-exempt interest, or capital gains, they will keep the same character in your hands for purposes of the tax treatment given those items. Report your dividends on line 9, Form 1040, and report your capital gains on Schedule D (Form 1040). The tax-exempt interest, while not included in taxable income, must be shown on line 8b, Form 1040. Report business and other nonpassive income on Schedule E, Part III (Form 1040).

The estate's personal representative should provide you with the classification of the various items that make up your share of the estate income and the credits you should take into consideration so that you can properly prepare your individual income tax return. See *Schedule K–1 (Form 1041),* later.

When to report estate income. If income from the estate is credited or must be distributed to you for a tax year, report that income (even if not distributed) on your return for that year. Report other income from the estate on your return for the year in which you receive it. If your tax year is different from the estate's tax year, see *Different tax years,* next.

Different tax years. You must include your share of the estate income in your return for your tax year in which the last day of the estate tax year falls. If the tax year of the estate is the calendar year and your tax year is a fiscal year ending on June 30, you will include in gross income for the tax year ended June 30 your share of the estate's distributable net income distributed or considered distributed during the calendar year ending the previous December 31.

Death of individual beneficiary. If an individual beneficiary dies, the beneficiary's share of the estate's distributable net income may be distributed or be considered distributed by the estate for its tax year that does not end with or within the last tax year of the beneficiary. In this case, the estate income that must be included in the gross income on the beneficiary's final return is based on the amounts distributed or considered distributed during the tax year of the estate in which his or her last tax year ended. However, for a cash basis beneficiary, the gross income of the last tax year includes only the amounts actually distributed before death. Income that must be distributed to the beneficiary but, in fact, distributed to the beneficiary's estate after death is included in the gross income of the beneficiary's estate as income in respect of a decedent.

Termination of nonindividual beneficiary. If a beneficiary that is not an individual, for example a trust or a corporation, ceases to exist, the amount included in its gross income for its last tax year is determined as if the beneficiary were a deceased individual. However, income that must be distributed before termination, but which is actually distributed to the beneficiary's successor in interest, is included in the gross income of the nonindividual beneficiary for its last tax year.

Schedule K-1 (Form 1041). The personal representative for the estate must provide you with a copy of Schedule K-1 (Form 1041) or a substitute Schedule K-1. You should not file the form with your Form 1040, but should keep it for your personal records.

Each beneficiary (or nominee of a beneficiary) who receives a distribution from the estate for the tax year or to whom any item is allocated must receive a Schedule K-1 or substitute. The personal representative handling the estate must furnish the form to each beneficiary or nominee by the date on which the Form 1041 is filed.

Nominees. A person who holds an interest in an estate as a nominee for a beneficiary must provide the estate with the name and address of the beneficiary, and any other required information. The nominee must provide the beneficiary with the information received from the estate.

Penalty. A personal representative (or nominee) who fails to provide the correct information may be subject to a $50 penalty for each failure.

Special Rules for Distributions

Some special rules apply for determining the deduction allowable to the estate for distributions to beneficiaries and the amount includible in the beneficiary's gross income.

Bequest

A bequest is the act of giving or leaving property to another through the last will and testament. Generally, any distribution of income (or property in kind) to a beneficiary is an allowable deduction to the estate and is includible in the beneficiary's gross income to the extent of the estate's distributable net income. However, it will not be an allowable deduction to the estate and will not be includible in the beneficiary's gross income if the distribution:

1) Is required by the terms of the will,

2) Is a gift or bequest of a *specific sum of money or property,* and

3) Is paid out in three or fewer installments under the terms of the will.

Specific sum of money or property. To meet this test, the amount of money or the identity of the specific property must be determinable under the decedent's will as of the date of death. To qualify as specific property, the property must be identifiable both as to its kind and as to its amount.

Example 1. Dave Rogers' will provided that his son, Ed, receive Dave's interest in the Rogers-Jones partnership. Dave's daughter, Marie, would receive a sum of money equal to the value of the partnership interest given to Ed. The bequest to Ed is a gift of a specific property ascertainable at the date of Dave Rogers' death. The bequest of a specific sum of money to Marie is determinable on the same date.

Example 2. Mike Jenkins' will provided that his widow, Helen, would receive money or property to be selected by the personal representative equal in value to half of his adjusted gross estate. The identity of the property and the money in the bequest are dependent on the personal representative's discretion and the payment of administration expenses and other charges, which are not determinable at the date of Mike's death. As a result, the provision is not a bequest of a specific sum of money or of specific property, and any distribution under that provision is a deduction for the estate and income to the beneficiary (to the extent of the estate's distributable net income). The fact that the bequest will be specific sometime before distribution is immaterial. It is not ascertainable by the terms of the will as of the date of death.

Distributions not treated as bequests. The following distributions are not bequests that meet all of the three tests listed earlier that allow a distribution to be excluded from the beneficiary's income and do not allow it as a deduction to the estate.

Paid only from income. An amount that can be paid only from current or prior income of the estate does not qualify even if it is specific in amount and there is no provision for installment payments.

An annuity. An annuity or a payment of money or of specific property in lieu of, or having the effect of, an annuity is not the payment of a specific property or sum of money.

Residuary estate. If the will provides for the payment of the balance or residue of the estate to a beneficiary of the estate after all expenses and other specific legacies or bequests, that residuary bequest is not a payment of a specific property or sum of money.

Gifts made in installments. Even if the gift or bequest is made in a lump sum or in three or fewer installments, it will not qualify as a specific property or sum of money if the will provides that the amount must be paid in more than three installments.

Conditional bequests. A bequest of a specific property or sum of money that may otherwise be excluded from the beneficiary's gross income will not lose the exclusion solely because the payment is subject to a condition.

Installment payments. Certain rules apply in determining whether a bequest of specific property or a sum of money has to be paid or credited to a beneficiary in more than three installments.

Personal items. Do not take into account bequests of articles for personal use, such as personal and household effects and automobiles.

Real property. Do not take into account specifically designated real property, the title to which passes under local law directly to the beneficiary.

Other property. All other bequests under the decedent's will for which no time of payment or crediting is specified and that are to be paid or credited in the ordinary course of administration of the estate are considered as required to be paid or credited in a single installment. Also, all bequests payable at any one specified time under the terms of the will are treated as a single installment.

A testamentary trust. In determining the number of installments that must be paid or credited to a beneficiary, the decedent's estate and a testamentary trust created by the decedent's will are treated as separate entities. Amounts paid or credited by the estate and by the trust are counted separately.

Denial of Double Deduction

A deduction cannot be claimed twice. If an amount is considered to have been distributed to a beneficiary of an estate in a preceding tax year, it cannot again be included in figuring the deduction for the year of the actual distribution.

Example. The will provides that the estate must distribute currently all of its income to a beneficiary. For administrative convenience, the personal representative did not make a distribution of a part of the income for the tax year until the first month of the next tax year. The amount must be deducted by the estate in the first tax year, and must be included in the gross income of the beneficiary in that year. This amount cannot be deducted again by the estate in the following year when it is paid to the beneficiary, nor must the beneficiary again include the amount in gross income in that year.

Charitable Contributions

The amount of a charitable contribution used as a deduction by the estate in determining taxable income cannot be claimed again as a deduction for a distribution to a beneficiary.

Termination of Estate

The termination of an estate generally is marked by the end of the period of administration and by the distribution of the assets to the beneficiaries under the terms of the will or under the laws of succession of the state if there is no will. These beneficiaries may or may not be the same persons as the beneficiaries of the estate's income.

Period of Administration

The period of administration is the time actually required by the personal representative to assemble all of the decedent's assets, pay all the expenses and obligations, and distribute the assets to the beneficiaries. This may be longer or shorter than the time provided by local law for the administration of estates.

Ends if all assets distributed. If all assets are distributed except for a reasonable amount set aside, in good faith, for the payment of unascertained or contingent liabilities and expenses (but not including a claim by a beneficiary, as a beneficiary) the estate will be considered terminated.

Ends if period unreasonably long. If settlement is prolonged unreasonably, the estate will be treated as terminated for federal income tax purposes. From that point on, the gross income, deductions, and credits of the estate are considered those of the person or persons succeeding to the property of the estate.

Transfer of Unused Deductions to Beneficiaries

If the estate has unused loss carryovers or excess deductions for its last tax year, they are allowed to those beneficiaries who succeed to the estate's property. See *Successor beneficiary,* later.

Unused loss carryovers. An unused net operating loss carryover or capital loss carryover existing upon termination of the estate is allowed to the beneficiaries succeeding to the property of the estate. That is, these deductions will be claimed on the beneficiary's tax return. This treatment occurs only if a carryover would have been allowed to the estate in a later tax year if the estate had not been terminated.

Both types of carryovers generally keep their same character for the beneficiary as they had for the estate. However, if the beneficiary of a capital loss carryover is a corporation, the corporation will treat the carryover as a short-term capital loss regardless of its status in the estate. The net operating loss carryover and the capital loss carryover are used in

figuring both the taxable income and the adjusted gross income of the beneficiary. In addition, the net operating loss carryover is used in figuring the alternative minimum tax.

The first tax year to which the loss is carried is the beneficiary's tax year in which the estate terminates. If the loss can be carried to more than one tax year, the estate's last tax year (whether or not a short tax year) and the beneficiary's first tax year to which the loss is carried each constitute a tax year for figuring the number of years to which a loss may be carried. A capital loss carryover from an estate to a corporate beneficiary will be treated as though it resulted from a loss incurred in the estate's last tax year (whether or not a short tax year), regardless of when the estate actually incurred the loss.

If the last tax year of the estate is the last tax year to which a net operating loss may be carried, see *No double deductions,* later. For a general discussion of net operating losses, get Publication 536. For a discussion of capital losses and capital loss carryovers, get Publication 550.

Excess deductions. If the deductions in the estate's last tax year (other than deductions for personal exemptions and charitable contributions) are more than gross income for that year, the beneficiaries succeeding to the estate's property can claim the excess as a deduction in figuring taxable income. To establish these deductions, a return must be filed for the estate along with a schedule showing the computation of each kind of deduction and the allocation of each to the beneficiaries.

An individual beneficiary must itemize deductions to claim these excess deductions. The deduction is claimed on Schedule A, Form 1040, as a miscellaneous itemized deduction subject to the 2%-of-adjusted-gross-income limit. The beneficiaries can claim the deduction only for the tax year in which or with which the estate terminates, whether the year of termination is a normal year or a short tax year.

No double deductions. A net operating loss deduction allowable to a successor beneficiary cannot be considered in figuring the excess deductions on termination. However, if the estate's last tax year is the last year in which a deduction for a net operating loss can be taken, the deduction, to the extent not absorbed in the last return of the estate, is treated as an excess deduction on termination. Any item of income or deduction, or any part thereof, that is taken into account in figuring a net operating loss or a capital loss carryover of the estate for its last tax year cannot be used again to figure the excess deduction on termination.

Successor beneficiary. A beneficiary entitled to an unused loss carryover or an excess deduction is the beneficiary who, upon the estate's termination, bears the burden of any loss for which a carryover is allowed or of any deductions more than gross income.

If decedent had no will. If the decedent had no will, the beneficiaries are those heirs or next of kin to whom the estate is distributed. If

the estate is insolvent, the beneficiaries are those to whom the estate would have been distributed had it not been insolvent. If the decedent's spouse is entitled to a specified dollar amount of property before any distributions to other heirs and the estate is less than that amount, the spouse is the beneficiary to the extent of the deficiency.

If decedent had a will. If the decedent had a will, a beneficiary normally means the residuary beneficiaries (including residuary trusts). Those beneficiaries who receive a specific property or a specific amount of money ordinarily are not considered residuary beneficiaries, except to the extent the specific amount is not paid in full. Also, a beneficiary who is not strictly a residuary beneficiary, but whose devise or bequest is determined by the value of the estate as reduced by the loss or deduction, is entitled to the carryover or the deduction. For example, such a beneficiary would include:

1) A beneficiary of a fraction of the decedent's net estate after payment of debts, expenses, and specific bequests;

2) A nonresiduary beneficiary, when the estate is unable to satisfy the bequest in full; and

3) A surviving spouse receiving a fractional share of the estate in fee under a statutory right of election when the losses or deductions are taken into account in determining the share. However, such a beneficiary does not include a recipient of a dower or curtesy, or a beneficiary who receives any income from the estate from which the loss or excess deduction is carried over.

Allocation among beneficiaries. The total of the unused loss carryovers or the excess deductions on termination that may be deducted by the successor beneficiaries is to be divided according to the share of each in the burden of the loss or deduction.

Example. Under his father's will, Arthur is to receive $20,000. The remainder of the estate is to be divided equally between his brothers, Mark and Tom. After all expenses are paid, the estate has sufficient funds to pay Arthur only $15,000, with nothing to Mark and Tom. In the estate's last tax year there are excess deductions of $5,000 and $10,000 of unused loss carryovers. Since the total of the excess deductions and unused loss carryovers is $15,000 and Arthur is considered a successor beneficiary to the extent of $5,000, he is entitled to one-third of the unused loss carryover and one-third of the excess deductions. His brothers may divide the other two-thirds of the excess deductions and the unused loss carryovers between them.

Transfer of Credit for Estimated Tax Payments

When an estate terminates, the personal representative can choose to transfer to the beneficiaries the credit for all or part of the estate's estimated tax payments for the last tax year. To make this choice, the personal representative must complete Form 1041-T, *Allocation of Estimated Tax Payments to Beneficiaries,* and file it either separately or with the estate's final Form 1041. The Form 1041-T must be filed by the 65th day after the close of the estate's tax year.

The amount of estimated tax allocated to each beneficiary is treated as paid or credited to the beneficiary on the last day of the estate's final tax year and must be reported on line 13a, Schedule K-1 (Form 1041). If the estate terminated in 1996 this amount is treated as a payment of 1996 estimated tax made by the beneficiary on January 15, 1997.

Form 706

You must file Form 706, *United States Estate (and Generation-Skipping Transfer) Tax Return,* generally, if death occurred in 1996 and the gross estate is more than $600,000.

If you must file Form 706, it has to be done within 9 months after the date of the decedent's death unless you receive an extension of time to file. File this form with the Internal Revenue Service Center listed in the form instructions.

Use Form 4768, *Application for Extension of Time To File a Return and/or Pay U.S. Estate (and Generation-Skipping Transfer) Taxes,* to apply for an extension of time. If you received an extension, attach a copy of it to Form 706.

Comprehensive Example

The following is an example of a typical situation. All figures on the filled-in forms have been rounded to the nearest whole dollar.

On April 9, 1996, your father, John R. Smith, died at the age of 62. He had not resided in a community property state. His will named you to serve as his executor (personal representative). Except for specific bequests to your mother, Mary, of your parents' home and your father's automobile and a bequest of $5,000 to his church, your father's will named your mother and his brother as beneficiaries.

One of the first things you should do, as soon as the court has approved your appointment as the executor, is to obtain an employer identification number. (See *Duties* under *Personal Representatives* earlier.) Next, you should notify the Internal Revenue Service center where you will file the tax returns of your father's estate that you have been appointed his executor. You should use Form 56, *Notice Concerning Fiduciary Relationship.*

Assets of the estate. Your father had the following assets when he died.

1) His checking account balance was $2,550, and his savings account balance was $53,650.

2) Your father inherited your parents' home from his parents on March 5, 1976. At that time it was worth $42,000, but was appraised at the time of your father's death to be worth $150,000. The home was free of existing debts (or mortgages) at the time of his death.

3) Your father owned 500 shares of ABC Company stock that had cost him $10.20 a share in 1980, but which had a mean selling price (midpoint between highest and lowest selling price) of $25 a share on the day he died. He also owned 500 shares of XYZ Company stock that had cost him $20 a share in 1985, but which had a mean selling price on the date of death of $62.

4) The appraiser valued your father's automobile at $6,300 and the household effects at $18,500.

5) Your father also owned coin and stamp collections. The face value of the coins in the collection was only $600, but the appraiser valued it at $2,800. The stamp collection was valued at $3,500.

6) Your father's employer sent a check to your mother for $11,082 ($12,000 minus $918 for social security and Medicare taxes), representing unpaid salary and payment for accrued vacation time. The statement that came with the check indicated that no amount was withheld for income tax. Since the check was made out to the estate, your mother gave you the check.

7) The Easy Life Insurance Company had given a check for $275,000 to your mother as the beneficiary named in the life insurance policy on his life.

8) Your father was the owner of several Series EE U.S. Savings Bonds on which he named your mother as co-owner. Your father purchased the bonds during the past several years. The cost of these bonds totaled $2,500. After referring to the appropriate table of redemption values (see *U.S. Savings Bonds acquired from decedent,* earlier in this publication), you determine that interest of $840 had accrued on the bonds at the date of your father's death. You must include the redemption value of these bonds at date of death, $3,340, in your father's gross estate.

9) On July 1, 1980, your parents purchased a house for $90,000. They have held the property for rental purposes continuously since its purchase. Your mother contributed one-third of the purchase, or $30,000 (from an inheritance), and your father contributed $60,000. They owned the property, however, as joint tenants with right of survivorship. An appraiser valued the property at $110,000. You include $55,000, one-half of the value, in your father's gross estate because your parents owned the property as joint tenants with right of survivorship and they were the only joint tenants.

Your mother also gave you a Form W-2, *Wage and Tax Statement,* that your father's employer had sent. In examining it, you discover that your father had been paid $9,000 in salary between January 1, 1996, and April 9, 1996, (the date he died). The Form W-2 showed $9,000 in box 1 and $21,000 ($9,000 + $12,000) in boxes 3 and 5. The Form W-2 indicated $2,305 as federal income tax withheld in box 2. The estate received a Form 1099-MISC from the employer showing $12,000 in box 3. The estate received a Form 1099-INT for your father showing he was paid $1,900 interest on his savings account in 1996 before he died.

Final Return for Decedent

Checking the papers in your father's files, you determine that the $9,000 paid to him by his employer (as shown on the Form W-2), rental income, and interest are the only items of income he received between January 1 and the date of his death. You will have to file an income tax return for him for the period during which he lived. (You determine that he timely filed his 1995 income tax return before he died.) The final return is not due until April 15, 1997, the same date it would have been due had your father lived during all of 1996.

Since the check representing unpaid salary and earned but unused vacation time was not paid to your father before he died, the $12,000 is not reported as income on his final return. It is reported on the income tax return for the estate (Form 1041) for 1996. The only taxable income to be reported for your father will be the $9,000 salary (as shown on the Form W-2) the $1,900 interest and his portion of the rental income that he received in 1996.

Your father was a cash basis taxpayer and did not report the interest accrued on the Series EE U.S. Savings Bonds on prior tax returns that he filed jointly with your mother. As the personal representative of your father's estate, you choose to report the interest earned on these bonds before your father's death ($840) on the final income tax return.

The rental property was leased the entire year of 1996 for $700 per month. Under local law, your parents (as joint tenants) each had a half interest in the income from the property. Your father's will, however, stipulates that the entire rental income is to be paid directly to your mother. None of the rental income will be reported on the income tax return for the estate. Instead, your mother will report all the rental income and expenses on Form 1040. Checking the records and prior tax returns of your parents, you find that they previously elected straight-line depreciation for the rental house with a 25-year life. They allocated $15,000 of the cost to the land (which is never depreciable) and $75,000 to the rental house. Salvage value was disregarded for the depreciation computation. Before 1996, $46,500 had been allowed as depreciation.

Deductions. During the year, you received a bill from the hospital for $615 and bills from your father's doctors totaling $475. You paid these bills as they were presented. In addition, you find other bills from his doctors totaling

$185 that your father paid in 1996, and receipts for prescribed drugs he purchased totaling $36. The funeral home presented you a bill for $6,890 for the expenses of your father's funeral, which you paid.

Because the medical expenses you paid from the estate's funds ($475 and $615) were for your father's care and were paid within 1 year after his death, and because they will not be used to figure the taxable estate, you can treat them as having been paid by your father when he received the medical services. See *Funeral and Medical Expenses* under *Income Tax Return of an Estate—Form 1041* and its discussion, *Exemption and Deductions*, earlier. However, you cannot deduct the funeral expenses either on your father's final return or from the estate's income. They are deductible only on the federal estate tax return (Form 706) as explained under *Funeral and Medical Expenses*.

In addition, after going over other receipts and canceled checks for the tax year with your mother, you determine that the following items are deductible on your parents' 1996 income tax return.

Health insurance	$1,250
State income tax paid	791
Real estate tax on home	1,100
Contributions to church	3,800

Rental expenses included taxes of $700 and interest of $410 on the property; in addition, insurance premiums of $260 and painting and repairs for $350 were paid. These rental expenses totaled $1,720 for the whole year.

Because your mother and father owned the property as joint tenants with right of survivorship and they were the only joint tenants, her basis in this property upon your father's death is $76,375. This is found by adding the $55,000 value of the half interest included in your father's gross estate to your mother's $45,000 share of the cost basis, and subtracting your mother's $23,625 share of depreciation (including 1996 depreciation for the period before your father's death), as explained next.

For 1996, you must make the following computations to figure the depreciation deduction:

1) For the period before your father's death, depreciate the property using the same method and the same basis and life used by your parents in previous years. The amount deductible for one-fourth of the year is $750. (This brings the total depreciation to $47,250 ($46,500 + $750) at the time of your father's death.

2) For the period after your father's death, you must make two computations.

a) Your mother's cost basis ($45,000) minus one-half of the amount allocated to the land ($7,500) is her depreciable basis ($37,500) for half of the property. She continues to use the same life and depreciation method as was originally used for the property. The amount deductible for three-fourths of the year is $1,125.

b) The other half of the property must be depreciated using a depreciation method that is acceptable for property placed in service in 1996. You elect to use the alternative depreciation system (straight-line method) with the mid-month convention. The value included in the estate ($55,000) less the value allocable to the land ($10,000) is the depreciable basis ($45,000) for this half of the property. The amount deductible for this half of the property is $797 ($45,000 × .01771). See chapter 3 and Table A–13 in Publication 946.

Show the total of the amounts in (1) and (2)(a), above, on line 19 of Form 4562, *Depreciation and Amortization*. Show the amount in (2)(b) on line 16c. The total depreciation deduction allowed for the year is $2,672.

 The use of certain types of accelerated depreciation would require you to fill out a Form 6251, Alternative Minimum Tax—Individuals. Use of the straight-line method does not require this.

Filing status. After December 31, 1996, when your mother determines the amount of her income, you and your mother must decide whether you will file a joint return or separate returns for your parents for 1996. Since your mother has no income in 1996 other than the rental income, it appears to be to her advantage to file a joint return.

Tax computation. The illustrations of Form 1040 and related schedules appear at the end of this publication. These illustrations are based on information in this example. The tax refund is $1,769. The computation is as follows:

Income:		
Salary (per Form W–2)	$9,000	
Interest income	2,740	
Net rental income	4,008	
Adjusted Gross Income		$15,748
Minus: Itemized deductions		7,071
Balance		$ 8,677
Minus: Exemptions (2)		5,100
Taxable Income		$ 3,577
Income tax from Tax Table		$ 536
Minus: Tax withheld		2,305
Refund of Taxes		$ 1,769

Income Tax Return of an Estate—Form 1041

The illustrations of Form 1041 and the related schedules appear at the end of this publication. These illustrations are based on the information that follows.

Having determined the tax liability for your father's final return, you now figure the estate's taxable income. You decide to use the calendar year and the cash method of accounting to report the estate's income. This return also is due by April 15, 1997.

In addition to the amount you received from your father's employer for unpaid salary and for vacation pay ($12,000) entered on line 8 (Form 1041), you received a dividend check from the XYZ Company on June 15, 1996. The check was for $750 and you enter it on line 2 (Form 1041). The estate received a Form 1099–INT showing $2,250 interest paid by the bank on the savings account in 1996 after your father died. Show this amount on line 1 (Form 1041).

In September, a local coin collector offered you $3,000 for your father's coin collection, and since your mother was not interested in keeping the collection, you accepted the offer and sold him the collection on September 21, 1996, receiving his certified check for $3,000.

The estate has a gain from the sale of the collection. You will have to report the sale on Schedule D (Form 1041) when you file the income tax return of the estate. The estate has a long-term capital gain of $200 from the sale of the coins. The gain is the excess of the sale price, $3,000, over the value of the collection at the date of your father's death, $2,800. See *Gain (or loss) from sale of property* under *Income Tax Return of an Estate—Form 1041* and its discussion, *Income To Include*, earlier.

TIP *Inherited property sold or disposed of by you within 1 year after the decedent's death is considered to have been held by you for more than 1 year.*

Deductions. In November 1996, you received a bill for the real estate taxes on the home. The bill was for $2,250, which you paid. Include real estate taxes on line 11 (Form 1041). (Real estate tax on the rental property was $700; this amount, however, is reflected on Schedule E (Form 1040).)

You paid $325 for attorney's fees in connection with administration of the estate. This is an expense of administration and is deducted on line 14 (Form 1041). You must, however, file with the return a statement in duplicate that such expense has not been claimed as a deduction from the gross estate for figuring the federal estate tax on Form 706, and that all rights to claim that deduction are waived.

Distributions. Under the terms of the will, you made a distribution of $2,000 to your father's brother, James. The distribution was made from current income of the estate.

The income distribution deduction ($2,000) is figured on Schedule B of Form 1041 and deducted on line 18 (Form 1041).

The distribution of $2,000 must be allocated and reported on Schedule K–1 (Form 1041) as follows:

Page 23

Step 1

Allocation of Income and Deductions:

Type of Income	Amount	Deductions	Balance of Distributable Net Income
Interest (15%)	$2,250	(386)	$1,864
Dividends (5%)	750	(129)	621
Income in Respect of Decedent	12,000	(2,060)	9,940
Total	$15,000	(2,575)	$12,425

Step 2

Allocation of Distribution to be reported on Schedule K–1 (Form 1041) for James:

Interest—

$$\$1,864 \times 2,000/12,425 = \qquad \$300 \quad \text{line 1}$$

Dividends—

$$\$621 \times 2,000/12,425 = \qquad 100 \quad \text{line 2}$$

Other Income—

$$\$9,940 \times 2,000/12,425 = \qquad 1,600 \quad \text{line 4a}$$

Total Distribution $2,000

Since the estate took an income distribution deduction, you must prepare Schedule I (Form 1041), *Alternative Minimum Tax,* regardless of whether the estate is liable for the alternative minimum tax.

The other distribution you made out of the assets of the estate in 1996 was the transfer of the automobile to your mother on July 1. Because this is included in the bequest of property, it is not taken into account in computing the distributions of income to the beneficiary. The life insurance proceeds of $275,000 paid directly to your mother by the insurance company are treated as a specific sum of money transferred to your mother under the terms of the will.

The taxable income of the estate for 1996 is $10,025, figured as follows:

Gross income:

Income in respect of a decedent	$12,000
Dividends	750
Interest	2,250
Capital gain	200
	$15,200

Minus: Deductions & Income Distribution

Real estate taxes	$2,250	
Attorney's fee	325	
Exemption	600	
Distribution	2,000	5,175
Taxable income		$10,025

Since the estate had a net capital gain and taxable income of more than $3,800, you use Part VI of Schedule D (Form 1041) to figure the tax ($3,050) for 1996.

1997 income tax return for estate. On January 6, 1997, you receive a dividend check from the XYZ Company for $500. You also have interest posted to the savings account in January totaling $350. On January 24, 1997, you make a final accounting to the court and obtain permission to close the estate. In the accounting you list $1,650 as the balance of the expense of administering the estate.

You advise the court that you plan to pay $5,000 to Hometown Church, under the provision of the will, and that you will distribute the balance of the property to your mother, Mary Smith, the remaining beneficiary.

Gross Income. After making the distributions already described, you can wind up the affairs of the estate. Because the gross income of the estate for 1997 is more than $600, you must file an income tax return, Form 1041, for 1997 (not shown). The estate's gross income for 1997 is $850 (dividends $500 and interest $350).

Deductions. After making the following computations, you determine that none of the distributions made to your mother must be included in her taxable income for 1997.

Gross Income for 1997:

Dividends	$ 500
Interest	350
	$ 850
Less deductions:	
Administration expense	$1,650
Loss	($ 800)

Note that because the contribution of $5,000 to Hometown Church was not required under the terms of the will to be paid out of the gross income of the estate, it is not deductible and was not included in the computation.

Because the estate had no distributable net income in 1997, none of the distributions made to your mother has to be included in her gross income. Furthermore, because the estate in the year of termination had deductions in excess of its gross income, the excess of $800 will be allowed as a miscellaneous itemized deduction subject to the 2%-of-adjusted-gross-income limit to your mother on her individual return for the year 1997, if she is otherwise eligible to itemize deductions.

Termination of estate. You have made the final distribution of the assets of the estate and you are now ready to terminate the estate. You must notify the IRS, in writing, that the estate has been terminated and that all of the assets have been distributed to the beneficiaries. Form 56, mentioned earlier, can be used for this purpose. Be sure to report the termination to the IRS office where you filed Form 56 and to include the employer identification number on this notification.

How To Get More Information

You can get help from the IRS in several ways.

Free publications and forms. To order free publications and forms, call 1–800–TAX–FORM (1–800–829–3676). You can also write to the IRS Forms Distribution Center nearest you. Check your income tax package for the address. Your local library or post office also may have the items you need.

For a list of free tax publications, order Publication 910, *Guide to Free Tax Services.* It also contains an index of tax topics and related publications and describes other free tax information services available from IRS, including tax education and assistance programs.

If you have access to a personal computer and modem, you also can get many forms and publications electronically. See your income tax package for details. If space permitted, this information is at the end of this publication.

Tax questions. You can call the IRS with your tax questions. Check your income tax package or telephone book for the local number, or you can call 1–800–829–1040.

TTY/TDD equipment. If you have access to TTY/TDD equipment, you can call 1–800–829–4059 to ask tax questions or to order forms and publications. See your income tax package for the hours of operation.

Index

*U.S. Government Printing Office: 1996 — 407-612

INDEX

NOTES

NOTES

NOTES

NOTES

NOTES

NOTES